P9-AGM-045

The Story
OF THE
Latter-day
Saints

Building the Nauvoo Temple, a 1975 painting by Gary Smith. (Courtesy the artist)

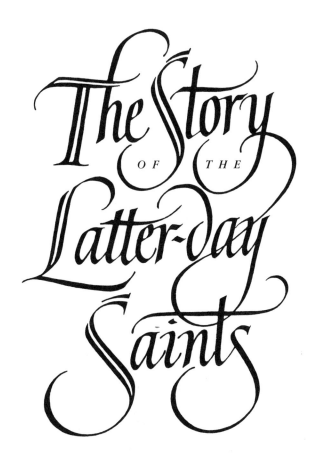

The Story of the Latter-day Saints

JAMES B. ALLEN AND GLEN M. LEONARD

SECOND EDITION, REVISED AND ENLARGED

Deseret Book Company
Salt Lake City, Utah

Library of Congress Cataloging-in-Publication Data

Allen, James B.
    The story of the Latter-day Saints / James B. Allen, Glen M.
Leonard. — 2nd ed., rev., enl., and updated.
        p. cm.
    Includes bibliographical references and index.
    ISBN 0-87579-565-X
    1. Church of Jesus Christ of Latter-day Saints—History.
2. Mormon Church—History. I. Leonard, Glen M. II. Title.
BX8611.A473 1992
289.3′32′09—dc20   92-33934
                                                           CIP

Printed in the United States of America

10   9   8   7   6   5   4   3   2   1

To Our Wives
Renée and Karen

Contents

List of Maps

Preface

The history of The Church of Jesus Christ of Latter-day Saints is constantly changing as new information becomes available and as each generation asks fresh questions about its past. It was because of the need to synthesize such new research for an audience of interested general readers that we first prepared *The Story of the Latter-day Saints* for publication in 1976. Now, after sixteen years, ongoing events in the Church's history and additional scholarship suggested the appropriateness of a revision.

In this second edition, our intent remains unchanged. We offer a compact, introductory overview, principally in narrative form. In order to provide an up-to-date look at Latter-day Saint history, we concentrate more heavily on events in the twentieth century than most other writers. And we attempt to explain the events with as much detail, interest, and meaning as possible while keeping in mind the broader trends as well as limitations imposed by the size of the book. In preparing this new edition, we reviewed the entire text, making changes as appropriate to reflect recent scholarship and to correct errors. We extensively rewrote the final chapters and brought them up-to-date. Similarly, we thoroughly revised the bibliography by eliminating older and less useful works and adding newer, more comprehensive books and significant recent articles.

There are many themes in the history of the Latter-day Saints, but four in particular influenced our interpretation.

First, we have tried to present the Latter-day Saints as a religious people. The first-person accounts of their religious experiences and daily lives convince us that they genuinely believed in the authenticity of their faith and were deeply concerned about sharing it with others. From the time of Joseph Smith's first vision, the Saints bore constant testimony that the Church was divinely inspired, directed by revelation from God. Even though the Saints and their leaders were constantly involved in political, economic, and other secular affairs, concern for these things was secondary to a quest for salvation and a concern for the spiritual well-being of all mankind. Only by understanding this motivation can we perceive what has led Latter-day Saints in all periods to sacrifice personal concerns so that the gospel message could spread to the people of the world. It was all done in the hope of preparing a righteous people for the millennial reign of Jesus Christ.

A second theme is that the Church has been influenced to some degree by the events of the world around it. We think it important to see the institution in the context of its environment, and where appropriate we have tried to demonstrate that relationship. The early persecution, the economic problems of the Saints, their choice of various places of refuge, and their changing religious and social programs were all related in some way to the broader setting. Understanding that relationship is essential to understanding the Church itself.

Third, The Church of Jesus Christ of Latter-day Saints has always seen its mission in universal scope. This religious body began in the northeastern United States as a tiny organization and expanded over the next 160 years to claim an international membership of over seven million. How and why that expansion took place is one of the essential themes of its history. The quest for a global presence was a continuing focus from the beginning; yet only in recent times, and only after the end of a policy of gathering to a central place of refuge, has the Church become a genuinely worldwide body. It continues at an accelerating pace its quest to carry the restored gospel to "all nations, kindreds, tongues, and peoples."

Finally, we are impressed with the dynamics of change within the Church. We have tried to suggest how and why new programs were adopted, old policies reevaluated and changed, and new doctrinal information presented to the Saints. We have also tried to suggest some of the things that have remained constant. The Church is based on the principle of continuing revelation, and as new conditions arise, the Saints are continually impressed with the importance of heeding the counsel of the living prophet. This central Mormon teaching helps explain the ready acceptance by most members of new programs and directions. How the Church maintained its constant commitment to certain central religious truths, and at the same time remained flexible enough to adapt to the ever-present but always changing challenges of the world, is an essential part of its history.

In the preparation of this book, and in its revision, we have relied heavily on the impressive body of new scholarship that has appeared in the last thirty-five years. We are most grateful for the contribution of scholars from many walks of life and diverse religious persuasions, all of them interested in expanding knowledge of the fascinating story of the Latter-day Saints. Of special help to us have been the standard historical works listed in the first section of the bibliography and the newer studies of specific periods in Mormon history. We owe respect and gratitude to such early scholars as B. H. Roberts, Joseph Fielding Smith, Orson F. Whitney, Hubert Howe Bancroft, Andrew Jenson, and others. We have also benefited greatly from conversations with other historians, including those who have recently published book-length studies of specific periods and places important in Church history. Many have generously provided materials and suggestions.

For ease of reading, we have avoided an abundance of footnotes. In general, they are used only to identify direct quotations that are not otherwise clearly identifiable from the context. Further, we have adopted the policy used by many textbook writers of not providing a footnote if the quotation is very short and used mainly for literary effect. Our basic sources are listed in the bibliographic essay at the end of the book. This listing, organized by chapters and topics, serves as well to suggest additional reading for those interested in pursuing topics in greater detail.

Although we bear full responsibility for the contents of the book, we are greatly indebted to many for their encouragement and support. Leonard J. Arrington, serving at the time as Church Historian and director of the History Division of the Church Historical Department, first suggested that we prepare the work. As we prepared the first edition, he shared much useful information and critiqued the manuscript, as did Assistant Church Historian Davis Bitton. Others who read that manuscript were Maureen Ursenbach Beecher, now at Brigham Young University, and Thomas G. Alexander, also at BYU. Sharon Swenson offered much additional editorial help. We especially appreciate the support given then by Earl E. Olson, Assistant Managing Director of the Historical Department, and Donald T. Schmidt, Church Librarian and Archivist, as well as the personnel of the department.

In addition to our extensive dependence upon published works acknowledged in the bibliography, we had the special assistance of

several researchers who sought out information and shared their find-
ings with us in the form of reports on various subjects. They include
Bruce D. Blumell, John F. Yurtinus, Evelyn Wendel, Craig Johnson,
Christian Thorup, Edward J. Thompson, John Bluth, Betty Barton,
Robert G. Mouritson, Richard L. Jensen, and Gordon I. Irving. Credit
for basic map work goes to Merrill K. Ridd and Burt Merkley. Valerie
Searle skillfully directed the process of typing and retyping the original
manuscript. She was assisted by Debbie Lilenquist, Karen Hulet, and
Kathleen Davidson. For the second edition, we give thanks to the world
of computer technology that provided us with the opportunity of scan-
ning the old text, putting it on our personal computers, and preparing
the revised manuscript ourselves. In the production of the first edition,
Wm. James Mortimer, Eleanor Knowles, and Michael Graves of Deseret
Book gave essential help, and Bailey-Montague and Associates created
the handsome design.

The second edition appears through the encouragement of Ronald
A. Millet, Eleanor Knowles, Sheri Dew, and their associates at Deseret
Book. This edition was designed by Richard Erickson. We had the
assistance of Bruce Westergren, Warren Metcalf, and J. Michael Allen
in collecting information for an expanded chapter 21. We also thank
our colleagues and readers churchwide for their interest and for encouraging a new edition. Their suggestions and comments made on
the first edition have improved the accuracy of our presentation and
kept us from many errors of fact and interpretation. In addition, the
forbearance and love of our wives and families have made this revised,
enlarged and updated edition possible.

James B. Allen
Glen M. Leonard

PART I

Laying the Foundations of Zion, *1820–1839*

This portrait of Joseph Smith, probably painted by W. Majors after the death of the Prophet, was painted in Nauvoo. It is thought to be the most authentic likeness of Joseph Smith extant. (Published by permission of the Reorganized Church of Jesus Christ of Latter Day Saints.)

IN 1990 FORTY THOUSAND full-time Mormon missionaries were actively proselyting in nearly ninety nations, attempting to acquaint their brothers and sisters around the world with the restored gospel of Jesus Christ. These missionaries included young men and women as well as mature couples of every race and nationality. Their common testimony was that in the modern world of strife and turmoil, God continued to give guidance, as he had in ages past, through living prophets. They told the story of Joseph Smith, the Book of Mormon, and the rise of The Church of Jesus Christ of Latter-day Saints, affirming that Joseph was the instrument in the hands of God for restoring to the earth the ancient church of Christ, with all the knowledge and authority necessary to bring about the salvation of mankind. Like the tiny stone that the prophet Daniel saw cut out of a mountain without hands, the restored church began as a small American body with a destiny to fill the world. Its universal gospel message was that Jesus Christ was the Savior of the world and that his gospel, restored through Joseph Smith, was the only road to world peace as well as to individual eternal salvation.

This was the same message the missionaries had taught for 160 years. They also taught that the United States was carefully prepared for its role in the restoration of the gospel, and that the times in which Joseph Smith lived were especially suited to receive that message. In the years immediately preceding 1820, the revivalistic fervor of western New York helped prepare young Joseph for his earliest spiritual experiences. Many seekers of true religion in the 1820s and 1830s believed in the necessity of restoring original Christianity as well as in temperance, miracles, spiritual manifestations, and the nearness of the Millennium. All this helped prepare prospective converts for the message of Mormonism, as it was soon called. The Book of Mormon proclaimed America to be a land of promise, "choice above all other lands," and the site of a New Jerusalem to be established in preparation for Christ's millennial reign. A revelation to Joseph Smith proclaimed the Constitution of the United States divinely inspired. With its protection of religious freedom, it was this, in part, that helped prepare America for the Restoration.

Within ten years after the Church's organization in 1830, scores of missionaries had covered many parts of the United States and gathered thousands of converts to Ohio and Missouri. The Saints made a valiant effort to establish ideal Christian communities in these two gathering places, but internal problems as well as conflict with non-Mormon neighbors resulted in their expulsion from both states. They never lost faith, however, that one day there would be a return to Missouri, where Zion, the New Jerusalem, would be built.

In 1839 about fifteen hundred members lived outside the United States, but the overwhelming majority of Saints were native-born Americans whose habits, values, and hopes were intimately connected with the land of their birth and whose faith in the gospel intensified their expectations of America's destiny. Because they were so intensely American, it may seem strange that the Latter-day Saints were unable to live peacefully with their American neighbors. Religious persecution, however, was not uncommon in that early period. Many Americans feared close-knit groups, suspecting subversive plots to overthrow their free and pluralistic society. Some even detected foreign influences in religion, particularly Catholicism, and often connected those influences with disloyalty. Others simply ridiculed the revivalists or other groups that claimed special spiritual manifestations. In short, America was a fluid, diverse society—some people accepted new ideas, others ignored them, and still others became actively involved in opposing new, hard-to-understand movements.

This formative period of Latter-day Saint history was dominated by the inspiring figure of Joseph Smith. As a leader he directed both temporal and spiritual activities, and suggested that actually there was little difference between the two. "All things unto me are spiritual," the Lord said to him in a revelation as early as September 1830, "and not at any time have I given unto you a law which is temporal." (D&C 29:4.)[1] From the beginning people came to "Brother Joseph" to ask the

---

[1] The Doctrine and Covenants of The Church of Jesus Christ of Latter-day Saints will be cited herein as D&C.

will of the Lord concerning them. Joseph instructed the Saints in the law of consecration, which envisioned the establishment of a series of ideal communities promoting temporal and spiritual equality. He led a small army from Ohio to Missouri, hoping to restore his followers to their homes, and he established both a banking enterprise and a temple in Ohio. The schools of Kirtland, the communities in Missouri, the printing houses in Ohio and Missouri, the publication of the Book of Commandments, and the willingness of thousands to uproot their lives and relocate were all results of the conviction that Joseph Smith was a prophet of God. His early vision of the Father and the Son, the appearances of Moroni and other angels, the translation of the Book of Mormon, the more than 120 revelations recorded by Joseph Smith, and countless incidents of healing, speaking in tongues, and other spiritual manifestations — all provided the strength of Mormonism in these early years. For believers, these things were "the substance of things hoped for, the evidence of things not seen"; they were the foundation of their faith.

CHAPTER 1

The Historical Setting for the Restoration

"This is my Beloved Son. Hear Him!"

These were the astonishing words heard by the fourteen-year-old Joseph Smith in the spring of 1820 as he knelt in fervent prayer in a grove of trees near his home in western New York, seeking guidance in personal religious questions. In vision he beheld two heavenly Personages, and the message he received from them was that he should join no church. Instead, he was to wait until the Lord saw fit, through him, to restore the ancient gospel of Jesus Christ. Young Joseph emerged from the grove a man of destiny whose story one day would be known and believed worldwide.

This profound experience was the first of many such events in the history of The Church of Jesus Christ of Latter-day Saints. But it was not just the beginning of the story of the Latter-day Saints. It was, as well, the culmination of a long historical process that included the establishment of religious freedom in America and the preparation of a political and social climate conducive to the spread of Joseph Smith's message. Part of America's divine destiny, the Saints believed, was to become the host society for the restoration of the original Christian faith. What follows in this chapter suggests some of the things that helped bring this about.

Early Christianity and the Protestant Reformation

The history of the Restoration through Joseph Smith actually began with the founding of Christianity itself. Jesus established his church among the Jews in Palestine, but frequently he foretold its spread throughout the world. "The gospel must be published among all nations," he declared, and his final instruction to his apostles was to "go ye into all the world, and preach the gospel to every creature." (Mark

13:10; 16:15.) Peter, Paul, and other early missionaries traveled extensively throughout the Roman world, planting churches wherever they went, though, as Christ also foretold, at the cost of bitter opposition, intense persecution, and often brutal death. Peter, for example, was imprisoned in Rome and there reportedly suffered death by crucifixion. Christianity nevertheless grew rapidly throughout the Mediterranean world, as the blood of the martyrs seemed to be the seed of the church, and in A.D. 313 Christians were finally granted complete freedom of religion by the Roman Emperor Constantine, who himself had become one of them. In 392 Christianity became the official religion of the empire.

Almost from the beginning the church was plagued internally with doctrinal dissension and controversy, particularly over issues such as the nature of the Godhead, the purpose and nature of baptism and other ceremonies, and the very nature of salvation itself. Sometime during the second century it began to be called the "Catholic" (meaning "universal") Church, but it continued to be racked by heresy and schism. It also developed a tightly knit ecclesiastical organization that, as it achieved political power, eventually served to strengthen its hold over the minds of the people as well as its influence on the affairs of state in every country of Europe and much of the Mediterranean world. The church did much good in spreading the message of Christ, but in its struggle for survival it also used every means at its disposal to protect its interests as an institution. By the Middle Ages its ability to both crown and excommunicate kings and princes brought to it a degree of political power unthought of by the ancient Christian fathers. Heretics were treated brutally, and by turning them over to the "secular arm" (i.e., the state) for punishment, the church had power even over life and death.

All this was accompanied by tragic wars and political controversies in the name of religion, where Christians often became the oppressors instead of the oppressed, and also by the development of elaborate ceremonies, forms, and dogma. By the sixteenth century no one doubted that much had changed since the days of Christ; but whether, through the centuries, the church had maintained the essentials of the faith originally delivered to the saints was a question raised often by heretics and less radical reformers alike.

In many places the time seemed ripe for a major reformation. As one author has described the situation in Germany:

Papal taxation and papal interference with churchly appointments were generally deemed oppressive. The expedition of clerical business by the papal curia was deemed expensive and corrupt. The clergy at home were much criticized for the unworthy examples of many of their number in high station and low. The trading cities were restive under clerical exemptions from taxation, the prohibition of interest, the many holidays, and the churchly countenance of beggars. Monasteries were in many places in sore need of reform. . . . The peasantry in general were in a state of economic unrest, not the least of their grievances being the tithes and fees collected by the local clergy. Added to these causes of restlessness were the intellectual ferment of rising German humanism and the stirrings of popular religious awakening, manifested in a deepening sense of terror and concern for salvation. It is evident that, could these various grievances find bold expression in a determined leader, his voice would find wide hearing.[1]

It was in this atmosphere that the great Protestant Reformation was precipitated by the German theologian Martin Luther, one of the few people whose life and work has profoundly changed the history of the world. A man of deep religious faith and unquestioning trust in God, his studies eventually led him to the conclusion that salvation came not through the forms and sacraments of the church but, rather, through faith in Christ which, alone, led to forgiveness of sins. Though he was not the first to criticize abuses in the church, he became notorious for his 1517 attack on the practice of selling indulgences (relief from the penalties of sin). This, together with other disagreements, eventually led to his trial for heresy. In 1521 he broke formally from Catholicism and, at the urging of certain German rulers, soon assisted in establishing the Lutheran Church.

Luther, however, had no intention of destroying Catholicism: he wanted only to purify it and return it to the ancient tenets of Christianity as he understood them. Many reformers followed, and though few if any could agree on just what those tenets were, they were generally dedicated to the proposition that somehow the simple truths and practices of the ancient church had been lost and that it was their role to bring Christianity back on course. Many did agree that the scriptures must be translated into the vernacular for the sake of the common

---

[1]Williston Walker, *A History of the Christian Church*, revised edition (New York: Charles Scribner's Sons, 1959), p. 301.

people, and the translation and widespread dissemination of the Bible became one of the major achievements of the Reformation era. The Reformation spread throughout the nations of Christendom, taking on political as well as spiritual significance as kings and princes supported it and established state religions of their own, partly to escape the domination of Rome.

In England, one of the least radical Protestant movements began after the Pope failed to sanction a divorce sought by King Henry VIII. Angered, in 1534 Henry proclaimed the English church independent of the papacy and established himself as the head of the Church of England, or Anglican Church. For many English reformers, however, Anglicanism did not go far enough, for it retained most of the forms and ceremonies they thought unnecessary to salvation. Some, who came to be known as Puritans and whose theology was influenced especially by that of John Calvin, a French Huguenot reformer in Geneva, spent their energies attempting to reform the church from within, while others advocated outright separation.

Religion and Society in America

When the first British colonists reached the shores of America in the early seventeenth century, they brought the Reformation with them. Jamestown, Virginia, was the first permanent settlement, and Anglicanism became the established faith in that colony. Certain Puritans, meanwhile, discouraged in their failure to purify Anglicanism at home, decided to seek refuge in America, where, they hoped, they could establish God's ideal community without political interference or opposition. It was their New England towns and villages that provided Joseph Smith's rich religious and cultural heritage.

The Puritans of New England inherited at least two distinctive concepts from Calvin: the doctrine of man's total depravity and the notion of predestination and election. Through the fall of Adam, they taught, man became utterly depraved—incapable of goodness and totally undeserving of anything but damnation. Salvation came only to those whom God, for his own purposes, had already "elected," or predestined, to be saved. Christ's atonement provided the power for this salvation, but it was only for those who had been so chosen.

The Calvinist-Puritan doctrine, however, compelled believers to adhere strictly to God's laws, as they interpreted them, and this helped create the high moral and ethical tone that characterized Joseph Smith's

South Royalton, Vermont, as it appeared in 1912, was representative of New England villages. (George E. Anderson photograph, Church Archives)

New England. Through faith and obedience to God's will, his "elect" could learn of their favored state. Further, he would bless the "elect" with success—particularly economic success—which led the Puritan fathers to emphasize thrift, industry, and hard work as characteristics of God's chosen people.

The Puritans saw themselves as a covenant people, commissioned by God to build a New Jerusalem, or a City of Zion, an exemplary community that all could observe and emulate. Each congregation consisted of a number of people who, through their lives and personal confessions of faith, had convinced the others that they were, indeed, among God's "elect," and who had joined together in a voluntary "covenant community" that agreed to obey the will of God. Children born to church members were said to be "born under the covenant." All things, including the selection of pastors and other church officers, were done by common consent of the congregation, and this became the basis for the development of Congregationalism in America.

As far as the relationship between church and state was concerned, the Puritans technically believed in separation. Ministers were forbidden to hold public office, and public officials had no authority over the selection of ministers or in other church affairs. In other ways, however, the influence of the church on public policy was direct and far-reaching.

Puritanism became the established faith in nearly all New England colonies, and at first only the "elect" (i.e., church members) could vote or hold public office. This, in effect, disfranchised most residents, for only a minority of the settlers had proven themselves to be among the "elect." Public officials were there to promote the will of God, and one result was the fact that initially no other religion was tolerated. After all, the leaders reasoned, it would be wrong in the sight of God to allow the existence of any false religion, and in Massachusetts, especially, heretics and preachers of other faiths were sometimes brutally punished and expelled. It was only in 1662 that Massachusetts officials were prohibited by Charles II from hanging Quakers.

But the Puritan way did not long remain the only way in New England. Roger Williams, for example, was a prominent dissenter who believed that the vitality of Calvinism could be maintained only by voluntary association, not by a state-imposed conformity. The formation of his and other dissenting congregations could not long be forestalled, even in Massachusetts, as population increased and as the younger generation demanded less rigid conformity to tradition. Within two or three generations the theological foundations of Puritanism had begun to wither, and this move away from an established church and from Calvinistic theology was an essential step in the preparation of many New Englanders for the restored gospel as taught to them by Latter-day Saint missionaries. Some elements remained, including the idea of a "covenant people," the hope for establishing Zion as a "light on a hill" that could not be hid, the emphasis on education, the desire to live according to the tenets of ancient Christianity, and the famous "Puritan ethic" of integrity, industry, and thrift. All these things found their counterpart in Mormonism, and those New Englanders who shared them but were purged of the extremes of Calvinism such as the doctrines of total depravity, predestination, and election, were part of the field that was "white already to harvest" when the missionaries came among them. It seems no accident that New England was one of the most fruitful fields for the Mormon harvest in the first few years of missionary work.

Anglicanism became the established faith in most colonies outside New England, but the Quakers, Presbyterians, Baptists, and Lutherans also gained sizable followings. The continuing immigration from Europe introduced a variety of smaller Protestant sects as well as a number of Catholic congregations; and by the time of the American Revolution, a significant religious diversity prevailed in all the colonies. Few people

Typical camp meeting at the time of the Second Great Awakening. (Library of Congress)

held formal membership in any church—an average of less than 10 percent—but religious values maintained a significant influence in colonial society.

Early in the eighteenth century a movement known as the Great Awakening swept America, reaching its peak in the 1730s and early 1740s. Essentially it was a fervent effort to restore righteousness and religious zeal, and in New England Jonathan Edwards attempted to restore the crumbling foundations of early Puritanism. Its most ambitious objectives were not achieved, but the Great Awakening nevertheless had some important long-range consequences. It kindled a warm glow of religious commitment that had not been felt in America for years, and gave rise to a new evangelistic pattern that resulted in itinerant preachers, especially Baptists, establishing many new churches along the frontier. It also helped promote greater participation by laymen in the affairs of organized religion, a pattern that would become essential to the church founded by Joseph Smith.

Another period of religious fervor, the Second Great Awakening, began in New England in the 1790s and spread throughout the nation. It was characterized by circuit-riding preachers, fiery-tongued evangelists, new grass-roots religious movements, fervent emotionalism, and in some cases the manifestation of certain physical excesses that demonstrated to new converts their divine acceptance. After the War of 1812, the revival swept the country in periodic waves, reaching a peak between 1825 and 1827.

Western New York was so intensely affected that it was called the Burned-over District. It was populated largely by former New Englanders, including the family of Joseph Smith, whose deep-rooted religious heritage made them especially sensitive to the call for a spiritual reawakening. One particularly intense series of revival meetings swept through the area during Joseph Smith's early years and had several important consequences that may have helped create an atmosphere conducive to the rise of Mormonism. The revivals enhanced the desire for perfection, or for bringing Christ into every aspect of one's life. They gave many people, especially youth, the feeling that they were "convicted of sin" and needed to find salvation. They helped along the revolt against Calvinism by enhancing the growing emphasis on free will. They gave many unchurched Americans the feeling that they must belong to a church, which gave rise to the quest by some for the "right" church and even a feeling of guilt if they did not belong. This, in turn, promoted sectarian conflict as ministers vied for converts and as many people, including young Joseph Smith, wondered who was right and who was wrong. The revivals also gave the future prophet of the Restoration ample opportunity, as a youth, to feel their fervor and to think seriously about his own salvation.

The early nineteenth century was a time of great social upheaval, and the revivals were only one manifestation of numerous changes taking place in American life. Another was the rapid growth of newspapers throughout the new nation, which not only enhanced communication between the people of the various states but also gave them greater choice of reading material, and thus a broader basis for forming ideas, opinions, and personal identity than the traditional sources of family, neighborhood, and community. All of this was part of the rapid democratization of America that, in turn, reflected the spirit of the Revolution itself. As people became convinced that they were capable of self-government, for example, they also became convinced that they were capable of self-improvement and of working out their own religious salvation. The fact that organized religion was in disarray did not reflect a lack of religious commitment, but only a lack of conviction that the traditional churches offered the way of salvation.

In addition, this was a period in which Americans seemed increasingly anxious to seek new forms of voluntary association, and in increasing numbers they joined almost every kind of group, including mutual aid societies, temperance organizations, various other kinds of reform movements, and Freemasonry. No longer, moreover, did the common folk stand in as much awe of college degrees, for while they continued to value good, basic education, they were also convinced that ordinary people could do just as many important things, and probably knew just as much about the things that really mattered, as the most learned among them. "For ye see your calling, brethren," the Apostle Paul had written, "how that not many wise men after the flesh, not many mighty, not many noble are called: But God hath chosen the foolish things of the world to confound the wise; and God hath chosen the weak things of the world to confound the things which are mighty." (1 Corinthians 2:26–27.) This was the spirit that prevailed among many humble seekers in the evangelical environment of the early nineteenth century, and they could easily relate to Jacob's lament in the Book of Mormon: "O the vainness, and the frailties, and the foolishness of men! When they are learned they think they are wise, and they hearken not unto the counsel of God, for they set it aside, supposing they know of themselves, wherefore, their wisdom is foolishness and it profiteth them not." (2 Nephi 9:28.) It seemed only natural to those who accepted the Latter-day Saint message that the prophet of the Restoration should be a young man with little formal education, one of the "weak things of the world" who was in tune with the Spirit rather than with merely the wisdom of men.

Another element in the religious and social milieu of the time was a continuing interest in various so-called "magical arts," such as the use of divining rods or stone gazing (sometimes called "glass-looking") in the quest for lost articles or buried treasure. Though by the early nineteenth century most of the well educated scoffed at such activities, a number of earlier intellectuals, including Isaac Newton, had taken some aspects of them seriously. In Joseph Smith's time these practices were still accepted as authentic among the common folk in upstate New York. Many respectable citizens included such beliefs in their religious world-view, and to them involvement in folk magic did not seem contrary either to nature or to Christianity.

The Quest for Freedom of Religion

Another element in the vibrant social and political evolution of America was the gradual achievement of freedom of religion, a departure from the tradition of established churches that had characterized Western civilization for over a thousand years. One early advocate of complete separation of church and state was the zealous Puritan minister in Salem, Massachusetts, Roger Williams. "Forced religion stinks in God's nostrils," he thundered, and after his banishment from Massachusetts he obtained a charter in 1643 for the establishment of the colony of Rhode Island, where complete religious freedom prevailed. Some forty years later, under the altruistic hand of William Penn, the colony of Pennsylvania was established; there, too, no state church was allowed and freedom of worship was guaranteed to anyone who believed in "one Almighty God." All the other American colonies, however, retained established churches, and complete freedom of religion did not exist.

Eighteenth-century America, nevertheless, was deeply influenced by the European Enlightenment, which contributed much to the philosophy of both the Declaration of Independence and the American Constitution. The authors of these two documents assumed that man was capable of discovering correct political principles for himself and formulating his own political institutions. Implicitly this meant that government should be free to respond to the needs of the people, uninfluenced by the pressures of organized religion, and that religion should be a matter of personal conscience with no one required, through payment of taxes, to support a church whose doctrines he did not believe.

Before the ink could dry on the Declaration of Independence, agitation for disestablishment began in several states. Thomas Jefferson was its foremost advocate, and the author of Virginia's famous 1785 Bill for Establishing Religious Freedom. By the time the Constitution was written in 1787 the sentiment against a religious establishment was so strong that, at least at the national level, it was prohibited. "No religious test shall ever be required as a qualification to any office or public trust under the United States," Article IV read. The First Amendment to the Constitution (1791) declared that "Congress shall make no law respecting the establishment of religion, or prohibiting the free exercise thereof." The remaining states soon followed the trend, and in 1833 Massachusetts became the last to sever completely the legal ties between church and state.

"I established the Constitution of this land, by the hands of wise men whom I raised up unto this very purpose," said the Lord in a revelation to Joseph Smith in 1833 (D&C 101:80), and Latter-day Saints believe that the separation of church and state was one of the Constitution's many wise provisions that helped prepare a fertile soil in America for the restoration of the gospel. The spirit that fostered disestablishment also encouraged the growth of new religious bodies, for society was becoming much more tolerant of religious pluralism. Equally important, the law itself protected the creation of new religious bodies in a way that it had never done before, either in America or elsewhere. While considerable toleration had developed even in those states with religious establishments, now there were no legal constraints on any church and hence no legal possibilities for restraining the rise of Mormonism, so long as it held to its own basic tenet of "obeying, honoring, and sustaining the law."

The Restoration Impulse

Even as the two Great Awakenings and the growth of religious freedom contributed to the development of diverse religious ideas in America and the multiplication of religious bodies, one impulse common to many movements, both old and new, was a desire for the restoration of the ancient teachings and practices of the New Testament church. As early as 1639 Roger Williams taught that the primitive church had been destroyed by apostasy and that the authority to perform ordinances had been lost. He thus became a seeker, looking forward to a time when the true church would be restored by special commission. The number of such seekers, often called "primitivists," or "restorationists," grew rapidly, some looking for a special restoration and others seeking for the simple New Testament church by moving in and out of the various sects and denominations of the day. By Joseph Smith's time the search for the restoration of original Christianity was common among Protestants both in America and Europe, and his declaration that "We believe in the same organization that existed in the primitive church . . . " would not fall on deaf ears among the seekers.

To many, if not most, seekers the restoration of the ancient gospel was a necessary precursor to the second coming of Christ. Millennialism — the belief that the Savior's second advent was imminent — was commonplace by the early nineteenth century, and many people fervently expected it within their own lifetimes.

Perhaps the most prominent restorationist group in Joseph Smith's time was the Disciples of Christ, or Campbellites. Thomas Campbell and his son Alexander were initially concerned with reforming the Presbyterian Church, but after Sidney Rigdon heard the younger Campbell discuss the "restoration of the ancient order of things," he persuaded him to join a liberal Baptist group. Campbell, in turn, later persuaded Rigdon to accept a call to head the First Baptist Church of

Pittsburgh in 1822. When Campbell decided to break with the Baptists, Sidney Rigdon's followers became the third group to declare itself a part of Campbell's new movement. Rigdon soon became popular among the Disciples of Christ, largely because of his eloquent preaching and profound biblical scholarship. As a restorationist he taught faith, repentance, and baptism, and promised the Holy Ghost to those who would believe. He was well prepared for the message of the Mormon missionaries when they came to him in 1830, and for a time he would be second only to Joseph Smith among the leadership of the Latter-day Saints.

Many other seekers were spiritually prepared for the gospel. Early in life Wilford Woodruff asked God in prayer to "restore the ancient Gospel, to restore the ancient gifts, to restore the ancient power,"[2] and he received assurance he would see it happen. At age fifteen Joel Johnson sat up all night reading the Bible and thrilling with a spiritual confirmation that someday he would possess the ancient gospel. Jesse Crosby at age sixteen wondered which of the churches was right, attended different denominations, and continually sought solitude in the woods to pray for guidance. Sarah Studevant Leavitt wrote in her autobiography that long before she heard of Mormonism she had read the Bible for herself and found that none of the denominations read it as she did; but, she wrote, "it was very evident to my understanding that they all came short of preaching the doctrine that Paul preached, but I was confident we should have the faith."[3] And as young Eliza R. Snow studied the New Testament, she too yearned for the spiritual gifts of which the ancient apostles testified.

John Taylor, a Methodist preacher in Canada, met regularly with a group that concluded that no existing religious sect was the church of Christ, and that all lacked divine authority. They sought a church with the same organization as the primitive church, including apostles, but disagreed on how to find it. Some felt they should ask God to commission them, by revelation, with the ancient authority of apostles and prophets, while others wondered if the Lord had not already ordained apostles somewhere in the world.

These and thousands of other seekers were soon attracted to and

---

[2]*Journal of Discourses*, 26 vols. (London: Latter-day Saints' Book Depot, 1854–86), 25:171.
[3]As cited in Kenneth W. Godfrey, Audrey M. Godfrey, and Jill Mulvay Derr, *Women's Voices: An Untold History of the Latter-day Saints 1830–1900* (Salt Lake City: Deseret Book Company, 1982), p. 27.

believed the message of the Mormon missionaries. When they joined, however, they discovered that Mormonism was much more than a simple reflection of popular primitivism. To be sure, they found in it a return to the Christian fundamentals they sought, but they also found new revelation and, of special significance, new scripture. The term "restoration of the gospel" soon took on a much broader meaning for the Latter-day Saints than for their contemporaries. It was not only the primitive Christian church that had been restored, but also the blessings and heritage of the Old Testament prophets. The priesthood, for example, was the same as that held by Abraham; Moses came to Joseph Smith and Oliver Cowdery in the Kirtland Temple and restored the "keys of the gathering of Israel"; and the visit of the prophet Elijah set the stage for the great genealogical and temple work that became an essential part of the LDS understanding of what the Restoration meant. In addition, many, if not most, early Mormons were converted through the Book of Mormon. This new book of scripture was an essential part of the "restoration of all things," for it not only restored a knowledge of God's dealing with ancient Israelites on the American continent, but also became an important new witness for the divinity of Christ himself.

The Smiths of New England

The family history of Joseph Smith, Jr., was a microcosm of the broader New England heritage. His ancestors on both sides migrated to Massachusetts in the seventeenth century. His paternal grandparents, Asael and Mary Smith, spent their early married years on the Smith family farm at Topsfield, where in 1772 their three children were baptized in the Congregational Church. Both Asael and Mary "owned the covenant," or made a personal confession of their faith. Asael, however, did not remain an active Congregationalist, for his religious views acquired some of the more liberal overtones of the Age of Enlightenment. Asael became an enthusiastic supporter of the American Revolution and enlisted in the army. His attitude toward America was not unlike that of other patriots of his day. He expressed it in a 1799 "address" written to members of his family:

> Bless God that you live in a land of liberty, and bear yourselves dutifully and conscionable toward the authority under which you

live. See God's providence in the appointment of the Federal Constitution.[4]

In 1778 Asael moved his family to Derryfield, New Hampshire, where he became prominent in civic affairs. His ill health, however, made it difficult for him to work his farm. Then in 1785 his father died, and the following year, with their eleven children, the Smiths returned to the family farm at Topsfield. Asael assumed the responsibility of paying the family debts, caring for his aged stepmother, and managing a hundred-acre farm. He began these tasks in the midst of a serious postwar depression. His success is an exemplary story of thrift and industry. After only five years he was able to settle all his father's debts. He later took his family to Tunbridge, Vermont, where he pioneered eighty-five acres of uncleared land, soon purchased more farms, and became a community leader. Sometime between 1810 and 1820 he moved to northern New York state, where he died in 1830, the year his grandson organized a new church.

On his mother's side, Joseph Smith's grandfather was Solomon Mack, son of the Congregational pastor at Lyme, Connecticut. Financial misfortune struck the Mack family when Solomon was only four, and he was apprenticed to a neighborhood farmer. He worked long, hard hours, with no opportunity for either education or religious training, and after he had served his apprenticeship he enlisted to fight in the French and Indian War. Later he followed several professions: merchant, land developer, shipmaster, mill operator, and farmer. He was apparently a model of the Puritan ethic in practice, for he was known for industry, hard work, honesty in business dealings, and generosity almost to a fault.

Although Solomon joined no church until late in life, his wife, Lydia, provided the family with strong religious training, which Solomon deeply appreciated. The daughter of a Congregationalist deacon, Lydia had been a schoolteacher before her marriage. When he was nearly eighty, Solomon turned to religion and, with his wife as his teacher, read the Bible, received some singular spiritual manifestations, and was converted. This seems to have had a miraculous influence on his health, and during the rest of his life he labored diligently to bring religion to others. He even wrote an autobiography designed to persuade his readers to Christianity.

---

[4]As quoted in Richard Lloyd Anderson, *Joseph Smith's New England Heritage* (Salt Lake City: Deseret Book Company, 1971), p. 128.

Lucy Mack, Joseph's mother, was the youngest daughter of Solomon and Lydia Mack; she was born at Gilsum, New Hampshire, in 1775. About twenty years later she met Joseph Smith, son of Asael, while she was visiting her brother at Tunbridge, Vermont. The two were married in 1796 and immediately took up farming in Tunbridge where, in 1798, the first of their nine children, Alvin, was born.[5] But farming in the rocky soil of Vermont was not prosperous, even though, as Lucy said, it was a "handsome farm," and after six years they rented their land and went into merchandising. Then Joseph learned of the large profits possible in raising ginseng root and selling it to China. He invested heavily in the enterprise, only to be disappointed when the son of his shipping partner absconded with the profits. The Smiths were forced to sell their farm and use Lucy's dowry to pay their debts. In 1804 they moved to Sharon, Vermont, where they rented Solomon Mack's farm, and there, on December 23, 1805, Lucy gave birth to their fourth child, Joseph Smith, Jr.

In Vermont, Joseph, Sr., worked the farm and taught school in the winter. In 1811 the family moved to Lebanon, New Hampshire. They looked ahead with optimism, but in 1813 they were struck by a devastating epidemic of typhus, which killed thousands in Vermont and New Hampshire. The Smith children all contracted the fever and recovered, except young Joseph who, two weeks after seeming to recover, was seized with an infection in his shoulder and another in his left leg. After failing to cure the leg, the doctors decided to amputate it. The seven-year-old boy and his mother refused to consent to this drastic step and persuaded them to try once more by cutting out the diseased bone. Because anesthetics were not yet in use, the doctors tried to tie Joseph down for the operation, but in an amazing show of will and stamina he refused. They tried to give him liquor to dull the pain, but this he also refused. Lucy then withdrew several hundred yards from the house in order to be out of reach of his screams, but when the surgeons removed the first piece of bone she heard them anyway and came running back in. Joseph sent her away again, and, after three pieces of bone were taken out, the horrible but successful operation was complete. Joseph was sent to recuperate at the home of his uncle

---

[5]Actually, Joseph and Lucy had eleven children, but the first was born prematurely about 1797 and lived only a few days and another, born in 1810, lived only eleven days. The nine Smith children generally referred to were those who lived beyond early infancy.

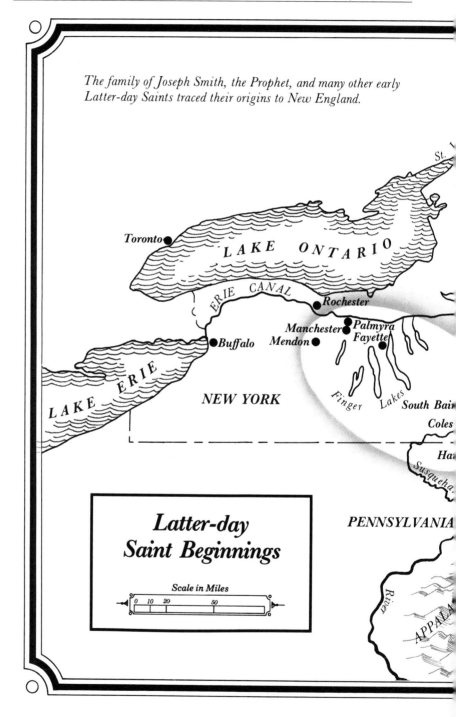

The family of Joseph Smith, the Prophet, and many other early
Latter-day Saints traced their origins to New England.

Latter-day Saint Beginnings

Scale in Miles

0 10 20   50

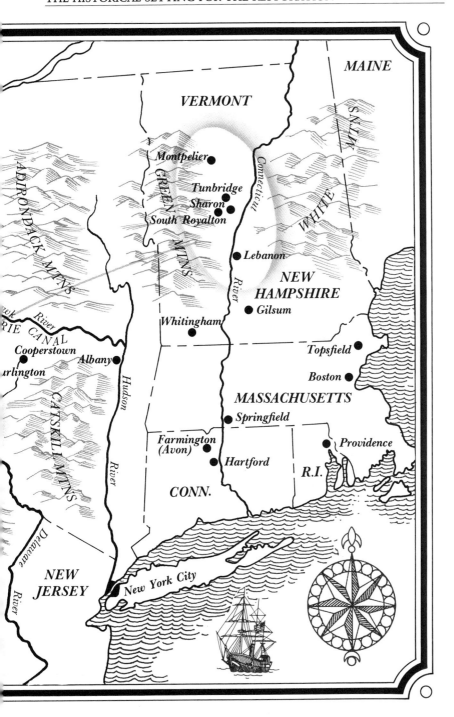

in Salem, Massachusetts, where he gradually regained his health, but he was on crutches for nearly three years afterward.

The epidemic took a heavy toll upon the Smith fortunes, as sickness continued in the family for nearly a year. Again they moved, this time to Norwich, Vermont, but three successive crop failures depleted their meager resources. The poor soil of Vermont was discouraging, but when snow fell in June of 1816 and frost killed the replanted crops in July, many Vermont farmers moved on. Emigration from Vermont reached a floodtide that year, and the Smith family was part of it.

The Smiths and the Westward Movement

The Smiths were latecomers to western New York. Shortly after the Revolution, land speculators, anticipating the inevitable settlement west of the Adirondacks, purchased all available state-owned land and then actively promoted the golden opportunities of the West. In western New York, especially, the land was rich, fertile, and easy to cultivate. All a prospective settler needed was enough money for a down payment and enough manpower to clear away the trees.

The emigration to western New York began as early as the 1790s, and by 1800 it had become a mass movement. By 1812, two hundred thousand people lived in the area, over two-thirds of them New Englanders. So great was the migration through the Mohawk Valley, in fact, that many of the more conservative New Englanders became alarmed. Not only did they see the rate of their population growth fall woefully behind that of the rest of the nation, but land values were declining, the social structure was threatened with disruption, and their best and youngest citizens were moving away. Newspaper propaganda bristled with alarming descriptions of danger on the frontier, as every effort was made to persuade the migrants to stay home. But the warnings were to no avail. Those who left were seeking better economic opportunity, and they were willing to risk the dangers and pay the price in work to find it.

In this atmosphere in the summer of 1816 Joseph Smith, Sr., left his family and headed west in search of new opportunities. Several weeks later he wrote and told them to follow him—not to Ohio, as they had expected, but to the vicinity of Palmyra in western New York. Lucy and her eight children, the youngest only a few months old, packed all they could into a wagon, used the last of their financial resources to pay off their creditors, and sometime during that winter joined Joseph, Sr., in Palmyra.

The township of Palmyra suffered from inflation at the time of their arrival. It had been settled for twenty-five years and boasted a population of nearly three thousand people. Only thirteen miles to the south was Canandaigua, the economic center of the region. Everyone expected the economic boom to continue, and immigrants, including the Smiths, paid highly inflated prices for their land. Unfortunately, the boom in the vicinity of Palmyra did not last. Before long many transplanted New Englanders found themselves once again moving west, to Ohio. The Smiths, however, decided to remain.

They rented a small home in Palmyra, and everyone old enough worked at odd jobs to help secure a livelihood. Joseph, Sr., was a cooper. He set about making the buckets and barrels in demand because of the abundance of maple trees in the area. Wooden containers were needed to store and collect the sap, which was made into sugar and syrup. He also knew enough masonry to case wells, cisterns, and basement walls. One such job came from Martin Harris, a well-to-do farmer, who hired him and his second son, Hyrum, to case a well. Alvin worked as a carpenter's helper. Lucy, meanwhile, set up a home business of her own. She painted and sold oilcloth table coverings and made and sold such sundries as gingerbread, pies, boiled eggs, and root beer. She did an especially lively business at public celebrations on the Fourth of July and other holidays. Within two years the family had saved enough to make a down payment on a hundred-acre farm in Farmington (later Manchester) township, a few miles south of Palmyra.

The family all continued to work in order to support themselves and pay for their land. During the first year Joseph, Sr., and his sons cleared thirty acres of timber and planted wheat. They also tapped twelve to fifteen hundred maple trees in order to draw the precious sap and make maple sugar. Though some antagonists later described the family as lazy and irresponsible, at least one neighbor, Orlando Saunders, recalled, "They have all worked for me many a day; they were very good people. Young Joe (as we called him then) has worked for me, and he was a good worker; they all were."[6]

The Smiths soon built a two-room log cabin with two attic bedrooms. Joseph was twelve years old when the family moved in. In mid-1821, needing additional sleeping quarters after their youngest child was born, they added a lean-to. Later they began to build a new and larger frame house, which was completed in the late fall of 1825.

---

[6]*Saints' Herald* 28 (1881): 165.

Young Joseph's educational opportunities were extremely limited. School terms normally lasted a maximum of three months, and children were taught little more than the basics of reading, writing, and arithmetic. Joseph attended school for only a term or two, but he also studied on his own. His mother noted that "he seemed much less inclined to the perusal of books than any of the rest of our children, but far more given to meditation and deep study."[7] He was also inquisitive and interested in contemporary news and issues. He regularly read the *Palmyra Register* and participated in a young people's debating club.

Joseph Smith was a "remarkably quiet, well-disposed child," his mother said. He admired and loved his parents, and was apparently an obedient son. Some of his contemporaries remembered him as "good natured, very rarely if ever indulging in any combative spirit toward anyone," as having a "jovial easy, don't care way with him and made him a lot of friends," and as "a real clever jovial boy."[8]

Until about 1820, none of the Smith family joined any religious denomination, though they were staunchly believing Christians. Like many other unchurched Americans, they were seekers and not eager to be too quick to join a particular church. Joseph's father was deeply spiritual, and Lucy later recorded several remarkable dreams and visions he experienced, which seemed to foreshadow the coming restoration of the gospel through their son. Under the tutelage of their father, the family studied the scriptures together and were led by him in family prayer. No pains were spared, the Prophet recalled later, in instructing him in the principles of Christianity. Young Joseph's life took on a clear religious direction, and his early search for God was later recalled in a blessing given to him by his father: "Thou hast sought to know his ways, and from thy childhood thou hast meditated much upon the great things of his law."[9]

Many things help shape the character and destiny of a man. From his family, as well as from the religious and social crosscurrents in early America, Joseph Smith received a heritage steeped in the Puritan

---

[7]Lucy Smith, *Biographical Sketches of Joseph Smith the Prophet and His Progenitors for Many Generations* (Liverpool: Published for Orson Pratt by S.W. Richards, 1853), p. 84.
[8]Pomeroy Tucker, *Origin, Rise and Progress of Mormonism* (New York: D. Appleton and Company, 1867), pp. 16–17; *Saints' Herald* 28 (1881): 167. For an insightful analysis of this general issue, see Richard Lloyd Anderson, "Joseph Smith's New York Reputation Reappraised," *Brigham Young University Studies* 10 (Spring 1970): 283–314.
[9]As quoted in Richard L. Anderson, "The Mature Joseph Smith and Treasure Searching," *Brigham Young University Studies* 24 (Fall 1984): 543.

ethic of thrift and industry, faith in God and a realization of man's dependence upon him, a longing for the establishment of God's ideal community, and belief that America was a land chosen for a divine destiny. By the time he came of age, America was a land of religious freedom, and although new movements were often ridiculed and scoffed at, no legal barriers barred their growth. His religious environment contained seeds of teachings that later became part of Mormon doctrine, but more importantly, it fostered a strong and active faith that one day the ancient order of things would be restored. The immediate vicinity of Joseph Smith's home burned with the fervor of the Second Great Awakening, and ministers and laymen commonly debated the question of which church was right.

But such historical forces alone would not produce a prophet. Not until he was determined and ready to open himself to the mind and will of God—to allow divine inspiration to help mold his character and destiny—would young Joseph Smith become different from what he was. By 1820 he was ready.

CHAPTER 2

The Restoration Commences, *1820–1831*

Joseph Smith could hardly avoid the spiritual awakenings of the Burned-over District. During a twelve-month period beginning in mid-1819, religious revivals took place in at least ten towns within a twenty-mile radius of his home. In July of that year the Methodists of the Genesee Conference held their annual meetings in Phelps Village (then called Vienna), about ten miles from the Smith farm. A hundred ministers met to deliberate policy, then began to hold camp meetings that sparked what one person called a "flaming spiritual advance" throughout the area. Methodists, Baptists, and Presbyterians all participated, and their churches showed uncommon membership gains.

In the midst of this religious excitement, the contemplative young Joseph was deeply touched.[1] His attendance at revivals while in his early teens, and his family's concern for religion, made his own quest for salvation urgent. He became seriously concerned for the welfare of his soul and began an intensive searching of the scriptures. No doubt he was somewhat torn when his mother, two brothers, and a sister joined the Presbyterians, while his father remained aloof from any church. Though Joseph began to lean toward the Methodists, he was still uncommitted, and he longed for the kind of emotional experience he witnessed in others. At one revival meeting, he later told a friend, he found himself with an intense desire to get religion, and he wanted to feel the spirit and shout like the rest.

---

[1]Joseph later dictated recollections of the memorable events of that year to scribes and confided more intimate details to close friends. On the basis of these accounts from the 1830s, we are able to reconstruct his remarkable story. In the following reconstruction, the direct quotations are taken from various accounts. The standard account is found in Joseph Smith, Jr., *History of the Church of Jesus Christ of Latter-day Saints*, ed. B.H. Roberts, 7 vols., 2nd ed. rev. (Salt Lake City: Deseret Book Company, 1964), 1:2–8. Other accounts are reproduced in various sources listed in the bibliography. The quotations referring to the visit from Moroni are all taken from the standard account.

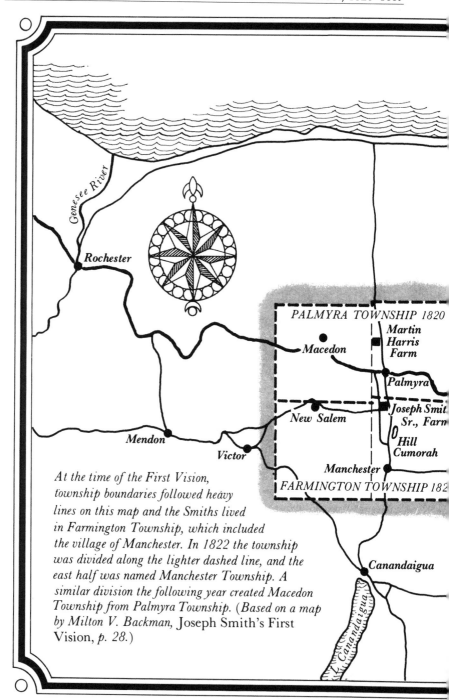

PALMYRA TOWNSHIP 1820

Martin Harris Farm

Macedon

Palmyra

Joseph Smith Sr., Farm

New Salem

Mendon

Victor

Hill Cumorah

Manchester

FARMINGTON TOWNSHIP 182

Rochester

Genesee River

Canandaigua

L. Canandaigua

At the time of the First Vision, township boundaries followed heavy lines on this map and the Smiths lived in Farmington Township, which included the village of Manchester. In 1822 the township was divided along the lighter dashed line, and the east half was named Manchester Township. A similar division the following year created Macedon Township from Palmyra Township. (Based on a map by Milton V. Backman, Joseph Smith's First Vision, p. 28.)

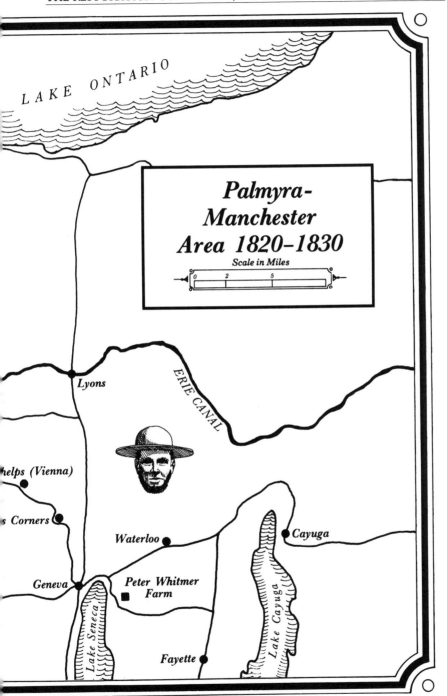

LAKE ONTARIO

**Palmyra-
Manchester
Area 1820–1830**

Scale in Miles

0   2   5

Lyons

ERIE CANAL

helps (Vienna)

s Corners

Waterloo

Cayuga

Geneva

Peter Whitmer
Farm

Lake Seneca

Lake Cayuga

Fayette

As the young seeker examined various denominations he became disillusioned, especially as he watched the intense competition for converts by the ministers. So contentious was this proselyting, he later wrote, that "great confusion and bad feeling ensued — priest contending against priest, and convert against convert; so that all their good feelings one for another, if they ever had any, were entirely lost in a strife of words and a contest about opinions." "I knew not who was right or who was wrong," he recalled in 1835, "but considered it of the first importance to me that I should be right."

At the same time, he began to suspect that perhaps none of the churches were right. Like so many others of his time who were seeking for the ancient truth, he observed that mankind "had apostatized from the true and living faith and there was no society or denomination that built upon the Gospel of Jesus Christ as recorded in the New Testament." His mind was soon drawn to James 1:5. "If any of you lack wisdom," he read, "let him ask of God, that giveth to all men liberally, and upbraideth not, and it shall be given him." He was ready for that message: "Never did any passage of scripture come with more power to the heart of man than this did at this time to mine. It seemed to enter with great force into every feeling of my heart. I reflected on it again and again, knowing that if any person needed wisdom from God, I did. . . . At length I came to the conclusion that I must either remain in darkness and confusion, or else I must do as James directs, that is, ask of God."

On a beautiful spring morning in 1820, Joseph went to a familiar spot in the woods near his home. At least three serious concerns were on his mind. Could he find forgiveness of sins and salvation for his soul? Secondly, what about the welfare of mankind? "I felt to mourn for my own sins and for the sins of the world," he later wrote. Finally, he longed to know which, if any, of the churches was right, and which he should join. For the first time in his life, he tried to utter a vocal prayer.

No one knows how long Joseph Smith remained alone in the woods, but before his objective was accomplished he experienced a desperate struggle. As he tried to pray, he said, "immediately I was seized by some power which entirely overcame me, and had such astonishing influence over me as to bind my tongue so that I could not speak." While he attempted to loose his tongue, several strange things happened. Distracting thoughts ran through his mind, threatening to keep him from his goal. At one point, he later recalled, "I heard a noise behind me like someone walking towards me. I strove again to pray, but could not; the noise of walking seemed to draw nearer. I sprang upon my feet and looked around, but saw no person, or thing." Presently "thick darkness" seemed to gather around him, and he felt that he was "doomed to sudden destruction" and must abandon himself to the power of "some actual being from the unseen world."

Despite his alarm, Joseph continued to pray inwardly for deliverance. It was then that he saw a pillar of light, which shone "above the brightness of the sun at noon day." It gradually descended until it enveloped him, and immediately he was freed from the invisible opposition. Within the light the astonished young man saw two persons who exactly resembled each other. They seemed to be standing above him in the air, the brightness of their presence defying all description. One of them called him by name, then pointed to the other and said, "This is My Beloved Son. Hear Him!"

As the solemn vision of the Father and the Son continued, Joseph received assurances concerning the religious questions that had perplexed him. "Joseph my son, thy sins are forgiven thee," he was told. He then began to gain a deeper understanding of the universal nature of salvation when the Savior testified in plainness that he had been crucified so that all those who believed in him might have eternal life.

Astounded at what was happening, Joseph nevertheless gained his composure enough to ask which of all the churches he should join. He was informed that all of them taught incorrect doctrines and none were acknowledged by God as his church. He was warned that certain professors of religion were "corrupt; that 'they draw near to me with their lips, but their hearts are far from me; they teach for doctrines the commandments of men: having a form of godliness, but they deny the power thereof.' " He was warned a second time against joining any of the existing churches, but received the firm assurance that "the fulness of the gospel should at some future time be made known" to him. He later confided to friends that he also saw "many angels" in his vision.

As the vision ended, Joseph again became aware of his environment. He found himself lying on his back looking skyward through the trees. Weak at first and unable to rise, he eventually regained enough strength to return home. His mother sensed that something was affecting him, but her first inquiries were met with, "Never mind, all is well—I am well enough off." Then he looked at her and said, "I have learned for myself that Presbyterianism is not true."

The heavenly vision had a profound effect upon young Joseph. His

Stained glass representation of Joseph Smith's First Vision, once located in the Adams Ward meetinghouse in Los Angeles, California, was one of the many fine artistic representations of this sacred event. (Church Archives)

An excerpt from Joseph Smith's 1832 account of the First Vision. This is the earliest known document in which the vision was recorded and the only one in the Prophet's own handwriting. (Church Archives)

mind, once agitated by uncertainty, was comforted, reassured by "a state of calmness and peace indescribable." In addition, he said, "my soul was filled with love, and for many days I could rejoice with great joy and the Lord was with me." In this spirit he began to relate his experience to selected friends and acquaintances, but he "could find none that would believe the heavenly vision." He was particularly disappointed with the reaction of a Methodist minister who had been active in the religious awakening around Palmyra. The preacher treated his story "not only lightly, but with great contempt, saying it was all of the devil, that there were no such things as visions or revelations in these days; that all such things had ceased with the apostles, and that there would never be any more of them."

It may seem strange that Joseph Smith should be so criticized when, in the intense revivalistic atmosphere of the time, many people claimed to have received personal spiritual manifestations, including visions; and their claims were often accepted by the ministers and populace alike as authentic results of their quest for forgiveness of sin and for personal salvation. But in addition to his report that he had seen both the Father and the Son, there was something else in Joseph Smith's story that the revivalist ministers did not like. The message that none of the churches were right, and that their creeds were an abomination in the sight of God, did not fall on friendly ears among those who were preaching the revivals and then contending with each other for converts.

The Sacred Grove, Palmyra, New York. (George E. Anderson photograph, Church Archives)

It was most likely this aspect of Joseph Smith's claims that became the catalyst for belittling his entire account.

Whatever the cause, the criticism became so intense that it seemed to young Joseph as though he were being attacked from every side. "Why persecute me for telling the truth?" he wondered. "Why does the world think to make me deny what I have actually seen? For I had seen a vision; I knew it, and I knew that God knew it, and I could not deny it, neither dared I do it; at least I knew that by so doing I would offend God, and come under condemnation." But his experience was deeply sacred, and perhaps because of this he finally decided it would be folly, even sacrilege, to keep on telling it publicly. Although he continued to share it privately with a few close associates, it was not until several years after the organization of the Church that he decided to prepare an account of the First Vision for publication, and then only to counteract the false and distorted reports that were circulating.

The Visit of Moroni

It was more than three years before Joseph experienced more spiritual manifestations. In the meantime, he grew up like other young men in western New York and was probably more fun-loving than many of his associates. In fact, he confessed later, "I was left to all kinds of temptation; and, mingling with all kinds of society, I frequently fell into many foolish errors, and displayed the weakness of youth, and the foibles of human nature; which, I am sorry to say, led me into divers temptations, offensive in the sight of God." This is not to say that he engaged in any gross misconduct. "I was guilty of levity," he explained, "and sometimes associated with jovial company, etc., not consistent with that character which ought to be maintained by one who was called of God as I had been. But this will not seem very strange to any one who recollects my youth, and is acquainted with my native cheery temperament." Lest anyone expected him to be more than human, never in his life did he claim perfection: rather, he recognized and, when he felt it appropriate, admitted his human failings.

On the night of September 21, 1823, Joseph Smith, now seventeen, retired to one of the sleeping rooms of the old log house. In bed he began to pray earnestly for forgiveness of his sins and follies and for further information on his standing before the Lord. Then, according to his own account, his room was filled with light, and appearing at his bedside, seemingly standing in the air, was a personage dressed in a brilliant white robe. Calling Joseph by name, the visitor announced that he was a messenger from the presence of God and that God had a work for the youth to do. The angel described an ancient record buried in a hillside not far from Joseph's home, a book giving an account of some of the early inhabitants of the American continent. The messenger, whose name was Moroni, was their last historian. He told Joseph that the book, written on "gold plates," contained the fulness of the gospel as it had been delivered by the resurrected Savior to these ancient people. With the record were "two stones in silver bows" which could be fastened to a breastplate. Called the Urim and Thummim, they were to be used in translating the book. The messenger told Joseph that when he obtained the plates, he should show them to no one. In vision he was shown where the plates were buried, and then the angel left as quickly as he had appeared.

As Joseph lay marveling at this experience, suddenly Moroni visited him again, repeating the same message. The messenger returned a third time, adding the caution that Satan would tempt him to use the plates to acquire wealth. He was admonished that the glory of God must be his only object in this work. Joseph had no sleep that night.

The next morning he went with his father to work in the fields as usual, but was so exhausted that Joseph, Sr., sent him home. Attempting to climb the fence at the edge of the field, the young man fainted. When he awoke he was again confronted by the angel Moroni, who repeated a fourth time the message of the night before and then instructed him to inform his father of the experience. He did so, and his father believed.

Joseph Smith, Sr., advised his son to follow Moroni's instructions, which he did. Proceeding immediately to the hill, he recognized the spot he had seen in vision. He soon located the plates, along with the breastplate and the Urim and Thummim, in a stone box buried in the hill. When he tried to take them, however, Moroni appeared again. He was not yet ready, he was told, and the angel chastised him for allowing thoughts of potential wealth to obsess him while traveling to the hill. As if to reiterate the awesomeness of his task, another vision was opened to his mind. First he saw the glory of the Lord resting upon him, and then the "Prince of Darkness" surrounded by his "innumerable train of associates." Moroni told the awestruck young man: "All this is shown, the good and the evil, and holy and impure, the glory of God and the power of darkness, that you may know hereafter the two powers and never be influenced or overcome by that wicked one." Joseph was then told that he must return to that spot each year for four years, where Moroni would meet him. He did so, and at each meeting, said Joseph, he received "instruction and intelligence . . . respecting what the Lord was going to do, and how and in what manner His kingdom was to be conducted in the last days." Finally, on September 22, 1827, Joseph was allowed to take the plates.

Four Important Years

Joseph Smith's activities between the ages of seventeen and twenty-one, when he removed the ancient record from the hill, are vague because of the dearth of authentic contemporary information. Yet this was a critical time in the life of the young prophet, as he developed from a teenage boy attracted to the wealth of the world into a young man who had overcome such desires and was entrusted with a sacred record.

Among other things, Moroni told young Joseph that both good and evil should be spoken of his name "among all people." Since then his detractors have emphasized every negative scrap of evidence, while others have countered with powerful evidence of his integrity and religious nature. From Joseph Smith's own viewpoint, he was not without fault, but was growing in his ability to live as God wished. While en route to Missouri just two years after the Book of Mormon was published, he wrote a tender letter to his wife. Recalling his earlier years, he poured out his soul:

> I have visited a grove which is Just back of the town almost every day where I can be Secluded from the eyes of any mortal and there give vent to all the feeling of my heart in meditation and prayer. I have Called to mind all the past moments of my life and am left to morn [and] shed tears of sorrow for my folly in Sufering the adversary of my Soul to have so much power over me as he has had in times past. But God is merciful and has forgiven my Sins and I rejoice that he Sendeth forth the Comforter unto as many as believe and humbleth themselves before him.[2]

This and other such heartfelt expressions from this early period confirm the genuineness of Joseph's religious conviction.

At first the religious activities of the Smith family remained unchanged by his experiences. Joseph, his father, and at least one brother, William, steadfastly refused to join any church. His mother and two brothers, Hyrum and Samuel, continued their membership in the Presbyterian church and evidently attended regularly until about 1828. On March 29, 1830, however, they were suspended for nonattendance, but that was only a week before they were to become members of the restored church.

In the meantime, the family struggled to get out of debt, pay off the mortgage, and complete their new home. The guiding hand in building the house was the oldest son, Alvin, but on November 19, 1823, he died of what his mother later described as an overdose of

---

[2]Joseph Smith to Emma Smith, June 6, 1832, as reproduced in *Brigham Young University Studies* 11 (Summer 1971): 519–20.

calomel to cure the "bilious colic." Almost his last thoughts were of the most important things in the Smith family life at the moment: the sacred record and the new home. "I want to say a few things which I wish to have you remember," he said to his brother Hyrum. "I have done all I could to make our dear parents comfortable. I want you to go on and finish the house." To Joseph he said, "I want you to . . . do everything that lies in your power to obtain the Record. Be faithful in receiving instruction, and in keeping every commandment that is given you."[3]

In the process of completing the house, the Smiths employed a carpenter by the name of Russell Stoddard, who apparently took a covetous liking to the commodious home. Unable to make their last payment on the property, the Smiths obtained an extension that would allow them to harvest their crops, get their wheat to the mill, and do other things to raise the money. When Joseph, Sr., and his son Joseph found work out of town, however, Stoddard and two neighbors used a legal technicality to accuse them of running away to avoid payment. On the basis of this false charge, the land agent gave Stoddard title to the property for the amount still owing. Friends of the Smiths heard of this deception, and Stoddard was soon forced to sell his title to a Mr. Durfee, the high sheriff of the county. Durfee then rented the home and farm back to the Smiths, but they never gained title to it.[4]

In the meantime, Joseph, Jr., continued to work with his father as well as hire out to other people. These included Joseph Knight, Sr., and Josiah Stowell (also spelled *Stoal*), both of whom lived nearly a hundred and fifty miles southeast of Palmyra. Knight lived in Colesville, Broome County, and operated several farms as well as carding machinery and a gristmill in the area, and he once said that young Joseph was "the best hand he ever hired."[5] Stowell, who lived in South Bainbridge (now Afton), Chenango County, ran several sawmills on the hundreds of acres of woodlots he owned in the area. He paid Joseph fourteen dollars a month plus room and board to work on the farm, and it was Joseph's work for Stowell that led him to one of his last money-digging experiences.

Sometime around 1822, before his first visit from the angel Moroni,

---

[3]Lucy Smith, *Biographical Sketches*, p. 88.
[4]The Calvin Stoddard who married Joseph's sister Sophronia in 1827 was a distant relative of Russell Stoddard, and in some histories he has been confused with the carpenter.
[5]As quoted in Bushman, *Joseph Smith and the Beginnings of Mormonism*, p. 69.

The Smith family home in Palmyra, New York, completed in the late 1820s, is maintained as a historic memorial by the Church. (Charles B. Hall engraving, Church Archives)

Joseph was digging a well with Willard Chase, not far from the Smith home, and he discovered a smooth, dark-colored stone, about the size of an egg, that he called a seerstone. He later used it to help in the translation of the Book of Mormon and also in receiving certain revelations.

Josiah Stowell, meanwhile, located what he believed to be the site of an ancient Spanish mine, where gold bars and many coins were reportedly buried. Late in 1825 he employed Joseph, Sr., and Joseph, Jr., along with some other men, to help him find the treasure. According to Lucy Smith, Stowell hired her son "on account of having heard that he possessed certain keys, by which he could discern things invisible to the natural eye."[6] Official articles of agreement were drawn up, and the Smiths were to share in the profits. All this happened during the crisis over the farm, which only enhanced the family's need for money and their willingness to work for Stowell. After less than a month, however, young Joseph saw that the enterprise was leading nowhere, and he persuaded Stowell to give it up. In mid-November he and his father returned home.

Such youthful experiments with treasure-seeking led to Joseph Smith's first experience with the law. Early in 1826 someone brought charges of disorderly conduct against him, and he was required to appear

---

[6]Lucy Smith, *Biographical Sketches*, pp. 91–92.

in court in Chenango County, New York. Because laws of the time defined actions by "persons pretending . . . to discover where lost goods may be found" as "disorderly," it is reasonable to conclude that the accusations involved money-seeking activities. According to one account, Joseph admitted that he had a stone through which he once looked for treasure and lost articles, but he said that he had since given up such activities and did not solicit this kind of work. Another account says that Joseph's father testified that "he and his son were mortified that this wonderful power which God had so miraculously given . . . should be used only in search of filthy lucre," and he expressed his belief that one day young Joseph would know more clearly the will of God concerning him. Joseph was acquitted of the charge.

Perhaps all this was part of Joseph Smith's maturing process as he gradually transcended his youthful involvement with treasure hunters and became more spiritually prepared to understand his own God-given destiny and to be entrusted with the sacred records denied him three years earlier.

These years also provided other important experiences for Joseph Smith. In 1826 he was back in southern New York, where he worked for both Stowell and Knight, and also attended school. In addition, he made some lifelong friends. Mr. Stowell himself testified in favor of Joseph at the 1826 trial and remained a friend and supporter. Joseph also became fast friends with Joseph Knight, Jr., and he told the Knight family of the visits of Moroni and of the sacred record. This association would eventually lead members of the Knight family, at great sacrifice, to follow Joseph from New York to Ohio, Missouri, and Illinois, and later to follow Brigham Young to Utah.

Joseph Smith also found romance that year. While working for Stowell, he boarded with the family of Isaac Hale, a locally famous hunter. There he met and began to court the gracious Emma Hale. Courtship was not easy, for Emma's parents had heard and believed the negative stories about the young prophet, and they refused to give their consent to the marriage. At twenty-two, however, she was of age and could legally marry without their permission. Seeing no other alternative, Joseph and Emma eloped and were married by a justice of the peace on January 18, 1827. Emma's father was later reconciled to Joseph and became a friend of the Church.

At length the time came for Joseph to receive the sacred plates from which he would translate the Book of Mormon. Immediately after his marriage he quit working for Josiah Stowell and took his wife to his father's home, where he helped with the farming. On September 20, 1827, Stowell and Joseph Knight, Sr., came to visit with the Smiths. During the early morning hours of September 22, Joseph borrowed Mr. Knight's horse and wagon and, taking Emma with him, drove to the Hill Cumorah. There he met Moroni again, and this time obtained the ancient plates. The angel also gave him a charge and warning. It was, Joseph wrote, "that I should be responsible for them; that if I should let them go carelessly, or through any neglect of mine, I should be cut off; but that if I would use all my endeavors to preserve them until he, the messenger, should call for them, they should be protected."[7] He would soon have cause to remember that warning.

The Sacred Records

Joseph Smith said that the ancient records

> were engraven on plates which had the appearance of gold, each plate was six inches wide and eight inches long, and not quite so thick as common tin. They were filled with engravings, in Egyptian characters, and bound together in a volume as the leaves of a book, with three rings running through the whole. The volume was something near six inches in thickness, a part of which was sealed. The characters on the unsealed part were small, and beautifully engraved. The whole book exhibited many marks of antiquity in its construction, and much skill in the art of engraving.[8]

Joseph Smith also described two stones, called the Urim and Thummim, which were deposited with the plates, but all he said about them was that they were "transparent stones set in the rim of a bow fastened to a breastplate." He implied that the "bow" was something like the rims of spectacles, which attached to a metal breastplate so that the person using it could concentrate and retain free use of his hands. Biblical writers also referred to an instrument called the Urim and Thummim, which somewhat resembled that described by Joseph Smith. Its precise use is not fully clear, but it is interesting that while the Israelites were wandering between Egypt and Palestine, the priestly

---

[7]*History of the Church*, 1:18.
[8]*History of the Church*, 4:537. There has been much speculation on how much such a book would weigh, for if it were pure gold it would be much too heavy for anyone to carry. The implication within the book, however, was that the metal was an alloy, hence Joseph's statement that it had the *appearance* of gold. It was not uncommon for ancient people to keep records on plates made of various metals.

Joseph Smith translated the Book of Mormon in various settings over a two-year period. Oliver Cowdery acted as scribe for a major portion of the work, shown here in an upstairs room at the Whitmer cabin at Fayette. (Oil painting by Earl Jones, courtesy LDS Church)

Levites wore as part of their sacred clothing a breastplate, or pouch, into which they were told to place the Urim and Thummim. It was apparently believed that this instrument would somehow assist them in receiving divine communications. When Moses consecrated his brother Aaron, he placed a breastplate on him and in it placed the Urim and Thummim. Aaron apparently used them to help receive inspiration in his role as a judge.

Joseph Smith left no firsthand description of how he used the Urim and Thummim in translation. Various associates left sometimes contradictory descriptions of the process, but Joseph Smith's simply states, "Through the medium of the Urim and Thummim I translated the record by the gift and power of God."[9] He also reported that he received several early revelations after inquiring of the Lord through the Urim and Thummim.

Because Joseph Smith obviously did not know the "reformed Egyp-

---

[9]*History of the Church*, 4:537.

tian" language in which the Book of Mormon was written, translation, with the aid of the Urim and Thummim, was a revelatory process. One key that clarifies how this worked came by revelation in April 1829. Oliver Cowdery had expressed a desire to translate, but after he was unable to do so, the Lord explained through Joseph Smith:

> Behold, you have not understood; you have supposed that I would give it unto you, when you took no thought save it was to ask me.
>
> But, behold, I say unto you that you, must study it out in your mind; then you must ask me if it be right, and if it is right I will cause that your bosom shall burn within you; therefore, you shall feel that it is right.
>
> But if it be not right you shall have no such feelings, but you shall have a stupor of thought that shall cause you to forget the thing which is wrong; therefore, you cannot write that which is sacred save it be given you from me. (D&C 9:7–9.)

This revelation clearly suggests that the translation process was not one in which words miraculously appeared, or a literal translation was placed in Joseph's mind. Rather, he was forced to concentrate deeply, attempting to determine the meaning for himself, and once he had the idea correct, he would know by divine confirmation that he was right. It must also be remembered that good translations are never literal, for words express ideas, and differing grammatical structures make it impossible to translate verbatim from one language to another. The finest translations convey the spirit and meaning of the material in the best possible form of the new language. They also carry the marks of the translator himself, who inevitably uses certain idioms and expressions characteristic of his training and background. For the faithful Latter-day Saint, this explains why the English version of the Book of Mormon carries unmistakable marks of the language of Joseph Smith's time, and why grammatical problems were not uncommon, especially in the first edition.

Briefly, the Book of Mormon gives an account of three groups of people who migrated to the American continent in ancient times. It focuses primarily on the family of Lehi, who left Jerusalem about 600 B.C. His descendants split into two groups, called Nephites and Lamanites, and the book traces their constant conflicts as well as the religion taught by their prophets. It also tells of the visit by the resurrected Christ to these ancient Americans, who were identified as some of the other sheep to which he alluded when he told his disciples in Palestine: "And other sheep I have, which are not of this fold: them also must I bring, and they shall hear my voice." (John 10:16; cf. 3 Nephi 15:16–17.) Within two hundred years after this visit, however, corruption and conflict again prevailed, and eventually the Lamanites completely overwhelmed and destroyed the Nephite people. Mormon was one of their last historians, and it was he who collected and abridged all available records. His son Moroni finished the work and buried the record in a hill, where it would rest until it came forth in the last days. Its primary purpose, as stated in the book's preface, was not just to tell the history of these people, but to be another witness of the divinity of Christ—"to the convincing of the Jew and Gentile that Jesus is the Christ, the Eternal God, manifesting himself unto all nations."

The Latter-day Work Begins

Joseph Smith's neighbors had mixed reactions to his claims, but some believed he actually possessed plates of gold. Rumors flew quickly, and it is not surprising that, in this area already saturated with stories of buried wealth, almost immediately various schemes were devised to get the plates from him. Some who had been associated with him in his early treasure-seeking were especially eager but, unfortunately, they thought of the plates only as a source of potential wealth. Constantly on his guard, Joseph changed the hiding place several times, on some occasions just barely before the arrival of a mob.

Some of those who hoped to steal the plates sought the help of a local clairvoyant, Sally Chase, who claimed that by peering into her personal peepstone she could tell where "Joe Smith kept his gold bible hid." She and her brother Willard were probably still involved in unsuccessful treasure-hunting ventures and, according to Joseph's mother, Willard was a "Methodist class-leader" at the time he led at least one group in search of the precious plates.

The Prophet despaired of proceeding with the translation while in such constant danger of losing the sacred record. He and Emma decided to move to Harmony, Pennsylvania, to live with her father, but they had no money to make the move. It was at that point that Martin Harris, a prosperous farmer in the area, unexpectedly gave them fifty dollars to help out. Harris had been acquainted with the Smiths for some time, had confidence in Joseph, and believed the account of the plates.

In Harmony, Joseph copied some of the characters from the plates and translated them. Martin Harris had previously agreed to take such a transcription to learned people in the East. Accordingly, he arrived in Harmony sometime in February 1828, then proceeded to New York City with the transcript in his pocket.

According to Martin Harris's own account, he first called on Dr. Charles Anthon, a professor of classical studies at Columbia College. A prolific scholar, Anthon produced at least one book a year for over thirty years and had a profound influence on the study of the classics in the United States. Harris also visited a certain "Dr. Mitchell," probably Samuel L. Mitchill, M.D., of New York City. Both scholars acknowledged that the translation of the characters seemed correct. The question arises, of course, as to whether either of them was qualified to make such a statement, since the Book of Mormon text was written in a language identified as "reformed Egyptian." They may have recognized the characters' resemblance to Egyptian or other ancient languages, but they probably could not verify the translation. In later years Professor Anthon denied having said the translation was correct, but whatever happened immediately swept away any doubts Harris may have had and, he said, Anthon signed a paper verifying the authenticity of the characters as well as the correctness of the translation. When he asked how Joseph Smith got the gold plates and Harris told him about the angel, however, Anthon said there was no such thing as ministering angels and tore up the certificate. He told Harris to bring the plates to him to translate, but when Harris said that part of the record was sealed, he replied, "I cannot read a sealed book."

The consequences of this journey for Martin Harris were momentous. At this time he was a well-respected farmer, trusted by Palmyra residents for his integrity. When he returned from New York City he was so certain of the authenticity of the Book of Mormon that he subsequently worked full-time to help in the translation, despite constant nagging from his unbelieving wife. He eventually lost the support of his wife, sold his farm to raise the money to publish the book, and generally subjected himself to public ridicule. But he also became honored in Church history as one of three chosen witnesses of the gold plates.

Martin Harris played another role in the story of the Book of Mormon. After his return from New York City he went back to Harmony to serve as a scribe for Joseph Smith. For two months he wrote as Joseph translated, and by June 14 he had recorded 116 pages of manuscript. Then the influence of Harris's nagging wife threatened the work they had so carefully put together. Mrs. Harris would apparently do anything to discredit Joseph Smith. In an effort to convince her that what he was doing was good and right, Harris repeatedly pressured Joseph to allow him to show her the manuscript. Twice the Prophet inquired of the Lord, and twice he received a negative answer. Finally, Joseph said the Lord had relented, and he loaned the manuscript to Harris on condition that he show it only to five specified individuals. But the harassed disciple did not restrain himself and soon began exhibiting it to almost every visitor. Whether his wife conspired to steal it is not certain, but the manuscript disappeared and was never recovered. Harris was crushed — so much so that he was afraid even to return to Harmony.

In the meantime Emma gave birth to a son who soon died, and Emma herself lay close to death for several weeks. This sorrow, together with the prolonged absence of Martin Harris, weighed heavily on Joseph. He finally traveled to Palmyra, where Harris reluctantly told him what had happened. Shocked, disillusioned, and feeling condemned for his own negligence, Joseph returned to Harmony. There he received a revelation that once again reminded him of his weaknesses, and chastened him for being careless with sacred things. He temporarily lost the power to translate, and the plates as well as the Urim and Thummim were taken from him.

This became another period of anguish, soul-searching, and repentance for Joseph. In a short time the plates and the Urim and Thummim were restored to him. He did not begin to retranslate the lost material but, instead, continued from where he had previously left off. In the summer of 1828 he received a revelation explaining that these recent events were part of a plan to thwart the designs of those who had stolen the manuscript. The thieves, according to the revelation, had altered the manuscript in a plot to destroy Joseph and his work. If he came out with another translation, they would produce the modified original, thereby demonstrating that Joseph did not really have the power to translate and was a fraud. He was told, therefore, that he was not to translate the same records twice. The plates in his possession contained two accounts of the lost material. One was Mormon's abridgment (from which Joseph had been translating), and the other was an original record written by Nephi and containing a "more particular" account of the religious teachings of Nephi and his people that shed greater light on the gospel. Joseph was to start over, but this time, instead of retranslating the lost material, Joseph was to translate from Nephi's account, until he came to the place where he and Martin Harris had stopped.

In the published Book of Mormon, then, all the material to and including the book of Omni (approximately the first one-fourth of the volume) is translated from the "plates of Nephi," and the balance is continued from Mormon's abridged history, plus the writings of Mormon himself and his son, Moroni. The translation from the plates of Nephi was apparently completed only after the rest of the book was finished.

The work of translation proceeded only intermittently during the fall and winter of 1828–29, with Emma acting as a scribe. In the meantime, a young man named Oliver Cowdery began teaching school in Palmyra and boarded with Joseph's parents. From David Whitmer, whom he met in Palmyra, he learned of Joseph's work, though Joseph's parents, reluctant to confide in someone who was still a stranger, hesitated to give much further information. He prayed earnestly for understanding, however, and after receiving his own witness that Joseph's work was divinely inspired, insisted on going to Harmony as soon as the school term closed. He arrived on April 5, in the company of Joseph's younger brother Samuel. Joseph Smith immediately recognized a godsend in Oliver Cowdery, and two days later the new arrival began working as his scribe. It was he who recorded the major portion of the Book of Mormon as the Prophet dictated.

These were days of tremendous spiritual growth and satisfaction for Joseph Smith. In the year following the loss of the first manuscript, he received fourteen of his recorded revelations, foreshadowing such important events as the appointment of three witnesses to view the Book of Mormon plates, the organization of the Church, the appointment of the Twelve Apostles, and the spread of missionary work. But the most memorable experience came on May 15, 1829, when Joseph and Oliver came upon a passage dealing with the ordinance of baptism. Immediately the question that had been asked repeatedly by other seekers came into their minds: Who had the authority to administer this saving ordinance? The two young men decided they must pray about such an important question, and they retired to a secluded spot in the woods on the banks of the Susquehanna River. Suddenly, as they prayed, they were visited by a heavenly messenger who announced that he was John the Baptist, sent to confer upon them the Aaronic Priesthood. Thus came another all-important step in the restoration of the ancient order of things, for as the heavenly messenger laid his hands upon their heads, he conferred upon them the same authority to baptize, as well as to administer other ordinances, that he had possessed in the days of Christ. As this was the lesser priesthood, it did not carry the power to confer the gift of the Holy Ghost by the laying on of hands. The angel commanded Joseph and Oliver to baptize each other, which they did in the Susquehanna River; then they ordained each other again to the Aaronic Priesthood.

John the Baptist told Joseph and Oliver that he was acting under the direction of Peter, James, and John, the ancient apostles who would later restore to them the higher, or Melchizedek, priesthood, which would give them authority to confer the gift of the Holy Ghost as well as administer in all the spiritual affairs of the kingdom of God. The date of their appearance is uncertain, but, as indicated in a subsequent revelation to Joseph Smith, sometime later they ordained and confirmed Joseph and Oliver as "apostles, and especial witnesses of my name, and bear the keys of your ministry and of the same things which I revealed unto them." (D&C 27:12.)

The importance of Joseph Smith and Oliver Cowdery's proclaiming the visits of John the Baptist and Peter, James, and John cannot be minimized in understanding the rapid rise of Mormonism in the 1830s. Joseph and Oliver declared not only that they were in the midst of restoring Christ's ancient church, but that they had received direct, divine authority to do so. Many restorationists had earlier raised the question of authority, and some, like Charles G. Finney, had solved the problem by receiving spiritual manifestations they believed were calls to preach. But none proclaimed so forcefully that they had received a personal visitation from one with divine authority who personally bestowed it upon them. For many seekers of the day, the claim of divine authority was a major attraction of Mormonism, and they were prepared both to test a prophet who made that claim and to follow him if they were convinced the claim was true.

Completion of the Book of Mormon, 1829–30

During the month of May 1829, Joseph and Oliver remained at Harmony steadily translating and writing. Other believers helped them in the process. Joseph Knight supplied them with provisions, and Isaac Hale protected them from antagonists who threatened violence. But they needed more peaceful surroundings and Oliver, possibly at the request of Joseph, wrote his friend David Whitmer asking if they might move to his father's home in Fayette, New York. Whitmer had received a testimony of the sacred work and soon arrived with a wagon to take them to Fayette, where the translation was completed.

The Three Witnesses to the Book of Mormon. (Charles B. Hall engraving, Church Archives)

Pressure continued on Joseph Smith to allow others to see the plates, and in the Book of Mormon he and Oliver found several passages indicating that certain witnesses would be allowed that privilege. (See 2 Nephi 11:3; 27:12; Ether 5:2–4.) Accordingly, on one memorable morning Martin Harris, Oliver Cowdery, and David Whitmer knelt with Joseph Smith in fervent prayer in the woods near Fayette, seeking a view of the plates. After each of the four had prayed twice with no result, Martin Harris, feeling that somehow he was to blame, withdrew from the others, who then knelt again and resumed their prayers. After a few minutes they saw "a light above us in the air, of exceeding brightness," and an angel standing before them. He had in his hands the sacred plates, and he turned the leaves one by one for them to see. "These plates have been revealed by the power of God," they heard a voice from out of the light saying, "and they have been translated by the power of God. The translation of them which you have seen is correct, and I command you to bear record of what you now see and hear." Joseph then went looking for Harris and, after more prayer, the two of them witnessed the same vision. " 'Tis enough; 'tis enough," shouted the elated Harris, "mine eyes have beheld."

Suddenly the faith of the three new witnesses was replaced with a dramatic certainty, but the experience also had a profound effect on Joseph Smith. Immediately he felt as if a huge burden had been lifted

The "Smith Press" owned by E. B. Grandin, on which the first edition of the Book of Mormon was printed, is shown here in a museum setting suggesting Grandin's shop. (Museum of Church History and Art)

from his shoulders. "They will have to bear witness to the truth of what I have said," he told his mother, "for they know of themselves. . . . I feel as if I was relieved of a burden which was almost too heavy for me to bear, and it rejoices my soul, that I am not any longer to be entirely alone in the world." Later Joseph was allowed to himself show the plates to eight other friends and family members: Christian Whitmer, Jacob Whitmer, Peter Whitmer, Jr., John Whitmer, Hiram Page, Joseph Smith, Sr., Hyrum Smith, and Samuel H. Smith. The signed testimonies of all eleven witnesses, which corroboration they never rescinded, are printed with the Book of Mormon.

In the meantime, Joseph secured the copyright on June 11, 1829, and began trying to make arrangements for publishing the book. He first went to Egbert B. Grandin, a Palmyra publisher, who initially refused the job, partly for religious reasons and partly because he doubted the economic feasibility of the project. Joseph tried other publishers, but Grandin was finally persuaded by friends that he could accept the job strictly as a commercial venture, with no implication of religious involvement. Martin Harris agreed to pay Grandin $3,000 for the work, and, much to the dismay of his wife, mortgaged his farm as security.

Joseph, meanwhile, returned to his farm in Harmony, leaving Oliver, Martin, and the Smith family to supervise the printing. Even this task, however, was beset with unforeseen problems. In September 1829, Abner Cole, under the pseudonym Obediah Dogberry, began a newspaper in Palmyra called the *Reflector*. He printed it on Sunday, using E. B. Grandin's press. After publishing several derogatory remarks about the forthcoming "Gold Bible," he announced that in January he would begin to print extracts from it. Because he was using Grandin's office, Cole had found access, albeit unauthorized, to the printer's manuscript, and some excerpts did appear in print. Hyrum Smith and Oliver Cowdery could not persuade him to desist, and finally Joseph, Sr., went to Harmony and brought Joseph, Jr., back with him. Even he could not persuade the belligerent Cole to cease, and only after the matter was submitted to arbitration was Cole obliged to stop violating the copyright.

But that was not the end of publication difficulties. A few residents of Palmyra were determined to block the project. They persuaded Grandin that he would never be paid if he proceeded with the printing. They threatened to boycott the book, and noted that without local sales the Smiths could hardly raise the money to pay their debt. Grandin stopped work, and only after Martin Harris convinced him that he would, indeed, be paid for his services did he resume printing the first edition of 5,000 copies. On March 26, 1830, a newspaper advertisement announced publication of the Book of Mormon. It was not a commercial success, however, and a year later Martin Harris, true to his word, sold his mortgaged farm and paid the $3,000.

The Restored Church

Joseph and Oliver, meanwhile, prayed anxiously for the fulfillment of the other promises they had received. Sometime during this period, said Joseph in his *History*, "we got together in the chamber of Mr. Whitmer's house, in order more particularly to seek of the Lord what we now so earnestly desired; and here, to our unspeakable satisfaction, did we realize the truth of the Savior's promise — 'Ask, and it shall be given you; seek, and ye shall find; knock, and it shall be opened unto you.'" They had been praying for only a short time when the word of the Lord came, commanding Joseph and Oliver to ordain each other elders in the Church of Jesus Christ, then to ordain others as directed from time to time. They were told ordinations should wait until those who had been or would be baptized could assemble to accept by vote Joseph and Oliver as their spiritual teachers. Among other revelations

A small log home on the Peter Whitmer farm was the setting for the organizational meeting of the Church on April 6, 1830. This reconstruction on the site was dedicated in 1980. (LDS Church)

of this period was one that designated the precise date on which the Church should be organized. (See D&C 20:1.)

On April 6, 1830, at least thirty believers met together in the log home of Peter Whitmer, Sr., in Fayette, New York. Some had already been baptized, and six of those present were officially listed as organizing members. After an opening prayer Joseph asked the members of the group if they would accept him and Oliver Cowdery as their teachers, and they consented by unanimous vote. Joseph then ordained Oliver Cowdery an elder of the Church, and Oliver ordained Joseph, after which the two leaders administered the sacrament of the Lord's supper by blessing and serving the sacramental emblems of bread and wine. Through the laying on of hands, they conferred the gift of the Holy Ghost on the new members and confirmed them members of the Church. Everyone in the little congregation seemed filled with the spirit, as some prophesied and "all praised the Lord, and rejoiced exceedingly." A new revelation (D&C 21) was given, other men were ordained to various priesthood offices, and after the meeting some people who had not been baptized came forward and asked to join the Church. That evening several people, including Joseph Smith's parents and Martin Harris, were baptized in a small stream nearby. So far as Joseph Smith was concerned, seeing his father and Martin baptized was one of the great joys of his life, and he was so overcome that he went out into the woods alone and sobbed. "He was the most wrot upon that I ever saw any man," Joseph Knight later recalled. "His joy seemed to be full."[10]

The newly organized group called itself the Church of Christ, and until 1834 members used either that name or the Church of Jesus Christ. The use of the term *Saints* came gradually, but as early as August 1831 Church members were referred to as Saints in a revelation. Nonmembers began to use the terms *Mormon* or *Mormonite* to designate the followers of Joseph Smith, sometimes in derision. On May 3, 1834, a conference of the Church in Kirtland, Ohio, accepted a resolution proclaiming that thereafter the Church would be known as The Church of the Latter-day Saints. Finally, on April 26, 1838, a revelation designated the name as The Church of Jesus Christ of Latter-day Saints. This has been the official title ever since.

The next few months were busy, hectic ones for Joseph and the infant church. In effect, even though the revivalism of the time had been a catalyst in their various religious quests, the Saints had rejected the kind of revivalistic pluralism that made converts feel it was all right to join just any church. Revival leaders preached the importance of being converted and coming to Christ but, even though they contended bitterly for people to join their own congregations, the specific church one joined was actually of little consequence so far as their understanding of salvation was concerned. The Latter-day Saints, on the other hand, taught that salvation could come only through the Church of Jesus Christ, for it was the only church with direct authority to baptize and administer other ordinances in the name of Christ. That authority had been restored through heavenly messengers, and thus constituted one of the essentials of the restoration of all things. The Saints also taught that the Millennium was close at hand, and that even church-going New Yorkers would suffer if they were not a part of the restored kingdom. "But those who harden their hearts in unbelief, and reject it," one of the revelations received by the Prophet said, "it shall turn to their own condemnation." (D&C 20:15.) This exclusive concept of salvation meant everything to the Saints, but it also led to ridicule, bitterness, and even violence from their neighbors. Twice during the summer of 1830 Joseph Smith was arrested and tried on charges of disorderly conduct. Numerous witnesses testified, but nothing sub-

---

[10]From Joseph Knight's "Manuscript of the Early History of Joseph Smith," as reproduced in Dean C. Jessee, "Joseph Knight's Recollection of Early Mormon History," *Brigham Young University Studies* 17 (Autumn 1976): 37.

stantial could be proven, and in both cases the Prophet was acquitted. In the meantime, persecution served only to further unify the believers.

The Church, meanwhile, began to grow. On Sunday, April 11, at the Whitmer home, Oliver Cowdery preached the first public discourse by a member of the Church, and on that day and the following Sunday he baptized thirteen people. Small pockets of Saints sprang up in various towns in western New York, including Colesville. There the Knight family provided the nucleus. On June 9 the first conference of the Church was held in Fayette, with thirty members and several prospective converts. Joseph Smith later expressed his ecstasy in the following words:

> To find ourselves engaged in the very same order of things as observed by the prophets of old; to realize the importance and solemnity of such proceedings; and to witness and feel with our own natural senses, the like glorious manifestations of the powers of the Priesthood, the gifts and blessings of the Holy Ghost, and the goodness and condescension of a merciful God unto such as obey the everlasting Gospel of our Lord Jesus Christ, combined to create within us sensations of rapturous gratitude, and inspire us with fresh zeal and energy in the cause of truth.[11]

The followers of Joseph Smith soon launched an energetic missionary effort. Every convert considered himself a missionary and was fired with a zeal to tell friends and neighbors. "Therefore, if ye have desires to serve God ye are called to the work," Joseph's father had been told by revelation as early as February 1829. "For behold the field is white already to harvest; and lo, he that thrusteth in his sickle with his might, the same layeth up in store that he perisheth not, but bringeth salvation to his soul." (D&C 4:3–4.) Within two months of the organization of the Church, missionary calls were formalized. Samuel Smith, brother of the Prophet, became the first missionary. He came home saddened by his lack of immediate success, but he had left copies of the Book of Mormon wherever possible. One of them eventually found its way into the hands of several people who subsequently joined the Church, including a carpenter named Brigham Young. In northern New York, Joseph Smith, Sr., and his youngest son, Don Carlos, described the restoration to their family, and most of the Prophet's uncles and aunts, as well as his grandfather, Asael, believed.

---

[11]*History of the Church,* 1:85–86.

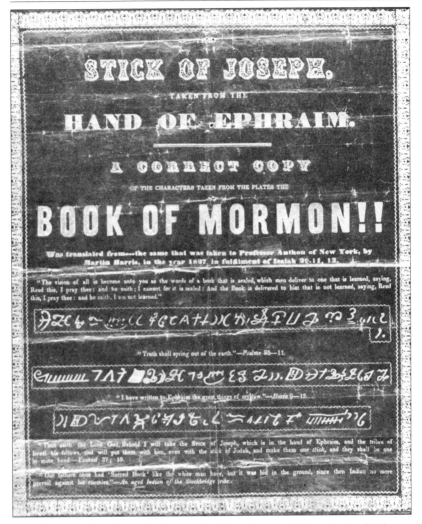

Broadside used in the early days of the Church to publicize the Book of Mormon reproduces the characters Joseph Smith copied from the plates. The broadside was printed in gold letters on black paper. (Church Archives)

These months also saw the foundation laid for various Church publications. Emma Smith was told by revelation to compile a hymn-book. She completed the work and finally published it in Kirtland in 1835.

Even in this early period, the Church did not escape misunderstanding and disagreement from within, and in the summer of 1830 Joseph had his first frustrating experience attempting to keep harmony among the faithful. The result, however, was a strengthening of his position as Prophet and undisputed leader. Oliver Cowdery challenged the use of certain words in a revelation, and in a letter from Fayette commanded Joseph to erase them. Disappointed and uneasy at such a challenge, the Prophet hastened to Fayette and found not only Cowdery but the entire Whitmer family rejecting his phrasing. With "labor and perseverance," he reported, he was able finally to persuade them that his wording harmonized with the scriptures, and thus he fortified his position as the only one authorized to receive divine revelations for the Church as a whole. Later Hiram Page, one of the eight witnesses, claimed to receive revelations for the Church through the use of a seerstone. Some Church members, including Oliver Cowdery and some of the Whitmers, believed him. Another revelation quickly set the matter to rest. Directed to Oliver Cowdery, it read, in part:

> Verily, verily, I say unto thee, no one shall be appointed to receive commandments and revelations in this church excepting my servant Joseph Smith, Jun. . . .
> And if thou art led at any time by the Comforter to speak or teach, or at all times by the way of commandment unto the church, thou mayest do it. But thou shalt not write by way of commandment, but by wisdom;
> And thou shalt not command him who is at thy head, and at the head of the church. (D&C 28:2, 4–6.)

It was clear that only one individual could receive revelation for the entire Church, but, unfortunately, even such clarity did not keep the problem from recurring.

Seekers Find Salvation

Even before the organization of the Church, Joseph and others recognized that they were experiencing the beginning of the restoration of all things. In March 1829, for example, a revelation had proclaimed that this was "the beginning of the rising up and the coming forth of my church out of the wilderness—clear as the moon, and fair as the sun, and terrible as an army with banners." (D&C 5:14.) The soldiers of the restored Christian army were to put on the whole armor of God, that they might be able to "withstand the evil day, having done all," and no revelation could more effectively fire their zeal than the one which urged them all to

> Stand, therefore, having your loins girt about with truth, having

on the breastplate of righteousness, and your feet shod with the preparation of the gospel of peace, which I have sent mine angels to commit unto you;

Taking the shield of faith wherewith ye shall be able to quench all the fiery darts of the wicked;

And take the helmet of salvation, and the sword of my Spirit, which I will pour out upon you, and my word which I reveal unto you, and be agreed as touching all things whatsoever ye ask of me, and be faithful until I come, and ye shall be caught up, that where I am ye shall be also. Amen. (D&C 27:15–18.)

And so the little army marched forth, small in number but, like Daniel of old, high in expectation.

Whom could they persuade to join their ranks? New Englanders with Puritan backgrounds might find a familiar note in such sentiments as "ye are called to bring to pass the gathering of mine elect; for mine elect hear my voice and harden not their hearts." (D&C 29:7.) Or perhaps the Mormon message would appeal to the Universalist, who insisted upon a rational faith, rejected the pessimistic doctrines of limited atonement and eternal damnation, and believed that man was largely responsible for working out his own salvation. How much more reasonable to him would be the revelation which explained that there was no such thing as endless punishment, for the term *endless punishment* merely meant God's punishment, since Endless was his name. (D&C 19:7–12.) Or perhaps it would appeal to the seeker who rejected all churches or went from church to church seeking a restoration of the ancient gospel.

Some of the new members, coming from such backgrounds, were also friends of Joseph, and closely associated with events preceding the organization of the Church. In Fayette, New York, Peter Whitmer, Sr., and his wife, Mary Mussselman Whitmer, were baptized on April 11. Mary and her family had been members of the German Reformed Church. Also baptized that day were Christian and Anne Schott Whitmer, Jacob and Elizabeth Schott (sister to Anne) Whitmer, Hiram and Katharine Whitmer Page, and Elizabeth Anne Whitmer — an example of the way the restored gospel often attracted entire families. Newel Knight, a youthful friend of Joseph's, had long been convinced that there had been an apostasy and that a restoration of the ancient gospel was needed. He attended the Church's early meetings, had numerous long and prayerful discussions with Joseph, and in April became the recipient of the first miracle done in the Church when, in the name of

Jesus Christ, the Prophet cast an evil spirit from him. Newel finally accepted the message of the restoration and was baptized in May by David Whitmer. In June, Joseph Smith, Oliver Cowdery, and John and David Whitmer went to Colesville, where Oliver baptized several people, including Joseph's wife, Emma, as well as Joseph Knight, Sr., and his wife, Polly Peck Knight, Newel's parents. Joseph Knight had previously accepted the doctrines of the Universalists, though he refused to join any religious group until this time. Polly's brother, Hezekiah, and his wife, Martha Long Peck, were also baptized that day, all amid the jeers of an abusive mob that lined the banks of a stream the Mormons had dammed up for the occasion. Also baptized about that time was Emily Coburn, a sister of Newel Knight's wife, Sally. The sisters had been Presbyterians, and Emily's pastor had put intense pressure on her ever since he realized she was beginning to believe the Mormons.

There were other new converts who had never known Joseph or his associates. At age eighteen Parley Parker Pratt had joined the Baptists, despite the feeling that he had not found the church of Christ. Four years later he heard Sidney Rigdon and was impressed that Rigdon and the Disciples of Christ were preaching the ancient gospel as it should be. He still wondered about their authority to administer the sacred ordinances, but he joined the movement anyway. In 1830, at age twenty-three, he was prompted to forsake his little frontier home in Ohio and travel east to preach as the Spirit directed. Not far from Newark, New York, he came upon the Book of Mormon, read it, and was so overwhelmed that he interrupted his mission to go to Palmyra seeking Joseph Smith. The Prophet was in Pennsylvania, but Pratt was up all night conversing with Hyrum Smith. Soon he became convinced that Mormonism was what he had been looking for—the ancient gospel restored, complete with proper authority. He interrupted his mission again to return to Palmyra where, about September 1, he was baptized by Oliver Cowdery. The next day he was ordained an elder of the Church and soon continued on his mission, a new and zealous recruit in the tiny Mormon band. Parley Pratt's younger brother, Orson, had been told by his father to use caution in accepting any denomination, and had refused to unite with any. When his brother brought news of the restoration of the ancient church, however, Orson also joined.

Such people were typical of the Mormon converts while the Church was yet in New York.

Looking Westward

Americans, meanwhile, were moving westward, as national prosperity, liberalized federal land laws, and beckoning economic opportunity pulled them to the maturing frontier. The tide of western migrants swelled enormously between 1815 and 1819, ebbed for a while as a result of the depression of 1819, then, in the late 1820s and 1830s, became a deluge. Ohio had become a state in 1803, and within two decades it boasted 600,000 residents. By then there were also six more new states west of the Appalachian Mountains: Louisiana (1812), Indiana (1816), Mississippi (1817), Illinois (1818), Alabama (1819), and Missouri (1821). The 1820s and 1830s saw a burst of road and canal building, often with the encouragement and help of states as well as the national government. Improved transportation routes not only hastened the westward flow but also linked East and West together economically.

Western growth was not without its complications, however, and in some ways what was happening in and near Missouri represented certain national problems that would soon affect the growth and progress of the Church. For one thing, the ever-present issue of slavery loomed ominously as a threat to the union of the American states, and the admission of Missouri seemed to serve as a portent of coming problems. When it appeared that Missouri was ready for statehood, both southern slaveholders and northern anti-slavery forces launched colonization drives to assure that the new state would adopt a constitution to their particular liking. Slavery won out, but Missouri was finally admitted to the union only after being paired with Maine, a non-slave state, in order to maintain a political balance in Congress. In addition, in what was really the most far-reaching provision of the famous Missouri Compromise of 1820, Congress defined an east-west line across the rest of the Louisiana Purchase, north of which slavery would be forever prohibited and south of which it would be protected. The aging Thomas Jefferson looked at all this with dismay. "Like a firebell in the night," he said, the Missouri issue filled him with horror, and he foresaw that it would eventually lead to disastrous consequences. "I considered it at once the knell of the Union," he wrote. "It is hushed, indeed, for the moment. But this is a reprieve only, not a final sentence."[12]

---

[12]Thomas Jefferson to John Holmes, 22 April 1820, as quoted in Dumas Malone, *The Sage of Monticello* (Boston: Little, Brown, 1981), p. 337.

The emotion-laden issue of slavery, which the Missouri compromise settled only temporarily, continued to plague the nation. By the time the Saints reached Missouri, the pro-slavery settlers looked at them, as well as other immigrating northerners, with great suspicion and deep mistrust. This, then, became one of many issues that created an atmosphere ripe for conflict even before the Mormons began settling there in 1831. It also created a political climate of deep division within the nation over the issue of states' rights, which directly affected the efforts of Joseph Smith to get national support for the Mormon cause after the Saints had been expelled from Missouri in 1838–39.

The westward movement created still another problem that affected LDS history, one that involved questions of race relations, politics, and human rights. As white Americans eagerly pushed into new areas, they often did so at the tragic expense of Native Americans. Many federal officials felt the only solution was to persuade eastern tribes to move west, beyond the ninety-fifth meridian (an area that, at the time, no white man wanted), where the government would help them begin anew and guarantee them a new home in the "permanent Indian frontier." After forcefully persuading the Native Americans already there to move further out on the Great Plains, the government offered the tribes east of the Mississippi various inducements to relocate. The process continued through the late 1820s and 1830s, usually accompanied by great discomfort and sometimes violence. Significantly, the "permanent Indian frontier," which eventually failed, was located on the western borders of the states of Missouri and Arkansas. The Shawnee of Ohio settled on a twenty-five-mile-wide reservation south of the Kansas River, not far from Independence, Missouri, and they were soon joined in 1829 by the Delaware, their former neighbors in Ohio, who accepted land immediately to the north. The Delaware were hardly settled in their new surroundings when the first Mormon missionaries to the American Indians appeared among them.

The Book of Mormon gave the Saints a special interest in doing missionary work among the Native Americans, and from the beginning Oliver Cowdery and others were anxious to know when it would begin. The same revelation that reminded Oliver that he was not to "command" Joseph Smith also called him to "go unto the Lamanites [i.e., descendants of the people in the Book of Mormon] and preach my gospel unto them." Later Peter Whitmer, Jr., Parley P. Pratt, and Ziba Peterson were called to go with him.

This mission to the cutting edge of the frontier was the Church's first official look westward, and it foreshadowed dramatic future activities. When Oliver Cowdery was instructed to go on the mission, he was promised that a site for building the city of Zion soon would be identified. Though the precise location was not specified, he was told that it would "be on the borders by the Lamanites" (D&C 28:9), and the implication was that his mission would have something to do with identifying the chosen place.

The four missionaries, eager to work among the Lamanites as well as to convert everyone else they could, set out for the Indian frontier about mid-October 1830. Before leaving New York they spent a day with the Cateraugus tribe, near Buffalo. They then headed for northeastern Ohio, where they spent several days with the Wyandot tribe, near Sandusky. No Indian converts were made. Joined by one of their Ohio converts, Frederick G. Williams, the missionaries then went on to Jackson County, Missouri, where they arrived in mid-December. Elders Peterson and Williams found work, while the other three crossed the Indian frontier. They spent one night with the Shawnee and then several days among the Delaware. Other Christian missionaries, however, quickly began to complain about their activities, which seemed to be having an effect upon the Delaware, and federal Indian agents ordered them to leave. They went back to Jackson County where they continued their missionary work, baptized several people, and prepared the way for the arrival of Joseph Smith and the migration of several families of Saints the following year. All but Elder Pratt remained until after the Prophet came.

The Foundation in Ohio

For Parley P. Pratt, his visit to northeastern Ohio in October 1830 was a fitting climax to the journey he had begun only two months earlier when he left the area to preach in New York. Now, as a Mormon elder, he called upon his friend and former pastor, Sidney Rigdon, leader of a congregation in Mentor, Ohio. When presented with a copy of the Book of Mormon, Rigdon was skeptical, but he promised to read it and find out for himself whether it was true. In addition, he gave the missionaries permission to use his meetinghouse, and Oliver Cowdery and Parley P. Pratt presented their message to his congregation. Rigdon warned his followers neither to accept nor reject without careful investigation. About two weeks later, after he had read the Book of Mormon and received a personal witness that it was true, Rigdon announced his own readiness for baptism. On Sunday, November 14, Rigdon spoke to a large congregation for nearly two hours, melting both himself and his listeners to tears as he confessed his past weakness and told of his conversion. It was probably the next day that he was baptized by Oliver Cowdery, and he then moved to Hiram, a short distance from Kirtland, where a little branch of the Church was soon formed.

The missionaries, meanwhile, preached throughout the vicinity, and converts, many of them former Campbellites, began to flock in. Suddenly Ohio's Western Reserve became a more fruitful field than the Burned-over District in New York. Before the missionaries left they had baptized approximately 130 new members. When Joseph Smith heard the good news, he sent John Whitmer to preside in Ohio, and by the summer of 1831 about a thousand people had joined.

Parley Pratt could not have approached Sidney Rigdon at a better time. For months Rigdon had been at odds with Alexander Campbell over various aspects of the restoration of the ancient order of things, including the gifts of the Holy Spirit and authority to perform ordinances. Some of Rigdon's followers also saw in the New Testament that the early Christians shared all things in common, and they wanted to establish a modern religious community that would exhibit this same brotherly love. Campbell objected, but Rigdon supported them as they formed themselves into a common-stock community called the "Family," under the leadership of Isaac Morley. Such differences finally led to a sharp break with Campbell's movement; when the Mormon missionaries arrived, Rigdon was struggling with the dilemma of whether his congregation should remain independent or join another group. He found his own answer in Mormonism. So did many of his disciples, for the entire "Family," as well as many others in and around Kirtland, soon followed him into the Church.

Rigdon, however, would not be satisfied until he met the Prophet, and in December he and a prosperous young hatter named Edward Partridge traveled together to New York. Partridge was not yet a member, and his main purpose was to learn for himself about the character of Joseph Smith. The two stopped at the Smith home in Manchester, and when they found no family members there they began to ask neighbors about their character. They were told it was unimpeachable, except on the subject of religion. They then proceeded to Waterloo, New York, where they met Joseph himself. After staying with the Smith family for a time, Partridge became convinced and was baptized by the Prophet. Joseph described him as "a pattern of piety, and one of the Lord's great men,"[13] and in less than a year he would become the first bishop in the Church.

Joseph Smith must have been as deeply impressed by Sidney Rigdon as were most people who heard him preach, and immediately the two were drawn together. Rigdon's years as an associate of Alexander Campbell had prepared him well to teach the doctrines of his new faith and to stand next to the Prophet in expounding them. A revelation through Joseph Smith soon confirmed this: "Behold, verily, verily, I say unto my servant Sidney, I have looked upon thee and thy works. I have heard thy prayers, and prepared thee for a greater work." He was sent forth like John the Baptist, he was told, to prepare the way for the Lord, thus assuring him of the correctness of most of what he had been teaching. Only one thing was lacking. "Thou didst baptize by water unto repentance, but they received not the Holy Ghost," but now, through him, they would also receive the Holy Ghost by the laying on of hands, "even as the apostles of old." The fulness of the gospel had been sent forth through Joseph Smith, the revelation went on, "and in weakness have I blessed him." Rigdon now was to strengthen Joseph, to "watch over him that his faith fail not," to write for him as he received revelation of ancient scripture, and to "preach my gospel and call on the holy prophets to prove his words, as they shall be given him." (D&C 35:3–6, 17, 19, 23.) Rigdon's years of preaching and his knowledge of the scriptures would be marshaled to demonstrate the truth of Mormon teachings. Almost immediately he began to help in Joseph Smith's inspired revision of the Bible, and in October 1833, he was designated by revelation as a "spokesman" for the Prophet. (D&C 100:9.)

The time was ripe for a move. The Prophet was being plagued by persecution and the Church was gaining members only slowly in New York, but it was growing by leaps and bounds in Ohio. No doubt Sidney Rigdon helped persuade Joseph that Ohio held great promise, in fulfillment of a revelation that had told him: "And now I say unto you, tarry with him, and he shall journey with you." (D&C 35:22.) Not long afterward, the two were told in another revelation that they should stop translating and go to Ohio, and the whole church in New York was told, "It is expedient in me that they should assemble together at the Ohio." (D&C 37:3; see also 38:32.)

By the end of the month Joseph and Emma Smith had left New

---

[13]*History of the Church*, 1:28.

York, accompanied by Sidney Rigdon and Edward Partridge, and early in February they arrived in Kirtland. There the Smiths were welcomed into the home of Newel K. Whitney, a merchant and former Campbellite who followed Sidney Rigdon into the new faith. Some New Yorkers were uncertain about the move, but during the rest of the winter they nevertheless prepared to participate in this first Mormon migration westward. In the spring several groups assembled and traveled from Colesville, Fayette, and Palmyra to the Erie Canal, where they took a canal boat to Buffalo. From there they went by steamer along Lake Erie to Fairport, Ohio, and from there a short distance overland to Kirtland.

The move to Ohio was, in one sense, a new beginning, but it was in New York that the foundations were laid and the direction set for the growth of Latter-day Saint doctrine. The restoration was by no means complete, for the body of doctrine continued to develop as new circumstances prepared the Saints for new instructions. Never, in fact, was it anticipated that Church doctrine would be static, and even today the Saints believe that God "will yet reveal many great and important things pertaining to the Kingdom of God." By the beginning of 1831, however, certain principles and doctrines had been established that would form a permanent base upon which later revelations and doctrinal expositions could build.

In summary, the Saints of these first months believed that Jesus Christ had established his church in its purity in New Testament times, that an apostasy had taken place over the centuries, and that they now belonged to the divinely restored Church of Christ. Divine authority to act in the name of God, the priesthood, had been restored by the ancient apostles and prophets themselves. For the time being Joseph Smith and Oliver Cowdery were called, simply, the first and second elders of the Church, but they were also designated as apostles, and the Saints believed that a quorum of twelve apostles soon would be appointed. The duties of various priesthood officers were outlined, and it was obvious from the beginning that the Church would be characterized by a lay priesthood. Joseph Smith was clearly in charge as the accepted prophet, seer, and revelator, and the doctrine of continued revelation was well established.

Along with the Bible, the Saints accepted the divinity of the Book of Mormon, and any doctrines it proclaimed were therefore part of the restored gospel. These included the principles of faith, repentance, baptism by immersion for the remission of sins (for all those who have reached the age of understanding), the laying on of hands for the gift of the Holy Ghost, miracles, spiritual gifts, and the sacrament of the Lord's supper in remembrance of his atonement. The Book of Mormon also taught the fall of man but rejected the Calvinist doctrine of total depravity. It testified of the reality of Christ's atonement and emphasized that man attained salvation by a combination of faith, good works, and the grace of Jesus Christ. It proclaimed mankind's free agency and the universality of the gospel. Also fundamental was the doctrine of millennialism: that Christ would return and reign for a thousand years in peace. Mormons expected this to happen soon and believed their mission was to prepare for his coming. These principles provided the foundation for more elaborate doctrines that would be proclaimed later, as the Saints were prepared to receive them.

CHAPTER 3

Unfolding Latter-day Zion, *1831–1836*

On August 2, 1831, a small group of Latter-day Saints recently transplanted from Colesville, New York, by way of northern Ohio, assembled at an isolated site twelve miles west of Independence, Jackson County, Missouri, to participate in a symbolic act of new beginnings. Twelve men representing the tribes of Israel solemnly placed the first log for a house, signifying the laying of the foundation of Zion. Assisting them was Joseph Smith, who had journeyed to the westernmost state of Jacksonian America to examine the site identified by revelation as the center place. There the Prophet envisioned a well-planned city built around a complex of sacred temples: the New Jerusalem — a city of refuge, a gathering place where the latter-day kingdom could be established in anticipation of the millennial reign of Jesus Christ.

Almost from the beginning, it seemed, the concept of the "gathering" tended to dominate the restored church. The righteous from all nations, sought out by proselyting elders, were to congregate in a place of refuge that would provide protection against wars, plagues, and other destructive forces of the last days. It was to be a place of righteousness and peace, and if the Indians beyond the boundaries of Missouri accepted the gospel, they, too, would help build the New Jerusalem, as promised in the Book of Mormon. But the realization of such plans always depends on people and circumstances, and in this case certain stresses developed that would make Jackson County only a brief wintering place on the trail of Mormon history. After three short years the Saints would unwillingly abandon their Zion, though with the expectation that one day they would return.

Two Places of Gathering

From the beginning, Church leaders realized that the proposed gathering place could not be peopled with Latter-day Saints all at once, but the effort would need support. So, while an advance contingent struggled to lay the groundwork for this millennial city on the frontier, other Saints remained in scattered branches eastward along the route to Zion. The greatest concentration was in northeastern Ohio, where Kirtland and nearby Hiram became nerve centers of the growing church. It was there, rather than in Jackson County, that Joseph Smith created a temporary headquarters.

This part of Ohio, designated by revelation as a gathering place "for a little season" (D&C 51:16), lay along the northern edge of the Allegheny Plateau, in an area known as the Western Reserve. It had been part of a royal grant to Connecticut, but during and after the American Revolution those states claiming western lands relinquished their titles to the national government. Some land was retained, however, to satisfy land bounties issued to state revolutionary militias, and Connecticut held on to nearly four million acres in northeastern Ohio for this and other purposes. Most of the land was soon acquired by speculators who surveyed it, sold it, and promoted settlement. Ohio became one of the most attractive destinations for the tide of westward-moving Americans, and by 1830 its population was nearly 938,000 — the fourth most populous state in the union. The Western Reserve consisted largely of New Englanders, who had brought their culture and religious sensitivities with them.

When the New York Saints arrived, they found hundreds of Church members ready to welcome them, and the law of consecration (discussed in detail later in this chapter) was soon introduced among them. Members of the Colesville Branch from New York followed Newel Knight to Thompson, Ohio, where they became "squatters" on land offered to the Church by Leman Copley's consecration. Frederick G. Williams and Isaac Morley of Kirtland and Philo Dibble, who lived near Mentor, also opened their farmland to the new arrivals. Bishop Edward Partridge and his assistants apportioned the consecrated lands to arriving Saints according to need, and additional property was purchased with funds obtained when the New York Saints liquidated private holdings. In September, Joseph and Emma Smith and the twins they had recently adopted took up residence with the John Johnson family of Hiram, thirty miles from Kirtland.

First, however, the Prophet made an important visit to Missouri. With Sidney Rigdon, Martin Harris, Edward Partridge, William W. Phelps, Joseph Coe, and A. Sidney Gilbert, he set out in mid-June to locate a settlement site and dedicate the land of Zion. Also heading west about this time were twenty-two elders assigned by the Kirtland conference of June 3–6 to travel in pairs, preaching along different routes toward Missouri. In addition, the entire Colesville Branch abandoned its site at Thompson, Ohio, after Leman Copley reneged on his agreement to share his property. Members of this congregation had been instructed in March to begin saving funds to purchase an inheritance in Zion; now they went to claim it. Arriving in Jackson County during the week of July 16, 1831, they settled in Kaw Township, later part of Kansas City.

The disciples had come to a remote frontier, largely undeveloped but not without promise. Shortly after their arrival, in fact, Joseph Smith received a revelation affirming that this place was "appointed and consecrated for the gathering of the saints . . . , the land of promise, and the place for the city of Zion." In addition, the specific location of the New Jerusalem was identified. "The place which is now called Independence is the center place," the Saints were told, "and the spot for the temple is lying westward, upon a lot which is not far from the courthouse." (D&C 57:1–3.) Their immediate task was to establish a claim to the area through the purchase of land.

Following the log-laying ceremony at Kaw Township, Sidney Rigdon dedicated the land as a permanent inheritance for the Saints. On the following day, August 3, on a spot one-half mile west of Independence, the Prophet set a cornerstone for a temple. Earlier he had issued instructions for establishing the law of consecration to govern Zion, and a revelation appointed Edward Partridge as bishop, Sidney Gilbert as land agent and merchant, William W. Phelps as printer, and Oliver Cowdery (who, unlike the other three, went back to Ohio) as editor. After the Prophet and his companions returned to Kirtland, those left in Missouri adjusted to frontier life. They harvested wild hay for livestock, sowed a little grain, and prepared land for cultivation.

A letter from William W. Phelps in July spoke glowingly of the sage-grass prairie and thickly timbered plain. So that the Church at large might know of Zion's potential, Sidney Rigdon prepared a similar description, boasting of the mild climate, fertile soil, and natural resources. He acknowledged the disadvantages that might be expected on a frontier—lack of industry, education, and the refinements of society—but both he and Phelps were impressed with "the rolling prai-

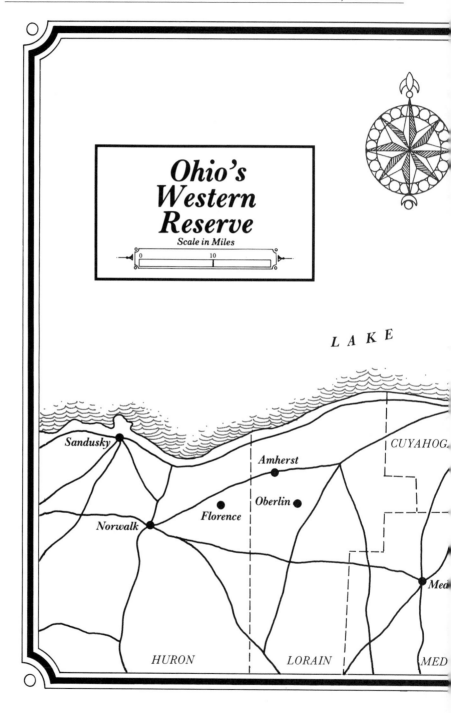

Ohio's
Western
Reserve

Scale in Miles

0   10

L A K E

Sandusky

Amherst

CUYAHOG.

Oberlin

Florence

Norwalk

Mea

HURON   LORAIN   MED

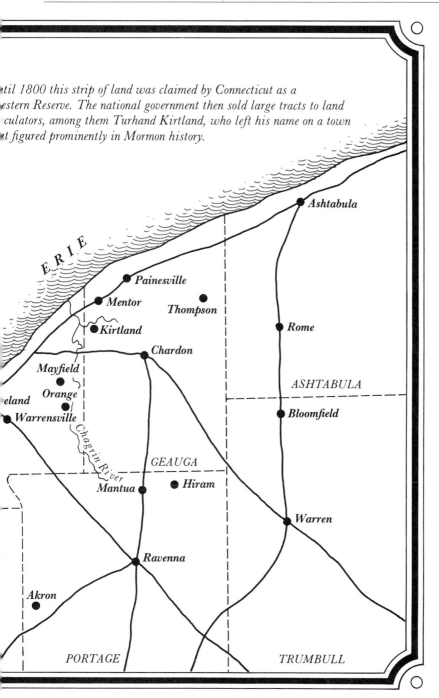

*til 1800 this strip of land was claimed by Connecticut as a
estern Reserve. The national government then sold large tracts to land
culators, among them Turhand Kirtland, who left his name on a town
t figured prominently in Mormon history.*

ries . . . decorated with a growth of flowers so gorgeous and grand as to exceed description."[1]

The optimism, nurtured by virgin land and by the Saints' enthusiasm for Zion, was soon tempered by the realities of pioneering. Within a year, after a poor harvest and other problems, the Church newspaper in Zion cautioned against bringing more settlers too rapidly: "Although Zion, according to the prophets, is to become like Eden or the garden of the Lord, yet at present it is as it were but a wilderness and desert, and the disadvantages of settling in a new country, you know, are many and great. Therefore, prudence would dictate at present the churches abroad, come not up to Zion, until preparations can be made for them."[2]

The Mormon population in Missouri thus remained intentionally small. By November 1832, *The Evening and the Morning Star* counted 830 gathered Saints preparing the land for additional immigrants. Those remaining in Ohio, meanwhile, concentrated on developing a secondary gathering place in a less remote region, closer to the field of potential converts and to the resources of the developed East. Thus two centers of Mormonism slowly gained strength—Zion, designated as the center place, though briefly left to its own resources, and Kirtland, a stake to Zion, a temporary headquarters where the Lord instructed the Saints to "retain a strong hold . . . for the space of five years." (D&C 64:21.)

A People of God and Their Quest for Community

The Latter-day Saints were committed to becoming true disciples of Christ and, in a yearning for Christian unity, they congregated in their designated places of refuge. There they hoped to find relief from the concerns of Babylon and to begin erecting the kingdom of God on earth.

One sign of the true faith was the outpouring of spiritual gifts, but in Ohio, unfortunately, it became the task of Joseph Smith to temper the excessive religious enthusiasm of some converts. A few young former Shakers, for example, persisted in participating in certain "spiritual operations" that even most Shakers had abandoned. John Whitmer reported:

Some had visions and could not tell what they saw. Some would

---

[1]*History of the Church*, 1:197. For reproductions of both letters, see Richard Lloyd Anderson, "Jackson County in Early Mormon Descriptions," *Missouri Historical Review* 65 (April 1971): 274–76, 285–87.
[2]*The Evening and the Morning Star* 1 (July 1832).

Emma Hale Smith,
wife of the
Prophet Joseph.
(RLDS Church)

Sidney Rigdon,
designated by revelation as
"spokesman" to the Prophet.
(Church Archives)

Edward Partridge,
first bishop
of the Church.
(Church Archives)

fancy to themselves that they had the sword of Laban, and would wield it as expert as a light dragoon; some would act like an Indian in the act of scalping; some would slide or scoot on the floor with the rapidity of a serpent, which they termed sailing in the boat to the Lamanites, preaching the gospel. And many other vain and foolish maneuvers that are unseemly and unprofitable to mention.[3]

Such manifestations, even when adapted to Mormon forms and terminology, were not considered acceptable spiritual experiences, and Joseph Smith denounced them. He had already defined the true and profitable gifts of the spirit: wisdom, knowledge, healing and other miracles, prophecy, discerning of spirits, and the gift of tongues. Church members received and exercised all of them, but the Prophet warned against excesses like those described above and against seeking after signs. "Behold, verily I say unto you," a May 1831 revelation declared, "that there are many spirits which are false spirits, which have gone forth in the earth, deceiving the world. And also Satan hath sought to deceive you, that he might overthrow you." (D&C 50:2–3.) The legitimate gifts, Joseph taught, would follow faith, and believing Mormons did witness such things as the miraculous healing of Mrs. John Johnson's paralyzed arm, the casting out of evil spirits during a June 1831 conference in Kirtland, and a miraculous parting of the ice at Buffalo harbor for the departure of the Colesville Saints.

---

[3]F. Mark McKiernan and Roger D. Launius, eds., *An Early Latter-day Saint History: The Book of John Whitmer, Kept by Commandment* (Independence, Missouri: Herald House, 1980), p. 62.

Among the most distinctive characteristics of Mormonism was its claim to modern revelation. Unlike many restorationists, the Saints did not view the Bible as the final, infallible source of religious authority. They agreed with the Campbellites that the King James Bible required correction, but they also claimed new revelation, through the Prophet, to restore lost truths. This claim was another challenge to contemporary Christian orthodoxy, and thus provided even more ammunition for critics of the new religion.

Nevertheless, Joseph Smith found it necessary again to clarify his preeminent role as prophet, seer, and revelator for the Church. In Ohio, for example, a certain Mrs. Hubble sanctimoniously claimed new revelations as a prophetess, and a servant on Isaac Morley's farm likewise asserted the right to direct the Saints. Against such interlopers the Prophet declared by revelation, as he had done before, that the Lord had appointed only one person to receive revelations and commandments for the entire Church. (See D&C 43.)

Among the many revelations Joseph Smith received were some that expanded the Saints' doctrinal understanding through the restoration of lost scriptures. The Book of Mormon spoke of other scripture hidden from the world, and Mormons were interested when newspapers reported the discovery of several supposedly lost books of the Bible. These included the books of Jasher and Enoch, which contained apocalyptic and communitarian messages, and a *Book of Enoch* published in English in 1821. Joseph Smith, however, gave to the Church his own restorations of the Prophecy of Enoch and the Visions and Writings of Moses, received by revelation between June 1830 and February 1831, and now published as the Book of Moses in the Pearl of Great Price. About the same time he formally began his inspired revision of the Bible, a project that continued for more than two years. As he neared the completion of this work, he cautioned the Saints against accepting the so-called lost books and specifically labeled the Apocrypha a mixture of truth and falsehood.

Except for selected segments, Joseph Smith's work on the Bible was not published in his lifetime. Nevertheless, the three-year project was a valuable learning experience. In addition, his intensive study raised questions whose answers were later included in the Doctrine and Covenants and other doctrinal expositions. Among the new insights were the vision of the degrees of glory, the separate identity of the Father and the Son as members of the Godhead, and man's place in the universe as an uncreated, premortal child of God. The Prophet also recorded important instructions on priesthood and prophecies of the second coming of Christ.

Another by-product of the Prophet's Bible revision and his general fascination with antiquities was an intensified interest in Hebrew and other ancient languages. All this quite naturally led to the purchase of certain Egyptian mummies and papyrus scrolls that had been displayed by Michael Chandler in Kirtland in 1835. Joseph Smith identified the scrolls as a record of Abraham, and he spent several weeks during that year working on a translation. He apparently progressed as far as the second chapter of the record later known as the Book of Abraham, but did not return to the task until 1842. It was first published that same year, and ultimately appeared in the Pearl of Great Price. It contained not only the story of the youthful Abraham's escape from Egypt to Ur of the Chaldees, but also many inspired truths about the relationship between God, man, and the universe.

The exact relationship between the ancient scrolls and the printed text of the Book of Abraham has been a matter of controversy. Only portions of the scrolls themselves are available for study. After the Prophet's death they, along with the mummies, were sold to non-Mormons and exhibited in various places, including Wood's Museum in Chicago. For years it was assumed that they all were destroyed in the great Chicago fire of 1871, but in 1967 eleven fragments were discovered in a New York museum and presented to the Church. Translations by LDS as well as non-Mormon scholars, however, made it clear that these were not the direct source of the Abraham text, though, as Church scholars were quick to observe, these and other fragments long held by the Church were only a small remainder of the much larger original collection of papyri. Speculation nevertheless persisted as to the process Joseph may have used in translating the book, including the possibility that even if the papyri were not contemporary with Abraham they contained material that, under inspiration, turned Joseph's mind back to ancient Egypt and opened it to direct revelation on the experiences of Abraham. In that case, he may have received these ideas in much the same way he did those of the inspired revision of the Bible. In that instance, acting without original documents, the Prophet's only claim was that by divine inspiration he was able to replace incorrect with correct ideas and restore the original biblical meaning. He studied Hebrew but never claimed fluency in ancient languages. Even the Book of Mormon was translated by the "gift and power of God" rather than through prior knowledge of ancient language. As

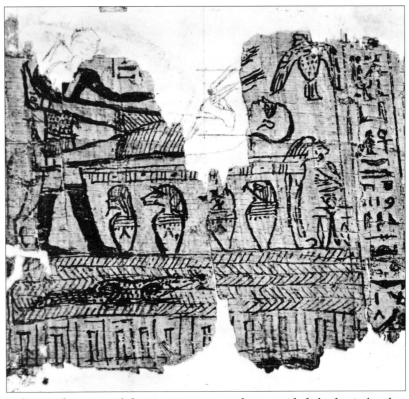

A damaged section of the Egyptian papyri that provided the basis for the Book of Abraham. (Church Archives)

Orson Pratt later recalled, "I saw him translating, by inspiration, the Old and New Testaments, and the inspired book of Abraham from Egyptian papyrus."[4] When applied by Mormons to Joseph Smith, the term *translator* thus has a special meaning.

From the first the Saints eagerly sought copies of the Prophet's translations and revelations. Recognizing this, as early as 1830 he began arranging the revelations in chronological order and making editorial corrections to prepare them for publication. In November 1831 six new revelations were incorporated, including a preface and an appendix to the proposed book. But the compilation did not go unchallenged. William E. McLellin, a teacher whom Joseph characterized at the time as "having more learning than sense," was critical of the lack of erudition in the language of the commandments. The Prophet invited him to

---

[4]Sermon of July 10, 1859, in *Journal of Discourses* 7:176.

write a revelation equal "to one of the least of the Lord's," and the humbled teacher soon discovered that he could not. In contrast, most of the elders at a special conference that October testified of the divine origin of the revelatory writings and offered their witness in a brief preface to the book.

Oliver Cowdery and John Whitmer personally carried the collection to Independence, Missouri, for printing, and during Joseph Smith's next visit these two and W. W. Phelps were authorized to proceed with publication. This they did, but when about two-thirds of the revelations had been set in type and sheets run off, a mob destroyed the press and scattered the printed forms. This interruption delayed publication another two years, though local members retrieved the printed sheets and bound a few copies of the incomplete volume, the Book of Commandments for the Government of the Church of Christ, which later became collector's items.

When finally published in the fall of 1835, the Doctrine and Covenants of The Church of Jesus Christ of Latter-day Saints had been enlarged, corrected, and rearranged by the First Presidency. Also included in the volume were several doctrinal essays, "Lectures on Faith," which were not revelations but had been used as lessons in a School of the Elders the previous winter. This important publication thus gave the Saints easy access to the Prophet's revelations, set forth the regulations or covenants of Church membership, and clarified doctrinal matters.

It is important to observe that, for the most part, the revelations of Joseph Smith did not come without some previous preparation, searching, and inquiring of the Lord on the part of the Prophet himself. Mormons believe, in fact, that revelation often comes in response to prayers concerning present concerns and specific problems, and much of Joseph Smith's new revelation was no different.

One concept probably first revealed during the Prophet's biblical studies in 1831 came in response to his prayer concerning how Old Testament prophets were justified by the Lord in their practice of plural marriage. He recorded the answer in 1843 as a revelation on the new and everlasting covenant of marriage (D&C 132). During the early 1830s rumors that polygamy was being practiced spread among the Saints and their detractors. Official pronouncements denied it, as the Prophet did not make this principle a matter of general Church doctrine or practice at that time. However, some members, told privately by the Prophet that a new marriage system eventually would be introduced, began to practice it without authorization. This led to some apostasy during the mid-1830s. The brief statement on marriage appended to the 1835 Doctrine and Covenants gave a direct answer to charges of immorality and polygamy among the Saints. Written by William W. Phelps, it asserted that the law of the Church at that time affirmed only the monogamous marriage relationship.

Whatever their validity, such rumors led to increased animosity towards the Church. Those speaking and writing against Mormonism — including ministers, editors, disaffected Mormons, businessmen, and local government officials — sometimes included charges of polygamy, among other accusations, in their scoffing diatribes. They also challenged the Prophet's revelations.

Eber D. Howe was one of the earliest newsmen in Ohio to revive the controversies the Saints hoped they had left behind in New York. In his Painesville *Telegraph*, Howe reprinted the earlier Dogberry articles and added his own ridicule. Others joined the chorus, but none so intensively as the Campbellites. The *Millennial Harbinger*, issued as the voice of this movement, denounced the Prophet as an imposter. This, of course, is understandable, for so many Campbellites were being converted to Mormonism that it threatened that movement's stronghold in Ohio. Alexander Campbell's sixteen-page *Delusions . . .* directly challenged the Book of Mormon and was the first of a steady stream of anti-Mormon books and pamphlets to issue from the Campbellite press.

The literary harassment reached its zenith in 1834 with the publication of *Mormonism Unvailed* [sic], an anthology that was the genesis of many later anti-Mormon works. A citizens committee sponsored this spurious collection, turning first to Doctor Philastus Hurlbut (Doctor was his given name), an ambitious convert and missionary to Pennsylvania who had been excommunicated for immorality and then turned to lecturing against the Church. Hurlbut's usefulness to the publications committee was weakened when a court in Chardon convicted him of threatening the Prophet's life, so the book was issued under Eber D. Howe's name. It contained a mixture of old and new charges against Joseph Smith's credibility and attempted to weaken the believability of the Book of Mormon by asserting a link with Solomon Spaulding's fanciful novel *Manuscript Found*, which told of Romans shipwrecked among the Indians in America. Joseph Smith, the theory suggested, was too unlearned to write the Book of Mormon himself, and so Sidney Rigdon wrote it for him by adding religious material to

Spaulding's narrative novel. This theory was discredited early, even by anti-Mormon writers.

Joseph Smith's response to this and other forms of literary harassment was restrained, and despite its claim to inside information, *Mormonism Unvailed* disappointed its sponsors. Few Mormons left the Church because of it, and anticipated sales to nonmembers were sluggish. The Church, meanwhile, continued to grow.

It was physical abuse that troubled the Prophet most. Here and there hecklers punctuated threats of beatings or tar and feathers by throwing eggs, inkstands, or books at preaching elders. Occasionally Latter-day Saint preachers created resentment themselves with unrestrained enthusiasm or dogmatic insistence on the superiority of their religion. "For these things," the Prophet wrote, "we are heartily sorry."[5] Certain residents of Hiram, Ohio, vented their personal feelings with mob action directed against the Prophet and Sidney Rigdon. Stimulated by whiskey and hidden behind blackened faces, a gang of more than two dozen men dragged Joseph from his bed during the night of March 24, 1832. Choking him into submission, they stripped him naked, scratched his skin with their fingernails, tore his hair, then smeared his body with tar and feathers. A vial of nitric acid forced against his teeth splashed on his face; a front tooth was broken. Meanwhile other members of the mob dragged Rigdon by the heels from his home, bumping his head on the frozen ground, which left him delirious for days. The Prophet's friends spent the night removing the tar to help him keep a Sunday morning preaching appointment. He addressed a congregation that included Simonds Ryder, organizer of the mob.

Newspaper reports of the mob action in Hiram strongly denounced it, but the Prophet's antagonists did not relent. When he left a week later on his second visit to Missouri, they pursued him three hundred miles to Cincinnati before he sought the protection of a steamer captain and safely completed the trip. He instructed his wife, meanwhile, to take refuge in Kirtland while he was away. Emma did so, still sorrowing over the death of Joseph Murdock, one of their adopted twins. The child, already weakened from a case of measles, died from complications of a cold probably contracted through exposure on the night of the Hiram mobbing. When he returned from Missouri in June, Joseph took up residence in Kirtland, where he was accompanied almost continu-

---

[5]*Latter-day Saints' Messenger and Advocate* 1 (September 1835).

THE EVENING AND THE MORNING STAR.

Vol. I.	Independence, Mo. June, 1832.	No. 1.

Revelations.

THE ARTICLES AND COVENANTS OF THE CHURCH OF CHRIST.

THE rise of the Church of Christ in these last days, being one thousand eight hundred and thirty years since the coming of our Lord and Savior Jesus Christ, in the flesh; it being regularly organized and established agreeable to the laws of our country, by the will and commandments of God in the fourth month and on the sixth day of the month, which is called April: Which commandments were given to Joseph, who was called of God and ordained an Apostle of Jesus Christ, an Elder of this Church; and also to Oliver, who was called of God an Apostle of Jesus Christ, an Elder of this Church, and ordained under his hand; and this according to the grace of our Lord and Savior Jesus Christ to whom be all glory both now and forever. Amen.

For, after that it truly was manifested unto this first Elder, that he had received a remission of his sins, he was entangled again in the vanities of the world, but after truly repenting God ministered unto him by an holy angel, whose countenance was as lightning, and whose garments were pure and white above all white-

The duty of the Elders, Priests, Teachers, Deacons and members of the Church of Christ. An Apostle is an Elder, and it is his calling to baptize and to ordain other Elders, Priests, Teachers and Deacons, and to administer the flesh and blood of Christ according to the Scriptures, and to teach, expound, exhort, baptize, and watch over the Church, and to confirm the Church by the laying on of the hands, and the giving of the Holy Ghost, and to take the lead of all meetings. The Elders are to conduct the meetings as they are led by the Holy Ghost. The Priests' duty is to preach, teach, expound, exhort and baptize, and administer the Sacrament, and visit the house of each member, and exhort them to pray vocally and in secret, and also to attend to all family duties; and ordain other Priests, Teachers and Deacons, and take the lead in meetings; but none of these offices is he to do when there is an Elder present, but in all cases is to assist the Elder. The Teachers' duty is to watch over the Church always, and be with them, and strengthen them, and see that there is no iniquity in the Church, neither hardness with each other, neither lying nor back-biting nor evil speaking; and see that the Church meet together often, and also see that all the members do their duty; and he is to take the lead of meetings in the absence of the Elder or Priest, and is to be assisted always, and in all his duties in the Church by the Deacons; but neither the Teacher nor Deacons have authority to baptize nor administer the Sacrament, but

Masthead of first issue of the first Mormon newspaper. The revelation is now published as section 20 of the Doctrine and Covenants. (Church Archives)

ously by a guard. Likewise, Sidney Rigdon sought protection, moving first to Kirtland, then Chardon. Other Saints also took precautions, even accelerating the manufacture of guns for defense.

Spreading the Gospel Message

Such troubles did not halt the Saints' efforts to publicize their message. In Missouri, the Church printing house commenced publishing the scriptures, hymns, and a newspaper. The first number of *The Evening and the Morning Star* appeared in June 1832, and the publication continued until the ransacking of its office less than two years later. The *Latter Day Saints' Messenger and Advocate* was then published at Kirtland until 1837. Church agents also issued two secular newspapers during this period, the *Upper Missouri Advertiser*, at Independence, and the *Northern Times*, published in 1835 at Kirtland. Although short-lived, these various papers provided a much-needed voice in the clarification of doctrine and Latter-day Saint views on matters of current interest.

Dispersal of the restoration message was not left to the printed media alone, for the disciples of Mormonism in the early 1830s exhibited a spontaneous missionary zeal. New members were fired with a desire to share the good news, to speak with a "warning voice, every man to his neighbor." Soon after the Church established itself in Ohio, the Prophet organized the missionary work. During conferences at Kirtland in June 1831 and at Amherst in January 1832, elders who had volunteered for service were assigned companions and in some instances directed to specific areas and routes of travel. Beginning in 1834 the missionaries were issued preaching licenses as authorized Church representatives. Missionaries heavily canvassed the communities close to their homes, for every departing set of elders was expected to preach along the way. Short-term missionary excursions were also common as elders traveled to nearby towns during slack seasons on the farm.

If Ohio was saturated with missionaries, other parts of the continent were not forgotten. By the end of the Kirtland period, people in every organized state in the Union, much of Upper Canada, the Fox Islands off the coast of Maine, and Great Britain had heard the message of the restoration. Wherever the missionaries went, they organized branches, and by the end of 1837 over sixteen thousand persons were baptized. Conversions were slowest in the southern states, where missionaries found difficulty penetrating the well-established traditions and dealing with the complications of slavery and rigid class structure. The work spread most rapidly along the corridor from New York and Pennsylvania through Ohio to the outpost in Missouri.

Wherever they were called to labor, these early missionaries preferred making contacts in public meetings — in courthouses, schools, churches, barns, homes, or on street corners. But they also went from door to door with Book of Mormon in hand. Their strongest opposition came from among the clergy, but they also encountered much difficulty from indifferent frontiersmen and jeering, mud-throwing pranksters and skeptics. The missionaries nevertheless displayed an overpowering optimism in a field ready for the harvest. Convinced that they were engaged in the Lord's errand of gathering the righteous out of Babylon, they found deep spiritual satisfaction in helping to establish Zion.

The Latter-day Kingdom: Economic Affairs

Many of the revelations and much of the preaching of the 1830s spoke of the kingdom of God that would be established in preparation for the second advent of Christ and his millennial reign. Its center would be Zion, the New Jerusalem, but its people would also require a righteous law and an ecclesiastical government. A revelation presented at the final conference in Fayette, New York, on January 2, 1831, gave the Saints the comforting promise that the Lord's law would soon be established among them:

> Wherefore, hear my voice and follow me, and you shall be a free people, and ye shall have no laws but my laws when I come, for I am your lawgiver, and what can stay my hand? . . .

And let every man esteem his brother as himself, and practice
virtue and holiness before me. . . .

And that ye might escape the power of the enemy, and be
gathered unto me a righteous people, without spot and blameless —

Wherefore, for this cause I gave unto you the commandment
that ye should go to the Ohio; and there I will give unto you my
law; and there you shall be endowed with power from on high.
(D&C 38:22, 24, 31–32.)

The promised law was not long in coming. On February 9, in the
presence of twelve elders in Kirtland, Joseph received a revelation that,
he said, embraced the "Law of the Church." It introduced among the
Saints an important new economic order, the law of consecration and
stewardship, which received fuller explanation and implementation in
later revelations and instructions. The Prophecy of Enoch, revealed to
the Prophet in June 1830, described a Zion people who were of one
heart and one mind and who dwelt in righteousness with no poor among
them. (Moses 7:18.) Similar societies, in which all things were held in
common, were the ideal Christian communities described in the Book
of Mormon and the New Testament. An effort to establish such a
system among the Latter-day Saints, therefore, was not only an attempt
to live the law of the Lord to its fullest, but also an important step in
the restoration of the ancient order of things.

The law of consecration and stewardship also met two practical
needs at the time. First, among the Ohio Saints were converts from
the communitarian orders of the Shakers and from Isaac Morley's
"Family" system. Joseph Smith disapproved of such communal systems in which everyone simply put their possessions together and all
had access to everything, and what he called "the more perfect law of
the Lord" became the alternative. In addition, it was anticipated that
the new law would provide land in Ohio for transplanted New York
Saints to farm and subsequently supply surplus funds to support the
poor and finance Church publications. It would also provide a living
for full-time officers, such as the bishop.

The new system, which would be developed more fully over the
next several months, was based on the assumption of unselfish devotion
to the kingdom and love for each other as fellow Saints. Each individual
was counted equal, for, as a later revelation noted, the goal was "that
ye may be equal in the bonds of heavenly things, yea, and earthly things
also, for the obtaining of heavenly things. For if ye are not equal in
earthly things ye cannot be equal in obtaining heavenly things." (D&C

78:5–6.) This was the great spiritual ideal, to be achieved voluntarily by those who would be the Lord's covenant people. All who entered the order were expected to consecrate their property and personal possessions to the Church "with a covenant and a deed which can not be broken."

This was the ultimate economic sacrifice, but at that point the new order departed from the practices of contemporary communal societies. After an initial consecration, each member then was entitled to receive an inheritance, or stewardship, "sufficient for himself and family." Each year all the faithful stewards were to make an accounting to the bishop, and to give their surpluses to the bishop's storehouse. These would be distributed to those without enough for their needs or used for other general improvements. The Saints were admonished to avoid debt, dress plainly in homespun, and avoid the Shaker practice of helping themselves to personal belongings of fellow members of the order.

Economically, the law of consecration and stewardship was designed to accomplish four related objectives. First, it would eliminate poverty and create an economic equality tempered by individual needs, circumstances, and capacities. Second, through the continuing consecration of excess production into the storehouse, there would be a sharing of surplus, creating capital for business expansion and for church programs. Third, the system relied heavily on individual initiative. Each steward operated under a system of free enterprise in the management of his own property. He was subject to profits and losses, the laws of supply and demand, and the price system. But beyond this, each steward also considered himself part of a united community working toward a fourth objective, group economic self-sufficiency.

In practice the imperfections of the Saints made it impossible for them to live in complete unity under the new law. The order inaugurated by the Colesville Branch at Thompson, Ohio, ended in confusion and lawsuits before it had scarcely begun in the spring of 1831. It dissolved when Leman Copley withdrew his offer of land for the common pool. The Colesville Saints then moved to Missouri, where other members were gathering for a second attempt to live the law.

These and other problems led to some important changes in the way the order functioned. The difficulties over land titles at Thompson suggested the need for legally binding, written documents to transfer property. In Jackson County, Bishop Edward Partridge prepared a deed of consecration listing as a perpetual conveyance all items transferred to the order. On another document he listed the items returned to the donor as a stewardship and spelled out the restrictions on this inheritance. Transmitted for life on condition of good behavior, the stewardship could be forfeited through transgression. In this case the steward would lose the real estate leased from the bishop but could retrieve his loaned personal property if he paid for it. The agreement included an insurance provision that bound the bishop to care for the steward's family in case of infirmity, old age, or widowhood.

More adjustments soon became necessary. Those not fully converted to the system interpreted their leases or stewardships as legal titles, irrevocable even if they apostatized, but in May 1833 a Missouri court ruled in favor of one member who sued for the return of a fifty-dollar donation. After this Bishop Partridge abandoned his attempt to establish a perpetual deed of consecration.

These adjustments in the law of consecration were incorporated into the revelations published in the 1835 edition of the Doctrine and Covenants. Under the modified plan, the donor, not the Church, retained personal ownership and stewardship of income-producing property and personal effects. Each year he was to decide for himself how much was surplus and consecrate it to the bishop, in a voluntary offering. Any inheritance given the poor was conveyed under a similar contract. All these changes were consistent with what Church leaders learned through experience, and with a revelation of August 1, 1831, that commanded members not to break the law of the land, "for he that keepeth the law of God hath no need to break the law of the land." (D&C 58:21.) Contemporary legal opinion tended to disapprove of churches holding property in trust, and the law of consecration was now harmonized with that view. For faithful Saints who wanted to live "the more perfect law of the Lord," their consecrations were just as sacred as if they were enforced by the law of the land, and real sacrifice and brotherhood were still required.

The eagerness of some Saints to gather to Zion and enjoy the benefits of the law of consecration created other problems. Too many wanted to gather before the order could accommodate them. To restrain the poor from coming too quickly, therefore, and to ensure an orderly migration, Joseph Smith issued regulations in 1831 and 1832 keyed to the ability of the Missouri bishop to provide for new arrivals. Before leaving Ohio, each candidate was required to obtain a certificate from three elders or the bishop, and only with this certificate would he receive a share of the common wealth in Zion.

The management of the new economic order required more than

handling consecrations of properties. The basic institution was the bishop's storehouse, which was responsible for storing and distributing consecrated goods. But the storehouses in both Kirtland and Independence also tended to double as mercantile establishments, where surplus consecrations and profits were handled as common property for the purpose of purchasing more land, paying for Church buildings, and caring for the poor. There was also a printing establishment in Zion, and in November 1831 a Literary Firm was established in Ohio. It consisted initially of six men who were appointed "stewards over the revelations and commandments" (D&C 70:3) and made responsible for all publishing activities. In addition, Newel K. Whitney was ordained a bishop in Ohio with authority to collect consecrations but not dispense inheritances. That duty remained with the bishop in Zion.

Administration of these economic affairs was complex, and in April 1832 the Prophet and others attempted to simplify it when they created a new administrative agency known as the Central Council. This council, in turn, immediately created the United Firm (sometimes called the United Order), consisting of Joseph Smith and a handful of other Church leaders in Ohio and Missouri. This was a joint-stewardship in which the members consecrated all their lands and business to the firm. They were to manage "all things pertaining to the bishopric" (D&C 82:12), supervise the establishment of stores in Ohio and Missouri, and use their profits not only for their personal living expenses but also for the economic needs of the Church, including assisting the poor. The bishop continued to administer the law of consecration, though under the firm's general supervision.

Clearly there were advantages to the new system, for it consolidated Church financial concerns and gave the Prophet and his Kirtland associates more strength in business affairs. Ultimately, however, heavy costs, burdensome debts, and other financial difficulties led to a dissolution of the original firm just two years after it was founded. It was reorganized in two divisions: Ohio and Missouri. The property of the Ohio United Firm was then divided among the seven officers as their stewardships and personal responsibility.

In Missouri, meanwhile, the imperfection of the Saints themselves as well as their persecutions led to the abandonment of the law of consecration there. After the brutal expulsion from Jackson County, a revelation made the responsibility of the Saints themselves uncomfortably pointed:

> Behold, I say unto you, were it not for the transgressions of my
> people, speaking concerning the church and not individuals, they
> might have been redeemed even now.
>
> But behold, they have not learned to be obedient to the things
> which I required at their hands . . . , and do not impart of their
> substance, as becometh saints, to the poor and afflicted among them;
>
> And are not united according to the union required by the law
> of the celestial kingdom. (D&C 105:2–4.)

In the same revelation they were told to purchase lands elsewhere in
Missouri and there institute the law again, but due to a variety of serious
problems their sporadic attempts to revive it in the new settlements
were never effective.

Despite their personal weaknesses, the efforts of the Saints to institute the law of consecration represented a noble and commendable
effort to bring themselves closer to Christlike perfection. In the end,
however, they could not attain the ideal of selfless economic equality.
Even when all they had to do was donate their annual surplus to the
bishop's storehouse, it was difficult to recognize what constituted "surplus." The ideal remained, but in the meantime participation in the
traditional American economic system, based on the profit motive and
private ownership, was the only workable alternative to the system they
believed was ultimately superior.

The Government of the Kingdom Grows

When the Church left New York, its ecclesiastical organization
consisted of elders, priests, teachers, and deacons, led by its first and
second elders, Joseph Smith and Oliver Cowdery. For over two years
the general government of the Church consisted simply of conferences
of elders that convened every three months. As the Church grew, so
did its organization. The office of high priest, not originally identified
in the revelation on church government, was soon added, and a clearer
distinction was made between the two main branches of the priesthood:
the Aaronic, or lesser, priesthood, and the Melchizedek, or higher, priesthood. By 1835 other important changes had been made that would
characterize the permanent ecclesiastical structure of The Church of
Jesus Christ of Latter-day Saints.

Originally the bishopric was the chief ecclesiastical office in Missouri, and whenever conferences of elders met to conduct church business, Bishop Partridge was usually named moderator of the session.
Sometime in the fall of 1832 the elders' role was assumed by a council

Engraving showing the Kirtland Temple and nearby buildings. (From the Illustrated American, *December 27, 1890, Church Archives)*

of high priests, but the bishop continued to be recognized as the head of the Church in Zion and to preside at high priests council meetings. This continued until the expulsion from Jackson County, after which the council of high priests was replaced by a newly formed high council at Far West, and the bishop's primacy as presiding high priest ended.

Bishop Partridge's primary responsibility in Jackson County was administration of the law of consecration. In September 1831, Newel K. Whitney became his agent in Ohio, and three months later Whitney was ordained a bishop. The bishops handled only questions of consecrations and inheritances, leaving the high priests to regulate spiritual matters. Church officials referred to the Prophet in Ohio those matters not provided for in already revealed guidelines.

On January 25, 1832, Joseph Smith was sustained at a conference at Amherst, Ohio, as president of the high priesthood, and he was so ordained by Sidney Rigdon. Shortly after that a new presiding quorum, the First Presidency, was organized, with Joseph Smith as president, and a statement dated March 8 recognized Sidney Rigdon and Jesse Gause as counselors. Gause, however, became disaffected and Frederick G. Williams filled the vacancy. The Prophet and his counselors held the keys of the kingdom and presided over the entire Church.

Another important development was the designation of Kirtland, in April 1832, as a "stake of Zion," the first such area to be so identified.

Stakes eventually became the basic units of regional Church admin-istration, each presided over by a presidency and consisting of several ecclesiastical wards, or congregations. Wards were not organized until the Nauvoo period, however, and until 1834 the affairs of the Kirtland Stake were handled by a council of high priests under the direction of the bishop. On February 17, 1834, the Kirtland high council was or-ganized. Acting under the direction of a presidency, this council con-sisted of twelve high priests and was to be the official judicial body for the stake. The First Presidency of the Church initially functioned also as the presidency of the Kirtland Stake, but after Kirtland was abandoned these functions were separated. In July 1834 a stake was also organized in Clay County, Missouri, with a presidency and a high council.

At the same time, Joseph Smith recognized the need for more help in the First Presidency. On December 5, 1834, Oliver Cowdery was named assistant president, and the following day Joseph Smith, Sr., and Hyrum Smith received the same calling. Although officially the First Presidency was a quorum of three, this action established the precedent for later leaders to call needed special assistants.

Another new office announced was that of patriarch. On December 18, 1833, Joseph Smith and his two counselors ordained Joseph Smith, Sr., as the first patriarch in the Church, responsible for giving individual patriarchal blessings to the members. Subsequently other patriarchs were called to serve in various stakes and missions, and the elder Smith served as patriarch to the whole Church.

In 1835, the basic hierarchy of the Church was completed with the organization of the Council of the Twelve Apostles and the First Council of the Seventy. On March 28, at a special meeting of the Twelve, the Prophet dictated a revelation that clarified the duties of many church officers and distinguished more clearly between the two priesthoods. Now section 107 of the Doctrine and Covenants, it is one of the basic references on the operation of church government.

As early as 1829 the three witnesses to the Book of Mormon had been instructed to seek out twelve apostles, but only at the urging of Joseph Smith did they finally accomplish this important task. After receiving proper authority from the First Presidency, Oliver Cowdery, David Whitmer, and Martin Harris ordained nine of the twelve on February 14 and 15, 1835, and the other three were ordained later. The primary function of the Twelve was to be special witnesses of Christ, although they also served as a traveling high council, authorized to set in order church affairs anywhere in the world outside the stakes of

Zion. In 1841 their authority was expanded to include conduct of affairs within the stakes.

The original Council of the Twelve was a dedicated body of young men. The president of the group was the eldest—Thomas B. Marsh, thirty-five. The youngest four were all twenty-four. All but three had served in Zion's Camp (discussed below) and, like the seventies who would soon be chosen, were told that this march had been a trial of their faith, a test that now qualified them for their new responsibilities.

The office of seventy was introduced into the Church by Joseph Smith about two weeks after the organization of the Twelve. Unlike other priesthood groups, this body was given seven presidents to preside over each quorum, and a First Council of seven presidents was to lead all the seventies. The seventies were to be missionaries; and the presidency of the Seventy, and eventually the First Quorum of the Seventy, were to become General Authorities of the Church. The revelation that delineated their duties indicated they were to form a quorum equal in authority to that of the Twelve Apostles, but it also said that they were to act under the direction of the Twelve in preaching and administering the gospel. The phrase "equal in authority" has been interpreted to apply only if something should happen to the entire First Presidency and the Twelve: the presidency of the Seventy was next in line to assume leadership.

By early 1835, nearly all the basic ecclesiastical units had been organized. The principal administrative responsibility was given to the First Presidency. The Twelve Apostles were traveling ministers, special witnesses of Christ authorized to set in order church business anywhere outside the stakes. The Seventy were to assist the apostles in this task, and sometimes were even called the "seventy apostles." The Patriarch had the special calling of giving blessings. These officers, along with the Presiding Bishopric, constituted the General Authorities of the Church.[6]

In addition, the organization of 1835 included two stakes of Zion, each presided over by a stake presidency assisted by a high council of twelve high priests. The high council was then basically a judicial body,

---

[6]For many years the presidency of the Seventy was referred to as the First Council of the Seventy. After the reorganization of the First Quorum of the Seventy in the 1970s that designation was changed. Also, the General Authority office of Patriarch to the Church was dropped, in favor of emphasizing the responsibilities and accessibility of local stake patriarchs. See chapter 21 of this volume.

Temple lot, Independence, Missouri, in 1907. (George E. Anderson photograph, Church Archives)

though it later assumed greater advisory and administrative functions under the direction of the stake president. Bishops in each stake presided over the Aaronic, or lesser, priesthood, whose basic responsibility was economic. The responsibilities of various priesthood positions would be augmented in years to come, but these offices remained basic to the Church's ecclesiastical administration.

The City of Zion and Disruptions in the Gathering

On June 25, 1833, the Prophet sent a plan for the city of Zion and its temple to his brethren in Zion. This ideal city was to be one mile square with ten-acre blocks divided into one-half-acre lots, one house to the lot, and with a complex of temples on two central city blocks. The ideal, according to Joseph Smith, was to fill this city, then another one next to it, and so on as needed to "fill up the world in these last days." Independence, Missouri, would be the Center Place.

But the Saints would have to postpone the building of Zion, for even as they anticipated it, conflict and persecution planted seeds that soon resulted in their forceful removal from Jackson County. Lack of adequate, unbiased sources makes the reasons for this conflict difficult to assess, but several differences between the Mormons and the old settlers of the area may be identified.

To the original settlers, one cause of conflict may have been economic. The law of consecration as well as the general cooperative nature of Latter-day Saint settlement required substantial land holdings to accommodate the anticipated gathering, and the Saints were rapidly buying property in Jackson County. At the same time Mormon merchants and tradesmen established stores and shops that competed with those of the old settlers and grasped a portion of the lucrative Santa Fe trade previously dominated by Missourians. Impressed by Mormon group solidarity, some old settlers expressed fears that the Mormons were determined to take over all their lands and businesses.

They also viewed the body of Saints as a political threat. Members in Jackson County did not form a separate political faction or party and held no public offices during their short stay, yet leaders in county government feared Mormon domination by sheer numbers. By July 1833 the population included about twelve hundred Latter-day Saints, nearly one-third the total population, and the Church was growing rapidly. Local citizens were suspicious of a religious zeal that predicted the imminent establishment of a millennial kingdom in which Latter-day Saints, under the King of kings, would rule the world from their Missouri capital. The Saints seemed to be religious aliens threatening political domination.

The gathering Saints also collided with their neighbors in matters of religion. Protestant ministers, challenged everywhere by the proliferation of new sects, resented the intrusion of a people they quickly tagged as fanatics. The religious views of the Saints on the gathering of Zion, consecration, millennial politics, and new revelation set them apart even from their Christian neighbors, who quickly agreed with the Mormons themselves that they were a "peculiar people."

Cutting across economic, political, and religious lines were two other issues important to the Missouri frontiersmen: Mormon attitudes toward Native Americans and slavery. The first Saints in Missouri had come to convert the Indians just beyond the western borders. Though they failed, the local citizens did not forget this strange interest in uniting two cultures in a religious venture of building the city of Zion.

Similarly, Missouri farmers suspected Mormon subterfuge among their slaves. Residents of the state shared a long-standing hostility toward free Negroes, for they seemed to threaten the institution of slavery. When Missouri was admitted to the Union under the famous

Compromise of 1820, restrictions were placed upon further entry of free blacks into the state. In 1830 fewer than six hundred lived in Missouri, and none in Jackson County. Rumors early in 1832 accused the Saints of attempting to persuade slaves to disobey their masters, rebel, or run away. The issue of free blacks soon triggered a confrontation that had been brewing for months in an atmosphere of religious intolerance.

The Saints themselves may not have been totally without blame in the matter. The feelings of the Missourians, even though misplaced, were undoubtedly intensified by the rhetoric of the gathering itself. They were quick to listen to the boasting of a few overly zealous Saints who loudly declared a divine right to the land. As enthusiastic millennialists, they also proclaimed that the time of the gentiles was short, and they were perhaps too quick to quote the revelation that said "the Lord willeth that the disciples and the children of men should open their hearts, even to purchase this whole region of country, as soon as time will permit." (D&C 58:52.) Though the Saints were specifically and repeatedly commanded to be peaceful and to never shed blood, some seemed unwisely to threaten warfare if they could not fulfill the commandment peacefully. In July 1833 Church leaders reemphasized the importance of legally purchasing land, but by then a combination of factors was leading to confrontation.

Whatever some unwise and imperfect Saints may have done, a revelation after their expulsion placed at least partial blame on them. "I, the Lord, have suffered the affliction to come upon them," rang the words that came through Joseph Smith, "in consequence of their transgressions. . . . Behold, I say unto you, there were jarrings, and contentions, and envyings, and strifes, and lustful and covetous desires among them; therefore by these things they polluted their inheritances. They were slow to hearken unto the voice of the Lord their God; therefore, the Lord their God is slow to hearken unto their prayers, to answer them in the day of trouble." (D&C 101:2–7.) The redemption of Zion must be postponed until Zion's people had become more perfect, but the same revelation promised that "Zion shall not be moved out of her place," and that one day her redemption would surely come.

Confrontation and Expulsion

Most of the Saints struggled to apply the principles of restored Christianity and live peacefully with their neighbors. But charges against them mounted, and the truth of the matter became unimportant: certain influential Missouri settlers simply did not want the Saints to live among them, and the indictments they spread were readily believed.

In April 1833 about three hundred leading citizens met in Independence to plan the removal or destruction of their unwanted neighbors. Nothing concrete was accomplished, but feelings on both sides were soon intensified. The Reverend Benton Pixley, a longtime missionary to the Indians, wrote anti-Mormon articles and made house-to-house visits denouncing the Saints. In July, William W. Phelps, editor of *The Evening and the Morning Star*, answered Pixley's charges with an article entitled "Beware of False Prophets."

The same issue of the Church newspaper carried a notice, entitled "Free People of Color," designed to warn free blacks who were members of the Church of the Missouri law that forbade them to enter the state unless they carried a certificate of citizenship from another state. The notice touched a nerve among the Missourians, who interpreted it as encouragement of immigration and therefore a threat to the slave system. In response, eighty prominent citizens signed a manifesto. Known as the "secret constitution," it denounced the Mormons and called for a meeting on July 20. The manifesto claimed that Mormons were tampering with slaves, encouraging sedition, and inviting free Negroes and mulattoes to join the Church and immigrate to Missouri. It openly declared the intent of the signers to remove the Mormons "peaceably if we can, forcibly if we must."[7]

When William W. Phelps heard of the secret constitution, he issued an "Extra" in an attempt to clarify the controversial notice. It was actually intended, he said, to halt the immigration of free blacks, and even to "prevent them from being admitted as members of the church." But the clarification failed. The "Extra" was ignored.

The meeting on Saturday, July 20, attracted four or five hundred citizens opposed to the Latter-day Saints. They released a public document repeating the assertions of the secret constitution and pronouncing a bitter ultimatum. Mormon immigration and settlement must halt, and the Saints must sell their land and businesses and leave the county within a reasonable time. All this must be accomplished under a pledge which, if broken, would justify the proponents in consulting again on further steps. Though the Saints were astounded, this un-

[7]*History of the Church*, 1:374.

believable mob proposal was soon presented to six Church leaders. Denied time to consider it, they rejected the plan. The impatient assembly, after waiting two hours for an answer, voted to take immediate action. About a hundred men proceeded to the Church printing office, kicked in the door, and evicted Mrs. Phelps and her children. They tossed the press from a second-story window, pulled off the roof, and tore down the walls of the building. Damages were estimated at about $5,000, and the attack halted the printing of the Book of Commandments and the two newspapers. The mob next attacked the store, the blacksmith shop, and two men, Edward Partridge and Charles Allen. They were hauled to the public square, partially stripped of their clothing, and, after failing to admit guilt or promising to leave, were covered with tar and feathers. Violence had erupted and would not cease until the Saints were gone.

The mob appeared again on July 23, carrying rifles, pistols, clubs, and whips, and compelled Mormon leaders to assemble in the public square. They were forced to sign a written agreement to leave the county, one group before January 1 and another before April, although John Corrill and Sidney Gilbert would be allowed to remain as agents in selling the property of the Saints.

This agreement allowed the Saints a little time to seek advice from Joseph Smith and consult with state officials. Oliver Cowdery was immediately dispatched to Kirtland, where a council met and sent a message to the Saints in Zion to seek redress under the law. A letter from Frederick G. Williams in October recommended that only those who actually signed the pledge should leave, and that no one should sell his inheritance in Zion. The Saints could hardly consider the agreement legally binding, for it was signed under mob duress.

The leaders in Zion, meanwhile, petitioned Missouri Governor Daniel Dunklin for help and protection. The state attorney general considered the request, criticized the citizens for lawlessness, and urged the Saints to seek both redress and protection under the laws by petitioning the circuit judge and justices of the peace. To pursue their case in the courts, the Church retained the legal firm of Doniphan, Atchison, Rees, and Wood in late October 1833. In addition, Church leaders ended their policy of passive resistance and counseled the Saints to arm themselves for the defense of their families and homes. A delegation to Clay County purchased powder and lead, and Church officials announced on October 20 their intent to defend themselves against any physical attack.

The Missourians quickly interpreted this as a violation of the Mormon promise to evacuate. They spread the word through the county, and on Thursday, October 31, the citizens took their first concerted action. That night forty or fifty men attacked the Whitmer settlement just over the Big Blue River, eight miles west of Independence, unroofed and demolished ten houses, and whipped several men as the Mormons fled. Church leaders sought a peace warrant against the captains of the raiding party, but after a justice of the peace refused it, the elders decided to post guards. Each branch was instructed to organize its own defense and be prepared to march at a moment's notice.

Violence continued throughout the county, and judges repeatedly refused to issue warrants against the mobsters. Early in November the Saints in Independence were forced to leave their homes and camp together on the temple lot under the protection of two or three dozen men. In another raid on a settlement on the Big Blue a Missourian was wounded, prompting his cohorts to organize for battle and the Saints, in turn, to congregate in even larger bodies for protection. On November 4 several Missourians captured a Mormon ferry on the Big Blue, and soon thirty or forty angry men from each side confronted each other in the fields. Shots were fired and the Missourians departed, with the Mormons in hot pursuit. Two Missourians were killed; on the Mormon side, Philo Dibble's injury crippled him for life, and Andrew Barber died of his wounds the following day.

Meanwhile, a few Mormon leaders were jailed in Independence, and rumors that the Mormons were planning to bring Indians against the town began to spread. More citizens rallied, but eventually the leaders either escaped or were freed from jail. By then, they had informed the sheriff of their intention to evacuate the county.

Lilburn W. Boggs, then lieutenant governor of the state, acted as intermediary between the two opposing groups and persuaded the Saints to surrender their arms and leave within ten days in order to avoid more bloodshed. The Saints understood that Boggs would also collect the arms of their enemies and that all would be returned to their rightful owners after they had evacuated. In this they were sadly misled.

The prisoners were released in a cornfield near Independence, and immediately they began planning for the exodus from Jackson County. But as if to reinforce their determination to rid themselves of their neighbors, the Missourians continued harassing Mormon settlements. Mounted bands threatened the Saints with physical violence, searched their homes for weapons, whipped some, and chased others from their property. One group of about 130 women and children, left alone while the men hunted wagons, were harassed by over one hundred armed men. When ordered out within two hours, they loaded supplies into four available wagons and moved across the river into Clay County.

A few of the Saints found refuge in Ray, Lafayette, and Van Buren counties, but the largest congregation assembled in Clay County, to open another chapter in the history of the Church in Missouri. The citizens of Liberty, the principal town of Clay County, offered work, shelter, and provisions. The refugees moved into abandoned slave cabins, built crude huts, and pitched tents. When spring arrived they rented land and found work splitting rails, grubbing brush, or working as day laborers. Women served as domestics and teachers. Because of their friendliness toward the beleaguered Saints, the helpful citizens of Clay and other counties were criticized by hostile elements in Jackson County and dubbed "Jack Mormons," a term applied widely in the nineteenth century to friendly non-Mormons.

The removal of the Saints from Jackson County deeply concerned the Prophet. Not only had it brought suffering to the Saints, but it had also interrupted a principal dream of the restoration. By revelation in October the Saints were assured, "Zion shall be redeemed, although she is chastened for a little season." Until that could be accomplished, the Prophet encouraged the eastern branches to continue gathering funds for land purchases in Jackson County and told the Missouri faithful to retain title to their lands and seek redress through constitutional means. These important instructions set the tone for Latter-day Saint policy toward Jackson County in following years, and the concept of redeeming Zion became a permanent part of Mormon millennial expectations.

Following the instructions of the Prophet, the exiled Missouri Saints made further attempts to recover their property and damages through the courts. They asked the governor to provide a military escort as they reoccupied their homes, and guards for witnesses who would testify in the Jackson County court. Governor Dunklin agreed to furnish arms if the Saints would organize themselves into a local militia, but, he explained to the dismay of the Saints, he would have to work through proper channels, meaning the Jackson Guard.

When the court of inquiry was finally held, the governor did authorize the Clay County militia, the Liberty Blues, to guard the witnesses. A circuit court hearing was held in late February, and a cadre of fifty Blues accompanied the Mormon witnesses across the river into

Jackson County. It soon became evident that the excitement of the Jackson County citizens made criminal prosecution impossible, so Church leaders decided to abandon the effort.

The Church next petitioned the president of the United States, Andrew Jackson, for a federal guarantee of protection once the lost property was regained. For the first time the Church encountered national politics and discovered that no matter how just their cause, other considerations made it impossible for the federal government to act. One of the great national debates of the day concerned the sovereign rights of states and the degree to which the federal government could intervene in a state's internal affairs. Just a year earlier the United States had come close to civil war when South Carolina had claimed the right to nullify an act of Congress within its borders. President Jackson went so far as to assemble troops, declare South Carolina in rebellion, and threaten to march on the state if it did not conform to the federal law. South Carolina backed down, but only with a strong proclamation that it was sovereign and had a right to do what it had done. Joseph Smith was so concerned by the issue that he had it recorded in his history of the Church, calling South Carolina's action a rebellion. Then, on Christmas Day in 1832, he received one of his best-known revelations, which predicted that "beginning at the rebellion of South Carolina," civil war would surely come to the United States.

When the Mormons presented their grievances to the United States, it was in an atmosphere charged with tension over the states' rights issue, and the general feeling was that the federal government had no authority to intervene in such matters. The Mormon question was referred to Secretary of War Lewis Cass, who replied on May 2, 1834, that the offenses listed as religious persecution appeared to be violations of state, not federal, law. According to the Constitution, the president could not call out the militia unless the governor declared a state of insurrection. Having just survived the nullification controversy, the Jackson administration was not prepared to intervene in another states' rights question.

Governor Dunklin continued efforts to help the Mormons, but the tense situation prevented effective action, through either the courts or the legislature. By 1834 he was complaining in despair to the legislature that "under our present laws, conviction for any violence committed upon a Mormon, cannot be had in Jackson County."[8] Mormon appeals

---

[8]As quoted in Warren A. Jennings, "Zion Is Fled: The Expulsion of the Mormons from Jackson County, Missouri" (Ph.D. diss., University of Florida, 1962), p. 238.

continued until well after the final expulsion from the state in 1838, but under the circumstances a fair court decision seemed impossible.

Zion's Camp

The Ohio Saints, in the meantime, were preparing to make a bold effort to rescue their beleaguered comrades: the march of Zion's Camp. Joseph Smith's revelations of December 16, 1833, and February 24, 1834, suggested direct action, though veiled in well-worded parable and hyperbole. (D&C 101:43–62; 103:15–22.) A parable of a nobleman and his vineyard was given "that you may know my will concerning the redemption of Zion." The Lord of the vineyard instructed his servant (i.e., Joseph Smith) to gather the young and middle-aged "warriors" and redeem the land that had been captured by an intruding enemy. By February, when the Prophet announced the intention to go to Missouri, he had enlisted more than thirty volunteers. The high council sent eight enlistment officers to the eastern congregations to seek out additional volunteers and contributions. It was not intended that this would be merely an invading army. The plan envisioned a return of the Saints to their homes in Jackson County through cooperation with state authorities and under state protection.

On the first day of May the advance guard of Kirtland volunteers began its thousand-mile trek. Additional units followed, and on May 6 the Prophet organized his 150 men into companies of twelve. Buying supplies as it traveled, the camp marched across Ohio, Indiana, and Illinois, adding volunteers from other branches until it grew to an estimated 205 members, including ten women (wives of recruits) who went along to help with the cooking and washing.

While the little Mormon army moved westward, the Clay County Saints proceeded to rearm themselves. On June 5 they informed Governor Dunklin that they were ready for a state escort for their return. But Jackson County citizens were also preparing by securing pledges from surrounding counties for support to resist reestablishment of the Saints in Jackson County. Rumors of imminent Mormon invasions across the Missouri during the last week of April brought a hasty mustering of the Jackson Guard, but when no invasion materialized, the Missourians vented their tension by burning the remaining Mormon houses. Then they slipped across the river in small groups to harass the settlers near the river.

Zion's Camp left its Salt River encampment June 12, having asked the Missouri governor for a military escort. Governor Dunklin, fearing that any attempts to cooperate with the Mormons would spark a civil war, withdrew his earlier offer to escort the refugees back to their homes and advised the Saints to sell contested lands and move elsewhere. Zion's Camp received word of the refusal with dismay, but the governor had already launched a compromise. Acting through Colonel John Thornton, a wealthy landowner in Clay County, the governor acknowledged the Mormons' right to live in Missouri, but concluded that their religious eccentricity made isolation advisable. Jackson County officials agreed to negotiate a peaceful solution, and the governor outlined the alternatives for the Latter-day Saints: sell out and leave the county, persuade the Missourians they should rescind their illegal resolves and abide by the law, or occupy separate territories and isolate themselves from their antagonists.

The two sides met at Liberty on June 16 in a crowded meeting at the courthouse. Judge John F. Ryland presided. After a tirade of inflammatory speeches by local citizens, a committee of ten proposed to buy out the Mormons if they agreed never to return. Prices would be established by disinterested arbitrators. Alternatively, the old residents said they would sell on the same terms if the Mormons wanted to purchase their holdings. Both offers were impractical, as neither side was actually inclined to sell to the other.

The meeting adjourned to allow the attending elders to seek the consensus of the Church. In the meantime, they promised to keep Zion's Camp outside Jackson County. The camp moved to a site between two branches of Fishing River, just east of the Clay County line, only to be warned that about three hundred armed mobocrats from several nearby communities were planning an attack. A fierce squall, however, prevented a clash, and the following day the Mormon army moved to a Mormon farm five miles away.

Church leaders soon rejected the Jackson County offer and proposed their alternative. They suggested that a committee of twelve, six from each side, be appointed to determine the value of the property of the citizens wishing to leave and the cost of damages. The Saints would use the credits for damages to buy out the old citizens and pay any differences within a year. The plan was rejected, however, and the stalemate continued.

The citizens of Jackson County, meanwhile, were still disturbed by the presence of the Kirtland militia on their borders. On June 22 the sheriff of Clay County visited the camp to secure a statement of

The arrival of Zion's Camp. This painting is one of a series begun by C. C. A. Christensen in 1869 to illustrate his lectures on Church history. The paintings were sewed together on a long wooden pole and unrolled as the artist talked. (From the Permanent Collection of Brigham Young University)

intent, as requested by Judge Ryland. "It is our intention," camp officials declared, "to go back upon our lands in Jackson county, by order of the Executive of the State if possible."[9] But the Saints lacked the necessary military support from the governor, although negotiations were in progress, and Joseph Smith soon recognized the impossibility of reoccupation without that support.

On June 22 the Prophet received a revelation at Fishing River declaring that Zion would not be redeemed at that time. The reason given was the failure of the Church as a whole to observe the law of consecration and to support Zion's Camp financially. The Saints were learning the difficult lesson that the Lord does not always fight their battles for them, and that political and physical realities often require that fulfillment of his commandments be delayed. Those who had met a trial of faith by responding to the call were promised a special endowment, and the Saints were urged to continue their efforts to obtain legal redress and to purchase Jackson County land. Zion would still, one day, be redeemed.

On June 30 the Prophet announced that the members of Zion's

---

[9]*Evening and the Morning Star* 2 (July 1834): 176.

Camp were discharged. Several had died of cholera; many drifted back to Kirtland in small parties, while others remained in Missouri. On July 7 the Prophet attended a conference which drafted an "Appeal to the American People," explaining the Latter-day Saints' refusal to accept the Missouri offer to buy them out and declaring that "to sell our land would amount to a denial of our faith."[10]

Kirtland: Way Station for a Season

Even while the Saints in Zion were suffering displacement, important developments occurred in Ohio. Particularly significant were Latter-day Saint involvements in the economic and political life of Geauga County, the establishment of an educational program, the demise of the United Firm, and completion and dedication of the Kirtland Temple. In addition, the printing agency was transferred to Kirtland.

Kirtland had been designated as a way station for five years, and many members willingly accepted the challenge to help the Lord "retain a strong hold in the land of Kirtland." (D&C 64:21.) Latter-day Saints crowded into Kirtland, overflowed all available houses, and then sought out abandoned shops, simple huts, barns, or wagon boxes for temporary living quarters.

In Ohio, as in Missouri, older settlers reacted negatively to the prospect of large numbers of Mormons living together in one place. Established communities were fully willing to allow the Saints to participate in their own religious practices and to share in the economic and political life of the community as long as they remained a scattered, integrated minority. But the policy of gathering—of congregating in self-contained, exclusive subcommunities—challenged the original citizens' traditions.

Many of the Saints were destitute of worldly possessions, but those with resources contributed generously toward land purchases, home building, and construction of the temple. The Saints had their own dry goods stores, inn, sawmills, gristmill, and fulling mill, plus various craftsmen. In this way, they contributed to the development of the community. Because of the general poverty of the Saints, however, older citizens feared the burden of charity might be shifted to the town. Their fears were compounded by the worsening economic conditions of 1835. Some non-Mormons wanted to force the Saints out of the Kirtland area,

---

[10]*Evening and the Morning Star* 2 (August 1834): 183–84.

and two leading businessmen refused to employ the newcomers in their factory and sawmill. When grain became scarce that summer, merchants expanded their boycott by refusing to sell to the Latter-day Saints, hoping to starve them out. But there were Mormon mills outside Kirtland, and other supplies were available fifty miles from the community.

The Saints in Ohio participated more broadly in public affairs than those in Jackson County, and Joseph Smith, who lived in Kirtland, took great interest in both local and national politics. The Mormons in general supported the national administration and gave allegiance to Andrew Jackson's Democratic party. But Ohio's Western Reserve was mixed politically, and the Whigs in Geauga County were suspicious of the potential political threat presented by a bloc of Mormon votes. Several Latter-day Saints in Kirtland, including Oliver Cowdery, Sidney Rigdon, and Frederick G. Williams, held elective offices, and the Whigs saw this as a possible first step toward Mormon control of local government. The unity of the Mormons thus created the potential for jealousies, even though the Prophet made no attempt to urge political conformity.

Already rumors were spreading that because of their exclusiveness Mormons were anti-American and part of a secret, autocratic society. To quash such tales, Frederick G. Williams founded the *Northern Times* in 1834. Another effort to quiet false political assertions was the statement on government, adopted in 1835 and printed in the first edition of the Doctrine and Covenants. This statement, probably written by Oliver Cowdery, emphasized freedom of religion, freedom of opinion, and the need for government free from the influence of any particular religion.

Contemporary Church leaders were not hesitant to speak out on many issues of both local and national concern. Through the *Northern Times* and other publications they denounced abolitionism, supported Andrew Jackson in his campaign against the United States Bank, and became involved in the question of changing the Geauga County Seat. Despite their religious exclusiveness, it was important to the Saints that they be recognized as part of the larger body politic in America and as loyal citizens.

Intemperance was an important social issue in Ohio and many other places in Jacksonian America, and the Mormon solution eventually played an important role in setting the Latter-day Saints apart as a distinctive people. By 1833, the year the revelation known as the Word of Wisdom was given, the temperance movement in America had five thousand local societies claiming over a million members. Temperance articles were regular fare in the public press. Diet, too, was receiving considerable attention, with stress on fruits, vegetables, and moderation in eating meat. Warnings against the use of tobacco also were beginning to appear.

The Owenites (a communitarian group) and the Campbellites had endorsed the temperance movement, and the Kirtland Temperance Society had been organized since October 1830. The society closed the local distillery, first by refusing to sell it grain and then, when the distillers imported grain, by pooling resources to purchase the business. A distillery at Mentor closed at the same time. Even though some Saints belonged to the society, critics complained of lack of Mormon support, and the society folded in October 1835.

During the height of the movement to close the Geauga County distilleries, the Prophet gave the Saints their own guidelines on temperance. This revelation, known as the Word of Wisdom, was another good example of divine guidance coming to the Church in response to inquiries about particular matters. Not only was there controversy among the region's populace, but, it appears, an immediate situation closer to home played a key role in calling forth the inspired code of health. Joseph and his family lived in rooms in Newel K. Whitney's store and, as Brigham Young reported many years later, the Prophet was influenced by happenings among the elders attending the School of the Prophets in an upstairs room above the store:

> When they assembled together in this room after breakfast, the first they did was to light their pipes, and while smoking, talk about the great things of the kingdom, and spit all over the room, and as soon as the pipe was out of their mouths a large chew of tobacco would then be taken. Often when the Prophet entered the room to give instruction he would find himself in a cloud of smoke. This, and the complaints of his wife at having to clean so filthy a floor, made the Prophet think upon the matter, and he inquired of the Lord relating to the conduct of the Elders in using tobacco, and the revelation known as the Word of Wisdom was the result of his inquiry.[11]

The Word of Wisdom denounced the drinking of wine, strong drink,

---

[11]Sermon of 8 February 1868, in *Journal of Discourses* 12:158. Brigham Young was not in Kirtland when the Word of Wisdom was given, so this famous story probably reflects his memory of what Joseph or someone else told him about the setting.

Joseph and Emma Smith lived in an upstairs room of the mercantile store operated by Newel K. Whitney and Company at Kirtland. While there, the Prophet received the Word of Wisdom and other important revelations. (George Edward Anderson photo, 1907, courtesy Church Archives)

and hot drinks. It declared that tobacco was not good for man, though it noted its value for medicinal purposes, advised moderation in the use of meat, and encouraged the use of grain and fresh fruits with thanksgiving. The "hot drinks" prohibited were later interpreted to mean specifically tea and coffee. At first written "not by commandment or constraint, but by revelation and the word of wisdom," this revelation eventually became a standard of health as well as a symbol of obedience to gospel principles among the Latter-day Saints.

In addition to such political and social concerns, the Church led Kirtland in education. One of the First Presidency's duties was to develop a training school for church officers — the School of the Prophets. According to the "Olive Leaf" revelation, recorded December 27, 1832, it was to be a temple school, conducted in the House of the Lord. One of its important tasks was to train prospective missionaries, but the Prophet also recognized the need for knowledge of temporal as well as spiritual matters. He had been urged by revelation to "study and learn, and become acquainted with all good books, and with languages, tongues, and people." (D&C 90:15.) With this philosophy, the School of the Prophets established divisions for secular education as well as theology classes, and participants discussed current issues and signs of the times along with the doctrines of the kingdom.

The School of the Prophets opened in January of 1833 but was disrupted in April. When it reopened in the fall of 1834 it had been divided into the Elder's School for theological training and the Kirtland School for temporal education. "Lectures on Faith," a series of lessons subsequently published with the Doctrine and Covenants between 1835 and 1921, was a basic text for missionaries. Burdick's *Arithmetic*, Kirkham's *Grammar*, and Olney's *Geography* guided nearly one hundred students in the secular division, where they were also tutored in the rudiments of penmanship by William E. McLellin. Both schools met during the winter of 1835–36 with increased enrollment and with new evening grammar classes. Beginning in late November the school sponsored a seven-week Hebrew class taught by Joshua Seixas of Hudson, Ohio. The classwork for both schools moved into the temple in January 1835 and a second term of Hebrew commenced. In November 1837 the Kirtland High School assumed the general education curriculum pioneered by the Kirtland School.

Except for the mob violence against Joseph Smith and Sidney Rigdon in March 1832, anti-Mormon activities in Ohio in the early 1830s remained at a relatively low pitch. But the Prophet found it necessary to employ guards, and the Saints were constantly harassed by threats and lawsuits. Joseph Smith spent thousands of dollars defending himself against various charges, many of which proved to be simply the venting of personal animosity.

At least some of the Prophet's troubles stemmed from internal problems. Sylvester Smith, for example, accused him of improper conduct as the leader of Zion's Camp, and this led to considerable difficulty between the two. In a Kirtland high council trial held in August 1834, however, the accuser acknowledged that he had misrepresented the facts, and he later made a voluntary public statement in the *Messenger and Advocate* to the effect that his accusations against Joseph Smith were in error. Such cases pitting one member against another often brought unwelcome publicity and were used by the Church's enemies to build a negative public image of Mormonism.

The Promised Endowment

Their admitted imperfections did not prevent the Saints from enjoying the outpouring of spiritual blessings, and they were still anxiously engaged in building the kingdom. Missionary work grew, the Prophet continued to receive revelations for spiritual guidance, and the Saints proceeded toward the fulfillment of a major goal: a temple in Kirtland.

When the Saints outgrew the log meetinghouse in Kirtland, a conference of Church leaders met to plan a replacement. Most assumed they would build another simple log or frame structure, but the Prophet had a grander plan in mind. In December the important "Olive Leaf" revelation not only spelled out significant doctrine, but also commanded the elders to establish a house, "even a house of prayer, a house of fasting, a house of faith, a house of learning, a house of glory, a house of order, a house of God." (D&C 88:119.) This would be the first Latter-day Saint temple. A later revelation specified that the lower floor would be a meetinghouse and the upper level a school. The building committee, composed of Hyrum Smith, Reynolds Cahoon, and Jared Carter, issued a circular, distributed to all branches of the Church, requesting money for the new project. Funds began to arrive from everywhere—even the beleaguered Zion in Missouri.

According to a revelation, the plans for this temple-school were to be "after the manner which I shall show unto three of you, whom ye shall appoint and ordain unto this power." (D&C 95:14.) Members of the First Presidency, with Frederick G. Williams as draftsman, were the three, and they created a plan resembling a modified New England meetinghouse. It was a striking building that utilized traditional motifs arranged in an unorthodox pattern, with two main doors instead of three, a vertically unaligned center window used to light both floors, and a second story replacing the more typical gallery. Inside, two sets of pulpits gave the assembly room an unusual double front. Four tiers of lavishly carved pulpits for the Melchizedek Priesthood were placed on the west (where other denominations placed a single pulpit), and pulpits for the Aaronic Priesthood were placed on the east. Veils or curtains lowered by hidden ropes and pulleys divided the room into quarters and covered the pulpits when the presiding officers wished privacy.

The temple was built of sandstone covered with plaster. The cornerstone was laid on July 23, 1833, and the project had an immediate impact on the Church and the community. It spurred a lagging economy and employed those unable to find work elsewhere, including refugees from troubled Missouri. When fund-raising fell short, Joseph Smith borrowed money to meet the estimated $60,000 cost. The project rallied members to a cause that demanded sacrifice and financial commitment and helped resolve some of the discord that had followed Zion's Camp.

Despite the Saints' difficulties in keeping the law of consecration, their cooperation on this project was exemplary. Typical of the enthusiasm they felt for building the temple was the experience of Vilate Kimball, who spent the summer spinning wool to provide clothes for those working on the project. She was supposed to receive half the wool as pay, but instead she gave it all to the workers. Many women participated in similar generous ways, and when the exterior coating was being applied to the sandstone walls, the women donated glassware to be crushed and worked into the plaster to give a gleaming appearance to the sacred building. To the Latter-day Saints the temple was more than a meetinghouse or a school. It was the visible symbol of the kingdom of God.

But once the building was complete, the Saints had something else to anticipate. Even before they left New York they had been promised that they would be "endowed with power from on high" (D&C 38:32), and by mid-1833 this special blessing was specifically promised as a function of the Lord's house. This was not the endowment later performed in the Nauvoo and other temples, but it was a special outpouring of spiritual manifestations resembling those of Pentecost.

Events surrounding the completion of the temple were a spiritual high point in the history of the Church in Kirtland. In January 1836, two months before the dedication ceremonies, Joseph Smith introduced among the leaders an ordinance of washing and anointing with oil, which symbolized the spirituality and cleanliness they desired. At an impressive meeting in the attic rooms of the temple, the Prophet and others reported visions of the celestial kingdom, and the Prophet saw his deceased brother Alvin in that kingdom. Marveling at how this could be, as Alvin had died before the restoration of the gospel, the Prophet received a revelation concerning the salvation of those who die without hearing the gospel, and this prepared the way for the Latter-day Saint practice of baptism for the dead.

On the day of the dedication, March 27, nearly half the crowd had to be turned away, though ceremonies were repeated on March 31 for those unable to crowd in for the original services. Morning and afternoon meetings were held; the sacrament of the Lord's supper was served; several powerful sermons and testimonies were heard; Joseph Smith gave the dedicatory prayer, which had been given to him by revelation and now constitutes Section 109 of the Doctrine and Covenants; a new hymn, "The Spirit of God Like a Fire Is Burning," which had been written especially for the occasion by William W. Phelps, was sung;

Appearance of the Savior in the Kirtland Temple, as depicted in a 1975 painting by Gary Smith. (Reproduced courtesy the artist)

and the spirit-filled services concluded with the whole congregation shouting together three times: "Hosanna, Hosanna, Hosanna to God and the Lamb, Amen, Amen, Amen."

But the day was not complete. That night members of the priesthood met in the temple to be instructed in the ordinances of washing of feet and anointing with oil. Suddenly, they reported, they heard the room filled with sounds of wind. People outside the temple also heard the sound and said they saw a shaft of light on the temple steeple. Inside, priesthood members spoke in tongues and, in that powerful atmosphere so reminiscent of the day of Pentecost, the Prophet admonished the Twelve to carry the gospel to the nations.

Two days later priesthood members spent an all-night session receiving washings and anointings, and on March 30 the Saints experienced another Pentecostal day. Several testified to visions of the Savior and of angels. A final outpouring of such experiences came on April 3 following two meetings attended by a thousand Saints. Joseph Smith and Oliver Cowdery dropped the curtains that surrounded the west pulpits and, after solemn prayer, received visions of the Savior and the ancient prophets Moses, Elias, and Elijah, each of whom restored certain keys pertaining to the last days.

Following these climactic events the temple was put to thorough use. This included regular Sunday meetings, fast meetings on the first Thursday of each month at 10 A.M. and 4 P.M. with Patriarch Joseph Smith, Sr., presiding, school classes during the week, and separate meetings for the Melchizedek Priesthood quorums on weekday evenings. Soon a new corps of missionaries left for various fields of labor, having received the "endowment from on high" promised when the Saints left their New York homelands to gather in Ohio. Within three years the same Saints would once again be uprooted from their homes, joining their Missouri brethren in a new attempt at community building in the westernmost corner of Illinois.

CHAPTER 4

The Saints Move On, *1836–1839*

On three successive nights in November 1833, the banks of the Missouri River north of Independence were covered with terrified, homeless refugees. Over twelve hundred Latter-day Saints were being driven from what they believed would be their place of refuge. Jamming the riverbank at Wayne Landing, they waited to board a ferry to cross into Clay County. Many distraught families had been separated, and even as they sought each other, their tormentors hunted them down, fired on them, and whipped them.

Among the harried group were the twenty-six-year-old apostle Parley P. Pratt and his wife, Thankful. About midnight on November 5 the two escaped their home on horseback. The next morning they crossed the river and camped with the growing number of Saints huddled among the cottonwood trees in the river bottoms of Clay County. Elder Pratt pathetically reported:

> Hundreds of people were seen in every direction, some in tents and some in the open air around their fires, while the rain descended in torrents. Husbands were inquiring for their wives, wives for their husbands; parents for children, and children for parents. Some had the good fortune to escape with their families, household goods, and some provisions, while others knew not the fate of their friends, and had lost all their goods. The scene was indescribable.[1]

The Latter-day Saints in Missouri were again seeking a place of refuge. They found it, temporarily, in Clay County, but within thirty months they would be on their way to another county; and finally, in another three years, they would find themselves completely driven from the state.

---

[1]Parley Parker Pratt, *Autobiography of Parley Parker Pratt*, ed. Parley P. Pratt, 3rd ed. (Salt Lake City: Deseret Book Co., 1938), p. 102.

In Kirtland, meanwhile, the Prophet himself would find little peace, and in 1838 he would join his exiled followers in northern Missouri, only to be imprisoned within the year and left behind as the Saints sought new refuge in Illinois. His distress would come not only from bitter anti-Mormons, but also from those within who would lose confidence in him, attempt to replace him, and fight against all he was trying to accomplish. By the end of the decade two of the three witnesses to the Book of Mormon, the president of the Council of the Twelve, and several other friends and close associates would turn against him. The last years of the 1830s, however, witnessed not only some of the most pathetic scenes in the history of the Church but also a surprising note of faith and optimism. This perseverance suggests a good deal about the Latter-day Saints, just as the reasons for their difficulties tell much about the society of western America in the 1830s.

Clay County Rejects the Saints

The Saints originally received a kindly reception from the citizens of Clay County, and for more than two years they lived and worked there, hoping for the day when Zion would be restored. Many became landowners in the new location, and members from other parts of the country swelled their numbers. But the citizens of Clay County considered the Mormon settlement there as only a temporary, humanitarian arrangement, and the same concerns that had disturbed their neighbors in Jackson County soon began to stir among them. Even though the Saints were peaceful in their conduct, the people of Clay County became increasingly apprehensive when it began to look as if they were planning to stay.

On June 29, 1836, a mass meeting of Clay County settlers was held in the Liberty courthouse. There the accusations leveled at the Saints in Jackson County were reiterated in four basic objections: their religious differences were exciting prejudice, they were easterners whose customs and even dialect were essentially different from those of the Missourians, they were non-slaveholders opposed to slavery, and they were constantly communicating with the Indians whom they proclaimed were God's chosen people who would inherit with them the land of Missouri. "We do not vouch for the correctness of these statements," said the report of the committee, "but whether they are true or false, their effect has been the same in exciting our community."[2]

---

[2]*History of the Church*, 2:450.

The committee believed that the very existence of such charges aroused hostility and, to avoid bloodshed, the Saints were asked to leave the county. The report made no direct threat of hostility, but committee members said the invitation to move would spare the county a civil war.

The accusations of Clay County spokesmen and the reply of the Saints reflect not only the stresses of frontier society but also the process by which tragic misunderstandings often occur. Deeply held sympathies for slavery had become part of the social structure in Missouri. As abolitionism gained momentum in the North and East, and sometimes reached extremes, Missourians looked at it with growing apprehension as something that seemed to threaten their social system. The Saints had unequivocally declared that they had no intention of interfering with slavery, and that they believed any interference would be both unlawful and unjust, but the fact remained that most Mormons were from the East, where abolitionism was strongest, and none of them was known to have held slaves. It seemed inconsistent that they would not oppose slavery and, despite Mormon denials, some Missourians were incapable of believing otherwise.

It was understandable, too, that the Missourians were wary of Indian uprising. The tribes along their western borders had only recently been transplanted there against their will, and the Missouri settlers knew all too well the smoldering resentment many Native Americans must have felt. The Indians probably posed no actual threat, but the settlers could never know for sure. The Mormons denied communications with the Indians and declared their readiness to assist in defense against any threatened uprising. To do otherwise would be sedition and rebellion, they said, and unbecoming them as citizens.

The Saints were sincerely attempting to be good citizens, but to the Missourians, circumstantial evidence to the contrary seemed strong enough to cause worry. The first Mormons to enter Missouri had come as missionaries to the Native Americans, and although they made no converts, one result of this mission was that Missouri was designated as the gathering place for the Saints. Besides, the Book of Mormon declared that the Indians were a choice people and actually promised that one day these descendants of the Book of Mormon people would assist in building the New Jerusalem. The Latter-day Saints had no thought of promoting violence or Indian rebellion, but anyone in Missouri who wanted to think otherwise at least had some basis on which to build. The totally different religious outlook of the Missouri Protestants, combined with the small element of truth in the generally false rumors about the Mormons, created a situation with the potential for misunderstanding and violence. Even if both sides had only the best intentions, which in this instance seemed to be the case, the situation was volatile and reflected the kind of tragic misunderstanding that persists all too frequently in human history.

The Saints recognized the accuracy of the Clay County citizens' assessment of the situation's explosiveness, and sadly but graciously acceded to their request. They agreed to discourage further Mormon immigration and to accept the friendly offer from the committee to assist them in selecting and moving to a new location. For once, at least, the Mormons could enjoy a peaceful exodus from their place of settlement.

The area selected was in the region of Shoal Creek, north and east of Clay County, and there the Saints began another gathering place. They petitioned the state legislature for organization of a new county, and suddenly it seemed that a possible solution to their problems had been found. That area was sparsely settled, and to the politicians it seemed appropriate for an exclusively Mormon county. Two new counties were quickly formed, Caldwell and Daviess counties, and there was a general understanding that Caldwell would be primarily for the Saints. This was simply a gentlemen's agreement, with no legal force, but the Saints happily accepted the understanding. Everyone already living in the new county who could be induced to sell to the Mormons did so, and the Saints agreed they would settle in other counties only with the consent of settlers already there. Soon Mormon settlements dotted both Caldwell and Daviess counties, but the major immigration was into Caldwell.

The most important settlement was at Far West, in Caldwell County. The site was chosen in the summer of 1836 by John Whitmer and William W. Phelps, who purchased it with money collected among Saints in Kentucky and Tennessee. Unfortunately a misunderstanding arose when these men acted independently of the high council in laying out the town and assigning to themselves the profits from the sale of lands, but after a hearing before the high council, the matter was settled. The profits from land sales on the townsite as well as other land titles were turned over to Bishop Partridge for the benefit of the Church.

The Saints poured in and within two years more than 4,900 of them lived in the county, along with a hundred non-Mormons. At Far West there were 150 homes, four dry goods stores, three family grocery stores, several blacksmith shops, two hotels, a printing shop, and a large schoolhouse that doubled as a church and courthouse. In the hard-drinking atmosphere of western Missouri, Far West was unique. The Mormons attempted to live temperate lives and in October 1837 even voted not to support any shops selling spirituous liquors, tea, coffee, or tobacco.

In Daviess County, meanwhile, another important settlement was located on the Grand River. This was Adam-ondi-Ahman, usually abbreviated "Di-Ahman," which Joseph Smith officially designated as a spot for settlement in May 1838. It came to hold a special place in the hearts of the Latter-day Saints, for the Prophet told them that here Adam had called his posterity together shortly before his death, and here he would someday return. A stake was soon organized, many residences and a store were erected, and a site was dedicated for a temple block. In 1838 there were approximately fifteen hundred settlers.

In addition to the religious symbolism of its location, Adam-ondi-Ahman was also strategically situated on the banks of the Grand River, which emptied into the Missouri fifty miles downstream. This provided the Saints with an important shipping route for agricultural products, as well as for immigration and other travel. Water transportation was necessary for a viable economy, as roads were few and poor in that frontier wilderness. In order to better control this economic lifeline, George M. Hinckle and John Murdock obtained permission from local citizens to create a settlement at the spot where the Grand emptied into the Missouri. This Carroll County settlement, named DeWitt, became a Mormon outpost amidst the non-Mormon settlements of Missouri. Once again the Saints were building a permanent, cooperative economy in western Missouri.

Difficulties at Kirtland

In Kirtland, meanwhile, problems were developing. By 1836 the Saints were in political control of Kirtland township and were numerically strong enough to decide county elections. The Whigs were irked at the fact that the Mormons apparently favored the Democratic party. Continued rumors that the Mormons were practicing plural marriage created another smoldering issue, even though Church authorities threatened to withdraw fellowship from anyone found guilty of such a practice. In addition, the intensity of Mormon preaching occasionally antagonized the Ohio settlers, who felt they were being condemned by

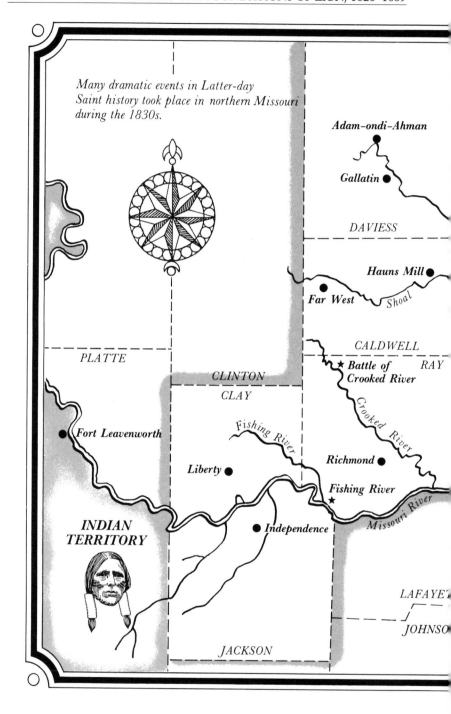

Many dramatic events in Latter-day Saint history took place in northern Missouri during the 1830s.

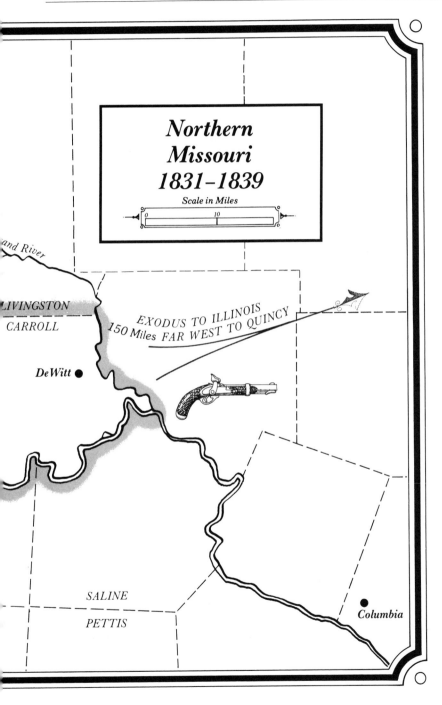

Northern
Missouri
1831–1839

Scale in Miles

0   10

and River

LIVINGSTON

CARROLL

EXODUS TO ILLINOIS
150 Miles FAR WEST TO QUINCY

DeWitt

SALINE

PETTIS

Columbia

certain overzealous missionaries. All these things, however, were only minor irritants and would not cause the Saints any major difficulty. The Mormons were not proclaiming that Ohio was Zion, and there was no likelihood of Missouri-style antagonism over either slavery or the Indians. The chief difficulty in Ohio was economic.

The economy of northern Ohio in 1836 and 1837 was in a state of flux, with high optimism for the future. The Ohio Canal had been completed in 1834, opening new trading opportunities for Ohio farmers. Population was still growing, especially with the immigration of Mormons to the vicinity of Kirtland, and land prices were rising rapidly. To most settlers, paying inflated prices seemed appropriate. Buyers were optimistic about the future and believed that the value of land would continue to rise, and businessmen were willing to lend money because they shared that belief. Credit and land mortgages were easy to come by.

Understandably, Joseph Smith and the Saints were caught up in the spirit of the times and incurred heavy debts in their efforts to build personal as well as community economic strength. In the 1830s, building lots in Kirtland jumped from $50 an acre to $2,000, and outside of town land prices rose from $10 an acre to $150. The Church undertook such projects as a steam sawmill, a tannery, and a print shop; and the building of the Kirtland Temple provided employment and some commercial activity. But the Saints, like other western settlers, had little liquid capital, and their business enterprises were begun on credit. Joseph Smith himself went into debt to purchase land. He also purchased merchandise on credit for his Kirtland store, and when he began the Kirtland bank, he borrowed money from other banks to help finance it. To some it may appear that he was borrowing too heavily, but the bankers, merchants, and land jobbers of the day would hardly have extended him such credit if they had not believed he had the potential to repay.

By late 1836 it was clear that something more was needed. The Prophet knew that he and the others could not borrow forever, and that somehow their assets must become more liquid. The answer seemed to be a bank that could print and circulate notes. If the notes were accepted at face value, a circulating medium would be created, debts paid, and the economy stimulated. On November 2, 1836, Church leaders organized the Kirtland Safety Society Bank. Orson Hyde was sent to Columbus, Ohio, to obtain a state charter, and Oliver Cowdery went to Pennsylvania to secure plates and printed bank notes.

Unfortunately for Joseph Smith's plans, Orson Hyde returned without the charter. At the time, the Prophet considered this as evidence of continuing prejudice against the Saints, but there was another reason the charter was not granted. Between 1830 and 1834 the number of banks in Ohio had jumped from eleven to thirty-one, and to some people this seemed too many. In 1834, however, the anti-banking wing of the Democratic party won control of the new legislature, which then began to refuse requests for new charters. In 1835 all such requests were turned down, and in 1836 only one of seventeen requested charters was granted. Thus the Saints were victims of a temporary political reverse, for their request came at exactly the wrong time.

Thus thwarted, Church leaders turned instead to a joint stock company that, while not officially a bank, could issue notes and take in money. The company was reorganized as the Kirtland Safety Society Anti-Banking Company, and the freshly printed notes of the Kirtland Safety Society Bank were stamped with "Anti-" and "-ing Co." in order to conform to the new name. The legality of such an enterprise was questionable, though other unauthorized banks existed in Ohio, and at the time it seemed the only solution to the money problem. On January 6, 1837, the new bank notes began circulating. About $20,000 had been acquired for purchase of stock, though it is not certain how much of this was in gold coin and how much merely some form of paper security.

Almost immediately Kirtland's economic life began to pick up as local citizens were able to turn their assets into cash. Townspeople began to borrow from the bank, often using land as collateral, and they received the Kirtland bank notes. These notes circulated at face value in Kirtland and some surrounding communities, and as long as people had confidence in this paper money, it could be used to purchase goods and to pay old debts.

But the boom ended almost before it began. Within three weeks the bank announced that it must stop redeeming its notes in specie (that is, gold coin). This signaled to those holding the notes that the company was in trouble. Reasons for these difficulties are hard to determine, but a few things are apparent. It is doubtful that the bank, as with other banks of the time, had enough gold coin in its vault to meet any sustained demand. In addition, there had been public criticism of the bank by non-Mormon editors cynical of its possibilities for success. Perhaps more important was the lack of a state charter. State law prescribed a heavy fine for anyone involved in banking without a charter

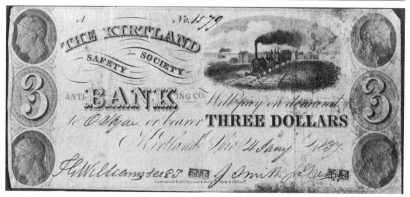

Kirtland Safety Society bank note, signed by Joseph Smith. The word "Bank" was changed to "Anti-Banking Co." when officials were unable to obtain a state charter. (Church Archives)

or in passing the notes of such a bank. Kirtland bank officers doubted the constitutionality of such law, and so argued in court tests, but they lost their case. In the meantime, major state banks refused to accept the Kirtland notes, probably because the bank had no charter. When this happened, the notes came pouring back into Kirtland. As they were presented to the bank for redemption in increasing numbers, Joseph Smith and other officers were forced to suspend specie payment. The notes were redeemable only in land.

For all practical purposes the Kirtland bank had failed even before the onset of the famous panic of 1837. In May, however, other economic forces combined to create the crisis that closed hundreds of banks throughout the United States. One factor was Andrew Jackson's Specie Circular of mid-1836, which declared that henceforth the federal government would sell public land only for specie. Suddenly both hard money and bank notes assumed new meaning, and when runs on the banks began in 1837, specie payments in the entire country ended and the less solvent banks began to fail.

The Kirtland bank struggled on through the spring and summer, with its notes circulating at greatly discounted values. Some members accepted them for goods and services in the belief that one day they would again be worth their face value. Joseph Smith did everything he could to build confidence and make the institution work, but early in the summer he recognized the inevitability of failure, and he resigned his position as cashier. By the end of the summer the bank was forced to close its doors permanently. Warren Parrish, who succeeded the

Prophet as cashier, was accused of absconding with a large amount of money, though the charge was never proved. The whole venture left the Saints shocked and bewildered, as many had lost both money and property.

Perhaps the greatest impact was on Joseph Smith and a few of the leaders. The Prophet was in debt for about $100,000, and when the bank failed, his creditors clamored for their money, threatening lawsuits if necessary. The Prophet controlled substantial assets or he could not have obtained the credit initially, but these holdings—particularly his store and land—could not be turned into ready cash. Besides, many of his notes had been cosigned by other men, complicating attempts to meet the demands of the creditors.

Unfortunately, some of Joseph Smith's closest associates failed to separate his role as prophet and religious leader from his activities in the temporal world, not recognizing that his business failure had nothing to do with the integrity of his religious experiences. Other honest men failed too, and so did much of the economy of western America in 1837. Nevertheless, throughout the summer the spirit of apostasy fomented within the Church, with economics as a central issue. On September 27 Joseph Smith and Sidney Rigdon left for a trip to Missouri, and in their absence the internal strife became so serious that the Church in Kirtland seemed threatened with dissolution. Even the temple became the scene of violent arguments as factions and bitterness grew. An attempt was made to replace the Prophet as head of the Church, and even some of the leaders began to turn against him as a fallen prophet. A number, however, remained firm in their convictions, and Brigham Young, especially, proclaimed loudly and publicly that Joseph was still the prophet and true leader of the Church. So forceful was Elder Young in his denunciation of those who were attempting to replace the Prophet that they turned their fury on him. On December 22, convinced that his life was in danger, he left his wife and children behind and fled on horseback toward Missouri.

Joseph Smith and Sidney Rigdon, meanwhile, returned to Kirtland and were dismayed to find the Church in disarray. Unable to reason with those who were now his enemies, Joseph had a hard decision to make. Threats were being made against his life, and he had reason to believe they would be carried out; creditors were pressing him from every side, and the most recent lawsuit seriously threatened imprisonment. Should he leave Kirtland, apparently running out on his debts, or should he stay and face prison and possible assassination? On the night of January 12, 1838, he and the ailing Sidney Rigdon finally decided that they must leave Kirtland to escape mob action, and they fled on horseback. Thus, Kirtland's brief period as the administrative center of the Church ended. Later the Prophet made a list of all his Ohio debts and employed an agent to help settle with his creditors. Though he made every effort, he was never able to fully meet these obligations.

Joseph Smith's trip to Missouri was both pathetic and dramatic. Heading west, the two leaders did not stop until they were at Norton, about sixty miles from Kirtland, where they waited for their families to join them. They then continued on in covered wagons. At Dublin, Indiana, the Prophet began looking for work cutting and sawing wood, but was unable to earn enough to meet his needs. There, however, he met Brigham Young and, to Brigham's great surprise, sought his counsel on what to do: "I am destitute of means to pursue my journey, and as you are one of the Twelve Apostles . . . I believe I shall throw myself upon you, and look to you for counsel."[3] Brigham advised him to rest, and assured him that he should have plenty of money to continue his journey. Not long after that a faithful Church member, a Brother Tomlinson, who had been trying to sell his farm finally did so and, at the urging of Elder Young, gave three hundred dollars to the Prophet to help him on his way.

The weather was cold that winter, and the travelers were still pursued by their enemies. Elder Rigdon was delayed because of the illness of his wife, but the Prophet and his family continued. At times they even had to hide in their wagons to elude pursuers armed with pistols and guns. In March they were in Missouri, and as they neared Far West they saw members of the Church coming to assist them with teams and money. On March 14 they entered Far West with their escort, and the Saints greeted them with open arms. It was a welcome sight after the disappointment and tragedy of Kirtland.

With the Prophet now living in Missouri, many of the faithful who remained in Kirtland wanted to follow him. On March 6, 1838, the seventies met in the temple to plan the migration. They extended the privilege of joining the exodus to all members of the Church. The result was the pioneer party known as Kirtland Camp, which left the city on July 6 with 515 people, 27 tents, 59 wagons, 97 horses, 22 oxen, 69

---

[3]Eldon Jay Watson, ed., *Manuscript History of Brigham Young 1801–1844* (Salt Lake City: Eldon J. Watson, 1968), p. 24.

cows, and 1 bull. Foreshadowing the later migration from Illinois, the party was divided into companies of tens, with a captain over each. As they traveled westward, the Saints were frequently hampered by muddy roads and by the need to work at odd jobs along the way in order to earn enough money to continue. Discouragement was great, and before reaching Springfield, Illinois, the group had been reduced to about 260 persons. On October 2, after traveling 866 miles, Kirtland Camp was met by Joseph Smith, Sidney Rigdon, and others and happily escorted into Far West. Two days later this group of Saints began to settle at Adam-ondi-Ahman.

Kirtland, meanwhile, did not immediately lose all its Saints. As late as 1841 there were still about five hundred there, but in October of that year Hyrum Smith wrote to the faithful in Kirtland to inform them that they were commanded to leave the town. It took a number of years, but eventually most of the former Kirtland Saints either migrated or joined schismatic groups.

Brighter Prospects

The troubles in Missouri and Ohio did not prevent the Church from growing elsewhere. Missionary work continued to be successful in various parts of the United States, and in 1836 and 1837 two especially significant missions by members of the Council of the Twelve Apostles remarkably demonstrated that prospects for growth had never been brighter.

In April 1836 Parley P. Pratt was sent to Canada, with a prophetic promise that this mission eventually would lead to the introduction of the gospel into England. Preaching in and around Toronto, he met John Taylor, a Methodist preacher originally from England. Taylor received him coolly at first but then decided to investigate. As he said to his friends:

> Mr. Pratt has come to us under circumstances that are peculiar; and there is one thing that commends him to our consideration; he has come amongst us without purse or scrip, as the ancient apostles traveled; and none of us are able to refute his doctrine by scripture or logic. I desire to investigate his doctrines and claims to authority, and shall be very glad if some of my friends will unite with me in this investigation. But if no one will unite with me, be assured I shall make the investigation alone. If I find his religion

John Taylor,
a Methodist preacher who became
an apostle and LDS Church
President. (Church Archives)

Parley P. Pratt,
a preacher of the Disciples of Christ
who became an LDS
apostle. (Church Archives)

true, I shall accept it, no matter what the consequences may be;
and if false, then I shall expose it.[4]

After three weeks of investigation John Taylor and his wife, Leonora,
were baptized, and within less than two years he became one of the
Twelve.

Elder Pratt converted others who had friends and relatives in England to whom they wrote letters about the restoration of the gospel.
Among them were Joseph Fielding, Isaac Russell, John Goodson, and
John Snyder, each of whom became especially anxious to proclaim the
gospel in England itself. Canada thus became the gateway for the opening of missionary work across the Atlantic.

In Kirtland, meanwhile, the Prophet found himself concerned not
only with the financial problems of the Church but also with dissent,
even among some members of the Quorum of the Twelve. In May or
early June of 1837, however, when it seemed as if the Church was
passing through its severest crisis yet, Joseph Smith declared that "God
revealed to me that something new must be done for the salvation of
His Church."[5] That "something new" was a long-anticipated mission
to England, the first mission outside the United States and Canada.

Already the groundwork had been laid, and apostles Heber C. Kimball and Orson Hyde both had displayed an interest in being among

---

[4]B.H. Roberts, *The Life of John Taylor* (Salt Lake City: Bookcraft, 1963), pp. 37–38.
[5]*History of the Church*, 2:489.

the first to go to a foreign land. In the spring of 1837 Elder Pratt had returned to Canada to discuss prospects for a mission to England with new converts there, and he found favorable response. By the time the Prophet received his revelation, enthusiasm was high, and he would have no difficulty in finding men to go. Early in June he called and set apart Heber C. Kimball to head the mission and Orson Hyde to accompany him. Elder Kimball's close friend Willard Richards was also sent, as were Elders Fielding, Russell, Goodson, and Snyder from Canada.

The missionaries left Kirtland in mid-June almost destitute, though friends and relatives gave them small amounts of money, which, together with sixty dollars in Kirtland Safety Society notes that John Goodson was able to exchange with a New York broker, provided money to purchase passage on the ship *Garrick*. The fare was eighteen dollars apiece, and they had to supply their own provisions. They arrived penniless at the port of Liverpool on July 20, 1837, yet by the end of their mission they had made friends and attained a success many would have thought impossible.

They began their work in Preston where, the day they arrived, a parliamentary election was in progress. They noted a political banner proclaiming in large letters: "TRUTH WILL PREVAIL." So appropriate did this seem to their work that they took it as their own motto. Joseph Fielding's brother, the Reverend James Fielding of Preston, at first opened his chapel to them, but when they began making converts, he accused them of "sheep stealing" and turned against them. They continued meeting in the homes of members of his flock, however, and on Sunday, July 30, they baptized their first nine converts in the River Ribble. All were from the Reverend Fielding's congregation, though the minister himself was never converted. Later the missionaries hired the local temperance hall, still known as the "Cockpit" because of its earlier use for the grizzly sport of cockfighting, where they continued to preach and make converts. They also spread the work to Bedford and other communities in the northwestern part of England.

The elders' methods were simple, plain, and sincere. They utilized friends and relatives as much as possible, preached in established churches when they could, and went door-to-door as a last resort. They were careful to give prospective converts only those points of doctrine for which they seemed ready, rarely mentioning the gathering to the new world, the law of consecration, or Joseph Smith's vision of the three degrees of glory. Elder Goodson actually slowed the work in Bed-

A TIMELY WARNING

TO THE PEOPLE OF ENGLAND,

Of every Sect and Denomination, and to every Individual into whose hands it may fall.

BY AN ELDER OF THE CHURCH OF LATTER DAY SAINTS, LATE FROM AMERICA.

PRESTON, 19th August, 1837.

First published in Toronto for distribution in eastern Canada and the United States, Orson Hyde's essay was published widely in England as a missionary tract of the Restoration. (Church Archives)

ford when he violated Heber C. Kimball's instructions and publicly read the vision from the Doctrine and Covenants. Such unfamiliar doctrine before the people were ready to hear it "turned the current of feeling generally, and nearly closed the door in all that region."[6]

Most converts were from the impoverished industrial classes. Orson Hyde wrote to his wife:

> Those who have been baptized, are mostly manufacturers and some other mechanics. They know how to do but little else than to spin and weave cotton and make cambrick, mull and lace, and what they would do in Kirtland or the city "Far West," I cannot say. They are extremely poor, most of them not having a change of clothes decent to be baptized in, but they have open hearts and strong faith. We have taught them nothing about the gathering for they have no means to bring them to America, let alone procuring them a place to live after they get there.[7]

The elders met little violent opposition, although many preachers spoke against the restored gospel, and in one instance one of Elder Kimball's converts was threatened with stoning. A few potential converts even refused baptism, fearing that when the elders returned to the United States they would be left alone to face persecution.

By April 1838 the missionaries had gained over four hundred members in Preston and more than fifteen hundred scattered throughout

---

[6]*History of the Church,* 2:505.
[7]*Elders' Journal of the Church of Jesus Christ of Latter-day Saints* 1 (November 1837): 19–20.

the western part of England. Heber C. Kimball alone was credited with more than a thousand converts. Elders Goodson and Snyder were the first to return to America, and on April 20 the two apostles and Elder Russell also sailed for home. Joseph Fielding was left in charge of the mission, with Willard Richards as first counselor and William Clayton, a convert from the industrial town of Penwortham, as second counselor. While the mission to England was not the salvation of the Church in Kirtland, it laid the foundation for the return of nearly the full Council of the Twelve two years later, which resulted in a massive immigration program that would be the main source of the Church's unprecedented growth in Nauvoo and in the American West.

Missouri Difficulties

Even as the missionaries in England enjoyed success and as Saints in America continued to flock to Missouri, the Church in Missouri experienced another period of ordeal in 1838 and 1839. Not even the leaders themselves were immune from disagreement and misunderstanding, and in February 1838 the presidency of the Church in Missouri—David Whitmer, W. W. Phelps, and John Whitmer—were tried by a general Church council and released. A major charge was that they had sold their land in Jackson County which, to some members, constituted a denial of the faith. David Whitmer was also charged with violating the Word of Wisdom, and the others with claiming money that belonged to the Church. This action was controversial, for it was not clear what body had proper authority to judge a stake presidency, but on April 6 Thomas B. Marsh was made stake president with Brigham Young and David W. Patten as counselors.

On April 7 even Oliver Cowdery was charged with a series of transgressions. He wrote a letter in reply but refused to appear before the high council. He, too, had sold his interests in Jackson County, and this was one of the original charges against him. It was dropped after he insisted in his letter that the Church could not dictate to him in such affairs, but his general disagreement with the Church's administrative procedures in Missouri, as well as his own request to withdraw from a society that claimed that degree of temporal authority, led to his excommunication. The same high council soon dropped from membership David Whitmer and Lyman E. Johnson, a member of the Twelve.

All three of these men had shown sympathy for the dissenters at

Kirtland and were publicly finding fault with Joseph Smith to the extent of justifying lawsuits against him. Their excommunication was, in effect, a purging from the leadership of those who could not work harmoniously. The action took two of the three witnesses to the Book of Mormon as well as an apostle. Within a year three more apostles would be excommunicated, and others would find their standing in the Church seriously jeopardized.

By the summer of 1838 conditions had reached an impasse within the Church. There were so many dissenters in Missouri that some who remained loyal felt threatened. Sidney Rigdon undoubtedly remembered the brutal beating he had received from apostates in 1832, and some Saints feared the dissenters would join with other enemies to intensify their Missouri troubles. It was a time of tension and pressure from both within and without.

On Sunday, June 17, Sidney Rigdon's feelings welled up and burst forth in a heated oration sometimes called the "salt sermon." He drew from the scriptural text, "Ye are the salt of the earth: but if the salt have lost his savour, wherewith shall it be salted? it is thenceforth good for nothing, but to be cast out, and to be trodden under foot of men." (Matthew 5:13.) In his direct and powerful way President Rigdon applied the test to the dissenters, and the implication was obvious: they must either leave or face the consequences.

Not long afterward a threatening document appeared, signed by eighty-four members of the Church. Addressed to the leading dissenters (Oliver Cowdery, David Whitmer, John Whitmer, W. W. Phelps, and Lyman E. Johnson), it pointedly ordered them to leave the county or face "a more fatal calamity." Apparently the ill-advised document was signed spontaneously, without the knowledge of Joseph Smith, and it contained neither his signature nor that of Sidney Rigdon. It nevertheless proved to be another embarrassment to the Church, for even though it prompted the dissenters to leave, it also fed the anti-Mormon hostility that was again gaining ground among the other settlers of western Missouri.

The impact of all this was only aggravated by the ongoing activities of Sampson Avard, the first signer of the document threatening the dissenters, and his associates among the more radical and hotheaded Mormons in a group known as the Danites. The origin of the Danites is still uncertain, and historians present widely diverse views on the subject. It is probable, however, that, except for those who followed Avard, the group was not as secret or insidious as some critics have argued. Rather, it was formed to protect the Saints and to perform community service for them. Organized into military-like groups of tens, fifties, and hundreds, at one time its members were not only bearing arms but also building houses, gathering food, caring for the sick, and gathering scattered Saints into the community. They called themselves "Danites," a contemporary Saint reported, "because the Prophet Daniel has said they shall take the kingdom and possess it forever."[8] This was consistent with frequent references by LDS writers in this period to the Book of Daniel. The Saints steadfastly believed that they were part of the kingdom represented by Daniel as the stone "cut out of the mountain without hands" that "shall never be destroyed . . . but it shall break in pieces and consume all these kingdoms, and shall stand for ever." (Daniel 2:34, 44–45.) It was this imagery that Joseph Smith used when, in dedicating the Kirtland Temple, he prayed "that the kingdom, which thou hast set up without hands, may become a great mountain and fill the whole earth." (D&C 109:72; see also D&C 65:2.)

Whatever their origin and purpose, the Danites in Missouri also became militant defenders of the Saints and rode out almost at a moment's notice when they heard a mob was coming or that a community of Saints had been attacked. Avard led some of them far beyond the limits of either legality or propriety and began not only to defend but retaliate. He skillfully persuaded some of his followers as well as the enemies of the Church that he had the backing of Church leaders and that the Danites were authorized to plunder, lie, and even kill to avenge themselves. They were bound together by oaths and had secret signs for identification and warning. Ruthless as well as hotheaded, Avard and others were finally arrested and brought to court after five months of terrorizing the territory. Avard accused Joseph Smith and Sidney Rigdon of being directly behind all that his misguided band had done.

Joseph Smith probably knew of the Danites and of their efforts to defend the Saints. He led out, in fact, in some such efforts, though it is not clear that they were all specifically Danite activities. He was unaware, however, of the extent of Avard's perfidy until the matter came to light in the courts. While in jail sometime later the Prophet wrote:

---

[8]Albert Perry Rockwood journal entry of 22 October 1838, in Dean C. Jessee and David J. Whittaker, eds., "The Last Months of Mormonism in Missouri: The Albert Perry Rockwood Journal," *Brigham Young University Studies* 28 (Winter 1988): 23.

We have learned . . . since we have been prisoners, that many false and pernicious things, which were calculated to lead the Saints far astray and to do great injury, have been taught by Dr. Avard as coming from the Presidency, and we have reason to fear that many other designing and corrupt characters like himself, having been teaching many things which the Presidency never knew were being taught in the Church by anybody until after they were made prisoners. Had they known of such things they would have spurned them and their authors as they would the gates of hell. Thus we find that there have been frauds and secret abominations and evil works of darkness going on, leading the minds of the weak and unwary into confusion and distraction, and all the time palming it off upon the Presidency, while the Presidency were ignorant as well as innocent of those things.[9]

The summer of 1838 was tense, and Joseph Smith was forced to make some difficult and harsh decisions. He hated violence, but once again such charges as fanaticism, disloyalty, conspiracy, and threatening economic domination were hurled at the Mormons. Violence was threatened, and yet the Saints had only begun their new communities in northern Missouri. Some had been driven from their homes four times within an eight-year period: from New York, Ohio, Jackson County, and Clay County. It seemed unthinkable that another relocation should be forced upon them. It was a wonder that some Saints restrained themselves as long as they did, and it is understandable that the Prophet apparently decided that this time, at least, they must stand and fight. This was no invitation to mob action on the part of the Saints or to excesses like those of Avard and his band, though in the hot summer of 1838 it could well be construed by the wily Avard as support for his own objectives. It could also be distorted by the enemies of Joseph Smith.

Independence Day, July 4, 1838, was crucial. At Far West the Saints celebrated the national holiday and laid the cornerstones of a temple. Orator for the day was Sidney Rigdon, who, despite recent illness, maintained the ability to whip feelings into high emotion. His speech, approved by Joseph Smith and other Church leaders, was a declaration of independence for the Saints from any further mob violence or illegal activity. He concluded his long and stinging oration with words that must have sunk deep into the heart of every listener:

[9]History of the Church, 3:231.

We take God and all the holy angels to witness this day, that we warn all men in the name of Jesus Christ, to come on us no more forever, for from this hour, we will bear it no more, our rights shall no more be trampled on with impunity. The man or the set of men, who attempts it, does it at the expense of their lives. And that mob that comes on us to disturb us; it shall be between us and them a war of extermination; for we will follow them, till the last drop of their blood is spilled, or else they will have to exterminate us: for we will carry the seat of war to their own houses, and their own families, and one party or the other shall be utterly destroyed. — Remember it then all MEN.

We will never be the aggressors, we will infringe on the rights of no people; but shall stand for our own until death. We claim our own rights, and are willing that all others shall enjoy theirs.

No man shall be at liberty to come into our streets, to threaten us with mobs, for if he does, he shall atone for it before he leaves the place, neither shall he be at liberty, to villify and slander any of us, for suffer it we will not in this place.

We therefore, take all men to record this day, that we proclaim our liberty this day, as did our fathers. And we pledge this day to one another, our fortunes, our lives, and our sacred honors, to be delivered from the persecutions which we have had to endure, for the last nine years, or nearly that. Neither will we indulge any man, or set of men, in instituting vexatious law suits against us, to cheat us out of our just rights, if they attempt it we say wo unto them.

We this day then proclaim ourselves free, with a purpose and a determination, that never can be broken, "no never! *no never!!* NO NEVER"!!![10]

The jubilant audience responded: "Hosannah, hosannah, hosannah! Amen. Amen. Amen!" and repeated it three times.

Much of Rigdon's oration was obviously heated rhetoric, but it represented the determination of the Saints to fight back. When distorted reports reached the mobs and other Missouri citizens, however, it provided a basis for charges of treason and violence against the Saints that were fostered by those who wanted to drive them from the state.

The rest of the long hot summer of 1838 was almost predict-

---

[10]The entire oration is reproduced in *Brigham Young University Studies* 14 (Summer 1974): 517–27.

able. The first blows of the so-called Mormon War were struck at Gallatin, in Daviess County. August 6 was election day, and William Peniston, a candidate for the state legislature and an old enemy of the Mormons, was determined to keep them from voting. Election days in the West were rarely orderly anyway, and when Peniston began to harangue the voters, many of whom were filled with whiskey, violence was inevitable. It broke out when a drunken citizen picked a fight with one of the Saints; as others ran to assist him, the fracas became general. Sticks, stones, clubs, and whips — anything available — were used by both sides, and although the Mormons claimed the victory, men were beaten and bloodied in both camps.

Reports, probably exaggerated, soon reached Far West, and immediately Joseph Smith and others armed themselves and rode to Daviess County. They met at the home of Lyman Wight in Adam-ondi-Ahman with several who had been in the battle, and there they learned with relief that no one had been killed. Tempers were high, but the Prophet and his companions did what they could to promote peace. They visited several old settlers in the vicinity, including Adam Black, the newly elected judge for Daviess County. Perhaps the fact that they were armed intimidated the judge, or perhaps he simply wanted to get rid of them; whatever the reason, he signed an affidavit certifying that he would not associate himself with any mob against the Mormons. By the end of August, however, he swore an affidavit against the Mormons alleging he had been threatened with death if he did not sign the document. Peniston, in the meantime, also brought charges against the Saints, and on the basis of these and other affidavits, warrants were issued for the arrest of Joseph Smith and Lyman Wight, charging them with insurrection.

Joseph Smith was willing to submit to arrest, but when the sheriff came, the Prophet requested that the trial take place in his own county. He feared a trial at Gallatin would be a pretext for lynching. A hearing was finally held before Judge King in Daviess County, and to the surprise of the Saints he ordered the Prophet and Lyman Wight to stand trial before the circuit court. They were released on $500 bond while awaiting the proceedings.

Rumors and exaggerated stories circulated on both sides, and false reports of Mormon uprising reached the desk of Governor Lilburn W. Boggs. Loath to help the Mormons (he had been an enemy earlier in Jackson County), Boggs chose to believe the worst and did little to quell the threats against them. He did, however, order General David R.

Atchison, of the state militia, and other generals to raise a force of mounted, armed men to stand ready to quell civil disturbances in Caldwell, Daviess, and Carroll counties. The Saints, meantime, enlisted in the militia of Caldwell County and began to act in self-defense. One group even intercepted and confiscated a shipment of arms intended for a mob in Daviess County.

The mob threatened to attack Adam-ondi-Ahman, where Lyman Wight and a contingent of Mormon militia prepared to defend themselves. Only the actions of Generals Alexander Doniphan and David R. Atchison prevented violence. At the same time, a committee of "old citizens" in Daviess County agreed either to buy all the property of the Saints there or to sell theirs to the Saints. Joseph Smith was informed, and he immediately sent messengers to Church branches in the East and South to try to raise the necessary money, but the continuing conflict made this tentative agreement impossible to fulfill.

In Carroll County, mob forces next besieged DeWitt. When Joseph Smith heard of it he rode immediately for DeWitt, which he had to enter secretly. He found the Saints in great distress, without food, and the mob growing daily. When it became apparent that even the militia supposed to protect them would probably side with the mob, there was nothing to do but capitulate and leave the county.

Encouraged by what they heard from DeWitt, the Daviess County mobs threatened the Saints at Adam-ondi-Ahman more seriously. Near Millport, a short distance from "Di-Ahman," several Mormon homes and haystacks were burned. General H. G. Parks instructed Lyman Wight, a colonel in the state militia, to put down mobs wherever he found them, and Wight immediately organized the Mormons into two companies of militia. Generals Parks, Atchison, and Doniphan knew that the Mormons only acted defensively against mobs, and they did all they could to persuade the governor that an action against the Saints would be unjustified. But Boggs remained unconvinced, as his later actions indicated.

As if such turmoil were not enough, another brutal shock from inside the Church awaited Joseph Smith. On October 24, Thomas B. Marsh, president of the Council of the Twelve but actually in a state of apostasy by this time, appeared in Richmond where he signed an affidavit that seemed to support the most damaging reports of Danite activities and accused the Prophet of promoting the violence. Orson Hyde, another member of the Twelve, also signed an affidavit saying that he knew most of Marsh's statements to be true and believed the others were. The tenseness of the summer and the confusing rapidity of incriminations had affected even the most prominent Church leaders. Marsh was excommunicated in March, and in May Orson Hyde was dropped from the Council. The latter was restored the following June, after a long, sad repentance and confession of his error. Marsh was rebaptized in 1857 and died in Utah a member of the Church, though he was never again a member of the Twelve. For the time being, however, the fact that two more apostles had turned against the Prophet only added fuel to the fire already raging against the Saints.

Captain Samuel Bogart was a Methodist minister in charge of a company of Caldwell County militia. On October 24 Bogart's men accosted at least two Mormon settlers in their homes, ordering them to leave the state, and took three Mormons prisoner. When word reached Far West, Captain David W. Patten, a member of the Quorum of the Twelve, took a small detachment of militia and marched on Bogart's camp at Crooked River to rescue the prisoners. It was ironic for two different companies of the same state militia to face each other, but such was the nature of the civil war developing in northern Missouri. A battle ensued in which Bogart's men were soon routed, one of them killed, and at least five wounded. On the Mormon side, Gideon Carter was killed and David Patten and their young non-Mormon guide, Patrick O'Banion, were mortally wounded. As Patten lay dying that afternoon he turned to his wife and pleaded, "Whatever else you do, O, do not deny the faith." He expired shortly thereafter—the first apostolic martyr of the restored church.

Highly exaggerated reports of these activities soon reached Governor Boggs, and it appeared to him that the Mormons were burning towns, driving old settlers from their homes, and generally undermining civil authority. The seeming proclivities of the Danites for vengeance did not help the Mormon cause. Finally, on October 27, heedless of any information he may have had about the Mormon viewpoint, Boggs issued his infamous "Order of Extermination." "The Mormons," he wrote to General John B. Clark of the state militia, "must be treated as enemies and *must be exterminated* or driven from the state, if necessary for the public good. Their outrages are beyond all description."[11] Clark was ordered to carry out his instructions immediately.

Events soon followed a predictable course. On October 30 more

---

[11]*History of the Church*, 3:175.

Haun's Mill Massacre of October 1838 as depicted by C. C. A. Christensen. (From the Permanent Collection of Brigham Young University)

than two hundred men of the state militia were involved in the most brutal massacre of the conflict. Jacob Haun, a Mormon, owned a small mill on Shoal Creek and had been joined there by about thirty families. They had made a peace treaty with militia leaders on October 28, but two days later about 200 to 250 troops, under the command of Colonel Thomas Jennings, attacked the tiny settlement. The Saints cried for peace but no respite was granted. Though men and women fled to a blacksmith shop or into the woods, the mob fired mercilessly. In all, eighteen Mormons were killed or mortally wounded, including one elderly man who was hacked to death with a corn cutter. Ten-year-old Sardius Smith was found trembling with fear in the blacksmith shop and summarily shot to death. His murderer bragged afterward, "Nits will make lice, and if he had lived he would have become a Mormon."[12] Twelve to fifteen more defenseless Saints were wounded in the massacre.

The next day the state militia was at Far West, and General Samuel

---

[12]As quoted in B.H. Roberts, *A Comprehensive History of the Church of Jesus Christ of Latter-day Saints*, 6 vols. (Salt Lake City: Deseret News Press, 1930), 1:482.

Lucas made four demands of the Saints: their leaders were to surrender for trial and punishment, Mormon property was to be confiscated to pay for damages, the balance of the Saints were to leave the state under the protection of the militia, and they were to yield their arms. Colonel George M. Hinckle, a Mormon militia officer, simply told Joseph Smith, Sidney Rigdon, Lyman Wight, Parley P. Pratt, and George W. Robinson that the militia officers wanted to talk to them. They consented in good faith and were shocked, therefore, when Hinckle turned them over to General Lucas as prisoners. Perhaps Hinckle thought this was the only way to end the violence, but Church leaders considered it treachery. Hyrum Smith and Amasa Lyman were taken prisoner the next day. The Mormons were required to give up their arms and they were defenseless as the unruly militia entered Far West, plundered the town, and brutally ravished some of the women. In addition, some five hundred Saints were forced to sign away their property in conformity to General Lucas's demands. It was a very uneasy peace that rested on Caldwell County.

The Prophet and the others arrested with him were treated with little mercy. They spent the first night in the rain on the cold ground, being verbally abused and ridiculed by their guards. The next day, in their absence, the militia officers held a hasty court-martial. This action was illegal, for none of the Mormon leaders were members of the state militia, but General Lucas apparently believed that only by trying and punishing them summarily could he convince the rest of the Saints of the severity of their so-called "crimes." The court-martial lasted until midnight, and its decision was that the prisoners should be shot the following morning. When the prisoners heard about the order they knelt together in fervent prayer, asking that it not be carried out. Lucas ordered General Doniphan to execute it, but Doniphan, indignant at the brutality and injustice of the whole affair, defied his superior and replied with a memo for which the Mormons would forever remember him:

> It is cold-blooded murder. I will not obey your order. My brigade shall march for Liberty tomorrow morning, at 8 o'clock; and if you execute these men, I will hold you responsible before an earthly tribunal, so help me God.
> A. Doniphan
> Brigadier-General[13]

---

[13]*History of the Church*, 3:190–91 note.

Alexander Doniphan statue, Richmond, Missouri. Doniphan has become a legendary hero to the Saints for his fearlessness in refusing an order to execute the Prophet. (Church Archives)

Doniphan's courageous response prevented the execution, and the next morning he marched his troops away. The same day Joseph, Hyrum, and other Church leaders were loaded into covered wagons to be hauled off to Independence, Jackson County. Joseph had been given the opportunity to say a tearful farewell to Emma and their children at his home, but when his mother was helped through the crowd to the wagon she was not permitted to see her two sons, who she believed were on their way to execution. Joseph and Hyrum reached their hands through the canvas and touched hers, and as they pulled away Joseph could only sob: "God bless you, mother."

November and December 1838 were months of relative calm, though the Saints knew that eventually they would have to leave the state. With Joseph Smith and his counselors in prison, responsibility to begin preparations for the exodus fell to Brigham Young as senior member of the Council of the Twelve. By January a committee to superintend the exodus had been appointed, and before the winter ended the threat of further mob activity finally forced the Saints to begin their wearisome march. In February Brigham Young was forced to flee from Far West for his life, and by April 20 nearly all the Saints in Missouri had crossed the Mississippi River and found refuge near Quincy, Illinois.

In the meantime, the Saints again sought relief from the Missouri legislature. Their grievances were clearly defined and much sympathy was shown by many of the lawmakers. A bill was introduced that would have initiated an investigation, but it was never acted upon. Instead, the legislature appropriated $2,000 for the relief of the citizens of Caldwell County, an act that actually provided little help. Later the lawmakers furnished the militia about $200,000 for the expenses of the conflict. The "Mormon War" in Missouri was officially at an end.

Five Months in Prison

Joseph Smith and those arrested with him on October 31 arrived in Independence on November 4. Four days later they were transferred to Richmond, Missouri, where they were turned over to civil authorities. Charged, among other crimes, with treason, murder, and arson, fifty-three defendants appeared at the courthouse for a preliminary hearing which began on November 13. It lasted for over two weeks, and the presiding judge was Austin A. King, whose dislike for the Mormons was clear and whose apparent aim was to see them brought to trial.

During that time Joseph, Hyrum, Sidney Rigdon, and four others were kept in an old log house where, chained together at their ankles, they slept on the cold floor. There they endured not only physical suffering but also a constant stream of vulgarity and verbal abuse from the guards. Later Parley P. Pratt vividly described one dreadful night in which the Prophet's outrage resulted in an awesome and never-to-be-forgotten rebuke. Their tormentors bombarded them until after midnight with filthy language, oaths, blasphemy, and boasts of horrifying abuses, including rape and murder, against the Saints. Then, as Parley recounted it,

> I had listened till I became so disgusted, shocked, horrified, and so filled with the spirit of indignant justice that I could scarcely refrain from rising upon my feet and rebuking the guards; but had said nothing to Joseph, or any one else, although I lay next to him and knew he was awake. On a sudden he arose to his feet, and

spoke in a voice of thunder, or as the roaring lion, uttering, as near
as I can recollect, the following words:

*"SILENCE, ye fiends of the infernal pit. In the name of Jesus
Christ I rebuke you, and command you to be still; I will not live
another minute and hear such language. Cease such talk, or you
or I die THIS INSTANT!"*

He ceased to speak. He stood erect in terrible majesty. Chained,
and without a weapon; calm, unruffled and dignified as an angel,
he looked upon the quailing guards, whose weapons were lowered
or dropped to the ground; whose knees smote together, and who,
shrinking into a corner, or crouching at his feet, begged his pardon,
and remained quiet till a change of guards.

I have seen the ministers of justice, clothed in magisterial robes,
and criminals arraigned before them, while life was suspended on
a breath, in the Courts of England; I have witnessed a Congress
in solemn session to give laws to nations; I have tried to conceive
of kings, of royal courts, of thrones and crowns; and of emperors
assembled to decide the fate of kingdoms; but dignity and majesty
have I seen but *once,* as it stood in chains, at midnight, in a
dungeon in an obscure village of Missouri.[14]

At the hearing, the evidence seems to have been stacked against
the Prophet. Sampson Avard, the first witness, accused him of responsibility for the wrongs of the Danites. Other witnesses were equally
bitter, but when the prisoners tried to get their own witnesses in court,
the individuals named were simply arrested and jailed by their old
enemy Captain Bogart, and not allowed to appear. Those few who did
appear in behalf of the prisoners were so abused and threatened that
they were unable to tell all they wanted. In the end Judge King dismissed
charges against over half the prisoners, but ordered twenty-four to stand
trial. Some were allowed to post bail while five, including Parley P.
Pratt, were sent to the Richmond jail pending their trial for murder in
connection with the Battle of Crooked River. Joseph and Hyrum Smith,
Sidney Rigdon, Lyman Wight, Alexander McRae, and Caleb Baldwin
were committed to jail in a Clay County town ironically named Liberty,
where they would remain for four-and-a-half months.

Liberty Jail was a small, twenty-two-foot-square building. Its heavy
stone walls were timbered inside with logs. The interior was divided
into an upper and lower room, or dungeon, very dimly lighted by two

---

[14]*The Autobiography of Parley Parker Pratt,* pp. 210–11.

small windows in the upper room. The prison fare was described as "so filthy we could not eat it until we were driven to it by hunger," and the general treatment given the prisoners was unfair. They were sometimes allowed visitors, however, and maintained contact with the outside world through letters. Twice they tried to escape, but both times their efforts failed.

Yet the months in Liberty Jail were of special significance to Joseph Smith and to the Church. They demonstrated the abilities of such men as Brigham Young, John Taylor, and Heber C. Kimball, who organized the exodus from Missouri and resettlement in Illinois. More importantly, the Prophet had time to pray and meditate about the Church and its meaning, time to formulate new ideas and put them into writing. Some of his most profound revelations and writings came from Liberty Jail. Surprisingly, his letters exuded optimism, though they also pointed to the weaknesses of the Saints and called for overcoming them. The Prophet displayed love and compassion along with sharpness.

On December 18 he wrote to Church members briefly reviewing their problems, condemning the actions of their enemies, and denying the charges levied against them. His letter also contained these words of counsel:

> Brethren, from henceforth, let truth and righteousness prevail and abound in you; and in all things be temperate; abstain from drunkenness, and from swearing, and from all profane language, and from everything which is unrighteous or unholy; also from enmity, and hatred, and covetousness, and from every unholy desire. Be honest one with another, for it seems that some have come short of these things, and some have been uncharitable, and have manifested greediness because of their debts towards those who have been persecuted and dragged about with chains without cause, and imprisoned. Such characters God hates — and they shall have their turn of sorrow in the rolling of the great wheel, for it rolleth and none can hinder. Zion shall yet live, though she seem to be dead.[15]

To his wife Emma the Prophet wrote these tender words on April 4:

> It is I believe now about five months and six days since I have been under the grimace of a guard night and day, and within the walls, grates, and screaking iron doors of a lonesome, dark, dirty prison. . . .

---

[15]*History of the Church*, 3:233.

I think of you and the children continually. . . . I want you should not let those little fellows forget me. Tell them Father loves them with a perfect love and he is doing all he can to get away from the mob to come to them. Do teach them all you can, that they may have good minds. Be tender and kind to them. Don't be fractious to them, but listen to their wants. Tell them Father says they must be good children and mind their mother. My dear Emma there is great responsibility resting upon you in preserving yourself in honor and sobriety before them and teaching them right things to form their young and tender minds, that they begin in right paths and not get contaminated when young by seeing ungodly examples.[16]

Toward the end of March, Joseph wrote a long letter to the Church, parts of which now appear as sections 121, 122, and 123 of the Doctrine and Covenants. These statements enjoined upon the Prophet, and all who read them, patience and long-suffering, the assurance of continuing revelation, a reminder that the powers of the priesthood should be exercised in righteousness, hope for the future, and the need to keep a record of all that transpired.

During all this, Joseph Smith still retained the uncanny ability to attract and impress people — even his avowed enemies. One of the most interesting descriptions of the Prophet in Missouri was later recorded by Peter H. Burnett, a non-Mormon attorney who helped defend him in the trial in Daviess County in early April:

Joseph Smith, Jr., was at least six feet high, well-formed, and weighed about one hundred and eighty pounds. His appearance was not prepossessing, and his conversational powers were but ordinary. You could see at a glance that his education was very limited. He was an awkward but vehement speaker. In conversation he was slow, and used too many words to express his ideas, and would not generally go directly to a point. But, with all these drawbacks he was much more than an ordinary man. He possessed the most indomitable perseverance, was a good judge of men, and deemed himself born to command, and he did command. His views were so strange and striking, and his manner was so earnest, and apparently so candid, that you could not but be interested. There was a kind, familiar look about him, that pleased you. He was

---

[16]Joseph Smith to Emma Smith, April 4, 1839, as quoted in Leonard J. Arrington, "Church Leaders in Liberty Jail," *Brigham Young University Studies* 13 (Autumn 1972): 22. Original at Yale University.

Jail at Liberty, Missouri. (C. C. A. Christensen painting, from the Permanent Collection of Brigham Young University)

very courteous in discussion, readily admitting what he did not intend to controvert, and would not oppose you abruptly, but had due deference to your feelings. He had the capacity for discussing a subject in different aspects, and for proposing many original views, even on ordinary matters. His illustrations were his own. He had great influence over others. As evidence of this I will state that on Thursday, just before I left to return to Liberty, I saw him out among the crowd, conversing freely with every one, and seeming to be perfectly at ease. In the short space of five days he had managed so to mollify his enemies that he could go unprotected among them without the slightest danger. Among the Mormons he had much greater influence than Sidney Rigdon. The latter was a man of superior education, an eloquent speaker, of fine appearance and dignified manners; but he did not possess the native intellect of Smith, and lacked his determined will.[17]

In February, Sidney Rigdon was released on bail. He hurried to Illinois, where he began making plans for an appeal to Washington and, rather unrealistically, to "impeach" the state of Missouri. In April

---

[17]Peter H. Burnett, *Recollections and Opinions of an Old Pioneer* (New York: D. Appleton and Co., 1880), pp. 66–67.

the remaining prisoners were ordered to Daviess County for trial. On the ninth a grand jury brought in a bill against them for "murder, treason, burglary, arson, larceny, theft, and stealing." The accused were unable to obtain a change of venue for trial on these charges, but as they were being taken to another county it became clear that the judge, the sheriff, and the guards had connived to allow their escape. A guard even helped them saddle their horses. With the sheriff and other guards filled with whiskey and asleep, Joseph and Hyrum rode the two horses while the others walked, and they escaped to Illinois. On April 22 Joseph arrived at Quincy to once again enjoy the embraces of his family and friends. Later Parley P. Pratt also escaped from prison, and before the year ended all the Missouri prisoners had left that state.

The exodus from Missouri was the end of an important period in the history of the Church. The years in Ohio and Missouri were marked by the building of a magnificent temple, new revelations of doctrine, the expansion of the Church overseas, and the designation of a land of Zion. They were also marred by financial tragedy, bitter persecution, apostasy, and the expulsion of the Saints from Zion. But something miraculous was happening. In the midst of all this trouble the Church was still growing, and even while the Prophet was in jail some ten thousand people followed him, figuratively speaking, across the frozen fields of Missouri to Illinois. For the fourth time in less than a decade they sought and began to build a place of refuge. A letter from Liberty Jail had struck the note of optimism:

> . . . and if thou shouldst be cast into the pit, or into the hands of murderers, and the sentence of death passed upon thee; if thou be cast into the deep; if the billowing surge conspire against thee; if fierce winds become thine enemy; if the heavens gather blackness, and all the elements combine to hedge up the way; and above all, if the very jaws of hell shall gape open the mouth wide after thee, know thou, my son, that all these things shall give thee experience, and shall be for thy good. The Son of Man hath descended below them all; art thou greater than he?
>
> Therefore, hold on thy way, the Priesthood shall remain with thee, for their bounds are set, they cannot pass. Thy days are known, and thy years shall not be numbered less; therefore, fear not what man can do, for God shall be with you forever and ever.[18]

---

[18]*History of the Church* 3:300–301; D&C 122:7–9.

PART II

New Directions, *1839–1856*

These views represent two new beginnings in this period of Mormon history. The engraving of a peaceful Nauvoo about 1848–1850 is by Herrmann J. Meyer, and the engraving of Great Salt Lake City in 1853 is by Frederick Piercy. The major building on the left of Salt Lake's Main Street is the Deseret Store and Tithing Office. (Church Archives)

THE EXODUS FROM MISSOURI was a sorrowful time for the Saints, but it opened an era of renewed vitality in the Church and provided a catalyst for the reorientation of Latter-day Saint economic, political, and religious life. At Nauvoo and again later in Utah the Saints built impressive communities based on the ideals of industry, cooperation, and self-sufficiency. The law of consecration was still the ideal, but practical realities made it impossible to maintain. For the first time the Saints negotiated with the federal government, although they received little cooperation until the Mexican War of 1846. In religious life, the Saints received many new insights concerning man's eternal destiny, expanded their organization, and adopted important new practices. Thus, in ways besides geographical displacement, the exodus of 1839 and the one that followed seven years later symbolized important new directions for the Church.

By this time even some of the language being used by the Latter-day Saints had special religious symbolism — a symbolism not fully understood by non-Mormons but resonant with meaning for the Saints themselves. They spoke of themselves not just as members of the restored Church of Jesus Christ but as modern Israel — partakers of all the blessings and promises given to Abraham, Isaac, and Jacob. At least two Old Testament prophets, Moses and Elijah, were part of the restoration process as they bestowed certain "keys" and blessings upon the modern prophet in the Kirtland Temple. Like Israel of old, the Saints also referred to themselves as a "covenant people," and often concluded correspondence with phrases such as "yours in the everlasting covenant." In thinking of themselves as Israel, they began to refer to non-Mormons as "gentiles," not in derision but as a symbol of their own special status. "I have sent mine everlasting covenant into the world," the Lord told them in 1831, "to be a standard for my people, and for the Gentiles to seek it." (D&C 45:9.) The term *Zion* also had a unique meaning for the Saints, and in the next five years even more distinctive concepts and word usage would be introduced among them.

At Nauvoo Joseph Smith reached the zenith of both his temporal and spiritual influence. As a secular leader he became mayor of one of the two largest cities in Illinois, editor of its newspaper, a leading entrepreneur, and a candidate for the Presidency of the United States. As a spiritual leader he announced important new doctrinal ideas, began the erection of a magnificent temple, introduced a sacred temple ceremony that helped increase brotherhood and spirituality among the Saints, and laid the foundation for expanding the gospel kingdom worldwide. His tragic martyrdom in 1844 became a rallying point for a greater spiritual unity among the Saints and strengthened the kingdom instead of destroying it as his antagonists had hoped.

The following years found the Saints inclined westward, where the Church under the firm hand of Brigham Young once again established a distinctive society, but outside the realms of American civilization in the somewhat foreboding Great Basin. The Saints were willing to help wrest that area from Mexico for the United States, and there they entrenched themselves with a determination never again to be driven from their homes.

In this new gathering place the Church faced its first direct conflict with federal officials, a challenge opening a political struggle that lasted until the end of the century. This friction was related to both the practice of plural marriage and the widely misunderstood participation of Church leaders in Utah's civil and business affairs. The foundations for these distinctive practices were laid in Nauvoo but they did not receive national attention until the 1850s.

Much of Church history in this period fit well the tempo of the times. In Great Britain, for instance, as in America, many humble Christians were searching for a restoration of the ancient order of things, and in this religious climate missionaries reaped hundreds of converts for the expanding Church. In fleeing to the Great Basin the Saints became part of the great American westward movement, a dominant theme throughout the nineteenth century. It began with steady settlement of the area from the Appalachians to the Mississippi; then in the 1840s pioneers began a series of jumps to widely separated places, skipping completely the Great Plains, which later became America's bread-basket. By the time the Latter-day Saints joined this movement in 1846–47, American settlers had established outposts in Oregon and in the Mexican province of Upper California. Other settlers were moving rapidly into Texas, which had just become a part of the United States. In the Great Basin the Latter-day Saints found themselves at a crossroads for other westering Americans and established an outpost that they envisioned as a self-sufficient place of religious refuge from the troubled world.

CHAPTER 5

Building the City Beautiful, *1839–1842*

The expulsion of the Latter-day Saints from northern Missouri re-opened the question of a single gathering place. Each time Mormon communities had been established as enclaves within existing societies it had resulted in conflict and expulsion. Some members thought these experiences proved that the policy of gathering should be abandoned. Joseph Smith retained the plan for a gathered community of the faithful, however, and over a seven-year period the Latter-day Saints expanded their missionary efforts and built an impressive city, one of the largest in Illinois at the time. These same years saw both Church doctrine and administration mature significantly.

A New Community for the Saints

As the beleaguered Saints scattered from Missouri during the winter of 1838–39, they moved eastward, uncertain of their final destinations. Some ranged as far south as St. Louis, a few went north into Iowa Territory. Most headed for the Mississippi River ferry at Quincy, Illinois, where they found temporary quarters just out of reach of their antagonists. Throughout the winter, companies of wagons, two-wheeled carts, and families on foot made the 150-mile trek to the Missouri border. Other families made the journey on river boats from Richmond. Levi Hancock's outcast family built a horse-drawn cart, filled it with corn, and set out from Far West through snow deep enough to half bury the young Mosiah. They carried few clothes or blankets and no household goods—Mosiah traveled barefoot. Eating roasted corn, elm bark, and herbs, and sleeping in the open, the family made its way to the river and crossed it early one January morning before the ice broke.

The mix of suffering and frustration on the one hand with unconquerable faith on the other was demonstrated in the story of Albert

Exodus of the Saints from Missouri, as depicted by C. C. A. Christensen.
(From the Permanent Collection of Brigham Young University)

Perry Rockwood and his family who, along with another family, left Far West on January 10. It rained or snowed every day as they tramped through mud and water, camped on the wet ground three nights, and arrived at the Mississippi on January 22. There they camped for three more nights waiting for the river to thaw so they could cross on a boat and go to Quincy, where they were received with sympathy and kindness. "We have meetings among the Brethren," Rockwood wrote to his father,

> but last night we heard that the Prophets advise for the Brethren to scatter, hold no meetings in this place & be wise servants that the wrath of the enemy be not kindled against us, we are a poor, afflicted & persecuted people, Drove to & fro, & when you come, you will have to share with us our afflictions. . . . The Saints have yet no continual abiding place but like the saints of old must wander about seeking shelter where we can find it. . . .
>
> It is thought by some that we shall not gather again in large bodies at present, still we do not know[.] our leader is gone, we have none to tell us what to do by direct Revelation, We want our Prophet & we feel we shall have him before our enemies triumph over us.[1]

---

[1]From the Albert Perry Rockwood journal, in Dean C. Jessee and David J. Whittaker, eds., "The Last Months of Mormonism in Missouri: The Albert Perry Rockwood Journal," *BYU Studies* 26 (Winter 1988), p. 34.

General supervision of the migration was handled by a seven-member relocation committee appointed in January with William Huntington as chairman. Its most urgent task was helping remove the poor. In response to a committee plea, at least four hundred Missouri Saints willingly committed their property to help the more destitute members. Headquartered at Far West, the committee directed the migration until mid-April, when mob pressure forced them to leave with the dispersing Saints.

The refugees received additional aid from non-Mormon citizens in Quincy. The town's Democratic Association quickly organized a sympathetic reception committee, which sponsored humanitarian relief measures, such as helping provide food, housing, and temporary employment. To emphasize their compassion, the Quincy citizens met on February 27 and adopted resolutions officially and bluntly denouncing the Missouri mobs and government officials. Soon Illinois Governor Thomas Carlin and others were encouraging the Saints to locate in the Prairie State, while across the river Iowa Territorial Governor Robert Lucas extended a similar invitation.

It was not a foregone conclusion that the Saints should continue to congregate in special gathering places. When a conference of elders debated the question in February, Bishop Edward Partridge and Far West's President William Marks argued that the Missouri persecutions left no choice but to scatter "to different parts." Initially their view prevailed, but when Brigham Young arrived in Quincy he proposed settlement by immigrant companies or branches as a better plan. Soon afterward Joseph Smith wrote a letter from Liberty Jail that promoted the spirit of gathering and suggested that the Saints "fall into the places and refuge of safety that God shall open unto them, between Kirtland and Far West . . . in the most safe and quiet places they can find."[2] Late in April, Joseph Smith presided at a conference in Quincy that affirmed the policy suggested by Brigham Young; the conference appointed the Prophet, Bishop Vinson Knight, and Alanson Ripley to select a relocation site.

In most respects the situation in Illinois and eastern Iowa favored the Latter-day Saints. In Illinois the government was underfinanced and the general economy still suffered from the panic of 1837. During the preceding decade tens of thousands of new residents had poured

---

2*History of the Church*, 3:301.

into the upper Mississippi River valley, spurring the sale of land, which was widely available though often at inflated prices. New citizens, including the Mormons, were welcomed in the hope they would stimulate the economy. Whigs and Democrats were about equally divided in Illinois, and office seekers considered new arrivals politically important as voters.

The selection of gathering sites in Hancock County, Illinois, and Lee County, Iowa, followed careful exploration and a thorough investigation of available land. One tract of 20,000 acres was offered at two dollars an acre on a twenty-year contract by land agent Isaac Galland, a resident of Commerce, Illinois. Galland's offer appealed to Joseph Smith, who wrote from Liberty Jail in late March encouraging both parties to close the deal. No action was taken until the Prophet arrived in Illinois; then he and other priesthood officers inspected lands in the Commerce area and Iowa's "Half Breed Tract." Beginning on April 30 with the purchase of a 123–acre farm from Hugh White and 47 acres near Commerce from Isaac Galland, Church leaders secured thousands of acres on liberal terms in the two counties fronting the Mississippi. A general conference May 4–6 sanctioned these purchases. On May 10 Joseph Smith moved with his family to a two-room log cabin, known later as the "Homestead," on the White farm about one mile south of Commerce.

Other purchases around Commerce included the 400–acre Horace Hotchkiss tract and Galland's 13,000–acre tract surrounding the Nashville townsite in Lee County, Iowa. Mormon land agents also bought the Montrose, Iowa, settlement where Fort Des Moines army barracks provided much-needed temporary housing for several families. But settlement was not limited to Nauvoo and Montrose, and in Illinois alone Latter-day Saints settled in at least nineteen different townsites.

Commerce was soon being promoted as the central gathering place. By summer it was unofficially renamed Nauvoo, a word that the Prophet said was derived from the Hebrew and suggested a beautiful place of rest. The following spring federal officials renamed the Commerce post office Nauvoo, and in December 1840 state legislators granted the city a charter. The original city plat of August 1839 contained about 660 acres, and the city council accepted another thousand acres to the east in eighteen separate transactions extending through April 1843. The burgeoning city of Nauvoo became the new headquarters of the Church, and gathering to that new place of refuge was soon vigorously encouraged among the Saints.

Joseph Smith, Jr., purchased this log home in Nauvoo and built the one-story addition. His son Joseph III added the frame portion and named the residence "The Homestead." (Church Archives)

It was not easy for the Saints to build a new gathering place along the Mississippi. The area near the river was swampy and unhealthy, and malaria was endemic in the region. As soon as the Saints began to settle, an epidemic struck. "It was a very sickly time," said Wilford Woodruff. "Joseph had given up his home in Commerce to the sick, and had a tent pitched in his dooryard and was living in that himself."[3] Calling upon the power of God, the Prophet went among the sick on both sides of the river, and many miraculous healings were reported. The following summer the epidemic hit again and many died. It reached such calamitous proportions in 1841 that at one point it became necessary for Sidney Rigdon to preach a "general funeral sermon" rather than have funerals conducted for every person who died.

An Appeal to Washington

As Church leaders attempted to resolve the issues that had forced them from Far West, the Missouri legislature rejected their petitions for investigation. Their next appeal was to the United States government. It was the Prophet himself with Judge Elias Higbee who made the trip to the nation's capital.

By this time Joseph Smith had learned some valuable lessons in

---

[3]Matthias Cowley, *Wilford Woodruff* (Salt Lake City: Deseret News, 1909), p. 104.

political astuteness. A few Mormons placed the blame for the Missouri persecutions on political parties, and in letters to the *Quincy Whig,* Lyman Wight had even extended the blame to the national Democratic party. On May 17 the First Presidency issued an immediate disclaimer. Clearly, it would be unwise to make redress a political issue, especially when the last hope for assistance lay with a Democratic administration in Washington.

In a political sense, the Latter-day Saint prophet's personal mission to Washington was significant. He revered the United States Constitution and while in Liberty Jail had written his disciples that it "is a glorious standard; it is founded in the wisdom of God. . . . It is like a great tree under whose branches men from every clime can be shielded from the burning rays of the sun."[4] He felt that the constitutional guarantees protecting freedom of religion, the right to petition the government for redress of grievances, and the right to property meant that, if necessary, the federal government could intervene within a state to protect a distressed people. His major goal was to win federal intervention in Missouri. His failure in this mission demonstrated how widely constitutional interpretations varied in that day. It so affected his own views that four years later he uttered his only recorded criticism of the Constitution:

> I am the greatest advocate of the Constitution of the United States there is on the earth. . . . The only fault I find with the Constitution is, it is not broad enough to cover the whole ground.
>
> Although it provides that all men shall enjoy religious freedom, yet it does not provide the manner by which that freedom can be preserved, nor for the punishment of Government officers who refuse to protect the people in their religious rights, or punish those mobs, states, or communities who interfere with the rights of the people on account of their religion. Its sentiments are good, but it provides no means of enforcing them.[5]

Joseph Smith and Elias Higbee arrived in Washington, D.C., on November 28, 1839, and the next day obtained an interview with President Martin Van Buren. They received little encouragement from him but contacted various senators and representatives. The Illinois delegation treated them especially well, and Illinois Senator Richard E.

----

[4]*History of the Church,* 3:304.
[5]*History of the Church,* 6:56–57.

Young promised to introduce their petition to Congress. Early in February they had another interview with Van Buren, who, according to the Prophet's report, listened reluctantly to their message and simply replied: "Gentlemen, your cause is just, but I can do nothing for you. . . . If I take up for you I shall lose the vote of Missouri."

Joseph Smith continued his quest and obtained interviews with other important political figures, including Senator John C. Calhoun of South Carolina, the leading advocate of states' rights. These interviews clearly reflected the national debate over the Constitution and states' rights that would culminate two decades later in civil war. The essential issue was sovereignty of the states, and the prevailing opinion, especially among southern politicians, was that questions like those raised by the Latter-day Saints were clearly state concerns. The Constitution provided no authority for national intervention. Joseph Smith's more liberal views resulted from the tragic experiences in Missouri but were expressed twenty years too soon. Only after the Civil War were guarantees of federal intervention more specifically written into the Constitution in the Fourteenth Amendment. For the time being the Mormon question was only one part of the constitutional debate that was already dividing the nation.

Disappointed, Joseph Smith returned to Nauvoo and joined the growing protest against the President. Van Buren was being blamed by his political enemies for the economic crisis of the late 1830s. To this criticism the Prophet added Van Buren's rejection of the Mormon plea. "May he never be elected again to any office of trust or power, by which he may abuse the innocent and let the guilty go free,"[6] Joseph Smith proclaimed. Not surprisingly, in that fall's national election the Mormons voted for the successful Whig candidate for president, William Henry Harrison. In their oppressed condition it was impossible for the exiled Saints to separate political from religious considerations.

Elias Higbee, meanwhile, remained in Washington for a time to see the Mormon petition through the Senate Judiciary Committee. But the unanimous committee report echoed feelings expressed earlier by Van Buren, Calhoun, and other political leaders. The appropriate places to seek relief, according to the report, were in the courts of Missouri or in the United States courts having jurisdiction within that state. The Saints were disappointed, for they had already tried unsuccessfully to plead their case in the Missouri courts.

---

[6]*History of the Church*, 4:89.

A general conference of the Church in April could do little more than adopt a resolution complaining that the committee report was both unconstitutional and subversive of freedom. The final appeal, the Saints acknowledged, must be to "the Court of Heaven." Frustrated by the unsatisfactory answers on this constitutional issue, Joseph Smith soon rejected the national leaders of both political parties, and in the presidential election of 1844 he declared himself a candidate for the U.S. presidency.

The Mission of the Twelve and the Gathering from Europe

On June 6, 1840, forty English Saints boarded the *Britannia* at Liverpool and sailed for New York. This first group of Mormon emigrants from Europe was organized by Brigham Young and Heber C. Kimball and led by Elder John Moon. Five months later, in a letter to family members in England, Moon favorably described the economic conditions in Nauvoo, expressed gratitude for his spiritual blessings, and encouraged his family also to take part in the gathering. He pictured Nauvoo as a "hiding place from the tempest of the last days," and said that "another reason for gathering the people of God is . . . that they may build a sanctuary to the name of the Most High."[7] Such expectations prompted 4,733 British Mormons to sail to America before the end of the Nauvoo period. Those who arrived boosted Nauvoo's population by over 25 percent.

This great movement of Latter-day Saints from Britain was a result of one of the most consequential missions in the history of the Church: that of the Council of the Twelve Apostles to the British Isles in 1840–41. On July 8, 1838, less than two months after Elders Kimball and Hyde returned from England, the Council as a whole was called by revelation "to go over the great waters" to preach the gospel. The revelation even specified a date (April 26, 1839) and a place (the temple site at Far West) for their departure. Before the appointed time, however, the Saints were driven from Missouri, and apostates taunted that this particular revelation could never be fulfilled. It seemed impossible that the apostles would actually return to a place where their lives were in so much danger. Nevertheless, before dawn on the appointed day Brigham Young, Heber C. Kimball, Orson Pratt, John E. Page, John Taylor, Wilford Woodruff, and George A. Smith assembled as commanded at

---

[7]*Millennial Star* 1 (February 1841): 253.

Far West and, with eighteen other members, held brief but impressive religious services. Wilford Woodruff and George A. Smith were ordained to the apostleship, filling the places of some who had fallen, other ordinations took place, several dissidents were excommunicated, and then the apostles each uttered a prayer. A song was sung, a cornerstone was placed at the temple site, and the apostles quickly left for Nauvoo. They had fulfilled both the spirit and the letter of the command.

Soon joined by Parley P. Pratt, who had escaped from jail in Columbia, Missouri, the apostles spent the rest of the summer preparing for their momentous mission. Their most pressing problems involved settling their families, but some still left their wives and children in temporary quarters. In addition, they spent considerable time in meetings with the Prophet and his counselors, who taught them important principles and designed to strengthen them in their responsibilities. Significantly, Joseph avoided discussions of administrative details and complex theological ideas. Instead, he talked to them of prudence, love, and humility, and of guarding against "self-sufficiency, self-righteousness, and self-importance." He urged them to "be humble, and not be exalted, and beware of pride, and not seek to excel one above another, but act for each other's good, and pray for one another . . . and not backbite and devour our brother."[8]

By mid-September all the apostles who had accepted the call were on their way. Some were seriously ill, left their families both ill and destitute, and, traveling without purse or scrip, made their way to New York only because of the goodness of Saints and friends along the way who were anxious to contribute to the mission.

The first to arrive in England were Elders John Taylor and Wilford Woodruff, accompanied by Theodore Turley. They docked in Liverpool on January 11, 1840, and immediately went to work in that vicinity and southward.

Elder Woodruff preached first in the Staffordshire Potteries, working among the friends of the Saints already there. One member with whom he worked closely was William Benbow. He preached in the Benbow home and spent several nights there. William told the apostle of his brother John, a prosperous farmer in Herefordshire who had joined a church known as the United Brethren. Like the seekers in America, they looked for a restoration of the ancient gospel of Christ. In early

---

[8]*History of the Church*, 3:383–84.

Brigham Young's license to preach in England, issued at Preston in 1840. (Reproduced from S. Dilworth Young, Here Is Brigham . . . , *p. 255)*

March, Elder Woodruff noted in his diary that "the Lord warned me to go to the South," and immediately he and his host journeyed to Herefordshire. Within two days after their arrival, John Benbow, his wife, and four friends were baptized, the first of a dramatic harvest.

In the Benbow home and some United Brethren chapels, Elder Woodruff preached the gospel to hundreds of willing listeners. The converted United Brethren soon formed the nucleus for many Latter-day Saint branches. Thomas Kington, superintendent of the local United Brethren organization, was baptized on March 21, ordained an elder the next day, and within three months presided over the Gadfield Elm Conference. When Elder Woodruff left Herefordshire to meet the other apostles early in April, he counted 158 converts, including 48 preachers, a former Anglican clerk, a constable sent to stop his preaching, and several wealthy farmers. Nearly 200 others awaited baptism. Before he finished his mission he had baptized more than 600 persons in a pool at the Benbow farm, and a total of more than 1,800 converts in southern England.

In April the second group of apostles arrived, and in a council meeting on April 14 they ordained Willard Richards, making a total of eight apostles in the British Isles. Two apostles, John E. Page and William Smith, had refused to go, Orson Hyde was preparing for a special mission to Palestine, and there was a continuing vacancy on the Council for nearly two years. They also sustained Brigham Young as "standing president" of their quorum. For the next year the Twelve and their coworkers preached in many cities and towns of England, Ireland, Scotland, and the Isle of Man.

Among the important consequences of this mission was its impact on the Twelve as a quorum. Before the mission the apostles seldom met as a group, and were frequently in disagreement with each other. Dissent and apostasy had affected their quorum as much as it had the Church membership, and they simply did not have the internal unity expected of a governing body of the Church. The moment they began to prepare for their mission, however, something miraculous seemed to happen, as they began to draw together in a way the quorum never had before. The hardships of just getting to England unified them even more. While there, under Brigham Young's leadership, they supported each other unfailingly as they shared the burdens and joys of their most difficult work, and their journals and letters reveal a love and concern for each other, as well as for the British people, almost without parallel. Truly on their own for the first time, without the Prophet and knowing the long-range consequences of success or failure, they were forced to depend not only on God but also upon each other. They sought Joseph's counsel on a variety of items, but they were often forced to make decisions before a response could come. The Prophet, however, eventually approved of all they did. By the time their mission was over, the Twelve were not only stronger as individuals, but they constituted a quorum more united than it had ever been before. Significantly, only those who went to Britain, plus Orson Hyde, remained in the quorum, which was now prepared to play an even more important role, next to Joseph Smith, in the leadership of the Church.

In January 1840, about 1,500 Saints lived in Great Britain, but when the apostles left fifteen months later, there were 5,814 members — and another 800 had emigrated to America. This remarkable success reflected not only the apostles' convincing testimonies, love for the people, and powerful preaching, but also the fact that they found a people well prepared to receive their message. Their greatest success came among the working classes, who were distressed by poor economic conditions, high food prices, and general urban poverty and unrest. The brotherhood and sisterhood of the gospel was more appealing to many of these people than the socialist utopias preached by certain reformers, and for some the doctrine of the gathering may have added to the appeal. Thousands of British citizens had already fled the country in search of economic opportunity, and in America the Mormon converts could find a better life as well as a chance to help establish the kingdom of God on earth. In addition, when the Mormon elders appeared among those, like the United Brethren, who were already seeking the restoration of the primitive gospel, conversion was often not long in coming.

The apostles also established an extensive publishing program. Under Brigham Young's direction, they printed 5,000 copies of the Book of Mormon and 3,000 copies of a hymnal in 1841. Under the editorship of Parley P. Pratt they inaugurated a monthly periodical, *The Latter-day Saints' Millennial Star*, which served the British Saints for 130 years. They also printed various pamphlets explaining and defending the faith, including Orson Pratt's important missionary tract, *Interesting Accounts of Several Remarkable Visions and the Late Discovery of Ancient American Records*, which contained the first printed account of Joseph Smith's first vision.

Along with preaching the gathering, the apostles soon established an orderly emigration system that required each emigrant to obtain a recommend from a local leader. As an expression of concern for the poor, the Twelve insisted that the more wealthy be denied recommends unless they assisted the needy. By the turn of the century the massive migration initiated in 1840 had transferred to America more than fifty-one thousand European Saints, including an estimated thirty-eight thousand from the British Isles.

Few stories illustrate the spirit and rigors of the gathering better than the account of William Clayton's migration, with two hundred Saints, in 1840. His eleven-week journey from Liverpool to New York included cold weather, storms, poor conditions aboard ship, and even a fire at sea. He traveled up the Hudson River, through the Erie Canal, through Lakes Erie, Michigan, and Superior to Chicago, overland across Illinois, then down the Rock River into the Mississippi, and finally to Nauvoo. The day he stepped ashore in the still rustic community of the Saints, he wrote in his diary, "We were pleased to find ourselves once more at home and felt to praise God for his goodness." Clayton had never seen the swampy peninsula on the Mississippi, but home was where the Saints were.

In April 1841 seven of the eight apostles returned to America, while Parley P. Pratt remained for another eighteen months with his family to supervise Church affairs. Amos Fielding was appointed supervisor of the trans-Atlantic migration, and the Twelve encouraged the Saints to travel in companies that could charter boats and purchase provisions wholesale. They were told to travel to Nauvoo via New Orleans instead of New York, for that was the less expensive route.

For the English Saints who arrived in the undeveloped countryside of Illinois, conversion changed their lives spiritually and brought them new and unexpected economic and political problems. Because homesteading on the frontier was often beset with hard work, deprivation, and illness, not to mention the unbrotherly behavior of some Mormons, the immigrants were bound to be disappointed if their expectations were too high.

William Clayton followed the advice of Hyrum Smith and took his family across the Mississippi into Iowa Territory to begin a new career as a farmer. There, in the cold month of January 1841, the former English bookkeeper found shelter in a rented house that had such poor ventilation that the family had to cook outdoors. He was disappointed to find that the Saints in Iowa held no regular religious services, and was discouraged even more when a fellow member presented a conflicting claim to his land and tried to drive him off. He had been induced to invest in a steamboat, but that venture failed. After frequent spells of illness and the destruction of his corn crop by cattle, he finally moved back across the river to Nauvoo. Some lesser men lost the faith.

The First Presidency anticipated such problems when they warned in a proclamation in January 1841:

> We would wish the Saints to understand that, when they come here, they must not expect perfection, or that all will be harmony, peace, and love; if they indulge these ideas, they will undoubtedly be deceived, for here there are persons, not only from different states, but from different nations, who, although they feel a great attachment to the cause of truth, have their prejudices of education, and, consequently, it requires some time before these things can be overcome. Again, there are many that creep in unawares, and endeavor to sow discord, strife, and animosity in our midst, and by so doing, bring evil upon the Saints. These things we have to bear with, and these things will prevail either to a greater or less extent until "the floor be thoroughly purged," and "the chaff be burnt up." Therefore, let those who come up to this place be determined to keep the commandments of God, and not be discouraged by those things we have enumerated, and then they will be prospered—the intelligence of heaven will be communicated to them, and they will, eventually, see eye to eye, and rejoice in the full fruition of that glory which is reserved for the righteous.[9]

---

[9]*History of the Church*, 4:272–73.

Although expansion of missionary work during the Nauvoo period centered in Great Britain, proselyting continued in southeastern Canada and the United States. In June 1843, Noah Rogers left Nauvoo accompanied by Addison Pratt, Benjamin F. Grouard, and Knowlton F. Hanks to establish a mission in Tahiti. Hanks died and was buried at sea, but the others succeeded in baptizing some sailors, English residents, and a few Tahitians. Additional missionaries carried the message of Mormonism to Australia, India, Jamaica, South America, and Germany. The work in these new areas was limited and resulted in only scattered conversions.

One of the most publicized special missions was Orson Hyde's call at the April 1840 conference to dedicate Palestine for the gathering of the Jews. His commission to visit the Jews took him to New York, London, Amsterdam, and then to Jerusalem, where on Sunday morning, October 24, 1841, with pen and paper in hand, he offered a prayer of dedication. He invoked a tempering of the sterile land and prayed for a gathering of the Jews, the rebuilding of Jerusalem, the creation of a Jewish state, and the rearing of a temple. As a symbol of these goals, Elder Hyde erected a pile of stones on the Mount of Olives and another atop Mount Moriah. Like his fellow apostles, whom he visited in England on the way to Palestine, he was responding to the call of the Church and doing his part to further God's designs for the latter days.

The Government of Nauvoo

The new gathering place encompassed several settlements in Hancock County and neighboring regions in Illinois and Iowa. Nauvoo, however, was the center place, and soon gained political and economic influence in western Illinois.

By September 1840 serious discussions on the form of government had begun. The arrival of John C. Bennett, quartermaster general of Illinois, precipitated positive action. Bennett offered his political support to the Saints and soon accepted baptism. In October, Bennett, Joseph Smith, and Robert B. Thompson were appointed to draft a bill incorporating the town. Bennett carried the proposal to the Illinois legislature, where both political parties cooperated in supporting it.

The Nauvoo charter was approved December 16, 1840, to become effective the following February 1. It encompassed an area three times the size of the original surveyed plat, though less than half of the added area was ever formally platted. The sixth city charter granted in Illinois,

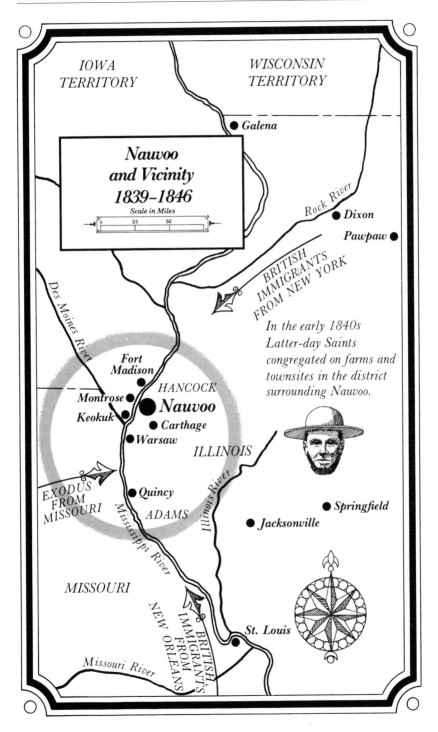

IOWA TERRITORY

WISCONSIN TERRITORY

● Galena

**Nauvoo
and Vicinity
1839–1846**

Scale in Miles

0   25   50

Rock River

● Dixon

Pawpaw ●

BRITISH IMMIGRANTS FROM NEW YORK

Des Moines River

In the early 1840s
Latter-day Saints
congregated on farms and
townsites in the district
surrounding Nauvoo.

Fort Madison

HANCOCK

Montrose ●

Nauvoo

Keokuk ●

● Carthage

● Warsaw

ILLINOIS

EXODUS FROM MISSOURI

Illinois River

Mississippi River

● Quincy

ADAMS

● Springfield

● Jacksonville

MISSOURI

BRITISH IMMIGRANTS FROM NEW ORLEANS

St. Louis ●

Missouri River

it was similar to the others; in fact, the city council's legislative powers were defined by verbatim references to the Springfield charter, issued ten months before. Church leaders considered it a "very broad and liberal" document, one designed to their advantage. Nauvoo's legislative and executive powers resided in the mayor, four aldermen, and nine councilors. The mayor and aldermen also served as judges of the municipal court, a change in the pattern of other chartered cities, so that five men controlled the legislative, executive, and judicial branches of government.

The first municipal elections, on February 1, 1841, made Bennett the mayor. Several Church leaders, including Joseph Smith, Sidney Rigdon, Hyrum Smith, and Williams Marks, were elected as aldermen and councilors, ensuring that local civil government would be friendly to the Church. While participation of Latter-day Saints in government was perfectly normal, the interlocking of church and state occasioned some criticism from neighbors who saw it as a violation of the American principle of separation of church and state.

The Nauvoo city council faced problems common to all towns and met them traditionally by appointing special officers and enacting laws. Two of the first laws passed guaranteed the right of peaceful assembly and freedom of conscience to all religions. A forty-member police force under Captain Hosea Stout enforced laws against the robbers, counterfeiters, horse thieves, confidence men, and renegades who were attracted to all Mississippi River towns. The city helped unemployed immigrants find employment in building stores, hotels, homes, and eventually the temple. It also planned to drain swamps in the lowlands and on the Mississippi River islands.

One important act of the city council was the creation on February 3, 1841, of the Nauvoo Legion. Most local militias in the state were organized at the county level, but the Nauvoo Legion was a city militia directly controlled by the mayor. By legislative amendment, enlistment was opened to all Hancock County citizens between the ages of eighteen and forty-five. The Legion enjoyed broad and unusual legislative power, for unlike other armies in the state, its court-martial could enact its own regulations. Although a branch of the state militia, with commissions issued by the governor and the Legion subject to the governor's call, the Mormon militia's internal government was independent of state interference. As the Legion's top officer, Joseph Smith held the unusual rank of lieutenant general. With the exception of George Washington, no other military officer outside Nauvoo held a rank that high until 1847. After Illinois officials approved Joseph Smith's election, he discovered that only a court-martial of his equals could remove him, thus assuring him lifelong tenure.

Major General John C. Bennett handled routine administrative affairs of the Legion. The two cohorts, or brigades, could accommodate more than five thousand men, but the Legion probably enlisted no more than two thousand members at its peak.

The Saints viewed the Nauvoo Legion as both a means of self-protection and a sign of their patriotism. "It will enable us," the First Presidency proclaimed, "to show our attachment to the state and nation, as a people, whenever the public service requires our aid."[10] But the showy trappings and bold talk of some Mormons created apprehension among non-Mormon neighbors. Comments about the Legion's activities became a standard part of anti-Mormon rhetoric as opponents of the Saints condemned stockpiling weapons, criticized the militia as an undemocratic concentration of military power, and accused the Prophet of becoming a "second Mahomet" who sought religious conquest by the sword.

Economics of the Kingdom

Although the Saints in Nauvoo were engaged in a cooperative enterprise to build the kingdom of God on earth, their economy was based primarily on private initiative, the profit motive, and free enterprise. In that respect it was different from the earlier law of consecration and the United Firms. In March 1839 Joseph Smith had written from Liberty Jail:

> And again, we further suggest for the consideration of the Council, that there be no organization of large bodies upon common stock principles, in property, or of large companies of firms, until the Lord shall signify it in a proper manner, as it opens such a dreadful field for the avaricious, the indolent, and the corrupt hearted to prey upon the innocent and virtuous, and honest.

> We have reason to believe that many things were introduced among the Saints before God had signified the times; and notwithstanding the principles and plans may have been good, yet aspiring men, or in other words, men who had not the substance of godliness about them, perhaps undertook to handle edged tools.

---

[10]*History of the Church*, 4:269.

Children, you know, are fond of tools, while they are not yet able to use them.[11]

This was not a rejection of the principle of consecration, but recognition that it may have been applied too soon. To provide funds to build the Nauvoo Temple and for other Church needs, a revelation given at Far West, Missouri, in July 1838 instructed members to tithe themselves, contributing one-tenth of all their possessions at first, then one-tenth of their annual increase. In addition, they were expected to labor one day in ten for the Church, and much of this tithing labor helped complete the temple.

Nauvoo's economy centered around the exchange of property, typical of the barter economy of the western United States. Its residents also looked forward to the possibility of commercial development. Primarily a religious, residential, and agricultural center, Nauvoo developed little major manufacturing or transportation. Land and buildings were its chief economic assets.

Because Joseph Smith had signed on behalf of the Church in its massive land purchases, in October 1839 the Nauvoo high council appointed him Church treasurer with responsibilities for property transactions. A conference fifteen months later elected him trustee-in-trust in conformity with the business transactions regulating most religious corporations. Consequently, during his first two years in Nauvoo he was directly involved in the land business, and evidently earned a living from it. Church officials urged all immigrants to purchase lots and farms through Church agents. Land could also be obtained through private investors, including Hyrum Smith, Brigham Young, Hiram and Ethan Kimball, Davidson Hibbard, and Daniel H. Wells.

Of greatest concern in the Nauvoo land business were the problems associated with land values and property titles. Speculation had inflated land prices, and in Nauvoo itself property values varied greatly. Special consideration was often given to the poor, who received land at little or no cost. Some refugees traded titles to abandoned Missouri land for lots in Nauvoo, and the Church used these Missouri titles as part payment on notes due to Galland, Hotchkiss, and others. In 1841 the Church began transferring deeds in Kirtland and other eastern Mormon properties that the Saints were urged to trade for Nauvoo property. For convenience in recording land transactions usually handled at the

---

[11]*History of the Church*, 3:301.

county seat in Carthage, Nauvoo created its own registry of deeds in the spring of 1842 and named Joseph Smith chief registrar.

The settlers established farms, homes, and businesses. Major farming was relegated to land outside the city, but garden plots flourished on one-acre lots inside city limits. Lots in Nauvoo included flower and vegetable gardens, orchards, fences, and outbuildings — summer kitchens, smokehouses, privies, barns, and stables. Construction quickly became Nauvoo's principal industry and employed hundreds of craftsmen. Early residents lived in temporary housing and then built log and block cabins. After several years, more impressive brick and frame homes in the tradition of New England and the Middle Atlantic states appeared.

Many small shops and factories in Nauvoo's pre-industrial economy directly served the building boom. Local businesses in the burgeoning city included sawmills, several brickyards, a lime kiln, a tool factory, a carpenter's and joiner's shop, and cabinetmakers. Nauvoo craftsmen produced matches, leather goods, rope and cord, gloves, bonnets, pottery, jewelry, and watches. Advertisements in local newspapers also identified a brewery, gristmills, a cast-iron foundry, a comb manufactory, a spinning wheel maker, a printing office and book bindery, a bakery and confectionery, and several tailors, weavers, cobblers, cordwainers, and wagoners.

Major industry, however, did not develop in Nauvoo. English emigrants seemed particularly interested in establishing corn mills, weaving enterprises, textile mills, potteries, and carriage manufactories, but such dreams did not materialize. "The difficulty is that men are not employed at what they ought to be," wrote John Taylor in a *Nauvoo Neighbor* editorial in May 1843. "Men that have been accustomed to manufacturing cotton goods are making ditches on the prairie," he lamented, "woolen manufacturers are carrying the hod, and working at day labor . . . and potters have been metamorphosed into builders and wood choppers."

To provide the lumber required to build a city where none existed before, the Church sent Bishop George Miller and a team of lumbermen to Wisconsin in 1842. The original intent was to provide materials for the temple and Nauvoo House, but large quantities were diverted for houses, barns, and other buildings.

The river offered opportunities for passenger transportation, and ferrying became a reliable business. In 1840, under a franchise granted to the First Presidency by the high council, Joseph Smith arranged to purchase a steamboat, the *Nauvoo*. Two years later Dan Jones and Levi Moffatt built the *Maid of Iowa* to transport converts from New Orleans. The Prophet obtained half interest in the *Maid* in 1843 and exclusive ferry rights between Nauvoo and Montrose, Iowa.

Considering contemporary economic conditions, the Saints at Nauvoo accomplished an amazing feat. The United States was in a depression during the late 1830s and early 1840s, and public and private credit was strained. In Illinois, the state was deeply in debt, two large banks failed, and the general economy hovered near collapse. In this setting, visitors to Nauvoo were amazed at the apparent economic vitality, a reflection of local construction and the influx of immigrants.

Despite the general appearance of prosperity in Nauvoo, the First Presidency carried heavy debts, including several thousand dollars in obligations from the years at Kirtland. Certain eastern creditors pressed for payment, but the October 1841 general conference instructed the trustee-in-trust to withhold payment. The conference resolved "not to appropriate Church property to liquidate old claims that may be brought forward from Kirtland and Missouri."[12] Six months later the Twelve encouraged general debt forgiveness within the Church and suggested that members voluntarily cancel debts to eliminate internal discord and animosity in preparation for temple blessings. Both actions eased the burden of indebtedness.

In a further effort to relieve the pressure of financial obligations, many Latter-day Saints tried another approach. A national Bankruptcy Act, effective February 1, 1842, allowed individuals to legally petition for relief. In April, Joseph Smith and several other leading Latter-day Saints engaged lawyers and filed bankruptcies under the untried law, hoping to eliminate debts and losses suffered in the removal from Missouri. Because of confusion over corporate and personal properties, the courts delayed Joseph Smith's appeal, and his debts were ultimately left for settlement by his estate after his death.

Education and Society among the Saints

Besides authorizing municipal government and a militia, the Nauvoo charter allowed establishment of the University of the City of Nauvoo and delegated the city council to select a twenty-three-man

---

[12]*History of the Church*, 4:427.

Joseph Smith's store, Nauvoo, Illinois. The upper floor served as a President's office and meeting hall, and the Relief Society was organized here in 1842. (Church Archives)

board of regents. In practice the council and school shared common leadership. Founded February 3, 1841, the university was governed by a chancellor, Mayor John C. Bennett, and a board of regents that included all city councilmen. The council soon gave regents responsibility for all common schools in the city. The First Presidency projected an educational system devoted to "knowledge and learning, in the arts, sciences, and learned professions," and hoped to make the university "one of the great lights to the world" for the diffusion of "that kind of knowledge which will be of practicable utility, and for the public good, and also for private and individual happiness."[13]

The university existed only on paper, and plans for a separate university campus were never realized. Some classes convened in homes, public buildings, the Masonic Hall, and the temple. Teachers offered secondary level classes in the sciences, philosophy, literature, history, music, and the languages. Orson Pratt taught mathematics and related subjects, Orson Spencer specialized in foreign languages, and Sidney Rigdon was appointed to teach religion.

---

[13]*History of the Church*, 4:269.

At the common school level, classes functioned in all municipal wards, with three wardens or trustees supervising the work. At least eighty different men and women served as teachers, utilizing standard contemporary texts selected from a list approved by the regents.

In addition to the enlightenment available through formal education, Nauvoo citizens enjoyed private lectures, debates, and social activities. Visiting dramatic companies and lecturers attracted audiences after Nauvoo became an established city. A circus visited in 1843, and phrenologists several times stopped to prepare head charts. Excursion boats regularly brought visitors to the river docks. These things, however, were only occasional parts of Nauvoo's social life. Local initiative created most leisure activities, and except for such voluntary educational organizations as the lyceum and the debate and literary clubs, the choir, and the bands, most fraternizing was carried out by families, at home or between households.

Entertainments for larger groups were held in the Concert Hall, north of the temple, or in the Masonic Hall. The Mansion House, an official residence built for the Church president in 1843, rapidly became a social center. Self-improvement was fostered by the Nauvoo Lyceum, organized in 1842 to conduct weekly debates on current issues, and by the Nauvoo Library and Literary Institute, founded two years later to encourage the reading of good books. University music professor Gustavus Hills helped create the Teacher's Lyceum of Music in December 1841 to foster improvements. The church choir offered occasional concerts, as did two brass bands, led by William Pitt and Domenico Balloo. The bands played for private parties, where dancing became a religiously acceptable practice among the Latter-day Saints. Useful pastimes included corn husking and rag and quilting bees. Young men enjoyed swimming and exploring small islands in the river. Horsemanship and sports, including running, jumping, wrestling, arm wrestling, stick pulling, and weight throwing, filled rare idle afternoons. For the Nauvoo resident seeking diversion from the routine of daily life, a great variety of homemade recreation was available.

Another voluntary activity opened with installation of a lodge of York Rite Freemasons in Nauvoo. Organized in December 1841, it filled a need for Freemason members of the Church. Hyrum Smith and Heber C. Kimball, for example, dated their affiliation with the Masons from the 1820s, and Newel K. Whitney, Lucius N. Scovil, George Miller, and many others had been Freemasons before settling at Nauvoo. But William W. Phelps and Ebenezer Robinson joined others who opposed the movement. John C. Bennett had been expelled from Ohio lodges but endorsed the solicitations in the early summer of 1841, which finally brought a dispensation for a Nauvoo lodge in mid-October.

The Nauvoo lodge grew rapidly. Within five months, the Mormons had more members than all other Illinois lodges combined. Latter-day Saints also organized the Rising Sun Lodge at Montrose, Iowa, in August 1842. The Mormon lodges began building a Masonic hall that year. About the same time, the Grand Lodge of Illinois launched an investigation of "irregularities" in Nauvoo. Fearful that Mormon members would soon control the fraternity in Illinois, a non-Mormon lodge at nearby Quincy petitioned state officers for an inquiry. The Nauvoo Lodge was temporarily suspended until October 1844, when recognition was formally withdrawn. In the meantime, two additional lodges – the Helm and Nye – had been created at Nauvoo. Ultimately most adult males in Nauvoo affiliated with one of the lodges, and despite the suspension, Freemasons in the city completed their Masonic Hall and dedicated it on April 5, 1844. Until this time lodge meetings had convened in the upper room of Joseph Smith's store and several other places. Now their own three-story building became a busy community center for social and cultural gatherings, city council meetings, schools, and surplus grain storage.

On March 4, 1842, during the same month that prominent men in the community were initiated into Freemasonry, several women met to organize their own society. Sarah M. Kimball and other women had expressed a desire to provide shirts for workmen on the temple. Those sharing this benevolent concern drafted a plan of government for their sewing group. When consulted, Joseph Smith offered to assist in forming an organization, not after worldly constitutional patterns, but "after the pattern of the priesthood." Under his direction, the Female Relief Society of Nauvoo was organized on March 17, with Emma Smith as its founding president. The Prophet counseled the women to "provoke the brethren to good works in looking to the wants of the poor, searching after objects of charity, and in administering to their wants – [and] to assist, by correcting the morals and strengthening the virtues of the community."[14]

The Relief Society was immediately popular. Attendance became too large for a single meeting, so under Emma Smith's direction sessions

---

[14]Nauvoo Relief Society Minutes, March 17, 1842–March 16, 1844, March 19, 1842, Ms., Church Archives.

were rotated through each of the city's four ecclesiastical wards. Membership by September 1842 was 1,142, and enrollment increased by another 200 during the next eighteen months. At these meetings, Emma Smith emphasized the society's charge to improve community morals by teaching sexual purity. Her counselors, Sarah M. Cleveland and Elizabeth Ann Whitney, typically addressed the need to seek out the poor, widows, and the sick. At each meeting, the sisters would donate to a central store of goods for use by the presidency in clothing and feeding those in need. Recipients of such compassionate service were identified during these same Relief Society gatherings in reports from those who had been assigned to visit the homes. The meetings also included reminders of the need to develop personal spirituality by studying the scriptures, praying, and living the commandments. The Nauvoo Relief Society was discontinued in the spring or early summer of 1844, but the organization was later revived in the Salt Lake Valley.

The Prophet's desire to have the Saints cooperate with impoverished members was also evident in remarks to an informal meeting of young people. At Heber C. Kimball's invitation, capacity gatherings of young men and women began to meet in homes or private halls in January 1843 to hear practical advice on the wise use of their time. The majority of the evening lectures, usually delivered by Elder Kimball, advised against excessive parties, dances, and entertainments. He contended that a young person would be better balanced with some nights devoted to scripture study, and the young people agreed.

When Joseph Smith addressed the informal Young People's Meeting, he encouraged them to organize not for self-improvement but for service to the poor. He particularly referred to an ailing English immigrant who had collected materials for a home but was too lame to build it himself. The Prophet challenged the young men to help the worthy convert. No report is available of the outcome of this project, but the youth did organize the Young Gentlemen and Ladies Relief Society of Nauvoo. This voluntary organization's focus, like the women's Relief Society, was charitable benevolence.

The Church: Expanding Settlement and Administration

Following the disruptive removal from northern Missouri, formal church programs were gradually reinstituted and then enhanced to meet the needs of an expanding membership. The general conference of October 1839 appointed a stake presidency and high council for Nauvoo and a similar organization for the Saints in Lee County, Iowa, later known as Zarahemla Stake. A bishop served Lee County as a stake officer, continuing an earlier pattern. But in Nauvoo the conference appointed three bishops for the city and gave them geographical jurisdictions: the upper, middle, and lower wards. Three years later, the high council created ten additional wards in Nauvoo and its outskirts to accommodate the increased population and appointed bishops for each ward. This introduced the bishop's ward as a geographical subdivision of the Church. In many American cities the term *ward* had been used to designate political precincts, and the first Latter-day Saint ecclesiastical wards were apparently created with this precedent in mind. Not yet a fully developed administrative unit, the bishop's ward was simply a convenient division for administering financial and welfare concerns. Preaching meetings remained as city-wide gatherings in one of the groves on the slopes surrounding the temple site, where the speakers were generally members of the First Presidency or the Quorum of the Twelve.

In the meantime, Latter-day Saint settlements were expanding. Church leaders initially encouraged gathering to central locations at Nauvoo and Montrose, where the Prophet had purchased land for resale to members. Other farm sites south of Nauvoo toward Quincy, in Adams County, and at locations surrounding Hancock and Adams counties soon attracted small congregations. In April 1840 Joseph Smith officially approved retention of these peripheral settlements, an action that brought several requests for stake organizations from the satellite communities. In July the Nauvoo high council approved a request to organize the Ramus Stake at the Crooked Creek settlement, twenty-two miles southeast of Nauvoo. The October conference re-established a stake at Kirtland, Ohio, and began procedures that soon resulted in eight more stakes in Illinois, five of them in Adams County.

At the same time, certain adverse conditions in the Nauvoo-Montrose area made it less attractive to many Saints. Nauvoo citizens had suffered greatly from malarial fever during the summers of 1839 and 1840, discouraging immigration and inducing some new residents to leave. Land speculators and squatters in Lee County, Iowa, were challenging Mormon ownership of lands purchased from Dr. Galland. Many Iowa settlers moved to Nauvoo when titles proved worthless in 1841. In addition, stake leaders disturbed some members with a debt repudiation policy in December 1839 and an attempt to instigate an unapproved system of consecration soon afterward. In Kirtland, meanwhile, stake president Almon W. Babbitt began encouraging European immigrants headed for Nauvoo to stop and help rebuild that partially abandoned Mormon community.

All this caused Church leaders to reconsider the policy of expanding settlements. During the early months of 1841 Joseph Smith decisively reestablished the importance of gathering to the twin settlements in Lee and Hancock counties. In January a proclamation from the First Presidency designated Nauvoo as the official site for a general gathering. It spoke glowingly of Mormon accomplishments there, the friendly reception among Illinoisans, and the expectations of improved health conditions. In revelations later that month and in March, the Saints were commanded to build a temple in Nauvoo and to establish cities in Iowa.

The small Mormon farming towns in Adams County, Illinois, were accepted as natural satellites of an expanding Zion for a time, because they were near Nauvoo. In contrast, Kirtland seemed to be rapidly mounting a schismatic challenge to Nauvoo's primacy. Gradually President Babbitt lost favor with other leaders of the Church as he continued to ignore their counsel on gathering. In May 1841 in the *Times and Seasons* the Prophet announced a First Presidency decision to discontinue all stakes except those authorized for Hancock County (Nauvoo, Warren, and Ramus) and Lee County (Zarahemla). This action came within a month after stakes had been organized in Philadelphia and New York City. It meant the end of a centrifugal movement, the official disorganization of the troublesome Ohio Stake, and discontinuance of eight stakes in Illinois. Babbitt was disfellowshipped in October for continuing to encourage European Saints to stop at Kirtland, which had been designated as a gathering place only for Saints from the eastern states.

At the beginning of 1841 Nauvoo held about three thousand inhabitants and was by far the Church's largest stake. The renewed effort to focus the gathering there rapidly increased its population, and the organization of Nauvoo into ten wards with three more on the outskirts of the city in August 1842 was an indication of its growth. Contributing further to Nauvoo's ecclesiastical ascendancy was the discontinuance of stakes at Ramus and Zarahemla in December 1841 and January 1842, though these areas were still approved for settlement. At the same time, in reconsidering the Kirtland question, the First Presidency authorized the reinstituted Almon W. Babbitt to proceed with caution. "Do what you can in righteousness to build up Kirtland," the instruction read, "but do not suffer yourselves to harbor the idea that Kirtland will rise on the ruins of Nauvoo."[15] The threatened dissolution of Nauvoo had been averted.

To guide Nauvoo's development, the Prophet called on the experienced Council of the Twelve and, in the process, significantly expanded the council's ecclesiastical authority. For nearly two years, until the municipal government became effective, the Nauvoo high council had managed city affairs. In addition, this and other high councils were authorized to handle all affairs within their own stakes, and at first not even the Twelve could intervene in their decisions. At a special conference on August 16, 1841, however, the Prophet announced it was time for the Twelve, who had so ably proved themselves in their British missions, to remain at home where they could support their families, relieve the First Presidency of some financial duties, and attend to the needs of immigrants. They would also continue to direct missionary work, but "the time had come," said the Prophet, "when the Twelve should be called upon to stand in their place next to the First Presidency."[16] Originally a "travelling high council," the apostles, under the direction of the First Presidency, were now given responsibility for the business of the Church within the stakes. The relationship between the stakes and the council was changed, and the authority of the Twelve became more general throughout the Church.

In their expanded role, the Twelve encouraged new arrivals to locate at Nauvoo and invited the Kirtland Saints to sign over their holdings to the Church in exchange for Nauvoo property. For British immigrants, the Twelve promoted a new and short-lived settlement at Warren, near Warsaw. Other converts were directed to Morley's Settlement, sometimes known as Yelrom. By the end of 1841 seven of the Twelve were serving as Nauvoo city councilmen; three others were elected later. The apostles became close advisers of the prophet-mayor and effective administrators of both church and civic programs. As active assistants to the First Presidency, they took a direct hand in the ecclesiastical decision-making process, issued missionary calls, and began assigning fields of labor, a task previously handled by other quorums. This close direction of affairs prepared Brigham Young and his associates to exercise the leadership of the Church after the death of Joseph and Hyrum Smith.

---

[15]*History of the Church*, 4:476.
[16]*History of the Church*, 4:403.

The Twelve also took a direct hand in the Church's publications program. Don Carlos Smith had established the *Times and Seasons* in November 1839 as a private business venture in partnership with Ebenezer Robinson. After Smith's death in 1841, Robinson inaugurated policies that the Twelve disliked. Robinson finally agreed to sell the paper to the Twelve if they would also buy his job printing business. On February 15, 1842, Joseph Smith's name appeared as editor and publisher of the *Times and Seasons.* John Taylor served as chief editorial assistant and after November as editor. Wilford Woodruff supervised the printing office and, in addition to publishing the newspaper, issued an edition of the Book of Mormon, three printings of the Doctrine and Covenants, a second edition of the hymnbook, and several private books and pamphlets.

One of the most important items published in Church periodicals was the Prophet's own history of the restoration. For years Joseph had been dictating his history to scribes and had directed the gathering of relevant documents by his associates. Various efforts had been made to prepare the history for publication, but in 1838 the Prophet began the final effort. Under his direction scribes and other committee members compiled the documents and wrote the history. By the time of his martyrdom in 1844 it was complete only through 1838; but the records were carefully packed before the exodus to the Great Basin, and the history was finally completed in 1856. Before the Prophet died, early portions of the manuscript were printed in the *Times and Seasons* and the *Millennial Star.* Eventually the completed work was published in six volumes as the *History of the Church of Jesus Christ of Latter-day Saints: Period I: History of Joseph Smith, the Prophet, by Himself.*

New Revelations and the Refinement of Church Doctrine

Much of Nauvoo's religious life centered around its Sunday meetings. There were no regular meetinghouses or chapels, and most preaching services were outdoor, city-wide affairs. Such large meetings had become regular by 1840, and they continued until the fall of 1845, when the temple was sufficiently completed that temporary seating could be provided indoors. Though small gatherings were held in homes, every Sunday at 10:00 A.M. the Saints in Nauvoo, across the river in Iowa, and in other nearby settlements knew that, weather permitting, an outdoor preaching meeting would convene. Joseph Smith was often the principal speaker.

As he preached to the Saints month after month, the Prophet explained the scriptures and introduced many important religious doctrines. In Nauvoo the teachings of the Latter-day Saints assumed the distinctive qualities that set them apart more clearly than before from other religions.

The Prophet still faced the necessity of explaining Mormon beliefs to the world in a way that those unfamiliar with Mormonism could understand. The famous Wentworth letter was a case in point. In the spring of 1842 John Wentworth, a Chicago editor, requested a short history of the Church. The Prophet complied and included several short statements of Latter-day Saint beliefs. These statements, later extracted from the Wentworth letter, became known as the Articles of Faith. Intended for non-Mormons, these articles were never meant to be a complete summary of the gospel, for they included none of the more advanced doctrines first presented to the Church in Nauvoo, nor did they contain such obvious practices as prayer or the sacrament of the Lord's Supper. The Articles of Faith were simply a summary of some of the most basic LDS beliefs, usually with respect to important contemporary religious issues, and in that sense they became a significant message to the religious world. Trinitarianism, the fall of man, predestination, election, Christian baptism, the restoration of the ancient church, spiritual gifts, millennialism, and other doctrines — all of which were frequently debated in nineteenth-century America — were approached in the Articles of Faith.

For the Saints, however, the Prophet opened new vistas. Things hidden from ancient times, he said, must now be taught as part of the restoration. He told the Saints they were living in the final dispensation of the gospel, in which all past knowledge and authority would be gathered together through the power of the priesthood. This idea was first suggested as early as 1836, when Moses, Elias, and Elijah appeared in vision to Joseph Smith and Oliver Cowdery in the Kirtland Temple and committed to them the keys of their own dispensations. On October 5, 1840, the Prophet expounded this doctrine more fully, marking the beginning of his efforts to open the minds of the Saints to some of the long-hidden mysteries of the gospel. A year later he told a general conference that "the dispensation of the fulness of times will bring to light the things that have been revealed in all former dispensations; also other things that have not been before revealed." As if to emphasize how revolutionary these new doctrines were, Brigham Young told the elders at the same conference that they must teach abroad "the first principles of the Gospel, leaving the mysteries of the kingdom to be taught among the Saints."[17]

Even for the Saints, some of the newly revealed doctrines were difficult to accept. Only five months before his death the Prophet preached a Sunday sermon to several thousand people in Nauvoo on salvation for the dead, but concluded with a discouraged recognition of how hard it was to accept such things. As recorded by Wilford Woodruff, the Prophet said:

> But there has been a great difficulty in getting anything into the heads of this generation. It has been like splitting hemlock knots with a corn-dodger for a wedge, and a pumpkin for a beetle. Even the Saints are slow to understand.
>
> I have tried for a number of years to get the minds of the Saints prepared to receive the things of God; but we frequently see some of them, after suffering all they have for the work of God, will fly to pieces like glass as soon as anything comes that is contrary to their traditions; they cannot stand the fire at all. How many will be able to abide a celestial law, and go through and receive their exaltation, I am unable to say, as many are called, but few are chosen.[18]

The doctrines of the nature of the Godhead, the eternal nature of man, and the relationship between God and man are fundamental to Latter-day Saint theology, yet these doctrines were not fully revealed until the 1840s. The "Lectures on Faith," published in 1835, had defined the Godhead as consisting of two persons, the Father and the Son, and the Holy Ghost as the combined mind of the Father and the Son. At a conference in Ramus, Illinois, in April 1842, Joseph Smith corrected this concept and declared by way of revelation:

> The Father has a body of flesh and bones as tangible as man's; the Son also; but the Holy Ghost has not a body of flesh and bones, but is a personage of Spirit. Were it not so, the Holy Ghost could not dwell in us.[19]

As early as 1833 Joseph Smith had taught by revelation that man was eternal and had existed from the beginning with God, but only in Nauvoo did he provide further insight into man's premortal existence.

---

[17]*History of the Church*, 4:426.
[18]*History of the Church*, 6:184–85.
[19]D&C 130:22.

In pre-earth life, he taught, God had created the spirits of all people—mankind literally became his offspring. One purpose of mortal life was to provide each spirit with a physical body and a testing ground. It was at this point that Mormon doctrine departed significantly from well-established religious tenets of the day. Presbyterians, Congregationalists, Baptists, and the reformed churches were still influenced by the Calvinist doctrine that man was helpless to determine his own salvation—he was predestined to be either saved or damned, according to God's will. In addition, they believed that fallen man was totally evil in the sight of God.

Joseph Smith taught that man, far from being an enemy or mere tool of God, was actually a god in embryo. The Father had achieved godhood only by going through the same experiences man is now enduring. Having successfully met all tests, he progressed in knowledge and power to become God. In turn, he instructed his spirit children in the plan of salvation before they came to earth and promised them that if they lived faithfully in their mortal life, one day they, too, might become gods. This was the doctrine of eternal progression, which became another hallmark of the restored gospel.

Especially important to Joseph Smith was the doctrine of agency. Even in his pre-earth life, man had the choice of accepting or rejecting the gospel plan, and in this life he still has that free choice. Such teachings totally rejected the doctrines of predestination and man's depravity. This view ennobled man and promised him a potential almost unthought-of elsewhere. It added new meaning to Christ's atonement, for the Saints were taught that the plan of redemption had been presented to them in pre-earth life.

Essential to all this was the teaching that certain principles must be accepted and certain ordinances performed by the power of the priesthood before any individual could attain exaltation, and only in the restored church was that priesthood found. What, then, would happen to those who died without a knowledge of the restored gospel? This question led to another hallmark of the Latter-day Saint faith: the doctrine of salvation for the dead. Joseph Smith first publicly discussed baptism for the dead in a funeral sermon in August 1840. The following month the Church began baptisms for the dead in the Mississippi River. Living proxies stood for dead ancestors in the belief that their loved ones would hear the gospel in the spirit world. Acceptance of the message in the spirit world would validate this earthly proxy ordinance. In January 1841 the Prophet announced by revelation that baptism for the dead was a temple ordinance. Even though the temple was far from completion, a temporary, oval baptismal font was hewn from pine and placed on the backs of twelve wooden oxen. It was dedicated in November 1841, and no more baptisms for the dead were performed in the river.

Many of the new doctrines taught in Nauvoo, including baptism for the dead, were directly related to temple ordinances. Back in Kirtland it had been clear that temples were to be a channel through which the Saints could receive great spiritual blessings. Now, in Nauvoo, a temple was to be built that would play an expanded role in the religious life of devout Church members. On January 19, 1841, the Saints were commanded by revelation to build a temple to perform baptisms and other ordinances for both the living and the dead; and if they failed, they were cautioned, "ye shall be rejected as a church, with your dead." Great blessings were promised if they completed it.

The temple was built at huge sacrifice. Financial problems and the persecutions of 1843 and 1844 continually interfered with its construction. In fact, only after the exodus from Nauvoo was well under way in 1846 was the temple completed and dedicated. Portions were dedicated earlier, however, and the important priesthood ordinances were performed.

One important temple ordinance was the endowment ceremony, in which special washings and anointings, symbolic signs, instructions, and sacred covenants gave the Saints new insight into their relationship with God, their eternal destinies, and their earthly responsibilities. So strongly did Joseph Smith feel about instituting the endowment that on May 3, 1842, he selected a small group of members and introduced it to them on the second floor of his brick store in Nauvoo. Other small groups received the endowment ceremony under his direction prior to his death in 1844.

By November 1845 the upper floor of the temple was nearing completion, and the Saints were anticipating this new spiritual experience with great enthusiasm. Church leaders and their wives provided drapes for the windows and canvas to divide the main hall into four rooms, borrowed carpets for the floor, and decorated the walls with borrowed paintings and mirrors. The Saints had been raising potted plants and shrubs in their homes during the winter, and these were taken to the temple, the House of the Lord, to create a setting of beauty and peace for the presentation of the temple ceremony.

Beginning December 11, 1845, the endowment ceremony was performed regularly for eager groups of Saints, and as soon as enough were familiar with it to help administer it to others, sessions were held around the clock. Sealings for deceased couples and the endowment ceremony in behalf of the dead were postponed until temples could be built in the Great Basin, but about five thousand members received their own promised endowments in Nauvoo and many married couples were sealed for eternity.

Perhaps the most controversial doctrines taught at Nauvoo were those relating to the sealing and plural marriage. According to the important revelation first committed to writing on July 12, 1843, no covenant or vow made between people on this earth is of force after death unless sealed by priesthood authority. This includes the marriage covenant. If marriage is performed or sealed by that authority, the marriage partners are promised that if they do not violate their sacred obligations, their marriage covenant will "be of full force when they are out of the world." This is the "new and everlasting covenant." In Nauvoo many husbands and wives were sealed by the power of the priesthood in the temple. Because the doctrine also provided that sealings could be performed in behalf of the dead, many whose spouses had passed on were sealed to them by proxy. For the most part, however, sealings for the dead had to wait until the move west.

The same revelation that clarified the sealing power also explained the doctrine of plural marriage. Under priesthood authority, it declared, ancient prophets had been given more than one wife, and if the Lord for any reason should command it again, the practice was right and valid when entered into under the direction of the priesthood. To Joseph Smith, this far-reaching doctrine was only one of several necessary parts of the restoration of the ancient order of things in the dispensation of the fulness of times.

Because of the controversial nature of this doctrine the Prophet initially taught it to only a few of his closest associates. Historical evidence suggests that he understood the principle as early as 1831 and may have begun taking plural wives as early as 1835. The first documented plural marriage came in 1841 when Louisa Beaman was sealed to the Prophet by Joseph Bates Noble. Then, after the Twelve returned from Great Britain, Joseph took them and other close associates aside individually and taught them the doctrine. All had difficulty accepting it, some more than others. Because of Orson Pratt's forceful rejection, he and his wife were excommunicated. Later, however, they were rebaptized, and in 1843 Elder Pratt was restored to the Council of the

Twelve. Nine years later he delivered the first public address on the subject, and he wrote most of the early Church literature explaining plural marriage.

Though several prominent men were sealed to additional wives, the practice remained confidential. Nevertheless, the widening circle of persons taken into the Prophet's confidence and the increasing number participating in the practice led to rumors and speculations. Apostates, especially, grasped distorted word-of-mouth reports in 1842 and 1843 and twisted them into sensational exposés and charges of adultery, attempting to discredit the Church. Joseph denied the charges of adultery, for the principle of plural marriage had been revealed as part of the new and everlasting covenant of the priesthood. Church members in general were not aware that polygamy was being practiced by some of the Saints, and it was not openly discussed until after 1852, when the revelation was published.

All this was only part of the rich development of doctrine that characterized the Nauvoo period. Little wonder the Saints congregated by the thousands to hear the Prophet each week, anticipating new insights. Such doctrines as the plurality of gods and man's potential for becoming like God excited the imagination and added meaning to life. Joseph Smith taught that spirit was not immaterial, but refined matter, and he explained that the creation of the earth could be understood as an organizing of already-existing matter rather than a creation from nothing. He expounded on the second coming of Christ, the resurrection, God's reckoning of time, the nature of angels, life in other worlds, and the nature of paradise and spirit prison.

The Nauvoo years, then, were of pivotal historical importance to the growth, organization, and doctrines of The Church of Jesus Christ of Latter-day Saints. A new gathering place was designated and a beautiful, influential city built. Responsibilities of priesthood leaders were expanded and clarified, and the Council of the Twelve gained its full authority in Church affairs. An expanded missionary program brought in new converts more rapidly than ever before, revitalized the Church in Britain, and laid the foundation for a vast emigration program. In addition, Joseph Smith expounded upon Church doctrines until the Saints' understanding of the gospel plan of salvation was greatly expanded.

These doctrines laid the foundation for the advanced religious outlook of the Latter-day Saints and accounted for such modern hallmarks of the faith as the temple endowment, marriage for eternity, salvation for the dead, genealogical research, understanding of the Godhead, and the doctrines of pre-earth life and eternal progression. But as the 1840s moved the Church forward in new directions, conflict and apostasy were leading to new tragedies.

Difficult Days: Nauvoo, *1842–1845*

The accomplishments that brought political influence and relative economic strength to Nauvoo during the early 1840s carried with them the possibilities of both peace and conflict. By 1842 Nauvoo so dominated Hancock County and surrounding areas that older residents feared its population was becoming a political threat. It was true that during the final two years of Joseph Smith's life politics became crucial and he and his close advisers became more politically active. In 1842 he accepted the Nauvoo mayorship. Two years later he became a candidate for national office. Other Latter-day Saints sought and won elective office in Nauvoo, Hancock County, and Illinois. The survival of the Church in Illinois seemed dependent upon its political strength, as the highly politicized climate of the mid-1840s revealed stresses within and jealousies without. But in mid-1844 a stunned membership suddenly found itself without its prophet-leader and facing complicated new challenges, including questions of leadership and threats of another exile. Politically the years between 1842 and 1845 were indeed difficult ones for the Saints in Nauvoo.

Political Events, 1842–1844

The difficulties between the Latter-day Saints and their neighbors around Nauvoo grew from the volatile politics of frontier Illinois. Party politics in the state were in the formative stage, and feelings were easily inflamed. In 1838, just before the Saints arrived in Commerce, progressive Democrats had elected Thomas Carlin governor and had won control of state government. The Whigs, a minority party statewide, had drawn substantial support from a region north and west of Springfield, including Hancock County. Local politicians were understandably concerned about the political attitudes of the growing Mormon community at Nauvoo, for it could have a pivotal influence on the fortunes of either party.

Until Joseph Smith's visit with Martin Van Buren in 1839, the Saints generally favored the Jacksonian Democratic party. This changed, at least temporarily, the following year. Even though the Prophet remained officially neutral in the election of 1840, he was known to favor Whig presidential candidate William Henry Harrison and the Saints probably cast an anti-Van Buren vote. In county balloting, the Mormon vote was divided, thus helping maintain a two-to-one edge for the Whigs, whose traditional concern for property rights elicited an appreciative response from the Missouri exiles. The unified votes in 1841 helped to elect a Whig congressman, but political allegiances remained fluid.

Not long after the 1840 election, political feelings in Hancock County began polarizing around religious issues, and the Saints found themselves deeply involved in state and local politics. Without this involvement, Nauvoo's existence as a political entity and a place of refuge seemed threatened. A small but vocal group of non-Mormons, alarmed at the concentration of political power at Nauvoo, formed an anti-Mormon party. Thomas Sharp's *Warsaw Signal* vocalized the resentment. In some county contests the new anti-Mormon alignment succeeded at the polls in August 1841.

Meanwhile, the Whigs lost ground with the Saints because of the party's opposition to granting the franchise to non-naturalized residents, including the growing British immigrant population at Nauvoo. Concern over this issue led some Whig newspapers to become openly anti-Mormon. Then the Democrats, with Mormon support, won control of the state legislature. After legalizing the vote for resident male aliens, the Democratic-controlled legislature reorganized the state supreme court. Governor Carlin was enabled to appoint five friendly justices willing to overturn Whig victories in the circuit courts.

Both parties had supported the Nauvoo charter, but the Democrats most actively capitalized on this support to gain the Mormon vote. In addition, Stephen A. Douglas furthered his political aims by patronage. A former secretary of state and an aspiring congressman, Douglas was a state supreme court justice in 1841. Through his influence, Nauvoo Mayor John C. Bennett was named master in chancery for Hancock County. Douglas also listened favorably when Joseph Smith brought some Missouri writs before him for a hearing. By 1842, therefore, Mormon leanings seemed Democratic, for in that party the Saints seemed to be finding their most effective friends. When the Democrats nominated as their candidate for governor Adam Snyder, who had befriended the Mormons in the state legislature, Joseph Smith immediately endorsed him. Attempting to reconcile such endorsement with continuing claims that the Church was nonpartisan, he wrote in the *Times and Seasons:* "In the next canvass, we shall be influenced by no party consideration . . . ; so the partisans in this county, who expect to divide the friends of humanity and equal rights will find themselves mistaken—we care not a fig for Whig or Democrat; they are both alike to us, but we shall go for our friends, our tried friends, and the cause of human liberty, which is the cause of God."[1]

Predictably, the *Quincy Whig,* the *Sangamo Journal* at Springfield, and other Whig papers denounced the Saints. To them, the Mormons were not ignoring party labels but were in collusion with the Democrats. Former governor Joseph Duncan, the Whig candidate for governor, campaigned on an anti-Mormon platform, pledging, if elected, to repeal the Nauvoo charter and drive the Saints from the state. The Saints were equally open in their criticism of Duncan. Joseph Smith indulged in a little political ridicule in July when he named his new horse "Joe Duncan." The Whig papers also eagerly published the shabby exposé written by John C. Bennett, recently disaffected from the Church. Charges of moral depravity and political conspiracy were hurled at the Mormons.

In May, when the Democratic candidate suddenly died, the party faced a difficult choice. With the anti-Mormon campaign gaining ground, anyone known as a friend of the Mormons would be a political liability. The Democrats made a shrewd choice—Illinois Supreme Court Justice Thomas Ford, who had not taken a public position on the Mormon issue. He could assure hesitant Democrats that he had never favored the Mormons, while in Nauvoo Douglas could assure the Mormons that the cause of liberty was safe in Democratic hands. Even though Ford actually supported repeal of the Nauvoo charter, the tactic worked. Ford won the election handily and the Saints' support helped him carry Hancock County.

Although the alignment of Mormon votes with friendly Democrats was not significant statewide, it had powerful emotional impact in Hancock County, where the anti-Mormon party was revived in Sep-

---

[1]*History of the Church,* 4:480.

State Representative William Smith.
(Church Archives)

Governor Thomas Ford of Illinois.
(Illinois State Historical Library)

tember 1842. At issue in the August election of 1842 was the candidacy
of the apostle William Smith, the Prophet's brother, who ran on the
Democratic ticket for the state House of Representatives. Some legislators were advocating repeal of the charters of all six chartered cities
in Illinois, including Nauvoo, and William Smith hoped to join those
in the state assembly opposed to the movement. His opponent was
Thomas C. Sharp, editor and publisher of the *Warsaw Signal*. To answer
Sharp's anti-Mormon comments, William Smith founded his own
weekly paper, the *Wasp*. Unlike the *Times and Seasons*, the *Wasp* was
exclusively secular. It carried advertising and general news and also
engaged in a lively editorial battle. With the Mormon vote behind him,
the apostle easily won the election, but this insured heightened tension
over the question of religious influence in politics.

Sharp's defeat only strengthened his antagonism. The hostile editor
broadened his attack against Mormonism and began criticizing Latter-
day Saints over a ten-county area. Realizing that no enemy of the
Mormons could win office while the Saints voted as a bloc, Sharp revived
the cry for extermination or expulsion.

The Prophet, uncomfortable with his brother's partisan editorial-
izing, persuaded William Smith to resign as *Wasp* editor in April 1843.
John Taylor succeeded as editor, enlarged the newspaper, and renamed
it the *Nauvoo Neighbor*. The new name was intended to reflect a nominally nonpartisan editorial stance.

When the question of charter repeal was debated in the state assembly in December 1842, William Smith cooperated with represen-

tatives of other threatened cities. He found the majority of Democrats supporting the Nauvoo charter, the Whigs evenly divided, and some from both parties seeking to replace the franchise with one less powerful. No conclusive action resulted, but the question would appear again.

Other stresses surfaced in the Church's political struggles in Illinois, some of them extending back to 1840. Reapportionment of legislative districts following publication of the 1840 census increased Latter-day Saint influence. The new boundary cut along the Hancock-Adams county line, placing substantial Mormon populations in both sections and making the Mormon vote important in both counties.

Actually, the Democrats were not always reliable in their support of the Mormons. Governor Carlin's Democratic administration rejected its first opportunity to assist the Saints when armed Missourians kidnapped four Mormons in Hancock County in July 1840. The small mob forced Alanson Brown, Benjamin Boyce, Noah Rogers, and James Allred across the river and detained them for several days. Rogers and Boyce were stripped and severely beaten and Brown was strangled to unconsciousness with a rope. Petitions to the Illinois governor for help went unheeded.

Two months later, when Missouri officers sought to extradite Joseph Smith and five others as fugitives from justice, Governor Carlin approved. The sheriff serving the papers failed to locate the wanted men, so the matter rested until the following summer. On June 4, 1841, Joseph Smith had what seemed to be a friendly interview with the governor. Immediately afterward, however, Carlin sent Adams County Sheriff Thomas King, accompanied by a Missouri officer, to arrest the Prophet. Judge Stephen A. Douglas heard the case in Monmouth the following week and ruled that the writ had become ineffective when the Hancock County sheriff returned it to the governor after failing to serve it the previous year. This favorable opinion reinforced the nonpartisan attitudes of Mormon officials. They had seen a lack of sympathy for their cause from the Democratic governor's office, yet friendliness from Democrat Stephen A. Douglas. The individual, not the party, earned their support.

In July 1842 former Missouri governor Lilburn W. Boggs appeared before a justice of the peace in Independence to charge Orrin Porter Rockwell, one of Joseph Smith's bodyguards, with attempted murder. Under an assumed name, Rockwell had been living in Independence with his in-laws while his wife awaited the birth of a child. On the rainy evening of May 6, an unknown assailant fired a pistol loaded with

*John C. Bennett, influential associate
of Joseph Smith. (From his book,
The History of the Saints)*

*Newspaper editor Thomas C. Sharp.
(Illinois State Historical Library)*

buckshot through the window of Boggs's home, severely injuring him. Shortly thereafter a bedraggled Rockwell arrived in Nauvoo. Rumors placed responsibility for the crime on the Mormons. The *Quincy Whig* reported that Joseph Smith had prophesied a year earlier that Boggs would meet a violent death. The Prophet quickly denied responsibility for the crime, but John C. Bennett urged Boggs to file a complaint. On August 8, on a warrant issued by Governor Carlin in response to a requisition from Governor Thomas Reynolds of Missouri, Joseph Smith was arrested as an accessory before the fact.

The extradition request contended erroneously that Joseph Smith had fled from Missouri following the shooting. Because the Prophet could readily establish his whereabouts in Illinois on the day of the shooting, he and Rockwell sought writs of habeas corpus through the Nauvoo municipal court. When Adams County officers challenged the court's jurisdiction, the city council enacted an ordinance broadening the court's powers. The arresting officers returned to Quincy disgruntled. Because the council's action was legally suspect, the Prophet secured a release from the master in chancery to be certain proper legal action had been taken. Then the two accused men went into hiding, the Prophet in the Nauvoo area, Rockwell in Pennsylvania and New Jersey.

It was during these uncertain months of 1842 that the Prophet apparently first looked seriously toward the Rocky Mountains as a place of refuge. A few could go at first, perhaps fifty pioneers, followed by others who would establish a stake, perhaps in Oregon. Increased immigration would eventually make the Saints a powerful people, united with the Indians of the Rocky Mountain West. But these vague ideas were shelved for a year while extensive legal efforts cleared the way for the Prophet's acquittal in the Boggs case.

Letters from Emma Smith, the Female Relief Society, and prominent Nauvoo citizens failed to persuade Governor Carlin of the impropriety of the extradition order. He offered a reward for the fugitives' arrest. To counter the tide of hostile public opinion, a special conference on August 29 prepared documents answering assertions being circulated by John C. Bennett and others. A volunteer force of 380 elders was appointed to carry them to public officials and Church members in various states. Meantime, a legal opinion from Justin Butterfield, the United States district attorney in Chicago, urged the Prophet to seek dismissal of the charges from the governor or state supreme court. In December 1842, the court advised newly elected Governor Thomas Ford that the writ was illegal. Upon Ford's recommendation, and with Butterfield as his defense attorney, Joseph Smith went before Federal District Judge Nathan Pope, who discharged him on grounds that the requisition and warrant of the two state governors went beyond the statements in Boggs's original affidavit and therefore lacked foundation.

A third attempt by Missouri officials to return Joseph Smith to Independence for trial occurred during the congressional campaign of 1843. In this instance John C. Bennett instigated the action in a grand jury hearing in Daviess County, Missouri. The hearing revived the old charge of treason and followed the usual legal channels of a requisition from Governor Reynolds and a warrant for extradition from Governor Ford. The Prophet and his family were visiting with Emma's sister near Dixon, Lee County, Illinois, when the warrant servers took him into custody. The prisoner was taken to Dixon, where he obtained counsel. At the same time, Stephen Markham, who had been sent from Nauvoo with William Clayton to warn of the arresting officers' approach, filed warrants against the two lawmen involved, Sheriff Joseph H. Reynolds of Jackson County, Missouri, and Constable Harmon T. Wilson of Hancock County, charging them with threatening Joseph's life and with false imprisonment. In this almost comic opera situation, all three indicted men sought hearings and headed toward Stephen A. Douglas's court in Quincy. Joseph, meantime, convinced his friends that the Nauvoo court had the power to try his case. Ushered into town by the mounted posse that had been sent to rescue him and by cheering

Hyrum Smith, Church Patriarch and brother to the Prophet. Oil painting by David W. Rogers, 1842. (Museum of Church History and Art)

citizens, this unusual party stopped in the Mormon city on June 30. Sheriff Reynolds refused to acknowledge the city court's jurisdiction or to present his writ for examination, but the court promptly released the Prophet on a writ of habeas corpus.

Disturbed by this development, the arresting officers proceeded quickly to Carthage and attempted to rouse public indignation. The sheriff sent a petition to the governor calling for a posse to retake the Prophet, but Ford honored the Nauvoo municipal court's decision. Meanwhile, certain Hancock County citizens protested the legal maneuvering in Nauvoo. Reacting precipitously, the city council made it illegal to arrest Joseph Smith on Missouri grievances and required the mayor's approval of all outside warrants. Both measures strained the city charter and weakened Latter-day Saint arguments in the courts.

One of the attorneys who defended the Prophet against this third extradition attempt was Cyrus Walker, a Whig candidate for Congress in 1843, who agreed to provide legal assistance in return for the Prophet's vote in the upcoming election. This pledge placed President Smith in an awkward position when it appeared that opposing candidate Joseph P. Hoge, a Democrat, would better represent Mormon interests. In January 1843 Governor Ford had advised the Prophet to avoid "all political electioneerings." The Church leader replied that he had not created the political unity of his people by his own initiative, but that the Mormons had been united by persecution. In the congressional campaign, he let it be known that he would vote for Walker, but that his brother, Hyrum Smith, felt differently. In this way the Prophet kept his promise to cast his personal vote for the Whig candidate, while Hyrum Smith and John Taylor's *Nauvoo Neighbor* advised the Saints to vote for Hoge. Both congressional candidates, uncertain of Mormon leanings, spent four days campaigning in Nauvoo. The Mormon vote decided the election in Hoge's favor.

Understandably, the Whigs viewed the 1843 voting as a misuse of corporate political power. Even Democrats, who benefitted from Mormon votes, joined the chorus of anti-Mormon feeling, for they saw that the power which worked for them might also work against them. Joseph Smith's attempt to keep the Church aloof from partisanship had been unsuccessful. Recognizing his own potential for political influence, he decided that he must use it wisely, though attempting to separate politics from religious doctrine. In February 1843 he told a group of workers on the Nauvoo Temple:

> It is our duty to concentrate all our influence to make popular that which is sound and good, and unpopular that which is unsound. 'Tis right, politically, for a man who has influence to use it, as well as for a man who has no influence to use his. From henceforth I will maintain all the influence I can get. In relation to politics, I will speak as a man; but in relation to religion I will speak in authority.[2]

---

[2]*History of the Church*, 5:286.

To many Saints, he also spoke with convincing authority in politics. To the non-Mormon citizens of Adams and Hancock Counties his authority had created an unwanted political voting bloc. The resulting fear and hatred would soon prove fatal to the Mormon community on the Mississippi.

Quest for Political Refuge

The ultimate aim of all Joseph Smith's political and legal activities was protection of himself and of the Church. In this search for refuge he considered many options, including a politically independent Mormon enclave. If working within the system would not prevent conflict, perhaps peace could be found in Mormon political independence. One manifestation of this was territorial; the Saints considered removing themselves from involvement in gentile political society and forming an independent government. Another option was the formation of a new national political party.

During the troubles of 1843 the city council considered creating an essentially independent city-state within Illinois. Recognizing the impossibility of achieving such a goal through state and local politicians, a committee was appointed to petition the U.S. Congress. The lawmakers would be asked to establish Nauvoo as a federal district, with rights similar to those of territories. The new enclave would be regulated under the existing municipal charter, and the Nauvoo Legion would be recognized as a federal army. This would provide a barrier of legal protection against non-Mormon intruders and a protective force to discourage mob invasions from Missouri. The city named Orson Hyde its delegate to Washington. Before his departure, however, other developments changed the nature of his mission.

In January 1843 Joseph Smith proposed an expansion of missionary work that would increase the gathering "by thousands and tens of thousands." Immigration of such vast numbers suggested new stakes, new settlements, and an enlarged concept of the physical boundaries of the kingdom of God. As early as 1839 Henry Clay had recommended a Mormon state in Oregon Country, an area then held jointly by the United States and Great Britain. That same fall the *Quincy Whig* and James Arlington Bennett, a New York friend of the Church, independently recommended creation of a self-governing Mormon empire in the Northwest. Other Americans, imbued with the spirit of Manifest Destiny, also looked west to California, Oregon, and Texas; and Mormon leaders exhibited an increasing interest in identifying possible sites beyond the Mississippi for an expanding Mormon community.

The first direct exploration of routes west came in July and August 1843, when Jonathan Dunham, accompanied by an Indian guide, examined lands in the western part of Iowa Territory. The following February, Joseph Smith instructed the Twelve to prepare another group of volunteers to examine sites in Mexican California, which extended eastward to the Rockies. Early in March 1844 Lyman Wight and George Miller presented an immediate colonizing plan. Their small company in the Black River Valley pineries of Wisconsin had produced sufficient lumber to complete the temple and Nauvoo House. Government agents were moving Native Americans onto the land, and these Indians had expressed an interest in joining the Mormon settlers for an expedition to the warmer climate of the Texas tablelands. The leaders of the Wisconsin Branch, therefore, proposed a Texas gathering place that would be an Indian mission and a colony for converted southern slaveholders. The latter would preserve southern culture and allow southern Mormons to make a unique contribution to the kingdom.

In response to the Wight-Miller proposal, Joseph Smith convened a special council on March 11, 1844, and charged it to study the plan. This council, called a "municipal department of the kingdom," was known as the General Council, or the Council of Fifty. It was a secular committee designed to relieve the First Presidency and the Twelve of temporal responsibilities, though many Church leaders actually belonged. Two non-Mormons were also part of the group. In addition to considering the immediate proposal, the council drafted petitions to Congress seeking Mormons' civil rights and considered ways to "secure a resting place in the mountains, or some uninhabited region, where we can enjoy the liberty of conscience guaranteed to us by the Constitution."[3]

On the Texas question, the General Council designated Lucien Woodworth as its agent to make arrangements for an independent Mormon state in southwestern Texas. He left for Austin in mid-March and six weeks later reported progress toward a partial treaty permitting settlement. Contemplating the establishment of western cities as satellites to the Nauvoo headquarters, the General Council drafted a memorandum to Congress asking permission to raise 100,000 vol-

---

[3]*History of the Church*, 6:261.

unteers as an army of settlers to protect those moving into uninhabited regions. The plan was presented as an economy measure to the government: the army would secure Texas for the Union and protect Oregon country against foreign intervention. It was this proposal that Orson Hyde finally carried to Washington, along with an alternative should Congress reject it.

By late April it was apparent to Elder Hyde that the Mormon plan was politically unacceptable. A better alternative, he told the General Council, would be to establish a base in Texas and then expand into California. In Congress, as expected, the Oregon proposal was rejected without a formal hearing. Stephen A. Douglas, meantime, provided the Latter-day Saint delegate with a map of Oregon and a copy of a report by John C. Frémont on his recent exploration of the country between the Missouri River and the Rocky Mountains. The report was not yet generally available but, as Elder Hyde wrote to the Prophet: "This book is a most valuable document to anyone contemplating a journey to Oregon."[4]

While Orson Hyde was discussing the Mormon dream of empire building with friendly congressmen, a general conference in April heard Joseph Smith proclaim a new definition of Zion that fit well with the Church's expanding political vision:

> You know there has been great discussion in relation to Zion — where it is, and where the gathering of the dispensation is, and which I am now going to tell you. The prophets have spoken and written upon it; but I will make a proclamation that will cover a broader ground. *The whole of America is Zion itself from north to south.*[5]

In the same conference both Brigham Young and Hyrum Smith emphasized this enlarged concept of Zion. After they received their temple endowments, the elders were to renew their missionary efforts, and the gathering was to take place all over both North and South America. Brigham Young called the plan "a perfect knockdown to the devil's kingdom," for the Church was to be built up in many places. Hopefully it would have enough political influence to create a more righteous nation.

These ideas may have been related to the Prophet's growing concept

[4]*History of the Church*, 6:375.
[5]*History of the Church*, 6:318–19.

of his own role in government, for three months earlier he had declared his candidacy for the presidency of the United States. At the April conference Brigham Young said: "It is now time to have a President of the United States. Elders will be sent to preach the Gospel and electioneer. The government belongs to God." Hyrum Smith optimistically remarked: "Don't fear man or devil; electioneer with all people, male and female, and exhort them to do the thing that is right. We want a President of the U.S., not a party President, but a President of the whole people. . . . Lift up your voices like thunder: there is power and influence enough among us to put in a President."[6]

The Prophet's Presidential Campaign

The decision to conduct a national political campaign was one aspect of the Prophet's search for ways to ensure the Saints' civil rights. Governor Ford had decided he could extend no executive protection without causing a local civil war, the national government had refused to involve itself, and Mormon political unity had alienated both political parties. In this setting the Prophet and his associates launched a full-scale effort to implement their ideal political concepts.

Implicit in the millennial concept of history held by most Latter-day Saints was the idea that the governments of men would ultimately fail, to be replaced by the just rule of the King of kings. Latter-day Saints during the 1830s and early 1840s often spoke of the establishment of this political kingdom. Sometimes they failed to distinguish between this anticipated government, which would rule people of all beliefs, and the existing priesthood, which would continue to regulate only the affairs of the Saints. Daniel's vision of a kingdom rolling forth to fill the earth was usually applied in a spiritual sense, but in the early 1840s it was increasingly given political interpretation. At least as early as 1842 those closest to Joseph Smith anticipated the establishment of a political entity outside the regular organization of the Church, although dominated by priesthood leaders. Known as the Kingdom of God, it would prepare politically for the coming of the Savior and the Millennium. The Council of Fifty, after its organization in early 1844, was the governing body of this political "kingdom." Though critics of the Church misinterpreted the actions of the council, its main concern was to influence the establishment of righteous government that would pro-

---

[6]*History of the Church*, 6:322–24.

tect the rights of all, including the Saints, and prepare for the Millennium. The presidential election year of 1844 seemed the right time to make the first great effort.

On October 1, 1843, the *Times and Seasons* printed an editorial asking, "Who Shall Be Our Next President?" and concluding that it must be a man willing to support the rights of the Saints. To ascertain the attitudes of five leading potential candidates on this question, Joseph Smith sent letters to John C. Calhoun, Henry Clay, Lewis Cass, Richard M. Johnson, and Martin Van Buren. The letter spoke of mistreatment of the Latter-day Saints, "who now constitute a numerous class in the school politic of this vast republic," and of their unsuccessful efforts to gain redress. It then pointedly asked, " *'What will be your rule of action relative to us as a people,'* should fortune favor your ascension to the chief magistracy?" Only Clay and Calhoun replied. Clay refused to make any commitment, while Calhoun echoed the arguments he and others had made in Washington in 1839 — that such affairs were state matters over which the federal government had no jurisdiction. Both prompted irate replies from Joseph Smith, who again emphasized his more liberal views of the federal government's powers. "Who shall be our next President?" echoed the *Nauvoo Neighbor* in its February 7, 1844, issue. The answer could only be: *"General Joseph Smith."*

Already, on January 29, the Twelve had decided to press for Joseph Smith's candidacy. On that date Joseph began working with William W. Phelps on a statement of his own "Views of the Powers and Policy of the Government of the United States." Soon available in pamphlet form, the Prophet's platform did not mention religion but focused on current political concerns and incorporated planks adapted from the leading political parties. He advocated presidential intervention when states refused to suppress mobs interfering with individual human rights. Further, he called for the abolition of slavery before 1850 under state initiative, but went beyond the abolitionist Liberty Party plank by suggesting federal compensation to slave owners. His economic policy followed Henry Clay's "American System." He endorsed a judicious tariff whose revenues might foster economic expansion, and a federally owned national bank. Bank profits, he said, would pay government expenses, and he hoped to reduce taxes by encouraging economy in government and drastically trimming the size of Congress. The Prophet's foreign affairs plank called for annexation of Texas, Oregon, and any liberty-loving people. As a social reformer, he advocated prison reforms, proposed making civil felonies punishable by labor on high-

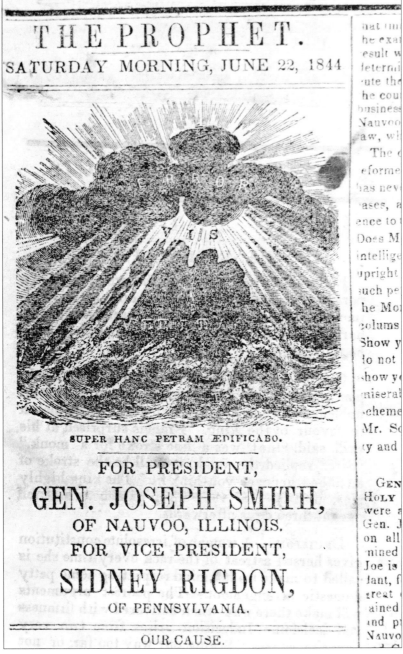

Campaign advertisement appearing in The Prophet, *Church periodical published in New York City. (Church Archives)*

ways or public works projects, and suggested imprisoning only those convicted of capital crimes. Even they would be encouraged to reform themselves in penitentiaries that would become "seminaries of learning." Overall, the Prophet's "Views on . . . Government" leaned heavily toward the conservative economic views of leading Whigs, but included broad interpretation of federal responsibilities in civil affairs conditioned by his past experiences and the important abolitionist and expansionist planks of the Liberty and Democratic parties. It was, in essence, an attempt to formulate a "union" program.

The platform was essentially a secular document. Joseph Smith offered himself as a candidate on his personal merits as an involved citizen and not as a religious leader with peculiar insights into national policy. The direction of his campaign fell to his advisory body, the General Council. Even so, the distinction between the political and ecclesiastical kingdoms blurred. The Prophet accepted the nomination on the condition that the machinery of church government would work for his election. At the April conference, speakers endorsed and the congregation unanimously affirmed Joseph Smith's candidacy. More than three hundred people volunteered to preach the restored gospel and campaign for him across the nation. The Council of the Twelve appointed elders to supervise these political missionaries in each state and set dates for a series of thirty-seven state and regional conferences. Sidney Rigdon, first counselor in the First Presidency, was named vice-presidential candidate. The National Reform party confirmed the nomination of its candidates in a state convention at Nauvoo on May 17 and scheduled a national meeting for Baltimore, Maryland, in mid July. The Council of Fifty adjourned on April 25 to join the campaigning. These political missions took the majority of Mormon leaders away from Nauvoo during the spring and early summer of 1844.

In their own view the elders of Israel went forth to win converts to the idea that the nation's strength lay in unity. Reacting against fierce partisanship, they supported a candidate who sought peace and justice. Joseph Smith envisioned an American government led by righteous men and ultimately a political kingdom under the Man of Righteousness himself. The candidate may have realized the unlikelihood of his actual election, but given the controversies that alienated him from all other parties, he felt that it was a necessary campaign.

The Martyrdom

The search for political and religious refuge ended abruptly for Joseph Smith in June 1844. While his supporters campaigned on a platform designed to unite factions under an inspired government ruled by good men, a disgruntled cabal plotted against him at home. Mormon apostates, influential men once close advisers to the Prophet, were setting in motion events that would lead to his murder.

The rumors that fed the fears of non-Mormons in Hancock County burgeoned after several key Latter-day Saints became disaffected and joined the opposition. The most prominent defector was John C. Bennett, whose much-publicized departure from Nauvoo in May 1842 created a sensation in both camps. The break had come gradually. Not long after Bennett's arrival in Nauvoo in September 1840, an old acquaintance wrote to Joseph Smith that the supposed bachelor had a wife and family in Ohio from whom he was estranged because of adulterous activities there. Affiliation with the Church in Nauvoo apparently did not reform him, for Bennett seduced at least one young woman there through a distortion of the doctrine of plural marriage. Church leaders privately confronted Bennett with his past in mid-1841, and the following spring began publicly refuting the argument he was using to cover his amours. At a parade ground maneuver of the Nauvoo Legion on May 7, 1842, Joseph learned that Bennett planned to assassinate him. Bodyguards foiled the plot, and ten days later Bennett resigned as mayor of Nauvoo. During the following month he and others confessed licentious conduct and pleaded for mercy. Expelled from the Church, he shortly left Nauvoo.

Immediately Bennett began publicizing his rift in area newspapers, accusing Mormon leaders of threatening his life, swindling local residents, committing immoral acts, and plotting the conquest of several midwestern states. His serialized exposé in the *Sangamo Journal* during the summer of 1842 was collected and published a few months later as *The History of the Saints; or, an Exposé of Joe Smith and the Mormons.* To counteract these scandalous accounts, Church leaders published an extensive review of the entire affair and sent special missionaries into neighboring settlements.

Bennett's distorted exposures caused some Saints to waver and a few to leave the Church. In April 1844 several of those who disagreed with the Prophet over the plurality of wives and other new doctrines withdrew and organized a reform church based on teachings as they had stood in 1838. The dissenters included William Law of the First Presidency, his brother Wilson Law, Austin Cowles of the Nauvoo high council, James Blakeslee, Charles G. Foster, Francis M. Higbee, and businessmen Robert D. Foster, Chauncey Higbee, and Charles Ivins.

The grievances of these men and about two hundred others who joined with them extended beyond polygamy. Joining the seceders, for example, were the land agents who had been chastised for selling lots in upper Nauvoo in competition with the more expensive Church-owned lots on the flat. Other leading participants claimed they had been unjustly excommunicated. Denouncing Joseph Smith as a fallen prophet, a political demagogue, an immoral scoundrel, and a financial schemer, these men publicized their charges in a newspaper inaugurated June 7, 1844, as the *Nauvoo Expositor*.

Reaction came quickly from those attacked in the paper. The city council met in long sessions on Saturday, June 8, and again the following Monday. The councilmen suspended one of their own number, non-Mormon Sylvestor Emmons, editor of the *Expositor*, and discussed the identity of the publishers and the intent of the newspaper. After analyzing legal precedents and municipal codes, the council decided the paper was a public nuisance that had slandered individuals in the city. Public indignation threatened mob action against the paper, they reasoned, and if the council failed to respond, the libelous newspaper would arouse anti-Mormon mobs. Early Monday evening the council acted under the nuisance ordinance. The mayor, Joseph Smith, then ordered the city marshal to destroy the press, scatter the type, and burn available papers. Within hours the order had been executed. The publishers, ostensibly fearing for their personal safety, fled to Carthage, where they obtained an arrest warrant against the Nauvoo city council on a charge of riot.

The council had acted legally in its right to abate a nuisance, though contemporary legal opinion allowed only the destruction of published issues of an offending paper, not destruction of the printing press itself. The city fathers had not violated the constitutional guarantees of freedom of the press, though they had probably erred in violating property rights. Witnesses affirmed that even this intrusion had been orderly, and, contrary to the publishers' claims, there had been no riot. Joseph Smith was released on June 13 following a habeas corpus hearing before the municipal court of Nauvoo. On the following day, as judge of the same court, he dismissed the other defendants.

Authorized only to hold a preliminary hearing, the Nauvoo court had exceeded its authority in deciding a riot case with finality. A few days later, to quiet public indignation and at the suggestion of the state circuit judge, Joseph Smith and fifteen others named in the complaint repeated the process of examination before justice Daniel H. Wells.

Well-known engraving of the Carthage Jail, made from Frederick Piercy's 1853 sketch. (Church Archives)

Again they were discharged, but again the inquiring judge was only a justice of the peace without authority to acquit. A few of the defendants later submitted to a trial before a circuit court jury and were legally acquitted. This release came too late to calm the storm that eventually claimed two lives at Carthage.

The brashness and swiftness of the city council's retaliatory action against the *Expositor,* and the easy release from trial of those responsible, gave those plotting against the Prophet's life ammunition for their scheme. Anti-Mormon newspapers called for the Saints' extermination. At Warsaw and Carthage, citizens' committees sustained this feeling with formal resolutions. In response, Joseph Smith mobilized his guards and the Nauvoo Legion, and on June 18 he placed the city under martial law. At the same time he furnished detailed information on the matter to Governor Ford and requested a thorough investigation. The citizens of Hancock County, meantime, importuned the governor to mobilize the state militia to ensure justice for the Nauvoo offenders.

So intense was the excitement on both sides that the chief executive published an open letter urging calmness, then personally traveled to Carthage to neutralize a situation that threatened civil war. At the county seat he found a large citizens' posse being formed. Ford obtained a pledge of strict legality and nonviolence toward the defendants. At the governor's request, Joseph Smith ordered the Nauvoo Legion to surrender its state arms in order to equalize forces and as a demonstration of good faith.

Governor Ford believed that the only way to settle the *Expositor* charges would be a trial at Carthage, the county seat. Therefore, on June 25, after negotiations over the legal procedures to be followed and after receiving a guarantee of protection from Ford, the fifteen men named in the riot charge voluntarily presented themselves to officials at the county seat. A justice of the peace reviewed the case and freed the defendants on bonds pending a trial at the October term of the circuit court. The Nauvoo party retired to the Hamilton House, a nearby hotel, but later that evening Joseph and Hyrum were jailed under an improperly issued writ granted by Robert F. Smith, a justice of the peace and captain of the Carthage Greys. The writ was issued in response to a warrant charging the Smiths with treason for declaring martial law. It was enforced without a hearing.

John Taylor, Willard Richards, Dan Jones, Stephen Markham, and John S. Fullmer accompanied Joseph and Hyrum to jail. When Jones, Markham, and Fullmer left on errands, they were refused reentrance. On June 26, Governor Ford visited the jail. In the discussion that followed, Joseph Smith defended his mobilization of the legion as a precautionary measure. He explained that he had no intention of invading non-Mormon regions as his accusers claimed. He also satisfied the governor concerning the city council's action and offered to pay for the property damaged if that would appease those plotting his destruction.

A week before leaving Nauvoo, Joseph had climbed atop the framing of an unfinished building to address the Nauvoo Legion. In his last public statement to an assemblage at Church headquarters, he noted that the *Warsaw Signal* had called for his death and for the expulsion of the Saints. With sword drawn, the Mormon leader had secured the militia's solemn pledge to fight with him, to the death if necessary, in defense of their rights. During the following week, when faced with arrest, and amid open threats against his life, the Prophet's first reaction had been to flee. On June 23 he crossed the Mississippi, intending to seek refuge in the safety of the Rocky Mountains, hoping that this would protect his life and save the Church further harassment. Some of his friends, however, believed mobs would drive the Saints from their homes despite the Prophet's departure. Pleas from them urged him to submit to the law, which he did. Uncertain that justice would be fairly administered in the hands of his enemies, he expressed hints of his fears to those on the road with him to Carthage. One of them remembered his words: "I am going like a lamb to the slaughter, but I am calm as a summer's morning. I have a conscience void of offense toward God and toward all men. If they take my life I shall die an innocent man. . . . "[7]

Now the death of Joseph Smith appeared certain. After his interview with the imprisoned prophet, Governor Ford disbanded the state militia at Carthage, except for two companies of the anti-Mormon Carthage Greys assigned to guard the jail. He took a third company with him to Nauvoo. Although warned of a plot to kill the Prophet, he paid little attention to the rumor and left for the city of the Saints on the morning of June 27, ignoring his promise to allow the prisoners to accompany him. Ford found Nauvoo alert but quiet.

At Carthage, meanwhile, a body of men from the disbanded Warsaw regiment daubed their faces with mud and gunpowder, rushed the jail, and quickly overpowered the cooperative guards, who had agreed in advance to load their guns without balls. The assailants rushed upstairs to the jailer's sleeping room where the four Latter-day Saint leaders waited. John Taylor and Willard Richards were armed with stout canes; the Prophet carried a six-barrel revolver and his brother a single-shot pistol.

Suddenly, shots from the narrow hallway punctured the thin bedroom door. One ball struck Hyrum Smith in the face; another from outside hit him in the back. He fell, mortally wounded. Opening the door partway, Joseph Smith shot into the hallway; three of the six barrels misfired. Two additional balls through the doorway punctured the dying Hyrum's chest and leg. Then, with bayonets and muskets threatening through the doorway, John Taylor moved toward an outside window. A ball from the doorway struck his leg; another, from outside, smashed into the watch in his vest pocket, knocking him to the floor. Elder Taylor was hit next in the wrist, then the knee. He rolled under a bed in the far corner, where he was hit a fifth time with a ball that tore away the flesh of his hip. Leaving Willard Richards alone behind the door, Joseph Smith tried the same escape. Two balls hit him from the open door, another from outside the window. Mortally wounded, he plunged through the window, exclaiming in a last plea for help, "Oh Lord, my God . . . "

---

[7]*History of the Church*, 6:555.

*"Last Public Address of Lieut. General Joseph Smith," an 1887 painting by
John Hafen. The painting is an idealization of the Nauvoo period and
incorporates a number of historical inaccuracies, such as the Nauvoo Legion
in full uniform and a tower that was not erected on the temple until after
Joseph's death. (Church Archives)*

Immediately the attackers inside the jail rushed outside to assure
themselves that the object of their attack was dead. Elder Richards and
the wounded Elder Taylor remained in the inner prison cell. Part of
the mob reentered the jail, but seeing only Hyrum at first glance, they
left amid cries from outside that a posse of Mormons was coming.
Though the rumor was untrue, the mobbers fled.

Of the four Latter-day Saints at Carthage Jail, only Willard Richards remained uninjured. Samuel Smith, who happened on the scene soon after the murders, helped Elder Richards arrange for removal of the bodies to the Hamilton House, where they also carried John Taylor. Elder Richards participated in the coroner's inquiry before Justice of the Peace Robert F. Smith, and wrote a quick note informing the Church at Nauvoo: "Joseph and Hyrum are dead."

A cannon's booming notified conspirators waiting in Warsaw and across the river in Missouri that the deed was accomplished. At about the same time, Governor Ford was addressing the Saints in Nauvoo. Cutting short his stay in the city, he was on the road toward Carthage when two messengers hurrying to Nauvoo informed him of the murders. Fearing retaliation from the Nauvoo Legion, Ford urged the citizens of Carthage to evacuate and ordered county records moved to Quincy for safety. Uncertain of further action by anti-Mormons, he also wrote a message to the citizens of Nauvoo urging them to prepare to defend themselves. Just before midnight he consulted with Willard Richards, who sent another message to Nauvoo urging the Saints to remain calm, stay in the city, and take precautions against a mob attack. Neither side, however, was disposed to be the aggressor, and the alarm soon quieted as the implications of the murders settled on those concerned. A melancholy calm pervaded Nauvoo.

On June 28 the bodies of Mormonism's two leading figures were transported by wagon to the city. A solemn crowd waited in the streets and along the road toward Carthage. The bodies lay in state the following day at the Mansion House while thousands filed silently past the coffins and William W. Phelps preached a funeral sermon in the grove. The next event displayed the tension of the times. Just before the scheduled burial on the temple block, the simple coffins were removed from their pine burial vaults. The vaults, weighted with sandbags, were interred before a sorrowing congregation. The coffins containing the bodies were destined for a secret midnight burial in the basement of the unfinished Nauvoo House to keep them from mutilation by the mob. A few months later Emma had the bodies secretly transferred to a spot behind the Homestead. Here they remained, in an unmarked grave, until 1928, when the two martyrs were reburied beside the grave of Emma Smith at Nauvoo.

Reactions of the Illinois press to the assassinations were mixed. Thomas C. Sharp of the *Warsaw Signal* applauded the deaths and reiterated his call for the Saints' removal. Many other local editors reacted with disbelief, astonishment, and disgust. Newspapers elsewhere in the United States generally echoed this denunciation. In their view the mob had violated the canons of justice by interfering with the due process of law in a cowardly act of cold-blooded murder.

Lists of persons believed implicated in Joseph Smith's murder were compiled by Sheriff J. B. Backenstos and Willard Richards. By late October indictments had been issued for eight men. Three of them left town, and a two-week trial the following May acquitted the remaining defendants. In June 1845 a jury gave a similar verdict to those accused of Hyrum Smith's murder. Contradictory evidence and the reluctance of guards to testify were key factors in the juries' decisions. Counsel for the accused argued that the murders had been a consensus of public opinion and thus no individual could be held responsible for what the populace decreed was legal. In essence, the murders had been justified by recourse to lynch law. Joseph Smith's opponents had turned vigilante, but in doing so they had misused even that extralegal means of popular justice.

At the death of the Prophet Joseph Smith, a universal sadness spread among the Saints, for he was revered as a man who had talked with God and who had guided the Church by revelation. His cheerful temperament, combined with his profound ability to impress and inspire, left a deep and permanent impact on the lives of those who knew him best. All this was accompanied by the creation of an impressive body of literature designed to perpetuate his memory and give recognition to his role as the Prophet of the Restoration. It was most profoundly expressed in an important essay, now part of the Doctrine and Covenants, which declared that "Joseph Smith, the Prophet and Seer of the Lord, has done more, save Jesus only, for the salvation of men in this world, than any other man that ever lived in it." (D&C 135:53.) It was also expressed in such hymns as "Oh Give Me Back My Prophet Dear," and "The Seer, Joseph, the Seer," by John Taylor, as well as "Praise to the Man Who Communed with Jehovah," by W. W. Phelps. Other hymns, such as "Oh, How Lovely Was the Morning" by George Manwaring and "I Saw a Mighty Angel Fly" by George Careless, found a permanent place among the Saints and helped keep alive in their consciousness Joseph's role in the restoration. Typical of the deep feelings of those who knew him best was a poem by Eliza R. Snow on "The Assassination of Generals Joseph and Hyrum Smith," part of which reads:

> For never, since the Son of God was slain
> Has blood so noble flow'd from human vein.

The Interlude: Energizing the Prophet's Program

The private war of Mormonism's chief opponents quieted briefly after the martyrdom. For Nauvoo there was an interlude of peace and an opportunity for renewed growth. The immediate question facing the Saints was one of leadership. The Prophet's role had been partly charismatic. Could his associates in the presiding councils fill the void? To whom did the leadership rightfully belong? To some Mormon-haters, Joseph Smith's death meant the end of Mormonism. To the Saints, life necessarily went on much as usual. With a commitment beyond the loyalty they felt to one man, they looked to the existing organization, expecting it to build upon the foundation Joseph had laid in his mission of restoration.

The question of leadership was complicated, partly because it had never been faced before; amid the many problems of the Church, it had not been thoroughly discussed. William Law of the First Presidency had been excommunicated in April 1844 and his position as second counselor not filled. The Prophet had intended to replace Sidney Rigdon with Amasa M. Lyman, but the nomination was never made because Rigdon's impassioned pleadings at the October 1843 general conference induced the congregation to retain him as first counselor, contrary to the Prophet's wishes. Even so, the unstable Rigdon's participation in church affairs had been minimal during the Nauvoo years, and at his own request he had been appointed to a local presidency in Pittsburgh.

President Rigdon was much less well known by the general membership in Nauvoo than were the active members of the Twelve. At the time of the martyrdom, however, all the apostles except John Taylor and Willard Richards were away on campaigning and preaching missions. When word of the murders reached them about mid-July, all except John E. Page and William Smith recognized the responsibility they must bear in continuing the Prophet's work, and they headed for Nauvoo. Brigham Young remembered his reaction to the news: "The first thing which I thought of was, whether Joseph had taken the keys of the kingdom with him from the earth; brother Orson Pratt sat on my left; we were both leaning back on our chairs. Bringing my hand down on my knee, I said the keys of the kingdom are right here with the Church."[8]

---

[8]Eldon J. Watson. ed., *Manuscript History of Brigham Young, 1801–1844* (Salt Lake City: Eldon J. Watson, 1968), p. 171.

On July 18 Brigham Young, Wilford Woodruff, Orson Hyde, Heber C. Kimball, and Orson Pratt held a tearful reunion in Boston. Then they issued an epistle instructing all priesthood leaders away from Nauvoo to gather there immediately.

Hyrum Smith had been second counselor in the First Presidency since 1837, but in 1841 his brother also ordained him both patriarch and assistant president. In Sidney Rigdon's mind, the latter calling could have given Hyrum a claim to the presidency, and this precedent encouraged Sidney, as first counselor, to advance his own claim. Arriving in Nauvoo on Saturday, August 3, Rigdon spurned an invitation to meet with the available apostles. He presented himself instead at the regular Sunday morning service in the grove. There he announced a June 27 vision outlining the need for a guardian to "build the church up to Joseph," and suggested that the ancient prophets had foreseen that Rigdon himself should step forth as "guardian" (meaning president and trustee). Rigdon asked stake president William Marks to call a special conference for Tuesday, August 6, to confirm selection of a new leader, but Marks called it for August 8. This providential delay allowed Brigham Young and three of his traveling companions to be present for the deliberations, joining the five members of the Twelve already in the city.

On the morning of the seventh, though weary from their long journey, the Twelve immediately began to fill the leadership gap. They called in the high council and high priests at the Seventies' Hall to hear President Rigdon's proposal. "Joseph sustains the same relationship to this church as he has always done," Rigdon said. "No man can be the successor of Joseph. . . . The martyred Prophet is still the head of this church. . . . I have been consecrated a spokesman to Joseph, and I was commanded to speak for him. The church is not disorganized though our head is gone." The senior apostle, Brigham Young, replied:

> I do not care who leads the church, even though it were Ann Lee; but one thing I must know, and that is what God says about it. I have the keys and the means of obtaining the mind of God on the subject. . . .
>
> Joseph conferred upon our heads all the keys and powers belonging to the Apostleship which he himself held before he was taken away, and no man or set of men can get between Joseph and the Twelve in this world or in the world to come.
>
> How often has Joseph said to the Twelve, "I have laid the

foundation and you must build thereon, for upon your shoulders the kingdom rests."[9]

Rigdon believed that a counselor to Joseph Smith was in direct line of succession. To Brigham Young, the counselor stood *beside* the President; not between him and the Twelve.

Despite their differences, the spokesmen for these two claims to leadership agreed that the priesthood of the Church should be assembled to rule on the matter. President Young suggested a solemn assembly for the following Tuesday, but as the call had already gone out for a meeting the next day, he attended. The gathering was larger than usual for outdoor meetings in Nauvoo, and the Saints strained to hear what was being said over the noises of the wind and the crowd. Speaking from a wagon box, President Rigdon rehearsed his claim for an hour and a half during the morning meeting. In the afternoon President Young discussed the nature of church government, the claim of the Twelve to the keys of the priesthood, and the authority of that quorum to ordain a new president if and when one would be chosen. "We have a head," he explained, "and that head is the Apostleship, the spirit and power of Joseph, and we can now begin to see the necessity of that Apostleship."[10] Following remarks by three other speakers, the congregation lifted its hands to sustain the Twelve as recognized leaders — specifically, to act in the office of the First Presidency. This sustaining action was repeated dozens of times as local conferences convened in quarterly sessions throughout the Church. To the satisfaction of most members the problem of leadership was resolved, though conflicting claims would later be advanced by others.

In other business, the Nauvoo conference voted to continue contributions for the temple, agreed to allow the Twelve to delegate management of church finances to bishops, and admonished the Twelve to select a new Church Patriarch. The membership also sustained President Rigdon in full fellowship. Several weeks later, however, the disappointed counselor asserted claims to an authority superior to that of the Twelve, and on September 8 he was excommunicated. He returned to Pittsburgh and the following spring organized a "Church of Christ" with apostles, prophets, priests, and "kings," which attracted a few who opposed the Twelve or who had rejected the private teaching on plural marriage.

---

[9]*History of the Church,* 7:229–30.
[10]*History of the Church,* 7:235.

For many who remained with the body of the Church in Nauvoo, Brigham Young's calling as President of the Twelve and presiding officer of the Church had been sanctioned by a divine witness. Some of the Saints in the congregation on August 8 had heard their new leader's voice as if it were the voice of Joseph Smith. "If I had not seen him with my own eyes, there is no one that could have convinced me that it was not Joseph Smith," Wilford Woodruff declared later in recalling the event.[11] The mantle of the Prophet had fallen upon a man who would direct the affairs of the Latter-day Saints for more than three decades. He began that task immediately.

The policies that Brigham Young and the Twelve endorsed in accepting the responsibility of the kingdom were those previously outlined by Joseph Smith. They put the missionary work in order, studied Joseph Smith's plan for an expansion of gathering places, and vigorously pushed industrial development and construction in Nauvoo, especially the erection of the temple. At the October conference the new leaders were formally sustained. Brigham Young's firm-handed approach and administrative skills were clearly evident in frequent councils with the apostles, the Council of Fifty, the city council, church trustees, and temple committees. Epistles over his signature on behalf of the Twelve instructed the Church frequently on matters of temporal and spiritual urgency.

These months were a time for setting the affairs of the Church in order. Amasa M. Lyman, who was serving as a counselor to the First Presidency when the Prophet died, and had been an apostle since 1842, was returned to the Quorum of the Twelve. In May 1845 the Twelve ordained William Smith to his inherited position as Church Patriarch. Wilford Woodruff was sent to preside in England, with jurisdiction over all of Europe. Supervision of affairs in North America was given to a committee of three who would become the First Presidency three years later: Brigham Young, Heber C. Kimball, and Willard Richards. Before year's end, Parley P. Pratt was called to New York as president, publisher, and immigration agent in the eastern states and provinces. To handle the managerial and clerical functions of the Church, the Twelve appointed senior bishops Newel K. Whitney and George Miller to the office of trustee, which Joseph Smith had held, freeing Brigham Young from details of financial affairs; Willard Richards continued as historian and recorder.

---

[11]*Deseret Semi-weekly News*, March 15, 1892.

Seventies Hall, Nauvoo, Illinois, rebuilt in early 1970s by Nauvoo Restoration, Incorporated. (Nauvoo Restoration, Inc.)

The administrative committee for the American continent, recognizing that administration of the hundreds of scattered branches needed to be tightened, decided to organize them after the pattern established by the Twelve in England and Scotland. The plan was to appoint a high priest over each congressional district in the United States and a bishop in each larger branch. Presiding elders in the smaller branches would be accountable to the district president at quarterly conferences. At the October 1844 general conference eighty-five names were presented as district presidents. Each president was instructed to move permanently to his assigned location and raise up a stake. Reuben McBride, for example, was assigned to Kirtland, Ohio, and George P. Dykes was established on a one-hundred-acre townsite named Norway, among the Norwegian Saints he had helped convert in LaSalle County, Illinois. Unfortunately, this ambitious design, a fulfillment of Joseph Smith's pronouncement that all of America was Zion, was curtailed by the evacuation of 1846.

At Nauvoo, the local priesthood received encouragement for greater activity. President Young urged the Aaronic Priesthood to visit regularly the homes of the Saints, and the deacons to fulfill their responsibility in assisting the bishops in their care for the poor. Within the Melchizedek Priesthood, the number of seventies multiplied rapidly. The sixty-three members of the first quorum became presidents over nine new quorums, and additional quorums were created under the supervision of the first seven presidents. By January 1846 at least thirty quorums were functioning—holding quorum meetings, participating in missionary work, and assisting in local assignments. In addition, the Seventies Hall was pushed to completion. To increase use of this two-story brick meetinghouse, George A. Smith of the Twelve urged the quorums to organize a preparatory school for missionaries.

The Twelve also gave attention to Joseph Smith's plans for western colonizing missions beyond United States boundaries, but they were simultaneously confronted with troublesome schisms and unauthorized western plans. Joseph Smith had authorized Elder Lyman Wight and Bishop George Miller to establish a stake in Texas, then an independent republic seeking to join the United States. Initially, the Twelve endorsed the still unrealized proposal, but when its sponsors' solicitations aroused talk of a general exodus, Church leaders reconsidered. By late August, Elder Wight was being counseled to limit his company to those with him at the pineries and to go north instead of south. He rejected this last advice and took the Wisconsin Saints on a long trek beyond the Red River to south central Texas, where he moved from place to place in successive settlement attempts. In April 1845 the Council of Fifty invited the Texas Saints back to Nauvoo, but Elder Wight, whom William W. Phelps had dubbed the "Wild Ram of the Mountains" because of his independent spirit, persisted in his separatist course. Refusal to cooperate with his colleagues led to his excommunication in 1848. He died in Texas ten years later.

Another man who led an expedition against the will of the Twelve was James Emmett, a member of the Oregon-California exploring party organized by the Prophet in February 1844. Without the sanction of the Twelve, Emmett left Nauvoo for the West about September with one hundred persons. He placed them under covenant to hold all property in common and to stand together in their venture. The Twelve on at least two occasions sent emissaries to consult with the migrating party, which Brigham Young's manuscript history labeled as excessively fanatic. Though Emmett confessed his error and sought forgiveness in the fall of 1845, he continued to disregard counsel, moved across Iowa into Sioux country, and finally was reprimanded by disfellowshipment two years later. Unlike Wight, Emmett was headed geographically in the right direction. In addition to being schismatic in religious practice, his journey toward the setting sun was ahead of its time.

Church leaders characterized those leading groups away from the City of Joseph as opponents of the Prophet's revealed program of building a city and a temple. If fear of hostile action or expectations of a better life elsewhere influenced too many members to scatter, the Twelve reasoned, the dispersion would endanger the incomplete projects at the central gathering place. It was important to build up branches in the East, but it was wrong to leave Nauvoo for premature settlements in the West.

The energetic direction of the Twelve launched Nauvoo into its most visible prosperity. Though foodstuffs remained scarce at times and industry failed to materialize, the city of log and frame residences acquired an impressive new look. Construction once again dominated economic life. Numerous new frame and brick homes were erected. Brigham Young added two wings on his house for an office and for his growing family late in 1844; Heber C. Kimball and Willard Richards built their two-story brick houses the following year; John D. Lee completed his residence; and the authorities bought a home for Lucy Mack Smith, widowed since the death of Joseph Smith, Sr., in 1840.

Public construction projects complemented the residential building boom. Besides the Seventies Hall, a Concert Hall was completed. The Twelve also attempted to implement the Prophet's plan for a large hotel, known as the Nauvoo House, facing Main Street and the river. In late 1845, brickwork commenced atop the stone foundations, only to be abandoned the following spring with part of the second-story walls erect. Another business enterprise left incomplete was the Mississippi River stone dike intended as a ship lock and waterhead for shops and machinery.

Both before and after the martyrdom, Nauvoo's most important building project was the Latter-day Saint temple, and the Twelve gave it priority over all other physical programs. Completion of the temple became a rallying point for those who retained their allegiance to the apostolic leadership. Brigham and the Twelve met frequently with temple committeemen Reynolds Cahoon and Alpheus Cutler and architect William Weeks. Relief Society sisters recommitted themselves to contribute a penny a week per member for glass and nails. Limestone blocks for the second story were laid by the fall of 1844, and the first

Charles B. Hall engraving of Brigham Young home at Nauvoo. (Church Archives)

of the large sunstones was raised into place. By late spring of the following year the trumpet stones and capstones had been positioned. The placing of the capstones was celebrated on May 24 with an appropriate ceremony accompanied by shouts of "Hosanna!" Workers next assembled the roof, finished the interior, removed the temporary baptismal font, and started carving a stone basin and oxen. Formal dedication was planned for April 1846.

Renewed Opposition and Removal

While this work proceeded, the peaceable détente in Hancock County fell apart. Stresses that had led to the death of Joseph and Hyrum Smith reappeared, eventually leading to the abandonment of Nauvoo. Latter-day Saint officials publicly spoke as if the Nauvoo settlement would be permanent, but at the same time they quietly laid plans for evacuation. They hoped to buy time to complete the temple before surrendering it.

In August 1844, as an election neared, Brigham Young informed the Saints he intended to avoid politics. Individual members, too, should remain aloof from the electioneering, he advised, although in this they had their agency. No national presidential candidate received Church endorsement. Locally, two of the three county commissioners elected in Hancock County were Latter-day Saints. Church members now controlled county government in cooperation with the sympathetic Sheriff Jacob B. Backenstos. The county also elected Mormon Representative Almon W. Babbitt to speak for it in the state assembly.

At Springfield, Babbitt faced revival of an effort to repeal the Nauvoo charter. Less radical elements hoped merely to amend it, to remove the power of the municipal court and clip the Legion's independent strength, but highly vocal opponents of Nauvoo's political strength advocated total repeal. When the issue came to a vote, the Democratically controlled legislature announced nearly two-to-one for repeal. The final tally on January 24, 1845, left Nauvoo without government.

The repeal of chartered government concerned the Saints most in matters of police protection and the courts. These arms of government, along with the Nauvoo Legion, had been effective in affording a defense against harassment. Recognizing an urgent need for continued defensive preparedness, Nauvoo militia officers initially decided to reorganize as an extralegal citizens' army, or "new police." During an organizational meeting in March, however, they evolved an unusual alternative. They gave their protective force quasi-legal standing by organizing it under the structure of the priesthood. Latter-day Saints outside Nauvoo joined in this body. Thereafter, a militia or police force composed of "quorums" of twelve men acting as "deacons" under the supervision of "bishops" patrolled the streets day and night and served as bodyguards for General Authorities. Brigham Young called this new interim government "The City of Joseph," a name approved at a special April conference.

In the meantime the Twelve asked Governor Ford about reorganizing the city under existing state legislation for towns. Ford was encouraging, and on April 16, 1845, citizens incorporated a one-mile-square section of the city, the maximum size allowed under the law, as a new town called Nauvoo. This government provided for justices of the peace, a council of five trustees, and other officers. The old police who had served faithfully under the charter were appointed en masse to serve the new town under their captain, Hosea Stout. Besides these regular officers, Nauvoo was watched by a "whistling and whittling brigade" of young men and boys armed with knives and sticks. Like a swarm of flies, they followed unwanted visitors as an unspeaking annoyance until the irritated persons left town. The brigade was a further protection for beleaguered Church leaders.

The disincorporated Nauvoo Legion, reorganized as the New Police, or Deacons, continued as an extralegal emergency force (under the priesthood) after the incorporation of the town of Nauvoo. Charles C. Rich had succeeded John C. Bennett as major general of the Nauvoo Legion, and Brigham Young had become lieutenant general. New titles were necessary when the municipal army became a priesthood-sponsored militia. Thus, in a letter in September 1845, President Young addressed Rich as "President of all the Organized Quorums of the Church of Jesus Christ of Latter-day Saints in Hancock County." Elder Rich was told to hold the quorums in readiness to act in response to threats against Morley's Settlement. This was consistent with Governor Ford's advice in April when he urged the Saints to prepare for self-defense.

Public cries against the Saints quieted after the martyrdom, but during the summer of 1845 antagonistic local newspapers again raised their voices. Thomas C. Sharp's *Warsaw Signal* revived its opposition to Mormon officeholders, reopening the debate over Mormon political activity and providing a smokescreen for a barrage of vandalism on Mormon property. Anti-Mormons and cooperating apostates hoped to drive the Saints from scattered settlements into Nauvoo and ultimately to force the entire religious community from Illinois.

Even before this direct harassment commenced, Church leaders reactivated plans for removing the entire membership beyond the borders of the United States. At a New Year's Day party in 1845 attended by several of the Twelve and their wives, and later the following week, the "Great Western Measure" was discussed. During consultations in February and early March, the Council of Fifty instructed Lewis Dana to lead a party of six or eight men to search for a settlement site. Dana, an Oneida Indian convert, had been recently installed as a member of the council. The party's departure in April was recorded in the official annals as "a mission to the Lamanites." Little is known of its efforts, except that the men were back in Nauvoo by summer's end.

The Latter-day Saint resettlement committees considered all three great western territories as potential sites: Texas, then an independent nation; Upper California, an ill-defined and loosely governed Mexican province; and Oregon, the entire American Northwest, jointly claimed by the United States and England. In early 1845 the Mormon leaders were privately favoring a central location somewhere in the middle Rockies or along the eastern rim of the Great Basin. At the same time they also asked non-Mormon friends and government officials for ad-

*Charles B. Hall engraving of Heber C. Kimball home, Nauvoo, Illinois.
(Church Archives)*

vice. Contacts in Illinois suggested asking Congress for a land grant
for exclusive Mormon use. Governor Ford, who had known for nearly
a year of Joseph Smith's colonizing plans, quietly proposed an independent Mormon government in California. He warned, however, that
the federal government would feel obligated to oppose any such invasion
of foreign soil if notified in advance. In March and April a Church
committee invited President James K. Polk and governors of states
outside Illinois and Missouri to propose solutions to the Mormon problem. The committee itself projected three alternatives: (1) the existing
state or federal governments should provide an asylum free from persecution for the Saints; (2) they should support the Mormon attempt
to seek redress for losses; or (3) the Church would find it necessary to
withdraw from American society and settle in a remote region. The
very few chief executives who responded favored this last alternative.

Private talk of abandoning Nauvoo did not interrupt public activities
to strengthen the city during 1845. Industrial development received
special attention from the Council of Fifty during these last months
in Nauvoo. With encouragement from John Taylor, a meeting of local
trade committees urged the development of manufacturing, home industry, and youth enterprises such as the weaving of straw hats and

willow baskets. In January 1845 Elder Taylor helped organize the Mercantile and Mechanical Association. The following month Nauvoo's Agriculture and Manufacturing Society began work on the long-envisioned Mississippi River dam.

Despite these activities and Church officials' quiet plans for the evacuation of the city, all surplus energies were directed toward completion of the temple. The edifice that the Saints had been commanded of God to build must be finished so that worthy members could participate in the sacred endowment ceremony before the exodus. Early in 1845 an appeal went out to scattered members for volunteers to work during the summer. Special missionaries visited the branches to collect tithing, and John M. Bernhisel was appointed traveling bishop. In May the capstone was laid, and the finishing touches were added to the attic story during late November. On December 10 the full ordinance of endowment was administered for the first time in a Latter-day Saint temple. This work continued steadily, with sessions for small companies of twelve continuing into the night and on Saturdays. By February 7 more than 5,600 ordinances had been administered to tithe-paying members. During that last month of feverish activity, officials performed numerous sealings, including new plural marriages.

Mormon leaders apparently did not reveal plans for the exodus until forced to do so in mid-September 1845 by the actions of their enemies. Public announcement of removal surprised many Saints, and some small factions within the Church openly opposed abandonment of the nearly completed temple and the physically expanding city. At the October general conference, held in the temple, officials assured the anxious Saints that the removal was a well-planned transplanting necessary to give the Church needed room for growth. The conference was largely devoted to assuring an orderly and unified departure, for the events of the previous few weeks had made it clear that Nauvoo would indeed be abandoned.

For three weeks before the conference, two emigration companies of one hundred families each had been in the process of formation. The first company included the apostles. Twenty-three other companies would now be created in a pyramidal organization resembling an army, with captains over tens, fifties, and hundreds. The assembly heard the Prophet's widowed mother, Lucy Mack Smith, declare her intention of joining in the orderly migration if her surviving children accompanied the Saints. In other action, the congregation appointed committees in each settlement to dispose of property and voted to discontinue Church newspapers. In a revival of the spirit of consecration that had aided removal of the poor from Missouri, the conference affirmed its intent to transport the entire membership to a new gathering place in the West. Latter-day Saints unable to attend the meetings were informed of plans by an epistle from the Twelve. They were advised to travel to Nauvoo for their endowments in the temple after its completion, projected for April.

Though Church authorities continually cautioned against haste, a spirit of anxiety pervaded Nauvoo. For more than a year, anti-Mormon forces had sporadically harassed the Saints. A rumored marauding, called a wolf hunt, against outlying settlements in September 1844 was thwarted when Governor Ford ordered the state militia to intervene. The mobsters then tried legal harassments. They swore out arrest warrants against settlers at Yelrom (Morley's Settlement), threatened Sheriff Jacob B. Backenstos with expulsion for his friendliness toward the Mormons, interfered with witnesses in the trials of the murderers of Joseph and Hyrum, and sought to incarcerate Brigham Young and several others on charges of treason.

In September 1845 the anti-Mormons under Colonel Levi Williams began burning Mormon homes, first at Morley's in southwestern Hancock County, then in other settlements. One after another, unprotected families were forced from their log farm homes to watch the vigilantes set the torch. In all, more than two hundred homes and farm buildings, plus many mills and grain stacks, were destroyed. The friendly Sheriff Backenstos vainly attempted to preserve order. He drove off the initial incendiaries with a posse of Mormon legionnaires; then, after occupying Carthage with his militia, he dispatched a number of scouting parties to protect frightened farmers against further raids. But the lives of Backenstos and other county officers who refused to sanction lawlessness were threatened. Confronted by several mobsters on the plains between Warsaw and Carthage, the sheriff fled toward Nauvoo, overtaking three Mormons, whom he immediately deputized. One of the pursuing horsemen raised his gun, and deputy Porter Rockwell fired. Frank A. Worrell, who had supervised the guard at the Carthage Jail on the day of the martyrdom, was mortally wounded. Rockwell and the sheriff were later indicted for murder, but acquitted on grounds of self-defense. Nevertheless, the act intensified hostile feelings in the county. Accordingly, Governor Ford sent General John J. Hardin with four hundred militia to supersede the sheriff. The state army was to act as an independent police force during the uncertain period of civil unrest. Hardin ended the Mormon posse's occupation of Carthage and halted plundering on both sides. As a mediator between the contending parties, he tried to please both sides and stall open confrontation until the Mormons could be evacuated.

Brigham Young's reaction to the home burnings was pacifistic. He ordered a total evacuation of all Latter-day Saints from rural areas and urged members to sell their property if possible, but cautioned against retaliation. In the move to Nauvoo he prohibited defensive measures. This policy, he hoped, would demonstrate to the many uninvolved citizens that the Mormons were not the aggressors. The governor's on-the-spot advisory committees included General Hardin, Mayor W. B. Warren, Attorney General J. A. McDougal, and Judge Stephen A. Douglas. This group concluded that, despite the mob's flagrant denial of property rights, nothing could be done to protect the Saints. The only solution was removal.

A group of Quincy citizens, at a meeting on September 22, issued a formal request to that effect. Two days later Church spokesmen replied, "We desire peace above all other earthly blessings."[12] The Saints revealed that they had already taken steps to evacuate between five and six thousand people in the spring, with thousands more to follow when ready. The Church committee asked for help in selling or renting Mormon property in order to procure supplies necessary for the migration. Both sides agreed to end legal prosecution and to promote an end to mobocracy. Representatives from the nine surrounding counties met at Carthage on October 1 and adopted similar resolutions. Citizens in Lee County, Iowa, meantime, echoed the call for removal. Neither of the Illinois citizens groups would promise to buy the vacated Mormon property, however, and the Carthage convention threatened to use force if necessary to assure a total evacuation.

Preparations for the exodus kept the artisans of Nauvoo employed throughout the fall and early winter. Each organized emigrant company established its own wagon shop by converting available shops or other buildings. Craftsmen in related fields joined the urgent task of wagon building. By Thanksgiving a published report identified 1,508 wagons ready to leave and another 1,892 under construction.

On August 23, 1845, the Council of the Twelve approved a pioneer expedition of 3,000 men to leave for the Great Salt Lake Valley in the

---

[12]Brigham Young, "Manuscript History," September 25, 1845, Church Archives.

One of the rare photographs of the completed Nauvoo Temple, taken from Lucian Foster's studio. (Church Archives)

spring. Later, the Council of Fifty, which was responsible for planning the expedition, resolved to send a smaller advance company of 1,000 men. These pioneers, traveling without their families, were to scout appropriate routes, locate sites, and plant crops.

Beginning with the October conference, public discussion of a precise relocation site seemed to center on Vancouver Island. Since the Great Salt Lake Valley was located in Mexican territory, it was recognized that the federal government would oppose any plan to locate there; that would violate Mexican sovereignty and might cause an international incident. Talk of Vancouver may have been a ploy to divert potential critics from a knowledge of the intended place of refuge west of the Rockies, but at least the island was under consideration as a place for a gathering of British Mormons. Late in 1845 Brigham Young asked the United States government for help in transporting the Saints into Oregon Territory. He proposed a contract to build blockhouses to help protect other pioneers or to carry the mail, but as before, the request for help fell on deaf ears.

Late in December 1845 several of the Twelve commenced reading John C. Frémont's report of his 1842 and 1843–44 explorations in the Rocky Mountains, Oregon, and California, and Lansford Hastings's

Emigrants' Guide to Oregon and California, both published earlier that year. Brigham Young carefully examined Frémont's map of the unsettled regions west of the Rocky Mountains, and three other maps hung from the walls of the temple. Officials were also familiar with the expeditions of Charles Wilkes and B. L. E. Bonneville. A Nauvoo high council circular in January, announcing the expected departure of the advance company in early March, said that the "resting place" would be sought "in some good valley in the neighborhood of the Rocky Mountains."[13] Those planning that expedition had narrowed the site to a few unclaimed valleys along the western slopes of the Wasatch Mountains.

In New York, meantime, Samuel Brannan was advertising for passengers for a five-month sea voyage to San Francisco Bay. He had been encouraged by Brigham Young in September to gather eastern Saints for the trip. The Nauvoo congregation had planned its overland trek for late spring, when water and livestock feed would be available on the plains, but mob pressures in Hancock County prompted an early departure. By coincidence, then, the eastern Saints and the Nauvoo Saints departed at the same time: as the ship *Brooklyn* sailed from New York harbor on February 4, the first contingent of Nauvoo refugees ferried across the cold Mississippi toward the rolling plains of Iowa. The Twelve had declared in their September epistle that the exodus West "forms a new epoch, not only in the history of the church, but of this nation. . . . Wake up, wake up, dear brethren, we exhort you, from the Mississippi to the Atlantic, and from Canada to Florida, to the present glorious emergency in which the God of heaven has placed you to prove your faith."[14] Beginning a new chapter in Mormon history, the exiles were heading west, as one pioneer put it, "to find a suitable place for a City of Refuge."[15]

---

[13]*Times and Seasons,* January 15, 1846.
[14]*History of the Church,* 7:478–80.
[15]Alfred Cordon, "Journal," October 6, 1845, Ms. in Church Archives.

CHAPTER 7

Exodus to a New Zion, *1846–1850*

From the eastern United States and Canada, from the American South, from Great Britain, and from scattered branches along the Mormon trail through upstate New York and northern Ohio came Latter-day Saints responding to the appeal of the Council of the Twelve for united action. They packed their trunks, sold their homes and farms, and loaded their wagons to join the trek to a new gathering place. For some this was the fourth move in less than sixteen years. But Parley P. Pratt was optimistic: "The people must enlarge in numbers and extend their borders," he told the general conference of October 1845; "they cannot always live in one city, nor in one county. . . . The Lord designs to lead us to a wider field of action." He compared the exodus to transplanting fruit trees from a small nursery to a field where they would have room to grow. "It is so with us," he said. "We want a country where we have room to expand."[1] That country was the unsettled American West, in a remote corner of Mexico's province of Upper California, near the eastern edge of the Great Basin.

The Mormon westward migration has been recognized as a major triumph in the settlement of the West. In the process, an entire religious society transplanted itself to a new place of refuge and spent a generation defending its institutions. While some of the scattered Saints who stayed behind attempted to restore a pre-Nauvoo variety of Mormonism, the larger congregation in the Great Basin labored to create a new religious society patterned after the one they had known in their abandoned Zion.

---

[1]*History of the Church*, 7:463–64.

The Mormons on the Move

The evacuation of the Saints from western Illinois was originally scheduled for sometime in April 1846. By then grass would be available on the plains to sustain livestock, and streams would be free from ice. During the winter the citizens of Nauvoo negotiated to sell their homes, shops, and farms and were busy stocking foodstuffs, building wagons, buying teams, and organizing emigrant companies. Suddenly, however, two new threats prompted an early and hasty exit.

An indictment issued by the U.S. District Court in Springfield against Brigham Young and eight other apostles was the first. They were accused of instigating and harboring a Nauvoo counterfeiting operation actually conducted by transient river traffickers. Government officials attempted to serve the warrants but failed when William Miller offered himself as a decoy to prevent President Young's arrest. Dressed in a cloak and wearing Brigham Young's cap, Miller left the temple, where the apostles were gathered, and stepped into the president's carriage. The waiting marshals arrested Miller and transported him the eighteen miles to Carthage before discovering the ploy. A second threat was contained in warnings reported by Governor Ford and confirmed in a letter from Sam Brannan. According to these unfounded reports, federal troops from St. Louis were planning to interfere with the orderly removal planned for spring.

Rather than risk such interference, the Twelve, the Church trustees, and others decided on February 2 to depart immediately. At least two thousand emigrants were prepared to go with them and thousands more could be ready within weeks. The first group, Church authorities and their families, crossed the Mississippi on February 4, utilizing skiffs and flatboats. In succeeding days, under the supervision of Nauvoo police, the evacuation rapidly gained momentum, and on February 24 the river froze, expediting the Saints' exodus. Within weeks several hundred exiles were assembled in temporary camps in Iowa. Late in February, Brigham Young joined his emigrating company at Sugar Creek, nine miles into Iowa.

Joseph Young, senior president of the First Council of the Seventy, was left to preside over the dwindling Mormon population at Nauvoo. His principal tasks were to hasten organizing for removal and to complete the temple for final dedication. During the late winter months, blacksmiths, carpenters, and cabinetmakers accelerated the forging of wheel rims and fashioning of wagon boxes, hubs, and spokes. The

Saints were also trying to sell their property, and before final evacuation they succeeded in disposing of 80 to 90 percent of their holdings.

The Saints were determined that nothing would hinder them in their religious obligation of completing and dedicating the sacred temple, even though they might never use it again. As artisans added finishing touches to the first floor of the building, Joseph Young conducted daily prayer meetings with small, selected groups. By April the temple was ready for dedication and simultaneous abandonment. On the last day of the month, in a secret session directed by Elders Wilford Woodruff and Orson Hyde, Joseph Young delivered the building over to the Lord. On the following day 300 people assembled for a brief public dedication. By this time at least 5,615 Saints had received endowments, but for those not so blessed Brigham Young had promised other temples in the West.

Subsequently, the temple was shamefully desecrated by mobs; finally, in October 1848, an incendiary set fire to that magnificent sacred structure. It was so weakened that the north wall came down, and after a tornado hit in May 1850, all but the front wall fell and the stones were hauled away to be used for other purposes.

By mid-May 1846, nearly twelve thousand Saints had crossed the river, and more than six hundred remained in Illinois. Some were detained by illness or poverty and a few sympathized with the seceders, but to some anti-Mormons it appeared that total evacuation might not be accomplished. This precipitated a final confrontation. Guerrilla warfare was revived against isolated settlers. Then, in June, the mobbers gathered four hundred volunteers, marched to Nauvoo, and demanded surrender. The remaining Nauvoo residents quickly united under former Nauvoo Legion officers and prevented an invasion, but the attacks against farmers in outlying areas continued. In late August Governor Ford responded to a Mormon petition for protection by dispatching an officer with ten men to organize a volunteer militia at Nauvoo. With both sides in readiness, the stage was set for battle.

In September the Carthage guerrillas under Thomas S. Brockman mustered about eight hundred men to enforce their ultimatum. Adequately armed, and with six cannons, they positioned themselves on the outskirts of Nauvoo and repeated the demand for all Mormons and Mormon sympathizers to leave. Inside the city about three hundred residents organized under Major Benjamin Clifford and Nauvoo Legion

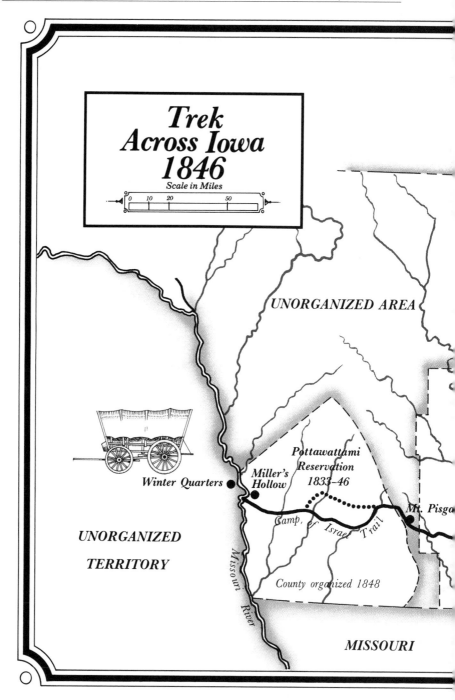

Trek
Across Iowa
1846
Scale in Miles

Mormon route westward from Nauvoo crossed the largely unsettled tablelands of Iowa, shown here with county boundaries established by the time of statehood in December 1846.

officers. For cannon they had five makeshift artillery pieces built from sawed-off steamboat shafts. The defenders positioned themselves behind barricades less than a mile from their challengers.

For two days the opposing forces exchanged gunfire in minor skirmishes, and on the third day, September 12, the invaders attacked in force. Flanking the defenders on the south, they headed for the city while the Mormons and their friends retreated to new positions behind stout blockades. Captain William Anderson, his fifteen-year-old son, August, and David Norris were killed when their "Spartan Band" attempted to cut off the attackers; several in the invading force also died.

Death, wounds, and the realization that further bloodshed was in the offing finally prompted both sides to seek a truce. A committee from Quincy mediated terms, and the holdouts in Nauvoo surrendered their arms and the city itself. In return, they were promised safety while crossing the river and allowed to designate a committee of five to remain long enough to sell their property. Those able to do so left immediately. Others were subjected to more plundering, harassment, and forcible expulsion in direct violation of the agreements.

Approximately 640 destitute Latter-day Saints were forced to cross the river in September. They crowded into makeshift tents on the river bottoms, where many contracted chills and fever in the cold September rains. Word of the condition of the "poor camp" reached the Twelve, and a relief company was sent with provisions, tents, and wagons. On October 9, still practically destitute, the "poor camp" organized for the journey west. On that day flocks of quail, exhausted from a long flight, settled for forty miles along the bottom lands. The hungry Saints easily and gratefully caught them with their hands. Food had been provided when it was badly needed, and the Saints thanked God for his goodness.

The Camp of Israel

Those who had departed earlier moved westward across Iowa. Despite extensive advance preparation, many had neglected to accumulate the suggested year's supply of food required for extended survival on the Iowa prairies. To supply themselves, some families drifted to St. Louis, which became an important outfitting depot. At numerous locations in Missouri the Saints chopped wood, split rails, built fences, and performed other labor in exchange for needed supplies. Supervisors of the emigrant companies purchased additional provisions, and families with adequate stocks shared their goods. Gradually even those who had started out amply provisioned were left with inadequate supplies.

On March 27, 1846, Brigham Young formed three new companies of one hundred families each among the Saints who had been separated from their intended companies and were gathered on the Chariton River. The military-style organization he established was not uncommon in westward travel and soon became the pattern for Mormon exiles. About fifty families comprised the basic unit of travel. Each fifty, sometimes subdivided into groups of ten, was led by a captain who supervised the march, maintained discipline, and oversaw the work of commissarians, guards, herdsmen, and other officers.

The homeless Saints dubbed themselves, symbolically, the Camp of Israel, and Brigham Young was their Moses. He originally planned that the three companies organized at the Chariton River would forge ahead to the Great Basin in 1846 and plant crops there. Muddy soil, a shortage of supplies, and cold weather plagued the camp for six weeks, though after mid-April the journey became easier.

It was under these conditions that William Clayton composed new words to a traditional English tune, "All Is Well." When the Saints left Nauvoo, he was assigned to act as scribe for Brigham Young, but he became discouraged when he could find little time or money to provide wagons and provisions for his family. In addition, one of his wives, the lovely but frail, teenaged Diantha, had been left behind in Nauvoo, for she was about to have a baby. Concern for her health weighed heavily on his mind. It had been a rainy, cool, and unhappy week for him when he received word on April 15 that Diantha had had her child and that both were well. His mood changed, and that evening he even held a long-distance christening party for his new son. A musician and poet at heart, he poured out his soul that day in words that have inspired Latter-day Saints ever since. "Come, come, ye Saints," he wrote, "no toil nor labor fear,"

> But with joy wend your way.
> Though hard to you this journey may appear,
> Grace shall be as your day.
> 'Tis better far for us to strive
> Our useless cares from us to drive;
> Do this, and joy your hearts will swell—
> All is well! all is well!

As the Camp of Israel proceeded west, the leaders searched out unclaimed land and appointed agents to establish farms. Two major encampments were located. At Garden Grove, about 145 miles west

A Mormon encampment on Mosquito Creek, about three miles east of Council Bluffs, Iowa. The original painting was by frontier artist George Simons, who once had a studio in Council Bluffs. The painting probably depicted a pioneer group of the 1850s. (Joslyn Art Museum, Omaha, Nebraska)

of Nauvoo, 715 acres were enclosed for grain and other crops, and an orderly village was laid out. Twenty-seven miles further on, William Huntington supervised a larger operation of several thousand acres. When surveying the area from a rocky knoll, Parley P. Pratt was reminded of the hill from which Moses first viewed the Promised Land, and thus named it Mt. Pisgah.

The important task of path-finding was delegated to Stephen Markham, who, with an advance party of a hundred men, scouted roads and campsites and built rough bridges when necessary. Following this route, Brigham Young and Heber C. Kimball reached the Missouri River in mid-June, with other travelers close behind. They established temporary headquarters on the lands of the Pottawattami Indians, and soon an estimated five hundred wagons had assembled along Mosquito Creek. Willard Richards's tent served as a post office for letters going east and as a meeting place for Church leaders.

The Twelve and Council of Fifty still anticipated that as many as four hundred men would be able to cross the mountains and plant fall wheat in the Great Basin that year. They sought information on routes west, supplies, Indian rights, and other information from the Indian agents and fur traders who knew the area. Their immediate concern, however, was getting the emigrants across the Missouri River, and they finally decided to build a ferryboat. They quickly mobilized the camp for this urgent task. As one crew hauled timber to the Pottawattomie sawmill ten miles away and returned with cut-to-order planks, another fashioned timber for framing. Along both sides of the river workmen prepared boat landings and cut dugways down the gullies and through the jagged bluffs to aid the wagon crossing. On the afternoon of June 29 four Nauvoo Legion cannons were floated across on the new Mormon ferry, and the work of ferrying emigrant wagons commenced immediately.

The Mormon Battalion

Even as the river crossing began, word arrived that Captain James Allen was en route from Mt. Pisgah seeking volunteers for military service. He was representing Colonel Stephen W. Kearny of the U.S. Army of the West, soon to be engaged in the war that Congress had declared a month earlier against Mexico.

In 1845 the United States had annexed Texas, but in the process had wounded the pride of Mexico, which still claimed much of Texas territory. War broke out after a skirmish between Mexican and United States troops in the disputed territory. The conflict was popular with American expansionists, for it meant the possibility of new territory for the United States. At the request of President James K. Polk, Congress authorized the enlistment of fifty thousand men to augment regular military forces. Within two years the Mexican provinces of Upper California and New Mexico would be added to the American Union. Upper California included the Great Basin, the destination of the Saints.

Captain Allen had gone first to Mt. Pisgah, where he presented his request for Mormon volunteers to Wilford Woodruff and the local high council. They studied his "Circular to the Mormons," but were suspicious of government intentions and unwilling to commit the Church to such an undertaking. They sent him to Brigham Young at the Mosquito Creek campground. Hosea Stout's reaction to Captain Allen's request for volunteers was typical of the feelings of many at Mt. Pisgah. The Saints were indignant, he said, and looked on it as another plot against them. If they did not comply, they could be denounced as enemies of the country, and if they did comply, the army would "then have 500 of our men in their power to be destroyed as they had done our leaders at Carthage. I confess that my feelings was uncommonly wrought up against them."[2] Though such feelings were understandable after so many previous rebuffs, the Saints had a false impression. They were unaware of efforts in Washington in their behalf.

To the surprise of many Latter-day Saints, Brigham Young immediately reacted in favor of the requisition. In a public meeting called to explain the government action, he supported the call as "the first offer we have ever had from the government to benefit us."[3] The men would serve one year and proceed at government expense first to Santa Fe and then to California. After discharge they would retain their arms and supplies. Meantime, the soldiers' pay would help transport their families west. Here was evidence, said President Young, that the government intended not to hinder but to help the Saints reach Upper California. In addition, the Mormons would be able to demonstrate their loyalty. Though President Young did not mention it, it was also a significant symbol for the Saints to help win for the United States the territory they were about to colonize.

If further assurance was needed of the sincerity of the government motives, it came with Jesse C. Little, who met Brigham Young and Heber C. Kimball on their way to recruit soldiers at Mt. Pisgah on July 6, and Colonel Thomas L. Kane, who arrived at Council Bluffs from Fort Leavenworth five days later. Both men had been directly involved in the negotiations in Washington, D.C., which led to the call of the Mormon Battalion.

Elder Little, who was the presiding Church officer in the East and official Church agent in Washington, had met Colonel Kane in Philadelphia in May while seeking means to transport the eastern Saints to Upper California by ship. Kane, a young adventurer who became an articulate, if self-appointed, guardian for the interests of the Saints, suggested the political tactic that Elder Little later used to persuade President Polk to aid the Mormons.

Armed with letters of introduction from Kane and others, Elder Little sought an audience with Polk. He had been told by Brigham Young to seek government contracts to build blockhouses and forts along the Oregon Trail. Failing that, he was authorized to embrace any

---

[2]Juanita Brooks, ed., *On the Mormon Frontier: The Diary of Hosea Stout*, 2 vols. (Salt Lake City: University of Utah Press, 1964), 1:172.
[3]Young, "Manuscript History," July 1, 1846.

offer that would aid the emigration. His first hope was for a shipping contract that would provide money as well as inexpensive transportation. His request was timely, for the government needed to send supplies around Cape Horn for its forces in California. Former Postmaster General Amos Kendall told Elder Little that he would urge the cabinet to authorize one thousand Mormons to travel by sea and another thousand overland to California.

When five days passed without a response, Elder Little addressed a personal letter to Polk. He threatened, as Kane had suggested, that lack of federal aid to help the Mormons migrate "under the outstretched wings of the American Eagle" might "compel us to be foreigners." This was indeed a clever ploy, for the Mormons had no intention of becoming disloyal. Yet the government had heard rumors of British interest in the Pacific Coast. An independent Mormon state that might gain the support of England was not an impossibility, and this would certainly complicate American interests in the West. Polk decided, however, to give the shipping contract to others, and he opted against marching a thousand armed Latter-day Saints into California. If they arrived before Kearny's forces, he reasoned, the Missourians in the Army of the West would be distraught, for he knew well the antagonism between the Mormons and the Missourians. Besides, he did not need additional soldiers. The existing Army of the West, supplemented by a thousand Missouri volunteers, could secure New Mexico and, if the season was not too late, still enter California.

As an alternative, Polk asked Little in an interview on June 5 if the Mormons would offer five hundred volunteers to enlist *after* the Mormon exiles reached California. This, the president confided in his diary, was a move to placate the Mormons and retain their loyalty. Kane's strategy was working. Little pressed for an immediate enlistment, but the request was turned down. Two days earlier orders had been sent to Kearny authorizing the Mormon enlistment, but in vague terms. Even though President Polk apparently intended the enlistment to take place in California, Kearny interpreted his instructions differently, and on June 19 he ordered the enlistment to take place immediately. Thus the way was paved for an important episode in Mormon history.

The provisioned conveyance west of five hundred men under salary from the government was the kind of financial aid Brigham Young had been seeking. He led the enlistment drive himself and promised that if they were faithful, the Mormon soldiers would not be required to fight. He also arranged for part of each volunteer's pay and his $42 clothing allowance to be returned to his family.

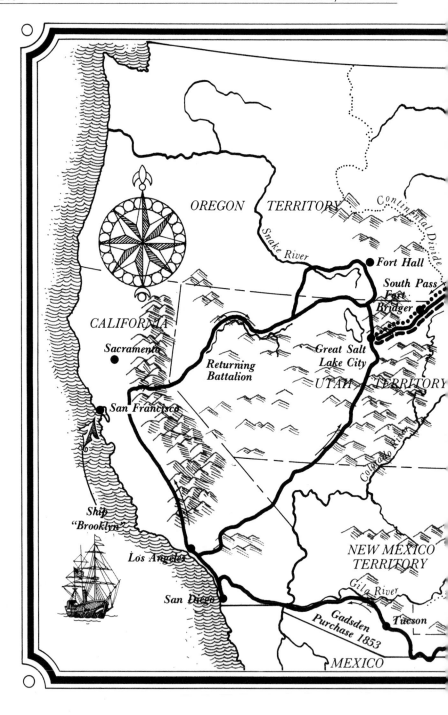

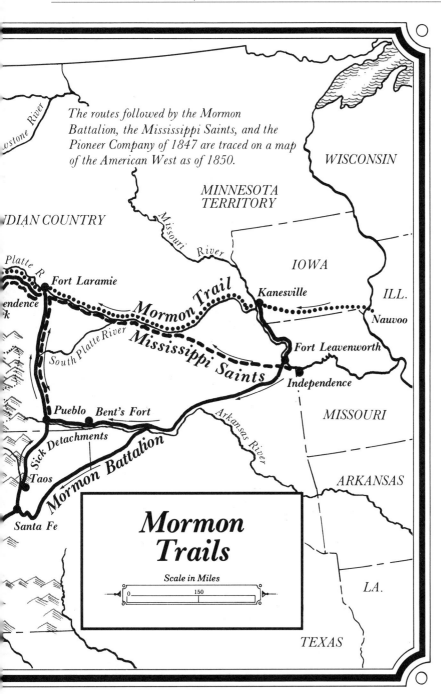

The routes followed by the Mormon Battalion, the Mississippi Saints, and the Pioneer Company of 1847 are traced on a map of the American West as of 1850.

Mormon Trails

Scale in Miles

0   150

The group that left Council Bluffs on July 20 included 541 soldiers and nearly a hundred other Latter-day Saints, including wives and children of some of the officers and twenty Battalion wives who served as laundresses. The Battalion consisted of five companies under Captain Allen, who was promoted to lieutenant colonel when he assumed command. Church leaders were allowed to choose the other officers. The Battalion was given a gala farewell on June 15. Later the officers met privately with six of the Twelve, who admonished them "to be as fathers to the privates, to remember their prayers, to see that the name of the Deity was revered, and that virtue and cleanliness were strictly observed." According to Sergeant William Hyde, "They also instructed us to treat all men with kindness . . . and never take life when it could be avoided."[4]

The new soldiers marched to Fort Leavenworth, where they were outfitted with muskets and supplies. Colonel Allen was suddenly taken ill and remained behind when the Battalion left the fort on August 12, and on August 23 he died. Allen was well liked by the Mormons, and his death caused great sorrow, which turned to bitter disappointment when Lieutenant Andrew Jackson Smith was named his successor. The Mormon soldiers disliked Smith, and seeds of tension were sown.

Lieutenant Smith pushed ahead more rapidly than the men thought proper. In addition, he imposed upon them his own military doctor, George B. Sanderson of Missouri. Sanderson clearly disliked the Mormons, and the feeling was quickly reciprocated. Evidence suggests that many of his medical treatments were less than adequate, and the Mormons accused him of not caring whether they lived or died. Another element of tension arose when Lieutenant Smith delegated Captain Nelson Higgins and ten men to convey most of the soldiers' families up the Arkansas River to Pueblo, Colorado, for the winter. The decision proved to be wise, as many of the women and children were clearly unprepared for the arduous journey ahead. Later, at Santa Fe, a second sick detachment and all but five of the remaining women were sent under the direction of Captain James Brown to join the earlier group at Pueblo.

At Santa Fe the remaining members of the Battalion were placed under the command of Lieutenant Colonel Philip St. George Cooke, whose leadership the men learned to appreciate and respect. Cooke had

[4]Daniel Tyler, *A Concise History of the Mormon Battalion in the Mexican War, 1846–1847* (1881; reprint ed., Chicago: Rio Grande Press, 1964), pp. 128–29.

The Mormon Battalion's only military action – a fight with wild bulls – is portrayed here in C. B. Hancock's panorama. (Church Archives)

orders to blaze a wagon trail from Santa Fe to California. The best available maps were of little use, but the company had the services of knowledgeable guides. Veering south, the Mormon soldiers at times followed Spanish or Mexican trails but generally cut new roads. This late-summer march also took its toll in sickness, and on November 10 a third detachment of worn and weakened men turned back. Lieutenant William W. Willis led them to Pueblo, Colorado, where the Mormon colony grew to about 150 men and their families.

About 350 officers and men remained, and on reduced rations they continued southward. For a month they struggled across the sandy valley of the lower Rio Grande, then, on November 21, turned toward Tucson. On the way they had an exciting encounter with a herd of wild cattle. Sixty of the beasts were killed by gunfire when the Battalion was attacked by enraged bulls. This "battle of the bulls" turned out to be the only battle fought in the entire expedition.

Beyond Tucson the Battalion soon rejoined Kearny's route along the Gila River. Guides arrived on December 23 to lead them beyond the Colorado River. The route lay across a trackless desert, where water was obtained only by digging deep wells. Beyond the desert they conveyed wagons through the narrow mountain passes of the coastal range with ropes and pulleys. On January 29, 1847, they reached Mission

San Diego at the end of their 2,030–mile march and reported to General Kearny at the nearby seaport settlement.

California had already surrendered, and the Mormon Battalion was not required to do battle. The men filled out the remainder of their enlistment as occupation troops, serving garrison duty in San Diego, San Luis Rey, and Los Angeles. On July 16 they were discharged, though eighty-one reenlisted for an additional six months. The others headed for the Great Salt Lake Valley. Some of these men spent the winter at Sutter's Fort, where employment was available, and thus several Mormons were at New Helvetia in January 1848 for the famous discovery that began the California gold rush. The following summer they abandoned their opportunity to get rich quick and joined their families and friends in the new gathering place of the Saints.

The Mississippi Saints

The sick detachments of the Mormon Battalion went to Pueblo, Colorado, specifically to join a company of Saints from Mississippi who were also on their way to the Rocky Mountains. This small group of emigrants came from Monroe County, where a group of perhaps 150 Church members was located. One of their number, John Brown, had moved his family to Nauvoo, and in January 1846, Brigham Young appointed him to carry a message back to Mississippi that the main body of the Saints would leave Nauvoo in the spring and intended to settle somewhere in the Great Basin, possibly the Bear River Valley. Eager to gather with the Saints, a small company of forty-three under the leadership of William Crosby left Mississippi on April 8, and by May 26 they had traveled 640 miles to Independence, Missouri. There they were joined by fourteen other persons and turned their wagons west.

On July 6 the migrating southern Saints reached Chimney Rock in Wyoming, about eight hundred miles from Independence. There they met some trappers returning from California, who informed them that there were no Mormons ahead of them. They were unaware that Brigham Young had decided to establish winter quarters in Nebraska. They soon decided to take up the offer of John Renshaw, a French trapper, who invited them to spend the winter near the trading post at Pueblo. They reached Pueblo on August 7 and soon learned where Brigham Young was spending the winter. They selected a site to build their own community, erected a row of simple cottonwood log dwellings, and planted crops: turnips, pumpkins, beans, and melons.

The three detachments from the Mormon Battalion arrived at Pueblo in November and December. Together with the Mississippi Saints, they constituted a community of about 275 Mormons camped more than a thousand miles further west than the main body of the Saints. They erected another row of eighteen cabins and completed a meetinghouse at the head of Main Street.

Life in the temporary little Mormon village was typical of life on the frontier. The Saints subsisted in part by trading as well as hunting venison in the forest. They were generally well supplied with goods obtained from Bent's Fort, and some were able to use their skills, such as blacksmithing, to obtain income. The Mormon Battalion members kept up regular military drills, and the Saints enjoyed frequent dances in the meetinghouse, which also doubled as a schoolhouse and community jail. Seven women gave birth to babies during the winter, and Indian wives of the mountain men assisted in caring for their families. Nine deaths were recorded during the winter, as well as one marriage. As spring approached, an advance party left Pueblo to meet the main pioneer company at Fort Laramie. The remainder arrived in the Salt Lake Valley a few days after Brigham Young's vanguard company.

Winter Quarters, 1846–47

While the Mormon Battalion was being organized in 1846, plans for the remaining exiles were in constant flux. The Battalion claimed many of the best teamsters and left large herds of cattle without manpower to manage them. For a time Brigham Young still hoped that a vanguard company could enter the Great Basin in 1846, but the needs of the stranded camps on the Missouri soon took precedence. The journey to the new promised land would have to wait another year.

In the meantime, Church officials secured permission from the Pottawattami Indians to winter on their lands in western Iowa. Several companies of Saints had already crossed the Missouri River, however, in anticipation of continuing farther west. There on the lands of the Omaha Indians they found equally desirable rangeland for their horses, mules, sheep, and an estimated thirty thousand head of cattle. In order to remain on friendly terms with the Indians, Church members helped them in various ways, including the occasional donation of a beef.

The temporary Mormon encampments on the west side of the river soon became the largest. By the end of September a town of 820 lots had been surveyed, and Winter Quarters came into being. Before Christ-

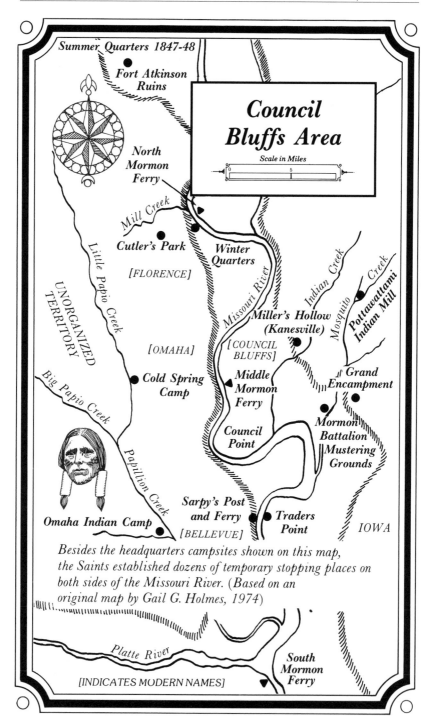

Summer Quarters 1847-48

Fort Atkinson
Ruins

**Council
Bluffs Area**

Scale in Miles

0   5

North
Mormon
Ferry

Mill Creek

Cutler's Park

Winter
Quarters

[FLORENCE]

Little Papio Creek

UNORGANIZED
TERRITORY

Missouri River

Indian Creek

Mosquito Creek

Pottawattami
Indian Mill

Miller's Hollow
(Kanesville)

[COUNCIL
BLUFFS]

[OMAHA]

Big Papio Creek

Cold Spring
Camp

Middle
Mormon
Ferry

Grand
Encampment

Council
Point

Mormon
Battalion
Mustering
Grounds

Papillion Creek

Sarpy's Post
and Ferry

Traders
Point

IOWA

Omaha Indian Camp

[BELLEVUE]

Besides the headquarters campsites shown on this map,
the Saints established dozens of temporary stopping places on
both sides of the Missouri River. (Based on an
original map by Gail G. Holmes, 1974)

Platte River

South
Mormon
Ferry

[INDICATES MODERN NAMES]

mas 700 log homes, roofed over with clapboards or with willows and dirt, were occupied by about 3,500 people. Other dwellings, including a few dugouts, were added before spring. The exiles on the Iowa side spread out their winter camps in all directions. Around one site, renamed Kanesville in 1848, grew the modern Council Bluffs. The winter of 1846–47, then, saw thousands of Saints located in a few large camps and many smaller ones on both sides of the Missouri River, and eastward along the trail from Illinois. For the time being, Zion was in the wilderness.

Even in these temporary locations the need for organization and civil government continued. At the principal encampments, high councils were created to superintend both ecclesiastical and municipal affairs. Winter Quarters was subdivided into thirteen wards, which were expanded to twenty-two by early 1847. The care of the poor was apportioned out, with two or three families accepting responsibility for each needy one.

Because of their dual functions, high councils in the emigrant camps were called municipal high councils and authorized to function like city councils. At Winter Quarters, for example, the high council levied a three-fourths percent property tax to support Hosea Stout's transplanted Nauvoo police force. It also encouraged the creation of schools and oversaw general discipline in camp through the town marshal.

To enhance their economic well-being, the wintering Saints actively traded with settlements in northern Missouri and in Iowa, offering unneeded goods or available cash for hogs, grain, vegetables, and emigrant supplies. Young men otherwise unemployed turned local resources into willow baskets, half-bushel measures, or washboards for trade. Under a franchise granted by the high council, Brigham Young organized a private company, which built a water-powered gristmill.

Diets in the camps were necessarily limited. One much-needed product obtained from Missouri was potatoes, but many Saints subsisted on little more than corn bread, salt bacon, a little milk, and a little fresh meat. The lack of fresh vegetables during the first summer caused many to contract scurvy, known among the Mormons as blackleg. The potatoes, horseradish discovered at old Fort Atkinson, and cold weather finally brought relief, but not before disease had claimed its toll. The numbers who died of scurvy, consumption, and chills and fever during that first summer were not recorded, but from August 1846 to July 1848 these ailments caused 361 recorded deaths at Cutler's Park and Winter Quarters. Unrecorded deaths may have brought the total to as high as 550 in the camps west of the Missouri between June 1846 and May 1848. Across the river in western Iowa, about 220 died. If the estimated 233 deaths at Mt. Pisgah, Garden Grove, and the Ponca Indian campsite two hundred miles upriver are added, more than a thousand Latter-day Saints sacrificed their lives during this period.

To some, the industry of the Mormon farmers raised the question of intent. Although announced as temporary way stations, the migrant wintering places were acquiring a look of permanence. Anyone inquiring about plans for removal, however, was quickly assured that an advance company would leave in the spring and that complete evacuation would follow as fast as possible in the next year or two. In the meantime, these villages would provide important rest and supply stations for those who followed the early companies on their way west.

Church leaders and the Council of Fifty turned again to plans for the westering venture as soon as they could. Corresponding frequently with the trustees remaining in Nauvoo, they endeavored to secure badly needed funds through the sale of the temple and remaining property, but without success. In the fall of 1846 a visit from Father Jean DeSmet, returning from five years among the Indians of Oregon Country, allowed camp leaders to gather firsthand information about the Rocky Mountains. DeSmet had traversed the Great Salt Lake Basin on his outward journey in 1841. The General Council considered the possibility of sending three hundred men to open farms at the headwaters of the Yellowstone, but discussion of a resting place still centered, as it had done for several years, on the valley of the Great Salt Lake and on nearby Bear River Valley.

On January 14, 1847, Brigham Young set forth "the word and will of the Lord" concerning the pattern of migration "to the place where the Lord shall locate a stake of Zion." Accepted by assembled priesthood quorums as a revelation to the Church, this document became a constitution governing the westward trek from Winter Quarters, reaffirmed the organizational scheme of emigrant companies already tested in the march across Iowa, and urged proper preparation. It reminded the Saints of their responsibility to care for the poor, widows, orphans, and Battalion families; advised the continuation of way stations; and required a covenant of obedience to principles of honesty, cooperation, diligence, and moderation. Comparing the migrating band to ancient Israel, the revelation recommended trust in God and promised divine protection:

> If thou art merry, praise the Lord with singing, with music, with dancing, and with a prayer of praise and thanksgiving.

If thou art sorrowful, call on the Lord thy God with supplication, that your souls may be joyful.

Fear not thine enemies, for they are in mine hands and I will do my pleasure with them.

My people must be tried in all things, that they may be prepared to receive the glory that I have for them, even the glory of Zion; and he that will not bear chastisement is not worthy of my kingdom. (D&C 136:28–31.)

A few emigrants declared themselves unwilling to undergo further refining in the wilderness. They returned to civilized comforts or remained in Iowa and disappeared into American society. Those who retained their commitment to a gathered Israel prepared to follow the vanguard, which recommenced its westward trek in April. They would make history.

Seagoing Mormons: The First to Reach the West

The Camp of Israel, the Mormon Battalion, and the southern Saints were not the only Mormons headed west in 1846. On February 4, the same day the first group from Nauvoo crossed the icy Mississippi, a company of Saints numbering 70 men, 68 women, and 100 children sailed out of New York harbor aboard the ship *Brooklyn*. Recruited by Samuel Brannan, they were headed for California with the expectation that they would help choose and establish the final destination for the thousands of Latter-day Saints who would cross the Great Plains.

Elder Orson Pratt of the Council of the Twelve was presiding over the Church in the eastern states when word arrived late in 1845 of the decision to hasten the departure from Nauvoo. Immediately he issued a dramatic call for the Saints in that area to join the exodus. Angered at the treatment the Church was receiving, he perhaps overstated the case when he declared: "We do not want one saint to be left in the United States" after the following spring. "Let every branch," he wrote, "in the East, West, North and South, be determined to flee out of Babylon, either by land or by sea."[5] Elder Samuel Brannan, publisher of the *Prophet*, the Church paper in New York, was appointed to charter a ship and direct a company that would go by sea as soon as possible.

By the end of December, Brannan had chartered the ship and begun to recruit passengers, offering the full voyage for $75 per adult, including

---

[5]*Times and Seasons*, December 1, 1845.

provisions, and half price for children. The company consisted of farmers and mechanics from the area, and they took with them all tools necessary for building a new society in the West, including the press on which the *Prophet* had been printed and a large quantity of schoolbooks.

The voyage of the *Brooklyn* was pleasant but eventful. It rounded Cape Horn; touched at Juan Fernandez, legendary as the Robinson Crusoe island; spent ten days in the Hawaiian islands; then arrived at Yerba Buena (San Francisco Bay) on July 29, 1846. On the way two severe storms were encountered, one in each ocean. Ten passengers died—nine were buried at sea and the other on Juan Fernandez Island—and two babies were born, one named Atlantic and the other Pacific, after the oceans where they first saw life.

When the *Brooklyn* Saints arrived at Yerba Buena, the American flag already flew over California. They found employment wherever they could and began looking for a site to establish a colony. The new settlement was called New Hope, and some members, unaware of the decision of Brigham Young and the Twelve to settle in the Great Basin, apparently hoped that it would become the basis for a permanent Mormon settlement in the West.

The voyage of the *Brooklyn* did not foreshadow a great Mormon migration by sea nor a headquarters for the Church in California, but it was a symbol of a remarkable saga that had begun in that important year of 1846. By the end of the year thousands of Saints had fled Nauvoo and were making camps in the Great Plains; the Mormon Battalion had marched through the Southwest to California; the sick detachments as well as a party of southern Saints were wintering in the Mexican village of Pueblo; the *Brooklyn* Saints had arrived at Yerba Buena; and in the East other Mormons were making provision to sell their homes and move. All over America one objective dominated the thoughts of Latter-day Saints: to leave whatever they were doing, wherever they were, and join the Twelve to help create a new refuge for themselves and the kingdom of God. In spirit all sang with William Clayton:

> We'll find the place which God for us prepared,
> Far away in the West,
> Where none shall come to hurt or make afraid;
> There the Saints will be blessed.

The Dissenters

Some, however, were not so sure. Though few in number, they illustrate the reality that diverse personalities and emotional influences remained that would lead even former close associates in several directions. Even as the Saints who remained loyal to the Twelve were looking toward a new gathering place in the West, some of those they had known best were creating rival groups elsewhere.

Sidney Rigdon, once appointed by revelation as spokesman for Joseph Smith, had rejected the Twelve and been excommunicated. In Pittsburgh he began publishing again the *Messenger and Advocate* in 1844 and established a rival organization called the Church of Christ. He was named "President of the Kingdom and the Church," but by 1847 his organization had almost disappeared.

A more successful leader was James J. Strang of Wisconsin, who had joined the Church only four months before the death of the Prophet. In August 1844 he presented a letter that, he claimed, had been written by Joseph Smith, appointing Strang as the Prophet's successor. The Twelve labeled it a forgery and excommunicated him, but the charismatic Strang gathered many believers and made a concerted effort to convert the rest of the Church to his claims. He was especially successful in the East, and finally established a headquarters on Beaver Island in Lake Michigan, where he was crowned king. By 1850, however, he had run into numerous economic and political difficulties, and in 1856 he was murdered by one of his own disaffected followers.

Most revealing of the misunderstandings of the time was the decision of the remaining members of Joseph Smith's family not to follow the Church west. William Smith, a member of the Council of the Twelve and the Prophet's only surviving brother, made his own claims to Church leadership and was finally excommunicated in 1845. For a while he was associated with James J. Strang, but later he began teaching that Joseph Smith's eldest son should, by right of lineage, inherit the presidency and that he, William, was to be a guardian and president pro tem until Joseph III was of age. His efforts at organization failed, and later he became nominally associated with the Reorganized Latter Day Saints.

There were others who refused to follow the leadership of Brigham Young and the Twelve. William Marks, former stake president in Nauvoo, was excommunicated in 1845, joined the Strangites for a while, moved to a group headed by Charles Thomson, then attached himself in 1855 to another group headed by former apostle John E. Page. Jason W. Briggs also joined Strang but later claimed divine guidance that Joseph Smith III should become the leader. Zenos H. Gurley had spiritual experiences similar to those of Briggs, and the two men joined their small followings in 1852. All three of these men were instrumental in 1860 in bringing about a new organization that became known as the Reorganized Church of Jesus Christ of Latter Day Saints. At its head was Joseph Smith III, son of the Prophet, and its membership included the Prophet's widow Emma, who had since married Lewis A. Bidamon. Members of the new organization were soon dubbed by the Utah Saints the "Josephites." They, in turn, called the Utah Saints "Brighamites."

Although it was distressing to see even a few former associates abandoning the main group of Saints, none of these groups posed a serious threat to the leadership of Brigham Young and the Twelve. On the other hand, Church leaders were delighted when one famous dissenter returned. Oliver Cowdery, who had assisted Joseph Smith in translating the Book of Mormon and had shared many of his most sacred spiritual experiences, had been excommunicated in 1838. In 1848 he was practicing law in Wisconsin when Phineas H. Young brought him the greetings of the Twelve. He decided to return to the Church, and on October 24, 1848, he appeared at a conference in Kanesville, Iowa, where he bore witness of his earlier experiences and of the truthfulness of the Book of Mormon, and asked for readmittance to the Church. On November 12 he was rebaptized, and he began to lay plans to migrate to the Salt Lake Valley with the rest of the Saints. His poor health, however, delayed his plans. On March 3, 1850, he died at the home of his friend and early Church associate, David Whitmer, who said he died "the happiest man I ever saw."

The Pioneer Company, 1847

The Saints in Winter Quarters and on the plains of Iowa waited out the winter of 1846–47 and laid plans for the momentous trek that would begin the following spring. It was decided that the vanguard company, including eight members of the Council of the Twelve, would consist only of able-bodied men who could travel fast and begin preparations for those to follow. Three women were included, so that the pioneer group consisted of 143 men, 3 women, and 2 children. They traveled in 72 wagons and took 93 horses, 52 mules, 66 oxen, 19 cows, 17 dogs, and some chickens. The pioneer company was fully provisioned to sustain itself for a year.

Plans for departure were carefully laid. A council in late February discussed the need for boats, seeds, maps, scientific instruments, and

Brigham Young. *Engraved by Charles B. Hall from a daguerreotype taken in 1855. (Church Archives)*

Heber C. Kimball. An early daguerreotype. (Church Archives)

Willard Richards. Engraved by Charles B. Hall from Marsena Cannon daguerreotype. (Church Archives)

farm implements, and considered the location for a city as well as the necessity of irrigating crops in the arid West. In April the group began to rendezvous. Brigham Young made a final visit to Winter Quarters, where he met John Taylor, Parley P. Pratt, and Orson Hyde, who had just returned from a short mission to England. They brought money contributed to the cause by the English Saints, a map based on John C. Frémont's recent expedition to the Far West, and instruments for calculating latitude, elevation, temperature, and barometric pressure.

The westward trail was not, of course, totally unknown. For years westering adventurers and pioneers had been following what came to be known as the Oregon Trail, along the south side of the Platte River. The Saints, however, wanted to keep their distance in order to avoid clashes over grazing rights, water, and campsites, so they selected a new route on the north side of the river from Winter Quarters to Fort Laramie. This segment of the journey took the vanguard company six weeks, from mid-April until June 1.

Because the pioneers were at first apprehensive of possible Indian danger, they formed a militia headed by Brigham Young and Stephen Markham. They also organized a night guard, traveled in close formation, and carried a cannon. Though they lost a few horses to Indians, they generally found them interested in trade and friendship.

The company suffered little unusual hardship, and the journey soon became almost leisurely. This seemed to nurture an attitude of flippancy and light-mindedness, which Brigham Young abhorred. On one occasion he roundly criticized the men for playing cards and dominoes and for boisterous dancing, urging them to conduct themselves in a way more befitting their serious mission. According to the camp diarist, there was some tearful repentance, but after that "no loud laughter was heard, no swearing, no quarreling, no profane language, no hard speeches to man or beast."[6]

William Clayton was an official camp journalist and was responsible for recording accurate mileage for later emigrants. For the first few days this meticulous record keeper monotonously counted the daily revolutions of a wagon wheel and calculated the mileage from that. Three days into the journey, however, he proposed a mechanical odometer, and on May 10 Brigham Young assigned Orson Pratt to design such a device. It was constructed by Appleton Harmon, an experienced woodworker, and thereafter Clayton could record the mileage with great ease and accuracy. West of Fort Laramie he marked the trail with signposts every ten miles.

At Fort Laramie the company halted for repairs, Brigham Young celebrated his forty-sixth birthday, and the camp was joined by a company of Mormon Battalionists and Mississippi Saints from Pueblo. The pioneers then followed the regular Oregon Trail, which took them to Jim Bridger's trading post, Fort Bridger, on the Black's Fork of the Green River. They made frequent contact with other travelers along the trail across the continent, including some at the crossing of the Platte, which could not be negotiated without a ferry. Anticipating this, the Mormon company had carried its own boat from Missouri. The Saints were able to cross with comparative ease, and the Missourians they met there paid $1.50 per wagon for the ferry. As the Saints went ahead, nine men remained behind to continue the lucrative ferry. The rest pushed on through South Pass, rafted across the Green River, and arrived at Fort Bridger early in July.

During the last week of June the vanguard company met Samuel Brannan, who had traveled east from California hoping to induce them to go on to San Francisco Bay. Brigham Young had already made up his mind, however, and California was not his final destination. The disappointed Brannan returned to the Bay area, where he shortly left the Church.

About the same time the company was joined by thirteen members of the sick detachment of the Mormon Battalion; the rest of the de-

---

[6]William Clayton, *William Clayton's Journal* (Salt Lake City: Clayton Family Association, 1921), p. 201.

To collect information for an emigrants' guide, William Clayton suggested an odometer to measure the mileage of the pioneer company. Orson Pratt designed and Appleton Harmon built one. Shown here is a full-scale museum replica of the 1847 instrument, which no longer exists, affixed to a wagon. (Museum of Church History and Art)

tachment was not far behind. After the group reached Salt Lake Valley the men were mustered out of the service and delegated Captain James Brown to go to California for their army pay. Brown accompanied Samuel Brannan back across the Sierra.

Meantime, the Saints were discussing settlement prospects in the Great Basin with everyone they met. Moses Harris was pessimistic because he thought timber was too scarce. To him, Cache Valley in the north was the best spot. On the other hand, Jim Bridger, who camped with them one night near his Wyoming trading station and advised them on the best routes, was most enthusiastic about the region around Utah Lake. He described a country filled with wild cherries, berries, timber, an abundance of fish, and plenty of good grass. The Indians there, he said, "raise as good corn, wheat, and pumpkins as were ever raised in old Kentucky."[7] Only the frost discouraged him, and he felt

---

[7]Clayton, *Journal*, p. 278.

Charles B. Hall engraving of the Salt Lake Valley in July 1847, after a painting by H. L. A. Culmer. (Church Archives)

that it might kill the corn. Miles Goodyear, whom they met after leaving Fort Bridger, already owned a trading post at the mouth of the Weber River, not far from the Great Salt Lake. He was most enthusiastic about the possibility of agricultural success.

The pioneer company arrived at Fort Bridger on July 7. Thereafter travel became more rugged, as they negotiated the mountain passes. They had received conflicting advice on which route to follow into the Salt Lake Valley but decided to follow the route blazed the year before by the ill-fated Donner-Reed party bound for California.

By the time they reached the valley, the pioneers had broken into three groups. Since crossing the Green River some of them had suffered from attacks of severe fever and delirium, which left them weak and listless. Brigham Young was struck with this same "mountain fever" (probably induced by wood ticks) soon after meeting Miles Goodyear. As a result, the company divided and a small sick detachment lagged behind. After July 13 a third division, under the direction of Orson Pratt, moved ahead to chart the route and prepare a wagon road through Emigration Canyon.

On July 21 Orson Pratt and Erastus Snow suddenly caught their first glimpse of the magnificent Salt Lake Valley and the broad waters of the Great Salt Lake, which "glistened in the sunbeams." After having been enclosed in the mountains for so many days and then beholding such extensive scenery, wrote Elder Pratt, "we could not refrain from a shout of joy, which almost involuntarily escaped from our lips the moment this grand and lovely scenery was within our view."[8] The two men took a twelve-mile circuit into the valley, then returned to camp.

The following day, July 22, was one of exploring. A delegation from the advance company went northward to the hot springs and found soil of "most excellent quality," abundant water, and green, "very luxuriant" vegetation along the streams. In other places the vegetation was dry for want of moisture, and large crickets swarmed in the foothills. That night the advance party camped in the valley.

The next day Orson Pratt dedicated the land to the Lord, then instructed his men to begin plowing and planting in order to preserve the seed they had carried from Winter Quarters. Some, like William Clayton, were "happily disappointed" because the lack of timber and the apparent scarcity of rainfall seemed foreboding. The soil, however, was fertile; all it lacked was water. While plowmen prepared the ground for potatoes and turnips, another group began to dam up the stream and dig the all-important ditches. From this crude beginning the Latter-day Saints would become experts in irrigation technology. When Brigham Young reached the mouth of Emigration Canyon, the pioneer camp was a beehive of activity.

On July 24 Brigham Young and the rest of the sick detachment zigzagged back and forth across a stream and made their way to the canyon mouth along a road freshly cleared of underbrush. "We gazed with wonder and admiration upon the vast rich fertile valley," wrote Wilford Woodruff in his diary. "President Young expressed his full satisfaction in the appearance of the valley as a resting place for the Saints and was amply repaid for his journey." In later years Elder Woodruff recalled the Church leader's words: "This is the right place, drive on."

For the next few days various companies scouted other nearby areas, but by July 28 the majority of the company had concluded that the site already selected was the best the valley had to offer. That afternoon Brigham Young identified the location for a temple and approved a city plan, and in a meeting that evening the location was unanimously approved by the company.

---

[8]*Historical Record* 9 (April 1890): 74.

Kanesville, or Council Bluffs, Iowa, in an engraving by Charles B. Hall. (Church Archives)

This was only the beginning of the task of conveying thousands of Saints to the new place of refuge, which continued through 1847 and into succeeding years. By December 1847, more than two thousand had completed the journey, and several hundred had returned east to bring families and friends. In 1850 census takers counted 11,380 residents in the Great Salt Lake Valley and settlements to the north and south. More than seven thousand Saints still waited in the semipermanent way stations in Iowa. They would be helped by William Clayton's *Latter-day Saints' Emigrants' Guide*, published in 1848 after he had remeasured the pioneer trail with a new odometer. He was among those who returned to Winter Quarters in August 1847 with Brigham Young.

Kanesville, Iowa, 1847–53

In August 1847 all the apostles who were with the vanguard company returned to the Missouri River camps with 161 other men. Traveling east to join their families, they met the first of nine westward-moving companies organized by Elders Parley P. Pratt and John Taylor. The historic Mormon trek was under way.

Meantime, federal Indian agents were complaining that the Mormons at Winter Quarters were stripping the country of timber and wild game. To avoid further misunderstandings, the Saints evacuated the camps west of the river in the spring, and Miller's Hollow, renamed Kanesville in honor of Thomas L. Kane, became the new headquarters. As a staging area for the migrating Saints, the community reached its peak population of five thousand in 1852. Another forty-five campsites, at least thirty of which became the basis for permanent towns in western Iowa, grew up in surrounding regions. Agriculture flourished, craftsmen pursued their trades, and schools were conducted. The principal newspaper was Orson Hyde's *Frontier Guardian*, established in 1849.

Kanesville's chief business was serving Church migration. Three Mormon-operated ferries met the needs of those who wished to cross the Missouri River near the staging center. They also helped an estimated 140,000 other pioneers traveling to Oregon and the California gold fields between 1848 and 1852. As the final abandonment of Kanesville approached in 1853, the Saints sold their land and improvements to other American frontiersmen, as they had done in Mt. Pisgah. The Mormon way stations had provided seven years of important service.

Early Mormon Settlements in Utah

As the Saints laid plans to build their new Zion in the valleys of the Great Basin, their first challenge was to select appropriate sites for settlement. Each new townsite was thoroughly investigated for its agricultural potential, the availability of water supplies and of wood for fuel and building purposes, and grazing lands for livestock. Most early settlements were located near the mouths of canyons, which provided easy access to timber in the mountains and streams coming from them.

The first homes in Salt Lake City were simple cabins built within a stockade. The original adobe fort was expanded twice in 1848 to make room for new arrivals; by that time families were beginning to occupy city lots.

Expansion beyond the original settlement began in 1848. Families located on every useful stream thirty miles northward to the Weber, and others moved southeasterly in Salt Lake Valley. Also that year Captain James Brown received authorization to use $3,000 of the Mormon Battalion pay, which he had been delegated to collect, to purchase the claims of Miles Goodyear on the Weber River. This cleared the way for the founding of Brownsville, later renamed Ogden. In 1849 thirty settlers moved south into Ute Indian country and established Fort Utah on the Provo River. That fall a dozen families pioneered Tooele Valley and 224 settlers accepted Ute Chief Walkara's invitation to settle in Sanpete Valley at a location soon named Manti.

In each of these locations the first arrivals lived for several months in crude dugouts or lean-tos while they laid out city plots, assigned the surrounding farmland, and began to build houses or cabins. Although some cabins were built of logs, timber was in short supply and many settlers used adobe bricks. Mud-and-straw adobe was also used for fences.

In all these areas natural resources were at a premium, but the Saints had their own system of resource development. Water, timber, and land were considered to be precious stewardships, and their use and distribution were regulated by bishops. The bishop distributed land according to each family's needs and abilities, and until the area was all assigned, newcomers were assured of property. These practices implemented Brigham Young's instructions of July 25, 1847, when he said that there would be no buying and selling of land—no speculating and no profit making on essential resources and commodities.

Supporting the infant farming communities were a number of basic industries that sprang up quickly in Salt Lake Valley and surrounding settlements. Gristmills, pit saws, and blacksmith shops were among the first established, for they were needed to produce the flour, timber, horseshoes, nails, and tools necessary to the pioneer communities. In addition, cabinetmakers, tanners, bootmakers, potters, and other skilled artisans soon appeared in every community.

The Saints were also at the mercy of natural forces. Though the first winter was relatively mild, flour was scarce, vegetables were generally unavailable, and meat from the overworked cattle was tough. As spring arrived the settlers found themselves turning to the sego lily and other roots and greens to save them from hunger. In March they began to plant seeds for the 1848 harvest, which would be especially critical, as the Saints arriving late that summer would not bring surplus food.

But 1848 was a dry year, and late spring frosts damaged many crops. Late in May the black crickets observed in the foothills the year before descended in swarms upon the winter wheat and maturing spring crops. Efforts to drown, mash, or burn the invading horde seemed futile. On Lorenzo Young's farm, he wrote in his diary on May 29, they destroyed in one day "3/4 of an acre of squashes, our flax, two acres of millet and our rye, and are now to work in our wheat. What will be the result we know not." The result was grim, but it would have been

In 1848 seagulls saved enough crops from invading crickets to enable the Saints to survive the winter. The Saints soon saw this as a sign of divine intervention, and the seagull story has been immortalized in music, drama, sculpture, and painting. This bronze relief at the base of the Seagull monument was executed by Mahonri Young in 1913. (LDS Church)

much worse had it not been for the flocks of seagulls from the islands of the Great Salt Lake that swept in and began gorging themselves on the crickets. The hungry gulls ate all they could, regurgitated the indigestible portions, then ate again and again. This continued for several weeks, and much of the crop was saved. Though the harvest was greatly reduced, the Saints were grateful for what was spared and for the proof that the untried soil of the valley could indeed produce crops.

The winter of 1848–49 was especially severe, and both settlers and livestock suffered heavily. Firewood was difficult to obtain and food supplies dwindled. Some turned to boiling rawhide for nourishment— "glue soup," it was called by one family. Those who had surplus shared with those who were less fortunate; and to prevent excess profit-making, voluntary controls were established on the price of such necessities as beef and flour. The colony survived, but empty stomachs, frostbitten feet, and an unfamiliar environment discouraged many pioneers. For some, California's milder climate became an increasingly attractive lure.

Money and the Gold Rush

Not long after the severe winter melted into spring, thousands of Americans rushing to the gold fields of California passed through the City of the Saints. The Saints were naturally interested, and "California fever" spread to some. Church leaders cautioned against going to the gold fields, lest overnight success and concern for worldly things interfere with the building of the kingdom.

Although most members followed counsel and stayed away from the mines, the gold rush had an important impact on their well-being. It supplied them with scarce commercial goods at surprisingly low prices. Merchant companies, organized to haul goods to California, learned when they reached Salt Lake City that food, clothing, implements, and tools sent by ship had beaten them to the marketplace. Rather than take an even heavier loss in California, they sold their goods at devalued prices in the Salt Lake Valley. California pioneers were equally eager to sell cheaply things that burdened them. In addition, the Saints operated ferryboats and blacksmith shops, turning handsome profits by providing these and other services. The gold rush of 1849 brought welcome hard cash into the Mormon commonwealth.

The Saints were influenced by the gold rush in other ways. A mint was established in Salt Lake City to process the gold dust brought in by travelers and returning members of the Mormon Battalion. And in 1849 Brigham Young called in several young men, mostly Mormon Battalion veterans, and sent them on a confidential mission to the gold fields of California. He did not want the Saints generally to rush for gold, but if these young men could bring back substantial amounts of dust, there would be gold for the mint to help establish an acceptable circulating medium in the territory. As it turned out, the returning gold missionaries brought little to show for their adventure when they returned—hard-won proof that Brigham Young was right in urging the body of Saints to stay home.

Political Patterns

Until Congress provided a territorial government for the Saints in 1850, they governed themselves, first through the ecclesiastical machinery of the high council and then through a provisional government, created by the Council of Fifty.

Before the apostles returned to Winter Quarters in 1847 they organized a municipal high council in the Salt Lake Valley, which presided for the next fifteen months. With John Smith, uncle of Joseph Smith, at its head, the council drafted laws, collected taxes, regulated prices, and conducted other public business. In January 1849 the Council of Fifty assumed the high council's municipal functions. This group of leading men drafted a plan for territorial government, which they later changed to one for state government, and while waiting for federal approval, they established the provisional State of Deseret.

The State of Deseret was the civil government of the Great Basin settlements for two years. It organized counties, granted rights to natural resources, regulated trade and commerce, established the Nauvoo Legion as an official state militia, and fulfilled all functions of a regular government. Brigham Young and his counselors were elected, respectively, governor, chief justice, and secretary. Members of the Council of Fifty and others, many of whom were prominent churchmen, filled other state offices and selected ward bishops as local magistrates. Church and state were clearly welded together through the persons of the officers, a precedent carried over from Nauvoo and Winter Quarters that later would bring severe criticism from the larger society. To the Saints, however, this seemed a natural expression of their needs.

Native American Relations

When the Mormon pioneers arrived in the Great Basin they confronted another problem—the people already there. Perhaps as many

*Mormon gold coins, 1849
and 1860. Initials on the
earliest coins stand for
"Great Salt Lake City Pure
Gold." "Holiness to the
Lord" appears in the Deseret
alphabet on the 1860 five-
dollar coin. (Charles B. Hall
engraving, Church Archives)*

as twenty thousand Native Americans of the Western Shoshoni, Ute, Southern Paiute, and Navajo tribes inhabited the area that is now the state of Utah. The Indians generally existed by gathering and hunting, with little cultivation of the land. They were also traders and sometimes ranged as far as California to dispose of horses and other goods stolen in raids along the Old Spanish Trail. The Salt Lake Valley was generally seen as Shoshoni territory, though the Utes also inhabited the area and many groups ventured into it for salt. In 1847 there were probably several hundred Indians in the valley.

Within a week of the pioneers' arrival, Indians had visited camp to trade for guns, ammunition, and clothing. These visits became frequent, and at times larger numbers gathered. After a squabble among different bands over a stolen horse, the pioneers resolved to trade with the Indians only at their own encampment, and appointed two men to handle all commercial dealings. As an expression of benevolent service, a number of Mormon women provided clothing for the Indians of Deseret.

Encounters between the newcomers and older residents during the first years were generally peaceful, although during the winter of 1849–50 Indians threatened war against the LDS farmers of the Provo River settlement, Fort Utah. The militia responded to the settlers' appeal, and in a series of battles over a ten-day period about forty to fifty Indians and one settler died. The confrontation effectively ended Indian resistance in Utah Valley and allowed the Saints to move out of their protective fort onto city lots and farms.

Lending assistance in the Fort Utah War was Captain Howard Stansbury, who arrived in August 1849 to conduct a government survey of the Great Salt Lake and Utah Lake. When the Saints first heard of Stansbury's expedition, they were apprehensive about its military and political implications, fearing another invasion of their rights. However, once the mission of the Army Corps of Engineers was made clear, Brigham Young cooperated fully and Albert Carrington, a Mormon, was hired by Stansbury to superintend the chain line. Stansbury's published report included the first accurate maps of the two valleys and much important scientific information about plant and animal life in the Great Salt Lake region.

Transplanting a Culture

The Saints brought with them to the Salt Lake Valley more than a concern for survival. They brought their social patterns, and much of their time in these early years was spent attempting to rebuild what they had enjoyed in Nauvoo. As in most pioneering settlements, there was a time lag before education, social life, and the arts could become what they were before, but the Saints did what they could even while they were establishing their pioneer communities.

In their concern for education during the early months of settlement, the pioneers conducted rudimentary schools around campfires on the plains and in wagon boxes, tents, and dugouts. In addition, they continued to enjoy parties, dances, picnics, and holiday celebrations. Most important, they brought with them their religion, and the religious system they knew in Nauvoo was quickly reestablished. The high council, organized in part to take care of the affairs of the community, was the only priesthood body in the valley until the Twelve returned in the fall of 1848.

In Winter Quarters the Twelve had become convinced of the need for reorganizing the First Presidency. On December 27, 1847, in the log tabernacle near Kanesville, Brigham Young was sustained as President. Members in the Salt Lake Valley sustained the action in April 1848. The familiar organization was reestablished. In February 1849 the Salt Lake Stake was organized and nineteen wards were established.

Buildings for Church administration and worship were provided as quickly as possible, including a small adobe building constructed as a church office in 1848, and a Council House, completed in 1850, which served as an important meeting place for various groups. The temple block was the site for immediate construction of a brush-covered bowery used for religious worship; it was soon replaced by a larger one and then, in 1851, by the "old" tabernacle.

In beginning again in the West, the pioneers were rededicating themselves to the religious goal of establishing Zion. As a symbol of their renewed commitment, the first arrivals were rebaptized by immersion in water. Many of those who followed shared the same experience. The Twelve proposed this renewal of covenants, not with any feeling that the prior baptism lacked validity, but rather as a symbol of thanksgiving and rededication. Like the pilgrims of earlier generations, the Saints had abandoned homes and farms in many places for the rigors of an untamed wilderness. Claiming it as their promised land, they hoped to reestablish themselves as a modern Israel, guided by a prophet and committed to the belief that the society they were building would one day become an ensign to all nations.

CHAPTER 8

Establishing an Ensign, *1851–1856*

On July 24, 1849, President Brigham Young attended an elaborate Pioneer Day celebration in Salt Lake City, the first celebration to commemorate the pioneers' arrival two years earlier. Bands played, a huge American flag was unfurled atop a hundred-foot liberty pole, bells rang, guns fired, an impressive parade was held, and when the Constitution of the United States was presented to the President he led the assembled throng in three successive shouts, "May it live forever!" Eight years later he attended another Pioneer Day celebration with several thousand Saints in Big Cottonwood Canyon. There he was informed that a major expedition of the United States Army was traveling to Utah, and he suspected their intent was hostile. Between these two events, the Latter-day Saints worked feverishly in their new place of refuge to create a self-sufficient community that could never again be forced to move. They grew in numbers, established civil government, and spread Mormon communities along the fertile eastern rim of the Great Basin. But they also saw the unfortunate beginning of new misunderstandings between themselves and their American neighbors. It was a time of high hope and accomplishment as well as one of trial, dominated by the energetic leadership of the great colonizer, Brigham Young.

Territorial Government for Utah: Organization and Seeds of Conflict

By 1851 more than 350 miles of Utah wilderness between Bear River in the north and the Virgin River in the south had been explored, and settlements were located along a 250–mile strip of the Wasatch Front sustaining a population of 15,000 Saints. The State of Deseret provided efficient government until 1850, when the territory was officially organized by the Congress of the United States.

267

When John M. Bernhisel was first sent to Washington to petition for territorial status, Colonel Thomas L. Kane astutely foresaw certain dangers and warned the Saints that they should press for full statehood. Only this, he argued, would assure them the right of self-government without interference from federally appointed officials who might not be sympathetic with their religious purposes. In 1849 he told them:

> You are better off without any government from the hands of Congress than with a Territorial government. The political intrigues of government officers will be against you. You can govern yourselves better than they can govern you. . . . You do not want corrupt political men from Washington strutting around you, with military epaulettes and dress, who will speculate out of you all they can. . . . You do not want two governments. You have a government now, which is firm and powerful, and you are under no obligations to the United States.[1]

The following year Brigham Young instructed Bernhisel to apply for statehood, but the Territory of Utah already had been created by Congress. The question of statehood had become part of the larger American controversy over the status of slavery in the territories recently acquired from Mexico. After a heated debate that almost tore the nation apart, the dispute ended with the famous Compromise of 1850. California became a state, with a constitution prohibiting slavery, and the territories of New Mexico and Utah were organized with the understanding that they could decide the issue of slavery for themselves. Disappointed, the general assembly of Deseret nevertheless resolved in March 1851 to "cheerfully and cordially" accept territorial status. The new territorial legislature soon adopted all the laws of the provisional State of Deseret.

As residents of a territory of the United States rather than a state, the Saints in Utah suddenly found themselves, as Thomas L. Kane had predicted, again under the threat of external political influence. As in the past, it would be impossible for them to avoid political conflict so long as their ideas and practices clashed with those of the men in power. They were unable to elect their own governor, judges, or executive officials, for these officers were appointed in Washington. They could send a delegate to Congress who could lobby, debate, and participate in committee work, but not vote. Happily for the Saints, some of the first territorial appointments were given to Church members. Brigham

---

[1]Brigham Young, "Manuscript History," November 26, 1849.

Mormon community of Fillmore, Utah, 1855, showing the old Statehouse. In 1851 Fillmore was designated as the location of the territorial capital, and the legislature met there in 1855 and 1856. Jules Remy, one of many visitors to Utah in this period, published this engraving in his book, Journey to the Great Salt Lake, *1861.*

Young was named governor, Zerubbabel Snow became one of the three federal district judges, and Seth Blair and Joseph L. Heywood were made U. S. attorney and U. S. marshal, respectively. On the other hand, the chief justice for the territory, the second associate justice, the territorial secretary, and two Indian agents were all non-Mormon appointees.

The stay of the first non-Mormon officials in Utah was both brief and controversial, sowing seeds of new misunderstanding. They did not arrive until late in August 1851, and the difficulties began almost immediately. At a special Church conference early in September, Justice Perry Brocchus requested and received permission to speak to the Saints. He expressed friendship for the Mormons, but some of his remarks were uncomplimentary, especially to the women in attendance. President Young was visibly irritated, and in defending the Saints he sharply criticized Brocchus and other government officials. Two weeks later, when the legislature opened, a disagreement developed over control of the $24,000 congressional appropriation that the territorial secretary had brought. Judge Brocchus was upset because the legislature did not choose him as Utah's congressional delegate. Before the end of the month the two non-Mormon judges, the territorial secretary, and an Indian agent had become so dissatisfied that they left the territory, taking the $24,000 with them. The accusations they carried to Washington were only the beginning of a series of unfortunate and distorted reports that would again result in misunderstanding and tragedy.

With two of the three federal judges gone, the territorial legislature quickly filled the judicial vacuum by granting criminal jurisdiction to the territorial probate courts. This created a unique situation that illustrates the unusual relationship between the Church and civil government in early Utah.

The chief legislative and executive body of the counties was the county court, which consisted of the probate judge and three selectmen. The probate judge also presided over the county probate court, which had jurisdiction over estates, guardianship, and other civil affairs. When criminal jurisdiction was added, the power of the judge was significantly broadened. He now held concurrent jurisdiction with the federal district courts in all criminal matters, so that even when a federal court was in session, those accused of crimes could proceed through the local probate courts instead.

The legislature's action in granting such jurisdiction created a situation loaded with potential misunderstanding, even though it had been done in other territories. In most cases the county probate judge, who was appointed by the territorial legislature, was also a local bishop or other church leader. To unsympathetic outsiders it could easily appear that the church and local government were one and the same. In cases where a bishop presided over the court, for example, the same man held executive, legislative, and judicial power within the county, as well as strong ecclesiastical influence. In the minds of most Latter-day Saints, this was both natural and desirable. To the non-Mormons, it appeared un-American.

As the settlement of the Great Basin proceeded, a close working relationship developed between the ecclesiastical units and local government. Before local government was officially organized, bishops as church officers directed the dispensing of land, building of roads, digging of ditches and canals, and other necessary projects. Even after civil government began to function, the county courts often used the Church to carry out important tasks. Bishops were the natural leaders and were often appointed as watermasters, herd ground overseers, and supervisors of roads and canyons. The Church was also often asked by the county court to assist in building schools, determining locations for roads, collecting certain taxes, and even in liquor control. The practical, beneficial result of this relationship was that the Church and civil government worked closely together in the many tasks necessary for building new communities.

Some non-Mormons in Utah were concerned with the unusual judicial authority given the probate courts. Whereas anti-Mormon federal judges were unwilling to grant citizenship to immigrating Latter-day Saints as long as the Church accepted the practice of plural marriage, the probate courts had the right to hear citizenship petitions and grant American citizenship. It also became apparent that many Saints distrusted the federal courts and did all they could to take their criminal cases to the probate courts. Ultimately, in 1874 the federal government removed the controversial jurisdiction by granting exclusive jurisdiction in both civil and criminal cases to the federal courts.

The Church helped promote order and justice in the Territory of Utah in another way. President Brigham Young and his counselors encouraged the Saints to avoid taking their personal disputes to courts of law. It seemed incongruous for a Saint to take his brother to court if the matter could be settled amicably some other way. Church leaders had little trust for most "gentile" lawyers, who seemed to them to value individual profit more than public well-being. As a result, church courts, especially bishops' courts, were often used to settle differences between members. They usually became courts of arbitration, and the Saints accepted the bishops' decisions. Church courts, relying more heavily upon an inherent sense of justice than upon technicalities growing out of legal precedent, gained such a reputation for fairness that non-Mormons sometimes took their claims there instead of to the territorial courts. In disagreements over property lines, ownership of livestock, and other matters that could be settled by arbitration, church courts were often the most effective dispensers of justice in the territory.

Utah's territorial legislature met annually. Members of the legislature were usually Church leaders, elected by the people of the various counties. In some ways they viewed their political responsibilities as an extension of their church activity, for they were all engaged in building a political community conducive to the success of the kingdom.

For a time, at least, the Council of Fifty had great influence on policymaking. Working informally and behind the scenes, it functioned as a kind of coordinating council between the Church and the political institution. Many of its members were also members of the legislature, others served as lobbyists, and some became heads of territorial government agencies. To the Saints, it seemed natural that the elected leaders of the territory should be the "chief men of Israel," and that an unusual degree of political harmony should prevail. This very unity, however, led to conflict with "gentile" appointees who resented their own lack of influence.

After the runaway officials of 1851 left the territory, a feeling of accord between other federal appointees and the Church prevailed for about four years. Then two new federal judges, George Stiles and W. W. Drummond, became particularly irritated by the jurisdiction of the probate courts and the territorial marshal. Drummond, in particular, ridiculed some of the practices of the Saints, and he soon left the territory. Arriving in Washington in the spring of 1856, he leveled a number of charges against the Saints, including the false accusation that they had destroyed federal court records in Salt Lake City.

Malicious reports against the Saints were also directed to Washington by David Burr, the territorial surveyor general. He criticized the legislature's action in granting certain leading Saints exclusive control or stewardship over water sites, timber, and grazing lands. This was actually done to assure equitable distribution and use of these natural resources, but to Burr it ran counter to American free enterprise and individualism. It may also have been illegal. The Saints also found themselves in conflict with Garland Hurt, a federally appointed Indian subagent. Brigham Young, as superintendent of Indian affairs, was his superior, but Hurt was suspicious of the Church's motives and worked to counteract Brigham Young's policies. The reports and accusations of these federal appointees unfortunately contributed to a misunderstanding that combined with political events to create the Utah War of 1857–58.

Expansion of Mormon Communities

The settlement of the Great Basin was a grand experiment in planned expansion. President Young was anxious for the Saints to occupy as much land as possible in order to provide for incoming converts. He also didn't want the Saints ever again to be driven from their homes because they were numerically overwhelmed by unsympathetic outsiders. Unlike most American colonizing activities, then, the unique Mormon commonwealth was the result of careful economic planning by Church leaders, authoritative direction in carrying out the plan, and the willing cooperation of members.

The chief economic activity of the Saints in Utah was agriculture, and in planning their settlements they chose areas most capable of sustaining farming. Brigham Young approved of mining for iron and coal, the raw products needed in building a new society, but opposed large-scale mining for precious metals. The boom-and-bust cycle of most mining would not provide the stability needed for permanent communities. Small-scale, family-oriented agriculture would offer the Saints steady employment and close proximity to each other. The major communities, of course, needed skilled artisans and craftsmen of all kinds, but the basic economy was necessarily agricultural.

The Saints considered a call to settle a new area as important as a call to serve on a proselyting mission. It was not uncommon for a man sitting in a conference meeting to suddenly hear himself called on a mission to locate a new community. This often meant leaving newly established homes and farms and starting over again in another strange and uninviting area. It was nevertheless a religious duty, and most Saints were willing to do as directed. They had the vision of being engaged in building the kingdom and were willing to make more sacrifice if it was necessary to that goal. To appreciate the unusual colonizing success of the Latter-day Saints, it is essential to understand that kind of discipleship.

Until 1850 Mormon colonies were generally confined to the vicinity of Salt Lake City, Ogden, and Provo, with outreach communities in Tooele and Manti. During the winter of 1849–50, the Council of Fifty sent out the Southern Exploring Company, which led to the establishment of Parowan in southern Utah in 1851. That fall, about thirty-five men skilled in mining and manufacturing were called from Parowan to establish an "iron mission" about twenty miles further south. There they founded Cedar City, began mining the rich iron ore nearby, and in less than a year had a blast furnace in operation. By 1853 nearly all the sites recommended by the Southern Exploring Company had been settled.

But Brigham Young had a larger plan in mind. Parowan, Cedar City, and the other communities along the Wasatch Front were part of what is sometimes called the Mormon Corridor. President Young announced as early as 1849 that the Church would build a string of settlements from Salt Lake City to the Pacific Ocean. Although he was reluctant to send many Saints to California, he did want an outpost near Los Angeles that would serve as a reception and outfitting post for immigrants. He could then encourage them to come by ship from Europe to California, even though it meant going around Cape

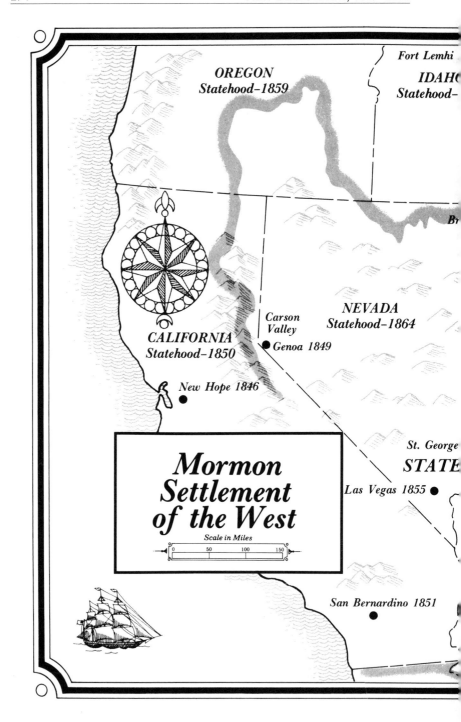

Fort Lemhi

OREGON
Statehood–1859

IDAHO
Statehood–

Br

NEVADA
Statehood–1864

Carson
Valley

CALIFORNIA
Statehood–1850

Genoa 1849

New Hope 1846

St. George

Mormon
Settlement
of the West

STATE

Las Vegas 1855

Scale in Miles

0   50   100   150

San Bernardino 1851

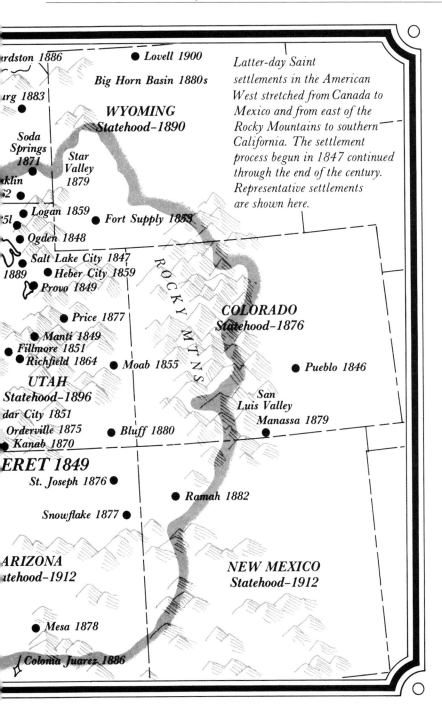

rdston 1886

● Lovell 1900

Big Horn Basin 1880s

Latter-day Saint
settlements in the American
West stretched from Canada to
Mexico and from east of the
Rocky Mountains to southern
California. The settlement
process begun in 1847 continued
through the end of the century.
Representative settlements
are shown here.

rg 1883
●

WYOMING
Statehood–1890

Soda
Springs
1871
●

Star
Valley
1879

klin
2 ●

5l ● Logan 1859 ● Fort Supply 1853

● Ogden 1848

● Salt Lake City 1847
1889 ● Heber City 1859
● Provo 1849

R
O
C
K
Y

M
T
N
S

COLORADO
Statehood–1876

● Price 1877

● Manti 1849
● Fillmore 1851
● Richfield 1864 ● Moab 1855

● Pueblo 1846

UTAH
Statehood–1896
dar City 1851
Orderville 1875 ● Bluff 1880
● Kanab 1870

San
Luis Valley
Manassa 1879
●

ERET 1849
St. Joseph 1876 ●

● Ramah 1882

Snowflake 1877 ●

ARIZONA
tehood–1912

NEW MEXICO
Statehood–1912

● Mesa 1878

Colonia Juarez 1886

Horn. They could then migrate overland along a route almost completely controlled by the Saints.

In 1851 President Young called apostles Amasa Lyman and Charles C. Rich to lead a group to California to select a site for settlement. They purchased a ranch and founded the community of San Bernardino. Within four years 1,400 Mormon settlers lived in the area — many more than the President had anticipated — and they were cultivating 4,000 acres.

The colony provided a port of entry for converts from the Pacific missions, a gathering place for California Saints generally, and a rest and supply station for missionaries. In 1857 the San Bernardino colony was officially discontinued, partly because of the approach of federal troops to Utah and also because the colony was experiencing internal dissension and problems with non-Mormon neighbors. Brigham Young had come to doubt the wisdom of having such a large Mormon center in California. After the recall some Saints remained in San Bernardino, although the majority responded to counsel and eventually returned to Utah.

The expansion of Mormon settlements was influenced by work among Native Americans. Soon after the founding of Cedar City, groups were sent to explore the Virgin and Santa Clara rivers of southern Utah, and in 1854 men were sent to work among the Indians of the region. The missionaries not only taught the Indians the gospel, but also tried to help them build homes and learn better agricultural methods. In the process they discovered that cotton could be grown in southern Utah, and in the late 1850s and early 1860s a "cotton mission" settled St. George and other colonies in Utah's Dixie.

During the 1850s several colonies developed beyond the perimeters of the initial Mormon Corridor. In April 1855 missionaries were called to teach Indians in a number of areas, including present-day Oklahoma. Missionaries were also assigned to establish Indian missions at Las Vegas, at Elk Mountain near present-day Moab, Utah, and at Fort Limhi in Idaho. None of these missions proved very successful. Elk Mountain was abandoned the year it began, while Las Vegas and Fort Limhi ended when Brigham Young recalled the settlers in 1857. A small Mormon settlement also grew up in Carson Valley in western Nevada, but because serious friction developed with non-Mormon miners in the area, the settlement was recalled in 1857. In each of these cases, as well as in the case of San Bernardino, the impending Utah War provided an official reason for withdrawing the Saints. It is also clear that some of

William Henry Jackson's painting of Fort Bridger. (Church Archives)

the settlements were having difficulties; they were too far from the central body of the Saints, and Brigham Young was impressed with the importance of maintaining strength in the mountain valleys of the central gathering place.

To supervise access to Utah from the East and to serve as supply stations for immigrants, two outposts were established along the Oregon Trail. Fort Bridger was originally owned by Jim Bridger, the famous mountain man and fur trader. It was there that Mormon pioneers often stopped to rest and purchase supplies before beginning the last hundred miles of their trip to the Salt Lake Valley. Unable to purchase Fort Bridger, colonists were sent out from Salt Lake City in 1853 to found Fort Supply, about twelve miles from Fort Bridger, and to do missionary work among the Indians. In 1855 the Church finally bought Fort Bridger and thus controlled that portion of the Oregon Trail. The two outposts provided supplies for both Mormon and non-Mormon travelers. The Saints burned Fort Bridger and Fort Supply in October 1857 as part of their effort to slow down the U.S. Army advancing toward Salt Lake City.

Despite a few failures, the accomplishment of bringing tens of thousands of immigrants from America and Europe and successfully settling them in new communities is truly astounding. By 1857 more than fifty settlements had been established along the western slopes of the Wasatch Mountains and approximately forty more in other places, with a total of forty thousand Saints. Though the settlement pattern was interrupted in 1857–58, it continued afterward until the end of the nineteenth century when more than five hundred settlements had been established by the Saints in the Mountain West.

The planting of each Mormon colony followed a similar pattern. First, exploring parties were sent out to identify sites with the greatest potential. Next, Church authorities called a leader and other colonists, making sure that various skills were represented so the colonists could create a smoothly functioning community. The group met in Salt Lake City or another major center, then traveled together to its destination. The traveling company was organized in groups of tens, fifties, and one hundreds, with captains over each.

Upon arrival, the settlers dedicated the land and immediately began working. The planning was frequently done in priesthood meetings. Some colonists were assigned to work on the stockade that would provide a temporary home and protect them against the Indians, while others built dams, dug irrigation ditches and canals, planted crops, built roads, hauled timber, and erected houses. Until the first homes were finished, they often lived in wagons and makeshift dugouts.

A typical Mormon community in the West was carefully designed to encourage close-knit community life and religious activity. The town was laid off in square blocks separated by wide streets. The blocks varied from five to ten acres, but each was divided into equal lots of about an acre, and a community drawing was held to determine ownership. Each family had sufficient acreage in town for a garden, a small orchard, and sheds for poultry and livestock, but the main agricultural activity took place outside the village. The center square was set apart for a meetinghouse, and usually the first public building erected was a combination church and school.

On the outskirts of the village was a large area known as the Big Field. It was divided into plots of several acres, depending on the amount of land available, and again each family received a section by drawing lots. The Big Field was used mainly for raising grain and hay, and it was fenced cooperatively by the community. Outside the fenced area was a common pasture for livestock, and men and boys would usually be assigned to take turns as herdsmen.

One key to the success of the Mormon communities was their peculiar combination of private enterprise and economic cooperation. In most cases each family head was considered owner of the property he had been assigned, but it was understood the land was to be cultivated and not held for speculative purposes. The land was free, but it was for the benefit of all, and in some cases if the man did not use the land it was transferred to someone who would. (Technically, no one held legal title until after the federal land office was set up in Utah in 1869.) The grazing lands and timber and water resources were considered community property, and everyone had equal access to them. Even though certain individuals were given control of the canyons and could charge for the use of roads into them, this was only to compensate for the expenses involved in building and maintaining the roads, and the fees charged were not excessive. When new settlers joined a community they were given land and community resources on the same basis as the original settlers. Thus Mormon community building was an exercise in both cooperative planning and free enterprise, regulated for the benefit of all by the authority of the Church.

The Latter-day Saint farmer continually had the problems of nature to combat. After the difficulties of 1848 and 1849, harvests were generally good until 1855 and 1856, when natural disasters brought near-famine. Rocky Mountain locusts caused serious damage in earlier years, and during 1855 a grasshopper plague was more destructive than during any previous year. In addition, this was a hot year, which cut down available irrigation water and caused a late-season drought. In some areas one-third to two-thirds of the crop was destroyed. Yet that same year 4,225 immigrants reached the Salt Lake Valley, more than any year since 1852. To add to the difficulties, an unusually severe winter in 1855–56 killed almost half the cattle in the territory, and during the next summer a damaging grasshopper invasion left another poor harvest.

Once again the organization and strength of the Church helped ward off utter starvation and disaster. Priesthood leaders instituted a rationing program and asked those with surplus to distribute it among the destitute. In addition, the Church inaugurated the practice of fast offerings, which has since become a fundamental practice among the Saints. During the winter of 1855–56 the Saints were asked to fast on the first Thursday of every month and to donate the food saved to the bishop's storehouse. These offerings were used for those most urgently in need.

Indian Policy

As Superintendent of Indian Affairs in the 1850s, Brigham Young generally maintained warm and cordial relationships, and gained the confidence of the Indians. He urged the Saints to be patient and kindly toward them, to feed rather than fight them, and to teach them peaceful agricultural pursuits. While this policy did not prevent some early skirmishes, or a small war in 1853–54, it was generally successful in maintaining peace.

One of the first difficulties arose over the Indian slave trade. Occasionally Indians voluntarily sold their own children into slavery to Mexican or other Indian traders, and often tribes raided each other for children and women to be sold. The Ute chief, Walker, was at first friendly with the Church, and even allowed himself to be baptized, but when differences on the slave trade became apparent, his amiability began to cool. The Saints were indignant about the slave trade but were unable to persuade the Indians it should stop. In 1852 the territorial legislature passed a law authorizing probate judges to purchase Indian women or children who had become slaves and assign them to suitable homes for care, protection, and education. Ironically, the Saints thus actually fostered a slave law in the territory, but its primary purpose was to liberate victims of Indian slavery.

The slave law angered the Native Americans, who saw in it the possibility of potential interference with a profitable business. Slave traders encouraged them to resist the law and supplied them with arms. This became an important factor in the outbreak of the Walker War in July 1853, when the Utes attacked various Mormon settlements beginning at Springville. The intermittent fighting lasted until May 1854, when Brigham Young and Chief Walker arranged a peace settlement.

The Walker War was followed by renewed missionary activity among the Indians. Often the missionaries would take their families to live in Indian villages, help the Indians learn to farm, work with them in the fields, and teach them the gospel. They baptized many and directed scores of Indian children who went to live in Latter-day Saint homes. The missionaries also worked among white Mormons themselves to get them to show more charity and understanding toward the native Americans. An attempt was made to establish Indian farms in a few central and southern Utah counties where the Indians would be taught farming methods as well as the gospel. Most of these farms were terminated by the 1870s though some, along with a few new ones, continued until nearly the end of the century.

However charitable in intent, Mormon policies toward the Native Americans led to friction with the federal government. In 1853 John

W. Gunnison, leader of a U.S. Topographical Survey unit, was killed in a tragic massacre. Because the Mormons were at peace with the Pahvants, some people accused the Saints of complicity in the affair. There was no basis to the charge. Moreover, certain federal Indian agents resented Mormon friendship with the Indians, for it undermined their own influence. Garland Hurt, for example, even though he cooperated briefly in the Indian farm experiment, disliked Mormon missionary activity, and especially disliked the distinction sometimes made by the Indians between "Mericat" and "Mormonee." His antagonistic reports to Washington caused the federal government to withhold part of the funds appropriated for territorial Indian programs.

Business and Financial Affairs among the Saints

Chief among Brigham Young's temporal goals for the Saints was the hope of economic self-sufficiency. As much as possible he wanted to end reliance upon outside interests and institutions for the needs of Mormon society. The plan called upon the Saints to develop their own manufacturing industries, largely as cooperative rather than private enterprise. Large sums of money needed to back these industries could not be obtained from the private sector, so the Church itself shouldered the principal responsibility. This meant that the Church needed a substantial source of income. In addition, it needed funds to support the building, administrative, colonization, and welfare activities that daily multiplied.

Although limited income was available from church properties and donations for special purposes such as the Perpetual Emigrating Fund, the basic source of funds was tithing. As a result, a tithing house, sometimes called the bishop's storehouse, sprang up in every community. About two-thirds of the tithing donated at local offices went to the General Tithing Office in Salt Lake City for general church needs; the rest was used at the discretion of local bishops.

In pioneer Utah tithing could be paid in several ways. Cash was always acceptable, but there was little available. Many people donated one day of labor in every ten toward various church projects. Most common, however, was payment of tithing "in kind." Pioneer farmers commonly brought chickens, eggs, cattle, vegetables, hay, grain, and goods they had manufactured themselves to the tithing houses. Uniform financial values were attached to these items, and the Church used them to pay its creditors as well as to distribute food and supplies to the Saints employed on its public works projects. The tithing house soon became a basic economic institution in every Mormon community. There local settlers would pay tithing, exchange one form of produce for another, and receive credit for surplus goods deposited. Tithing scrip was printed and issued to those who received credit, and this scrip, though not an official currency, became an important circulating medium in Utah in the 1850s. The tithing houses served almost every economic need in the community, even providing a postal system, as mail was taken in and forwarded by tithing labor. Through these activities the Church was thoroughly involved in the economic life of its members.

But the Church needed increased capital to finance public works, support immigration and colonization, and develop industry. One approach to the problem was a brief effort, beginning in 1854, to reinstitute the law of consecration. It was strictly voluntary, but those who wished to comply were asked to deed their property to the Church, in return for which they would be assigned inheritances according to their needs. The result, ideally, would be not only a stronger pool of capital to further the work of building the kingdom, but also greater equality and unselfishness among the Saints. By 1856 about 40 percent of the family heads in the territory had signed forms deeding their property to the Church, but in the end the Church did not assume control and the plan was not implemented.

The main hope for further economic development lay in industry, and in 1851–52 the Church commenced a systematic program to develop manufacturing. Such industry would provide work for the rapidly increasing population and help combat the high cost of importing eastern goods. The iron mission, for example, was designed to provide Utah ore to support the manufacture of iron products in the territory. That project, however, was beset with such major difficulties—inadequate fuel and water, as well as the problems of the Utah War—that by 1859 it had closed.

Other manufacturing enterprises during the 1850s met similar fates. A pottery plant was abandoned in 1853, although a more successful private business was set up three years later. The attempt to establish a lead smelter at Las Vegas in 1856–57 also failed. In 1851 Elder John Taylor purchased machinery in Paris for a woolen factory, but it did not arrive in Utah until 1862, which meant that until then no major woolen factory existed among the Saints. Similarly, the effort to establish sugar manufacturing failed for technical reasons, although

Deseret Store and Tithing Office, about 1858. The Utah Building presently stands on this spot. (David A. Burr photo, Church Archives)

local farmers demonstrated they could grow sugar beets. More successful was the establishment of a paper mill in the 1850s as part of the Church's public works program. This process required the continuous gathering of rags for conversion into paper, and for a time bishops sponsored extensive "get out the rags" campaigns. One faithful Saint was even called on a "rag mission" in 1861 and for three years traveled among the people collecting rags for the paper project.

The failure of these early manufacturing projects did not mean economic disaster for individual Mormons. Since these were cooperative Church-sponsored ventures, the losses were sustained primarily by the Church. These various manifestations of the search for economic self-sufficiency are important as an illustration of the Church's wide-ranging activities in attempting to build the kingdom of God in the West. When one experiment failed, persistent leaders tried another, for they believed it was important to the kingdom to promote both the spiritual and the economic well-being of the Saints.

Very early, the rapid influx of converts created a major surplus of labor in the territory; in response, the Church inaugurated a Public Works Department in 1850. The new department had the dual advantage of being able to provide employment for immigrants as well as needed laborers for public building projects and experimental manufacturing enterprises. Supported by tithing funds, it kept between two hundred and five hundred men on its rolls. Several important projects were supported by the public works program. Of special significance was the Endowment House, finished in 1855, which provided the only place for the performance of temple ordinances until the completion of the St. George Temple in 1877. Workers built a wall around Temple Square and helped with the temple itself. They labored in the sugar, wool, and paper manufacturing experiments, in a machine shop and foundry, and manufactured adobe bricks, the territory's major building material.

Church leaders also attempted to launch an overland freight business. They were displeased that unfriendly merchants controlled transportation of goods from the East and seemed to be reaping exorbitant profits. As early as 1852, Church spokesmen petitioned Congress for a coast-to-coast railroad that would run through Utah and reduce the cost of transportation. In 1856 Hiram Kimball, acting for the Church, received a contract for hauling mail from Independence, Missouri, to Salt Lake City; it was hoped he could also haul freight more cheaply than outside merchants. Then, in 1857, the Church organized the Brigham Young Express and Carrying Company, better known as the Y. X. Company, designed to operate between Salt Lake City and Independence. Forty settlements were planned along the route to act as supply stations. More than $100,000 was invested in the enterprise, but just as prospects looked hopeful, the federal government canceled the mail contract, a chief source of revenue for the company. Antagonists criticizing Church action in Washington had succeeded not only in stopping the mail contract but also in inaugurating the Utah War.

Life among the Pioneer Saints

All was not work and worry for the Saints in pioneer Utah. On the contrary, visitors were often impressed by the good humor and enjoyment of life that marked every community. Singing, dancing, drama, and other wholesome recreation characterized Latter-day Saint life. The Nauvoo Brass Band, under William Pitt, was reinstituted in Salt Lake City, and later Domenico Ballo, an Italian immigrant, organized and conducted an even more famous band. Brigham Young himself regularly led the dancing at parties held by the Saints wherever he went. Holidays were times of special celebration, characterized by picnics, parades, dances, and good times in general. In 1852 the Deseret Dramatic Association was organized, and the following year the Social Hall in Salt Lake City was dedicated. It became the center for dramatic productions in the Mormon capital. The much larger Salt Lake Theater was completed in 1862. Non-Mormon visitors often observed that such social activities were accepted parts of the LDS religion, remarking with interest that social events were always opened with prayer.

Nor did the Saints forget the importance of education, although during the earliest years their efforts were somewhat limited. During the first winter in Salt Lake City a single school class for children was taught in a tent; by 1854 schools had been established in every ward. Usually the first building erected in a new community was a combination school and meetinghouse, but before such buildings were ready, some classes were conducted in the homes of the teachers. The University of Deseret (later renamed the University of Utah) was created by the legislature of the State of Deseret in 1850, although it ceased operation temporarily after the first five years. The Deseret Agricultural and Manufacturing Society was formed in 1856 to instruct farmers in better farming techniques. Educational opportunities were limited, but the difficulties of forming a new community did not cause the Saints to ignore them completely.

Serving as a substitute for adult education was the Polysophical Society, organized during the winter of 1852 by Lorenzo Snow, who wanted to encourage young men and women to cultivate literary talents. Begun in the Snow home, the society moved to public halls and then spawned similar organizations in Salt Lake City and surrounding settlements. A forerunner of the Mutual Improvement (or Retrenchment) Associations of the 1860s, this popular educational organization featured essays, debates, musical numbers, and other expressions of the heart and mind. It gradually ceased operation after Elder Snow moved to Brigham City during the religious retrenchment of 1856.

In general, social life centered around the ward. Ward socials, dances, and dramas, and even some music clubs, contributed to the feeling of community among the Saints.

Religious life also centered around the ward. By the end of the 1850s there were only four stakes in Utah, but each community had its ward. Wards, first organized in Nauvoo, began to assume a religious significance. They varied in size and were without auxiliaries except for a few Sunday Schools for children. Nevertheless, the bishop assumed the religious leadership of the community, and the wards began to hold preaching meetings each Sunday as well as fast meetings one Thursday each month. In addition, block teaching helped create a greater cohesiveness among ward members. This was basically an Aaronic Priest-

A huge crowd gathered for the groundbreaking ceremony for the Salt Lake Temple, February 14, 1853. (Marsena Cannon daguerreotype, Church Archives)

hood responsibility involving mostly adults. Because those holding the lesser priesthood were few in number, bishops began to assign Melchizedek Priesthood holders as acting teachers to visit all ward families monthly and to exhort them to good works.

In the 1850s general conferences of the Church held semiannually in Salt Lake City also acquired greater significance. From the beginning these conferences had been a time of religious instruction, but in the West, because the Saints often traveled for hundreds of miles to attend, they also became a time of reunion and socializing. The conference became one of the great symbols of Mormon unity as well as a cohesive force in building a sense of community. As one eastern correspondent good-naturedly observed, the general conference became "the post office, newspaper, legislature, Bible, almanac, temporal, spiritual, and social director of the people."[2]

Perhaps the most controversial aspect of Latter-day Saint religious and social life was the practice of plural marriage. Even though the doctrine had been privately taught and practiced by Joseph Smith and other Church leaders in Nauvoo, it was not announced publicly until August 29, 1852, at a conference in Salt Lake City. Elder Orson Pratt

---

[2]*Harper's* 2 (December 4, 1858): 781.

of the Council of the Twelve was chosen to give the first public sermon on plural marriage, and among other things, he said that it would provide the opportunity for the righteous Saints to raise up a numerous posterity in the true principles of the gospel. He added that polygamy was a religious practice and the Constitution guaranteed freedom of religion. In later years some federal legislators and judges emphatically disagreed.

Though plural marriage became one of the major focal points for legal and political action against the Church, it played a relatively small role in the total life of most Mormon communities. Most Saints accepted it in principle but did not practice it. Exactly how many people entered into plural marriage is difficult to determine. Perhaps as many as 20 percent of the families in pioneer Utah were involved. Local leaders were sometimes encouraged to take multiple wives in order to set the example, but two-thirds of the men who married a second wife did not take another.

Nevertheless, plural marriage had some unusual social dimensions for those who practiced it. According to accepted guidelines (usually but not always followed), a man must receive the permission of both his first wife and the leaders of the Church before marrying a second wife, and Church permission depended upon his spiritual worthiness. Often a first wife would actually select her husband's second wife; frequently she would be a sister or close friend. Whether or not both families lived in the same house varied. Stresses naturally arose, but it is also true that in many plural families the wives lived together as affectionate, mutually helpful sisters. Many entered out of a firm conviction that it was part of the restoration of the ancient gospel and that it would help ensure a large posterity and the blessings of eternal exaltation.

One significant religious event of the 1850s was the reformation of 1856–57. Sparked by the preaching of Jedediah M. Grant, second counselor in the First Presidency, the reform was an effort to persuade the Saints to renew their dedication to righteous living. The leaders, deeply concerned about what appeared to be signs of a moral and spiritual decay, traveled around the territory preaching repentance with unprecedented fervor. Members were called upon to repent and rededicate themselves fully to the work of the Lord and to seal this rededication with rebaptism.

Political problems, economic reverses of previous years, plus the evidence of moral laxity contributed to the apparent need for reformation. Some members possibly felt that the zeal with which it was preached became at times almost excessive. The result, however, was that thousands of Saints rededicated themselves to the building of the kingdom. All this may have accounted for the fact that the following year the Saints were emotionally prepared to confront the army of the United States en route to Utah. So thorough was the reformation that on December 30, 1856, the entire membership of the all-Mormon territorial legislature was rebaptized for the remission of their sins, and all were confirmed by the laying on of hands of the Twelve. "This was a new feature in the Legislature," wrote one member. "We believed if we could get the Spirit of God we could do business faster and better than with the spirit of the Devil, or the spirit of the World."[3]

Missionary Work and the Gathering

Regardless of the tremendous tasks the Saints faced in building a new community in the Mountain West, few things were more urgent than spreading the gospel and preparing for the gathering of the Saints. Even though it appeared that Europe, especially the British Isles, was the most fruitful field for converts outside North America, leaders hoped to spread the gospel worldwide. They sent missionaries to Latin America, the islands of the Pacific, India, Asia, and South Africa. The Church was hardly a world church, but the nascent spirit of worldwide influence was present. The missionaries took literally the prophecy of Daniel: the latter-day kingdom would begin as a stone cut out of a mountain, then would roll forth and eventually fill the whole earth. The kingdom had been established in the tops of the mountains, and the Saints intended to start moving it toward its international destiny. In 1852, for example, of the 159 missionaries set apart—the most in a single year since 1844—only 22 were assigned to work within the United States.

Although most converts during this period came from Britain and Scandinavia, the work of the missionaries in other areas illustrates the scope of what the Saints were attempting. In 1851 the first elders arrived in India. These missionaries, originally British converts, began working among British citizens. Within a short time they had baptized several people, and when Brigham Young heard of their success, he called nine more elders to India. They arrived in April 1853 and spread throughout the subcontinent.

---

[3]Wilford Woodruff, "Journal," December 30, 1856, Ms., Church Archives.

The British-born missionaries baptized several natives, but neither they nor the American-born elders understood the native languages and customs of India well enough to succeed. Therefore, the missionaries worked primarily among British citizens at military bases, until they ran into trouble with chaplains of the Church of England; then they tried unsuccessfully to work among the natives. They translated the Book of Mormon into one of the Hindu tongues, but it was never printed. A number of the Caucasian converts immigrated to Utah.

At the same time Hosea Stout, a former police captain in Nauvoo, and two companions attempted to open a mission to China. The political situation of the country prevented them from venturing inland, so they remained in Hong Kong. They could find no one to teach them the native language, and the reception they received from the English-speaking people was generally hostile. After fifty-six days of almost total discouragement, they headed home. Wrote Elder Stout in his journal shortly before departure: "We feel that we have done all that God or man can require of us in this place. We have preached publickly and privately as long as any one would hear and often tried when no one would hear. . . . And thus it is this day we do not know of one person in this place to whome we can bear our testimony of the things of god or warn to flee the wrath to come."[4]

In South America, Elders Parley P. Pratt and Rufus Allen landed in Valparaiso, Chile, in 1851. They were hampered by a disruptive revolution and their lack of fluency in Spanish. Equally important, they could not use the standard missionary approach of working through families and friends, or preaching to large gatherings. These methods had worked well in England, but in South America Catholicism seemed to have an unbreakable hold on the social customs of the upper classes. The lower classes and pure-blooded Indians were uneducated and dominated by the landowners, making communication difficult. As in both China and India, the missionaries were unprepared to cope with economic and social conditions vastly different from anything they had known, and they sailed for home in less than a year.

In northern Europe, and especially in Great Britain, success was phenomenal. The Scandinavian Mission, organized in 1850, baptized about a thousand converts each year during the decade, mostly in Denmark. About 25 percent of these immigrated to the United States.

---

[4]Brooks, *On the Mormon Frontier*, 2:482.

Latter-day Saints emigrating from Europe frequently rode Mississippi riverboats upstream from New Orleans to an outfitting post, where they would prepare for the trek across the plains. (A Frederick Piercy engraving in Route from Liverpool to Salt Lake City, *1855)*

Missionary work was also opened in France, Italy, and Switzerland in 1850, although success there was minimal. From the British Isles, however, more than 15,000 converts left for Utah between 1849 and 1857. In addition, several hundred emigrated from France, Italy, and Germany. Missionary work outside Britain and Scandinavia temporarily languished after missionaries were called home by Brigham Young in 1857 and 1858 because of the Utah War.

The migration of thousands of Saints to Zion demanded organization. When the first companies left England in 1840, they were assisted in their planning by the Council of the Twelve, but generally, once in America, they had to organize and arrange for their own supplies and transportation. In the next few years various attempts at organization were tried. In 1845 Reuben Hedlock, just released as British Mission president, organized the Mutual Benefit Association. Designed to bolster the economy of Nauvoo, it was actually a private business venture, though endorsed by the Church. At the same time it assisted the British Saints and provided land and goods for them in America. This commercial aspect of emigration did not last long, and Hedlock's company was dissolved in 1846.

Following relocation of the Saints in the Rocky Mountains, the Church's involvement in emigration became more needful. In 1849 Church leaders attacked the need of some eight thousand refugees from Nauvoo still camped on the Great Plains. A special call in conference brought $5,000 and several yokes of oxen to help them to Utah. This was the beginning of the Perpetual Emigrating Fund (PEF), and the following year the Perpetual Emigrating Company (later called Perpetual Emigrating Fund Company), which administered funds and supervised migration, was formally incorporated under the laws of the State of Deseret.

The accomplishments of the new company have been recognized as unique in the history of immigration. PEF agents were employed in England to charter ships and assemble and instruct prospective emigrants. The agent was located in Liverpool; all applications went through him, and he informed the Saints when they should arrive. Some emigrants could pay their own way completely; others needed some help from the fund, while others were so poor their trip required total financing. The fund was maintained by donations of cash and property from the Saints in the Great Basin as well as by the agreement that those who were helped would repay as soon as possible. Some, of course, did not repay their indebtedness — an irritant to Brigham Young, on whose shoulders rested the responsibility of raising sufficient funds. In 1856, for example, the indebtedness to the fund totaled $56,000, and the disgusted President declared, "I want to have you understand fully that I intend to put the screws upon you, and you who have owed for years, if you do not pay up now and help us, we will levy on your property and take every farthing you have on the earth."[5] This was simply rhetoric, for the debtors were never abused, even though the Church constantly tried to persuade them to repay.

The Liverpool PEF agent sometimes chartered ships exclusively for the Saints, but if this was not possible, he arranged to have the ship partitioned into separate sections for Mormons and non-Mormons. The emigrants were noted for their heavy luggage, having been encouraged to take tools and equipment with them, and some captains were heard to complain that their ships were an inch lower in the water than usual.

Once aboard ship, the Saints were usually organized into wards or branches, with a presidency of returning missionaries presiding over each. The daily routine included morning prayer, cleaning the ship, religious classes, and evening prayers, with special religious services on Sunday. Charles Dickens said the captain of one such ship told him, "They came from various parts of England in small parties that had

---

[5]*Journal of Discourses*, 3:6.

never seen one another before. Yet they had not been a couple of hours on board, when they established their own police, made their own regulations, and set their own watches at all the hatchways. Before nine o'clock, the ship was as orderly and as quiet as a man-of-war."[6]

Mormon emigrating companies shared the experiences of other groups plus some that were unusual. They saw romance and marriages, births and deaths, and burials at sea. At the same time, the Saints were missionary-minded and made many conversions at sea; on one occasion they even converted an entire ship's crew after a storm. In one instance baptisms were performed in a large barrel filled with sea water, which had to be entered from a ladder. At another time a platform was suspended from the side of the ship and the convert was baptized in the ocean.

At first the emigrants sailed to New Orleans, where another PEF agent met them and booked passage up the Mississippi River to St. Louis. Then a third agent arranged transit up the Missouri River about 500 miles to an outfitting post, where a final agent prepared them for the overland journey to the Great Basin. Later, after the railroad reached St. Louis, when cholera was taking an unfortunate toll along the river, the Saints were routed to New York, Boston, or Philadelphia, whence they traveled by railroad to St. Louis and then continued on to the outfitting posts. The total journey usually required eight or nine months.

Even with donations from the Saints, the PEF found itself in financial difficulty, and Church leaders sought to cut costs. In 1855 Brigham Young revived a plan that had been considered once before but never instigated. The worthy poor were instructed to walk from the end of the railroad to Zion and to carry their possessions across the plains in handcarts. Some nineteen hundred European Saints volunteered, and they were divided into five companies for emigrating in 1856. Each group arriving at the railway terminus in Iowa City was outfitted with handcarts and supplies, along with a few wagons to carry heavier baggage. Then began one of the most heroic treks in the history of Mormon migration. The first three companies reached Salt Lake City safely and were greeted with joy and enthusiasm by the Saints. "As I gazed upon the scene," wrote Wilford Woodruff, "it looked to me like the first hoisting of the floodgates of deliverance to the oppressed millions.

---

[6]Quoted in William Mulder and A. Russell Mortensen, *Among the Mormons* (Lincoln: University of Nebraska Press, 1958), p. 336.

Handcart pioneers at a campsite on the plains. (Painting by C. C. A. Christensen, Museum of Church History and Art)

We can now say to the poor and honest in heart, come home to Zion, for the way is prepared."[7]

Joy soon turned to sorrow with the tragic experience of the Willie and Martin companies. When they arrived at the railroad terminus they found their handcarts not yet prepared. Some observers wisely suggested that they postpone crossing of the plains until the following year, as the season was getting late. Determined to join the Saints as soon as possible, however, they waited until their carts (some hastily made of green wood) were finished, then headed west. After reaching Wyoming they were caught in an early snowstorm.

When leaders in Salt Lake City heard that a thousand Saints were still on the plains, they were shocked. October conference was about to convene, and Brigham Young quickly calculated what would be needed to rescue them. He and other leaders devoted their conference addresses to the task of delivering the handcart pioneers, exhorting the Saints in the valley to donate food, clothing, teams, and wagons for their relief. Even though the Saints had little surplus, their response

---

[7]Wilford Woodruff to Orson Pratt, September 3, 1856, *Millennial Star* 18 (1856): 795.

was warm and overwhelming. On October 7 an advance group of twenty-seven men with sixteen mule teams was on its way eastward with provisions, and more were to follow. Both companies were rescued, though only after more than two hundred had frozen to death. The last group struggled into Salt Lake City at the end of November. In all, some eight thousand Saints arrived in Utah between 1856 and 1860, and just under three thousand in ten handcart companies had walked. But 1860 was the last year for handcarts.

When new immigrants arrived in Salt Lake City, they were usually met as they emerged from Emigration Canyon and escorted to a block appropriately named Emigration Square. After being greeted by President Young or some other Church leader, they were treated to a celebration feast by the wards of the city. Then they were placed with families or in campgrounds until they could be permanently located. Some were sent to distant settlements or assigned to help colonize new areas, while others were given land and work in the Salt Lake City area or found their own way through contact with friends and relatives. The Public Works Department often provided temporary employment until the immigrants could be relocated. Such planning was an important key to the success of the entire colonization program. One "gentile" visitor to Salt Lake City was highly impressed with what he saw when an immigrant train rolled in. Presiding Bishop Edward Hunter was instructing other bishops in their responsibilities:

> An emigrant train had just come in, and the bishops had to put six hundred persons in the way of growing their cabbages and building their homes. One bishop said he could take five bricklayers, another two carpenters, a third a tinman, a fourth seven or eight farm-servants, and so on through the whole bench. In a few minutes I saw that two hundred of these poor emigrants had been placed in the way of earning their daily bread.[8]

By 1856, less than a decade after the first pioneers entered Salt Lake Valley, almost forty thousand Latter-day Saints had arrived in Utah. They had founded many communities, established a permanent agricultural society in a difficult environment, begun to develop a small industrial potential, created the basis for a more permanent religious community than anything they had yet known, sent numerous mis-

---

[8]William Hepworth Dixon, *New America*, 2 vols. (London: Hurst and Blackett, 1867), 1:252–53.

Salt Lake Temple stone quarry, Little Cottonwood Canyon. (C. W. Carter photograph, Church Archives)

sionaries throughout the world, and organized a vast and successful program for immigration. To most Latter-day Saints the Great Basin Zion was becoming an ensign to the nations, a New Jerusalem from which the kingdom would eventually roll forth to fill the world. When faced with serious problems and reverses, the Saints took them in stride, believing that strength can come through adversity. They also realized that misunderstanding with the rest of the nation, or with the federal government, could not be avoided even though they were trying to act as honorable and upright citizens. Nevertheless, they were amazed in July 1857, while celebrating their tenth anniversary in the Great Basin, to hear that an American army was approaching their place of refuge.

PART III

Defending the Kingdom, *1857–1896*

This view of Temple Square and vicinity was taken in 1892, at the laying of the capstone of the Salt Lake Temple. It represents the near-completion of much of what the Saints were seeking in the latter half of the nineteenth century. (C. R. Savage photograph, Church Archives)

DURING THE LAST HALF of the nineteenth century the American people witnessed momentous events that changed the course of their nation's history. The same events were also of consequence for the history of the Latter-day Saints.

In July 1854 fifteen hundred anti-slavery enthusiasts congregated at Jackson, Michigan, antagonized by congressional acceptance of the Kansas-Nebraska Act. Engineered by Senator Stephen A. Douglas of Illinois, that measure organized two new American territories and permitted the people of those territories to decide for themselves whether or not they would allow slavery. This grant of local option was called popular sovereignty, and it eliminated federal prohibitions against slavery in parts of the Louisiana Purchase north of 36°30' north latitude. Lands considered closed to slavery since the Missouri Compromise of 1820 were now opened to that controversial institution. Popular sovereignty angered abolitionists in both the Whig and the Democratic parties, for it apparently meant that Congress had relinquished its right to prohibit slavery in the territories. In response, the Jackson convention adopted a free-soil platform and created a new political coalition called the Republican party. Over the next thirty-five years it was this new party that also constantly played the role of antagonist against the Mormons.

In 1856 the Republican party made an impressive showing at the polls in its first national election. The campaign that year turned upon a catchy phrase linking polygamy and slavery as "twin relics of barbarism." Four years later the nation elected a Republican president, Abraham Lincoln, and, fearful of what he might do to slavery, the South left the Union. Secession touched off the Civil War, for President Lincoln believed that no state had the constitutional authority to withdraw, and he felt obligated, if necessary, to prevent this illegal act with military force.

Few Latter-day Saints left their isolated refuge in the Rocky Mountains to participate in the Civil War, but the dreadful battles caused them to remember Joseph Smith's 1832 prophecy on war and to wonder if the war foreshadowed the Millennium, when the kingdom of God would be fully established on the earth. The war did not trigger that anticipated climax, yet important changes swept the nation in the postwar reconstruction era and some, including a powerful reforming zeal, had a direct effect on the history of the Saints. The main objective of the radical Republican reformers was to restructure the South politically and socially, and though it was not achieved at that time, the goal was full civil and political rights for the freed blacks. Among the other institutions challenged by the reformers was the Latter-day Saint practice of plural marriage. It was a Republican president who signed the first anti-polygamy bill in 1862 and Republican congressmen who spearheaded the political campaign against the Church that lasted until 1890.

While defending themselves against intrusions, the Saints in these years were influenced by other affairs in the expanding nation. In their mountain haven they found themselves peculiarly fitted to profit economically from the continuing westward movement. In the 1850s they provided goods and services for California-bound emigrants, and later sold agricultural products to adventurers in nearby mining towns. They even profited from the unwanted presence of federal troops sent to Utah in 1857–58 and again during the Civil War.

Completion of the transcontinental railroad in 1869 changed economic patterns and institutions in the nation and among the Saints. For the United States, coast-to-coast travel and the more rapid shipment of goods between East and West generated an economic revolution. It increased settlement of the plains states, filled in other areas, and stimulated industrial development. For the Saints, it meant an end to their unrealized goal of economic self-sufficiency and fostered instead a strengthening of ties with the national economy. The Saints participated directly in constructing the railroad and profited through investments in related enterprises. The arrival of the iron horse also hastened immigration, an important element in their continuing efforts to build Zion in the tops of the mountains.

The half-century under territorial government in Utah was generally a time of defensiveness for the Saints. Very early they confronted an American army that they mistakenly thought was sent to drive them from their homes. The tone of their public preaching during these years was one of indignation toward their detractors. Their economic activities were often designed to strengthen them against the growing "gentile" influence within the boundaries of their western commonwealth. Through it all, the ultimate goal of the Saints continued to be building the kingdom of God on earth in preparation for the coming Millennium; if anything, their millennial expectation increased over the years. The Saints also continued their determination to create an ideal and exemplary community, a Zion that would convince impartial observers of the strength and goodness of the Latter-day Saint way of life.

As the century drew to a close, the Saints reached a compromise with the federal government that seemed satisfactory to all. The sanction of plural marriage was abandoned as church policy, and the long-sought goal of statehood, which meant local self-government without the interference of federal overseers, was finally achieved. Forty years of important accomplishments through a period of watchful defensiveness prepared the Saints and the Church at the end of the century for a new era of more rapid growth and a more friendly relationship with their American neighbors.

In the National Spotlight, *1857–1863*

Thirty miles southwest of Salt Lake City lies the tiny settlement of Fairfield. Just west of town is a military cemetery with eighty-four graves, almost incongruous against its isolated desert background. To the casual visitor it is hard to believe that this was once the location of the third largest city in Utah. The military base, Camp Floyd, housed three thousand American soldiers, and the satellite town of Fairfield accommodated seven thousand civilians. Today the cemetery stands as a desolate symbol of the unhappy consequences of misinformation, misunderstanding, and miscalculation.

The years between 1857 and 1863 were, indeed, years of tragic misunderstanding. The Mountain Meadows Massacre, which contributed to the distorted image of the Saints throughout the nation, was the result of imprudent words and actions by certain California-bound travelers and overzealous responses from a few Latter-day Saints. The wasteful military expedition to Utah in 1857 was the result of poor information and lack of investigation by the president of the United States, and the unfortunate soldiers spent a freezing winter in Wyoming because the Mormons misinterpreted their mission. Within ten short years after their exodus from the United States, the Saints once again realized that their place of refuge was not a place of isolation, and their efforts to build the kingdom would have to be conducted in the presence of others, under the watchful eye of the nation.

The "Mormon Question" in National Politics

In the distorted reports that reached the American public in the 1850s, two themes stood out: the Mormon belief in plural marriage and the firm control of the government of the Territory of Utah by Church leaders. Both practices seemed to conflict with traditional Amer-

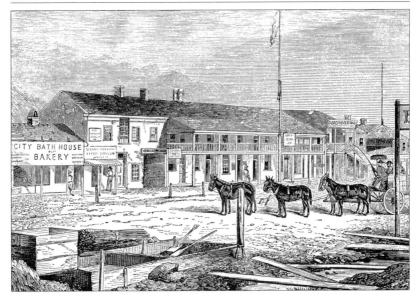

Evidence of new construction and varied economic activity can be seen in this portrayal of Salt Lake City's Main Street. The engraving appeared in Richard Burton's book, City of the Saints *(1861).*

ican values. Many people considered plural marriage a violation of Christian morality; it seemed impossible to them that Mormon women who entered it could accept the principle without coercion, that good men could entertain the thought of more than one wife, and that the reason for the practice was religious commitment rather than moral depravity. Critics saw church influence in territorial affairs as the antithesis of American political pluralism, and they could not believe the system would produce anything but political tyranny. It was hardly surprising that the Mormon question entered national politics in the 1850s.

It was not a major question, but it was present, and the national political climate seemed right to consider it. This was the decade in which the so-called Know-Nothing party became temporarily important by spreading ill-founded rumors of a conspiracy by Catholics to take over America and by charging that immigrants threatened the American way of life. Even though the party never turned its attention officially to the Saints, the charges of murder and subversion that it made against Catholics and aliens were strikingly similar to the irresponsible indictments others were making against the Saints. The fact that Mormon society consisted heavily of immigrants made the charges even more plausible to those who sympathized with the Know-Nothings.

More significant was the involvement of the Mormon question in the national presidential campaign of 1856. It was tied to the bitter debate over slavery and popular sovereignty, which would soon drive the nation into civil war. Defenders of slavery believed not only that each state was fully sovereign and therefore had the right to decide for itself on the issue of slavery, but also that Congress should positively protect slavery in the territories. A compromise, adopted in forming the territories of Kansas and Nebraska in 1854, was the idea of popular sovereignty. This allowed the people of a territory to decide the issue of slavery for themselves, though it was unclear at what point they could decide: when they were ready for statehood, or anytime previously. When the opponents of slavery joined together in the newly formed Republican party with the goal of keeping slavery out of the territories, they used the Territory of Utah as a bad example of what might happen under popular sovereignty. If the people of a territory could pass legislation protecting slavery, even before their territory became a state, then the Latter-day Saints in Utah could practice their peculiar marriage system without congressional interference. The Republicans thus attempted to build upon anti-Mormon attitudes in order to foster their campaign against popular sovereignty and slavery.

In 1856 a number of antipolygamy resolutions appeared for the first time in Congress, and Utah made another bid for statehood. It did not take the Mormon delegates long to discover that this was the wrong time politically. That same year the Republican party entered its first national campaign and nominated the popular John C. Frémont as its presidential candidate. The party's official platform included a resolution that "it is both the right and the imperative duty of Congress to prohibit in the Territories those twin relics of barbarism — Polygamy and Slavery."

The Republicans lost the election, but the anti-Mormon activities of 1856 had an important effect. Forced to disclaim any partiality for the Saints, the new Democratic president, James Buchanan, felt under obligation to do something to clear both himself and his party from any lingering suspicion that they supported the Mormons in Utah.

Buchanan Sends the Utah Expedition

Shortly after his inauguration in March 1857, President Buchanan appointed Alfred Cumming of Georgia governor of Utah, to replace Brigham Young. At the same time, in the mistaken belief that the

Mormons were in rebellion against the government, Buchanan sent along a large military force to ensure the new governor's acceptance and authority.

The President's decision to send the Utah Expedition was based on misinformation fed to him by disgruntled federal officials who had left the territory. The most influential was W. W. Drummond, who had been appointed an associate justice of the Utah territorial supreme court in 1854 and had come into open conflict with the Saints almost immediately. He first attacked the jurisdiction of the probate courts, which the Saints considered their most important legal defense against attacks from their enemies, for it included jurisdiction in criminal cases. In addition, he joined other federal appointees in writing letters to Washington decrying the Church. In March 1857 he wrote a letter of resignation that probably became the most important factor in forming the Buchanan administration's image of the Church. Buchanan did not realize that, even as he was berating the Saints, Drummond's own conduct was far from exemplary. He had deserted his wife and children, for example, and had taken with him to Utah a prostitute who occasionally sat beside him in court. Even territorial chief justice John F. Kinney, another non-LDS federal appointee, urged Drummond's removal from office because he was immoral and "entirely unworthy of a place upon the bench."

Drummond's letter charged that the Mormons looked to Brigham Young, and to him alone, for the law by which they should be governed, and considered no law of Congress binding. Further, he claimed, there was a secret, oath-bound organization among male members of the Church created to resist the laws of the land and acknowledge no law except the priesthood. He also charged the Church with murder, destruction of federal court records, harassment of federal officers, and slandering the federal government. He concluded by urging the president to appoint a governor who was not a member of the Church and to send with him sufficient military aid to enforce his rule.

The image created by Drummond and others was both distorted and ludicrous. Some critics claimed that the Mormons were held virtually in bondage, unhappy with the rule of Brigham Young. They ignored the fact that each year a flood of immigrants poured into Utah, that only a trickle left, and that the Church certainly could not have held them long if very many really wanted to leave. The Saints were charged with harassing federal officials, yet in most cases those officials (such as Judge Drummond), whose appointments had been injudicious in the first place, actually were guilty of harassing the Saints. The Mormons were accused of disloyalty to the government and of promoting separatism, yet an impartial observer would have seen that their very actions belied such charges. They constantly appealed for statehood, and each July 4 they celebrated American Independence Day with an intense patriotism that would have been exemplary in any community. Like most other Americans, they often criticized officers of the government, sometimes in severe language, but they never criticized the Constitution or the form of the national government itself. Buchanan, however, did not look beyond the anti-Mormon reports that came to his desk. Twenty-five hundred officers and men were ordered to escort the new governor to the territory.

Buchanan blundered further; he failed to notify Brigham Young, governor of Utah Territory, that he was to be replaced or that a military expedition was on the way. When President Young learned of the approaching troops, therefore, he acted on the assumption that they had no legal authority to enter the territory and that, as governor, he must use the best means available to him of opposing them. The potential for conflict had not been greater for over a decade.

Buchanan issued his general orders on May 28, designating General William S. Harney as commander and ordering the troops to assemble at Fort Leavenworth, Kansas, to begin the march. It took time to make adequate preparations, for it was no easy matter to take that many men across the Great Plains, along with thousands of cattle and all the other food, supplies, and equipment they needed. Finally, on July 18, the first contingent left Fort Leavenworth.

Coincidentally, on that same date nearly six hundred miles to the west, three Latter-day Saints were leaving Fort Laramie on a hasty ride to Salt Lake City to inform the Saints that the expedition was on its way. Abraham O. Smoot, mayor of Salt Lake City, had taken the June mail to the states and along the way had noted signs of military activity and had seen several heavily laden government supply trains. At Independence he had talked to William H. Russell, a partner in the freighting firm of Russell, Majors, and Waddell, and learned that Russell's freight trains were hauling supplies to Salt Lake City for government troops. He also learned the disappointing news that the mail contract the Y.X. Company was depending upon had been canceled. Smoot and those with him, therefore, turned back toward Salt Lake City, disbanded the company stations along the way, and took along the company livestock. They also met Porter Rockwell, who was carrying the July mail eastward but, upon hearing the news, decided to go back with them. At Fort Laramie, Smoot, Porter Rockwell, and Judson Stoddard decided to push on with their news as fast as possible and, hitching two of their best horses to a small spring wagon, they raced the 513 miles to Salt Lake City in the incredibly short time of five days. Arriving on July 23, they found the city almost lifeless.

Brigham Young and twenty-five hundred Saints were camped nearly twenty-five miles away, at the head of Big Cottonwood Canyon where, the next day, they would celebrate with parades, brass bands, and many other festivities the tenth anniversary of the Saints' arrival in the valley. It no doubt seemed a bitter irony, then, that about noon on July 24, the day of the anniversary, the three weary travelers rode into camp and informed the Church leader of the approaching army. He had been anticipating something like this, and for weeks had been warning of possible conflict, so he was not surprised at the news. He waited until the celebration was over, however, then calmly announced it to the Saints that evening.

The Saints' reaction was just what might be expected. With no official word of the expedition's purpose, it was easy for most of them to believe that once again hostile forces would attempt to drive them from their homes. Recalling the persecutions of earlier years, the settlers easily accepted the rumor that spread among them, and many feared the worst. Sermons of Church leaders and editorials in the *Deseret News* did little to allay their fears, and for the next few months the spirit in Utah was one of indignant preparation for defense. The federal government, of course, was not bent on driving out the Mormons or even on beginning hostilities, although some of the soldiers harbored hatred of the Saints and were heard to brag of designs to rid the country of them permanently. This was not the expedition's purpose, however, and Governor Cumming was far from disposed to begin hostilities. But just as Buchanan's misunderstanding of the Mormon system led to sending the expedition in the first place, so Mormon misunderstanding of the army's mission created apprehension and led to elaborate military preparations in Utah.

On August 1 word of the approaching army was circulated to all units of the Nauvoo Legion, and immediately they began quiet but definite preparations for defense. Latter-day Saints were advised to save their grain, for an ample supply of food would be essential. In an effort to consolidate and strengthen the Saints should they have to defend themselves, Church leaders called home colonists who had gone to San

Bernardino, Carson Valley, and other scattered settlements. Missionaries also were called home. Finally, patrols of the Utah militia were sent out on the plains to protect, if necessary, the immigrants headed for Zion and to report on the progress of the federal troops. On one occasion two Mormon militiamen actually mingled with the troops, representing themselves as California immigrants. They heard firsthand the anti-Mormon braggadocio of some soldiers who claimed they were going to "scalp old Brigham." Such attitudes could only make the Mormons more apprehensive about the approaching confrontation.

As the expedition plodded westward, General Harney was detained in Kansas and his replacement, General Albert Sidney Johnston, was unable to catch up with his troops until early November, after all hope of making it into Utah before winter had disappeared. On July 28 Captain Stewart Van Vliet was sent ahead to make whatever arrangements were necessary to accommodate the troops in Utah, for no one expected at this point that the Saints would resist so strongly. He arrived in Salt Lake City on September 7.

Van Vliet was the first official contact regarding this expedition that Brigham Young and the Saints had received. They treated him kindly and with personal respect, but their attitude toward his approaching comrades was made clear. Previous experience persuaded the Saints that the government had only evil designs against them, and the surprised and frustrated captain found it impossible to convince them otherwise. They informed him that they had made their last retreat and were now prepared to fight to defend their homes. He attended Sunday services, heard emotional speeches, and saw the Saints raise their hands in a unanimous resolution to guard against any "invader." He returned to the army sobered, realizing for the first time that it would be impossible to obtain supplies or any other form of help from the Mormons in Utah. He feared the possibility of conflict if the army proceeded too boldly, and advised that it should not push into Salt Lake City that season.

Captain Van Vliet was an astute and observant officer, and his report demonstrated a clear understanding of what the Mormons were ready to do. Every person he interviewed told him the same thing—if the government should continue in its course, the Latter-day Saints were prepared to burn their homes, destroy their crops, and make Utah a desert before the troops arrived. They would take to the mountains and there defy any power that came. Further, Van Vliet predicted, the Saints would not resort to actual hostilities until the last possible mo-

Alfred Cumming, who replaced Brigham Young as governor of the Territory of Utah in 1858. (Church Archives)

ment. Rather, they would burn grass, cut up roads, and stampede army animals in an effort to delay the troops until snowfall made it impossible for them to proceed. The lateness of the season, he said, would then make it dangerous for the troops to force their way in, for snow was already falling at Fort Bridger, and it would soon fill up the mountain passes.

Van Vliet's predictions were completely accurate. On September 15 Brigham Young issued a proclamation that declared martial law in the Territory of Utah and forbade the entry of armed forces. He ordered the Nauvoo Legion to make itself ready for the invasion, and in nearly every Utah community defensive preparations were accelerated. In a letter to bishops and other leaders in the territory, Brigham Young and Daniel H. Wells, commander of the Nauvoo Legion, gave some significant instructions that demonstrated the spirit of their preparations.

They expected the "big fight" would take place in another year, and they were to be ready to lay to waste everything that would burn if hostilities actually occurred. They were to leave nothing for the army but, rather, were to "waste away our enemies and lose none."

Tragedy at Mountain Meadows

As if one source of trouble were not enough, the year 1857 brought a disaster that not only intensified national feelings against the Saints but was also a dreadful tragedy in its own right. The same week that Captain Van Vliet appeared in Salt Lake City to negotiate with the Saints, two hundred miles south a band of Indians and a few ill-informed and overzealous settlers murdered a company of emigrants on their way to California. Though the Church itself cannot be held responsible, the massacre at Mountain Meadows became a tragic stain on the history of these tense and difficult times.

The ill-fated Baker-Fancher company from Arkansas was only one of several groups of Americans migrating to California in search of new economic opportunities. It was not unusual that they should pass through Utah, and late in the season they took the southern route to avoid early snows in the Sierra Nevada. The Arkansas train, led by John T. Baker and Alexander Fancher, was the first to take this route in the 1857 season.

It was unfortunate that this group of emigrants should arrive in Utah during a time of unusual tension and high emotion. Because of the approach of Johnston's Army, nearly every able-bodied man in the territory had been mustered into the militia, and regular military drills were beginning. The Saints anticipated serious trouble, and they looked upon all strangers with suspicion. Normal trading activities had ground to a halt, for the Saints' efforts to preserve food meant that they would not sell it to outsiders. This was especially hard on the emigrant companies of that year, and it angered them. In southern Utah, priesthood leaders from Salt Lake City, especially Elder George A. Smith, had preached military preparedness and the possibility of conflict. The feeling ran to extremes among some local Saints, and Elder Smith noted in his report, even before he knew of the massacre, "There was only one thing that I dreaded and that was a spirit in the breasts of some to wish that vengeance for the cruelties that had been inflicted upon us in the States."[1] He realized that people were remembering the massacre of

---

[1]As quoted in Juanita Brooks, *The Mountain Meadows Massacre* (Norman: University of Oklahoma Press, 1962), p. 39.

the Saints in Missouri and the martyrdom of Joseph and Hyrum Smith. It would have been a tense situation for any outside party, but some of those attached to the Baker-Fancher company were overheard threatening the Saints and boasting that they had participated in the Missouri and Illinois outrages. Trouble began as soon as the migrants passed Salt Lake City, and the feelings of hostility intensified as they traveled south toward Cedar City.

Complicating the picture was the Indian problem in southern Utah. The Saints had been cultivating good relations with local Native Americans, but the relationship was by no means perfect. The Mormon-Ute Indian Walker War had ended only three years earlier. In addition, the Indians had few good feelings for the "Mericats," as they called non-Mormon travelers in the territory. At the same time the pending military "invasion" made it seem imperative to Mormon leaders that if fighting should break out, they must have the Indians on their side. Aware of the increasingly hostile feelings between the Saints and the "Mericats," the Indians perhaps felt less restraint as they began to raid emigrant companies, stealing their cattle and supplies. The southern Paiutes were hostile against the Baker-Fancher party, whom they accused of poisoning their springs and of giving them poisoned meat. They also threatened some of the small communities of the Saints, who felt themselves risking greater danger if they acted openly to restrain them.

The Arkansas company stopped at Mountain Meadows, but settlers in the area refused to sell them food. Frustrated, the migrants began to help themselves. The Indians attacked the party on September 7 and laid siege to the encampment for the rest of the week. John D. Lee, who had been working with the Indians as a farmer, was unsuccessful in his efforts to calm them. After a tense meeting of officials at Cedar City, a messenger was sent to Brigham Young on September 6 asking for advice concerning the emigrant train. President Young sent word back immediately by the same messenger, instructing the settlers of southern Utah to "let them go in peace."

The message arrived too late. An emigrant fleeing for help had been killed by local settlers, implicating the Saints in the attack. Therefore, without waiting for the messenger's return, local militia leaders in southern Utah ordered the destruction of the company. The Indians were to kill the women and older children, the militia the emigrant men. By the morning of September 11, all was in readiness. Agreements were made with the Indians, and on that tragic morning the militia decoyed the besieged emigrants from their encampment under the

In a spirit of reconciliation, descendants of victims and participants in the Mountain Meadows Massacre dedicated a memorial to the victims in September 1990. Joining hands in a symbol of unity and forgiveness are (from left) J. K. Fancher, Rex E. Lee, Roger V. Logan, Jr., and J. E. Dunlap. (Nancy Rhodes photograph, courtesy Daily Spectrum*)*

promise of protection. At a prearranged signal, both Indians and white militia turned on the company, and about 120 people were slain. When some militiamen refused to follow orders, the Indians did the work of destruction for them. Only eighteen children survived, and they were cared for in nearby communities until the U.S. military located and returned seventeen of them to friends or relatives.

When the affair was reported to Brigham Young, he was told simply that it was an Indian massacre. Only gradually did the truth filter out. A few local Church officials, suspected of having ordered the massacre in their capacities as militia leaders, were released from their church positions. Despite Brigham Young's encouragement to Governor Cumming to pursue a civil investigation, the territorial official declined. Twenty years later, John D. Lee was tried and executed for his part in the crime, but the others were never brought to justice.

When word of the tragedy reached the LDS settlements, there was only horror and disgust. None would condone the massacre, and even its perpetrators wept. Inevitably, there were also wider repercussions. Coming, as it did, while the Utah Expedition was marching toward the territory, the massacre only added fuel to the already inflamed public opinion against the Saints.

The Bloodless War

Johnston's Army, meanwhile, still without its leader, continued pushing westward. The temporary commander did not as yet even know the expedition's purpose. Mormon scouts hovered in the hills watching the movements of the troops and hearing threats from the soldiers about what they would do once they arrived in Utah. When the officers of Utah's Nauvoo Legion learned that the army intended to disregard Governor Young's proclamation forbidding its entry into the territory, they decided to enforce the order. About eleven hundred men were sent to Echo Canyon, east of Salt Lake City, on the most direct route into the territory. At a narrow point in the ravine they built stone walls and dug trenches from which they planned to act as snipers. They also loosened boulders that could easily be sent crashing down to damage and block the moving columns, and constructed ditches and dams in the valley that could be opened to send water across the army's path. There was no doubt about Mormon determination.

The most colorful and daring activities of the Mormon militia were the exploits of Major Lot Smith and his "raiders" on the plains of Wyoming. Had the circumstances been less serious, they would have been almost comic in effect. On the night of October 5, Smith and twenty of his followers rode up to a wagon train carrying freight for the army. Smith noted as he rode into the light of the campfire that he could not see the end of his line of troops, which made it appear that he had more men behind him than was actually the case. The captain of the wagon train was duly impressed when he was ordered to evacuate his men from the wagons. After taking enough supplies to outfit themselves and after providing a group of Indians with some canvas, flour, and soap from the train, Smith and his men set torches to the wagons and rode off into the night, leaving them ablaze. In all, fifty-two wagons in two wagon trains were burned that night, and the oxen and cattle accompanying them were driven off.

Such exploits succeeded so well in delaying the progress of the army that when General Johnston finally joined his command in November, he realized that it was too late to enter the valley and they must winter at Fort Bridger. By this time the army's situation was desperate. It took fifteen days to push thirty-five miles through storms and below-zero weather, cattle died by the hundreds, and the soldiers arrived at the fort only to discover that the Mormons had burned the wooden buildings. The stone walls were intact, however, and provided partial shelter for the winter, and the army had enough cattle and supplies to see it through. A major military engagement would have been impossible. Thus ended the only hostilities of the Utah War.

The Occupation

Back in the states the difficulties of the army were becoming known, and Buchanan was being severely criticized. He was chided in particular for sending the expedition without first thoroughly investigating the charges and for sending it so late in the season that it could not get through the mountains before snowfall. At this point Thomas L. Kane, a longtime and influential friend of the Saints, offered to go to Utah as a mediator, and his offer was gratefully accepted. It was a near-heroic journey for him. Unable to enter Utah through the mountains because of the heavy winter, he took a ship to Panama, crossed the isthmus, took another ship to southern California, and went overland through San Bernardino to Salt Lake City, arriving late in February 1858.

After persuading President Young that the Saints should let the new governor enter the territory unmolested, Kane traveled eastward through bitterly cold weather to Fort Bridger. He persuaded Governor Cumming to return with him to Salt Lake City without a military escort, assuring him that the Saints would accept him peacefully. When Cumming arrived he found that Kane was right, for he was treated with dignity and respect. He administered his office with tact and diplomacy and soon won the respect and confidence of the people.

Equal tact on the part of the President of the United States nearly a year earlier might have averted the unfortunate confrontation with the Saints altogether. The Saints still did not completely trust the army and, recognizing that military resistance would ultimately end in tragedy, they decided to adopt, if necessary, a scorched-earth policy. Even before Governor Cumming arrived they had begun preparations for a move south, and they organized themselves magnificently. Between the end of March and mid-May some thirty thousand settlers from Utah's northern towns moved south to the vicinity of Provo, leaving behind only enough men to care for fields and crops. If it appeared that the army intended to occupy their homes, these men were to set fire to them.

Thomas L. Kane,
friend of Brigham Young and the Mormons.
(Church Archives)

It was an extraordinary operation. As the Saints moved south they cached all the stone cut for the Salt Lake Temple and covered the foundations to make the site resemble a plowed field. They boxed and carried with them twenty thousand bushels of tithing grain, as well as machinery, equipment, and all the Church records and books. The sight of thirty thousand people moving south was awesome, and the amazed Governor Cumming did all he could to persuade them to return to their homes. Brigham Young replied that if the troops were withdrawn from the territory, the people would stop moving, but that they would rather spend the rest of their lives in the mountains than endure governmental oppression.

Momentarily at least, Brigham Young even entertained the possibility of a permanent exodus of the Saints from their Wasatch Front settlements to a new place of refuge further west. In the spring of 1858 he sent an expedition from southern Utah into the largely unexplored White Mountain region of what is now southwestern Utah and southeastern Nevada. Divided into two companies, under the leadership of George W. Bean and William H. Dame, the expedition explored this desolate, forbidding country in the hopes of finding a huge but isolated oasis where the Saints could establish another gathering place. By the time the leaders made their unfavorable report to President Young, peaceful negotiations were under way and the Church leader had long since abandoned any thoughts of permanent relocation. The expedition was not without significance, nevertheless, for it resulted in some important achievements in the exploration of the Great Basin, and demonstrated once again the Saints' willingness to follow their leader in whatever seemed necessary for building the kingdom.

Colonel Kane, meanwhile, ill from the months of difficult travel, took the overland trail eastward to report to President Buchanan. Before Kane arrived, Buchanan had decided to send a peace commission to the Saints, and on June 7 the two commissioners, Ben McCullock and Isaac Powell, arrived in Salt Lake City, carrying an offer of pardon if the Saints would reaffirm their loyalty to the government. The Saints were indignant at the idea that they needed to be pardoned, for they had never been disloyal, but they accepted it in order to establish peace. Thus "Buchanan's blunder," as people were beginning to call it, was effectively whitewashed by an unnecessary pardon carried by a peace commission following an army of occupation that never needed to be sent.

On June 26 the army entered Salt Lake City, which was almost ghostly quiet and deserted except for those left behind to set the torch to it if the troops did not respect Johnston's pledge to leave their property alone. That night the army camped on the banks of the Jordan River, and soon General Johnston began to erect a permanent base in Cedar Valley, west of Utah Lake. On June 30 the Saints were told they could go back to their homes. Brigham Young himself led the return.

The campaign had taken its toll, and most of the Saints were beset with poverty and frustrated by the confusing chain of circumstances that had interrupted their plans for building Zion. As Leonard Arrington has summarized the end of the Utah War:

> A decade and more of achievement and social independence, in the face of hostile nature and hostile humanity, had ended in poverty and disappointment. The picture of 30,000 pioneers trudging back to their hard-won homes, farms, and orchards, with their skimpy and ragged suits and dresses, driving their pigs and family cows, to the accompaniment of jeers from "the cream of the United States Army" would live long in the hearts and minds of the pioneer leaders. None would have dreamed that within three years Babylon itself would be engulfed in a terrible fratricide as the result of which the tables would be reversed: Soldiers would be pulled out of Utah leaving to the Saints the spoils.[2]

Johnston's Army remained in Utah for three years, until it was

---

[2]Leonard J. Arrington, *Great Basin Kingdom* (Cambridge: Harvard University Press, 1958), p. 194.

recalled because of the Civil War, and the occupation meant several things for the Saints. Their ten-year period of relative isolation was clearly at an end, for the army symbolized the fact that, for whatever reason, growing numbers of "gentiles" would come to live among them. At the same time, the supporting community of some seven thousand people in Cedar Valley, in addition to the soldiers, proved a definite advantage to the economy of the Saints, who found a market there for agricultural and other goods. In addition, when the army finally abandoned Camp Floyd in 1861 it provided a windfall for the Saints, as some four million dollars worth of surplus goods were sold for a fraction of their value. The blessing was mixed, however, for all the vices of civilization also were introduced and nurtured by the army and its satellite community.

The Saints and the Civil War

The retirement of Governor Cumming in 1861 was the result of America's greatest tragedy: the outbreak of civil war. Cumming was from Georgia, and when the southern states seceded from the Union, he felt it his duty to return to his native state. The same was true of General Johnston, who joined with the Southern Confederacy and was killed at the Battle of Shiloh in 1862.

The Saints viewed the American Civil War with mixed emotions. They were firm believers in the Constitution, and in general they supported the cause of a united nation. On the other hand, they saw in the dissolution of the union the fulfillment of Joseph Smith's December 1832 prophecy, in which he not only predicted civil war but also said that this ultimately would result in war being "poured out upon all nations." (D&C 87:3.) Some believed this meant that the Millennium was very close at hand, and that soon Christ would return to earth, the Saints would return to Zion, and the kingdom of God would be established and take precedence over all other governments. Such considerations made their attitude toward the war appear ambivalent.

Nevertheless the Saints had definite feelings about the political issues that divided North and South. Because of their own experiences with federal interference, they supported the idea of local sovereignty and therefore had some appreciation for the southern position. But they did not seriously consider supporting the Southern Confederacy, and they repeatedly affirmed their loyalty to the Union. It was significant that when Brigham Young was given the privilege of sending the first message from Salt Lake City on the newly completed transcontinental telegraph in 1861, he chose to say to the president of the telegraph company, "Utah has not seceded, but is firm for the constitution and laws of our once happy country." Acting Governor Frank Fuller wired President Lincoln the same day: "Utah, whose citizens strenuously resist all imputations of disloyalty, congratulates the President upon completion of an enterprise which spans a continent."

The first opportunity the Mormons had to demonstrate their loyalty to Lincoln came in 1862. With the federal troops gone from Utah, the overland mail and telegraph needed protection. Significantly, the president wired Brigham Young, who was no longer governor of the territory, authorizing him to raise a company of cavalry for ninety days' service along the southern Wyoming route. In response, a company of 120 men under the command of Major Lot Smith was raised to perform the service. Ironically, Major Smith, along with Daniel H. Wells and Robert T. Burton, had only five years earlier led forces against the federal troops as officers in the territorial militia; now they were serving the government.

But the citizens of Utah went even further, for in 1862 they made their third attempt to gain statehood. They chided their critics by pointing out that, while many states were trying to leave the Union, they were trying to get in.

The statehood petition was denied but, in the meantime, a constitution was drafted for the proposed State of Deseret and the people elected a full slate of officers, with Brigham Young as governor. These men actually continued to meet for several years and, as they were also members of the territorial legislature, the decisions they made as a "ghost" government of Deseret usually became law when the legislature met officially. It was just such unusual political activity that continued to arouse antagonism in Washington.

The Mormon militia guarded the mail route for only a short time. In October 1862 Colonel Patrick Edward Connor arrived in Salt Lake City at the head of the Third California Volunteers, who were ordered to take over the guard duty from the Mormons. The Saints were taken aback, first because this seemed to impugn their own ability, and second because the presence of Connor and his troops seemed to cast new doubt upon their loyalty. Connor believed the accusations of Mormon disloyalty and made it clear that one of his assignments was to keep them under surveillance. The Saints expected he would take his men to the post recently vacated by Johnston's Army, but instead he chose

Barracks at Fort Douglas, several years after its founding. (Church Archives)

a site in the foothills directly east of Salt Lake City from which he could look down on the capital city. This new military post was named Camp Douglas (later Fort Douglas). As a military officer Connor led his troops well and was later acclaimed for a battle against the Indians on the Bear River—in reality a massacre of innocents—but as an individual he joined with those who were doing all they could to force the Mormons to relinquish their influence in Utah and change their way of life.

In Washington, meanwhile, efforts at anti-Mormon legislation were finally successful when Congress passed the Morrill Anti-Bigamy Act of 1862. Applying specifically to the Territory of Utah, this act levied penalties against anyone practicing plural marriage, disincorporated the Church, and limited the value of real estate which it could hold to $50,000. Any amount of property above that figure could be confiscated by the government.

President Abraham Lincoln signed the bill on July 8 but did not push for its enforcement. He was fair-minded with regard to the Mormon question and tried to steer a middle ground between the Saints and their most vocal opponents. He expressed his feelings to one member of the Church in a manner typical of his good will. When he was a boy on a farm, he said, there was a great deal of timber that had to be cleared away. Occasionally they came to a log that was "too hard to split, too wet to burn, and too heavy to move," so they plowed around it. That, he said, is what he planned to do about the Mormons. "You go back and tell Brigham Young that if he will let me alone I will let him alone."[3] This attitude won him the respect of the Saints, and they genuinely mourned his assassination in 1865.

Some of Lincoln's appointees were not so impartial. Governor Stephen S. Harding continued to accuse the Saints of disloyalty, despite their continued protests against such charges. When Harding and two federal judges attempted to set aside the powers of the probate courts and the territorial militia, the Saints finally petitioned the president for their removal. Attempting to be fair, Lincoln replaced the governor, but to placate non-Mormons he also removed the one judge the Mormons considered their friend, John F. Kinney, and territorial secretary Frank Fuller. Harding's replacement, Governor James Duane Doty, promoted Lincoln's policy by showing genuine impartiality, and thus gained the Saints' friendship and support.

But the Church Goes On

Despite the stress and strain, the troubles and excitement, and the continuing challenges to their goals and aspirations, the lives of the Saints went on. Immigrants continued to arrive each year, though their numbers diminished during the Civil War. The handcart pioneers came until 1860, eager and enthusiastic to join the Saints in a home they had never seen. Even though the problems they might confront were known to the immigrants before they left their native lands, the spirit of gathering to Zion remained firm. The converts fully believed that they were on the Lord's errand in trying to build a righteous kingdom in the West. The spirit is well illustrated in the "Handcart Song":

> Ye saints who dwell on Europe's shore
> Prepare yourselves for many more,
> To leave behind your native land,
> For sure God's judgments are at hand.
> For you must cross the raging main
> Before the promised land you gain
> And with the faithful make a start
> To cross the plains in your handcart.
> *Chorus:*
> For some must push and some must pull

---

[3]This and other anecdotes are found in George U. Hubbard, "Abraham Lincoln as Seen by the Mormons," *Utah Historical Quarterly* 31 (Spring 1963): 91–108.

LDS missionaries in Echo Canyon east of Salt Lake City, in 1867. (C. W. Carter photograph, Church Archives)

As we go marching up the hill;
So merrily on our way we go
Until we reach the Valley-o.[4]

The Saints continued to send missionaries abroad, even though in 1857 they were temporarily called back because of the impending conflict with federal troops. In Europe some areas were left largely to the management of local leaders between 1858 and 1860. Swedish-born Carl Widerborg, for example, presided over the Scandinavian Mission during these two years, and in 1858 reported over a thousand baptisms. In 1860 Elders Amasa M. Lyman, Charles C. Rich, and George Q. Cannon of the Council of the Twelve were appointed as the presidency of the European Mission. The result was an impressive number of new converts and emigrants to America. As in earlier years, missionary work was most successful in Great Britain and in the Scandinavian countries. The missionaries were barred from France in 1864, and the French Mission was not reorganized until nearly fifty years later.

More than four hundred missionaries were sent out between 1855 and 1864, most of them going to European countries. They were re-

---

[4]Thomas E. Cheney, *Mormon Songs from the Rocky Mountains* (Austin, University of Texas Press, 1968), pp. 64–65.

sponsible for paying their own way, and usually traveled without purse or scrip, relying on the people they met for sustenance. Few missionaries had means to support themselves, and often they left wives and families at home, depending on the priesthood quorums to help provide for their needs. In 1857 seventy-six elders left from Salt Lake City and pushed handcarts as far east as Florence, Nebraska. If the converts could come west by handcart, why shouldn't the missionaries use them going east? On the first night out Elder Phillip Margetts wrote a song that poignantly caught the spirit of how the missionaries viewed themselves:

No purse no script, they bear with them, but cheerfully they start
And cross the plains a thousand miles, and draw with them a cart.
Ye nations list! The men of God, from Zion now they come,
Clothed with the Priesthood and the Power, they gather Israel home!
Chorus
Then cheer up ye Elders, you to the world will show,
That Israel must be gathered soon, their oxen are too slow.
. . . .
Some folks would ask, Why do you start with carts, come tell I pray?
We answer: When our Prophet speaks, the Elders all obey;
Since Brigham has the way laid out that's best for us, we'll try,
Stand off ye sympathetic fools, the handcarts now or die.[5]

In general, the Saints were an amazingly united people but, just as in Nauvoo, there would always be those who disagreed, and some would even claim that they had been called of heaven to instruct the leaders. Such a man was Joseph Morris, who wrote to Brigham Young in 1857 claiming authority to be prophet, seer, and revelator to the Church. President Young decided that the best course was simply to ignore such claims. In 1860 Morris began promoting his revelations in earnest and a few people believed him. The following year Morris and seventeen followers were excommunicated, but this made little difference. Morris soon began to prophesy that the second coming of Christ would occur late in 1861. His followers joined him at a place called Kingston Fort near the Weber River south of Ogden to await the event, and even took his advice not to plant or harvest crops. Several times between December 1861 and February 1862 Morris announced specific dates for the advent of the Savior, and with each disappointment he would receive explanatory revelations and predict another date. Several hundred persons

---

[5]*Mormon Songs from the Rocky Mountains*, p. 67.

remained loyal to him, even though his prophecies were unfulfilled and they were suffering shortages of food and inadequate housing. Finally, when one dissenter tried to leave the group with his property, he was caught and held prisoner by Morris and his followers. Chief Justice Kinney then issued a warrant for the arrest of Morris and some of his lieutenants and, when they refused to submit, a posse led by Robert T. Burton was sent to capture them. The unhappy result was that Morris, determined never to surrender, called his followers to take up arms and follow him even to death. Shots were fired, and Morris and three of his disciples were killed. The remainder settled at Soda Springs, Idaho, and later in Montana.

Visitors among the Saints

Although disgruntled politicians and businessmen sought to undermine the image of the Church, other visitors to Utah were impressed quite differently. On the one hand, few critics were as opinionated as Mrs. Benjamin G. Ferris, who arrived with her husband in October 1852. Ferris had been appointed secretary of the territory, but in less than a year he and his wife were gone. Both published stinging denunciations of the Saints. In Mrs. Ferris's book, published in 1856, she could say nothing kind about any of them, but described the Mormon capital as full of "wretchedness, abominations, and crimes."

An opposite point of view came from Elizabeth Cumming, wife of Governor Alfred Cumming. Like her husband, she took time to try to understand the Saints and developed great sympathy for them. In one candid letter she told her sister that although her husband did not like Mormonism, he liked the Mormons; their courage, intellect, and "admirable horsemanship" he had never seen equaled. She described the Church leaders as polished in their manners and able to conduct interesting conversations. The Mormon community, she said, was peaceable and well disposed. After several months in Utah she had never heard noise or oaths in the street and had seen only one Mormon man intoxicated. Of the women she said, "The Mormon ladies talk a great deal about their religion. They live it. They feel it. Every act almost of their lives is Mormonized. They talk much of their happiness in having found the only true gospel."[6]

Other visitors also came – some of special note in both America

---

[6]Letter reproduced in Mulder and Mortensen, *Among the Mormons*, pp. 303–15.

and Europe. In 1855 Jules Remy, a French botanist, and Julius Brenchley arrived in Salt Lake City for a month's stay. Remy published his observations in Europe in 1860, and while the book was critical of the Mormons in some respects, in general it was more friendly than accounts by many Americans. Remy gave a particularly interesting description of an October conference meeting. The Saints were still meeting in the Bowery, and the travelers were invited to sit on the stand with Church leaders:

> Everywhere were to be seen rustic wagons, drawn by mules, oxen, or horses, going on fast or slow, and filled with Saints of both sexes, whose costume—varied without any attempt at show, picturesque in its simplicity—would have attracted the pencil of an artist. . . . At each meeting, the religious exercises began as soon as the president announced that the business of the day was to begin. Then the choristers and band belonging to the choir executed a piece of one of our greatest masters; and we feel bound to say that the Mormons have a feeling for sacred music, that their women sing with soul, and that the execution is in no notable degree surpassed by that which is heard either under the roof of Westminster, or the frescoes of the Sistine chapel. The music finished, the officiating priest extemporizes a prayer, often long enough, in which he returns thanks to God for his mercies, and makes known to him the wants of his people. At the end of the prayer all the faithful respond "Amen." Then the choir sing a hymn, after which one or more sermons follow.[7]

Another notable visitor was Richard Burton, a famous world traveler who arrived in 1860 and later published a book entitled *The City of the Saints*. It was sympathetic toward the Mormons and became the century's most widely read travel book about them.

One of the most instructive pieces of contemporary observation came from an ordinary soldier who arrived at Camp Floyd in 1858. His name has not been preserved, for he signed his letters to the Philadelphia *Daily Evening Bulletin* simply "Utah." But his observations on some aspects of Mormon society poignantly revealed to eastern Americans a side of the Mormons they had seldom read about.

On the way to Camp Floyd, "Utah" and his company passed through Provo Canyon, where they took a road the Saints had built.

---

[7]Significant portions of this are reproduced in Mulder and Mortensen, *Among the Mormons*, pp. 279–80.

Salt Lake City, 1865. On Temple Square the foundation of the temple, the old Tabernacle, and the pillars of the new Tabernacle can be seen.

Without exception, the young soldier reported, it was the best piece of road he had seen since Fort Leavenworth. "The builders had great difficulties to overcome, but notwithstanding the narrowness of the passage, the hardness of the rock and the almost perpendicularity of the mountainsides, they succeeded in making a road fit at any time for a railroad track." There could be little better tribute to the pioneer skill and industry of the Saints. He described them as very friendly, and endorsed their criticism of Judge Drummond. As he traveled to Utah he was determined to reveal all the evils of the Mormon people he had heard so much about. After being among them for a while, however, he could only say: "Uncle Sam had not a more faithful, loyal, liberty-loving people within his proud domains than they; and from my association with them I am convinced that they are not liable to the charge of false pretense. Some of the more ignorant and bigoted of the soldiery are continually berating them, calling them all manner of hard names, and telling what they 'would have done if the Mormons hadn't caved in!' but the thinking and intelligent portion (a very small minority, I am sorry to say), appreciate their worth and treat them accordingly." Then, writing of a local bishop for whom he sometimes worked on the side, "Utah" reported, "Last Sabbath I heard him preach one of the most eloquent and powerful sermons it has ever been my lot to listen to. . . . There was nothing of fanaticism or bigotry in his address, but an earnest heart-stirring appeal to all to rally around the up raised standard of Jehovah, and fight the good fight. . . . And when

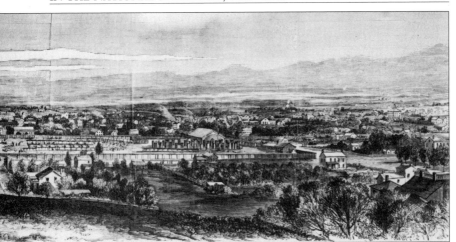

The engraving is from a photograph by Savage and Ottinger. (Church Archives)

he prayed it was not for the success of Mormonism or the glory of 'our Church,' but for all mankind, be they what they may. Had you heard him, you would have agreed with me that those who rant about the ignorance, bigotry and fanaticism of the Mormons are merely slanderers of the lowest grade."[8]

The years from 1856 to 1862 were indeed years of stress and trial for the Latter-day Saints. Most of them lived their religion well, and impressed those who observed them, but a few sometimes made mistakes that marred the Church's public image and acceptance. The period was one of mutual misunderstanding and misinformation between the Saints in Utah and the government in Washington. As a result, these years saw Brigham Young replaced as governor, the morality and loyalty of the Saints drawn into question nationwide, an army dispatched to Utah, thirty thousand Saints leaving and preparing to burn their homes if the invasion took place, a brutal massacre by a handful of overzealous Saints, and a second military unit occupying the territory at the beginning of the Civil War. Yet the Church not only survived but continued to grow. Its isolation, however, was ending, and ensuing years would see the Saints respond with redoubled efforts to build a kingdom that could not be shaken in either its spiritual strength or its economic and political influence.

---

[8]Harold D. Langley, ed., *To Utah With the Dragoons and Glimpses of Life in America and California* (Salt Lake City: University of Utah Press, 1974), pp. 91, 101–2.

CHAPTER 10

Challenges and Cooperatives, *1864–1872*

As the American Civil War drew to a close, the Latter-day Saints had reason for being optimistic that at last they could work to build the kingdom in relative peace. Abraham Lincoln had treated them impartially, and the Church was beginning to adopt economic policies designed to achieve a greater degree of self-sufficiency.

The coming of the transcontinental railroad, however, brought important changes to Zion. It led the Saints into new economic programs, was instrumental in introducing renewed political and judicial crusades against the Church, and was the catalyst for the outbreak of a rash of religious challenges in the heart of the kingdom itself. Nevertheless, the spiritual strength of the Saints and the dynamics of the Church meant continued growth in numbers and a strengthening of the organization. Total membership in the decade following 1860 grew from approximately 80,000 to 110,000 and the number of missionaries almost doubled.

Continuing the Quest for Economic Self-Sufficiency

During the 1860s the Saints continued to work toward economic independence, which was just as much a spiritual objective as it was a temporal one. Building the kingdom of God on earth, with a righteous people ready to meet the Savior when he came again, was their ultimate goal, and creating a self-sufficient society in the Great Basin, where they could worship the Lord and practice their religious principles in peace, was an essential element of that goal. As Brigham Young declared in 1865, when he visited the Saints in several communities to encourage them in personal righteousness, self-sufficiency, and unselfish cooperation: "To build up the kingdom of God is our business; we have nothing else on hand."[1]

Brigham Young sought a self-sufficiency based primarily on agriculture, supplemented by manufacturing and trade, and not on the speculative mining booms that characterized other western settlements. For this reason he vigorously opposed the efforts of Colonel Patrick E. Connor, who encouraged his soldiers to prospect for precious metals in the mountains near Salt Lake City and tried to promote a mining boom. Ores bearing silver and gold were discovered southwest of the city in 1863, and the *Daily Union Vedette*, an anti-Mormon newspaper founded by Connor, actively promoted Utah mining opportunities. Connor hoped to attract enough non-Mormons to overwhelm the Saints at the ballot box and wrest control of the territory from them. His efforts failed to spark the anticipated rush, but Connor himself remained in Utah after his military discharge in 1866 and became a respected business leader.

Church leaders, meantime, were not opposed to all mining, for the development of some resources was important to their plans for economic self-sufficiency. A mission sent to Minersville in 1859, for example, produced large amounts of lead for use in molding bullets and mixing paint. Coal was also essential, and in 1860 settlers were sent to what is now Coalville on a coal-mining mission. This enterprise not only provided a substitute for scarce timber fuel but also helped hundreds of men find employment.

One of the most ambitious efforts to exploit and develop the natural resources of the region was the cotton mission, begun in 1861. Settlers were sent to St. George, in the southern area known as Utah's Dixie, with the hope of producing enough cotton for all the Saints. By 1864 the experiment was floundering but, determined to make it succeed, Church leaders furnished thousands of dollars in cash, merchandise, tools, and equipment. They also provided the settlers with a cotton factory, which began operation in 1869. It seemed, however, that every problem imaginable conspired to hamper the enterprise. Poor soil, grasshopper and cricket plagues, alternating floods and drought, and other difficulties caused some settlers to leave. Many of those who remained found other crops more profitable than cotton, and eventually it was alfalfa, which provided feed for livestock and better nutrients for the

---

[1]Brigham Young, summary of instructions given on his visit to Utah, Juab, and Sanpete Counties, June and July, 1865, *Journal of Discourses* 11: 115.

soil when crops were rotated, that revolutionized the agriculture of Dixie.

In the meantime, between 1865 and 1867 about two hundred families were called to establish three communities along the Muddy River, a few miles southwest of St. George. These agricultural missionaries were supposed to produce cotton and other farm products, such as molasses and figs. Unfortunately, they also had problems with the forces of nature, as well as with Native Americans, and these were compounded in 1870 when a government survey placed their settlements just outside the Territory of Utah. The Nevada government promptly assessed the surprised settlers back taxes, demanding payment in specie. But hard money was scarce, and in 1871 Brigham Young advised these Mormon farmers to abandon their claims, which they did.

Each of these activities was part of a major effort in the 1860s to develop the agricultural potential of southern Utah. Another was the calling of a group of Swiss immigrants to raise grapes and other fruits at Santa Clara, Utah, near St. George. These hard-working Saints soon developed a flourishing business in dried fruits and wine, which was sold in Utah as well as to outside settlements. Santa Clara wine was also used for the sacrament service in many wards until the practice was officially ended near the close of the century.

Also intended to bolster the agricultural colonies of Utah's Dixie was a plan to use the Colorado River for shipping. In 1864 Anson Call was called by Church leaders to locate a road from St. George to the Colorado River, where he was to build a settlement and establish a landing and warehouse. Call's Landing was founded in December 1865, about fifteen miles above the present site of Hoover Dam. According to the plan, ships steaming up the Colorado from a point 150 miles below Call's Landing would bring both immigrants and freight, which could travel via the Muddy River colonies to St. George and then to Salt Lake City. Little business was actually conducted on the route, and in 1869 the expensive enterprise was abandoned.

From one perspective, the history of these economic enterprises was a history of almost impossible dreams and successive failures. From another perspective, the failures generated positive by-products. St. George, Santa Clara, and other southern Utah settlements remained permanent communities for the Saints. Even though their economies developed in a different direction than planned, the towns in Mormon Dixie contributed to the widening of the physical perimeters of the

Latter-day Saint commonwealth. Brigham Young's plan for building a western Zion was not achieved in every detail, but without his vision the Saints would have achieved far less. From still another perspective the dream became a test of faith and a challenge to the Saints, who saw themselves as tools in the hand of God in building his kingdom on the earth. The trials of pioneering the hot, desolate country surrounding St. George, for example, at the expense of leaving well-established homes elsewhere, dramatically revealed not only their fortitude as pioneers but also their willingness to sacrifice personal ambitions because of faith in something larger than self.

The story of these settlements offers a rich treasure trove of pioneer tales, folklore, and songs that illuminate the settlers' spirit, dedication, disappointments, and sense of humor. In October 1861 John Pulsipher was called to the cotton mission:

> This news was very unexpected to me. Volunteers were called for at conference to go on this mission, but I did not think it meant me, for I had a good home, was well satisfied and had plenty to do.
>
> But when Apostle Geo. A. Smith told me I was selected to go I saw the importance of the mission to sustain Israel in the mountains—we had need of a possession in a warmer climate, and I thot I might as well go as anybody. Then the Spirit come upon me so that I felt to thank the Lord that I was worthy to go.[2]

A pioneer song written about 1870 jabs humorously at the hard life in St. George. One verse reads:

> The sun it is so scorching hot
> It makes the water siz, Sir,
> The reason why it is so hot
> Is just because it is, Sir.
> The wind like fury here does blow
> That when we plant or sow, Sir,
> We place one foot upon the seed
> And hold it till it grows, Sir.
> *Chorus:*
> Mesquite, soap root, prickly-pears and briars,
> St. George ere long will be a place that everyone admires.[3]

---

[2]As quoted in [Juanita Brooks], "The Cotton Mission," *Utah Historical Quarterly* 29 (July 1961): 207.
[3]*Mormon Songs from the Rocky Mountains*, pp. 114–15.

Eventually St. George became a lovely, viable community, set in a gorgeous red-hilled landscape with a beautiful white temple dominating the skyline. For a time it was almost a second headquarters of the Church, for Brigham Young loved it and during his later years spent most of his winters there.

In their drive for self-sufficiency the Saints seemed indefatigable, and despite some disappointments Brigham Young remained the incurable optimist. He began to decry the use of any items the Saints could not grow or manufacture themselves. "We can produce them or do without them," he exclaimed on one occasion. This attitude gave fresh emphasis to the nonuse of tobacco, another step toward more uniform compliance with the Church's health code.

To further promote husbandry, the Deseret Agricultural and Manufacturing Society was revitalized in the 1860s. It immediately encouraged self-sufficiency with such products as cane sugar, molasses, flax, hemp, sheep, and silk. The society maintained its own experimental farm in Salt Lake City and went to great lengths to provide agricultural information to settlers in every Mormon town.

One especially interesting experiment was the attempt to establish a silk industry in Utah, which created the need for an abundance of mulberry trees. Silkworms hatched from just one ounce of eggs, for example, consumed as much as one hundred and twenty pounds of chopped mulberry leaves per feeding, eight feedings per day, by the time they reached maturity and were ready to spin their cocoons. As early as the mid-1850s, at Brigham Young's suggestion, immigrants were bringing mulberry seeds and silkworm eggs into Utah, and between 1865 and 1868 the Church leader personally directed transplanting some one hundred thousand mulberry trees throughout the territory. George D. Watt was called on a "silk mission" to spread the "gospel of silk" among the Mormons, but eventually it was the women who did most of the work. Zina D. H. Young, president of the Relief Society, was personally revolted at the sight of hordes of tiny, wriggling silkworms, but she nevertheless took seriously the mission given her by the President of the Church, learned sericulture, and crisscrossed the territory teaching other women. In 1875 she became head of the newly organized Deseret Silk Association, set up to dispense information on the subject. The women learned to nurture the worms, feed them (which included spending untold hours chopping up mulberry leaves), prepare sticks on which they would spin their cocoons, dry the cocoons, reel them into thread, and, ultimately, weave the thread into fine silk cloth.

The interior of the Provo Woolen Mills, taken some years after this cooperative enterprise was established. (C. W. Carter photograph, Church Archives)

The Relief Society sponsored silk projects in nearly 150 communities, and many lovely dresses, handkerchiefs, and other items were produced. In 1892 Elise T. Forsgren was called by Church leaders on a four-month mission to the World's Fair and won a gold medal for her silk reeling. The exhibit from Utah also won several other awards and, as a result, Emmeline B. Wells was asked to speak on sericulture before the National Council of Women. By the end of the century, however, it was clear that the silk industry was not really viable in Utah and it, too, succumbed to external competition.

The quest for economic well-being in the 1860s included development of trade with western mining communities. Products grown by the Saints were marketed in Colorado, Idaho, Montana, and Nevada.

Commerce with outsiders was not particularly encouraged, but when Mormon farmers participated in it anyway, the Church helped them regulate prices to ensure the highest possible return for their produce. After general conference each April and October, the leading farmers were invited to a price convention in Salt Lake City, where each pledged to support the established prices, eliminating hurtful competition. In 1866 these Church-sponsored conventions were succeeded by the Utah Produce Company, an organization that regulated the marketing of surplus products.

At the general conference of October 1860, John W. Young preached an unusual sermon on "the science of Ox-teamology," which inaugurated another part of the self-sufficiency program, the Church team trains. Every year but two between 1861 and 1868 the Church sent ox teams from Salt Lake City to the Missouri River where the teamsters, who were considered missionaries, sold Utah-produced goods and picked up immigrants. The result was a great boon to the Latter-day Saints, for transportation west became less expensive, food for the immigrants was provided from Utah rather than purchased in the East, and profits were made from goods sold. The Church trains brought more than sixteen thousand Europeans to Utah at a total cost of about $2.4 million, most of which was met by voluntary donations of labor, teams, and supplies. The enterprise was an outstanding example of the success of Church cooperative activity. The need for Church teams ended with the coming of the railroad in 1869.

Another example of Church cooperative enterprise was the Deseret Telegraph line. After the transcontinental telegraph was completed through Salt Lake City in 1861, the Church launched a program to construct auxiliary lines. Under priesthood direction, a five-hundred-mile system from north to south was completed in 1867, much of it by tithing labor, and in later years more lines were added. After its incorporation, the Deseret Telegraph Company was fully owned and controlled by the Church. The kingdom was growing, and a worthwhile communications network aided materially by directly connecting outlying settlements with headquarters.

The Black Hawk War

During all this time relationships between the Mormon settlers and Native Americans continued to fluctuate: sometimes friendly and at other times tense—even hostile, but with Brigham Young still reminding the Saints to avoid conflict whenever possible and to treat the Indians with kindness. The remaining tensions were largely a reflection of the larger story of Indian-American relations, and there seemed to be no way that Mormon settlers could totally avoid problems and actions similar to those of their contemporaries elsewhere.

From the perspective of the Indians, the coming of the whites also meant encroachment upon their traditional grazing, hunting, and gathering areas. It was a devastating clash of cultures, as fences, farms, towns, and white man's laws and customs were simply not compatible with Indian ways. From the standpoint of the new arrivals, the solution was seen in federal laws and treaties "extinguishing Indian title" to the land and requiring the Indians to move onto reservations. Conflict inevitably resulted as the Native Americans resented not only their loss of sustenance but also the loss of their ancestral homelands and their way of life.

In Utah, despite the peaceful efforts of the Mormons, the pattern was unavoidably repeated. In 1864 a reservation was created in Utah's Uintah Basin. In June 1865, Indian Superintendent O. H. Irish invited Brigham Young to attend treaty negotiations with the Utes at Spanish Fork, and it was President Young's prestige that persuaded the Indians that they should give up their lands and move to the reservation. The treaty was rejected four years later by the United States Senate, but in the meantime the Utes lost more territory, some began to move to the reservation, and all became even more destitute.

It is not surprising that hostilities broke out again, beginning in April 1865. Under the prodding of a Ute leader named Black Hawk (one of those who did not attend the June treaty), bands of Indians periodically raided Mormon settlements in central and southern Utah, mainly seeking food and stealing cattle and horses. It is estimated that between 1865 and 1867 they stole five thousand head of cattle and killed perhaps ninety settlers and militiamen. At the height of the raids some 2,500 men were enrolled in the territorial militia. Several Mormon towns and villages, including such major settlements as Richfield, Circleville, Panguitch, and Kanab, were abandoned. Hostilities did not abate until 1868, and occasional raids continued for another few years after that. Ironically, in 1870 Black Hawk himself toured several settlements, speaking to LDS congregations, asking forgiveness, and trying to explain his motives. It was the starvation of his people, he said, that forced the raids. In the end, the Utes gradually moved to the reservation,

The end of isolation: A Mormon wagon train meeting the newly completed Central Pacific Railroad near the Great Salt Lake. (Utah State Historical Society)

and the Black Hawk War was the final outbreak of hostilities against the Mormon settlements of Utah.

Defensive Economy: The Challenge of the Railroad

The economy of the United States was changing in the years following the Civil War, and one of the most significant symbols of change was completion of the transcontinental railroad in 1869. Consumer goods, mail, and passengers suddenly could go from coast to coast in days instead of weeks or months. Marketing of cattle and farm products was revolutionized as auxiliary lines expanded into all parts of the West. In addition, the railroad contributed greatly to the growth of goods processing, oil production, manufacture of consumer goods, and, in general, rapid industrialization. The tracks from east and west were joined at Promontory Summit in Utah, heralding not only an important economic milestone in America but also significant changes for the Saints in Utah and the West. As Church leaders contemplated what all this meant for the kingdom, they anticipated not only new challenges to Mormon self-sufficiency and isolation but also new opportunities for growth and profit. They would try to deal with both in appropriate ways.

Church leaders naturally were apprehensive that the railroad would bring a flood of non-Mormons who would undermine Latter-day Saint principles and attempt to destroy the Mormon way of life. It also appeared that Zion's economic self-sufficiency was in jeopardy, for an influx of cheap goods from the East could undercut local agriculture and industry and leave many Saints unemployed. The possibility also loomed that the railroad would stimulate a massive expansion of Utah mining.

Despite such potential problems, however, Brigham Young and other leaders welcomed the railroad. It would stimulate immigration by making it easier and cheaper to bring converts across the continent, and it would encourage other economic activities that, if properly controlled, could greatly improve conditions in the Great Basin. Said President Brigham Young in 1867:

> Speaking of . . . this railroad, I am anxious to see it, and I say to the Congress of the United States, through our Delegate, to the Company, and to others, hurry up, hasten the work! We want to hear the iron horse puffing through this valley. What for? To bring our brethren and sisters here.[4]

The anticipated arrival of the railroad was one reason for the organization in 1867 of the School of the Prophets, a confidential forum of leading high priests who discussed religious doctrines, economic policies, and political problems. Schools were formed in various communities, but the Salt Lake City school became the leading body.

Under the direction of the First Presidency, the School of the Prophets formulated plans to counteract the social and economic influence a rapid influx of non-Mormons might bring. One of its first projects was to sponsor a contract in the name of Brigham Young for construction of the railroad within the Territory of Utah. This would have the dual advantage of keeping out transient, possibly undesirable, workers and simultaneously providing employment and income for Latter-day Saint laborers. Contracts were signed with both the Union Pacific and the Central Pacific, and Mormon men either volunteered or were called to become railroad workers. In effect, it was another cooperative Church enterprise, and the men worked in ward groups. It was probably the most unusual situation in the history of western railroad building: the majority of the laborers were active Mormons, most of them refrained from swearing and drinking, there was no work on Sunday, and each

---

[4]*Journal of Discourses*, 12:54.

man paid a faithful tithe. Latter-day Saint workers joined in the festive ceremonies at Promontory Summit on May 10, 1869.

Church leaders also initiated construction of a connecting network of railroads within Utah. The Utah Central, Utah Southern, and Utah Northern were all completed in the early 1870s, thus linking Mormon settlements throughout the territory into the national transportation system. In each case the railroad was financed, at least in part, by private individuals who were prominent in the Church, and the profits went back to them. In reality, they acted in behalf of the Church, but because the Anti-Bigamy Act of 1862 had prohibited the Church from owning more than $50,000 worth of property, it was necessary for the leaders (particularly Brigham Young) to carry much Church business in their private accounts.

Beautifully symbolic of what the Saints were trying to achieve were the dedication ceremonies of the Utah Central Railroad, which tied Salt Lake City to the national line at Ogden, on January 10, 1870. All the work had been done by Mormon labor. The last spike, driven at the ceremony, was made of native iron, and it as well as the steel mallet used by Brigham Young to drive it were engraved with the words "Holiness to the Lord." In his address to the fifteen thousand Saints attending the ceremonies, the President of the Church took the opportunity to emphasize the theme of self-sufficiency:

> Since the day that we first trod the soil of these valleys, have we received any assistance from our neighbors? No, we have not. We have built our homes, our cities, have made our farms, have dug our canals and water ditches, have subdued this barren country, have fed the stranger, have clothed the naked, have immigrated the poor from foreign lands, have placed them in a condition to make all comfortable and have made some rich. We have fed the Indians to the amount of thousands of dollars yearly, have clothed them in part, and have sustained several Indian wars, and now we have built thirty-seven miles of railroad.[5]

A potential problem related to the coming of the railroad concerned landholdings. Even though the Saints had occupied Utah for over twenty years, they could neither purchase nor homestead their land legally without a federal survey, and no federal land office existed in the territory. The coming of the railroad made a land office essential, if only

[5]*Deseret News*, January 11, 1870, as cited in Arrington, *Great Basin Kingdom*, pp. 272–73.

to distribute federal land grants to the railroad companies. Anticipating possible conflicts of interest, the School of the Prophets set up a committee to work with government authorities and the settlers. Eventually most Mormon land titles were confirmed.

The Saints became increasingly convinced that the continuing influx of "gentiles" could undermine them and their way of life, and they sought ever new ways to defend themselves against such a possibility. This was well illustrated at the October conference of 1868, when several leading brethren discussed the potential threat and urged the Saints to new cooperation. Brigham Young reminded them that they were building both a spiritual and a temporal kingdom; then, in the rather forceful language appropriate to the day, he asked: "But if this is the Kingdom of God and if we are the Saints of God . . . are we not required to sustain ourselves and to manufacture that which we consume, to cease our bartering, trading, mingling, drinking, smoking, chewing and joining with all the filth of Babylon? . . . We want you henceforth to be a self-sustaining people. . . . What do you say brethren and sisters? All of you who say that we will be a self-sustaining people signify it by the show of your right hands." Everyone in the new Tabernacle raised his or her hand, confirming the beginning of a renewed drive for economic cooperation. "Let us govern our wants by our necessities," he said toward the end of his address, "and we shall find that we are not compelled to spend our money for nought. Let us save our money to enter and pay for our land, to buy flocks of sheep and improve them, and to buy machinery and start more woolen factories. We have a good many now, and the people will sustain them."[6]

President George Q. Cannon also warned the Saints of the threat to their institutions, then asked: "Will we sustain the Kingdom of God or will we not? Will we sustain the priesthood of God, or will we not? This power of which I have been speaking, or more properly, this antagonistic class in our midst, flatter themselves with the idea that when it comes to the test this people will desert their leaders and cleave to something else. This is an illusory hope. The Latter-day Saints know too well the source of their blessings."[7]

The result was a new cooperative movement, directed largely by the School of Prophets and avowedly defensive in nature. In addition to the railroads, the Saints continued cooperatively to build fences,

---

[6]*Journal of Discourses*, 12:284–89.
[7]*Journal of Discourses*, 12:290–91, 297.

At right is one of many Mormon-owned stores that became part of the ZCMI chain during the cooperative movement of the 1860s. John K. Trumbo, non-Mormon businessman who responded bitterly to Mormon economic policies, seems to be lampooning Brigham Young's religious-economic influence in the sign above his door. (C. W. Carter photograph, Church Archives)

canals, roads, and public buildings in their various communities. Also, more emphatically than at any time since Missouri, Church leaders stressed cooperative stores and factories rather than individual enterprise, and before long nearly two hundred separate cooperatives were founded in the Mormon commonwealth.

The most controversial part of the plan was the proposition that Latter-day Saints should not trade with outsiders. If they were to keep the kingdom from being too strongly influenced or controlled by non-Mormon merchants, they must support their own cooperative institutions, and from 1868 until 1882 Church leaders encouraged the Saints to boycott "gentile" merchants and trade only with Mormon-owned establishments. In retrospect this may seem harsh and unfriendly, but most Latter-day Saints genuinely felt that incoming non-Mormons posed a threat to their economic well-being, and there was evidence that some outside merchants actually were trying to undermine the Church. At the very least, then, they felt justified in refusing to contribute to the profits of such people.

The program of cooperative buying and selling revolved around a parent company organized in October 1868 as Zion's Cooperative Mercantile Institution (ZCMI), originally a wholesale house. Its first supply of goods came from leading Mormon merchants, who were encouraged to subscribe their goods in exchange for cash or stock in the new company. Stock was sold widely to others in the territory, making the ownership of the company broadly based. The plan was to establish a system that would benefit the LDS community as a whole, rather than just a few private wholesalers. When it began to make a profit, the company tithed its profits first and then distributed the rest to the stockholders.

Cooperative retail stores were soon established in nearly every community in the territory. The parent institution did not own these outlets, but they all purchased their goods from it, and it maintained control over prices. These retail outlets also absorbed the business of local Mormon storekeepers, paying either cash or stock, and they sold stock widely. Brigham Young expressed sympathy for Mormon retailers who thus went out of business, but he explained that it was for the larger good of all. He encouraged those with money to invest in other kinds of agricultural or manufacturing activities.

Both ZCMI and the local cooperatives expanded their operations by establishing cooperative manufacturing enterprises for boots, shoes, clothing, furniture, and other small items. They also promoted cooperative livestock herds and dairy activities, and they shared their products with each other, widely distributing the benefits of their specialties.

While only partially successful, the cooperative program was another dramatic demonstration of the Saints' determination to become self-sufficient. ZCMI itself was an outstanding financial success and became a permanent retail institution, but the various local outlets gradually declined as cooperatives. The controlling stock found its way into fewer and fewer hands, so the stores again assumed the flavor of limited individual enterprises. Finally, in 1882, President John Taylor opened the way for the growth of more privately owned retail stores by officially declaring an end to exclusive Church support of local cooperatives.

Other cooperative activities inaugurated during this period of defensive economic activity included an iron works in southern Utah, various cooperative textile factories, and a bank (Bank of Deseret).

Some Saints objected to economic regulation by the Church, and, unfortunately, the most extreme forms of objection led, as in earlier

Zion's Cooperative Mercantile Institution, Salt Lake City, about 1885. (C. R. Savage photograph, Church Archives)

days, to apostasy. The most vigorous opposition came from a group calling itself the New Movement, though better known as the Godbeites. Its founders, William S. Godbe and E. L. T. Harrison, were already involved in both doctrinal dissent and spiritualism. Their dissatisfaction with what they perceived as the Church's effort to control business in the territory only helped strengthen their dissent and direct it toward apostasy and excommunication. Godbe and Harrison were joined by a few other LDS businessmen and intellectuals who sided with non-Mormon businessmen in calling for a return to uncontrolled free enterprise in the territory and lauding the economic value of mining. The outlet for their opinions was the *Utah Magazine*, founded in 1868, which was succeeded by the *Mormon Tribune* in 1870. Its name was soon changed to the *Salt Lake Tribune*. Even one apostle, Amasa M. Lyman, joined the New Movement, but he and the other Godbeite leaders were excommunicated in 1869, and the movement was short-lived.

The Spiritual Kingdom: Growth and Development

While Church economic activities were designed primarily to strengthen the earthly kingdom of God, growth and development were also taking place in many other ways. Five new stakes were organized in Utah in 1868 and 1869, bringing the total to nine. Missionary work continued to expand as 417 new missionaries were sent out between

1865 and 1869, compared with 222 during the previous four-year period. New missions were opened in the Sandwich Islands (Hawaii), the Netherlands, and the Eastern States, though the latter was shortly closed.

The mission to Hawaii was of particular interest. It had been opened earlier, but the missionaries were called home in 1857 because of the Utah Expedition. Not long after that, the eccentric Walter Murray Gibson, a traveler and soldier of fortune, arrived in Salt Lake City and was converted to the Church. When he suggested that the Saints move to the islands of the East Indies, Brigham Young rejected the idea. But, impressed with Gibson's enthusiasm, the President sent him alone to the Pacific to do missionary work.

Gibson arrived on the Hawaiian island of Lanai in July 1861, and soon his ego and flamboyancy overwhelmed whatever understanding he may have had of how the Church should operate. Far exceeding the bounds of his instructions, he soon gained virtual control of the native Saints, proclaimed himself "Chief President of the Islands of the Sea and of the Hawaiian Islands for The Church of Jesus Christ of Latter-day Saints," and began practices completely foreign to Church policy. He gathered the Saints at a six-thousand-acre plantation and set up an elaborate hierarchical system. He sold priesthood offices (some not even authorized in the Church, such as archbishop), wore a white robe, and even required the Saints to crawl in his presence. Apparently he planned eventually to unite all the Hawaiian Islands into one grand empire, with himself as king, by converting as many natives as possible and using his army to bring in the others.

Such unauthorized and irresponsible activity could not long go unchallenged. Some twenty-five native Saints finally wrote to headquarters in Salt Lake City, with the result that Elders Ezra T. Benson and Lorenzo Snow of the Council of the Twelve were sent to the islands, accompanied by Elders Joseph F. Smith, Alma L. Smith, and William W. Cluff. They excommunicated Gibson, and subsequently all his followers among the Hawaiian Saints deserted him. One helpful incident occurred when two of the elders walked on a certain rock, even though Gibson had warned that anyone who did so would be struck dead, for, he said, it was a sacred shrine. When they did not die, Gibson's prestige began to wane. Joseph F. Smith remained for a time as mission president, and under his direction the Church began to develop a plantation at Laie, which eventually became mission headquarters and the home of many native Saints.

The Sunday Schools were also revitalized in this era. The first Sunday School had been established in 1849 by Richard Ballantyne, but as the movement spread, each Sunday School was an independent unit with no central direction. By the 1860s Sunday School leaders were discussing the need for adopting a uniform system. In 1866 Elder George Q. Cannon began publishing the *Juvenile Instructor*, which eventually became the official Sunday School publication, and the next year a central, coordinating body known as the Parent Sunday School Union was formed. On August 2, 1872, Elder Cannon, a member of the Council of the Twelve, was selected as general superintendent of the Deseret Sunday School Union, and a unified churchwide Sunday School program was inaugurated. Intended mainly for the benefit of young people, it was not until the twentieth century that the Sunday School held adult classes on a churchwide basis.

During this era other auxiliaries were either revitalized or initiated. The Women's Relief Society was reorganized in 1867, when Eliza R. Snow, secretary of the Nauvoo Relief Society and perhaps the most influential woman in pioneer Utah, became the president. In a way, the new emphasis on Relief Society work was part of the reaction to the coming of the railroad, for in addition to aiding the poor, the sisters were asked to assist in the operation of cooperative stores and to support home industry. They were also encouraged to be frugal and avoid buying luxuries.

The Relief Societies helped stimulate the organization of "retrenchment" societies among the young ladies. This movement began in 1869, when Brigham Young called together his wives and daughters and gave them instructions in economy and modest living. Concerned about the extravagance and vanity that seemed to be taking hold, he wanted to bring about a reform and to have his own daughters set the example. The following year Mary Isabella Horne was assigned by President Young to assist Eliza R. Snow in forming Retrenchment Associations. Members participated in all kinds of practical economic and cultural activities. In 1872 they began publication of the *Woman's Exponent*, which disseminated news, practical information, and editorials of the women's viewpoints throughout the territory.

Special emphasis was placed on fashions for two reasons. Brigham Young wanted the women to cease buying from outsiders in order to stimulate self-sufficiency, but he also wanted them to learn frugality. He especially decried the vanity and extravagance that led to showy

Four of the leading women of Zion (left to right): Zina D. H. Young, Bathsheba W. Smith, Emily P. Young, and Eliza R. Snow. (Church Archives)

dresses made of several yards of material. One 1872 sermon colorfully portrays some of his practical instructions:

> If I were a lady and had a piece of cloth to make me a dress, I would cut it so as to cover my person handsomely and neatly; and whether it was cut according to the fashion, or not, custom would soon make it beautiful. I would not have eighteen or twenty yards to drag behind me, so that if I had to turn around I would have to pick up my dress and throw it after me, or, just as a cow does when she kicks over the milk pail, throw out one foot to kick the dress out of the way. That is not becoming, beautiful or convenient — all such fashions are inconvenient. Take that cloth and cut you a skirt that will be modest and neat; that does not drag in the dirt nor show your garters; but cut it so that it will clear the ground when you walk.[8]

The young men also began to organize themselves for purposes other than priesthood and work. Several independent mutual improvement and literary societies sprang up in various LDS communities, but in 1875 Junius F. Wells was called by President Young to organize the young men on an official Church basis. The Young Men's Mutual Improvement Association was inaugurated on June 10 in the Salt Lake

---

[8]Quoted in Mulder and Mortensen, *Among the Mormons*, p. 388.

City Thirteenth Ward, and within a year it too had become a churchwide movement.

The growing strength of the Church was also symbolized by its building program. The most famous of the new edifices was the Salt Lake Tabernacle, begun in 1865 and sufficiently completed by October 1867 that it could accommodate the general conference. Finally dedicated in 1875, this unique structure was built largely under the direction of the Church's public works program. It became famous for its self-supporting dome, outstanding acoustics, and the fact that part of the construction was accomplished without metal nails. The original pipe organ, designed by Joseph H. Ridges, was built of native materials by Mormon craftsmen.

The first conference in the Tabernacle, which began on October 6, 1867, was in many ways a fitting representation of the faith, enthusiasm, and practical nature of the Saints. Crowds of people lined up outside long before the doors were opened, and when the conference began at 10:00 A.M. there were still hundreds unable to find seating. Several choirs sang at the conference services, which lasted four days. On Monday, October 7, President Brigham Young outlined several topics he wanted the speakers to deal with, and the sermons preached on that single day dramatically revealed the wide variety of concerns characterizing the lives of the Saints in the 1860s. One was the need to subscribe money to aid the Perpetual Emigrating Fund. Another was education, and the Saints were told to teach their children the ways of the Lord and to introduce both scriptures and phonetics into their schools. Young ladies were encouraged to study arithmetic, bookkeeping, and other aspects of business so they could tend stores and operate the telegraph offices, freeing men to labor in the canyons, build houses, work farms, and more fully support their families. Five hundred teams were requested to haul rock from Little Cottonwood Canyon for the Salt Lake Temple, and the Saints were told that they could prolong their lives best by living frugally and temperately. In addition, 163 missionaries were called to establish settlements in southern Utah.

Brigham Young's emphasis on learning was complicated by the presence of many immigrants who neither read nor spoke English. As early as 1853, in an attempt to simplify the language, the board of regents of the University of Deseret had appointed a committee to create a phonetic alphabet. The committee included Parley P. Pratt and Heber C. Kimball from among the General Authorities, and George D. Watt, a man skilled in shorthand, who transcribed many of the major ad-

This historic photograph, probably taken in the early 1870s, shows both the old and new tabernacles, as well as construction work taking place on the Salt Lake Temple. (C. W. Carter photograph, Church Archives)

dresses of Church leaders for the *Journal of Discourses*. Interest in the unique new Deseret Alphabet of thirty-eight characters was revived in 1868, when it was used for printing two readers. The following year Orson Pratt used it in publishing part of the Book of Mormon. Public interest was not widespread, however, and the experiment soon ended.

The Non-Mormon Religious Challenge

The Latter-day Saints could hardly hope to create their own religious society without some challenge from other churches. They were becoming even better known throughout the nation than they had been in the days of Joseph Smith, and ministers and missionaries offended by Mormon teachings (or by what they thought were Mormon teachings) would continue to attempt to reform them.

One of the most publicized challenges came from Dr. John P. Newman, chaplain of the United States Senate. In April 1870 he gave a sermon in Washington, D.C., against the practice of plural marriage, and in June he traveled to Utah, where he challenged Brigham Young to a debate. President Young refused to enter into such a public spectacle over what he considered a sacred religious practice, but after great pressure he allowed Elder Orson Pratt to debate Newman on the subject, "Does the Bible sanction polygamy?" The well-publicized and well-attended debate was held in the Tabernacle and extended over three days, June 12–14. As in most such debates, neither side convinced the other, and the followers of both were confirmed in their own opinions, but Elder Pratt's mastery of the scriptures and his knowledge of Hebrew stood him well against Newman and greatly surprised the Senate chaplain.

More important to the life of Utah was the fact that by the end of the 1860s other faiths were beginning to establish themselves in the territory. In the spirit of religious freedom and tolerance, the Church made no effort to keep them out, and sometimes even cooperated by letting them use Mormon chapels until they could build their own meeting places.

Among the first non-Mormons in Utah were Jews, some of whom came as merchants and businessmen as early as 1854. Strong friendships grew between the Jews and the Mormons, and more than once Brigham Young made Mormon church buildings available for Jewish religious services.

Roman Catholics came to Utah in 1862 as members of the California Volunteers. In 1866 when the Reverend Edward Kelly was looking for a place to celebrate mass, he was allowed to use the old tabernacle, and Brigham Young helped him obtain a clear title to land for a church in Salt Lake City. Though the Catholics and the Latter-day Saints had little in common theologically, they maintained general good will. The Reverend Lawrence Scanlan arrived in Utah in 1873, eventually became a bishop, and remained until his death in 1915. He established parishes wherever possible, and on one occasion in 1873 was invited by Mormon leaders in St. George to use their tabernacle for worship. Fearful that part of the service would have to be omitted because it called for a choir singing in Latin, he learned to his surprise that the leader of the St. George Tabernacle choir had asked for the appropriate music, and in two weeks the choir would sing it in Latin. On May 18 a Catholic high mass was sung by a Mormon choir in the St. George Tabernacle, symbolizing the good will that existed between Father Scanlan and the Saints.

Other groups came to Utah with the express purpose of converting the Mormons. The first was the Reorganized Church of Jesus Christ of Latter Day Saints, headed by Joseph Smith III, who sent missionaries to Utah in 1863. Six years later two younger sons of the Prophet Joseph Smith, Alexander and David, also appeared as missionaries, though their mission was less successful. Eventually, a branch of the Reorganized Church was established in Salt Lake City.

In later years the Congregationalists, Episcopalians, Presbyterians, Methodists, Baptists, and Lutherans all came among the Saints. In many cases these churches established mission schools, partly for the purpose of attracting Mormon children and becoming tools for pulling them away from the Church. With educational facilities sometimes better than those found in most LDS communities, the challenge presented by such schools eventually led the Saints to reemphasize excellence in their own schools and to pay more attention to the establishment of Church-sponsored academies (high schools). The Church also began to support more fully the idea of free, tax-supported elementary schools, and in 1869 the first free public school in Utah was opened in American Fork.

The Judicial and Political Crusade Begins

The late 1860s saw the beginning of an intensified judicial and political crusade against the Church that not only presented new difficulties to the Saints in their efforts to build the kingdom, but also served as a rallying point for increasing unity. By giving them little respite from external pressure, it constantly reminded Church members that God's people would always have differences with the outside world, and that sometimes they must sacrifice for the sake of those differences.

The political conflict manifested itself in many ways. One was the aftermath of the 1866 murder of two prominent non-Mormons: Newton Brassfield, who had won the affections and married the wife of an absent LDS missionary, and King Robinson, a surgeon at Camp Douglas who had challenged some of the Saints on certain land titles. Both murders remained unsolved, but members of the "gentile" community made every effort to blame them on the Saints.

Another manifestation of conflict was the 1867–68 contest over the election of a territorial delegate to Congress. In February 1867 William H. Hooper, the Mormon incumbent, defeated his challenger, William McGorty, by the resounding margin of 15,068 to 105. A year later McGorty challenged the election before a congressional committee, claiming that it was improper because the people of Utah had an antirepublican form of government and because, through the practice of plural marriage, they were violating the laws of the United States. He also charged that Hooper had taken a secret religious oath that disqualified him. Actually, most such charges referred to the sacred endowment ceremonies, in which only faithful Saints could participate, but uninformed and suspicious non-Mormons wrongly interpreted such participation as evidence of a secret conspiracy against the government.

McGorty lost his appeal, but such disagreements soon resulted in a new political alignment in Utah that placed the Saints on one side and the "gentiles" and a number of dissatisfied and apostate Mormons on the other. In 1870 the leaders of the Godbeite movement joined prominent members of the non-LDS community to form the Liberal party, which would oppose not only Mormon marriage practices but also the Church's political and economic influence. In response, the Saints took what seemed to be the only reasonable alternative and formed their own party, the People's party. The Liberal party was not fully united, for some members, such as the Godbeites, were not eager to completely disrupt Mormon family relationships. In 1871, therefore, the most extreme anti-Mormon faction formed the Gentile League of Utah, which became even more extreme in its avowal to destroy Mormon "theocracy."

While all this was taking place in Utah, renewed anti-Mormon sentiment appeared in the national capital. In its larger context, the campaign to eliminate plural marriage was probably one manifestation of a harsh general reform program inaugurated by Radical Republicans after the Civil War. The Radicals controlled Congress and, in their efforts to change the social structure of the South, passed legislation designed to promote civil and political rights for the blacks just freed from slavery. Some of the same Radicals who were working so hard to reform the South were among those who sought also to reform the social structure of Utah. Among them was Senator Benjamin F. Wade of Ohio, author of the stringent Wade-Davis bill that would have disfranchised all former officials of the southern Confederacy and made it difficult for the southern states to return to full partnership in the union. The bill was vetoed by President Abraham Lincoln, but its intent was carried out by later congresses.

Clearly indicative of the growing national hostility toward the Latter-day Saints were three bills introduced in Congress by such reformers in the late 1860s. In 1866 Senator Wade introduced a bill designed to destroy not only plural marriage but, in fact, the very strength of the Church in Utah. It was unsuccessful, but was soon followed by the Cragin Bill, which would have eliminated trial by jury in Utah in cases involving polygamy. In 1869 a different approach was

Photograph taken in 1895 shows many of the Utah women who were
active in the suffrage movement about 1870. Seated on the front row, third
from the right, is Susan B. Anthony, national women's rights leader.
(Church Archives)

tried in the House of Representatives through the Ashley Bill, which proposed completely dismembering the Territory of Utah and dividing the area among surrounding states and territories.

The legislation that came closest to passing was the Cullom Bill of 1870, which would have required that all cases involving plural marriage be prosecuted exclusively by federal judges, and that juries be selected by federally appointed marshals and attorneys. When news reached Utah that it had passed the House, three thousand Latter-day Saint women held a massive protest meeting in the Salt Lake Tabernacle, demonstrating to surprised people throughout the nation that the women in Utah supported plural marriage. In addition, certain prominent newspaper editors and legislators, feeling that the proposed law could lead to civil war with the Mormons, argued that such drastic measures were not needed. These voices of moderation helped finally to defeat the bill.

Another approach to the Mormon question was the effort of some members of Congress to establish female suffrage in Utah, under the impression that if the women had the vote they would destroy plural marriage at the ballot box. Utah's delegate to Congress gave the measure such enthusiastic support, however, that its sponsors changed their minds and dropped it. Ironically, just at this time, on February 12, 1870, Utah's territorial legislature passed a women's suffrage bill, and seventeen years later the federal Congress itself outlawed women's suffrage in Utah as part of the effort to fight polygamy!

Even the new president of the United States, Ulysses S. Grant, and his vice-president, Schuyler Colfax, joined in denouncing Mormon practices. Strongly influenced by Colfax and by J. P. Newman, as well as his own sense of Victorian morality, Grant adopted a get-tough policy, reflected in the nature of those he appointed to office in Utah Territory.

General J. Wilson Shaffer, who had served the aims of the Radical-controlled government well in helping establish federal rule in the South, was appointed governor in 1870. "Never after me," he boasted, "shall it be said that Brigham Young is governor of Utah." Though he died within the year, Shaffer's actions displayed his bias and contributed to a renewed tension between the Saints and federal officials. His home became virtual headquarters for the anti-Mormon group that conspired to destroy the Church's power. He was influential in securing removal of the territorial chief justice, Charles C. Wilson, which paved the way for Grant to appoint James B. McKean to that office. In addition, Shaffer effectively immobilized the territorial militia, the Nauvoo Legion, when he appointed Patrick E. Connor as commander, ignoring the previous election of Daniel H. Wells to that position. Shaffer also suspended the annual musters of the legion, forcing it into inactivity until its official disbandment seventeen years later.

Simultaneously, starting in 1869, a new judicial crusade was pursued by Associate Justices O. F. Strickland and C. M. Hawley, who attempted to strip the Mormon-dominated probate courts of their criminal jurisdiction, and thus of their right to original jurisdiction in polygamy cases. The major power in this crusade, however, was Chief Justice McKean, who was sent to Utah by President Grant with instructions to root out polygamy by strictly enforcing the law.

McKean accepted his assignment with a sense of mission that seemed almost as great as the dedication of the Mormons themselves, and his four-year tenure became a notable study in conflicting value systems. The Saints firmly believed that the federal law against plural marriage was unconstitutional, for it violated their religious freedom. McKean, on the other hand, believed just as firmly that the law was right, that "the Mormon system" was wrong, and that he must pursue his goal with every means at his command. In his zeal he wrote to Louis Dent, the president's brother-in-law, in 1872: "Judge Dent, the mission which God has called upon me to perform in Utah, is as much above the duties of other courts and judges as the heavens are above the earth, and whenever or wherever I may find the Local or Federal laws obstructing or interfering therewith, by God's blessing I shall trample them under my feet."[9] To him it was not a matter of religion, but of upholding federal authority against "polygamic theocracy."

Ignoring the fact that he was subject to judicial procedures established by the territorial legislature, the zealous Judge McKean allowed the U.S. marshal to impanel juries (thus effectively keeping Mormons off the juries) and he denied criminal jurisdiction to the local probate courts. Indictments, convictions, and prison sentences soon multiplied. In addition, McKean took aim at the Saints in the matter of naturalization of aliens by granting citizenship only if the applicants agreed to abide by the Anti-Bigamy Law of 1862. He even denied citizenship to people who had taken plural wives before the law was passed, as well as to some who, though they did not practice plural marriage, admitted they believed the principle was right.

McKean's major target was the entire Latter-day Saint system, but Mormonism's greatest symbol was Brigham Young. For his participation in plural marriage, President Young was indicted on a charge of adultery. While awaiting trial, he and several others were also indicted on a flimsy charge of murder, brought by an anti-Mormon acting United States district attorney and based on nothing more than the testimony of a notorious gunman. The Church leader appeared in court on January 2, 1872, and was released on bail to await trial.

The trial was never held, for on April 15 some of McKean's judicial errors caught up with him. In an earlier case Paul Englebrecht had violated city ordinances by operating a liquor store without a license. Acting under city law, officials had confiscated and destroyed his stock of liquor, and Englebrecht brought suit against them. Judge McKean allowed the jury to be impaneled by the United States marshal rather than by the territorial marshal, as required by law, and this excluded Mormons from the jury. Englebrecht won his case in McKean's court, but it found its way to the United States Supreme Court, which ruled that the jury had been illegally drawn. The result was a blow to Judge McKean, for it not only set aside the Englebrecht ruling, but it also released from custody about 130 prisoners who had been tried during the previous eighteen months before similar juries. The Supreme Court

---

[9]Edward W. Tullidge, *Life of Brigham Young* (New York: [n.p.], 1876), pp. 420–21.

also quashed all other indictments pending, including the charges against Brigham Young.

Though a rebuff to the career of Judge McKean, the Englebrecht case did not long hold back the mounting pressure against the Church. In the next few years Judge McKean would be heard from again, and new federal legislation against the Mormons would pass, but the Saints themselves would show increased determination to stand firmly for the principles they believed were true and for the right to build an ideal community in the West that would be acceptable as the earthly manifestation of the kingdom of God.

Close of a Career, *1872–1877*

Brigham Young was President of the Church for thirty years, longer than any other man in its history. "Brother Brigham," as he was affectionately called by the Saints, believed his task was to build on the foundation laid by Joseph Smith and to see that the gospel was carried to all nations. He directed the westward movement of the Church, inspired the establishment of four hundred communities, promoted numerous economic and social programs designed to make the Saints self-sufficient, and led in firm defiance of all harmful external forces.

One of his great attributes as a leader was his confidence in the ultimate accomplishment of his goals and his willingness to try whatever programs seemed necessary to achieve them. At the same time, he seldom, if ever, pronounced his programs perfect—many of them were frankly provisional, and if they did not work, he tried something else. This constant looking forward with hope rather than backward with dismay was a trait that inspired and impressed both Saints and non-Mormons. During the last four years of President Young's life, the Saints continued to suffer political hardships and saw important changes in their society. Politically, they were still governed by federal appointees, the majority of whom were antagonistic toward the Church and its doctrines, and they were the target of national legislation that resulted in new political restrictions. Despite these problems they overcame the most severe effects of an economic depression, expanded their cultural and educational activities, established important new colonies, and dedicated their first temple in the Rocky Mountains. In addition, Brigham Young led a significant reform in Church government.

Confrontation and Expansion in Education

In the early days of settlement the Saints made every effort to establish elementary schools in each community and ward. These were private schools, in which teachers' salaries were paid by tuition, with little subsidy from either the Church or the territorial government. Gradually, however, public schools were established throughout the territory, even though opposed by certain Church leaders and other Saints who were fearful that non-Mormon teachers would be unsympathetic toward Church principles and might undermine the faith of the children. At the same time, scattered Protestant mission schools began to provide better educational opportunities than the Mormon-controlled, poorly financed community schools, and a few Saints sent their children to them. The time was right for the Church to reevaluate its educational politics, and gradually its leaders shifted their support to the free, tax-supported public schools.

This policy raised new questions, as Church leaders become concerned with another movement that seemed to strike at the very heart of their attempts to establish the kingdom. If they were to create a righteous society, the Saints believed, they must teach its principles in the public schools, at least so far as Bible reading would promote them. Some non-Mormons, on the other hand, objected. Their concerns reflected the growing nationwide movement to free public education from denominational influence. The Constitutional principle of separation of church and state, it was argued, was at the heart of the American tradition, and it required that tax-supported schools should not promote the viewpoint of any one religious group. Bible reading in public schools was considered a violation of that principle. In 1875, in an effort to promote public education as such, President Ulysses S. Grant went so far as to recommend unsuccessfully that all church property in the nation be subject to taxation for the support of public schools. The Saints were dismayed at the suggestion, as were many American Catholics, who foresaw that such a policy could tax their extensive school system out of existence. Non-Mormons in Utah, meanwhile, continued to urge elimination of Bible teaching from schools not just because it was a national trend, but also because they thought it would help undermine Mormon influence.

A related issue was the hiring of teachers. By the 1870s the Saints were becoming concerned that their influence in education would diminish in proportion to the growing number of non-Mormon teachers, while "gentiles" continued to resent the obvious Mormon dominance. Governor George L. Woods expressed the typical anti-Mormon view by implying that the Church had usurped the government's function in education. He argued that not even a majority had a right to control school revenues to suit their own religious faith (i.e., to hire mostly Mormon teachers), for governments were "not established for the benefit of majorities, but for the purpose of protecting minorities. Individual rights, and not collective rights, constitute the true foundations of all just governments."[1]

Church leaders had some sympathy for the need to protect minority rights, for they vividly remembered when the Saints themselves were in the minority in other places. They nevertheless objected to the governor's views, and they could point to some significant differences now that they were in the majority. They had no intention of destroying any other religion or way of life, driving anyone from their midst, or destroying property. They believed, however, that they had the right to insist at least that the Bible be taught in the public schools and that teachers be selected from among their own people. In 1877 Elder John Taylor was elected territorial superintendent of district schools, and he openly defended this position. "See that they are men and women who fear God and keep his commandments," he declared in a general conference in 1879. "We do not want men or women to teach the children of the Latter-day Saints who are not Latter-day Saints themselves. Hear it, you Elders of Israel and you school-trustees! We want none of these things."[2] Saints and non-Mormons continued to see differently on the subject, and the issue was not fully resolved.

During these same years the need for better schools, especially secondary schools, was becoming more apparent. Brigham Young was convinced of the need for a broad, well-balanced education, and he followed with great interest, therefore, the progress of the private Dusenberry School in Provo, founded by two brothers who were initially non-Mormons but soon joined the Church. This school was eventually absorbed by the University of Deseret but, despite this help, was discontinued in 1875 because of financial problems.

One of President Young's primary goals was to create a school that would train teachers for LDS youth. As early as 1871 he commissioned John R. Park to study educational systems in the eastern United States and several European countries, and in 1873 preliminary plans were laid for the establishment of a college. In 1875, the year the Dusenberry School closed, President Young selected a group of trustees and set aside

---

[1]As quoted in James R. Clark, "Church and State Relationships in Education in Utah" (Ed.D. thesis, Utah State University, 1958), pp. 209–10.
[2]*Journal of Discourses*, 20:179.

"Brigham Young's Back Yard." This interesting scene was painted by Dan Weggeland, prominent Utah artist, in 1868, then copied by the artist himself in 1915. The original Eagle Gate may be seen, spanning what is now State Street. To the left is the schoolhouse built by Brigham Young for his children, and to the right is the Beehive House, President Young's official residence. (Museum of Church History and Art)

some of his Provo property as the basis for a school, which became known as Brigham Young Academy. The new school began operation the same year, and Karl G. Maeser, a German-born convert and educator, became principal. The academy's early students were mostly in the elementary grades, but in later years it became a secondary school, a teacher training college, and finally Brigham Young University. President Young also founded Brigham Young College in Logan, which began operating in 1876 and continued until 1926.

These two schools exemplified Brigham Young's educational ideals and established a precedent for future Church education. Both emphasized the liberal arts, high moral and ethical principles, and sound factual knowledge, and both made room in their curricula for religion. President Young constantly advised the Saints to involve themselves in every field of learning, and on one occasion he emphasized his broad perspective by saying, "'Shall I sit down and read the Bible, the Book of Mormon, and the Book of Covenants all the time?' says one. Yes, if you please, and when you have done, you may be nothing but a sectarian after all. It is your duty to know everything upon the face of the earth, in addition to reading those books."[3] The schools he founded

---

[3]*Journal of Discourses*, 2:93–94.

were forerunners of a more widespread academy movement that would characterize Church education well into the early twentieth century.

The Courts and Politics – An Ongoing Struggle

The judicial and political crusade against the Church seemed to heighten in the mid-1870s. Chief Justice James B. McKean was not the only federal officer attempting to destroy plural marriage, but his court became a rallying point for all anti-Mormon activity. The most widely publicized case was that of Ann Eliza Webb Young, Brigham Young's last and youngest plural wife. In 1873, at the urging of some members of the non-LDS "Utah ring," she sued for divorce, charging neglect, cruel treatment, and desertion. The suit placed Judge McKean in a dilemma: he wished to embarrass President Young and force him to pay the costs and alimony requested, but if he granted the divorce he would be recognizing the marriage, thus admitting the legality of the very system of plural marriage he was trying to destroy. Despite this, the judge ordered President Young to pay $3,000 in court fees and a $500 monthly maintenance to Ann Eliza.

Acting upon his lawyers' advice, President Young declined to pay the fee, pending an appeal to a higher court. Because of this, the judge ordered him to face charges of contempt of court. The President did not intend to treat the order of the territorial supreme court with contempt, and if he lost his appeal he would pay, but he believed he had the right to the appeal. McKean, however, found him in contempt of court, fined him twenty-five dollars, and sentenced him to the penitentiary for one day.

The spectacle of the aging President of the Church being sent to prison was immediately publicized in the national press. So blatantly irresponsible were McKean's actions that many newspapers sympathized with Brigham Young. Five days later President Grant removed McKean from office. Other reasons prompted the unseating, including charges of judicial corruption and poor judgment, but the man who seemed most to symbolize the challenge to Mormon autonomy was finally out of the territory.

In spite of what might be said about the corruption or irresponsibility of many enemies of the Saints, it must be observed that much of the conflict in these years centered around honest differences of opinion among people of good character. It was difficult for the Saints to understand the increasing determination of federal officials to destroy

plural marriage, for example, because to them this was the fulfillment
of a religious principle. Those who opposed it, on the other hand,
although often people of honor and integrity, could not understand the
religious motivation behind the practice. They considered it not only
a violation of federal law but also morally reprehensible. President Grant
shared these feelings, and even though desire to be fair was demonstrated by his recommendation that Congress legitimize all children
born prior to a certain fixed date, he also wanted laws that would result
in the "ultimate extinguishment of polygamy."[4]

It was to be expected, therefore, that Grant should appoint federal
officers for the Territory of Utah who were sympathetic with his goals.
Some of them, however, harassed the Saints beyond the limits of judicial
propriety. In 1872, for example, Judge Cyrus M. Hawley of the Second
Judicial District Court was obviously trying to discredit the Saints when
he charged that it was almost impossible to dispense justice in southern
Utah because of their antagonism and asked that a military post be
established at Beaver. The secretary of war approved the request in
September 1873, and Fort Cameron was soon constructed. The Saints
of Beaver did not object to the presence of the troops, for it helped them
economically, but they saw no need. They were not, after all, disorderly
citizens. The fort was maintained until 1883, when the troops were
withdrawn.

The Saints' antagonists were not without fault. It was soon dis-
closed that Judge Obed Strickland had actually purchased his office
from his predecessor, and that Judge Cyrus Hawley was guilty of bigamy.
It was also charged that McKean had been allowed to write editorials
in the *Salt Lake Tribune* supporting his own judicial decisions. George
C. Bates, United States district attorney, became so disgusted with the
general nature of federal justice in Utah that he wrote President Grant:

> Your entire administration of affairs in Utah, your special Mes-
> sage to Congress, and many of the most important appointments
> made by you here, have all been the result of misrepresentation,
> falsehood, and misunderstanding on your part of the real condition
> of affairs in this territory. . . .
>
> In other communications, soon to be made, in every instance
> accompanied by the evidence, I will demonstrate how other dis-
> tinguished officers have bought their offices, how you were made

---

[4]James D. Richardson, ed., *A Compilation of the Messages and Papers of the Presidents,
1789–1897*, 10 vols. (Washington: Government Printing Office, 1896–1899), 7:203.

a mere catspaw, by corrupt Senators and Representatives, to send officers here whom you would not have trusted among your horse blankets in the executive stable.[5]

Despite the ineptness of President Grant's appointments, when he visited the territory in 1875 he received a grand welcome. He was the first American president to visit Utah, and when he arrived, many territorial and Church officials, including President Brigham Young, courteously greeted him. Compliments were exchanged, and impressive crowds cheered him as his carriage moved along the streets. He arrived in Salt Lake City on a Sunday, and well-dressed Sunday School children, waving happily, lined the streets. It is said that he inquired whose children they were and was answered by the governor, "Mormon children," after which he was silent for a while, then quietly remarked, "I have been deceived."[6] After his return to Washington, however, the President continued his attack on Mormon practices.

Congress Acts Once Again

In the meantime, the failure of McKean's judicial crusade reemphasized to Utah "gentiles" the need for more national legislation if their attack on polygamy and on the political influence of the Church in Utah was to be successful.

A number of measures aimed directly at Mormon practices were introduced in Congress unsuccessfully in 1873. In 1874 a bill sponsored by Representative Luke P. Poland of Vermont passed both houses of Congress and was signed by the president. Adding strength to the Anti-Bigamy Act of 1862, the new law extended federal jurisdiction in both criminal and civil cases by abolishing the controversial original jurisdiction in these areas that had been given to the territorial probate courts nearly twenty-five years earlier. No longer would it be so difficult for polygamy to be prosecuted in the federal courts of Utah. The law also did away with the offices of territorial marshal and attorney general, whose powers had overlapped those of the United States marshal and district attorney.

The debates in the House of Representatives over the Poland Bill were especially interesting, for among the participants was Elder George

---

[5]*Millennial Star* 35 (1873): 241–43.
[6]Orson F. Whitney, *History of Utah*, 4 vols. (Salt Lake City: George Q. Cannon & Sons Co., 1892–1904), 2:778.

Q. Cannon, Utah's representative to Congress. Poland argued vehemently that federal officials simply were not able to exercise their authority in Utah because they were effectively supplanted by Mormon officials. He was particularly irate that the territorial legislature was filled by Mormons, and he was incensed that so many probate judges were Latter-day Saint bishops. Delegate Cannon ably defended Utah and argued that the main reason these courts held the unusual jurisdiction in the first place was that justice could not be obtained in the federal courts. He demonstrated the impartiality of the probate courts by producing a list of eighty-four civil cases that had been tried in Salt Lake City involving Mormons and non-Mormons. Fifty-nine of these were decided in favor of non-Mormons or dissenting Mormons, while only twenty-five were decided in favor of the Mormons. Elder Cannon then presented a powerful justification of Utah's unique ecclesiastical situation that summarized the peculiar needs and attitudes of the Saints:

> Sir, there is probably no officer in the Utah Territory, if he belongs to the Mormon people, who does not hold some position in the Church. The Mormon people do not believe in salaried preachers; but they believe it to be the privilege of every worthy man of the organization to be an elder, and, when called upon, to make himself useful in preaching. Doubtless many gentlemen about me who have visited Utah Territory will recollect, if they passed a Sabbath there, that elders were very frequently called from the body of the congregation to preach from the stand without any preparation whatever. Bishops, probate judges, men of different vocations in the community, are thus called upon to speak to the people, so that if you say that a man must not exercise political functions in Utah because he is an officer in the church you exclude from all offices in the Territory every respectable Mormon.[7]

Despite his logic and eloquence, Elder Cannon's pleadings were in vain, and the long sought anti-Mormon legislation became a reality.

Prosecution and the Reynolds Case

As soon as the Poland Bill became law, the federal judiciary began criminal proceedings against plural marriage under the Anti-Bigamy Act of 1862. Like the American revolutionaries a century earlier, the

---

[7]United States Congress, House, *Congressional Record*, 43 Cong., 1 sess., 1874, vol. 2, pt. 5:4471.

Saints believed that a higher law compelled them to violate one they considered unjust, and especially one they believed ultimately would be declared unconstitutional.

The most significant case was that of George Reynolds, who was actually designated by Church leaders to be the subject of a test case. Reynolds, private secretary to Brigham Young, was arrested in October 1874 and voluntarily gave evidence against himself. He was found guilty of bigamy but his conviction was overturned on a technicality by the territorial supreme court. In October 1875 he was indicted a second time; his trial resulted in another guilty verdict, a $500 fine, and two years of hard labor. On July 6 the territorial supreme court upheld the conviction, and an appeal was quickly made to the United States Supreme Court.

Before the Supreme Court, Reynolds's attorney presented several technical arguments about the nature of the jury and the testimony that convicted Elder Reynolds, and argued that plural marriage was not intrinsically evil. It was, rather, part of the social and religious life of Utah, and should be left alone as an exercise in freedom of religion. The court turned a deaf ear to all these arguments and ruled that polygamy constituted an offense against society and, as such, was a valid matter for legislation. On January 6, 1879, therefore, with only one dissent, the lower court's decision was upheld and the Anti-Bigamy Act of 1862 was affirmed as the constitutional law of the land. The court believed, however, that the penalty imposed on Reynolds was too severe and remanded the case to the lower court with instructions to lighten it.

Needless to say, the decision of the Supreme Court stunned Church leaders. Brigham Young had passed away two years earlier, and was thus spared a severe disappointment, but those who remained faced a cruel dilemma. Should they continue to preach and practice what they believed was a divine law, or should they now conform to the constitutional law of the land? It had taken many of them a long time to accept the principle of plural marriage in the first place. It is little wonder that it would take another eleven years to become prepared for a revelation that would bring it to an end as a Church-sanctioned practice.

The United Orders of Zion

During the last five years of his life, President Brigham Young continued to fight the influences of outside competition that seemed to threaten the economic independence and solidarity of the Saints. The railroad had made possible a mining boom, and inevitably the territory was becoming dependent upon the prosperity of the mining industry. In addition, the railroad brought to Utah consumer goods that could often be sold less expensively than those produced in the territory. This was the situation when the United States was suddenly hit by the famous Panic of 1873. The financial failure of Jay Cooke and Company caused many depositors to lose confidence in the nation's banks and begin to withdraw their funds. Bank failures quickly multiplied, the circulation of money slowed, movements of some agricultural products were halted, credit declined, people hoarded cash, consumer spending dropped, unemployment rose, and the panic was on. In Utah, bank deposits dropped by more than 30 percent in a year; the mines closed, causing a decline in retail business; shops, factories, the agricultural market, and two major banks failed. Despite their efforts at independence, the Saints in Zion were clearly affected by the economic rhythm of the nation.

This was proof enough to many Latter-day Saints that they were still too entangled in economic alliances with the world. Church leaders tried to soften the effects of the panic by reemphasizing home industry and reaffirming their teachings on unity and brotherly love. They also began to instruct the Saints in the United Order of Enoch.

The move into the United Order was not sudden, for it had found expression in the cooperative movement of the late 1860s. "This co-operative movement," President Young declared in 1869, "is only a stepping stone to what is called the Order of Enoch, but which is in reality the order of Heaven."[8] The next step, the actual establishment of United Orders throughout the territory, was inspired in part by the impressive success of the Brigham City Cooperative, which had weathered the disastrous Panic of 1873. Lorenzo Snow had founded a cooperative mercantile establishment in 1864, and it soon branched out into some forty cooperative departments. Brooms, hats, molasses, furniture, a general store, a tannery, a woolen mill, sheep, milk cows, hogs, flax, all phases of the building trades, and specialized farms were all part of the Brigham City Cooperative. It was owned by approximately four hundred shareholders who represented nearly every family in this village of two thousand, and the profits from its activity were paid to

---

[8]Sermon of April 7, 1869, in *Deseret News*, June 2, 1869.

A Brigham City manufacturing cooperative. Lorenzo Snow, founder of the town's cooperative movement, stands at the end on the right. (Church Archives)

shareholders in kind (goods and services) rather than cash. The panic left the cooperative almost untouched, and the reputation of Brigham City spread as far as England and impressed social reformers everywhere. It was reported later that Brigham Young had said that "Brother Snow has led the people along, and got them into the United Order without their knowing it."[9]

When Brigham Young took his annual winter trip to southern Utah in the winter of 1873–74, he began to preach the need for improving community economic efforts. He envisioned a society in which the people would make and raise all they needed to eat, drink, or wear, and still realize a surplus for sale to outsiders. Such a dream was, of course, idealistic, and no one knew better than Brigham Young that a true Zion never would be created in this world until the people overcame every vestige of selfishness and were prepared for the millennial reign of Christ. But the ideal was worth striving for, and the economic problems of the territory provided the impetus for bold new efforts.

The new program had both spiritual and economic ramifications, and it is significant that it should emerge at the same time that various

[9]As quoted by Lorenzo Snow in a sermon of April 21, 1878, *Journal of Discourses*, 19:347.

economic reform measures were attracting attention throughout the nation. The newly industrialized American society had recorded some incredible achievements, but it had also created economic inequality, poverty, and lack of opportunity for many rural and urban workers alike. As a result, political reformers were beginning to advocate stricter government controls to ensure a more even distribution of America's new wealth. The Latter-day Saints clearly opposed the idea, advocated by some reformers, of a socialist state in which all means of production and distribution would be owned outright by the government. The same problems that concerned the reformers, however, made the Saints willing to try to establish communities based on cooperation and equality, grounded in the religious belief that the earth's abundance belonged to God and that in building their ideal communities they were furthering the cause of the kingdom of God on earth. Consisting of cooperative enterprise based on individual, voluntary association, their communities would exist side-by-side with the larger society and would engage in trade with it, but they would also be economically self-sufficient and not dependent upon the outside in times of emergency.

The settlement at St. George was particularly in need of an economic boost in the winter of 1873–74, and it was there that Brigham Young organized the first United Order. Nearly three hundred people, most of the adults in the city, pledged their time, energy, ability, and economic (i.e., income-producing) property to the order and became subject to the direction of an elected board of management. In return for property, each person received a commensurate amount of stock. Stockholders pledged themselves to boost local manufacturing, stop importing goods, and trade only with members of the order. The whole community constituted a single economic enterprise that operated various agricultural and business activities, including the nearby Washington cotton factory. Members received wages and dividends depending upon the amount of labor and property contributed. The order was also to be a spiritual union, and a long list of rules for Christian living was drawn up. Each person entered the order by being rebaptized and pledging to obey all the rules.

That winter Brigham Young established the order in about twenty communities in southern Utah, and as he traveled back to Salt Lake City the following spring he organized each settlement along his way. In all, about 150 United Orders were established, and most of them adopted constitutions similar to the pioneer model at St. George.

In addition to promoting the self-sufficiency of the kingdom, an equally fundamental reason given for establishing the new system was to protect the Church from the internal schism that could be caused by the development of separate wealthy and poor classes among the Saints. In a pamphlet published in 1875 the First Presidency decried class distinctions and labeled them as a primary reason behind the original cooperative movement:

> Years ago it was perceived that . . . a wealthy class was being rapidly formed in our midst whose interests, in the course of time, were likely to be diverse from those of the rest of the community. The growth of such a class was dangerous to our union; and most of all people, we stand in need of union and to have our interests identical. Then it was that the Saints were counseled to enter into co-operation.[10]

Brigham Young realized that the United Order must be flexible enough to accommodate a variety of community needs as well as a variety of Saints. Some people, for example, simply were less willing than others to enter into the most "advanced" cooperative activity. As a result, the term *United Order* was defined loosely enough that it could apply to various kinds of associations throughout the LDS commonwealth.

St. George represented one of four general types of United Orders, and most orders of this type lasted little more than a year, however. As might be expected, problems arose regarding fair distribution of benefits. As a result, many decided that they were not ready to live the plan. The St. George order itself was dissolved in 1878.

A second type of United Order followed the Brigham City plan. It did not require members to consecrate all their economic property and labor to the order but, rather, emphasized community ownership and operation of particular enterprises. In Hyrum, Utah, and Paris, Idaho, for example, the cooperative activity began with a general store, which used its profits to establish cooperative sawmills, blacksmith shops, tanneries, and herds. Each participant retained his own private property in addition to the stock he held in the cooperative businesses. Some of these orders lasted into the 1880s, and the Brigham City order operated until 1885, when several natural disasters, economic restrictions by federal officials, and the fact that Elder Snow was sentenced to the penitentiary for practicing polygamy made it difficult to function.

---

[10]James R. Clark, ed., *Messages of the First Presidency of the Church of Jesus Christ of Latter-day Saints, 1837-1964*, 6 vols. (Salt Lake City: Bookcraft, 1965-1975), 2:268.

Deseret currency represents a number of important aspects of Mormon economy in nineteenth-century Utah, including the development of local cooperatives and the emphasis on home industry. (Church Archives)

A third variation was designed for larger cities: Salt Lake City, Ogden, Provo, and Logan. Each ward organized its own cooperative enterprise, and all ward members were expected to help finance it. The Logan First Ward, for example, built a foundry and machine shop, while the Second Ward organized a woodworking shop, and the Third Ward managed a dairy. Like the Brigham City type, most of these co-ops lasted until the mid-1880s, when the federal government's anti-polygamy activities combined with other problems to compel their abandonment. Most of the business activities were continued as private enterprises.

The best-known United Orders were those of the type established at Orderville, Utah. Most were small communities, with populations ranging from 50 to 750 in size. Settlers retained no private property at all, shared equally in the community's production, and lived and ate together as a well-regulated family. This was the ultimate in economic cooperation, for no one could live in the community without becoming part of the order. This was also the closest the Saints came to the ideal community established by the New Testament apostles among the Christians in Jerusalem and by the people of the Book of Mormon who "had all things common among them."

Orderville was founded in 1875 by twenty-four families, consisting of 150 people, though within five years there were seven hundred people in the town. By cooperative labor they built all the apartment units, shops, bakeries, barns, and other buildings needed for a well-regulated community. Each family had its own apartment, but at first everyone ate together in a large dining room with the women taking turns at kitchen duty. They operated farms, orchards, dairies, livestock projects, and various manufacturing enterprises. They produced an excess of furniture and sold it to surrounding communities in exchange for funds for expansion. They wore the same kind of clothes, all manufactured at Orderville, and no member of the community could improve his situation unless all were likewise improved. The self-discipline and dedication to serving the needs of each other demonstrated during the ten years the order functioned was indeed remarkable.

As might be expected, various human problems caused difficulty. The generous Saints were perhaps too ready to allow new members to join, and consequently, Orderville became too crowded for effective cooperation. In addition, the young people of the community became restless as they compared themselves with the youth of surrounding towns. As the whole region became more wealthy in the late 1870s, the old-fashioned jeans, shoes, and straw hats they wore, as well as their very small apartments, became objects of ridicule. In one instance the young men of Orderville became so enamored with the new style of trousers worn by the boys of surrounding communities that they took to wearing out their own sturdy, "everlasting" jeans by placing them on the community grindstone! The result was that the community manufactured new trousers for all. In addition, natural disagreements over the equitable distribution of goods and credits arose, and some people began to chafe under the rigid regulation necessary to keep the community going. When the accelerated anti-polygamy campaign of the 1880s drove many of their leaders into hiding or placed them in the penitentiary, the people of Orderville were counseled by Church authorities to dissolve the order.

The Saints reacted in various ways to life in these cooperative communities. Some were long-suffering and uncomplaining, seeming to find unusual joy in attempting to live a selfless life. Others complained of the regulation, and still others simply left the communities. For the most part, those who worked to build Orderville later looked back with genuine nostalgia for the happy feelings it gave them to live in a well-ordered Christian community.

The United Orders did not achieve all their economic goals, but they counted some notable accomplishments. For the time being, at least, there were fewer imports, production increased, local investment was stimulated, and progress was made toward diminishing economic inequality among the Saints. The orders promoted thrift and industry as well as more rapid development of local resources. For a while, and probably when it was most crucially needed to assist in pursuing the other goals of the kingdom, the United Orders helped the Saints maintain a degree of economic independence from the East. In addition, they aided significantly in building the temples at St. George, Logan, Manti, and Salt Lake City, by furnishing both labor and materials.

The Settlements on the Little Colorado

The Saints, meanwhile, continued to enlarge the perimeters of their commonwealth. The most important area of expansion in the 1870s was along the Little Colorado River in Arizona. The establishment of the Little Colorado colonies was a fitting climax to the career of the "great colonizer," Brigham Young.

The Church had long been collecting data on northern Arizona, and as early as the 1850s LDS explorers had penetrated the region. In addition, from 1858 until the early 1870s, Jacob Hamblin and a handful of his associates designated as Indian missionaries made periodic visits to the mesa villages of the Hopis. They became well acquainted with the deserts of northern Arizona, though they probably did not explore much of the Little Colorado. The Saints also learned much about that country through close contact with John Wesley Powell and other government explorers. They cooperated with official surveyors and profited by an exchange of information.

In 1870 the Navajos, who had conducted intermittent raids along Utah's southern frontier since 1865, were pacified, enabling the Church to resume the southward movement, which had long been an important element of Brigham Young's design for a great Latter-day Saint commonwealth in the intermountain region. Between 1870 and 1873 settlements were established at Kanab, Pipe Springs, Paria, and Lee's Ferry, and these soon served as the approach to Arizona.

The eventual settlement of the Saints in Arizona was actually the result of an even more ambitious plan conceived by Brigham Young and Thomas L. Kane, the longtime friend of the Mormons. The two men spent the winter of 1872–73 together in St. George and laid plans for a second gathering place for the Saints in Sonora Valley, Mexico. The settlements in Arizona were to form a connecting link between Utah and Mexico.

Daniel P. McArthur, St. George Stake president, baptizes a Shivwits Indian, about 1875. Standing on the rock is Sheriff Augustus P. Hardy, who, along with Jacob Hamblin, helped establish the Santa Clara Indian Mission in 1854. (Church Archives)

The first effort to colonize along the Little Colorado River was discouraging. In December 1872, an exploring company under the leadership of Bishop Lorenzo Roundy was sent into the region. His report, written in March, was perhaps too optimistic, and immediately about 250 missionaries were called to move south, as soon as weather permitted, under the leadership of Horton D. Haight. The first group crossed the Colorado River at Lee's Ferry on April 22, 1873, but soon became almost totally discouraged. The arid, broken countryside was difficult to traverse, the river seemed to be drying up, and an advance exploring party that went 120 miles further upstream found the area a desert. A messenger was sent to the telegraph office in southeastern Utah for instructions, but when no word came, the advance party turned back and the mission was abandoned.

At this point the amazing optimism of some of the Saints again became significant. Belatedly, Brigham Young had sent word to the struggling company of missionaries that they were to stay in Arizona, and he made clear his belief that no matter what the obstacles were, a company of determined Saints could establish a successful outpost.

At the same time, other leaders proclaimed that such formidable, un-inviting territory was actually a blessing, for there the Saints could settle without fear that anyone else would try to take it away. "If there be deserts in Arizona," said George Q. Cannon, "thank God for the deserts. . . . The worst places in the land we can probably get, and we must develop them. If we were to find a good country how long would it be before the wicked would want it and seek to strip us of our posses-sions?"[11] Even some of the unsuccessful missionaries were not certain the enterprise was a total failure. After one group inscribed on a rock "Arizona Mission Dead – 1873," a more visionary writer countered by composing a poem that began, "Thou Fool, This Mission is not dead, it only sleeps," and went on to emphasize the lack of wisdom and understanding of those who despised this land, created by God. Saints of this persuasion looked upon the hardships as challenges and the mission as the will of God to further strengthen the kingdom.

During the next two years more thorough exploration was under-taken by various groups of Saints, including missionaries to the Indians, and early in 1876 Lot Smith led the first successful Mormon settlement in the lower valley of the Little Colorado. That year four regular Mormon villages were founded, in addition to a community to support mis-sionary work among Native Americans in Arizona and another in New Mexico. As in earlier colonization activities, the Saints in Arizona built their villages by community cooperation, working together in erecting dams, constructing irrigation ditches, clearing the land, and harvesting their crops.

A second group of settlements was founded during the next two years along Silver Creek, a major tributary of the Little Colorado. Here other settlers had already attempted to establish farming and livestock communities, but several of their holdings eventually fell into Mormon hands. One group of LDS settlers departed from the normal pattern of the time and did not adopt the United Order. Under the leadership of William J. Flake, they were encouraged by Elder Erastus Snow of the Council of the Twelve, and the successful village was aptly named Snowflake. Eventually it became one of the major Mormon centers in Arizona. Finally, in 1879 and 1880 a third group of settlements was begun at St. Johns and the area near the headwaters of the Little Col-orado. The basis for strong Latter-day Saint influence in Arizona had been laid.

---

[11]*Journal of Discourses*, 16:143.

Lot Smith was prominent for activities in the Utah War and later as a leader of pioneer Mormon settlements in Arizona. (Church Archives)

All this, however, did not immediately result in a push further south—the Mexican colonies were established later and for different reasons. The success of the Arizona settlements nevertheless demonstrates once again that many significant achievements in this era were the result of even more ambitious dreams, and that without such dreams less would have been accomplished. In 1873 George Q. Cannon proclaimed that "the time must come when the Latter-day Saints . . . will extend throughout all North and South America, and we shall establish the rule of righteous and good order throughout all these new countries."[12] Another hundred years would see at least a partial fulfillment of this prediction, but it would come through missionary work rather than colonization.

The St. George Temple

Important and time-consuming as they were, the political problems, economic activities, and colonization ventures of the Church were the least of Brigham Young's concerns during the last years of his life. Uppermost in his mind was the perfecting of the Saints, the most direct way to build a truly acceptable kingdom of God on earth. His deep love

---

[12]*Journal of Discourses*, 16:144.

for the Saints was readily apparent, even as he criticized their weaknesses, and his devotion to everything the gospel meant dominated all he did. "I sometimes feel that I can hardly desist from telling the Latter-day Saints how they should live," he quipped to a congregation in Logan about a year before his death, "but my talking organs will not permit me to say as much as I wish to." He nevertheless delivered a rich sermon that reflected many of his most important spiritual values. "The Celestial Kingdom of God is worth seeking for," he said, "and there are times when I see the importance of the people living their religion that I almost feel to cry aloud and spare not, if I had the strength to do it." As he had done so many times in over forty years of preaching, he decried the tendency to seek worldly riches before the "riches of eternity" that come only after "having done all the Lord requires of us, towards perfecting ourselves, and assisting him in the work of the salvation of the human family." With reference to the United Order, he dramatized its spiritual nature by proclaiming that, in reality, the Lord cared nothing for a man's property. "But what does the Lord want of this people? It is written in the Bible, and is said to be the words of the Lord, 'Son, give me thine heart.' Without it, you are not worth anything; with it, he has your gold and silver, your houses and your hands, your wives and your children, your all. . . . We do not want your property, we want you." He also touched on missionary work, immigration, donating to the poor, tithing, and the importance of keeping all the commandments in order to achieve the greatest possible blessings in the glories beyond this life. "Our Christian religion," he concluded, "incorporates every act of a person's life. We never should presume to anything unless we can say 'Father, sanction this, and crown the same with success.' If the Latter-day Saints live so, the victory is ours."

Perhaps the most important physical symbol of the establishment of the kingdom in the tops of the mountains was the building of temples, and at the heart of this 1876 sermon was a powerful reminder of the duties of the Saints in that regard. "We have a work to do just as important in its sphere as the Savior's work was in its sphere," the prophet reminded his people. "Our fathers cannot be made perfect without us; we cannot be made perfect without them. They have done their work and now sleep. We are now called upon to do ours; which is the greatest work man ever performed on the earth. . . . All I want is to see this people devote their means and interests to the building up of the kingdom of God, erecting Temples, and in them officiate for the living and the dead."[13]

Temple building in Utah was inaugurated when the site for the temple in Salt Lake City was chosen just four days after the Saints entered the valley, though actual construction did not begin until 1853. A large granite quarry in Little Cottonwood Canyon provided the building material, and as the work progressed ox teams were constantly engaged in hauling the stone to the temple site, where sometimes more than a hundred stonecutters were at work.

The first Utah temple to be completed, however, was in St. George. Ground was broken in November 1871, and construction soon began. The workers opened rock quarries, hauled timber eighty miles, and donated one day in ten as tithing labor. Some worked for a pittance in the quarry after walking five miles each day to work, then donated half their wages to the temple. Others donated food, clothing, and other goods to those who were working full-time. The beautiful white structure was finally completed and dedicated on April 6, 1877, with President Daniel H. Wells offering the prayer. Sites for the Logan and Manti temples were dedicated the same year, and these temples were completed in 1884 and 1888 respectively.

The St. George Temple symbolized many things to the Saints. First, of course, it demonstrated their continued dedication to temple work, and here they began for the first time to perform endowments in behalf of the dead. In addition, no sealings in behalf of the dead had been performed since the days of Nauvoo, and it was in the St. George Temple that this practice was renewed. The fact that this sacred work was moving forward again after thirty years reflected the determination of Brigham Young and the Saints to carry out all that had been established through the Prophet Joseph Smith.

The temple also symbolized other things for Brigham Young. The dedication of the Saints in building it was exemplary, as was their craftsmanship. Like all the temples of the nineteenth century, it was a labor of love, and a striking example of the painstaking handwork of pioneer artisans. In addition, it represented the self-sufficiency and independence the Church leader had idealized. Built entirely by the labor of the Saints from native materials, it was a monument to President Young's great concern for the development of local industry and

---

[13]*Journal of Discourses*, 18:212–17.

The first temple to be completed in Utah was the St. George Temple, shown here in process of construction. Groundbreaking took place in 1871, and it was dedicated in 1877. The original spire was replaced later with a much taller one. In the early twentieth century the interior of the temple was redesigned to provide separate lecture rooms for the various stages of the endowment ceremony. The temple was rededicated in 1975 after another major interior renovation. (Church Archives)

lack of dependence upon outside sources. Even the decorations were produced in Utah: the Provo Woolen Factory made carpet and the local sisters made rag carpets for the hallways. Fringe for the altars and pulpits was made from Utah-produced silk. Finally, the April 1877 general conference was held in the St. George Temple at the time it was dedicated. This was to be President Brigham Young's last conference.

Administrative Reform

During these same years the General Authorities took time to examine how the administrative structure of the Church had developed since Nauvoo, and they found need for some changes. As the Church had grown the administrative burdens on President Young had become heavier, and he sought to relieve himself of some of them. In April

Typical church service in the new Ephraim, Utah, tabernacle about 1900. In this important photograph today's Latter-day Saint will note a number of interesting differences between Church practices today and those of a century ago. The painting of murals in chapels was more commonplace; few young children attended preaching services; the sacrament was administered and distributed by mature men (possibly "acting" priests); and people offering public prayers often raised their hands in a worshipful attitude. (Church Archives)

1873 he resigned the office of trustee-in-trust and named his first counselor, George A. Smith, to succeed him. At the same time a dozen men were named assistant trustees. In addition, he selected five men as counselors, besides the two counselors already serving in the First Presidency. The precedent for this had been set earlier by Joseph Smith, and as Brigham Young advanced in years he felt the need to do the same thing.

A more basic decision concerning Church leadership was the question of seniority among the presiding authorities. It had not been fully clarified, and by June 1875 two apostles held positions within the Council of the Twelve contrary to President Young's understanding of seniority. Elders Orson Hyde and Orson Pratt had been excommunicated because of misunderstandings in the days of Joseph Smith, but both had been reinstated to their earlier positions in the Council of the Twelve, even though other men had been ordained and sustained in the meantime. With the full support of the Twelve, President Young ruled that seniority was to be held by those with the longest continuous position in the quorum. John Taylor, Wilford Woodruff, and George A. Smith were placed ahead of the other two as a result of this ruling, and thus the order of seniority was clearly defined and accepted by the leaders of the Church.

In the last year of his life President Young also inaugurated changes directly affecting the operation of the Church on the local level. Membership growth in the Rocky Mountain stakes had created a need for a general reform of some practices, but they had been neglected amid the problems of colonization, economic planning, and political conflict. Before he left St. George for the last time in the spring of 1877, he reorganized the officers of the stake, then proceeded to do the same in other stakes. Some that had become too large and unmanageable were divided, increasing the number of stakes from eight to eighteen. Members of the Council of the Twelve who had been presiding in stakes were released from local positions. In addition, stake presidents were instructed to hold stake conferences each quarter and to begin to hold monthly priesthood meetings.

Priesthood quorums were also affected by the reform. Elders quorums were instructed that they must be properly organized with ninety-six elders in each, even if it meant that two wards must join together to form a quorum. The quorums were encouraged to involve themselves in welfare services and to work closely with the United Orders then being established.

Equally important, the organization and administration of wards was tightened. In some areas acting bishops were serving without having been ordained, and some bishops were serving without counselors. A *Circular of the First Presidency* issued July 11, 1877, directed that henceforth all bishops were to be ordained high priests, and they were to have two counselors who were high priests. It was also emphasized that bishops were the presiding high priests in their respective wards. Previously there had been some differences between bishops and priesthood quorum leaders about who was the presiding authority.

All this was a significant representation of what had happened to the organization of the Church since the days of Nauvoo. The bishops' responsibilities had greatly expanded beyond their original economic functions, and the ward was becoming a fundamental part of the church administrative structure. Ward bishops also began once again to handle temple donations, and their responsibility to preside over priests quorums was reemphasized. Aaronic Priesthood quorums were clearly given ward status, where before many had functioned as stake units rather than as ward units. One of the most significant aspects of the developing organization was the emphasis placed on the ward as the primary local unit of church activity and the expanded role of bishops as heads of wards. These developments would be further augmented in the twentieth century, but by 1877 the ecclesiastical ward had come of age.

Another important move was the introduction of more youth into the Aaronic Priesthood. Brigham Young declared that the priesthood would be good training for young men and that they needed it much earlier than they had customarily been receiving it. No ages were set for receiving priesthood offices, but from that time more young men than ever before began to receive the Aaronic Priesthood.

In the October 1877 conference, Elder George Q. Cannon commented on the significance of the reform:

> I do not believe myself that President Young could have felt as happy, as I know he does feel, had he left the Church in the condition it was in when he commenced his labors last spring. I am convinced that it has added greatly to his satisfaction; it has been a fitting consummation to the labors of his long life that he should be spared to organize the Church throughout these valleys in the manner in which it now is organized.[14]

The closing years of President Young's life were a fitting conclusion to a remarkable career. True to his reputation as a colonizer, he had directed the opening of new colonies in Arizona. Known for his excellence in planning and administration, he had devised and promoted new plans for economic cooperation for the Saints. Never one to resist change if he believed change was needed, he had encouraged the founding of auxiliaries as well as the further development of stake, ward, and priesthood organization. At the same time, he was convinced that he was only building the kingdom upon the foundation laid by Joseph Smith. On August 29, 1877, Brigham Young died. His last words were simply: "Joseph! Joseph! Joseph!"

---

[14]*Journal of Discourses*, 19:232.

CHAPTER 12

A Turbulent Decade, *1877–1887*

Brigham Young was spared the shock of the Reynolds decision but his successor, John Taylor, was not so fortunate. During his leadership the Church continued to grow in numbers, expand its colonies, and refine its religious programs to meet the spiritual needs of the Saints, but it faced more intense legal challenges than ever before. For a time the Saints in both Utah and Idaho were disfranchised as new national legislation provided a more effective basis for legal attacks upon the Church, men and women alike among the Saints were jailed because of their beliefs, Church leaders were imprisoned or went into hiding, and the President of the Church went into exile. The ten years after 1877 constituted a turbulent decade.

The Second Apostolic Presidency

President Brigham Young's death left no question, as there had been at the death of Joseph Smith, about who should lead the Church. It was clear that the duties of the First Presidency devolved upon the Council of the Twelve, and the only question was when a new First Presidency should be organized. The Twelve disagreed on whether this should be done immediately, and until a unanimous agreement could be reached the Council itself functioned as the presidency of the Church. John Taylor was senior member of the Council, which meant that he was also its president and, in effect, presiding officer over the entire Church. Daniel H. Wells and John W. Young, who had been Brigham Young's counselors but were not members of the Twelve, were sustained as counselors to the Twelve Apostles.

The Twelve continued the administrative reforms initiated by Brigham Young and encouraged the expansion of church programs. The auxiliaries received special attention. In 1878 a central committee was established in each county of Utah to direct the work of the Young Men's Mutual Improvement Association. In 1880 its role in providing cultural and recreational activities had grown to such proportions that a general superintendency for the entire Church was named from among the Twelve. Wilford Woodruff became superintendent and Joseph F. Smith and Moses Thatcher were his counselors.

The women's organizations also received attention. The name of the Retrenchment Association was changed to the Young Ladies' Mutual Improvement Association by Eliza R. Snow, and in 1878 she began organizing stake boards. This reform proceeded rapidly during the next two years and finally, in 1880, a churchwide organization was created, with Elmina S. Taylor as president. On the same day, Eliza R. Snow again became general president of the Relief Society, but she continued in an advisory role to the YLMIA under a new calling as "president of woman's work of the Church in all the world."

About this time, in the summer of 1878, Eliza R. Snow visited Aurelia Spencer Rogers in Farmington, Utah, where their discussion turned to the needs of children. Both were concerned that more be done for their cultural, moral, and spiritual development than was being accomplished in the home and through the schools. On August 11, after Eliza Snow had consulted with President John Taylor and obtained permission from the bishop of Farmington Ward, Aurelia Rogers gathered together the parents in that ward and organized the first Primary Association in the Church. Two weeks later the children met for their first meeting. Eliza Snow spread the work throughout the territory, and soon the Primary organization was publishing its own manuals and songbooks and carrying out a remarkable program. Its activities included learning Church doctrine, reciting poetry, and participating in drama, crafts, and public speaking. The children in many wards published manuscript newspapers. Each year a Primary Fair also allowed the "little Saints" to display the results of their handiwork. In 1880 a churchwide organization was formed with Louie B. Felt as president.

One method adopted by Church leaders to encourage participation in these auxiliary organizations was special missionary work. In 1878 a group of missionaries was called to promote membership in the Deseret Sunday School Union, and in 1880 several Mutual Improvement Association missionaries were called to strengthen that program. They were to help stake leaders perfect the organization, encourage the establishment of libraries and reading rooms, and extend the circulation of the *Contributor*, the official MIA publication. The successful MIA missionary program continued for twenty-five years. In addition, auxiliaries were soon extended to other areas. The first Relief Society and MIA in Denmark were organized at Copenhagen in 1879, for instance, and other groups were soon organized in the rest of Scandinavia.

One of the complicated administrative problems facing the Twelve was the disposition of Brigham Young's estate. Because the anti-bigamy law of 1862 had made it illegal for the Church to own property valued at more than $50,000, Brigham Young as well as other Church leaders had felt it prudent to mix many Church accounts with their own. Brigham Young's apparent wealth actually consisted of bonds and property he was holding for the Church, but after his death it was difficult to sort out the holdings accurately. It was finally determined that his estate was worth approximately $1,626,000, but obligations of more than a million dollars to the Church plus other debts and executors' fees reduced the family's claim to $224,000. When seven of his dissatisfied heirs challenged this settlement, however, the matter was settled out of court and the Church agreed to give the heirs an additional $75,000.

One interesting item included in Brigham Young's estate was the magnificent, though uncompleted, "Gardo House." Designed originally as a private home, it was also envisioned as an official residence for the President of the Church, where visiting dignitaries could be appropriately entertained. With the encouragement of the Twelve, Elder George Q. Cannon suggested more than once that John Taylor make it his residence, but each time President Taylor declined. In April 1879 Elder Cannon presented the matter to the general conference, which approved President Taylor's use of the mansion as a kind of Mormon "White House." A man of simple tastes and not given to ostentation, President Taylor only reluctantly accepted the offer. After his death this beautiful home was rented out, then sold, and in 1925 it was razed to make way for a federal reserve bank building.

Economically, the Church seemed financially sound, despite federal restrictions on how much property it could hold. Its revenues in 1880 amounted to over $1,000,000, with $540,000 coming from tithing and the rest from donations to temples, contributions to the Perpetual Emigrating Fund, and income from various Church enterprises. Its major expenditures that year included $235,000 for temple construction, $91,000 for general administrative needs, and $28,000 for relief to the poor and to the Indians.

The imposing Gardo House was built as an official residence for Church presidents. This view of South Temple in 1879 also shows Brigham Young's office, between his Lion House and Beehive House, his steepled, family schoolhouse, and a rear view of George A. Smith's residence and the adjacent Historian's Office. (Church Archives)

Jubilee Year

In 1880, fifty years after its organization, the Church celebrated a Year of Jubilee, following the ancient Hebrew custom of observing every fiftieth year as a jubilee. At the April general conference President Taylor made some dramatic proposals, again suggested by Hebrew anniversary practices. Many individuals still owed money to the Perpetual Emigrating Fund, but the indebtedness of the "worthy poor" was struck from the books. This amounted to $802,000, or half the total deficit. "The rich can always take care of themselves," explained President Taylor, "that is, so far as this world is concerned."[1] In addition, half the unpaid tithing was forgiven the poor on the same principle. President Taylor also proposed distributing a thousand head of cattle and five thousand sheep to the poor. Further, the Relief Society had been storing grain for years while a number of Saints had ignored similar advice and were without grain after a drought in 1879. The Relief Society was asked to loan nearly 35,000 bushels to the less fortunate farmers, to

---

[1]Roberts, *Life of John Taylor*, p. 334.

be returned the next year without interest. All this was accepted, and President Taylor raised his voice in a dramatic exclamation: "It is the time of Jubilee!"

The Saints were asked also to be generous with one another in their financial obligations. In an official circular President Taylor urged the well-to-do to forgive their debtors as much as they would desire if their circumstances were reversed, "thus doing unto others as you would that others should do unto you. . . . Free the worthy, debt-bound brother if you can. Let there be no rich among us from whose tables fall crumbs to feed a wounded Lazarus. . . . The Church of Christ has set us a worthy example, let us follow it, so that God may forgive our debts as we forgive our debtors."[2]

In the meantime, President Taylor became especially anxious that the First Presidency be reorganized so that the Church would be fully organized according to the accepted revelations. In October 1880 the Council of the Twelve discussed the matter for two days and came to a unanimous conclusion that it was the will of the Lord that this should happen. At the general conference held that month, John Taylor was sustained as President, with George Q. Cannon and Joseph F. Smith as his counselors.

Church Publications

The Church was involved in a variety of activities as it observed its fiftieth anniversary, and in some ways its several publications represented that variety. The *Deseret News* continued as the official newspaper of the Church, reporting both national and local news, and the *Woman's Exponent* remained a powerful organ representing women's views and interests. Some of the improvement and literary associations established in various wards began to publish the works of their members, and the *Amateur*, which appeared in Ogden in 1877, was a good example. Two years later the first edition of the *Contributor* was issued. This periodical, edited by Junius F. Wells, became the official publication of the Mutual Improvement Associations and got its name from its announced purpose of encouraging young people to contribute their works for publication.

That same year the Sunday School began publishing readers for the children, and in 1884 it issued the *Deseret Sunday School Union Music*

---

[2]Roberts, *Life of John Taylor*, p. 337.

First Presidency, 1880–1887: President John Taylor, with George Q. Cannon, first counselor (left), and Joseph F. Smith, second counselor (right). (Church Archives)

Book. This replaced the music cards previously used and provided a broader range of music for the fife and drum bands the Sunday Schools were organizing to help develop the talents of youth.

This period also saw renewed interest in publishing modern scriptures. The Book of Mormon was published in Swedish in 1878. In 1879 the first edition of the Doctrine and Covenants to include extensive cross-references and explanatory notes was issued. Prepared by Elder Orson Pratt, who had divided the book into chapters and verses three years earlier, this new edition, published in England, was expanded to include 136 sections. It was re-canonized by a vote at the general conference of October 1880, when the Pearl of Great Price also was formally accepted as scripture. As a result, the Church now had four standard works of scripture: the Bible, the Book of Mormon, the Doctrine and Covenants, and the Pearl of Great Price.

The Mormon People after Fifty Years

As the Church celebrated its fiftieth birthday, Church membership stood at nearly 134,000, with approximately 114,000 Saints located in Utah and constituting about 79 percent of the territory's population.

Despite the turbulence of the times, there was every evidence of vibrancy and vitality among the Saints.

More than anything else, life among the Mormons centered around the family. Not unlike the attitudes of many others in the society around them, the Saints believed that the position of the wife and mother in the home was fundamental, for she was the one who had the most influence in shaping the minds and hearts of future generations. The husbands were charged with the responsibility for the spirit of the home. Brigham Young urged the men to control their tongues and passions, and he pleaded with parents to discipline their children not with the whip but with patience and forbearance. "Kind looks, kind actions, kind words, and a lovely, holy deportment towards them," he preached in 1864, "will bind our children to us with bands that cannot easily be broken; while abuse and unkindness will drive them from us, and break asunder every holy tie that should bend them to us and the everlasting covenant in which we are all embraced."[3]

At the same time, building strong and vital homes was not the only role of women in LDS society. In rural communities, especially, they often worked side-by-side with their husbands taking care of the farm and doing all the tasks necessary for the economic well-being of the family. Plural wives often had their individual homes to care for, and sometimes, especially after their husbands were cast in prison or fled their communities in order to escape prosecution, had to earn the entire living for their families. Beyond that, some women felt that plural marriage even tended to "free" them for greater participation in the political and economic affairs of the community, and it is significant that many of those who led out in directing various programs for social improvement in Utah were, in fact, the plural wives of prominent Latter-day Saint priesthood leaders. These included Eliza R. Snow, Zina D. H. Young, Presendia L. Kimball, Elizabeth Ann Whitney, Sarah M. Kimball, Bathsheba W. Smith, Mary Isabella Horne, and Phoebe Woodruff. Another of their number, Emmeline B. Wells, even argued in the *Woman's Exponent* of May 1, 1879, that "[plural marriage] gives women the highest opportunities for self-development, exercise of judgment, and arouses latent faculties, making them more truly cultivated in the actual realities of life, more independent in thought and mind, noble and unselfish."

---

[3]*Journal of Discourses*, 10:361.

Brigham Young urged that women should go beyond the home and contribute in a variety of ways to the well-being of the community. "We believe," he said, "that . . . they should stand behind the counter, study law or physic [medicine], or become good bookkeepers and be able to do the business in any counting house, and all this to enlarge their sphere of usefulness for the benefit of society at large. In following these things they but answer the design of their creation."[4]

Mormon women, then, were found in almost every aspect of community life. They built and managed cooperative stores, ran the silk industry, operated a grain-storage program, did the welfare work, developed home industries, taught the children, organized and ran a variety of charitable and other public-spirited organizations, promoted the cultural life of the community through leadership in civic organizations and cultural associations, encouraged young women to go to medical school, and got deeply involved in the quest for women's suffrage. They maintained steady contact with national women's organizations, and with important national leaders such as Susan B. Anthony and Elizabeth Cady Stanton.

Latter-day Saint families, meanwhile, sometimes faced unusual problems. Conversion to the Church often meant separation from family, either through estrangement or because only part of a family could afford to emigrate. In Utah, married men with families were not immune from mission calls, and fathers therefore sometimes were absent for extended periods, in a few cases as much as six years. While these constituted only a tiny portion of all married men at any given time, over the years a number of families had such an experience. Loneliness and sometimes economic hardship could result, though in the long run most families declared that the father's missionary service only enhanced their spiritual well-being.

The Mormon view of the family was governed in part by the unique LDS doctrine of the eternity of marriage and family relationships. Marriages performed by the authority of the priesthood were to last "for time and all eternity," and children born to those marriages became part of an eternal family. In addition, the doctrine of the premortal existence of all human beings, as spirit children of God, provided another religious basis for having large families, as by doing so the parents were providing the opportunity for unborn spirits to take up their mortal

---

[4]*Journal of Discourses*, 13:61.

existence more quickly. The birthrate among the Mormons was usually higher than the national average,[5] and the death rate was consistently lower. The Saints seemed to feel a special closeness to their families, and establishing family organizations and holding family reunions became an increasingly common occurrence in the Mormon community. Some family reunions, especially those in families of plural marriages, were amazingly large.

A New Look at Economics

In 1878 Church leaders established a new economic organization, Zion's Central Board of Trade, designed to supplement or, if necessary, replace the failing United Orders but still maintain Brigham Young's objective of economic independence for the Saints in Zion. With John Taylor as president and various leading businessmen throughout the territory as members, the Board of Trade became a powerful coordinating agency that held considerable influence because of its direct association with the Church. It was intended to promote business activities that would benefit the entire territory, seek new markets, disseminate information to farmers and manufacturers, prevent competition harmful to home industry, and, when necessary, regulate wages and prices for community benefit. Boards of trade were also created in each stake, to function under the coordination of the central organization.

The board promoted a variety of economic activities. Through regulating competition, it actually began to increase private enterprise in the territory and work toward completion of a comprehensive plan of resource development. It seemed to strike a satisfactory balance, at least for a time, between the need to maintain private enterprise and initiative and the need for group economic planning. Unfortunately, it was forced to disband in 1885 as a result of the anti-Mormon raid that reached its peak that year.

---

[5]An exception to this rule may have occurred during some of the last 30 years of the nineteenth century, when, for some unexplained reason, the statistical data shows the LDS average somewhat below the national average. See Dean L. May, "A Demographic Portrait of the Mormons, 1830–1980," in Thomas G. Alexander and Jessie L. Embry, eds., *After 150 Years: The Latter-day Saints in Sesquicentennial Perspective*, Charles Redd Monographs in Western History, no. 13 (Provo: Charles Redd Center for Western Studies, 1983), pp. 37–70.

W. Woodruff.   L. Snow   E. Snow   F. D. Richards

B. Young.   A. Carrington.   M. Thatcher   F. M. Lyman.

J. H. Smith.   G. Teasdale.   H. J. Grant.   J. W. Taylor.

Council of the Twelve in the 1880s: Wilford Woodruff, Lorenzo Snow, Erastus Snow, Franklin D. Richards, Brigham Young, Jr., Albert Carrington, Moses Thatcher, Francis M. Lyman, John Henry Smith, George Teasdale, Heber J. Grant, John W. Taylor. (Church Archives)

Zion's Borders Expand

Even though Brigham Young was gone, his dream of expanding the kingdom's perimeters was very much alive. Arable farmland in Utah was filling up, which led many Saints, with Church encouragement, to seek opportunities elsewhere. In the four-year period from 1876 to 1879, at least a hundred new settlements were founded outside Utah and more than twenty within the territory. Settlements in Arizona expanded rapidly, and other new areas were opened up. In August 1878, a small company of Saints that included the apostles Moses Thatcher and Brigham Young, Jr., visited Salt River Valley, later called Star Valley, in western Wyoming. There, in a tender scene typical of the Saints' deep spiritual feelings about such new colonies, the valley was dedicated as another gathering place. As recalled later by Elder Thatcher, "Kneeling down in the midst of this most Sweet and beautiful Valley on a lovely Sunday morning, with all nature smiling round, we humbly dedicated it, the surrounding mountains, timber and streams to the Lord our God for the use of the Saints." The prayer was offered by Elder Young, but as Elder Thatcher thought back on the occasion he could not help but write: "Oh may his richest blessings ever rest upon it and the Saints who may reside there. How I would rejoice if I could be permitted to return there with my family each summer for a rest. . . . But my calling is not one of rest or ease."[6] It was in the early 1880s that Saints from Utah began to migrate to this beautiful valley. In 1879 and 1880 Bunkerville and Mesquite, Nevada, were settled, and in the 1880s the Snake River Valley in southeastern Idaho was colonized. The Saints also expanded into Castle Valley in eastern Utah, as well as into the rugged San Juan River country of southeastern Utah. Beginning in 1878, they located settlements in south-central Colorado, populated by converts from the southern states and Saints from southern Utah.

In the mid-1880s the borders of Zion were expanded even further as a result of mounting antipolygamy prosecution. The pressure had become so intense by 1884 that President John Taylor instructed Christopher Layton, president of the St. Joseph Stake in Arizona, to lead his people into Mexico, if necessary, to defend themselves against their persecutors. "Better for parts of families to remove and go where they can live in peace," President Taylor wrote, "than to be hauled to jail and either incarcerated in the territory with thieves and murderers and other vile characters, or sent to the American Siberia in Detroit to serve out a long term of imprisonment."[7]

President Taylor himself, along with several other Church officials, visited Mexico in 1885, and by the end of the year hundreds of colonists,

---

[6]Moses Thatcher Journal, December 14, 1880, as cited in Dean L. May, "Between Two Cultures: The Mormon Settlement of Star Valley, Wyoming," *Journal of Mormon History* 13 (1986–87): 129–30.

[7]As quoted in Thomas Cottam Romney, *The Mormon Colonies in Mexico* (Salt Lake City: Deseret Book Co., 1938), p. 52.

mostly from Arizona and New Mexico, were pouring into the Mexican state of Chihuahua. They were disappointed, however, when they were unable to purchase lands and the acting governor of Chihuahua ordered them expelled from the province. Apparently he was influenced not only by anti-Mormon propaganda from the United States but also by certain Mexican officials who believed that the arrival of the Mormons was part of a Yankee effort at conquest.

The beleaguered colonists met their new challenge with faith and action. Sunday, April 12, 1885, was set aside as a day of fasting and prayer, and the colonists were told by their leaders that in spite of what was happening they were to plow and plant on their rented lands. In the meantime, Elders Moses Thatcher and Brigham Young, Jr., made a hurried trip to Mexico City, where they met with President Porfirio Diaz and other officials. Surprised at the expulsion order of the acting governor, Diaz revoked it and the Saints were allowed to remain in Mexico.

Settlement was not easy. The committees negotiating for land purchases seemed blocked at every turn, and the colonists continued to live in wagon boxes, tents, and caves. Negotiations were finally successful early in 1886, and on March 21 the happy colonists held a grand celebration and named their new settlement Colonia Juarez, in honor of a Mexican folk hero born on that day. Late that spring, however, their hopes were dashed again when they received word that an error had been made in describing the boundaries of their purchase, and their legal location was about two miles to the north. They were allowed to harvest their crops but were forced to move to the narrow, rocky valley of the Piedras Verdes River, where the soil was poor and the water scarce. Chances for success seemed bleak. In the spring of 1887, the water level of the Piedras Verdes fell even lower than usual, and on May 7 an earthquake hit the region. The Saints watched with despair as rocks tumbled from the mountains and forest fires burned for days. It was not long, however, before they became aware that, miraculously, the earthquake had opened fissures that increased the river's water by a third. As the colonists put it, "The Lord was in the earthquake," and the Mexican colony was saved.

In less than a decade more than three thousand Saints moved into Mexico. Three main settlements were established—Colonia Juarez, Colonia Dublan, and Colonia Diaz—and until 1895 George Teasdale, a member of the Council of the Twelve, presided over them. On December

Townsite of Colonia Juarez, Mexico, looking northwest. (Church Archives)

9 of that year a stake was organized, marking the success of the new place of refuge.

Even as some pushed south seeking refuge in Mexico, Charles Ora Card, president of the Cache Stake in Logan, Utah, was instructed by John Taylor to seek out a place of "asylum and justice" in Canada. In September 1886 a small group of explorers went into Canada and identified the vicinity of Cardston, Alberta, as the northern gathering place. The following spring a number of settlers from Cache County arrived, and soon settlements spread. By 1895 the body of Saints in Canada was large enough to warrant a stake in Alberta, the first to be organized outside the United States. Both Canada and Mexico became important gathering places for the harassed Saints who chose to leave the United States rather than face prosecution and disruption of their families.

Missionary Work and Immigration in a Time of Stress

Even as the Church devoted attention to expanding its colonies, it continued to augment its missionary activities — sometimes with impressive success and often in the face of serious obstacles.

The first proselyting efforts in Latin America since 1852 began in 1876 when a group of missionaries went into northern Mexico. They took with them a partial translation of the Book of Mormon that had been done by two of their number, Meliton G. Trejo, a former Spanish army officer who had joined the Church in Salt Lake City, and Daniel W. Jones. The group soon felt discouraged, though in 1877 other missionaries did make a few converts. A copy of the Book of Mormon left by the 1876 missionaries eventually fell into the hands of Plotino C. Rhodacanaty, a Greek resident of Mexico City, who wrote President John Taylor asking for more information. Moses Thatcher of the Council of the Twelve and Elders Trejo and James Z. Stewart were quickly sent to Mexico City. There a small group already studying LDS literature became the basis for a mission. In April 1881 Elder Thatcher dedicated Mexico for the preaching of the gospel, and Elders Trejo and Stewart finished their translation of the Book of Mormon. Only a few missionaries were called to Mexico, but between 1879 and 1889, when the mission was closed, 242 converts were baptized. After that most of the branches collapsed and Juarez Stake remained the sole Latter-day Saint outpost in Mexico.

In New Zealand a branch was organized among the Maori people in 1883, and a native chief, Manihera, was ordained a priest and made president of the branch. At the same time, the number of missionaries in Europe continued to increase. In December 1884, Jacob Spori opened the Turkish Mission, which included the land of Palestine. Later Elder Spori and his companion, Joseph M. Tanner, preached to a small colony of Germans at Haifa, and on August 29, 1886, George Grau became the first person baptized in Palestine.

Over 2,300 missionaries were called in the 1880s, and in some cases Mormon women from Utah even accompanied their husbands on missions. Between 1850 and 1900, for example, eighty-nine such women served with their husbands in the Polynesian islands. Much of their time was spent in the drudgery of caring for mission homes, but many of them also did such things as organize schools, conduct meetings for native women, teach sewing and other domestic arts, and work with local Relief Societies (which were presided over by native women).

Missionary work continued uninterrupted throughout the United States, though sometimes with bitter opposition. Perhaps the most brutal treatment received by the missionaries in this era occurred in the South, which was still suffering the indignities of political reconstruction and seemed unwilling to tolerate any preventable outside influence. In this bitterly charged atmosphere Mormon missionaries were mistrusted not just because of the distorted image spread everywhere about them, but also because, to southern whites, they represented an external intrusion. In addition, after the Southern States Mission was organized in 1875, many converts emigrated from Tennessee, Arkansas, Georgia, Alabama, Mississippi, and Virginia, mostly to Colorado and Arizona, and such signs of Mormon successes angered many local citizens. Irate mobs, encouraged by southern ministers and congregations, drove the missionaries from their communities, and many elders were tied to trees, severely beaten, and threatened with death if they returned.

On July 21, 1879, Joseph Standing, presiding elder in the vicinity of Varnell's Station, Georgia, was shot to death by a mob. Surprisingly, his companion, Rudger Clawson, was allowed to leave the scene to secure help in removing the body. A coroner examined the body and gave a verdict of murder. Georgia state officials arrested three suspects, but these men were acquitted by the local jury despite the positive identification and eyewitness testimony given by Elder Clawson.

The Standing murder proved to be only a precedent as persecution mounted. The most flagrant act was the 1884 massacre at Cane Creek in Tennessee. There a mob interrupted religious services at the home of James Condor and demanded the surrender of the elders. Shooting ensued, and two missionaries, two investigators, and the leader of the mob were killed and a woman was crippled for life. The mission president had gone to Salt Lake City and had left the mission in charge of B. H. Roberts, soon to become a member of the First Council of the Seventy. Risking his own life, Elder Roberts went to Cane Creek in disguise, secured the bodies of the murdered elders, and sent them to Utah.

Because missionary activity continued to result in immigration from Europe, the Mormon question created a minor international episode. As early as the 1850s efforts were made to discourage foreign countries from allowing Mormon converts to flock to Utah, and in 1858 President James Buchanan even commented to Lord Clarendon, British secretary of foreign affairs, "I would thank you to keep your Mormons at home."[8] In 1879 both President Rutherford B. Hayes and Secretary of State William M. Evarts were convinced that they must try to halt Latter-day Saint immigration. On October 9 Evarts issued a proclamation to the American ambassadors in England, Germany, Norway, Sweden, and Denmark asking them to seek the aid of these governments

---

[8]William Mulder, "Immigration and the 'Mormon Question': An International Episode," *Western Political Quarterly* 9 (June 1956): 416.

in stopping any further Mormon departures to the United States. This was justified, in Evarts's mind, on the grounds that they were "potential violators" of the laws against polygamy.

The reaction in Europe was mixed. By this time considerable anti-Mormon sentiment colored public opinion, and distorted accounts of the Church in the American West were becoming widespread. Such things, however, could hardly justify a barrier against emigration, even though the Scandinavian countries promised to discourage it if they could. In England, Secretary Evarts was ridiculed by the press. The *London Times*, for example, denounced the very idea of curtailing the emigration of those "who have contravened no law," and the *London Examiner* took him severely to task.

The gathering to Utah, meanwhile, continued uninterrupted. Annual figures fluctuated greatly according to various economic conditions, but the average remained at about 1740 per year. A majority continued to come from Great Britain, although after 1855, Scandinavians, along with a few French, Italian, and German Saints, constituted an increasingly larger portion. As immigration continued to swell the LDS population in Utah, however, it naturally depleted the population of the Church elsewhere. In Great Britain, for example, membership dropped from 30,747 in 1850 to 2,770 in 1890, but during that same period of time 37,710 people had emigrated.[9]

Various factors affected the immigration process, one of which was the technology of the industrial revolution. Steamships were becoming more plentiful, and by the end of the 1860s most immigrants were using them. They were faster, the Church used its powerful bargaining position to negotiate exceptionally reasonable costs, and the mortality rate on steamships in 1872 was only one-twenty-fifth that of sailing vessels in 1867. After the completion of the transcontinental railroad in 1869, steamship travel combined with rail travel brought the Saints to Utah in dramatically reduced time. The first steamship company of 1869, for example, made its way from Liverpool to Salt Lake City in twenty-four days: a far cry from the three to five months required in the old days of sailing ships, stagecoaches, riverboats, and wagon trains. In 1877 a new record of seventeen days was set.

---

[9]See tables in V. Ben Bloxham, James R. Moss, and Larry C. Porter, eds., *Truth Will Prevail: The Rise of the Church of Jesus Christ of Latter-day Saints in the British Isles 1837–1987* (Printed in Cambridge: The Church of Jesus Christ of Latter-day Saints, 1987), pp. 214, 442.

Immigration for those who could not afford completely to finance themselves, which consisted of from 20 to 50 percent of the immigrants, was still supported, in part, by the Perpetual Emigrating Fund Company; but by far the largest amount of help came from private sources: friends, relatives, and a few instances of contract labor agreements. In 1880, for example, Simon Bamberger, a non-Mormon, helped five men emigrate from Great Britain to Sanpete County in Utah, where they agreed to work for him for a year producing coke. The cost of their migration was deducted from their wages.

The Continuing Crusade

For many Saints, the 1879 Supreme Court decision in the Reynolds case was a shattering blow to their confidence in the ultimate protection of the law. President John Taylor's relationship with his plural family, for example, was based on mutual love and respect as well as religious obligation. How, then, could he abandon wives who had already endured so many hardships for the sake of religious principle, and what could he say to his children who would thus seem disowned? The seventy-year-old Church leader had fought too long for the principle to give it up immediately, despite court decisions. His inward struggle must have been traumatic as he considered his options, but the principle remained the law of God until revoked by God.

President Taylor could not advise the Saints to abandon the law of God, for he had received no revelation authorizing him to do so. He could only advise them either to hide from law enforcement officers, face prosecution, or flee to new gathering places outside the United States. His attitude was boldly expressed to a federal official in Utah shortly after the Reynolds decision. The United States Constitution forbade interference with religious affairs, he declared. "I do not believe that the Supreme Court of the United States . . . has any right to interfere with my religious views, and in doing it they are violating their most sacred obligations." Then, in a powerful response to the common accusation that polygamy was immoral, he added,

> We acknowledge our children, we acknowledge our wives; we have no mistresses. We had no prostitution until it was introduced by monogamy, and I am told that these other diabolical deeds are following in its train. The courts have protected these people in their wicked practices. We repudiate all such things, and hence I consider that a system that will enable a man to carry out his

Elder B. H. Roberts in disguise. In 1884 he found it necessary to dress this way in order to enter the region of Cane Creek in Tennessee to obtain the bodies of two murdered missionaries. (Church Archives)

professions, and that will enable him to acknowledge his wife or wives and acknowledge and provide for his children and wives, is much more honorable than that principle which violates its marital relations, and, whilst hypocritically professing to be true to its pledges, recklessly violates the same and tramples upon every principle of honor.[10]

---

[10]*The Supreme Court Decision in the Reynolds Case: Interview between President John Taylor and O.J. Hollister,* reported by G.F. Gibbs (Salt Lake City: n.p., 1879), pp. 4,7.

The Latter-day Saints were not, by nature, violators of the law. They firmly believed that the Constitution of the United States was divinely inspired, and the Articles of Faith required them to honor, obey and sustain the law of the land. The decision to defy the Reynolds decision was a painful exception to an otherwise firm commitment to the rule of law and order.

Significantly, however, in choosing to defy the law, the Latter-day Saints were actually following in an American tradition of civil disobedience. On various previous occasions, including the years before the Revolutionary War, Americans had found certain laws offensive to their fundamental values and had decided openly to violate them. One of the most famous was Henry David Thoreau who, in 1846, willingly went to jail rather than pay taxes in support of the War with Mexico, which he considered immoral and unjust. Imprisonment, for him, was the symbol of obedience to a higher law, and it became the catalyst for his famous essay, "On the Duty of Civil Disobedience." "Must the citizen even for a moment, or in the least degree, resign his conscience to the legislator?" he asked. His answer was a resounding NO, for, he declared, "under a government which imprisons unjustly the true place for a just man is also a prison." While the Saints in Utah did not call upon Thoreau as a precedent for their own civil disobedience, their attitude was similar. Even though declared constitutional, the law was still repugnant to all their values, and they were willing to face harassment, exile, or imprisonment rather than bow to its demands.

These considerations counted little with any but the Saints. Instead, the crusade against them intensified. In September 1878 the *Boston Watchman*, a Baptist newspaper, suggested steps for a new anti-Mormon campaign, and to some degree these proposals actually foreshadowed the events of the next decade: Utah was to be prevented from becoming a state until polygamy was abandoned; Congress was to repeal women's suffrage in Utah; all those involved in plural marriage, including husbands, wives, and children, were to be disfranchised; and the public schools were to be "rescued" from Mormon control.

The following month two hundred non-Mormon women met in Salt Lake City and drafted an appeal to "the Christian Women of the United States," asking them to join in urging Congress to take stronger action against the Saints. Even Mrs. Rutherford B. Hayes, wife of the president of the United States, was enlisted in the crusade. A week later two thousand Latter-day Saint women held a counter-demonstration in the Salt Lake Theater and passed a resolution endorsing plural marriage as a religious practice. It was clear to the public that Mormon wives and daughters fully supported their religion.

The attacks on polygamy came from every direction. Women and women's groups were often in the forefront; prominent religious groups throughout the country also joined the crusade, though none of them attacked with more bitterness than certain Protestant churchmen in Utah. Perhaps the most revealing evidence of the saturation of the American mind with anti-Mormon sentiment was the fact that every president of the United States in this entire era joined the crusade and made it a point of public discussion.

The motives behind the anti-Mormon crusade were mixed. Some people were seeking political advantage, others sought public attention or financial gain, and still others simply were outraged at a system they did not understand and took little time to investigate. Some were well-meaning reformers whose only objective was to require the Saints, as American citizens, to conform to the marriage practice they considered the foundation of Christian society. The clash between people who were otherwise men and women of goodwill displays one tragedy of the conflict. Another was in the lives of those families who suffered as a result of the raids of the 1880s.

The Edmunds Act

Mounting political pressures finally resulted in congressional approval of the Edmunds Act of 1882. The new law provided punishment for both polygamy and unlawful cohabitation, and a person could be tried for both offenses at the same time. Anyone who had a husband or wife living and then married another was guilty of polygamy and could be sentenced to a $500 fine and five years in prison. In addition, the law made it impossible for anyone practicing polygamy to perform jury service. It declared vacant all offices in the Territory of Utah connected with registration and election duties, and established a board of five commissioners, to be appointed by the president, to assume these functions. The law also disfranchised and barred from public office anyone guilty of polygamy or unlawful cohabitation. Finally, the Edmunds Act provided that children born of polygamist parents before January 1, 1883, were legitimate, and the president of the United States was authorized to grant amnesty to those who had previously entered into plural marriage, provided they complied with whatever conditions he should set. The long-awaited "teeth" for the old anti-bigamy act had been provided.

Federal commission appointed under the Edmunds Act of 1882 to supervise election procedures in Utah. These men attempted to be fair but firm in their execution of the law. (Church Archives)

The new law was put into effect almost immediately. The Utah Commission, appointed on June 16, consisted of men who proved to be generally honest and fair, but who were determined to uphold the law. Their main function was to supervise all election procedures, and they interpreted the law to mean that anyone who had ever practiced plural marriage could be excluded from voting. New registration and voting officials were appointed throughout the territory, and anyone wishing to vote was required to take a test oath affirming he was not in violation of the law. As a result, more than twelve thousand Saints in Utah were disfranchised in the first year of the commission's existence. In 1885, much to the relief of the Latter-day Saints, the U.S. Supreme Court declared the Utah test oath unconstitutional.

First to be prosecuted under the new law was Rudger Clawson. His case was also the first to be brought before Charles S. Zane, the newly appointed federal judge in Utah and the major judicial force in the final battle against plural marriage. In the Clawson trial of 1884 the nature of the two opposing forces was clearly revealed. Unlike many earlier federal officials, Judge Zane was recognized as a man whose personal integrity was above reproach. Numerous cases outside the realm of polygamy demonstrated his commitment to fair play and justice before the law. Now that the Edmunds law was in effect, however, he was adamant about its enforcement. He demonstrated leniency toward those who would agree to comply with the law and abandon plural marriage, but he felt the need for severity toward those who refused to conform.

The twenty-seven-year-old Rudger Clawson, on the other hand, was equally determined to obey the law of God. He was convicted of both polygamy and unlawful cohabitation, but when Judge Zane allowed him to make a statement before being sentenced he only replied, "Your honor, I very much regret that the laws of my country should come in conflict with the laws of God; but whenever they do, I shall invariably choose the latter. If I did not so express myself, I should feel unworthy of the cause I represent." Clawson's sincerity was self-evident, as was his boldness, but he was sentenced to pay an $800 fine and serve four years in prison. After three years, he was pardoned by President Grover Cleveland.

For some Saints, however, the matter was not so simple. They faced a difficult dilemma: whether to obey the law of the Church that required them to continue in plural marriage, or to obey the law of the land. A few, for reasons of their own, decided that the better part of valor was to obey the constitutional law of the land and agree to give up their plural wives.

Thus the judicial crusade began, and it created a new way of life for many Saints. Otherwise law-abiding men suddenly found themselves on the underground—that is, going into hiding, and frequently moving from place to place to escape the marshals who were hunting them. Hideouts were prepared in homes, barns, and fields to serve as way stations for the fleeing "cohabs," as they were nicknamed by their pursuers. Secret codes were invented that could be sent between towns to warn of approaching deputies, and Mormon spotters became proficient at detecting the hunters and spreading the alarm. Not to be outdone, the scores of federal officers brought into the territory to conduct this all-out raid disguised themselves as peddlers or census takers in order to gain entry into homes and hired their own spotters to question children, gossip with neighbors, and even invade the privacy of homes. Ten- and twenty-dollar bounties were offered for every Latter-day Saint violator captured.

Even at its mildest the raid caused much distress. With husbands away, wives and children tended the farms, but often they, too, were forced to flee. Wives were required to testify against their husbands, and some were sent to prison for refusing. Some went on the underground, more often than not in places separate from their husbands. Babies were born on the underground, and wives and mothers suffered long periods of deprivation and fear. In all, between 1884 and 1893 more than a thousand judgments were secured for unlawful cohabitation and thirty-one for polygamy. At least one man, Edward M. Dalton, was killed by a pursuing deputy in 1886, adding to the bitterness of the Saints against the federal marshals' relentlessness.

In the meantime, the Supreme Court slowly clarified the legal technicalities of prosecution for polygamy. In 1885, responding to Mormon claims that they could not be prosecuted for marriages entered into prior to the passage of the law, the court ruled that illegal cohabitation was a continuing violation, so that if it continued after the law was passed a person could be prosecuted. On the other hand, the same decision provided some comfort to the Saints by declaring the test oath unconstitutional. Later the same year, in a far-reaching decision confirming the conviction of Angus M. Cannon, the court defined cohabiting as providing food and shelter on a regular basis for more than one woman. Such a definition made it difficult even for Saints who tried to live the law but felt obligated to continue to care for their plural wives. In 1886, however, the court overturned a particularly harsh decision of Judge Zane, who had developed a so-called segregation rule in which he assumed that the time a man lived in polygamy could be divided into years, months, or even weeks, that each period of time thus constituted a separate offense, and that the man could be tried for each offense. In the case of Lorenzo Snow, the court ruled that since cohabitation was "a continuous offense," dividing it into segments for the sake of separate convictions was arbitrary and wrong. This was small satisfaction for the Saints, who felt they should not be tried at all.

Prosecution was not limited to the Territory of Utah. The legislature of the Territory of Idaho also established a test oath that disfranchised the Saints, and an equally intense crusade was conducted by the federal marshals and judges there. In Arizona, too, the same thing happened, and when the prisons in these places became too crowded, the convicted "cohabs" were escorted to the federal penitentiary in Detroit, some two thousand miles away. This led to President Taylor's 1885 visit to the Saints in Arizona and his decision to advise them to flee to another country. After also visiting Mexico, President Taylor detoured to San Francisco on his way home. There he received word that it would be unsafe for him to return to Salt Lake City, for the federal authorities

$800 REWARD!

JOHN TAYLOR.   **GEORGE Q. CANNON.**

To be Paid for the Arrest of John Taylor and George Q. Cannon.

The above Reward will be paid for the delivery to me, or for information that will lead to the arrest of

JOHN TAYLOR,

President of the Mormon Church, and

George Q. Cannon,

His Counselor; or

$500 will be paid for Cannon alone, and $300 for Taylor.

All Conferences or Letters kept strictly secret.

S. H. GILSON,

22 and 23 Wasatch Building, Salt Lake City.

Salt Lake City, Jan. 31, 1887.

This reward poster appeared in the late 1880s when President Taylor and many other General Authorities of the Church had gone underground in order to escape prosecution under the Edmunds-Tucker Act. (Church Archives) had decided that he, too, should be arrested. The aging Church President decided, however, that his place was in Utah, and he arrived back in Salt Lake City on January 27, 1885. On February 1 he preached his last public sermon. Clearly indignant at what he considered judicial outrage, he criticized all that was taking place and explained his own refusal to submit to arrest willingly. He would submit to the law, he said, "if the law would only be a little more dignified," but until then he had no intention of being arrested. That night he disappeared from public view and, like so many of his followers, went into hiding on the underground.

The crusade disrupted many normal church activities, including the custom of holding general conference in Salt Lake City. Between 1884 and 1887 Church leaders considered it prudent to hold these meetings in Logan, Provo, and Coalville in order, if possible, to relieve those who attended from pressures of possible arrest. Federal officers, nevertheless, continued to show up at conference sites in the hope of apprehending fugitives, though they usually left empty-handed. The conferences were sparsely attended by Church officials, for most were in hiding. Apostle Franklin D. Richards, immune from prosecution by special arrangement with the government, presided over some of them. Guidance to the conferences came in the form of general epistles, signed by President Taylor and his first counselor, George Q. Cannon. Joseph F. Smith, the second counselor, was in Hawaii as a missionary. To the Saints, continuing to hold conferences even without their leaders bolstered their faith and eloquently testified of their continued opposition to any surrender to the government.

Meanwhile President Taylor moved from place to place and continued to direct the Church by writing letters. Hundreds of other Saints were also being pursued and hounded as the raids continued. As 1886 ended, nearly every settlement in Utah had been raided by federal marshals, hundreds of Saints had sought refuge in Mexico or Canada, and nearly all the leaders were in hiding. The situation was critical, but in the following year it would become even worse.

CHAPTER 13

The End of an Era, *1887–1896*

In general conference on the morning of October 6, 1890, the Church approved an official declaration, usually called the Manifesto, announcing that plural marriage had been discontinued. In an atmosphere charged with both disappointment and faith, George Q. Cannon, first counselor to President Wilford Woodruff, explained why the long-resisted move had finally been made. His sermon was based on portions of a revelation given to Joseph Smith in 1841, after the Saints had failed to build the city and temple they had been commanded to erect in Jackson County:

> Verily, verily, I say unto you, that when I give a commandment to any of the sons of men to do a work unto my name, and those sons of men go with all their might and with all they have to perform that work, and cease not their diligence, and their enemies come upon them and hinder them from performing that work, behold, it behooveth me to require that work no more at the hands of those sons of men, but to accept of their offerings. (D&C 124:49.)

The application to the principle of plural marriage was obvious. "It is on this basis," said President Cannon, "that President Woodruff has felt himself justified in issuing this Manifesto."[1] The Saints had fought to carry out the Lord's commandments, but as they entered the 1890s circumstances were changing. The Manifesto was only one of many events symbolizing the end of an important era and foreshadowing the adjustment of the Church to new challenges in the political and economic milieu of the twentieth century.

---

[1]Full discourse is in *Deseret Weekly*, October 18, 1890.

Another Change in Leadership

Beginning in early 1885, President John Taylor remained on the underground for nearly two-and-a-half years, separated from family and friends except for a few companions who shared his voluntary exile. His official residence, the "Gardo House," was continually watched and raided by United States officers bent upon his capture, but he was constantly on the move, accepting the hospitality proffered by trusted friends who felt honored at having the prophet beneath their roofs. So well kept was the secret of his whereabouts that squads of deputy marshals more than once approached the very house where he was staying, never suspecting how near they were to their objective. President Taylor's health began to fail in mid-1886, and on July 25, 1887, he died at his hiding place in Kaysville.

The death of President Taylor dissolved the First Presidency for the third time in the history of the Church, and again there was discussion as to whether it should be reorganized immediately. The Twelve presided over the Church for another two years, with Wilford Woodruff as their President and therefore head of the Church.

Wilford Woodruff's first public appearance after the death of President Taylor was heartwarming. Accompanied by Elders Lorenzo Snow and Franklin D. Richards, he entered the Salt Lake Tabernacle just before a general conference meeting on the afternoon of Sunday, October 9, 1887. The white-haired leader was immediately greeted with warm applause, which did not subside until he arose from his seat and waved to the multitude. No attempt was made to arrest him, but since it was unwise to remain "off the underground" for long, he went into retirement again after the meeting.

At the general conference of April 1889, the First Presidency was reorganized. President Woodruff retained George Q. Cannon and Joseph F. Smith as counselors. Members of the Twelve who earlier questioned President Cannon were reconciled with him. President Woodruff was concerned that at some future time failure to organize the First Presidency could cause serious problems. After considerable thought and prayer he instructed Lorenzo Snow, President of the Twelve, and other leaders that it was the will of the Lord that in case of the death of a President, a new First Presidency should be organized without delay. This was the last time the Council of the Twelve would be left to preside for any extended period.

The First Presidency under Wilford Woodruff. President Woodruff retained the men who had been John Taylor's counselors, and this group led the Church during the early years of transition after the "Manifesto." (Church Archives)

The Edmunds-Tucker Law and National Politics, 1887–89

It was clear to national political leaders in 1887 that the Latter-day Saints had no intention of changing their policies, despite intensified prosecution under the Edmunds law. They prepared a new measure, therefore, the Edmunds-Tucker Act, which seemed designed to destroy the Church itself.

Throughout this period the Church maintained several influential lobbyists in the nation's capital to plead its cause. In 1887 they included John T. Caine, Utah's delegate to Congress; John W. Young, a railroad promoter; Franklin S. Richards, the Church attorney; and George Ticknor Curtis, a non-Mormon attorney associated with Franklin Richards. These men were fully aware of the implications of the proposed law and did all they could to block it. Their most novel plan was to persuade Congressman William L. Scott of Pennsylvania to sponsor an amendment that would give Utah time to draw up another state constitution that outlawed polygamy, then apply for statehood before the Edmunds-Tucker Act went into effect. Mormon agents felt the only way to escape the perils of the forthcoming legislation was to persuade the public that plural marriage could be eliminated without it.

In Utah, some Church leaders were not so sure about the merits of the Scott amendment. At first President John Taylor was adamant in his refusal to consider it seriously. It would give the appearance, he felt, that the Saints intended to surrender plural marriage, and this he could not endorse unless God revoked the principle. He also believed that the move was politically unwise, for congressmen would be skeptical of a Mormon-supported anti-polygamy constitution and would reject it anyway. Others, however, suggested that there was a way to adopt such a constitution without denying their religious principles. It would outlaw polygamy in Utah, but it would be up to Utah itself to define the term, and this might be done in such a way that celestial marriage, at least, was not part of the definition. Furthermore, even if the more limited definition were not adopted, state courts would be more lenient in their prosecution of polygamy than federal courts.

The Scott amendment failed to pass and the Edmunds-Tucker Act went to President Grover Cleveland for approval. The president disliked its harsh provisions and was reluctant to sign it, especially if there was any chance the people of Utah would accept the spirit of the Scott amendment and present a petition for statehood based on an anti-polygamy constitution. But he was caught in a dilemma: if he signed the bill, he jeopardized his future negotiations with the Church; if he vetoed it, he would be in trouble with both political parties, clearly endangering his own political future. He finally allowed the bill to become law without his signature.

When Church leaders received word that the Edmunds-Tucker Bill had passed, President Taylor took a second look at the alternative proposal and decided to accept it if it would mean a complete settlement of the issue as far as the government was concerned. It would be clearly understood that the Church was not abandoning its teaching, even though its members would be voting for a constitution outlawing polygamy. At the end of June a constitutional convention in Utah drew up such a document, and it was almost unanimously approved by the electorate in August. A statehood petition was presented to Congress, though after nearly two years it failed to pass. This was Utah's sixth attempt to become a state but, as President Taylor had suspected earlier, national politicians would not accept a halfway measure in their effort to curb polygamy.

Partly in an effort to support the proposed constitution of 1887, Church leaders deemed it prudent to remain silent on the issue of plural marriage. Beginning in 1887, they rarely if ever discussed the principle in public discourse. They counseled Church publications to refrain from bringing it up at that particularly crucial time. The Endowment House on Temple Square was torn down in 1889. The battle for statehood was lost, however, and the cruel consequences of the Edmunds-Tucker Act were being felt. It would be only a short time before President Woodruff, as a result of his quest for divine guidance, would make the agonizing decision necessary to save the Church from virtual destruction.

What the Law Provided

The Edmunds-Tucker Act officially dissolved The Church of Jesus Christ of Latter-day Saints as a legal corporation and directed the attorney general to institute proceedings to accomplish this end. It also required the Church to forfeit to the United States all property in excess of $50,000. The chief agency for immigration, the Perpetual Emigrating Fund Company, was dissolved and its property escheated, and the territorial militia, the Nauvoo Legion, was disbanded.

To assist directly in the prosecution of polygamy, the law required compulsory attendance of witnesses at trials and stipulated the legality of testimony from a legal wife against her husband. County probate judges in Utah henceforth were to be appointed by the president of the United States, for these local officers helped empanel juries.

Other provisions struck at political rights and Mormon influence in the public schools. Women's suffrage was abolished in Utah and a new test oath was incorporated into election procedures. No one could vote, serve on a jury, or hold public office unless he signed an oath pledging obedience and support of anti-polygamy laws. Congress further ordered that territorial voting districts be redefined so that voting results could be controlled more effectively. The office of territorial superintendent of schools was eliminated, and schools were placed under the control of the federally appointed territorial supreme court and a court-appointed commissioner. In addition, the act required that all marriages be certified in the probate courts. Children born of plural marriages more than one year after the act was passed were disinherited.

In Hiding and in Prison for Conscience' Sake

Meanwhile, harassment by federal officials bent on arresting and imprisoning Mormon leaders continued. President Woodruff was one of those on the underground, and often used St. George as his head-quarters. Not far from the town was the tiny, out-of-the-way settlement of Atkinville, inhabited mainly by members of the William Atkin family who willingly accepted the Church leader in their home when he fled to avoid arrest in St. George. If any strangers approached Atkinville, word came rapidly through various lookouts and he departed immediately for a nearby wilderness area where thick undergrowth would protect him. The eighty-two-year-old Wilford Woodruff remained busy writing letters and conferring with trusted Church members, and as long as he remained in Atkinville young Will Thompson carried messages back and forth between him and the Saints in St. George.

One of the most important arrests of the period was that of George Q. Cannon. As first counselor to President John Taylor, President Cannon went into hiding with him in February 1885, and for an entire year federal marshals searched for both of them. In February 1886 a poster appeared offering a $300 reward for information leading to the arrest of President Taylor and $500 for President Cannon. Immediately the tempo of the hunt stepped up and on February 13 President Cannon was arrested in Nevada and returned to Utah for trial. Four days later,

Prisoners for conscience' sake. When George Q. Cannon and other Saints were serving time in the territorial penitentiary for their refusal to abandon their religious principles, they sometimes had their pictures taken for posterity, showing them in prison garb. Elder Cannon is seated in the center of the photograph. (Church Archives)

at a hearing conducted in Salt Lake City, he was required to post $45,000 bail in order to go free until the trial. When the case was called up for trial on March 17, he had again retired to the underground and the bail was forfeited. The search continued with another reward offered for his arrest but on September 17, 1888, when it appeared likely that a newly appointed judge would pronounce a more lenient sentence, he gave himself up. He was sentenced to 175 days in prison and a $450 fine. His entering prison, he said, had at least one good effect, for "it proves that the leading men are willing to suffer but not to concede." He was discharged from the Utah penitentiary on February 21, 1889.

As the most distinguished guest of the Utah penitentiary, President Cannon was able to transact a great deal of church and personal business, for his visitors were allowed to come and go freely. Among other things he supervised the Sunday Schools and finished writing a book on the life of Joseph Smith. In addition, the mere presence of a member of the First Presidency seemed to lift the spirits of other Latter-day Saint prisoners.

The "cohabs" enjoyed an unusual fraternity. They held regular religious services, often with outside speakers and musical numbers, including on one occasion the Tabernacle Choir. Many kept prison journals and autograph books in which they recorded original prose and poetry reflecting their feelings. One such verse was written in 1888 and, poor as it may have been, aptly represented the deep religious convictions of a proud people:

> Though confined in this prison, you are for a while,
> Keep cheerful and greet all your friends with a smile,
> The time will soon come when we all will be free,
> And the judgments of God on the wicked we'll see.
> We will pity them then and remember how they
> Sought to take both our rights and our families away.[2]

The Utah Commission reported with some dismay in 1890 that the prisoners were regarded as martyrs and that in some instances when they were released they were met at the prison gates by brass bands, escorted to their homes in a parade, and "toasted, extolled, and feasted as though it were the conclusion of some brilliant and honorable achievement."[3] So far as the Saints were concerned, it was exactly that.

Enforcement of the Edmunds-Tucker Act

Arrests and imprisonments alone were no real threat to the Church, for they could be endured by the Saints without disrupting its ability to operate as a legal institution in its day-to-day business. Temple building, missionary work, welfare activities, publishing, and general administrative affairs could continue, though somewhat curtailed. What did hurt was the Church's inability to acquire and hold the funds necessary to do these things, and the destruction of the political rights of many of its members, which meant they would have no influence on public policy in the territories in which they resided.

Despite the 1862 law that limited Church property holdings to $50,000, by 1887 it had acquired real and personal property worth possibly $3 million. There had simply been no way to enforce the restriction, which was generally thought to be unconstitutional. The Edmunds-Tucker Act changed this, for it called specifically for escheatment of Church property and the appointment of a receiver.

The Church would not part with its property lightly. Even before

---

[2]Quoted in Gustive O. Larson, The "Americanization" of Utah for Statehood (San Marino: The Huntington Library, 1971), p. 199.
[3]"Americanization" of Utah, p. 186.

the act was passed, the trustee-in-trust (President Taylor) and other General Authorities began a plan of action that they hoped would keep Church property from government control if the proposed measure became law. As Brigham Young had done earlier, they asked several prominent individuals to take over certain properties in their private accounts, holding them in trust for the Church. Since legally these properties would appear to be private property, there would be no need to forfeit them. Included in the transfer was the Church Historian's Office, which was the actual headquarters of the Church at the time—the place where most Church business was transacted. Separate non-profit associations were organized to hold property, such as the three Utah temples. Stake ecclesiastical associations received local meeting-houses, tithing houses, and stock in community herds of livestock.

The most important of all these financial transactions concerned tithing property, which was consigned to the ecclesiastical associations of the stakes before the new law became effective. Included were cattle, horses, sheep, grain, furniture, building materials, dairy products, and other items valued at approximately $270,000. Much of this property was used by the stakes to help establish academies.

Frank H. Dyer, the U.S. marshal in Utah and an active opponent of the Church, was appointed federal receiver for Church property and for the Perpetual Emigrating Fund. Immediately he confiscated all property that had not been sold or turned over to private individuals or other associations, then rented back to the Church certain properties, such as the Temple Block in Salt Lake City. He next attempted to obtain the property already deeded to other people, arguing that it actually belonged to the Church and therefore ought to be escheated. By the middle of 1888 more than $800,000 worth of property had been taken by the receiver, including a promissory note of $475,000 in cattle or cash to compensate for the tithing property turned over to the stake ecclesiastical associations.

Church leaders believed that the confiscation of property under the Edmunds-Tucker Act was unconstitutional, and in January 1889 they succeeded in bringing their case before the United States Supreme Court. On May 19, 1890, however, in a 5 to 4 decision, the Court upheld the constitutionality of all the government had done under the new law. The Saints were shocked, but there seemed to be little they could do to ward off the impending economic destruction of the Church.

This economic crusade was matched by the continuing political crusade. The Liberal party in Utah was hard at work in its effort to undercut all Church influence, and in 1889 it gained political control of the city of Ogden. Then, in the municipal elections of 1890, the Liberals gained control of Salt Lake City government. By that time some twelve thousand Utah citizens had been disfranchised because of the provisions of the Edmunds-Tucker Act, and because it was impossible for new convert immigrants to obtain citizenship in the territorial courts, they too were unable to vote. The bitter bias of at least one judge was displayed in his remark that an alien who was a member of the Church was "not a fit person to be made a citizen of the United States."

But this was not enough. In Idaho a test oath written by the territorial legislature disfranchised practically all Latter-day Saints by requiring them either to swear they did not believe in or belong to a church that believed in plural marriage, or to lose their voting rights. In 1888 a number of members in Idaho went so far as to have their names withdrawn from the records of the Church so they could legally vote. Their main objective was to defeat Fred T. Dubois, anti-Mormon federal marshal, who was running for territorial delegate to Congress. Their strategy did not work and Dubois was elected. While Utah Mormons looked on with a fearful eye, in February 1890 the Supreme Court of the United States upheld the constitutionality of the Idaho law.

The decision on the Idaho test oath encouraged Utah Liberals to seek one just like it and thus disfranchise even more Latter-day Saints. A representative was sent to Washington and soon a new measure, the Cullom-Strubble Bill, was introduced.

The Church quickly sent a delegation to Washington, headed by George Q. Cannon, in an effort to ward off the fearsome legislation. While there, the delegation received news that the Supreme Court had upheld the Edmunds-Tucker Act. The temporal strength of the Church had been dealt a crushing blow, and now, if the Cullom-Strubble Bill passed, its political influence would be equally devastated. In Utah the Saints organized a defense fund, gathering contributions from the wards and stakes in support of what they considered one of the most pivotal battles they had yet waged in the American capital. They were fighting not only to save the Church but also for one of the basic rights of citizens in a free society—the right to vote in their own local elections.

One of the men who worked hard in Washington to defeat the bill was Frank J. Cannon, son of George Q. Cannon. He represented, in many ways, "Young Utah"—the second and third generation of Utah Saints, most of whom, although loyal to the Church and its ideals, had not entered plural marriage and were quite willing to pledge that they would not do so. They felt it blatantly unfair that those who had not violated the law should be disfranchised because of what others had done, yet this is what the bill would have achieved. Young Cannon pleaded:

> The young men of the Mormon faith have accepted the special conditions imposed by the Government. They are giving every reasonable pledge that they will not disobey the laws of Congress relating to polygamy; and will not aid or abet others in disobeying such laws. It is a poor reward that this bill proposes to bestow — to inflict the same political deprivation on the men who are obeying the law as have been imposed upon offenders.[4]

The delegation met with little encouragement, however, and returned to Salt Lake City confident that nothing short of a declaration by the Church that plural marriage had ended would prevent approval of the Cullom-Strubble Bill or assure statehood for Utah.

President Woodruff had already been thinking about this possibility for months, discussing it with Church leaders and others and praying earnestly. Finally, and in no uncertain manner, he received the divine guidance he sought, and on September 25, 1890, he issued the Manifesto. Among other things, this important action forestalled passage of the Cullom-Strubble Bill.

President Woodruff's Revelation and the Manifesto

The Manifesto was not simply a political document. It represented many deep-rooted religious principles, some of which were more important to the Latter-day Saints even than the principle of plural marriage. One of these was their firm belief that through Joseph Smith the kingdom of God had been established in preparation for the second coming of Christ and the establishment of the Millennium. The political aspects of the kingdom (as represented by the old Council of Fifty) were no longer functioning, but to allow the spiritual kingdom, the Church, to be destroyed would be, in President Woodruff's opinion, the greatest failure possible. Above all else, even if it meant withdrawing approval for new plural marriages, the Church must be preserved to meet the Savior when he came. President Woodruff did not pretend to know when the Millennium would arrive, though he believed it was

---

[4]Whitney, *History of Utah*, 3:732.

imminent and that it would result in the political ascendancy of the kingdom of God, with Christ at its head, over all the earth. He was careful to avoid the unwise speculation of some Saints that this would happen in 1890, but on December 31, 1889, he wrote in his diary:

> Thus ends the year 1889 and the word of the Prophet Joseph Smith is beginning to be fulfilled that the whole nation would turn against Zion and make war upon the Saints. The nation has never been filled so full of lies against the Saints as today. 1890 will be an important year with the Latter Day Saints and the American nation.

Another essential principle to the Latter-day Saints was revelation. Despite any political or economic pressure that could be mustered, Church leaders would not have accepted the momentous decision on plural marriage had they not been assured that it came by revelation. How President Woodruff received the revelation, and how he let it be known, is an essential part of the history of the Manifesto.

Early in September 1890, President Woodruff made a trip to California, where he met with Isaac Trumbo and other political and business leaders, and then returned to Salt Lake City on September 21. There is no record of what they discussed, but clearly the problems of the Church weighed heavily on the President's mind, and he was concerned with the views of these men on Utah's chance for statehood, as well as the possibility of easing the Church's political and financial burdens. Immediately after his return he met with his counselors and members of the Council of the Twelve to discuss the policies that he now knew he must follow. "In broken and contrite spirit," he told them, he had sought the will of the Lord, and it had been revealed to him that the Church must relinquish the practice of plural marriage. There was a long and serious discussion in which some of the brethren at first resisted the inevitable, but one by one they acknowledged his decision as revelation. That same day, September 24, the Manifesto was issued to the press in the form of a reply to recent accusations that polygamous marriages were still being performed. Authorization for plural marriage had already been withdrawn, but this was the first official announcement that the Church would now fully conform to the law of the land. When questioned later, President Woodruff made it clear that the prohibition would apply throughout the Church, even in places where the law did not forbid the practice, and it would therefore be uniform Church policy. On September 25 he made the following poignant entry in his journal:

> I have arrived at a point in the history of my life as the President of the Church of Jesus Christ of Latter-day Saints where I am in the necessity of acting for the Temporal Salvation of the Church. The United States government has taken a stand and passed laws to destroy the Latter-day Saints upon the subject of polygamy or patriarchal order of marriage. And after praying to the Lord and feeling inspired by his spirit I have issued the following procla- mation. . . .

The Manifesto was simply an official declaration that the Church had already halted the teaching of plural marriage and was not allowing anyone to enter into the practice. In it President Woodruff said he intended to submit to the laws of the land and that there "is nothing in my teaching to the Church or in those of my associates, during the time specified, which can be reasonably construed to include or en- courage polygamy and when any elder of the church has used language which appeared to convey such teaching he has been promptly re- proved."

About two weeks later, on October 6, 1890, the Manifesto was presented to a general conference of the Church and approved. This action helped convince skeptics that the membership at large accepted the new position. Most Saints readily accepted the new direction. At the same time, a few die-hard opponents of the Church accused the Saints of insincerity and continued their attacks, but for the most part the Manifesto was accepted in good faith by non-Mormons and the path toward statehood and home rule was cleared. The Manifesto was finally incorporated into the Doctrine and Covenants in 1908.

Unfortunately, a few Latter-day Saints could not accept the Man- ifesto as revelation, for it reversed an earlier command. Some were not even persuaded by President Cannon's powerful sermon on October 6 reminding them of what the Lord had said through Joseph Smith: He would not require the Saints to fulfill a command when it became impossible because of persecution from their enemies. Yet the very principle of continuing revelation, one of the foundations of the Latter- day Saint faith, meant that changing circumstances would inevitably require new instructions. Joseph Smith once remarked that "that which is wrong under one circumstance, may be, and often is, right under another."[5] The Saints in all ages have heard sermons about the im-

---

[5]*History of the Church*, 5:135.

portance of following the *living* prophets, and this was the essential principle involved in accepting the Manifesto. As President Woodruff told a group of Saints in Logan in 1891:

> The Lord showed me by vision and revelation exactly what would take place if we did not stop this practice. . . . He has told me exactly what to do, and what the result would be if we did not do it. I have been called upon by friends outside of the Church and urged to take some steps with regard to this matter. They knew the course which the government was determined to take. . . . I saw exactly what would come to pass if there was not something done. I have had this spirit upon me for a long time. But I want to say this: I should have let all the temples go out of our hands; I should have gone to prison myself, and let every other man go there, had not the God of heaven commanded me to do what I did do; and when the hour came that I was commanded to do that, it was all clear to me.[6]

Aftermath and Statehood

The Manifesto left some problems still unresolved, but in general the atmosphere changed and the Church entered a new era of cooperation and understanding. One question was the status of those who became plural wives before the Manifesto; it was generally understood that husbands would not be required to reject them or their children. Even though some enemies of the Church were skeptical of the Saints' sincerity, most federal officials demonstrated faith in their intentions and leniency in administering the laws. Judge Charles S. Zane, for example, who earlier had been extremely harsh, demonstrated that his only concern was in upholding the law, not in punishing the Saints or destroying the Church. He was lenient with those who were now brought before his court and charged with polygamy, and he even signed a petition asking that an official pardon be given to Church members. Such action antagonized some anti-Mormons, but it heralded the approach of a new era of understanding. In one instance Judge James C. Miner heard the case of a Saint indicted on two counts of polygamy and asked him if he accepted the Manifesto and considered it valid. When the defendant said yes, the judge dismissed the case with a fine of six cents. In January 1893 retiring President Benjamin Harrison issued amnesty to all the Saints who had been in compliance with the

---

[6]*Deseret Evening News*, November 7, 1891.

Statehood for Utah was finally achieved in 1896. This photograph, showing the statehood star still in place above the Tabernacle organ, was taken in 1900 when the Church celebrated the Scandinavian Mission Jubilee. (Church Archives)

law since 1890, and in September 1894 President Grover Cleveland issued a more general amnesty.

Meanwhile, the quest for statehood continued. Before this could be achieved the Church political party in Utah had to be eliminated, and the only way to do this convincingly was to divide the Saints along national party lines. Accordingly, in June 1891 the People's party was formally dissolved. Two years later the Liberal party disbanded. So serious were Church leaders about the Saints aligning themselves with both national parties that they even preached it in stake conferences. Traditionally the Saints leaned toward the Democratic party, for the Republicans had been blamed for most anti-Mormon legislation. When it seemed, therefore, that the balance in Utah might favor the Democrats so heavily that it would appear as another Church party, the leaders encouraged some members to join the Republicans.

At the same time, national Republican party leaders looked with increasing favor on Utah statehood, and the Democrats, once thought to be the friends of the Mormons, seemed to be dragging their feet.

Church leaders were forming increasingly close friendships with Republican political leaders and businessmen, and it was due to a series of astute political moves by Republicans in Congress that the Utah enabling act was finally passed in 1894. It was signed by the Democratic president, Grover Cleveland, on July 16. Utahns immediately began writing a constitution that specifically prohibited plural marriage and ensured the complete separation of church and state. On January 4, 1896, Utah became a state, nearly fifty years after Brigham Young first began to seek that goal.

Inevitably, there were disagreements and some misunderstandings within the Church over political matters. In 1892, Elder Moses Thatcher of the Council of the Twelve, Elder B. H. Roberts of the First Council of Seventy, and Charles W. Penrose of the Salt Lake Stake presidency campaigned openly for the Democratic party, assuming that their church positions did not prohibit them from participating, as individuals, in partisan politics. The prevailing opinion among the leaders was that it would be unwise for such high officials to take to the political stump at that time. After being reprimanded, the three brethren in question confessed themselves in error.

In 1895 the matter came up again when Elder Thatcher accepted the nomination of the Democratic party for senator from Utah and B. H. Roberts agreed to be candidate for congressman. Again they were disciplined for having accepted the nominations without prior consultation with Church leaders. This did not mean that they could not be active in their respective political parties, President Woodruff explained in a public statement of October 19, but simply that they must get proper permission before running for office.

Neither man was elected, and the following year the General Authorities issued a formal statement, known as the "political rule of the Church." Designed to avoid similar controversies in the future, it reaffirmed that before accepting any position that would interfere with the discharge of his ecclesiastical duties, a leading Church official should apply to proper authorities to determine whether he could function adequately in both positions. "To maintain proper discipline and order in the church," the announcement read, "we deem this absolutely necessary." The document was signed by all General Authorities except two. One was in Europe and the other, Elder Moses Thatcher, refused. Because of his disharmony on this and other matters, Elder Thatcher's name was not presented with the other authorities sustained in the general conferences of 1896, and on November 19 he was officially dropped from the Twelve.

Church Activity in a Still Troubled Time

The Manifesto was issued partly to enable the Church to resume its normal activity, but other affairs had not been ignored in the meantime. Missionary work continued to expand, new stakes and wards were organized, auxiliary programs were augmented and refined, and increasing attention was paid to education.

Perhaps no President has been more known for his devotion to missionary work than Wilford Woodruff, and during his administration this Church activity was not neglected. Between 1890 and 1900, for example, 6,125 missionaries were called and set apart, nearly triple the number of the previous decade. Between 1888 and the end of the century, eleven new missions were opened.

Much of the new missionary activity centered in the South Pacific. In Samoa a mission was formally organized in June 1888. The mission president, Elder Joseph H. Dean, had been proselyting in Hawaii, where he had gone to escape prosecution under the Edmunds-Tucker Act. Upon arrival with his family in Samoa, he was received by Samuela Manoa, a Latter-day Saint from Hawaii, who helped him become acquainted and served as an interpreter. By the end of the year thirty-five people had been baptized, a meetinghouse constructed, and a Sunday School and Relief Society organized. Missionary work has been continuous in Samoa since then.

Missionaries were sent to Tonga in 1891. The elders quickly erected a mission home and purchased a thirteen-foot boat for travel among the various islands. Their success was limited, and the mission closed in 1897, not to reopen until 1917. At the same time, other elders were finding greater success among the Maori people of New Zealand and among the Australians. Both areas were part of the Australian Mission, but in 1898 the two were organized into separate jurisdictions.

Though immigration into Utah was declining in the 1890s and most immigrants still came from Europe, a number of converts from the South Pacific also wanted to emigrate. In 1894, for example, seven Maoris left New Zealand with a group of missionaries returning home, the beginning of a small but steady migration.

An effort by Pacific islanders to establish themselves in Utah became one of the most unusual colonizing experiments in Church history. This was the colony of Iosepa, in western Utah's Skull Valley. In 1889 the Church purchased a 1,290–acre ranch in this arid valley for the benefit of Hawaiian Saints who wanted to be near the Salt Lake Temple. The name, Iosepa, was the Hawaiian word for Joseph, and the settlement was named in honor of Joseph F. Smith, who had been prominent in spreading the gospel in the Hawaiian Islands. It must have seemed strange indeed to see these Hawaiian settlers begin farming and raising stock in an environment so different from their tropical island home. But with the aid of the Church they survived. They had many problems in adjusting; several people became discouraged, and in the end a plague of leprosy struck the settlement. By the time the colony was abandoned they were beginning to show a profit. The experiment ended in 1917 after the Church announced it would build a temple in Hawaii and offered to assist those interested in returning to their native land. Today the tiny, lonesome graveyard of the Hawaiian Saints seems paradoxical in its Utah desert setting. It is a fitting though pathetic reminder of the faith and determination of one group of Polynesian Saints, as well as lingering evidence of international efforts in the nineteenth century.

Missionary work began in California in 1892 and reopened in the eastern United States in 1893. In Asia, missionary work began in Turkey about 1885, under the direction of Jacob Spori, though it proceeded very slowly. The same year the first converts in Russia were baptized by a traveling elder from the Scandinavian Mission. Russia was officially dedicated for preaching the gospel in 1903 by Elder Francis M. Lyman, though missionaries were unable to work in that country until nearly ninety years later. In no area of the Near East did missionary work take hold permanently, but the efforts represented the Church's continuing interest in expanding its work worldwide.

The Church continued to make converts in its organized European missions, and many continued to emigrate. In general, however, the flow to Utah declined in the 1890s, dropping to half that of the previous decade. One reason was the dissolution of the Perpetual Emigrating Fund Company under the Edmunds-Tucker Law. Another was that the Church itself began to change its policy toward immigration. The colonization era was over, and economic opportunities for immigrants in Utah were becoming more limited. The original purpose of immigration, filling the region with Latter-day Saints so that the kingdom could not be shaken loose again, had been fulfilled. By the end of the decade Church leaders were beginning to encourage the Saints abroad to realize that emigration would not solve their economic problems. In 1898 President George Q. Cannon remarked in October conference that they had been counseling the Saints in other lands to "remain quiet for a while; to not be anxious to break up their homes to gather to Zion." With changing times and changing needs, this and other policies of the Church were also changing. Henceforth more attention would be paid to building Zion in other lands and in the hearts of the Saints, as the closing of the pioneer era foreshadowed greater efforts at internationalization.

To strengthen Zion in the wards and branches, the Church continually reassessed its auxiliary programs. In 1889 annual conferences were begun in Salt Lake City for Relief Society and Primary workers. This considerably reduced the load of general officers in these auxiliaries who earlier had tried to visit the stakes and wards regularly to give instructions. Representatives from the stakes could now carry the instructions back from the conferences.

The Sunday School was particularly active in the search for new and better ways to accomplish its mission of teaching the gospel. Sunday School missionaries continued to work in the stakes to create new interest. In November 1892 Brigham Young Academy opened a Sunday School normal training class, taught by the faculty but directed by the Deseret Sunday School Union board. By the end of the year nearly 150 Sunday School workers had been called to take this teacher training course, and they responded as if they had been called on missions. In 1894 the Sunday School also began to establish model Sunday Schools, which were conducted by prominent educators and served as examples to other Sunday School workers. To help support all these new efforts, in 1891 the auxiliary began an annual "Nickel Day" in the Sunday Schools, with members invited to make voluntary contributions of five cents or more. In later years "Nickel Day" became "Dime Sunday," and for years this annual collection was an important Sunday School tradition. In 1893 the Sunday School Union board began holding Sunday School conferences in each stake to better coordinate and promote the work. With these and other innovations, the auxiliaries helped provide continued spiritual instruction and growth.

The Church also expanded its programs of formal, weekday education, both religious and secular. Under the Edmunds-Tucker Act the funds appropriated from the Church were redirected to strengthen the tax-supported public schools in Utah, where religious education would, of course, be excluded. As Utah's children attended public schools in

A Utah schoolroom of the late nineteenth century. (Church Archives)

larger numbers, the Church soon began to hold religion classes in various ward meetinghouses after school, where religious training could take place without violating separation of church and state. In addition, academies were founded by the Church in most larger settlements. Between 1888 and 1891 at least thirty-one academies were started in Utah, Idaho, Arizona, Canada, and Mexico, and in 1907 and 1909 two more were begun in Colorado and Wyoming. Under the direction of a Church board of education, appointed in 1888, these academies were financed partly by the Church and partly by local stakes. Some began as elementary schools, but most soon became secondary schools and emphasized classical and vocational education as well as religious instruction.

Most symbolic of the Church's spiritual strength as the pioneer period closed was completion of the Salt Lake Temple. After forty years of construction, it was officially dedicated on April 6, 1893, though daily dedicatory services were held until April 18 in order to accommodate the crowds wanting to attend. Special services were held later for children under eight, and it was estimated that ultimately more than seventy-five thousand people attended the programs.

Among other things, the completion of the Salt Lake Temple represented the Saints' renewed determination to seek after the names of

Salt Lake Temple, dedicated in 1893, forty years after Brigham Young broke ground. This photograph of the Celestial Room was taken in 1911 and published the following year, along with photographs of other rooms of the temple, in James E. Talmage's The House of the Lord. *(C. R. Savage Company photograph, Church Archives)*

their dead ancestors and perform vicarious saving ordinances in their behalf. At the same time, the nature of the sealing ordinances was clarified by President Woodruff. Since the days of Joseph Smith the Saints had performed vicarious baptism in behalf of their dead loved ones. In addition, some members had themselves and their families sealed to prominent Church leaders under what was known as the "law of adoption," and by 1893 about thirteen thousand such "adoptions" in behalf of the dead had taken place. Members believed that by linking themselves and their immediate progenitors to prominent priesthood leaders, they would be assured in the next life of being attached to families holding the priesthood. By 1894 Church leaders had given this practice a great deal of reconsideration. In the April general conference

President Woodruff announced that he had received a revelation on the subject, and this revelation ended adoption in favor of vicariously sealing family groups together. In announcing the new revelation President Woodruff emphasized the importance of every person being adopted or sealed to his or her own parents, and so on back, "not to Wilford Woodruff, nor to any man outside the lineage of his fathers. That is the will of God to this people." If this should be done faithfully, he declared, the Saints would be doing "exactly what God said when he declared He would send Elijah the prophet in the last day."[7]

The results of the new revelation were impressive. Previously little genealogical work had been done among the Saints and few sealing ordinances had been performed beyond two or three generations. Now President Woodruff told them to trace their genealogies as far as they could and perform the appropriate sealings to "run this chain through as far as you can get it." The following month the Genealogical Society of Utah was formed under the Church's sponsorship, providing powerful stimulus to genealogical work. In the nineteenth century much of the Church's energy was absorbed by colonization, community building, and strengthening the temporal roots of Zion, but in the twentieth century a consuming dedication to genealogical research and temple work would replace some of the Saints' earlier concerns.

In this period of reevaluation and change, Church leaders also examined other long-standing practices. The custom of holding a special fast day and meeting on the first Thursday of each month, for example, was beginning to interfere with employment of Saints who could no longer drop their work in the middle of the week. Accordingly, in 1896 the First Presidency issued instructions that henceforth fast day would be observed on the first Sunday of each month.

Another nineteenth-century practice that was reexamined was rebaptism. For many years it had been common for members to recommit themselves to building the kingdom through rebaptism. This practice was not considered essential to salvation, but was a symbol of rededication. On other occasions the Saints were baptized as a symbolic gesture related to blessings for their health, entry into the United Order, preparation for marriage, and even for going to the temple if they had not been there for some time. So common, in fact, was rebaptism that printed forms introduced in 1877 for ward membership records con-

---

[7]*Deseret Evening News*, April 21, 1894.

Until dedication of the new Church Office Building in 1917, the old Church Historian's Office served as a headquarters building. It also housed the Genealogical Society of Utah, formed in 1894. Pictured here in the upper story genealogical library are, left to right, Nephi Anderson, Lillian Cameron, Joseph Christensen, Joseph Fielding Smith, and Bertha Emery. (Church Archives)

tained columns for recording it, and these forms were not replaced until 1900.

In 1893 the First Presidency instructed stake presidents not to require rebaptism for Saints wishing to attend the Salt Lake Temple dedication, for "the Lord will forgive sins if we forsake them." In 1897 the practice was discontinued altogether. As explained by President George Q. Cannon, the possibility of frequent rebaptism led many people to think of it as an easy way to obtain constant forgiveness of their sins. "It is repentance from sin that will save you," he reminded them, "not rebaptism."[8]

The End of an Era

As the nineteenth century ended, a number of long-standing temporal policies were disappearing and changing conditions were suggesting new directions for the future. Economically, the Church had ended its boycott of "gentile" merchants in 1882, opening retailing and manufacturing in Utah to private enterprise more widely than before. This meant that the Church would have less direct control over

---

[8]*Conference Report*, October 1897, p. 68.

the region's economy, even though most of the proliferating businesses were owned and operated by individual Latter-day Saints. Most Church-owned concerns were sold to private interests or adopted the competitive policies of private enterprise. Just as the elimination of polygamy and the alignment with national political parties had brought the Saints closer to the mainstream of American social and political life, so these economic changes helped facilitate their more rapid assimilation into the national economic system. This did not mean that the Church divorced itself completely from business enterprise. Rather, the few businesses it retained were operated independently as income-producing ventures rather than as shared community cooperatives. At the same time, the Church consciously promoted establishment of certain basic industries in the region and even, in some cases, loaned money to help them become established. This included beet sugar manufacturing, salt refining, hydroelectric power, and certain mining and transportation facilities.

Even while the Church promoted the region's well-being, its own financial situation was distressing. In 1894 its escheated personal property was returned and in 1896 the real estate came back, but it was less than what had been confiscated and did not greatly aid in settling the debts. In addition to the damage done by escheatment in the first place, the Church was hurt by the drop in tithing income when members felt it would only be confiscated by the government receiver and therefore saw no purpose in donating their income to that source. The nationwide depression of the 1890s probably also contributed to the loss of income. At the same time, the Church attempted to aid the families of those in prison, maintained a large defense fund for legal expenses, and faced the costs of finishing the Salt Lake Temple, expanding the educational program, and assisting in the development of industry. It had to operate on credit, and by 1898 the total debt amounted to more than $1,250,000. President Woodruff attempted to relieve the debt by issuing bonds and selling them to eastern financiers, but these negotiations fell through. It would remain for his successors, Lorenzo Snow and Joseph F. Smith, to find more successful ways of removing heavy financial burdens.

In a very real sense the year 1896 was both a culmination and a new beginning for the Church. The long struggle for statehood and home rule in Utah was ended and the chief causes of tension with the larger society were left behind. At the same time, important doctrines and practices were being clarified and a variety of programs expanded

World Room in the Manti Temple, which was dedicated in 1888. The Logan Temple, dedicated four years earlier, was first to include in its original plans separate rooms for each stage of the sacred temple ceremony. It soon became the practice to commission prominent artists to paint murals in some of the rooms of the temples to represent what those rooms symbolized. Near the end of the century a number of artists were sent to Europe for the express purpose of improving their skills and, upon their return, painting temple murals. This impressive mural in the Manti Temple was completed in 1948 by Minerva Teichert. It symbolizes the people of the world in many times and places, and in the background may be seen the peaceful valley where the temple itself is located. Temple mural art was once one of the distinctive art forms of Mormonism, and within the walls of these temples are the works of some of the Church's most distinguished artists, as well as a few important non-Mormon artists. The Los Angeles Temple, completed in 1956, was the last to be designed according to the traditional pattern and the last to include extensive murals. (Church Archives)

to provide greater spiritual and moral direction to the lives of the Saints. Despite all the changes, the Church had not lost sight of its major goals and the reason for its existence. The 1890s saw a reaffirmation of the faith that the kingdom of God had indeed been restored to earth through Joseph Smith, that divine priesthood authority existed within the Church, that the destiny of the Church was still guided by revelation, and that the fundamental principles received through Joseph Smith, the Book of Mormon, and the other scriptures were true. In doubling their efforts at missionary work and augmenting their dedication to genealogical and temple work, the Saints also demonstrated their basic faith that the gospel was for both the living and the dead, and that priesthood authority provided the means to save both. In the years to come they would continue their accommodation to the realities of the world around them, as well as their efforts to remain a "peculiar people," even while sharing their unique religious principles with all who would listen.

PART IV

A New Era, *1897–1950*

The Church Office Building (now called the Church Administration Building), completed in 1917, symbolized the transition of the Church from the problems of the nineteenth century to the security and prestige of the twentieth. (Church Archives)

AS THE TWENTIETH CENTURY dawned on New Year's Day, 1901, the venerable Lorenzo Snow attended a special service in the Tabernacle in Salt Lake City and presented a greeting to the world. The gentle, white-bearded prophet had lived through the entirety of Mormon history and now, eight months before his death, he looked forward to the new century as an era of dramatic possibilities:

> The lessons of the past century should have prepared us for the duties and glories of the opening era. It ought to be the age of peace, of greater progress, of the universal adoption of the golden rule. The barbarism of the past should be buried. War with its horrors should be a memory. The aim of nations should be fraternity and mutual greatness. The welfare of humanity should be studied instead of the enrichment of a race or the extension of an empire.[1]

President Snow's hope for universal peace and brotherhood reflected the Saints' continuing faith in the eventual establishment of the Millennium. But that was not to come in the immediate future. Instead, the first half of the new century saw the tempo of war accelerate around the world, along with new evidences of political corruption, greed, poverty, and social injustice.

The President's comment on the "enrichment of a race or the extension of an empire" was an oblique reference to the Spanish-American war recently ended, a war for an American empire justified in part by ill-perceived concepts of racial superiority. But the United States was not alone in its imperialistic ambitions, and by the outbreak of World War I in 1914, Western powers had extended their influence to nearly all parts of the earth. After the war most world leaders banded together in the League of Nations, hoping to create a force for peace. The United States, however, refused to join for fear of undermining its own sovereignty, and while this was not the only reason for the league's failure, it contributed. At the end of the 1930s war again engulfed the world as the totalitarian states of Germany, Italy, and Japan attempted to expand their political perimeters. After Japan attacked Pearl Harbor,

---

[1] *Deseret Evening News*, January 1, 1901.

the United States joined with England and the Soviet Union, a former German ally, to defeat the three major aggressors. After the war another world organization, the United Nations, tried anew to find a path to continuing world harmony, this time with full American support.

Though permanent peace was not forthcoming, the progress Lorenzo Snow envisioned came in other ways. The world saw amazing scientific and technological achievements. The radio, the automobile, and the airplane all brought the people of the world closer together. In medicine, improved anesthesia, better drugs, and new surgical developments prolonged life and improved health. Scientists registered significant attainments in chemistry, electronics, and atomic science, which had great potential for human happiness as well as for tragedy.

At the same time, world affairs became more and more a part of the story of the Latter-day Saints. Although always influenced by the forces around them, they felt the nature of that influence change in subtle and important ways. In the nineteenth century they had attempted to build the kingdom somewhat apart from the society that seemed to be working against them. In the first half of the twentieth century they abandoned separatism and became more directly involved in the broader political and economic life of the world around them, especially in that of the United States. The willing participation of American Saints in America's wars, as well as encouragement by Church leaders for non-American Saints to be loyal to their own countries, demonstrated that building the kingdom was basically nonpolitical. The Saints were influenced by and contributed to certain reform movements that swept America, particularly those, like prohibition, with direct application to gospel principles. They became active participants in American economic and political life, and a number of prominent Latter-day Saints made important contributions to the American scene while helping to create a positive image for the Church in the minds of their constituents. One was Reed Smoot, a member of the Council of the Twelve who served in the United States Senate for thirty years and had great influence on American economic policy. Another was J. Reuben Clark, Jr., a prominent international lawyer who held several important federal offices. After serving on international claims commissions and arbitration boards and as undersecretary of state and ambassador to Mexico, he retired from public service in 1933 when he was called into the First Presidency.

Other prominent Latter-day Saints in government during this period included James H. Moyle, assistant secretary of the treasury from 1917 to 1921, Edgar B. Brossard, member and then chairman of the United States Tariff Commission, William H. King, senator from 1917 to 1941, and William Spry, commissioner of public lands from 1921 to 1929. In addition, the man who was President of the Church from 1918 to 1945, Heber J. Grant, was a successful, respected American businessman. These individuals represented the new reality that Mormonism was more a part of American political and economic life than ever before.

The pattern of Church history in the twentieth century reflected the changing status of the Church itself. Gone was intensive immigration and, for the most part, planting new settlements in uninhabited areas. Gone also was the possibility of being continually driven from place to place, conflict with federal authority, and imprisonment for the sake of conscience. Instead, the Church found itself dealing with the problems created by a rapidly growing population, educational concerns, the need for more social and cultural programs, and constant consideration of necessary administrative reforms. While these concerns differed from the adventures of the nineteenth century, they were nevertheless as significant to the progress and development of the kingdom.

Even as the Saints were moving toward greater integration with the broader society, they attempted to remain aloof from the sins and destructive forces in that society. Their objective was to influence the world with the gospel, and to do so, they must remain in the world though not of it. Between 1900 and 1950 membership grew from 268,300 to over a million. The Church took advantage of new technological advances to enhance its programs. It continued to adjust its internal organization to meet the needs of a growing membership, and placed new emphasis upon the importance of building up the Church throughout the world rather than emigrating to Zion. Stakes were organized outside the Mountain West and new missions were opened.

The Church also confronted the challenge of new scientific and secular thought that, in some cases, seemed to challenge religious assumptions. With nationally and internationally respected scientists and educators such as James E. Talmage, John A. Widtsoe, and Joseph F. Merrill listed among its General Authorities, the Church assured its members that scientific truth would never really conflict with fundamentals of the gospel. Finally, the economic forces that produced the great Depression of the 1930s led the Church to adopt a new program of economic security for the Saints that became one of its most publicized features.

As the last prophet of the nineteenth century looked forward in 1901 to the new era, he concluded his message with a moving summary of the Saints' real objective for the world:

> I hope and look for grand events to occur in the Twentieth Century. At its auspicious dawn, I lift my hands and invoke the blessings of heaven upon the inhabitants of the earth. May the sunshine from above smile upon you. May the treasures of the ground and the fruits of the soil be brought forth freely for your good. May the light of truth chase darkness from your souls. May righteousness increase and iniquity diminish as the years of the century roll on. May justice triumph and corruption be stamped out. And may virtue and chastity and honor prevail, until evil shall be overcome and the earth shall be cleansed from wickedness. Let these sentiments, as the voice of the "Mormons" in the mountains of Utah, go forth to the whole world, and let all people know that our wish and our mission are for the blessing and salvation of the entire human race. May the Twentieth Century prove the happiest as it will be the grandest of all the ages of time, and may God be glorified in the victory that is coming over sin and sorrow and misery and death. Peace be unto you all![2]

---

[2]*Deseret Evening News*, January 1, 1901.

CHAPTER 14

A Time of Transition, *1897–1907*

The celebration of statehood was barely forgotten when a second public observance attracted the attention of the Saints in Utah. This was the Pioneer Jubilee of July 20–24, 1897 — in one sense a symbolic rite of passage from the old era to the new — and it presented two significant themes. One looked back and honored Utah's pioneers, while the other marched forward from 1847, applauding progress. These same themes would reveal themselves continuously in the coming years.

The turn of the century was a time of transition; the pioneering past gone, new challenges lay ahead. In 1897 only a few of the founding fathers of Mormonism remained. President Wilford Woodruff died September 2, 1898, and Lorenzo Snow became president eleven days later. In another three years, on October 10, 1901, President Snow passed away and his place was taken by Joseph F. Smith. Presidents Woodruff and Snow were the last of the first generation of Mormon leaders; President Smith, the son of Hyrum Smith, represented a second generation of leaders, for he was the first president to have been born in the Church. Other positions of leadership were also being filled by sons and grandsons of earlier stalwarts. Between October 1897 and 1907 eleven new apostles, two new members of the First Council of the Seventy, a new Presiding Bishop, and three Presiding Bishop's counselors would be chosen; of the whole group, only one was born before the Saints migrated to Utah. In addition, four auxiliaries would have new general presidencies.

At least six important themes may be identified as a new generation of leaders helped guide the Church into the twentieth century. First, and of particular significance under the new political détente achieved at Utah statehood, was a series of challenges to the Saints' political integrity. At least three times during the following decade their status as patriotic, law-abiding citizens was tested. Next, out of a past that had been discredited in the public mind, the Saints were newly awakened to their heritage of sacrifice and honor and began to place new emphasis on establishing this creditable heritage before the world. Third, the burden of financial indebtedness and the obligations of economic development received special attention. A fourth area of concern was the Church's contribution to family life and education, and a fifth involved a revitalized effort to carry the gospel to all the world. Finally, the Church was concerned with perfecting the Saints and launched a significant reform movement that affected both its priesthood and its auxiliary programs.

The Saints and American Politics

The agreements that led to statehood anticipated that in the future the Church would refrain from direct involvement in political affairs. This did not mean that individual leaders could not participate, but only that they would not exercise their influence as if they were speaking for the Church. It was also assumed that the Saints would demonstrate their political loyalty to the American system by upholding the laws against plural marriage. The Spanish-American War gave the Saints an opportunity to demonstrate a supportive attitude toward America in wartime, and the struggles over seating two General Authorities in Congress brought to light several political questions left dangling since 1896. In a sense, each of these events was a test of the Saints' political adaptability as they emerged into a new era.

In 1898 the United States declared war on Spain, culminating a months-long campaign promoted by American expansionists and journalists. The brutal treatment of Spanish political prisoners and others in Cuba was one of the most publicized complaints, but it was also clear that many expansionists hoped for war in order to grab the Philippines and other Spanish possessions for the United States. When it appeared that Spain was responsible for sinking the American battleship *Maine* in Havana Harbor, the popular clamor practically pushed America into war.

Although the Spanish-American War was generally popular, there were some Americans who decried it as evidence of American imperialism. In Utah, too, there were various opinions. The Church-owned *Deseret News* criticized the idea of American militarism, and Joseph F. Smith told a Salt Lake Stake conference he deplored the war spirit.

Mormon volunteers who participated in the Spanish-American War returned to Salt Lake City for a hero's welcome and parade along South Temple Street. (Savage and Ottinger photo, courtesy Church Archives)

Nevertheless, most Church leaders felt it important to stand with the American government, and for this reason they supported the war.

Brigham Young, Jr., a member of the Council of the Twelve, held a minority view. He counseled young men against enlistment and preached in the Tabernacle against the call for volunteers. The First Presidency requested him to stop his personal campaign against the war, which he did, and on April 28 they issued a formal statement in support of the war effort. Utah's volunteer quota was five hundred men — a number that brought immediate comparison with the Mormon Battalion. Official encouragement from the Church and the speed with which Utah's volunteer units were filled demonstrated that the Latter-day Saints in Utah were loyal to the American government and would support its military efforts. If former critics doubted Mormon patriotism, this response should have helped persuade them.

As the Church worked to disengage itself from direct involvement in matters of politics and government, members were urged to exercise their freedom in political activities and to put principle ahead of party in electing good men to public office. "I do not care whether a man is a Republican or a Democrat," said Wilford Woodruff in 1897, "but it is your duty to unite in electing good men to govern. . . . Unite together within your party lines and appoint good men."[1]

In this spirit, in 1898 Elder B. H. Roberts obtained permission from the First Presidency to seek the Democratic nomination for a seat in the House of Representatives. Elder Roberts had entered into plural marriage before the Manifesto and was still living with his plural wives. By informal agreement arranged after the Manifesto, it was assumed—though not written into law—that in such cases men would not be punished so long as they entered into no new plural marriages. Most Utah political leaders felt that polygamy was therefore a dead issue and that Elder Roberts would be accepted as a law-abiding citizen, as entitled to election as anyone else. The contest became an important test of that assumption.

Elder Roberts won both the nomination and the election, but the ensuing opposition was unexpected. Protestant ministers in Utah accused him and the Church of a breach of faith on the issue of polygamy, and after he was elected they promoted a nationwide campaign against him. Numerous protests were sent to Washington, including a petition claiming seven million signatures. Having failed to prevent his election, his opponents were determined to keep him from being seated.

For six weeks after Elder Roberts presented himself in Washington, a specially appointed committee investigated the charges against him. In the end the House voted 268 to 50 not to seat him. His place was later filled by William H. King, a Democrat and a monogamous Mormon. After 1890 Elder Roberts was never accused in the courts of violating the laws against polygamy, but his expulsion from the House of Representatives demonstrated that the nation at large was still wary of Latter-day Saint motives and that the Church had not yet completed the transition to widespread public acceptance.

Four years after the Roberts case another General Authority, Reed Smoot of the Council of the Twelve, was elected to the United States Senate as a Republican from Utah. Even though Elder Smoot could categorically deny any involvement with plural marriage, he spent nearly five years defending the legality of his election in a Senate investigation that once again exposed the Church, its leaders, and its doctrines to the scrutiny of the American public.

---

[1] *Conference Report*, October 1897, p. 71.

Prior to Elder Smoot's election the Church had made every effort to calm the continuing tempest over polygamy. In response to a national campaign for anti-polygamy amendments to the American Constitution, President Lorenzo Snow issued a statement in 1900 reaffirming the Church ban and declaring that any Latter-day Saint who contracted an unlawful marriage must "bear his own burden." At the same time, leaders made a quiet effort to have repealed a territorial unlawful cohabitation law that had been inadvertently codified into state law. Even though there was general agreement that former plural marriages contracted before the Manifesto could be continued, it was still possible for anti-Mormons to bring embarrassing action under that law whenever they wished. When opponents of the Church interpreted this move as a step toward reinitiating the practice, Church leaders attempted to quiet the agitation by publicly approving Governor Heber M. Wells's veto of the legislation that would have repealed the law.

A more pervasive problem was politics. A general, though unwritten, understanding provided for dividing important public offices somewhat equally between Mormons and friendly non-Mormons, but a few influential opponents of the Church felt left out. Their irritation led to the formation of the hostile American Party, which dominated Salt Lake City's municipal government from 1905 to 1911. They charged that too much Church involvement still persisted in politics. The Church's position that Latter-day Saint voters should place a candidate's personal qualifications above party label had subtle implications that contributed to this feeling. Joseph F. Smith, first counselor in the First Presidency, advised the Saints that before voting they should "get the word of the Lord as to who is the right man."[2] Even though the President of the Church still avoided taking an official stand on individual candidates, such statements along with the obvious personal interest Church leaders took in public issues gave partisans grounds for charging that Mormon leaders had not abandoned their involvement in political affairs.

Prominent Latter-day Saints were optimistic that these conflicts were only minor difficulties and that the Church was entering a new era of public acceptance. It was in this setting that Elder Reed Smoot announced his candidacy for the Senate in May 1902. Immediately there was a wave of opposition from the Salt Lake Ministerial Association,

_____

[2] *Conference Report*, October 1900, p. 48.

protesting it as a violation of the principle of separation of church and state. But on January 20, 1903, the Republican-dominated Utah legislature overwhelmingly elected him.

By the time Senator Smoot reached Washington, a number of protests were already there. The Senate voted to seat him, but the Committee on Privileges was given the responsibility of conducting a full investigation of the charges. The hearing opened in January 1904, and in the next thirty months over three thousand printed pages of testimony accumulated.

Objections to Senator Smoot took many forms. The extreme charge that he had plural wives and was therefore a lawbreaker was easily refuted. More serious was the accusation that he belonged to a self-perpetuating fifteen-member ruling body that controlled Utah's elections and economy. Church leaders, including Elder Smoot, were also charged with secretly continuing to preach and permit plural marriages. In addition, he was accused of taking a secret pledge of disloyalty to the American government.

Senator Smoot's opposition was indeed impressive. Attorney Robert W. Tayler called as witnesses not only leading sectarian ministers and missionaries but also important Church leaders, who were subjected to rigorous cross-examination. Tayler was effectively assisted by Fred T. Dubois, Idaho's leading crusader against the Mormons, and Frank J. Cannon, who had once helped fight for the Mormon cause but who was now politically embittered against the Church. Senator Smoot, on the other hand, had competent attorneys helping him, as well as a Church-appointed task force whose able spokesman was James E. Talmage. He had the backing also of several influential senators on the committee.

In reply to the charges against him, Senator Smoot emphasized the legality of his election and said he could be unseated only if he had been convicted of violating the law against polygamy or if he had taken an unpatriotic oath. Neither of these conditions existed. The hearings gave Elder Smoot's defenders opportunity to counter charges of Church control of politics by explaining the internal operations of the Church. Witnesses on his behalf asserted that the Church operated by common consent at all levels and that its members had their free agency in all things.

In December 1903 the First Presidency issued a statement clarifying the use of the term "Kingdom of God" and denying that the Church constituted a political kingdom. When the "political rule of the

Church," which required leaders to get permission before they ran for public office, was questioned, Church witnesses replied that this was merely a reasonable housekeeping regulation and that the Church had made no attempt to control state elections. With regard to plural marriage, a Church census was displayed showing that in 1902 there were only 897 polygamous families, as compared with 2,451 families twelve years earlier: clear evidence that the practice was dying out. Perhaps the most dramatic point in the investigation was when President Joseph F. Smith appeared as a witness. He testified regarding the nature of revelation and Church doctrine, free agency in the Church, and the discontinuance of polygamy. He had no firsthand knowledge, he reported, of any plural marriages being performed since 1890, for he had neither witnessed, performed, nor authorized any. Some men, including himself, were still living with plural wives whom they had married before the Manifesto, but this was not in violation of the understandings reached earlier. He also observed that half the Twelve and both of his counselors were monogamists.

In response to questions concerning what statements or literature could be considered Church doctrine, President Smith asserted that authoritative doctrine could be found only in the standard works and that any other writings or speeches were not binding. This was intended to satisfy the public that Latter-day Saints were free agents and not bound by some dictatorial system to accept every declaration that came along from high Church officials.

In the end, Senator Smoot retained his seat, despite the majority committee report which recommended his expulsion. He went on to serve a distinguished thirty-year career in the Senate, becoming highly respected among his colleagues for his personal integrity and hard work. He was most influential in economic affairs, especially as chairman of the Senate Finance Committee.

Additional Consequences of the Smoot Hearings

The Smoot hearings once again exposed the Church to national scrutiny, but they also had significant consequences within the Church. In 1904, for example, President Smith responded to charges of continuing polygamy with a new "Official Statement" denying that any marriage violating the law had taken place "with the sanction, consent or knowledge of the Church," and declaring that any known transgressors would be excommunicated. This statement, sometimes called the "Sec-

IN 1950

First Man—Who's the elderly looking Senator?
Second Man—That's Senator Smoot, the grand old man from Utah. They're
still taking his seat away from him.

This cartoon, friendly in spirit, was published in the Washington Herald
*during the three-year investigation concerning the seating of Reed Smoot in
the United States Senate. (Church Archives)*

ond Manifesto," was a clear public signal that further plural marriages, in or outside the United States, would be ended. In Canada and Mexico the practice was illegal, but the laws against it had not been strictly enforced.

No matter how one feels about the idea of plural marriage, it must be remembered that many Saints, both men and women, in the nineteenth century were deeply devoted to it. It had been preached, practiced, and defended for over a half-century as the will of God. Such an institution simply could not fade away overnight, even after the Manifesto, which was accepted by the Church generally as also the will of God. It was only to be expected that well into the twentieth century there would be continuing differences of interpretation on how and when to implement the new policy.

A few Church authorities had adopted a literal interpretation of the Manifesto, despite President Woodruff's statement that it applied everywhere, and had continued to authorize and perform plural marriages outside Utah. Some interpreted President Woodruff's statement as "policy," rather than doctrine, and felt personally justified in continuing privately to perform new marriages. The new declaration was a definite indication that the practice must stop. Even then, two apostles, John W. Taylor and Matthias F. Cowley, could not accept this interpretation. In October 1905 they finally submitted letters of resignation, and at the following April conference they were dropped from the Council of the Twelve.

Another result of the Smoot hearings was that President Smith directed that President Woodruff's 1890 Manifesto be published in the Doctrine and Covenants. This satisfied critics who had pointed out that this book of scripture contained the revelation authorizing plural marriage but no revelation terminating it.

Finally, in 1907 the First Presidency published *An Address: The Church of Jesus Christ of Latter-day Saints to the World*. Prepared with the help of an eight-member study committee, this sixteen-page document was an important reply to the charges made in Washington during the previous four years. Written in a conciliatory spirit, the address restated the basic religious beliefs of the Church and affirmed that it had no intention of dominating the state, was politically loyal, and had abandoned plural marriage. It was adopted unanimously by the general conference of April 1907. The difficult problems of political transition were not resolved, but at least the Church was making progress toward eliminating public misunderstandings.

First Presidency and Council of the Twelve, September 1898. Front row, left to right: Brigham Young, Jr., Franklin D. Richards, President Lorenzo Snow, George Q. Cannon (first counselor), Joseph F. Smith (second counselor), Anthon H. Lund. Back row: Matthias F. Cowley, Abraham O. Woodruff, George Teasdale, Francis M. Lyman, John Henry Smith, Heber J. Grant, John W. Taylor, Marriner W. Merrill. When Lorenzo Snow became President of the Church in September, a vacancy was left in the Council of the Twelve, which was filled the following month by Rudger Clawson. (Church Archives)

Creating a New Image

Throughout the nineteenth century the Church and its members were presented to the public in popular magazines and novels that stressed the sensational. Many readers gained their only conception of Mormonism from articles condemning polygamy or criticizing the leaders as autocrats and denouncing the Church as un-American. The image changed little during the decade of the Roberts and Smoot investigations, though some members received positive recognition for their practical accomplishments in economics and education. The tone of periodical literature seemed to be moving from hostility toward neutrality, but fictional accounts retained the proven format of money-making sensationalism. The literature was often lurid, combining sensualism and violence, and it even found its way into the European press. Missionaries almost anywhere in the Western world might encounter people who said they had "read *all* about Mormonism" but who really knew only the inaccurate, sensational stories.

More favorable comments were volunteered on occasion by people who took time to observe the Saints seriously. To encourage and promote the spread of positive statements, Church leaders often referred to them in public speeches, and Church magazines often cited them. The *Improvement Era*, for example, was understandably pleased in 1904 when G. P. Putnam's Sons published *Scientific Aspects of Mormonism* by BYU Professor N. L. Nelson. According to the *Era*, it was the first friendly book written by a Mormon to be published by a prominent Eastern house. More directly, non-Mormon Charles Ellis wrote a pamphlet in 1899 entitled *Mormons and Mormonism: Why They Have Been Opposed, Maligned and Persecuted*. It was eventually reprinted by the Church for missionary use.

To counteract the generally negative image still being promoted, a program was established for disseminating information to tourists. Heretofore visitors to Utah commonly received their information from cab drivers who made storytelling a profitable business. As early as 1898 Benjamin Goddard suggested the need for a local missionary program aimed at visitors, and in 1901 LeRoi C. Snow discussed the suggestion with the general board of the YMMIA. The matter soon reached the First Council of the Seventy, and, with the approval of the First Presidency, the Seventies established a Bureau of Information and Church Literature on Temple Square. It opened on August 4, 1902, in a small octagonal building measuring about twenty feet across, costing less than six hundred dollars.

Staffed with about two dozen volunteers, the bureau distributed Articles of Faith cards and thousands of free tracts. By the end of the year 150,000 tourists had heard the Mormon story from the Mormons themselves. So pleased were Church leaders that in 1903 they authorized the opening of a branch center at the Saltair resort on the Great Salt Lake, and the following year a new $9,000 building was provided for the bureau on Temple Square.

The new information center became a significant force in building goodwill toward the Latter-day Saints. Eastern newspaper editors were among the thousands who went away impressed and so reported to their readers. In addition, the free guided tours of Temple Square helped promote the fame of the Tabernacle organ and the Salt Lake Tabernacle Choir. In the summer of 1906 daily recitals on the enlarged and rebuilt organ were begun and soon became a regular feature offered to tourists. By the late 1920s annual visitors numbered 200,000.

Recapturing the Past

Church leaders were concerned not only with the Church's public image but also with helping the Saints themselves gain a better collective memory and personal appreciation of their heritage. They supported numerous historical celebrations in which members participated during these years, as well as the formation of a number of historical organizations in the 1890s. These included the Genealogical Society of Utah (1894), the Utah Society of the Sons of the American Revolution (1895), the Utah State Historical Society (1897), and the Sons and Daughters of the Utah Pioneers (1898), later organized separately.

By the turn of the century the work of the Church Historian's Office was becoming increasingly important in providing the means by which the Saints could become acquainted with their history. Church Historian from 1889 to 1900 was Elder Franklin D. Richards of the Council of the Twelve, who was deeply concerned with carefully scrutinizing all history in order to achieve the "strictest accuracy." One of those working under him was Andrew Jenson, an avid compiler of historical sketches, manuscript histories, and chronologies, and the one who supervised the work of compiling the massive "Journal History of the Church." In 1898 he was sustained as Assistant Church Historian, and in 1899 he brought out a second edition of his popular *Church Chronology*. Unlike the first edition, this volume was sponsored by the Church and its sale was urged through circular letters to local authorities. In 1900 Elder Anthon H. Lund was named Church Historian, and after he was called into the First Presidency in 1902, Orson F. Whitney, A. Milton Musser, and B. H. Roberts were added to the roster of assistant historians. In May 1901 President Joseph F. Smith appointed B. H. Roberts to edit Joseph Smith's *History of the Church* for republication. Meanwhile, Elder Roberts's own study of the Missouri persecutions was compiled from a series of *Contributor* articles of fifteen years earlier and issued as a book in 1900. Orson F. Whitney was also making an important contribution with his well-known four-volume *History of Utah*, published commercially between 1892 and 1904. John Henry Evans published a popular *History of the Church* for the youth in 1905.

The Church was also interested in recording contemporary history, and around the turn of the century a major program was inaugurated to improve record keeping. Instructions were sent to wards and stakes detailing the kinds of historical records they should maintain. Individual members were encouraged to trace their priesthood authority and keep their own records of ordinances and ordinations. Missionaries were instructed to keep diaries, and members who owned pioneer diaries or manuscripts were urged to lend them to the Church for copying or to donate them for safekeeping. "We want to make you all historians," said Andrew Jenson.

In 1903 President Joseph F. Smith began to authorize the purchase of Church historic sites. Two of these acquisitions, the Solomon Mack homestead in Vermont and Carthage Jail in Illinois, marked the beginning and the end of the life of Joseph Smith the Prophet. Purchase of a twenty-five-acre parcel adjacent to the Independence Temple lot in Missouri underscored continuing Latter-day Saint interest in the Center Place of Zion. Along with the opening of the first Bureau of Information in 1902, these purchases marked the beginning of a new educational and proselyting thrust through the management and interpretation of historic sites.

Because the birthplace of the Prophet held special significance for the Latter-day Saints, Junius F. Wells was asked to direct the construction of a memorial cottage around the hearthstone of the original Mack family home. He also supervised the hauling of fifty tons of native stone for an impressive granite monument on the site. The central spire was thirty-eight-and-one-half feet high, a foot for each year of Joseph Smith's life. Donations from members helped pay for the project, and both the cottage and the monument were completed for the hundredth anniversary of Joseph Smith's birth, December 23, 1905.

Church Finance in a Time of Transition

At the turn of the century the Church was still heavily in debt, which concerned its leaders greatly. In 1899 President Snow initiated a retrenchment policy designed to help balance income and expenditures. The Church stopped borrowing for investments, consolidated its debts through a million-dollar bond issue, sold its controlling interest in a number of businesses, and launched a major campaign that stressed a new dedication to the principle of tithe paying—"the Lord's law of revenue."

Remembering the failure of his predecessor to sell Church bonds in the East, President Lorenzo Snow determined that the Church should borrow money "among ourselves" rather than "go into the world." Two local bond issues of $500,000 were both purchased quickly. President Snow also established an annual "sinking fund" which would accumulate until the debt was paid. Half the bonds were redeemed in December 1903 and the balance three years later.

To help relieve financial pressures, the Church continued to reduce its involvement in business investments, though it retained control of some businesses and a minority interest in others. In addition, in 1899 it regained control of the daily *Deseret News* and reinstated Charles W. Penrose as editor. Subscriptions increased by nearly seven thousand in one year and the newspaper business became profitable. The Deseret News Bookstore, predecessor of the Deseret Book Company, was purchased a year later from the Cannon family. The Church also began a new business in 1905 when President Smith encouraged formation of the Beneficial Life Insurance Company. Within five years this enterprise became a major Utah financial institution, with the Church holding controlling interest.

During this period of returning prosperity special emphasis was laid not only on getting the Church out of debt but also on the evils of individual indebtedness. The simple formula, "get out of debt," was stressed again and again. In addition, Church leaders advocated a diversified regional economy, although they reemphasized the value of agriculture as a vocation. They warned the Saints against flocking to overcrowded cities where day laborers and office workers were severely affected by times of depression and unemployment.

At the same time many young families were leaving Utah cities and marginal farmlands after becoming discouraged with the urban job market or poor agricultural prospects. They headed for new colonies in the Big Horn Basin, Wyoming; Alberta, Canada; Grande Ronde Valley, Oregon; and southern Arizona. "The days of colonizing by this people are by no means past," observed Elder Abraham O. Woodruff, who until his death in 1904 directed the final organized Mormon settlement efforts. The Saints were cautioned against joining the outward movement too hurriedly, without the counsel of local priesthood leaders, and those who did leave were urged to gather in designated colonies. The strength of the Church lay partly in its communities, and if the Saints became too scattered, the sense of community could diminish.

The Church's unsettled financial conditions during the raid and the depression of the 1890s had led to a great decline in tithe paying. In 1899, therefore, Church leaders saw the opportunity to achieve a spiritual reform and simultaneously help deliver the Church from financial bondage. At the April conference no fewer than seven speakers mentioned the subject, although official inauguration of the reform was announced by President Snow in May.

The aged Mormon leader was on a preaching tour in southern Utah, where a severe drought was causing great concern for the future. At a special conference in St. George he suddenly preached on a topic he had seldom mentioned before. "The Lord requires me to say something to you," he said. "The word of the Lord to you is not anything new; it is simply this: The time has now come for every Latter-day Saint . . . to do the will of the Lord and pay his tithing in full." He then made a dramatic promise to the people of southern Utah that if they would pay an honest tithe they would be blessed with rain and a satisfactory harvest. Journeying northward, President Snow preached tithing everywhere, and in June the annual conference of the Mutual Improvement Association voted to accept the new emphasis as "the present word and will of the Lord unto us."

The tithing reform caught hold throughout the Church, and southern Utah got its rain and a reasonable harvest. For the next two years general conferences resounded with the tithing message, and local priesthood leaders soon reported satisfying progress. The percentage of full tithe payers rose dramatically, and President Snow remarked with satisfaction that it was "a reformation . . . that is perfectly marvelous."

Also changing was the ratio of cash to tithing paid in kind. Cash accounted for two-thirds of the tithing receipts in 1901, a significant change from 1890 when about two-thirds was paid in produce and livestock.

An increase in the payment of tithing plus better returns on business investments made it possible for the Church to wrest itself free from debt. It was a proud day for President Joseph F. Smith when he could announce in general conference in April 1907, "Today the Church of Jesus Christ of Latter-day Saints owes not a dollar that it cannot pay at once. At last we are in a position that we can pay as we go."

Social and Humanitarian Concerns

The turn of the century ushered in a complex period in America often called the Progressive Era. Progressives were concerned with reform in American politics, economic life, and social institutions, and generally believed that both national and local governments must broaden the scope of their activities to bring about needed reform. In the social realm, reformers looked with dismay at the evils of crowded

Riverdale Ward, Weber Stake, early twentieth century. This little rock meetinghouse was typical of chapels in many Mormon communities in the nineteenth and early twentieth centuries. (Church Archives)

cities which seemed to foster poverty, crime, ill health, and general lack of opportunity for the underprivileged.

The Church, too, was concerned with the social ills of the early twentieth century, though it did not necessarily urge its members to become involved with the active reform groups that were attracting national followings. Neither did it criticize those who did, but the ideal was to work on improving individuals who would then improve society. Later the Church would espouse a few nationally organized reform movements such as prohibition and the anti-cigarette movement, but in the first few years of the new century its social and humanitarian efforts were concerned with emergency welfare and health care, family relationships, and wholesome activities for youth.

The Church's humanitarian impulse was demonstrated in 1906 when it sent shipments of food and supplies to aid those left homeless in the huge San Francisco earthquake and fire. The Relief Society sent flour, and wards contributed food, clothing, and quilts, some of which were collected at benefit concerts. Members also contributed aid to the families of two hundred miners killed in eastern Utah's Scofield mine explosion of 1900, and when word came of famine in China the Relief Society contributed a carload of flour. The Latter-day Saints were at last in a position to look beyond their own needs and help others in times of tragedy and misfortune.

Concern for adequate health care in Utah was visibly expressed by Church leaders during this period through the construction of the Groves LDS Hospital in Salt Lake City. It was built with a donation of $25,000 from the estate of Dr. William S. Groves, a $10,000 donation from the Fifteenth Ward in Salt Lake City, and the balance of $175,000 from general Church funds. Opened in 1905, it was the first modern Latter-day Saint hospital and served many families in the Intermountain West. The Church counseled its members on personal health care, warning them against unproven patent medicines and other products of medical quackery.

One of the most debated national health questions of the day was that of vaccination for smallpox, and after a mild epidemic in 1900–1901 it became a major public issue in Utah. When schoolchildren were required by the State Board of Health to be vaccinated, strong protests arose throughout the state and the *Deseret News* took an editorial stand against compulsory vaccination. The First Presidency, however, issued a statement recommending voluntary vaccination, and this approach eventually became Utah law.

Another concern was the changing life-style of the times that seemed to pose threats to the family life so important to Mormon culture. Young people had more leisure, and many who left the farms and headed for the cities found themselves in a new and unfamiliar environment that led to various forms of self-indulgence. In addition, the trend toward small families, often achieved by birth control or abortion, worried Church leaders. This led to many sermons and much advice in which youth were encouraged to dress modestly, marry within the Church, and avoid any temptation to postpone the responsibilities of marriage and children. Parents were reminded that teaching the gospel was primarily *their* responsibility, not that of the auxiliaries, and they were encouraged to set aside regular times for family activity.

In addition, the Church paid increasing attention to sponsoring appropriate youth activities. The ward was the center of the Mormon community, and ward recreation committees began to plan youth activities more regularly than before. Leaders urged young people to remain aloof from Sunday sports, pool halls, card games, and non-LDS dance halls, and actively encouraged wholesome activities such as theatricals, picnics, concerts, dances, team sports, music, and properly chaperoned excursions. Summer youth conferences and field days organized by the MIA included excursions to recreation resorts. Church-sponsored activity for the youth had come a long way from the Retrenchment Associations of a quarter of a century earlier.

Educational Adjustments

An expanded commitment to education, both secular and religious, characterized these years of transition, as funds for Church schools became the fastest growing portion of the Church budget. It had become compulsory for Utah children to attend schools; as a result, free public elementary schools had become available in most communities. The Church then moved out of the elementary school program, and its academies began to offer high school training. Public high schools were beginning to grow in Utah, but for several years the academies offered the only secondary training available in many communities.

As the Church moved out of elementary education, the religion class program was expanded. Often these classes were held in public school buildings; but in 1905, responding to public criticism, the First Presidency advised that they move elsewhere. Not all members enthusiastically supported religion classes, saying they duplicated the Primary, but by 1908 some thirty thousand Latter-day Saint students were enrolled in this program of weekday religious instruction for elementary school children.

At the college level, the greatest need was for the training of teachers. The Church was especially concerned that its own young people be prepared to teach in Utah's public schools and retain some Latter-day Saint influence on the training of youth. Brigham Young Academy at Provo, therefore, began to move slowly in the direction of providing a better normal course (teacher training) as it advanced from a secondary school curriculum to higher education. Its name was changed to Brigham Young University in 1903. In addition, the Brigham Young College at Logan and the Latter-day Saints' College in Salt Lake City also began to teach college courses, though all three remained basically secondary schools. The Salt Lake school expanded its offerings in 1902 and became one of the largest schools of business in the intermountain area. Under a new name, Latter-day Saints' University, and with a new campus on part of the block east of Temple Square, it served as the principal Church-owned institution of higher education until 1907, when that honor went to Brigham Young University.

Expanding Horizons: The Church's Worldwide Mission

As the new era dawned President Lorenzo Snow felt the need to make some administrative course corrections in order to move the Church more clearly toward its worldwide goal. The pioneering age, in which Church leaders were necessarily involved in the problems of building and governing new communities, was gone, but President Snow was concerned that members of the Quorum of the Twelve were still spending too much time dealing with affairs just as easily handled by local officers. It was the business of the apostles and the seventies, he said, "by the appointment of the Almighty, to look after the interests of the world,"[3] and he instructed local leaders to depend less upon top authorities. The commission given the apostles was to see that the gospel was preached throughout the world, in preparation for the approaching Millennium.

Under President Snow's prodding, the Twelve began to expand their activities. An early step was the opening of a mission in Japan in 1901, under the direction of Elder Heber J. Grant and a few handpicked associates. "The Lord has not revealed to me that they will succeed," said the President at a farewell reception, "but he has shown me positively that it is their duty to go." The enthusiasm of the missionaries was soon dampened as they grappled with a new and difficult language and a culture they did not understand, but at least the mission was a beginning in a renewed effort to fill the earth. Elder Grant soon returned, but one of the missionaries accompanying him, Alma O. Taylor, remained in Japan for nine years and translated the Book of Mormon into Japanese.

This was the only new mission established in these early years of the new century, but it did not exhaust the possibilities. "The eyes of the Twelve have been roaming over the habitable globe," said Elder Brigham Young, Jr., in 1901, "and they have looked upon Turkey, Austria, Russia, and especially South America. . . . As Brother Heber J. Grant has gone, so others will go when the Spirit indicates the place and the time."[4] The Mexican Mission was reopened in 1901 as an anticipated first step into Latin America, and two years later Mormon elders returned to South Africa after an absence of nearly forty years. In these areas, too, there were difficulties and little success, though in

[3]*Conference Report*, October 1901, p. 61.
[4]*Conference Report*, October 1901, p. 66.

Sunday School conducted by missionaries in Sapporo, Japan, about 1907. Seated in the foreground are Elders Justus B. Seely and J. Preston Cutler. (Church Archives)

Mexico, Elder Ammon M. Tenney was able to reestablish several former branches.

At the same time, the Church strengthened established missions by contributing funds for meetinghouses and mission headquarters. This helped ensure permanent branches and supported Church efforts to discourage emigration to Utah. "We desire it distinctly understood," said President Smith in 1903, "that 'Mormonism,' as it is called, has come to the world to stay."[5]

The missionary force declined slightly in the first few years of the century, and the nature of the missionaries changed. It became increasingly common in the late nineteenth century for young, unmarried men to be called, and by the 1890s they formed the bulk of the missionaries. The first sister missionaries were called in 1898. They were relatively few in number, twenty-seven out of 866 missionaries called in 1902, but it quickly became apparent to mission presidents that the sisters were as effective in the work as the elders. Most of the new missionaries, men and women, were better prepared than their predecessors. Before being called they were carefully interviewed, to identify

---

[5]*Conference Report*, October 1903, p. 4.

health problems and to attest to spiritual preparation, and after 1899 increasing numbers took the special missionary training courses offered at six academies and colleges in Utah and Arizona.

The missionaries were introduced to proselyting techniques that differed in some ways from those used by their fathers and grandfathers. They no longer relied as heavily on street meetings or on traveling without purse or scrip, for legal restrictions had arisen against both. On the other hand, they distributed literature as their fathers had done, relying principally on a new series of tracts, *Rays of Living Light*, written by Charles W. Penrose. The effectiveness of missionary work varied greatly from place to place. In the United States the greatest success was in the Midwest; in Europe, it was in Great Britain and Scandinavia.

Administrative Refinements

In his message admonishing the apostles to remember their calling as "special witnesses unto the nations of the earth," Lorenzo Snow gave a parallel charge to local presiding officers. Henceforth they would receive less help from the General Authorities. They were urged to "be lively" in their own "wonderful responsibility" of working with the Saints, a timely plea in an age when "reform" was on every tongue. This reawakening soon extended from the highest to the lowest priesthood offices, and into the auxiliaries.

One significant new development concerned the Patriarch to the Church. Heretofore his duties had been limited largely to giving blessings, but President Joseph F. Smith felt that the prestige and importance of his position should be enhanced in the minds of the Saints. Beginning in 1902, therefore, Patriarch John Smith was invited to address the general conference. In addition, his name was added to the fifteen General Authorities customarily sustained as "prophets, seers, and revelators." President Smith encouraged the Patriarch to travel among the Saints, believing such action necessary to give the office the primal position outlined in the Doctrine and Covenants.

The general move to decentralize priesthood responsibility had direct implications at the local level. Nineteen new stakes were created, thirteen of them carved from long-established units that had become so large they were unwieldy. Some had memberships of from ten to twenty thousand. The average stake after the reshaping consisted of five or six thousand members and about ten wards. Similar action was taken at the ward level. But the reform went further than mere reorganization. More clearly than before, stake presidents and ward bishops were identified as the key links in the jurisdictional chain between members and General Authorities, and members were counseled to go to these local officers before taking their problems higher. Decentralization thus enhanced the importance of local priesthood leaders. At the same time, bishoprics and quorum presidencies were given advice on how to function more effectively. They were to hold regular preparation meetings. They were reminded that they were administrators, not preachers, and should not make unauthorized, authoritarian doctrinal pronouncements. Stake high councils also felt the impact of the reform movement as President Snow prodded them to go beyond their traditional roles as priesthood courts. Soon high councilors were undertaking regular monthly speaking assignments to the wards, a practice that has continued to the present day.

These administrative reforms had the desired effect of involving more Saints in local church affairs. Reports from the stakes indicated increased attendance at church, but, more importantly, smaller units allowed bishops and other leaders to give closer attention to individual needs. In October 1907 Elder Francis M. Lyman, president of the Council of the Twelve, reported that decentralization had succeeded and local officers were doing such an effective job of handling affairs in the fifty-five stakes of Zion that appeals to the First Presidency were becoming rare. Though decentralization tended to place members another step from central leaders, the growth in membership made it necessary. It also had the advantage of bringing into activity many more people, enhancing spirituality, and providing important leadership experience to thousands.

The organization of new stakes and wards and the slowed pace of construction during the preceding two decades created a pressing need for many new meeting places. As the building program expanded, Church architects introduced changes in meetinghouse design, began using concrete and steel, and experimented with a variety of styles. Sunday School officers requested that ward meetinghouses include partitioned classrooms in basements or annexes, rather than the curtained dividers commonly used, and ward recreation committees stressed the need for amusement halls. The Relief Societies, meanwhile, continued to build separate halls for their own meetings and granaries for their wheat-storage program. In the early years of the twentieth century, building proceeded at an unprecedented rate.

Auxiliary Reform

The reform in the auxiliaries started with what Elder Francis M. Lyman called "the re-baptism of Mutual Improvement." Beginning in 1897 the Young Men's Mutual Improvement Association, recognizing the need for many local units to awaken from comparative lethargy, revitalized its program in such a way that other auxiliaries took note and the general reform movement soon became all-inclusive.

In general, the auxiliary reformation exhibited three common trends, though the degree differed from one organization to the other. One tendency was the greater application of contemporary educational methods, as other auxiliaries followed the lead of the Sunday School in structured gospel education. Next, an increasing reliance on central planning developed, strengthening the auxiliaries' general hierarchy. This did not lessen local responsibility, but rechanneled it along lines more clearly determined by general officers. Finally, the auxiliaries began developing a common curriculum based on the standard works and Church history rather than on secular subject matter. In a sense, though each auxiliary maintained separate functions, the result of these common trends was to soften the distinctions between them.

Profiting from the experiences of the Sunday School, by 1903 the Mutual Improvement Associations and the Primary had incorporated graded classwork or departments into their programs. They developed better recruitment policies and demonstrated a new awareness of the need for teacher training activities. There was also an increased use of officers' handbooks, uniform curricula, and centrally prepared lessons. In these matters the authority of the general auxiliary officers was enhanced and the local organizations were drawn more tightly under their direction.

The reform of the young men's organization included several innovations. A new training program for local leaders was introduced in 1900: the annual stake convention, held jointly each fall with the young women's leaders. The MIA missionary program was abandoned after 1903 because local workers were relying too heavily on the missionaries to perform their own administrative duties. The YMMIA developed a religious course of study that replaced the greater variety of topics, both secular and religious, that had been taught earlier. They also began holding opening exercises at each weekly meeting in conjunction with the young women. These and other changes were all part of the greater degree of churchwide uniformity in the YMMIA. In addition, this or-

Mutual Improvement Association missionaries, 1899–1900. Seated on the bottom row are J. Golden Kimball, W. S. Baxter, Heber J. Grant, and Matthias Cowley. (Church Archives)

ganization introduced a new magazine in 1897: the *Improvement Era*. As the official organ of the YMMIA, it consisted of a format designed to uplift young men and inform them on important subjects relating to the gospel and current affairs. The editor was Joseph F. Smith, whose "Editor's Table" provided a forum for opinions on pressing religious and social questions. Associate editor B. H. Roberts's running history of the Spanish-American War and other features kept readers abreast of world affairs.

The Young Women's MIA was naturally affected by what happened to the Young Men, but in 1896 and again in 1902 its officers soundly rejected a proposal that the two organizations be merged. They accepted joint preliminary exercises, conferences, training sessions, and meeting times, but the young ladies wanted to maintain their independence in other areas. Consolidation, they said, was too reminiscent of a dating bureau. Reforms in the YWMIA were similar to those in the young men's organization and consisted of more uniform direction from the top, a graded instruction program, and continuation of the *Young Women's Journal*, which was founded in 1889. The curriculum offered by the young women included literature, history, physical culture, physiology, and ethics. Its attractively illustrated journal offered practical help on the arts of homemaking, such as recipes, home furnishings, and sewing, and included mind-expanding features such as poetry, fiction, articles on literature and the arts, and travel features.

The Sunday School also published its own journal, the *Juvenile Instructor*, which was purchased from the Cannon family in 1900. It had been owned and edited by George Q. Cannon since its founding, albeit specifically for the benefit of the Sunday School. As part of the reform movement, the Sunday School attempted to increase its membership and improve the quality of teaching. In some wards it seemed at cross purposes with the MIA, as both vied for the best teachers. The Sunday School, long the leader in adapting educational methods to religious instruction, adopted a system of effectively grouping children in classes by age group, and in 1902 this became standard practice churchwide. About the same time the Sunday School adopted uniform courses of study, based on outlines published by the general officers. A new program of teacher training was introduced in 1902. Stakes began to hold stake "union meetings" — training sessions for teachers under the new stake boards, organized along departmental lines. The most significant innovation, however, was the parents' class, introduced churchwide in 1906 after a successful two-year experiment in the Weber and other stakes. Organized initially around discussions of child rearing, the classes immediately became popular and were the beginning of a regular adult program in the Sunday Schools.

The reform in the Primary was clearly influenced by what was happening in the other auxiliaries and imposed greater uniformity in the Primary programs. This included strengthening the central board, implementing graded classwork, and introducing a uniform, churchwide curriculum. The Primary also developed its own magazine, the *Children's Friend*, which first appeared in January 1902. Originally a magazine for the benefit of Primary teachers, it soon added a section for parents. Once it was in the homes, parents began to pressure Primary leaders to make it useful for children as well. In 1905 the magazine announced its intention to include children among its readers.

The introduction of the Parents' Department in the *Children's Friend* in 1903 was part of a broader program intended to strengthen ties between the auxiliary and the home. Earlier many wards had instituted special mothers' meetings to coordinate teaching between the Primary and the home. These changes demonstrate the Church's involvement in the widespread national interest in child development and its continued commitment to home and family.

The new attention to revitalizing organizations naturally created a few administrative conflicts. The Primary, for example, felt that the week-day religion classes competed with it and proposed an amalgamation. This was not approved. In 1903 the Primary also proposed that it be merged with the MIA. With the upper age-limit for Primary and the lower age-limit for MIA both set at fourteen, some Primary leaders felt the organization functioned as a junior class of the MIA. Certainly it was a "feeder" to the MIA membership, and General Primary President Louie B. Felt, at least, believed the organizations would function better if joined. The idea of integrating a junior MIA, however, did not appeal to the leaders of the YMMIA and the YWMIA, and though they co-operated in other things, the proposed merger did not take place.

In 1901 Bathsheba W. Smith became president of the Relief Society and directed the ensuing reforms in that organization. These changes were not as sweeping as those in the other auxiliaries, and the Relief Society tended to retain greater independence of action. The Relief Society existed not just to serve its members and build their spiritual well-being, but also to render public service. It was affiliated with the National Council of Women and participated in such national activities as the women's rights movement. Its quasi-official magazine, the *Woman's Exponent*, reported regularly on national women's activities and other public affairs. After 1900 the activities of the Relief Society turned gradually away from national crusades, though it was still very much involved in local public activities affecting the Saints' well-being.

The Relief Society's reforms were all associated with the Church's changing needs. It attempted to revitalize itself by bringing in younger women and developing new programs to meet their needs. These efforts had encouraging results. In 1905 the Relief Society established an employment bureau to aid the young women who were flocking to cities seeking work. In educational efforts in 1902 the society launched its first eight-month course in nursing, designed to help its members more fully assist the needy sick. The course continued until 1920, with many stakes sending representatives to the successive training sessions. Another new program of 1902 was the mother's class, which became a feature of all the Relief Societies in the Church. Structured to assist in child training, this innovation became the first uniform classwork offered in regular Relief Society meetings and was the forerunner of a broader curriculum that appeared a few years later.

The Relief Society also maintained some important long-standing programs. Wheat storage, for example, received continued emphasis and included flour and beans. Another agricultural carryover from the nineteenth century was the effort to raise silkworms. In addition, Latter-day Saint women continued to participate in public movements, such as the Mother's Congresses and the peace movement.

Revitalizing the Priesthood Quorums

President Joseph F. Smith looked forward to a period when the priesthood would completely fulfill its proper function, thus, he believed, eliminating the need for auxiliaries. At the time, however, the quorums hardly seemed capable of assuming such responsibility, for even though they displayed remarkable brotherhood, they were characterized by a disappointing lack of activity. But they were not immune from the reforming spirit of the age, and the key word in reform was "activation." The major goal, as announced by Elder Abraham O. Woodruff in 1900, was "a renewal of interest in all the quorums."

Only about half of those who had received the priesthood were actively magnifying their callings, and Church leaders believed that at least one reason for this was the growing popularity of fraternal lodges. They complained that membership in such organizations interfered with weeknight priesthood meetings and that lodge dues sometimes took precedence over Church contributions. In urging priesthood holders not to affiliate with these lodges, Church leaders pointed out that such affiliation tended to divide the allegiance of the brethren. The Saints were reminded that "everything necessary for their salvation, both temporal and spiritual," including brotherhood, was to be found within the kingdom of God. In some cases local auxiliaries excluded members of these societies from leadership positions. Some leaders also questioned the affiliation of some members in radical labor unions, though it was primarily the compulsory nature of certain union memberships that disturbed them.

One way to stimulate activity among the young men of the Aaronic Priesthood was to encourage them in their obligations to visit families in the ward. Beginning in 1902 Presiding Bishop William B. Preston authorized bishops to call Melchizedek Priesthood holders to accompany each priest or teacher on his rounds. These older men were dubbed "acting priests" and "acting teachers," for they were acting in the revealed duties of the lesser priesthood, but they were charged as tutors

The Coalville Tabernacle, dedicated in 1899, was representative of the numerous fine pieces of architecture erected by the Church in the late nineteenth century. These distinctive buildings added a special flavor to their communities and some still stand to help remind the Saints of their heritage. Though unfinished at the time, this building was the site of the October 1886 general conference.

of the young men. In earlier years the older men had, themselves, performed these tasks, but now that young men were regularly being ordained to the priesthood it was important to train them in their duties. This was only the beginning of a major priesthood reform that blossomed during the last decade of Joseph F. Smith's presidency.

By 1907, then, the Church had begun to take on a new aura, both publicly and internally. While it was still not widely praised, it had demonstrated its accommodation to some American norms by proving that it had indeed abandoned its misunderstood marriage practices and that its people were loyal to country. Some of its leaders were beginning to gain impressive public acceptance, and Senator Reed Smoot, a member of the Council of the Twelve, was beginning a distinguished career of public service. Economically the Church had shaped its involvement in business to the pattern of the broader American society and, most importantly, was out of debt. In addition, it was anxiously devoting itself to spreading the gospel worldwide, improving its image in the public eye, discovering and promoting its inspiring heritage, and re-forming all its programs to meet the challenges of growth and other modern problems.

In 1906 President Joseph F. Smith looked optimistically at the current reforms and the possibility that one day every priesthood council would fully magnify its responsibility. "When that day shall come," he told the Saints, "there will not be so much necessity for work that is now being done by the auxiliary organizations, because it will be done by the regular quorums of the Priesthood. The Lord . . . has made provision in the Church whereby every need may be met and satisfied through the regular organizations of the Priesthood."[6] In the spirit of this hope, the next decade would witness continued internal reform as well as growth and progress in spiritual and economic affairs.

---

[6]*Conference Report*, April 1906, p. 3.

CHAPTER 15

Consolidating for Growth, *1908–1918*

At the close of the stress-filled hearings over the seating of Reed Smoot in the United States Senate, President Joseph F. Smith left Salt Lake City for a much-needed working vacation in Europe. He took with him a small group of family members as well as his close friend Charles W. Nibley (soon to be named Presiding Bishop). Wherever they went President Smith met with the Saints in special conferences and shared with them his personal warmth and his insights into gospel topics. Four years later, in 1910, he returned to Europe and again met with members and missionaries in several countries.

Joseph F. Smith was the first President of the Church to visit Europe while in office, and his personal concern over the well-being of the Latter-day Saints there reflected an increasingly significant attempt to build up the Church outside the American West. During his presidency he also made several visits to the Hawaiian Islands and toured Canada and Mexico as well. Everywhere he encouraged the faithful to remain in their homelands, even though the full program of the Church was not yet available to them. His intent was to move toward that goal as rapidly as possible.

Economic Policy in a Decade of Prosperity

The last decade of Joseph F. Smith's presidency was one of general prosperity for the United States as well as for the Latter-day Saints. Most Church members still lived in Utah, Idaho, and Arizona, where agriculture remained the mainstay of the economy. The key to Church economic policy was no longer isolation and cooperative self-sufficiency, but economic cooperation with the larger society, in which private enterprise was fully espoused and non-LDS capital was turned to good purposes under commercial arrangements only indirectly involving Church members.

The Church's relationship with the sugar industry typified the changing nature of its economic activities. Sugar was Utah's most viable agricultural product, and stable prices enabled Mormon sugar beet farmers to reap generous profits. The Utah-Idaho Sugar Company, formed in 1907 through the merger of three Utah and Idaho companies, vigorously expanded its ability to process sugar by establishing many new factories. Church leaders continued to hold influential positions in the new company, even though the Church remained a minority stockholder. Mormon farmers provided most of the raw products, but the key to success was the combination of church and private funding. Much of the investment capital came from Henry O. Havemeyer of the American Sugar Refining Company. The Utah-Idaho Sugar Company shared the refining business in the area with the Amalgamated Sugar Company, dominated by the Eccles interests. The company did well for a time, but in the 1920s it found itself in serious financial difficulty.

One of the most sharply debated investments was the elegant Hotel Utah in downtown Salt Lake City. Designed to help the area around Temple Square and the Church offices remain a vital part of the city's business district, it was built with space for several small businesses. The Church hoped to attract influential visitors to that part of town, where they would be close to Temple Square and could be more easily introduced to the Church and its programs.

Some persons criticized the First Presidency for the venture, especially when the Hotel Operating Company, which leased the facility from the Church-backed Utah Hotel Company, opened a bar. Shortly after the hotel opened for business, President Smith defended Church involvement at the October 1911 general conference. He explained the financial arrangements that made it possible and reminded the congregation of his unsuccessful attempt to influence Salt Lake City voters to declare the city dry. But since it was not dry, visitors expected "something to wet up with," and if they couldn't get it at Hotel Utah they would stay elsewhere. He also reminded Church members of Joseph Smith's revelation authorizing construction of the Nauvoo House — a hotel to entertain important visitors to the Mormon capital of the early 1840s. This explanation satisfied most members. Hotel Utah became widely known for its fine food and first-rate accommodations.

Construction of the Hotel Utah also represented a shift away from President Lorenzo Snow's policy of selling controlling interest in Church-founded businesses. Times were prosperous and it was believed that a conservative investment policy could create a reliable income for the Church in addition to its increasing tithing receipts. The Church resumed control of the Provo Woolen Mills, became the major stockholder in Beneficial Life Insurance Company, and reacquired control of Utah-Idaho Sugar Company in 1914, when federal trustbusters dissolved the Havemeyer monopoly. The Trustee-in-Trust reacquired about one-fourth of the ZCMI stock and maintained its control of the Salt Lake Theater, Zion's Savings Bank & Trust Company, *Deseret News*, and Deseret News Bookstore, while continuing to hold stock in several other companies. In 1919 the Deseret Sunday School Union Bookstore was merged with the Deseret News Bookstore, and the combined facilities became Deseret Book Company. In none of these instances did the Church intend to establish monopolies or hurt non-Church private enterprise, even though critics later accused it of doing so. They were simply considered sound investments in order to help the Church in its other financial needs and to maintain a degree of influence in the economic development of the region.

The greatest benefit to the Church of such commercial ventures was the realization of income that could be expended to support other important purposes. Some of the Church's income helped subsidize charitable institutions, such as hospitals. In 1913 a wing was added to the Groves' Latter-day Saints Hospital in Salt Lake City, doubling its capacity to 250 beds, and in 1915 the Church purchased the Thomas D. Dee Memorial Hospital in Ogden, an institution that the local stakes had operated for three years.

New Building Programs

The Church's brightened economic outlook was reflected in several new and badly needed building projects. First to gain approval was a Central Women's Building, and in 1901 a site was selected, but Church leaders later decided to consolidate in one building the offices of the women's organizations, the Primary, the Presiding Bishopric, and Young Men's MIA. This move naturally disappointed those who had contributed toward the separate women's auxiliary building, but in 1910 the new Bishop's Building, as the combined facility was called, was completed and dedicated on the block immediately east of the Salt Lake Temple. The same year a new recreational facility, the Deseret Gymnasium, was also opened on that block.

Seven years later the five-story Church Office Building was com-

"Bishop's Block," Salt Lake City, about 1909. This photograph suggests the transition taking place in Utah and the Church at the beginning of the twentieth century. The Old Deseret Store and Tithing Office, formerly located on the corner, is in the last stages of demolition, while behind it the Bishop's Building nears completion. The new building housed the Presiding Bishopric and Church auxiliaries, and the modern architecture suggests the strength and permanence the Church had achieved by this time. In the first stages of construction is the Deseret Gymnasium. New streetcar tracks surround the statue of Brigham Young, sculpted by Cyrus E. Dallin. It was placed at this intersection in 1897, a symbol of the unity between the past and the present. (Utah State Historical Society)

pleted at 47 East South Temple. It housed the First Presidency, the Church Historian, and the Genealogical Society library, and for the first time provided central offices for the Council of the Twelve, the First Council of the Seventy, and the Patriarch to the Church. The handsome Grecian Ionic-style granite structure with native marble and fine wood interiors was a fitting symbol of the Church's newfound prosperity and increasing acceptance in the world. In addition, the attic and basement storage areas provided much-needed archival space for historical records, which had been housed previously in facilities without fire protection.

To make room for these and other new buildings, it was necessary to raze the old Deseret Store and other structures related to the Presiding Bishop's Office. The removal of the tithing barns and warehouses was particularly significant, for in 1908 the Church ended its general policy of receiving tithing in kind. Cash rather than home produce was rapidly becoming the medium of exchange, and when this change was announced, more than three-fourths of all tithing was being paid in cash. The transition that had begun in the early 1890s was virtually complete.

The change in economic patterns also affected local building programs. Bishop's tithing offices and granaries in local wards fell into disuse, and the bishops were provided offices in ward meetinghouses. Separate Relief Society halls were no longer built, and ward recreation halls were increasingly incorporated into the consolidated ward buildings. For twenty years architects had been experimenting with different styles for ward meetinghouses, and in 1910 the first truly modern Latter-day Saint buildings were constructed. They were largely the work of Harold W. Burton and Hyrum C. Pope, who introduced to the Church the prairie-style architecture of Frank Lloyd Wright, a noticeable contrast to the earlier mixture of Gothic and Classical design. These two men were also selected as architects for new temples in Canada and Hawaii.

The decision to build the first temples outside the continental United States reflected not only the Church's newfound ability to erect more buildings but also its de-emphasis on gathering to the Mormon heartland. Membership was sufficient in Alberta and Hawaii to justify temples that would serve broad areas in the American Northwest and in the Pacific. A site for a temple at Cardston, Alberta, was dedicated in July 1913 and construction began soon afterward. President Smith dedicated a site at Laie, on the island of Oahu, during his visit to the Hawaiian Islands in June 1915.

Continuing Challenges to the Public Image

One characteristic of the Progressive Era in the early twentieth century was a public reexamination of most of America's basic economic, political, and social institutions. Especially active were the so-called muckrakers, who spared no efforts in the press to ferret out embarrassing information about illegal and otherwise corrupt business and political practices. Though they often did considerable good in providing the impetus for important reform legislation, such as the Pure Food and Drug Act of 1906, they also produced a great deal of sensa-

This anti-Mormon illustration was one of many in a series of attacks on the Church published in Cosmopolitan Magazine *in 1911. Seldom since then has the Church been the brunt of such distorted imagery in the public press.*

tionalist literature based on distortion and exaggeration. In this climate the Church did not escape renewed criticism and a revival of many old charges.

The most direct attack came in the years 1910 and 1911 in such popular magazines as *Pearsons, Everybody's Magazine, McClure's,* and *Cosmopolitan*. Though primarily intending to discredit Senator Reed Smoot, who was easily reelected by the Utah legislature in January 1911, the muckrakers also attacked the Church and continued their articles well beyond the election. A *Cosmopolitan* series entitled "The Viper on the Hearth," by Alfred Henry Lewis, accused the Church of laying plans to subvert the family structure of America and take over the country both politically and economically. It was so vicious that both author and publisher were censured by their colleagues. Nevertheless, many newspapers picked up the themes of polygamous living and Mormon domination of politics and economics and joined the dissonant chorus. The net effect was the spread of considerable misinformation about Latter-day Saint life and the unfortunate reinforcement of negative images.

Reports from the magazine campaign in the American muckraking press hit Great Britain during a time when many conservative political and religious leaders were speaking out against the erosion of Victorian moral standards. In this they had the sympathy of Latter-day Saints, who themselves denounced trends toward smaller families, abortion, unchastity, and increasing divorce. Nevertheless, certain overzealous crusaders decided to let Mormonism represent the evils of immoral living, and rumors of the survival of plural marriage became a central theme in their lectures, rallies, movies, and novels. A typical plot in the popular novels of Winifred Graham (Cory), for example, followed the trials of the naive British heroine who at the last moment would be rescued from the deceit of a crafty American missionary.

The anti-Mormon crusade in England attracted little general support except in certain regions in the north and in East Anglia, but emotions in those areas were aroused to such an extent that anti-Mormon rallies turned to violence. Chapels in Birkenhead and Nuneaton were pelted with rocks and mud, a branch leader was tarred and feathered, and missionaries were harassed and asked to leave town. The missionaries were also expelled from Germany and rumors circulated that other European nations were considering sanctions against proselyting.

These hindrances to missionary work had temporary adverse effects. In England, baptisms since 1900 had been double those of the previous decade, with only a 25 percent increase in missionaries. During the renewed anti-Mormon agitation, while the number of missionaries dropped by a third, convert baptisms slid from 963 in 1910 to a low of 363 in 1912.

Church leaders were not reluctant to respond. In Europe the mission president, Rudger Clawson, answered the agitators with letters to sympathetic newspapers. The London *Evening Times* published a response from the First Presidency, in which Church teachings were outlined and policies on emigration and plural marriage explained. Responses were also published in American newspapers, and the April 1911 general conference approved an official statement which received wide circulation in pamphlet form.

A persistent rumor was that plural marriages were continuing in the Church. The First Presidency reminded stake presidents and bishops in 1910 and again four years later of their obligation to try offenders for their membership. Problems continued with the two members of the Council of the Twelve who had resigned from office in 1905; Elder Matthias Cowley was disfellowshipped and Elder John W. Taylor excommunicated. (Both were later restored to full membership, Elder

Cowley in 1936 and Elder Taylor, posthumously, in 1965.) These actions and similar ecclesiastical sanctions at the local level helped demonstrate the Church's continuing commitment to sustaining the law.

At the height of the anti-Mormon magazine crusade the Tabernacle Choir accepted an invitation to sing at the American Land and Irrigation Exposition in New York City in 1911. It also performed four dozen additional concerts in twenty-five cities in the Midwest and East. Critics of the Church circulated flyers and attempted to prevent the appearances in larger cities, but only in Buffalo, New York, were they successful. The choir sang for ten days at Madison Square Garden and on the return trip presented a special concert in the East Room of the White House for President and Mrs. William Howard Taft and invited guests. Music critics were generally pleased with the quality of these western voices, and their positive comments helped remold the popular image of the Latter-day Saints.

Also helping to counter misinformation about the Church was a series of articles on Church history written for *Americana*, a magazine of history, by Elder B. H. Roberts. He initiated the series to correct information published earlier in the magazine, and so pleased were the editors that they invited him to prepare a more thorough explanation of the Church's origins. The magazine devoted much of its space between 1909 and 1915 to the articles, which were later revised, expanded, and republished in book form during the Church's centennial in 1930 as the six-volume *Comprehensive History of the Church*. In April 1911 *Colliers* printed a letter from former President Theodore Roosevelt refuting allegations of Mormon polygamy and charges of secret political deals, and applauding the strength of Mormon families and their adherence to high standards. These comments, and an investigation in Great Britain instigated by Home Minister Winston Churchill to quell unfounded reports there, added voices of influence to the Latter-day Saint plea for a fair hearing and were indicative of better times ahead for the Church in the popular press.

Adjustments in Church Programs

In the last decade of President Smith's administration numerous additional program changes demonstrated a continuing ability to adapt to the fluctuating needs of a growing church in a changing world. The historical significance of all these changes is that when they were complete they established new, quite different patterns of local administration and activity that met the needs of the twentieth century. Children growing up in the new era would become familiar with a church quite different, in many ways, from that their grandparents knew; but all this only demonstrated the adaptability and dynamic vitality of the Church itself.

In the Melchizedek Priesthood, the changes began with the seventies quorums. The primary responsibility given to the seventies was missionary work, and in the nineteenth century it was a general custom to ordain men to the office of seventy when they were called on missions. By 1912, however, only about 18 percent of the full-time missionaries held that office. This reflected the increasingly common practice of calling younger men without families on missions and a reluctance to ordain young men to the office of seventy. At the same time, other men were often ordained to the office of seventy even if they had not been on missions, and in 1915 only half the members of the 192 seventies quorums in the Church had been on full-time missions.

The seventies were encouraged to serve as home teachers and home missionaries in the stakes, though the emphasis continued to be on preparation for full-time missionary service. With this in mind the First Council of the Seventy inaugurated a "new movement" focused on gospel study. Beginning in November 1907 seventies quorums began holding weekly meetings on Sunday mornings and studying a special manual, *The Seventies Course in Theology*, prepared by Elder B. H. Roberts of the First Council of the Seventy. Because these meetings conflicted with Sunday School in most wards, bishops were instructed to release seventies from Sunday School work wherever possible. The new program was launched with a general conference of seventies — the first since 1844 — and the *Improvement Era* began carrying monthly helps in a special seventies column.

The successful "new movement" was a catalyst in the revival of Melchizedek Priesthood activity generally. Traditional summer vacations from priesthood meetings were eliminated in most stakes, quorum members attended their meetings more faithfully, and the systematic approach to gospel study created lively discussions. The First Presidency soon appointed a Priesthood Committee on Outlines to prepare lesson manuals for all other priesthood quorums. These were introduced in 1909, and the seventies agreed to move their meeting back to the traditional Monday night so that all priesthood quorums could meet together in an opening exercise before separating for quorum instruction. But Monday nights were not always convenient and some stakes soon began to experiment with other times. Many found that Sunday morning was the best time for priesthood meeting, and eventually, with the approval of the First Presidency and the Twelve, this became church-wide practice. The result was improved attendance not only in priesthood meetings but in Sunday School as well. The *Improvement Era* was designated the official organ for the priesthood quorums as well as for the Young Men's MIA. In 1914 all Melchizedek Priesthood quorums began studying the same lesson manual. Soon afterward enrollment procedures were simplified so that a person moving into a ward was no longer required to present a written recommend from his former priesthood leader before he could be added to quorum rolls. Such changes in administrative policy may seem minor in perspective, but their significance lies in the fact that when they were complete they established new, quite different patterns for local priesthood activity that lasted, except in the case of the seventies,[1] throughout the century.

The Aaronic Priesthood was also revitalized in an effort to stimulate young men to greater activity and more effectively train them as leaders. Since 1877 it had been a general suggestion that boys be ordained to the office of deacon when they turned twelve, but this was not always followed. In the early years of the twentieth century the policy was urged on the wards again, and in the October 1906 general conference President Francis M. Lyman of the Council of the Twelve laid out specific procedures. All worthy boys were to be ordained at age twelve and then serve for three years in each Aaronic Priesthood office: deacon, teacher and priest. President Joseph F. Smith felt that through the priesthood the training of young men could be substantially improved, and he expressed his concern in the April 1907 conference:

> The bishops should take especial charge of the lesser priesthood, and train them in the duties of their callings — the priests, teachers and deacons. Our young men should be looked after. The boys, as soon as is prudent, should be called to take part in the lesser priesthood. If it were possible to grade them, from the deacon to the priest, and from the priest upward through all the offices that will eventually devolve upon them, it would be one of the best things that could be done.[2]

---

[1]See chapter 21.
[2]*Improvement Era* 10 (May 1907): 545.

In this spirit, Church leaders began more clearly to identify duties for each office. Deacons, for example, were invited to assist in caring for ward cemeteries and meetinghouse grounds, act as ushers, distribute special notices, pump organs at meetings, chop wood for widows, collect fast offerings, and so on. Similar lists gave teachers and priests appropriate opportunities for service. At the same time, as bishops adopted the systematic advancement program, teachers and priests quorums were built up, and the number of over-age deacons in the wards was substantially reduced.

The general reform had a direct impact on ward teaching. Districts were reduced in size and more adults were called as ward teachers. Regular visits — summer months included — were stressed and reporting procedures were standardized. These changes increased the ratio of families visited each month from 20 percent in 1911 to 54 percent four years later and 70 percent by 1921.

The net effect of the priesthood reform movement was to enhance the educational role of priesthood quorums and multiply the number of priesthood-sponsored activities. The pursuit of more gospel knowledge and better performance of priesthood duties gave the quorums a noticeable new vitality. At the same time, it raised new questions of overlapping responsibilities, for priesthood quorums were now joining the earlier revitalized YWMIA in the work of religious education, thus invading a field long dominated by the Sunday School. This multiplication of programs for studying the gospel created a need for a closer correlation between organizations and led General Authorities to sponsor a series of coordination studies that would continue over the next half century.

One immediate result was the decision to eliminate theological studies from the Mutual Improvement Associations. The youth auxiliaries turned increasingly to music, drama, sports, dance, and other activities, and away from doctrinal classes. The ward recreation committee, which had functioned as an agent of the bishop in controlling amusements within ward boundaries, became an MIA committee, and the MIAs took up the task of providing wholesome entertainment and recreational activities for ward members of all ages.

Weekday programs designed for twelve- and thirteen-year-olds were also reexamined. These age groups had been the responsibility of the Primary Association and religion classes, but many young people in these transitional years attended MIA meetings under an arrangement that allowed them that option. In 1913 the MIA adopted the program

In 1913 the Church adopted the Boy Scout movement as an official part of its program. (Church Archives)

of the Boy Scouts of America and also tried the national Campfire Girls program. These innovations firmly committed the MIA to serving boys and girls of twelve and thirteen. Scouting met Church needs adequately, but after a year's trial the girls' program was dropped in favor of the Beehive class, an adaptation of the Campfire Girls. The Primary, meantime, dropped its classes for these age groups.

In 1914 the Relief Society was the last auxiliary to adopt standardized lessons. For twelve years it had offered a mothers' class, but the lessons on child rearing were prepared independently in each stake to meet local interests and needs. Occasional lectures on other topics paved the way for a definite educational offering that filled a vacuum created when the YWMIA dropped its study of secular subject matter. Organized around a four-week lesson format, the new lessons were published first in a monthly *Bulletin* and, commencing in 1915, in the *Relief Society Magazine*, which replaced the independently owned *Woman's Exponent* as the official Relief Society organ. Under the new class schedule one week in each month was set aside for a work and business meeting, another for theology lessons and testimony bearing, a third for genealogy and literature or art, and a fourth for home economics. This pattern in Relief Society classwork has continued, with variations, since that time.

Other evidences of uniformity appeared between 1914 and 1916 as stake board meetings and union meetings (i.e., meetings of auxiliary workers) were introduced, ward Relief Society meetings were moved to a uniform Tuesday schedule, a *Circular of Instructions* was issued, record books were standardized, and visiting teachers were provided with standard messages. At the same time, the Relief Society did not forget its charitable obligations. In 1913 it opened a boarding home for working girls who came to Salt Lake City from rural areas with no relatives or friends to take them in. This home continued for nearly eight years until it was replaced by the Young Women's Mutual Improvement Association's boardinghouse in the Beehive House. The Relief Society also operated an employment office, adoption services, and a clearinghouse for Latter-day Saint transients.

The inclusion of a regular genealogy lesson in the Relief Society curriculum in 1914, and an optional course along similar lines as much as seven years earlier, signaled a broadening interest in educating members in genealogical research. The initiative in this educational effort centered in the women's committee of the Genealogical Society. Beginning about 1907 this committee sponsored a series of lessons on genealogy taught by Susa Young Gates at the Lion House. This led to written lessons, which were published in 1912; but in the meantime, requests for the classes came from many stakes outside the Salt Lake area. The society sponsored union meetings or conventions in several locations to fill the need.

In 1909 Joseph Fielding Smith, secretary of the Genealogical Society, and Bishop Joseph Christensen visited genealogical societies in the eastern United States to study their libraries and programs. In a report of their findings to Genealogical Society president Anthon H. Lund they suggested the need for a magazine, and this proposal was approved. Launched in 1910 as a quarterly, the *Utah Genealogical and Historical Magazine* published articles on research helps, family pedigrees, and local history, and continued until 1940. Another boost to genealogical work was the designation in 1912 of an annual Genealogy Sunday, during which sacrament meetings in all wards considered the doctrinal basis of genealogical and temple work. The practice continued through the 1930s. All these efforts increased activities in genealogical research, and in the temples several endowment sessions were scheduled each day, where before only one had been conducted.

These were only a few of many far-reaching program and administrative changes in the first two decades of the new century. Others included the inauguration of a better system of budgetary control; a redefinition and further clarification of the nature of Church courts, including the elimination of the practice of members going there instead of to civil courts to arbitrate debts; and a strengthening of the record-keeping program in the wards, particularly with respect to membership records.

The Challenge of Secular Knowledge

One of the Church's continuing concerns was the education of its youth. In the early twentieth century the challenges presented by the rapid expansion of secular education became particularly complex. With the continued growth of tax-supported public schools in Church-dominated areas, for example, it seemed increasingly illogical to ask members also to support Church schools, so by 1910 the Church had largely vacated the field of elementary education. Its basic concern was that students receive religious instruction along with their secular training. This was provided for in once-a-week religion classes and in the Primary.

At the secondary level, the Church continued to operate its stake academies, which in Utah accommodated about half the secondary school students. As tax-supported public high schools received better financing and became more available statewide, however, the Church was faced with the dilemma of whether it should continue pouring money into academies, though it was unwilling to abandon them until an alternative way could be found to provide religious instruction. The result was a new approach to religious education that would have important and far-reaching consequences.

The initial suggestion came from Joseph F. Merrill, a professor of engineering at the University of Utah and a member of the Granite Stake presidency in Salt Lake City. He proposed a program of religious instruction to be offered to Granite High School students on a voluntary basis, with "released time" being granted by the school. If successful, such seminaries could provide religious training for LDS students at a fraction of the cost of maintaining church schools. In 1912 he persuaded the Granite School District to approve the establishment of an experimental LDS seminary near the school, and seminary classes began that fall. By the end of the decade they had spread to other schools. Church leaders worked closely with state education officials, and in January 1916 the state board of education provided an important boon to seminary enrollment by granting limited high school credit for released-time classes in Bible history and literature.

In the meantime, the state superintendent of public instruction urged the Church to withdraw completely from secondary schools, observing that the money saved could be used to establish good normal schools for teacher training, a serious and growing need in the state of Utah. The Church was already sympathetic with this idea, and especially concerned that public school teachers not only be well prepared in their academic subjects but also be in tune with the spiritual and moral ideals of the Church. Academies were not eliminated at the time, but between 1916 and 1918 the Dixie, Snow, and Weber academies became normal schools and joined Brigham Young University, Brigham Young College at Logan, and the Latter-day Saints University in Salt Lake City in offering college courses along with high school work.

At the college level, Brigham Young University was named the official Church normal school as early as 1908, and it was soon competing with the Latter-day Saints University for the honor of becoming the major Church university. Both were expanding but BYU won out, partly because Church leaders saw no need to compete in Salt Lake City with the University of Utah. The Latter-day Saints University eventually became a high school, though two of its collegiate departments became the basis for two new institutions: the LDS Business College and the McCune School of Music. Brigham Young College at Logan, meanwhile, deemphasized its teacher training to specialize in liberal arts and "practical subjects."

Already President George H. Brimhall had launched a concerted effort to enlarge Brigham Young University and enhance its prestige. As enrollment expanded he scoured the country in search of more well qualified, high quality teachers with master's and Ph.D. degrees. Such scholars would both enhance the faculty and strengthen the curriculum. As a result, the first Ph.D. ever to teach at BYU, Joseph Peterson, was hired in 1907 to teach psychology. He had been trained at the University of Chicago. His brother, Henry, who had a master's degree from Harvard, became head of the education department. Ralph Chamberlin, a Ph.D. from Cornell, came in 1908 and headed the biology department, and the following year his brother William, who had received advanced training at the University of California and the University of Chicago, joined the faculty to teach ancient languages and philosophy. Other outstanding teachers and scholars were added in the next few years, including Alice Louise Reynolds in literature, Joseph B. Keeler in accounting, and Harvey Fletcher, who earned his Ph.D. in physics *summa cum laude* from the University of Chicago in 1911.

*The Maori Agricultural College, near Hastings, New Zealand, represented
the Church's continuing interest in education for its members in the early
twentieth century. (Church Archives)*

These and other dynamic new teachers worked actively to enhance
the academic stature of BYU by providing greater intellectual challenges
to students. It was not long, however, before questions were raised
about the religious orthodoxy of a few of them. The result was an
important reflection of the secular trends that were affecting the larger
society, especially in religion and higher education, and also of the
uncomfortable problems often faced when secular learning and religious
faith appear to come in conflict.

At the heart of the matter was the nature of secular, scientific
learning itself, and its relationship to the LDS understanding of God,
man, and revelation. Two issues, however, stood out: "higher criticism"
and the teaching of the theory of organic evolution. Higher criticism
was an approach to Bible study that went beyond simply trying to
determine the accuracy of the text. Scholars also asked where the authors of the texts acquired their ideas in the first place, and the role
that tradition, environment, and other influences may have had on their
writings. For some people this raised questions about the inspiration
and literal truth of the scriptures. The theory of evolution suggested
that the origin of life was a natural process and the creation of man
was the result of "natural selection" and evolution from lower forms
of life.

In November 1909 the First Presidency responded to the doctrinal
implications of the theory of natural selection by publishing in the
Improvement Era a statement entitled "The Origin of Man." The

statement clearly reaffirmed certain basic doctrines essential to the faith of the Latter-day Saints: the human race was created by God, and in the image of God; the spirits of all people existed in a premortal state and came to the earth to "undergo an experience in mortality"; Adam was the "the first man of all men" (Moses 1:34) and the "primal parent of our race"; and, as the "undeveloped offspring of celestial parentage," a person is capable in due time, "by experience in ages and aeons, of evolving into a God." Significantly, the question of *how* Adam and Eve were created was not discussed, but after more questions arose concerning it the editors of the *Improvement Era* (i.e., President Joseph F. Smith and Edward H. Anderson) responded in the April 1910 issue with a mention of several possibilities but a strong caution that these "are questions not fully answered in the revealed word of God."[3]

Among those at BYU who both accepted and taught the principles of higher criticism as well as the theory of organic evolution were the Peterson and Chamberlin brothers. To them these ideas did not conflict with the fundamentals of the gospel, but they taught them with such effectiveness that they stirred up unusual interest among the students and caused concern among many people in the community. The controversy came to a head when stake presidents began complaining that students were becoming disturbed, and the professors were charged with raising doubts concerning the historical accuracy of portions of the Old Testament.

Horace H. Cummings, Church superintendent of schools, initially supported the professors, but he concluded late in 1910 that the matter should be brought before the Church board of education. He visited the campus, encouraged the teachers to avoid dogmatic presentations of their views, and made a report to the board. During the ensuing investigation the Peterson brothers and Ralph Chamberlin were quizzed extensively in a hearing in Salt Lake City and in the end they were asked either to desist in the way they were teaching or to resign. They chose the latter course.

Most of the publicity centered on the theory of evolution, but the main problem, it seems, was not the theory itself but the dogmatic, uncompromising way it was taught. Officially the Church took no position on the question, beyond the statements in the *Improvement Era*, and other teachers expressed favorable attitudes toward it, though

---

[3]*Improvement Era* 13 (November 1909): 75–81; 13 (April 1910): 570.

not as unequivocally as those who were dismissed. In April 1911, President Joseph F. Smith explained the decision in an editorial. "In reaching the conclusion that evolution would best be left out of discussions in our Church schools," he said, "we are deciding a question of propriety and not undertaking to say how much of evolution is true or how much false." He also warned against too much intellectual speculation on the manner of the Creation for, he felt, this could lead to a "theological scholastic aristocracy in the Church, and we should therefore not enjoy the brotherhood that now is, or should be common to rich and poor, learned and unlearned among the Saints."[4] Those able to harmonize in their own minds scientific findings with Church teachings were free to do so, but they were not to push their views upon students who were unprepared for the challenge and could not perceive the harmony.

Further Elaborations on Doctrine

During these same years other gospel questions arose, some related to the expansion of secular knowledge and others simply as a result of extensive inquiry into questions not fully answered in the past. The Church turned to some of its best-trained minds for help, and a number of capable scholars within the leadership produced studies that survived the period to become important Church works. One was James E. Talmage, whose book *A Study of the Articles of Faith* was published in 1899 under the auspices of the First Presidency. It has gone through more than fifty printings and still stands as one of the most widely read doctrinal works in the Church. Talmage also published other works, such as *The House of the Lord* (1912) and *Jesus the Christ* (1915), which remain well known. Other important books of the period included John A. Widtsoe's *A Rational Theology* (1915) and David O. McKay's *Ancient Apostles* (1918), both originally prepared as lesson manuals. Each of these men, avid students of both the gospel and so-called "worldly" learning, were ideal examples of the ability to combine secular knowledge with deep religious faith in their continuing search for truth and understanding, as suggested in an 1832 revelation to Joseph Smith: "Seek ye out of the best books words of wisdom; seek learning, even by study and also by faith." (D&C 88:118.)

At the same time, many articles on Church doctrine appeared in

---

[4]*Instructor* 46 (April 1911): 209.

the *Utah Genealogical and Historical Magazine* as well as in other Church magazines, and these together with enhanced gospel study in the Church's auxiliaries helped create a growing interest among members in more theological discussion, and a need for amplification and/ or clarification of many doctrinal questions. It was in this setting that two particularly important additional doctrinal statements appeared.

The first was issued on June 20, 1916. Some confusion existed among the Saints over the use of the term *Father* in scripture, especially in view of the Latter-day Saint teaching that Jesus Christ was the Creator of the earth and the Jehovah of the Old Testament. Some clarification was needed, and in their official exposition, "The Father and the Son," the First Presidency and Council of the Twelve noted that the term *father* was used in four different ways in scripture: referring to God as the literal parent of the spirits of all men, to Jesus as Creator or Father of the earth, to Jesus as the father of those who abide in his gospel, and to Jesus as one invested with the authority of the Father while on earth. Widely published, this clarifying statement has taken its place among the important documents of the Church. In 1921, to further lessen confusion over the nature of the Godhead, the "Lectures on Faith" were eliminated from the Doctrine and Covenants. This unofficial series of lessons, dating back to 1835, contained some ideas, particularly with reference to the Holy Ghost, that were no longer totally consistent with LDS doctrinal understanding as it had grown "line upon line" over the years.

A second important doctrinal statement came in a document entitled "Vision of the Redemption of the Dead." On October 3, 1918, President Joseph F. Smith was pondering the scriptures related to the atonement of Christ. He was especially impressed with Peter's discussion of the Savior preaching to the "spirits in prison" during the three days that his physical body lay in the tomb. "For this cause was the gospel preached also to them that are dead," he read, "that they might be judged according to men in the flesh, but live according to God in the spirit." (1 Peter 3:18–20; 4:6.) Then, said President Smith, "As I pondered over these things which are written, the eyes of my understanding were opened, and the Spirit of the Lord rested upon me, and I saw the hosts of the dead, both small and great." He also saw the Savior visiting the spirits of the dead and organizing missionary work among them, and he was given to understand that since that time missionary work had been conducted continually in the spirit world and that faithful elders of the modern era who had died were participating in that important work. He had the experience recorded and submitted to the other General Authorities, who unanimously accepted it. It was published in the December 1918 issue of the *Improvement Era*, giving the Saints new insight into the nature of missionary activities in the spirit world and a fresh incentive to do temple work on behalf of the dead. In April 1981 it was added to the Doctrine and Covenants as Section 138.

Political Issues in the Progressive Era

In its 1907 "Address to the World" the Church affirmed its commitment "to the doctrine of the separation of church and state; the non-interference of church authority in political matters; and the absolute freedom and independence of the individual in the performance of his political duties."[5] Nevertheless, in the next half dozen years some political issues arose that the Church found difficult to avoid: in some cases simply because Church leaders, as individuals, felt strongly enough to speak out, while in other cases certain fundamental principles were involved.

So long as the anti-Mormon American party continued to control the politics of Salt Lake City and often made the Church a political issue, Church leaders could hardly avoid political responses. In 1911, however, the party's strength collapsed, and about the same time the *Salt Lake Tribune* discontinued its harsh editorial voice against the Church and against Senator Reed Smoot. The most open surviving political hostility was at an end, even though Church leaders did not remain aloof from partisan issues.

One issue centered around President Joseph F. Smith's personal endorsement of William Howard Taft as the Republican candidate for the American presidency in 1912. It was a mild endorsement at best, but critics reacted strongly. Their main complaint was that his endorsement had been printed in Church publications and would therefore unduly influence members who gave special credence to the political statements of their leaders. President Smith quickly issued a second statement emphasizing that his published editorial was merely an expression of his personal views. The discussion carried over into the general conference of October 1912, when various leaders expressed

---

[5]The entire "Address to the World" may be found in Clark, *Messages of the First Presidency*, 4:143–55.

views concerning the importance of exercising freedom in political judgments but also of relying on prayer to help make those judgments.

One of the most intense political issues of the Progressive Era was prohibition, and here the Church faced a dilemma. It opposed the sale and use of alcoholic beverages, but there was a question as to which of three governmental approaches, if any, it should support: a national prohibition amendment, state prohibition laws, or state laws that allowed local option for each community. Both President Smith and Senator Smoot initially supported local option. They were aware that if the Church officially campaigned for a statewide prohibition law, it would run the risk of alienating many of the senator's supporters and perhaps of losing his seat in the Senate. In addition, when the Church had so recently been accused of controlling politics to its own ends, they did not want it to appear that a prohibition law was simply another religious bill being pushed through the state legislature. With the support of Senator Smoot, therefore, a state prohibition bill was defeated in 1909, and later Governor William Spry, a valiant Church member, vetoed similar bills.

Not all Church leaders agreed, and some of them did all they could to bring about mandatory statewide prohibition. Elder Heber J. Grant, especially, was active in the movement, and he was supported in his campaign by Elders George Albert Smith and David O. McKay. In 1911 a local option bill passed. Even though these men joined in urging Utah communities to eliminate liquor, they considered it only a first step.

In 1916 President Smith finally threw full Church support behind both statewide and national prohibition. He had reached the conclusion that the question was of national import and one in which the Church must participate fully. Prohibition appeared as planks in both national party platforms. General conference speakers pleaded for its passage, the MIA adopted a theme calling for state and national prohibition, and the *Improvement Era* lent its pages to support the campaign. In August 1917 Utah became the forty-first "dry" state in the Union and in 1919 the national prohibition amendment passed. Although they had disagreed on the methods for achieving that result, Church leaders were uniformly pleased with the outcome of the prohibition movement: it had been an exercise in both political liberty (i.e., the right to disagree) and brotherhood in pursuit of a common cause.

War and the Saints Abroad

Such political questions centered in western America, but as membership increased outside the United States the affairs of the Church became increasingly affected by international affairs. Two significant upheavals, the Mexican revolution of 1911–12, and the World War of 1914–18, directly touched members living in other countries and prompted discussion of the Church's attitude toward war.

Latter-day Saint colonies in Mexico were prospering, and the full Church program was being carried out in Juarez Stake. All this was disrupted, however, with the outbreak of a revolution against Mexican dictator Porfirio Diaz in 1910, and for the next seven years the political situation remained unsettled. Revolutionary forces under Francisco I. Madero sought military support from the American government and from Latter-day Saint colonists, who were mostly American citizens. But the United States maintained a noninterventionist attitude, and when Church officials in Mexico declared their intention to remain neutral, the Saints were threatened, robbed, and expelled from their homes and farms, and several were killed.

In 1912, with little advance notice, the Saints were suddenly forced to leave Mexico. Women and children left first on a train for El Paso, Texas, and nearby border towns, and the men followed on horseback shortly afterward. A few Saints disagreed with the decision to leave and returned to their homes in Chihuahua, but most became permanent exiles in the United States. The U.S. Congress granted emergency supplies for all American refugees, and the First Presidency asked Elder Anthony W. Ivins of the Council of the Twelve, a former stake president in Mexico, to handle resettlement plans for the Saints. The Juarez Stake was officially disorganized, freeing officers and members to find new homes elsewhere.

Eventually fewer than half the Saints returned to their homes in Chihuahua, and none were able to reclaim their property in Sonora, though they did receive payment from the Mexican government. A new Mexican constitution adopted in 1917 required that all ministers be native-born. This interfered with the reestablishment of missionary work and prevented the return of missionaries as presiding officers in the native branches around Mexico City. During the revolution, mission president Rey L. Pratt maintained contact with local priesthood officers through correspondence. He visited them in 1916 and reorganized the branches under Mexican leaders. American missionaries entered the country in small numbers after 1921, but when the constitution began to be rigidly enforced five years later, they were again deported and the mission business was conducted by mail from headquarters in Los Angeles.

The expulsion of the Latter-day Saints from Mexico was purely political in nature, even though the official Church position was one of neutrality. At the same time, pressures building up in Europe would soon involve members of the Church on both sides of an international conflict. In this case neutrality was no longer possible.

In August 1914, Germany and Austria-Hungary declared war on Serbia, Russia, and France. Britain entered the war that same month when Germany invaded Belgium, but the American president, Woodrow Wilson, declared impartiality in the conflict; his decision to keep the country out of war aided in his successful campaign for reelection in 1916. Church officials in the United States supported their government's decision and urged members to do likewise. At the October 1914 general conference members joined in a special prayer for peace. But American trade with the Allies angered the German government, and submarine attacks on ships carrying American goods and passengers finally brought the United States into the war in 1917.

Missionaries had been evacuated from western Europe in 1914 at the first outbreak of hostilities. Some people were disappointed when the elders, who had presided in branches, left, but the Church continued to function under local leadership and with native missionaries. The president of the Swiss-German Mission remained in Switzerland during the war, keeping in touch with the Saints by mail and through *Der Stern*. This mission magazine was sent to German members serving in the armed forces of their nation and, until it was restricted by the German government in 1916, it kept members informed of Church news. German membership actually increased from about seventy-five hundred to eight thousand during the war.

A pertinent question raised by the conflict was the attitude of Church members toward their enemies, including Latter-day Saints on the opposite side of the conflict. In a classic statement reflecting the perplexities of war, President Joseph F. Smith encouraged American Saints not to think ill of their German counterparts. "Their leaders are to blame, not the people. Those who embrace the gospel are innocent of these things and they ought to be respected by the Latter-day Saints everywhere."[6] As an expression of that respect, American members were encouraged by the First Presidency in 1915 to contribute to a Zion's Emergency War Fund to aid needy members in Europe. The German

---

[6]*Conference Report*, April 1917, p. 11.

Saints themselves lent moral support to their branch members in the armed forces by writing letters and sending packages to the soldiers. About seventy-five Saints died in service to the German government.

Latter-day Saints in the United States exhibited a similar patriotism. Church leaders felt it particularly crucial that members support the war effort so critics would not accuse the Church of disloyalty. With the encouragement of the Church, members in Utah oversubscribed their quotas for enlistments, and more than twenty-four thousand donned the uniform of their country. Of these, 544 were killed in service. Latter-day Saints at home contributed generously to the Red Cross and surpassed the goals set for the purchase of Liberty bonds. The Church and its auxiliaries alone bought $1.4 million in bonds, and the Relief Society sold its store of more than two hundred thousand bushels of wheat to the government for wartime use.

One unfortunate problem in the United States was the bitter prejudice sometimes expressed toward German immigrants. The Church looked toward all men as brothers, and President Smith encouraged members in the United States to accept such immigrants on that basis. In his opening address at the April 1917 general conference, as the distinct possibility of American entry into the war loomed, he also spoke on the spirit that Latter-day Saints should manifest in war: "the spirit of humanity, of love, and of peace-making, that even though they may be called into action they will not demolish, override and destroy the principles which we believe in . . . ; peace and good will toward all mankind, though we may be brought into action with the enemy." He encouraged soldiers to serve as "ministers of life and not of death; . . . in the spirit of defending the liberties of mankind rather than for the purpose of destroying the enemy."

The peace the Saints worked and prayed for was achieved in the armistice of November 11, 1918. Eight days later, and only six days after his eightieth birthday, President Joseph F. Smith died. Though an epidemic of influenza prevented the Church from honoring him with a public funeral, thousands showed their respect as a private funeral cortege proceeded along the city streets to the cemetery. Respected by the Saints, President Smith had endured a life of much public hostility against him and the Church but had lived to see that attitude mellow. He had presided over an important period of transition and had led the Church in marshalling its resources and revitalizing its programs for the challenges ahead.

CHAPTER 16

Change and Continuity in the Postwar Decade, *1919–1930*

The man who headed the Church when it celebrated its hundredth anniversary was Heber Jeddy Grant. Born in 1856, he was the only son of Jedediah M. Grant, counselor to Brigham Young, and Rachel R. Ivins. As President Grant began his administration in 1918, the Church was entering a new era of prosperity and popularity. Bankruptcy and the attacks of politicians and muckrakers were generally things of the past. Early leaders, to be sure, had looked with trepidation at such a time, fearing that it might become too easy to be a Latter-day Saint or that lack of hardship could diminish the unity and faith that had been bolstered by adversity. In 1918 a Protestant minister described the subtle new challenge as well as anyone. Though opposed to the Church, he recognized that Mormonism was no real threat to American institutions. But he believed that the Church's spiritual strength was waning, and that if Americans would simply stop opposing it, it would die a natural death. "The way to oppose Mormonism is not to throw mud upon it," he said. "A campaign of detraction only helps it grow. The thing to do is to treat it with candor and fairness. . . . It must fall of its own weight if it is to fall at all."[1] By the end of its first century, however, it showed no signs of falling.

President Grant: Symbol for His Age

Many things about Heber J. Grant's life represented significant facets of LDS history, particularly with respect to the transitions being experienced by the Church when he became its leader. He was the first

---

[1]As quoted in Roberts, *Comprehensive History of the Church*, 6:551.

President of the Church born after the exodus from Nauvoo. Before the Manifesto he had married three women, and afterwards he personally experienced the difficulties involved in changing from the old ways to the new. A successful businessman, he had been instrumental in getting the beet sugar industry on a firm footing in Utah and Idaho, representing the transition from the old economics to the new. Politically he was a Democrat, even though most of his associates were Republicans, but he consistently refused to impose his politics on members, demonstrating the Church's efforts to separate itself from political partisanship in the twentieth century. At the beginning of the century he had opened missionary work in Japan, foreshadowing the Church's increasing international commitment in the new era. He was literally a man of two centuries who knew he was leading a dynamic church that was becoming more widely appreciated as the new century progressed. But in 1920 he was hardly prepared for the reception he received when he spoke to the Knife and Fork Club of Kansas City, Missouri. He arrived thinking that he would be called upon to defend his faith before critics. Instead, he heard nothing but praise and admiration for the Church.

There was another, more subtle, way that President Grant's administration represented a new age. In 1921 Church leaders ended years of discussion on interpreting the Word of Wisdom by making adherence to this important principle a requirement for admission to the temple. Since the days of Joseph Smith, the revelation known as the Word of Wisdom had been revered as the Lord's instructions regarding health, and Latter-day Saints had been particularly enjoined to refrain from the use of tea, coffee, alcoholic beverages, and tobacco. The doctrine was stressed more firmly in some periods than in others, and some early leaders, including Brigham Young, had declared that it was to be considered a "commandment." They did not, however, make adherence a specific requirement for office holding or temple attendance. In the early twentieth century General Authorities stressed the principle regularly, suggesting that those who did not obey it should not be advanced in the priesthood or recommended for the temple, and it was a significant culmination to all their efforts when they felt inspired to formalize the policy. It was also significant that this should happen as the United States entered a period of national prohibition as well as one of intensive anti-tobacco campaigning. Church policy both complemented and augmented important national efforts at reform.

Between 1918 and 1930 Church membership grew from less than 500,000 to more than 630,000, the number of organized stakes in-

President Heber J. Grant inaugurates broadcasting on the Deseret News radio station (later KSL), May 6, 1922. With him (from left) are Nathan O. Fullmer, George Albert Smith, Mrs. Grant, Salt Lake Mayor C. Clarence Neslen, and George J. Cannon, and (in the doorway) Anthony W. Ivins, a radio operator, and B. F. Grant. (Church Archives)

creased from 79 to 104, new temples were constructed, and significant changes continued to affect the priesthood, the auxiliaries, the educational program, the missionary program, and public relations. But change was accompanied by continuity, and President Grant was again the perfect symbol. The traditional emphasis on temperance, sobriety, thrift, tithe paying, and setting an example of Christian living continued, even intensified, during his administration. The distinctive Latter-day Saint doctrines of priesthood authority, salvation for the dead, and the importance of the restoration of the gospel through Joseph Smith continued to be emphasized. Missionary work was stepped up dramatically, and President Grant's commitment to spreading the gospel to all the world was illustrated in a conference address in 1927: "I want to emphasize that we as a people have one supreme thing to do and that is to call upon the world to repent of sin, to come to God. And it is our duty above all others to go forth and proclaim the gospel of the Lord

Jesus Christ, the restoration again to the earth of the plan of life and salvation. . . . We have in very deed the pearl of great price."[2]

The Dispersion of Modern Israel: A Beginning

In the decade following World War I America continued the trend toward urbanism that had begun shortly after the Civil War. By 1930 over 56 percent of the population lived in cities, and though the rest lived in areas designated as rural, only 25 percent of all Americans lived on farms. Economically, even though the 1920s was a decade of general prosperity, farmers remained in a state of comparative depression.

All this had implications for the Latter-day Saints, for in 1920, 76 percent still lived in Utah or the surrounding intermountain states and 79 percent of all the stakes were predominantly rural in their economic orientation. The agricultural depression of the early 1920s was hard on the rural Saints, and many families from Utah, Idaho, Nevada, Arizona, and Wyoming headed toward the urban areas of those states or toward the West Coast in search of work. Some leaders, including President Grant, imbued with the Jeffersonian ideal of the nobility of agriculture as a way of life, looked with misgiving upon the social problems inherent in the city. They urged members to stay on the farm if possible rather than seek so-called easy jobs in the city, though they put no religious sanctions upon the idea of moving. Between 1920 and 1930 the percentage of members living in the intermountain region dropped from 76.1 to 72.3, while the percentage on the West Coast increased from 2.6 to 6.2. Though small, this change was an indication of the beginnings of an important trend.

At the same time two shifts in policy culminated in the 1920s. One was official discouragement of all immigration from abroad. Saints in Europe were still eager to migrate to Utah, for members were few in their homelands, and opportunities to mingle with the Saints and marry in the faith were extremely limited. Church leaders were nevertheless reluctant to encourage them to make a move they might later regret. Work opportunities in Utah were limited, and assimilation into the new society would be more difficult than in the days when the state was being filled with immigrants. Immigration had been discouraged since before the turn of the century, but the dream of a better life in America persisted. In a statement issued on October 18, 1921, the First

---

[2]*Conference Report*, April 1927, pp. 175–76.

Presidency urged the missionaries to stop preaching emigration. The Saints, they said, could be more useful to the Church by strengthening the kingdom in their own lands, rather than sacrificing to emigrate to Zion where "their hopes will not be realized." The gathering definitely had "great meaning in our history," the Presidency said, "but we must realize that times and conditions change and that therefore the application of the principles and teachings must change."[3] The Saints in Europe were promised that one day temples would be built in their homelands so temple work could be accomplished without uprooting them.

Even in America there was no effort to encourage the Saints elsewhere to move to Utah, or, despite the advice to remain on farms instead of going to cities, to encourage Utah Saints to stay in Utah for the sake of the Church itself. In 1922, for example, the president of the Central States Mission made an extra effort to persuade the Saints to remain and help build up the Church where they lived rather than "move to the stakes of Zion, where through their inability to obtain employment they might get discouraged or even apostatize." In 1921 the Saints in the area of Santa Monica, California, wrote President Grant asking about the truth of rumors that the leaders were opposed to Mormons' moving to California. When he visited them in October, President Grant declared that permanent settlement in these areas was in full accord with Church policy.

By the 1920s, then, the Church was implementing a policy of expanding Zion's borders by encouraging the Saints to build up the Church wherever they were. It was the beginning also of a modern dispersion of Israel. The gathering of former years had emphasized the importance of strengthening Zion in Utah, but that need had been fulfilled. No longer were young Latter-day Saints reluctant to leave the mountains in search of opportunity elsewhere. The reality of this change was emphasized in 1923 when the first stake outside the nineteenth-century settlement regions of the intermountain west, Canada, and Mexico was created in Los Angeles, California. In 1927 the second and third such stakes came into being in Hollywood and San Francisco. For the time being the dispersion was chiefly toward the West Coast, though there was also evidence it was moving east. In 1934 there were

---

[3]This document is included in Douglas Dexter Alder, "The German-speaking Immigration to Utah, 1850–1950," Master's thesis, University of Utah, 1959, pp. 114–18.

enough Saints in New York City and surrounding areas to create a stake in the state where the Church was originally organized.

Continuing Organizational Reform: Study and Implementation

These years saw additional studies of the Church's growing programs and implementation of more important changes that tended to streamline the administrative process, strengthen the priesthood, and further define the proper roles of the auxiliaries. In November 1918, for example, President Grant announced that members of the First Presidency would no longer serve as auxiliary heads: these assignments were given to other General Authorities. To more effectively handle the increasingly complex activities related to managing taxable and other nonecclesiastical Church property, Zion's Security Corporation was created in 1922, and the following year the Corporation of the President was organized to hold and administer all ecclesiastical property.

Among the auxiliaries, in 1919 the Relief Society established a Social Welfare Department, to help handle problems of unwed mothers and adoption. In 1921 it implemented a new monthly lesson sequence that included theology, literature, social service, and a business and work meeting. Mutual Improvement Association programs were gradually developed for young men and women ages seventeen to twenty-one, and were adopted churchwide in 1921 as the M-Men and Gleaner programs. In 1922 the Primary Association completed its Primary Children's Hospital in Salt Lake City, evidence of the Church's increasing commitment to social welfare concerns. This hospital eventually became one of America's major pediatric clinics.

This was an era in which social problems of all sorts seemed more regularly to affect the well-being of Latter-day Saints, who were less isolated from the world than ever before. It was also an era in which the Church undertook intensive studies in an effort to determine what more it could do, administratively or otherwise, to deal with such problems. Not all the resulting recommendations were implemented, but the fact that they were made at all suggests the growing complexity of the challenges facing the Church.

In 1916 the Social Advisory Committee was organized, consisting of board members from the general boards of all the auxiliaries and chaired by Stephen L Richards of the Council of the Twelve. Among other things, it promoted cooperation between the Church and various

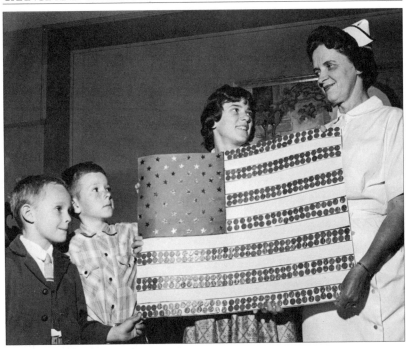

After completion of the Primary Children's Hospital, the Primary "penny parade" became a tradition among children of the Church. Birthday pennies helped care for children in the hospital. (Church Archives)

public welfare agencies, as well as cooperation with the legislature on a variety of social welfare concerns, including social standards, assistance to the indigent, juvenile delinquency, and motion picture censorship.

In 1920 the Social Welfare Committee was merged with the general Church Correlation Committee, and the combined committee was asked by the First Presidency and the Council of the Twelve to review the relationship between the priesthood and the auxiliaries with a view toward eliminating gaps as well as overlaps in educational and social responsibilities. In April 1921 it submitted an extensive report and recommended a number of far-reaching changes, some of which were similar to recommendations made by another committee as early as 1907. It identified an overlapping of theological instruction and suggested that all such instruction in the wards become the responsibility of the Sunday School. The Primary and the MIA were to be responsible for organizing recreation, the Relief Society was to assist the bishop in social welfare programs, and the Church School System was to continue to operate daily religion classes. In addition, new correlation committees were to be set up at the ward, stake, and general levels to assess needs and coordinate programs.

After more than a year of study the First Presidency decided not to implement some of the committee's most sweeping recommendations, particularly the plans for exclusive Sunday School control of theological instruction and for correlation committees. However, many of the ideas in its report so clearly reflected problems in local church administration that in 1923, the year after the committee was released, the First Presidency sent circular letters to stakes making some very pointed suggestions. Auxiliary organizations were not to become independent entities but were to operate under the direct supervision of stake and ward authorities. Stake presidencies and bishoprics were advised to hold monthly planning meetings with their respective stake and ward officers (an idea that became institutionalized in the 1960s with the official organization of ward and stake councils). The MIAs were assigned sole responsibility for recreation, and training its own teachers was the duty of each auxiliary. Aaronic Priesthood quorums were instructed to work toward better preparation of missionaries.

As a direct result of the correlation committee's study, the Young Women's Mutual Improvement Association became wholly an activity program and began to sponsor, among other things, a summer camp program for girls. In 1929 the MIA magazines were combined into one, the *Improvement Era*, ending forty years of independent operation of the *Young Woman's Journal*. That same year the weekday religion classes for children, which seemed to compete with the Primary, were eliminated. In addition, more men and boys than ever before were active in the priesthood, especially in ward teaching.

As in earlier years, a continuing goal of reform was to strengthen the priesthood, but this centered in encouraging priesthood activities such as ward teaching rather than in providing gospel instruction. Despite the First Presidency's rejection of some features of the correlation report, the idea that the Sunday School be given sole responsibility for gospel teaching did not die. Some persons still felt there was too much duplication when the priesthood, MIA, and Sunday School all sought to give weekly gospel lessons.

A new study committee consisting of Elders David O. McKay, Stephen L Richards, and Joseph Fielding Smith of the Council of the Twelve recommended that the teaching of the gospel take place in a unified Sunday School that would include the priesthood quorums. In

October 1927 the First Presidency announced the adoption of such a program, with priesthood business being handled in a monthly quorum meeting. By 1928 the Sunday School had become the teaching arm of the priesthood for theological and doctrinal instruction. A separate weekly priesthood meeting was scheduled each Tuesday night in connection with MIA; this session was designated, for a time, as the Priesthood-MIA.

Despite such changes, the ideals of correlation were not achieved in this decade. The auxiliaries did not become helps of the priesthood as intended; rather, they were influences tending to mold the priesthood into their own pattern of organization. In addition, the plans did not always meet the needs of outlying, scattered branches. Study committees continued to work on ways to improve coordination. The 1930s would see a permanent reinauguration of weekly priesthood meetings and the end of the unified Sunday School.

Changes in Education

The Church also reevaluated its secular education program in the postwar decade. Educational costs continued to soar, and the advisability of continuing all the academies and colleges, which accounted for the major portion of the Church budget, was seriously questioned. Horace Cummings, superintendent of Church schools, reported in 1918 that federal funds, particularly for vocational education, were aiding Utah schools, and Church schools would have an even more difficult time competing successfully.

In 1919 the Council of the Twelve authorized several significant changes in the administration of the school system. A member of the Council of the Twelve, David O. McKay, was made Church commissioner of education, for the first time placing a General Authority in direct charge of the education program. This was part of an overall effort to centralize the direction of Church activities, and it had important consequences for education by involving the Twelve more directly. Stephen L Richards and Richard R. Lyman, also members of the Twelve, became assistant commissioners.

By 1920 about twenty seminaries were in operation and it was clear that this program, begun as an experiment in 1912, was succeeding. It was also clear that there were enough public high schools to accommodate the needs of all Latter-day Saint youth in the intermountain area. Accordingly, the Church commissioner of education recom-

By the 1920s the seminary movement had proved itself and become a permanent part of the Church educational program. This is the Payson, Utah, seminary, January 13, 1926. (Church Archives)

mended that eight academies be eliminated that year, and by 1924 all academies except the one at Colonia Juarez, Mexico, had been closed or turned over to the states to be operated as secondary schools. At the same time, the seminary program was expanded so that weekday religious instruction could continue to supplement the secular education of the Church's youth. Between 1922 and 1932, seminary enrollment increased from 4,976 to 29,427. At a much smaller cost per student, many more were being reached than could have been reached through the academy program.

The new seminaries were successful partly because of the willingness of school boards to grant released time to students for the purpose of taking private religious instruction and their willingness to grant high school credit. Ironically, the Salt Lake City board refused to grant either released time or credit, and in the city of the Church's headquarters students were required to take their seminary training either before or after school. As a result, seminary enrollment in Salt Lake City in the 1920s was only about 10 percent, compared with an average of 70 percent in released-time areas.

In 1930 the state high school inspector raised questions about the constitutionality of the released-time program. It violated the constitutional principle of separation of church and state, he said, because public school buses were used by pupils who also attended religious classes, and seminary teachers were sometimes being used by the public schools to supervise study periods, assist in registration, and even conduct some regular high school classes. The following year the state board of education ordered total disassociation of seminaries and their facilities from the schools. At the same time, the board rejected a resolution that would have denied credit for seminary work. In later years attempts to challenge the system in the courts continued, but a judicious and complete separation of the seminaries from the public schools helped maintain the released-time arrangement. In the 1980s, however, the limited high school credit was withdrawn as a result of a court decision.

In the 1920s the Church also reevaluated its college programs. In addition to Brigham Young University, it continued to operate Brigham Young College at Logan, Dixie College at St. George, Weber College at Ogden, Snow College at Ephraim (all in Utah), and Ricks College at Rexburg, Idaho. These schools still offered secondary training, but were strengthening their programs in post-high-school work. The major need in the intermountain area was the training of public school teachers; in 1920, therefore, at the same time that he recommended abandonment of the academies, the Church commissioner of education proposed that each of these colleges be authorized to establish a two-year normal course. He recommended further that Brigham Young University should develop a complete college course leading to a four-year degree. The proposals were accepted, and these Church schools moved closer to becoming exclusively institutions of higher education.

Because the state of Utah was also moving into the junior college field, it became necessary to resolve the question of whether the Church should continue to operate a competing system. To some it seemed like a needless expense when equivalent education was becoming available in public institutions. In 1926 the Church board of education explored the issue in great detail. There was considerable disagreement among board members, but in the end they recognized that the Church must ultimately withdraw. Immediate action was taken with regard to Brigham Young College, which held its last commencement in May 1926. Its buildings were turned over to the city of Logan to house a public high school. Two years later the Church made known that it favored establishment of junior colleges by the state of Utah, and in 1930 it announced its decision to turn its Utah colleges over to the state. The transition was completed in 1933, though in the transfer the Church stipulated that if the state should ever cease operating educational facilities on any of the properties, they should be returned

Ricks College in Rexburg, Idaho, was one of the few Church academies that survived as a junior college. This is the gymnasium building on the Ricks campus as it appeared sometime after 1913. (Church Archives)

to the Church. In Idaho, the Church made the same offer with respect to Ricks College, but the offer was rejected and the Church decided to continue operating the school.

The centralization of college-level programs at Ricks and BYU left a gap in religious instruction elsewhere, which was filled by the establishment of institutes of religion adjacent to college campuses. The first institute was opened for students at the University of Idaho at Moscow in 1926, after LDS professors and other Church members in the community had called to the attention of Church leaders the need for a student center adjacent to the campus. J. Wyley Sessions became the pioneer institute director. From the beginning the program had four goals: religious instruction, student counseling, social activities, and worship. The experiment in Idaho gradually won student acceptance, and soon faculties were appointed and buildings provided adjacent to other campuses attended by significant numbers of Latter-day Saint students.

Missionary Work

With some exceptions, between five and seven hundred missionaries were sent out each year during the 1920s. At the same time,

In 1922 a film entitled Trapped by the Mormons *was produced in England and circulated widely, contributing to the negative image of the Church. It was later rereleased as* The Mormon Peril. *(Utah State Historical Society)*

General Authorities continued the earlier trend toward reducing the number of seventies, and most missionaries were drawn from the ranks of young, unmarried elders. In North America missionary work prospered and Church membership in the 1920s increased by nearly 25 percent.

In some areas missionary work was difficult. In England, for example, distorted images and vicious stories and accusations persisted. An anti-Mormon film, *Trapped by the Mormons*, portrayed the missionaries as mesmeric villains who would stop at nothing to delude the fair young women of England and lure them away to Utah. Missionaries were still sometimes harassed and beaten, yet in this decade LDS membership in Europe increased by about four thousand, in addition to those who emigrated.

For reasons other than persecution, times were difficult for the Saints in Europe. The tragedies of World War I had left devastation and poverty. To aid needy members in Europe, Zion's Emergency War Fund was organized, and in 1919 the Church also purchased food from the American Expeditionary Force in France. Wishing to escape poverty, and still clinging to the tradition of gathering to Zion in America, many European Saints ignored the admonitions against emigration. Except for the period immediately after World War II, the years between 1922 and 1930 saw the greatest German LDS emigration in the Church's history. The decade also saw substantial numbers of British Saints emigrate to Utah, as well as some from other countries. Members distant from the Church's population center could not easily shake off the ideal of gathering that had been instilled in them for three or four generations. Despite this exodus, by 1930 there were about 29,000 Saints scattered throughout Europe. During this time a number of missions were reorganized or divided, and a new mission was opened in Czechoslovakia.

In Latin America the Church experienced different kinds of difficulties. Rey L. Pratt continued as president of the Mexican Mission, but after 1913 political problems in Mexico kept him and other American missionaries from returning to live in the country. Through letters and personal visits, however, he kept in touch with native leaders until his death in 1931. In 1919 he was sent to El Paso, Texas, where he set up a headquarters in exile for the mission and established a number of branches in American border towns with large Spanish-speaking populations.

Political conditions calmed enough in 1922 to allow American missionaries to enter Mexico again, though President Pratt was never able to take up residence there. The returning elders found local members had done a great deal of proselyting on their own, and the Church was growing. In 1926, however, the government began to enforce the constitutional provision against foreign-born ministers and the American missionaries were required to withdraw again. Despite these political difficulties, the membership in Mexico grew from 2,300 to 4,700 Saints in the 1920s.

There were few members elsewhere in Latin America, though in 1925 the South American Mission was officially opened. This resulted from an invitation to work with German immigrants in Argentina, rather than optimism that missionary work among the Spanish-speaking people would prosper. After World War I the Friedrichs and Hoppe families, who had joined the Church in Germany, migrated to Argentina. They soon began to share the gospel with other German families and in 1924 wrote the First Presidency asking for elders to assist in missionary work and other Church activities. Their request was favorably received, and in 1925 Elder Melvin J. Ballard of the Council of the Twelve was sent to Argentina as president of the new South American Mission. Rulon S. Wells and Rey L. Pratt of the First Council of the Seventy accompanied him. Elder Wells spoke German and Elder Pratt was fluent in Spanish. Their success was limited, although they did baptize some German people already converted by Wilhelm Friedrichs and others. They departed after six months, leaving a German convert, Reinhold Stoof, in charge. Elder Stoof visited southern Brazil in 1927 and later assigned permanent missionaries among the German colonies there. The Church had virtually no success among the Spanish-speaking population in this period. By 1930 there were 751 members in Argentina and Brazil, practically all German-speaking. Only after World War II would there be substantial expansion in South America.

In Asia, the work of the Church did not go well at all. In 1924 President Grant decided to close the mission he had opened in Japan in 1901. Linguistic and cultural differences seemed to be at the heart of the problem, and by the time the mission closed only 174 converts had been baptized. The handful of active Japanese Saints made every effort to maintain an organization, however, and a month after the closing Elder Fujiya Nara of Tokyo and a few others organized the Japan Mutual Improvement Association. On January 1, 1925, they began publishing a small magazine for the Japanese Saints that continued sporadically until 1929. When Nara went to Manchuria in 1933, he was replaced as Church leader in Japan by Taken Fujiwara, who had attended BYU in 1927 at the invitation of President Franklin S. Harris. The Church in Asia continued to dwindle, though a few Saints remained active during World War II and were there to begin meeting with the many LDS servicemen who arrived in 1945.

An important assurance of the Church's worldwide interests came in 1920 and 1921 when David O. McKay of the Council of the Twelve traveled nearly 56,000 miles, on assignment by the First Presidency, in a worldwide survey of missions. On this tour he dedicated China for the preaching of the gospel. In Hawaii he was so impressed by a group of small children at a flag-raising ceremony at Laie that he was moved to predict that this location would eventually become an important religious and educational center for the Church. He visited many other areas in the South Seas and Asia, as well as India, Egypt, and Palestine, and returned home via Europe. In many places he was the first General Authority the Saints had ever seen. After that, visits of General Authorities to the missions became more frequent.

Church Buildings, Historic Sites, and Public Relations

Three new temples were dedicated in this era: the Hawaii Temple, smaller and less costly than the others, in 1919; a million-dollar temple

Elder David O. McKay's world tour in 1920–21 symbolized the growing worldwide commitment of the Church. Here he and Elder Hugh J. Cannon (left) and Mission President George S. Taylor (right) are surrounded by a group of Maori leaders in April 1921. (McKay Scrapbooks, Church Archives)

at Cardston, Alberta, Canada, in 1923; and the Arizona Temple, in Mesa, in 1927. Architecturally each of these sacred buildings represented a distinct departure from the four Utah temples of the nineteenth century. None had spires or assembly rooms, and each was characterized by simple though elegant exteriors reflecting design concepts borrowed from Mesoamerica and the work of Frank Lloyd Wright. The Alberta Temple, especially, has been praised as one of the finest examples of the adaptation of Church architecture to modern design. It was planned by Hyrum C. Pope and Harold Burton, who were selected in an architectural competition in 1913.

The modern trend in Church architecture evident in the design of these three international temples and in many meetinghouses of the 1910s disappeared in the 1920s in favor of a return to neoclassical and colonial lines. The revival of colonial designs seemed to mark a recognition of the Church's New England heritage. In 1919 Willard Young was appointed superintendent of the church building department, and under his direction the Church began to standardize plans for ward and stake buildings. Several basic patterns were developed in which chapels, recreation halls, Relief Society rooms, Scout rooms, classrooms, and bishops' offices were combined under one roof, and a ward needing a new building was simply provided with an existing plan. It was not long, however, before local architects began to complain that such a practice was unfair because it curtailed their opportunities, and in 1924 President Grant changed the policy so that, if they chose to do so, wards and stakes could hire local architects.

The Church also continued in its efforts to preserve its heritage through further purchases and development of historic sites and monuments, especially in the region of Mormon origins. In 1926 it purchased and began to improve the Peter Whitmer, Sr., farm, where the Church was organized, and in 1929 it purchased the Hill Cumorah. Here a monument to the Angel Moroni was erected in 1935, and two years later a bureau of information was established. In 1927 the Church cooperated with the Utah State legislature in erecting a monument to the Mormon Battalion on the grounds of the Utah State Capitol. Such efforts were designed both to enhance appreciation for the Mormon heritage and to create the kind of interest that would help the Church present its message to the world.

In its effort to reach the world, the Church did not hesitate to take advantage of technological developments in the early twentieth century. In 1913, for example, Church leaders commended the release of a silent film, not produced by the Church but nevertheless sympathetic, entitled *One Hundred Years of Mormonism*. A grandson of Brigham Young even played the part of his illustrious progenitor. The film countered the impressions commonly gained by moviegoers of a depraved people under a despotic church government. Another developing medium was radio, first heard by members in the early 1920s. The Church was quick to see its advantages. In March 1922, experimental transmission demonstrated a listening radius from Salt Lake City of a thousand miles, and the *Improvement Era* speculated that in three years the voice of President Grant would be heard simultaneously by congregations in every part of the region. A Church-owned radio station, the forerunner of KSL, was dedicated in 1922, and two years later general conferences were first broadcast. Later that year plans were instituted for a regular Sunday evening program. In 1925 the Tabernacle Choir began broadcasting some of its performances, and four years later it began weekly network broadcasts.

Despite stepped-up efforts at public relations, the Church's image in America did not become fully positive during the 1920s. Some journalists still looked for the sensational and others were still unfriendly.

Commemorating the pioneer heritage, the first This Is the Place Monument was dedicated in the Diamond Jubilee celebration in 1922. Standing near the monument are President Heber J. Grant and Lorenzo Zobieski Young, last survivor of the original pioneer company of July 1847. (Church Archives)

Some writers pointed to the exodus from Utah as evidence that the Church was beginning to lose its younger generation. Others played up the fact that certain people claiming allegiance to Mormonism still practiced polygamy. So-called Fundamentalists still insisted that they were right in performing new plural marriages. When they were discovered, they were cut off from the Church, but the publicity naturally linked them in the public mind with the Church. The First Presidency responded to the continuing criticism by emphasizing that the practice was restricted to an overzealous clique. In 1924 another official statement denounced as disloyal those who entered into new polygamous marriages, but the issue continued to plague the Church for years.

A curious public was also interested in the new financial position of the Church, and while some applauded, others criticized it as a great wealth-gathering institution. On the other hand, the Church's conservative financial policies as well as the influence of Reed Smoot in the U.S. Senate helped it gain greater respectability among businessmen of the nation. Heber J. Grant, acknowledged as an astute business leader, was often invited to address important conventions of business and public officials. In the 1930s the changing public image would become predominantly positive.

The Church and Public Issues

Whether it wanted to or not, the Church still could not avoid having its name associated with political issues. It remained dedicated to the principle of separation of church and state, and President Grant was adamant that members in the United States should be active in political parties of their choice. As individuals, Church leaders did not hesitate to speak out on issues of public importance, although they tried to separate their own opinions from any official Church position. At the same time, there were a number of issues that Church leaders believed went beyond politics and on which the Church took sides.

One question that affected the Church's public image nationally, but on which it took no official stance, was the League of Nations controversy. In 1919 the president of the United States, Woodrow Wilson, attempted to persuade the American people that the only way to keep the peace just won in the Great World War was to ratify the treaty that would make the United States part of the League of Nations. Senator Reed Smoot disagreed and joined the powerful group of Republican "reservationists" who were attempting to block the president's program. The Church became involved when Elder Smoot went so far as to suggest that even the Book of Mormon opposed the idea of the League of Nations. His attitude became a matter of public comment in many parts of the country. In Utah the debate raged heavily, with B. H. Roberts avidly supporting the League and declaring that Mormon scripture supported the idea. Unfortunately, as the debate intensified in Utah, rhetoric on both sides sometimes implied that it was reflecting the Church's position. Among Church leaders, most tended to support the League, though a few were outspoken against it. Finally, on September 21, President Heber J. Grant made his own position known as he addressed a quarterly conference of the Salt Lake Stake. He firmly endorsed the League of Nations, but in doing so he made it abundantly clear he was speaking as an individual, not as a church leader. This issue should not divide the Church, he emphasized, and neither side represented an official Church position. He also made it clear that latter-day scriptures were not to be used on either side of the argument. In the end, American membership in the League of Nations was blocked in the United States Senate.

More important than the League of Nations controversy itself was the fact that subsequent events proved that President Grant did not allow differences of opinion on political matters to change his assess-

The Hill Cumorah, purchased early in the twentieth century by the Church, became an important tourist attraction by the 1940s. (Church Archives)

ment of any of the discussants as religious leaders. He was still a friend and admirer of Reed Smoot, and supported his reelection in 1920 and subsequent years. He called another League opponent, Charles W. Nibley, to be his counselor in 1925, and two others, J. Reuben Clark, Jr., and David O. McKay, to be counselors in 1933 and 1934. In the modern world, he declared, it was to be expected that men of integrity and strong will would be found on both sides of political issues, but this did not diminish their ability to function as brothers in the priesthood. Such political latitude was clearly the rule in the 1920s, as Church leaders openly expressed differing political views on practically every major issue and supported opposing candidates.

The year 1930 was the centennial of the Church, and the general conference that convened in April was largely devoted to memorializing this important milestone. To highlight the occasion, a number of special events took place. The Salt Lake Temple was officially illuminated by floodlights. In the conference meeting of April 6, members participated in the "Hosanna Shout," usually reserved for temple dedications. Elder B. H. Roberts presented his six-volume *Comprehensive History*, covering the first century of the Church, to the conference. A memorable pageant, *Message of the Ages*, was presented throughout conference week. These and other activities represented appreciation for past progress and optimism for the future.

The Church had come a long way in a hundred years and had seen many changes. Each change was designed to better equip it to improve the lives of the Saints and proclaim the restored gospel throughout the world. The Church could not claim perfection, for its people were not perfect, and it would continue to examine and adapt its programs to strengthen them spiritually.

One economic problem of immediate importance was scarcely recognized at the centennial conference. The world was in the first stages of the Great Depression, and the Saints would be as deeply affected as anyone. In the 1930s, in response to the problems of that depression, they would welcome a formalized program that would carry the Church in an important new direction.

CHAPTER 17

The Church and the Great Depression, *1930–1938*

As President Heber J. Grant led the Church into its second century, he faced the problem of guiding it through the most severe economic depression in American history, and one that threatened the financial well-being of many Latter-day Saints. The Church's response was the Security Plan of 1936, later known as the Church Welfare Plan, designed to restore economic confidence. The 1930s also saw more challenges in education, expansion of missionary work, and continuing emphasis on the Word of Wisdom. Translation of the Book of Mormon into Braille and other languages along with greater use of the radio helped expand the scope of missionary activity. Continuing efforts to preserve historic sites built appreciation for the past. In addition, the implementation of the Security Plan and greater public awareness of the high ideals of the Latter-day Saints helped create a new, more positive, public image.

The Church Responds to the Great Depression

In the 1920s many farmers in the United States endured serious financial depression. One result was increasing migration from country to city as the unemployed sought jobs. On the other hand, American businessmen saw a period of sustained economic growth. There were more jobs, higher incomes, and the growth of what seemed to be permanent economic well-being. At the same time, the rapidly growing economy encouraged stock market speculation and highly extended credit. During these years Church leaders strongly counseled against the bondage of debt and condemned waste, extravagance, and speculation. They urged members to be industrious, frugal, and to live within their means.

*Planning welfare activities in the Church, April 1939. Before he became a
General Authority, Harold B. Lee (left) was responsible for managing the
welfare program. Here he meets with other men involved in welfare
planning. Standing is Henry D. Moyle, who also later became an apostle;
seated are three members of the Council of the Twelve, Elders Albert E.
Bowen, Melvin J. Ballard, and John A. Widtsoe. (Church Archives)*

Then came the dark days of the Depression. Following the stock
market crash in October 1929, previously wealthy men became poverty-
stricken. Fortunes were wiped out. Factories, businesses, and banks
closed their doors. Industrial expansion ceased and agricultural markets
dried up. During 1929 and 1930 national farm income, already low
from the failure to recover from the postwar collapse in 1921, dropped
15 to 20 percent, followed by another drop of 20 percent during 1932
and 1933.

As business adjusted to depressed conditions and agriculture reduced its labor force, millions were thrown out of work. The number
of unemployed Americans jumped from 1,499,000 in 1929 to
12,634,000 in 1933, encompassing over one-fourth of the labor force.
During the 1920s many had lived extravagantly, failing to provide for
hard times. When they lost their jobs during the 1930s, they had money
for neither rent nor food. Breadlines formed; want, hunger, and despondency became rampant. To alleviate some of the suffering and
distress, the federal government instituted numerous programs for the

unemployed and destitute, pouring millions of dollars into make-work projects and other ameliorative measures.

With the Depression worsening and no promise of respite, Church leaders began considering the Church's role in providing relief and ending the economic crisis. They realized that temporal and spiritual well-being were intimately related. Accordingly, the general conference of April 1931 offered much practical and familiar advice: keep out of debt, patronize home industry, pay tithes and offerings. Elder George F. Richards of the Council of the Twelve reminded the Saints of their responsibility to give fast offerings for the poor. He said that if members had lived fully the law of tithing and fast offering, they would have no need for government relief. To the question, "Can the Depression be cured?" Church authorities responded affirmatively, stressing that "despondency and pessimism will never better the situation." Prosperity would return, they said, when selfishness, strife, and bitterness were discarded and genuine brotherhood was established in economic relations.

Recognizing that much of the Mormons' economic achievement in the past had come from their willingness to work together, authorities urged cooperation among the Saints. They felt that "every person who wants work should be able to find it" and directed priesthood quorums to assume responsibility for helping their members find employment. The Presiding Bishop urged each ward bishop to appoint a ward employment committee composed of a high priest, a seventy, an elder, and a representative from the Relief Society, to function in conjunction with a proposed stake employment committee.

Early in the Depression, Church leaders disapproved of spending money to provide food, clothing, and shelter as outright gifts, believing that efforts would be more wisely directed toward providing work for the unemployed. As a result, government programs providing relief in the form of a dole aroused considerable concern. Church authorities received reports of able-bodied Latter-day Saints on government relief who had sufficient cattle, hay, and chickens to provide for their own needs. President J. Reuben Clark, Jr., remarked that "the thought [among the Latter-day Saints] that we should get all we can from the government because everybody else is getting it, is unworthy of us as American citizens. It will debauch us."[1]

---

[1]*Conference Report*, October 1933, p. 102.

Federal work relief programs, on the other hand, received full Church support. But as early as 1933, the First Presidency began to fear that these programs would be curtailed, placing a considerable burden on Church relief organizations and an increasing reliance upon the dole. They did not know how long government aid would last or how sufficient it would be. They began, therefore, urging members to prepare to shoulder the burden of providing for their own welfare. "The cries of those in distress must be hushed by our bounty. The words of the Lord require this from us. A feeling of common humanity bids it from us. . . . If we shall fully observe that law, the Lord will pour out His richest blessings upon us; we shall be better and happier than ever before in our history; and peace and prosperity will come to us."[2]

In 1933 the First Presidency began to plan a more comprehensive Church relief program by requesting each stake president to conduct a survey, indicating resources available, areas of need, and employment opportunities. "The Lord will not hold us guiltless if we shall permit any of our people to go hungry, or to be cold, unclad, or unhoused during the approaching winter," the message emphasized. "Particularly he will consider us gravely blameful if those who have heretofore paid their tithes and offerings to the Church when they had employment, shall now be permitted to suffer when the general adversity has robbed them of their means of livelihood."[3]

Results from the survey enabled the First Presidency to issue instructions for relief work during the coming year. The brethren were especially impressed that no new organization needed to be established. Under priesthood direction, and properly coordinated by bishops and stake presidents, the organizations already established could function successfully as relief agencies. The First Presidency urged the leaders of wards and stakes to develop private, community enterprises in which able-bodied members could find employment. They were careful to stress that relief should not be extended as a handout, except to the worthy sick, infirm, or disabled. Faithful Saints were "independent, self-respecting and self-reliant" and did not desire such aid. Each bishop and stake president was directed to provide the less fortunate in their wards and stakes with food supplies and other materials.

In these ways Church authorities delegated responsibility for pro-

---

[2]"A Message from the First Presidency Concerning Preparation for Relief Measures," in Clark, Messages of the First Presidency, 5:333.
[3]Clark, Messages of the First Presidency, 5:331.

viding relief to local units without at first setting up a coordinated program. Each stake acted independently in aiding members within its boundaries. Left to their own resources, many stakes and wards devised truly innovative programs. Pioneer Stake in Salt Lake City, with more than half of its adult members unemployed in 1932, instituted a program to provide wood, blankets, quilts, clothing, and canned food to its estimated 2,500 needy. It also found jobs in private industry for more than seventy-five men upon recommendations from their bishops. Other unemployed members were put to work renovating chapels, cutting wood, and helping farmers harvest crops. In order to store goods that were donated to the stake, leaders rented the Bamberger Electric Train Company warehouse in Salt Lake City at a cost of $100 per year. A portion of goods from the warehouse was given to the needy and the rest sold to members who could afford to pay. The receipts were placed in a fund to purchase items the stake could not produce for itself. At one point, Harold B. Lee, president of the stake, even obtained permission to keep tithing revenues within the stake, making it almost entirely self-sufficient.

Other stakes implemented their own programs for taking care of their poor and unemployed, with varying degrees of success. Between September 1931 and June 1932, ten Salt Lake City stakes distributed a total of $177,438 for relief. By 1935, however, it appeared that many local wards had fallen short of earlier expectations, and about the same time the federal government announced its intention to shift the burden of relief to the states and localities. That year a churchwide survey to ascertain actual relief conditions showed that almost 18 percent of the membership (88,460 persons) were receiving either Church or government relief. Further study revealed that between 11,500 and 16,500 of these persons did not actually need this relief.

Alarmed that many active members depended upon government handouts, and concerned that the government might soon discontinue its program, the First Presidency decided to act immediately. After studying the experimental plans devised by various stakes, the General Authorities formulated the Security Plan and formally launched it during the April 1936 conference. They urged that all members endeavor to make themselves independent and self-supporting, that the destitute and unfortunate be provided for through collective effort within the Church, and that immediate steps be taken by the wards and stakes to lay in stores of food, fuel, and clothing for the winter in order that those who were worthy of charity would not suffer or become public

An LDS Relief Society president in 1938 picks up a welfare order from a bishop's storehouse in Salt Lake City. (Church Archives)

charges. In October, President Grant clearly stated the program's objective: "Our primary purpose in organizing the Church Security Plan was to set up a system under which the curse of idleness will be done away with, the evils of the dole abolished, and independence, industry, thrift, and self-respect be once more established among our people. The aim of the Church is to help the people help themselves. Work is to be re-enthroned as the ruling principle in the lives of our Church members."[4]

Called to head the expanded welfare program was Harold B. Lee. It was a momentous assignment, and one that took him completely by surprise. As he recalled thirty years later,

> There I was, just a young man in my thirties. My experience had been limited. I was born in a little country town in Idaho. I had hardly been outside the boundaries of the states of Utah and Idaho. And now to put me in a position where I was to reach out to the entire membership of the Church, worldwide, was one of the most staggering contemplations that I could imagine. How could I do it with my limited understanding?

---

[4]Quoted in Henry D. Moyle, "Some Practical Phases of Church Security," *Improvement Era* 40 (June 1939): 354.

The young stake president sought inspiration during a walk and private prayer in Rotary Park in Salt Lake City. In particular he was concerned with what kind of new organization should be set up. Then, he said, it came to him: " 'There is no new organization necessary to take care of the needs of this people. All that is necessary is to put the priesthood of God to work. There is nothing else that you need as a substitute.' "[5]

The Security Plan, designated the Welfare Plan at the April 1938 conference, was organized on that assumption. It was not a new philosophy; it simply revived the idea of a bishop's storehouse and adapted it to the needs of members in a new age. Priesthood leaders received important new assignments, but no new auxiliary was established. The program functioned through regular priesthood channels, becoming part of the Church's longtime effort to strengthen the priesthood.

A general welfare committee, headed by Elder Lee and supervised by the First Presidency and the Presiding Bishopric, was responsible for formulating plans and directing operations. Each stake established an executive coordinating committee that exercised authority over the wards. Presidents of adjoining stakes formed councils to cooperate on a regional basis. This multi-stake cooperation established a precedent adopted decades later for ecclesiastical administration.

Priesthood quorums and Relief Societies within the wards were charged with carrying out details of the program. The bishop had the responsibility of discovering where need existed. He appointed special committees from among the quorums and the Relief Society to study the problems of needy families, determine the extent of their economic distress, provide for their immediate needs, and then plan cooperatively for their permanent rehabilitation.

Each ward gave attention first to emergency cases. Women in the Relief Society sewed quilts and clothing and organized canned foods for distribution to the needy. Priesthood quorums leased land and obtained farming equipment to provide gainful employment for the needy as well as help them produce food for themselves. In some cases an exchange system was worked out between wards so that surpluses of one item might be traded for something more urgently needed.

To help employable members become self-supporting, bishops appointed special employment committees and work directors. The

[5]*Conference Report*, October 1972, p. 124.

Zion Park Stake Welfare Store House and Cannery, in the 1930s. (Church Archives)

Church Welfare Committee also established special employment offices. One particularly innovative scheme involved vocational education for unskilled workers. Under this program apprentices were placed in businesses to learn new trades. After a training period they were qualified to be placed in commercially operated institutions. The Church also cooperated with school authorities in conducting training classes in bricklaying, carpentry, plumbing, and other trades.

There were not enough jobs to go around, however, so new projects had to be developed. Each priesthood quorum had the responsibility of organizing and maintaining at least one project for unemployed members of that quorum. These make-work projects included constructing homes and church buildings, sewing, repairing clothing and shoes, manufacturing furniture, logging, producing cement blocks, mining coal, and refining molasses. Those employed on such projects received work receipts that could be presented to the storehouse where goods could be drawn on the basis of need.

The mainstay of the welfare program was agriculture. As long as there was idle land there seemed no need for idle people. Contrary to the federal policy of attempting to create scarcity in order to raise farm prices, Church leaders believed an abundance of farm produce offered the best means of alleviating distress. On both purchased and donated land stakes and wards took up farming programs as community enterprises. As the welfare program enlarged, it came to include an unpaid agricultural committee that assisted private farmers in solving production problems.

During the first summer of its operation the welfare program made impressive strides toward accomplishing its goal. Nearly fifteen thousand needy Saints were transferred from government to church relief and more than one thousand were placed in jobs. Sufficient food, clothing, and fuel were collected to provide for practically all needy families through the coming winter.

The welfare program provided immediate and positive publicity for the Church. Some journalists published exaggerated reports of its effectiveness. Its detractors, on the other hand, showed that Utah was still high on the list of states receiving government aid. Even though the goal of complete self-sufficiency was not reached, after two years the results were impressive. By 1938 approximately twenty-two thousand Latter-day Saints had been taken off federal relief rolls and more than thirty thousand others had received some kind of aid. Private employment had been found for an additional twenty-four hundred.

With the effectiveness of the welfare program established in the minds of the General Authorities, it was decided early in 1937 to continue it in order to enable every able-bodied member to become self-sustaining. That same year several leaders began speaking of the imminence of a more severe depression than the one the country was passing through. On September 19, 1937, the First Presidency asked members to observe a special fast and give the monetary equivalent toward construction of a regional warehouse for storage of the just-harvested bumper crops. The welfare program soon became an established part of the program of the Church.

The Word of Wisdom, Prohibition Repeal, and Politics

Perhaps no doctrine was preached more enthusiastically by President Grant or stressed more in Church literature during his administration than the Word of Wisdom. In the fall of 1930 the Church set up its first Word of Wisdom exhibit at the International Hygiene Exhibition at Dresden, Germany. Another exhibit was displayed in 1931 at the June Conference of the MIA in Salt Lake City. Lectures, charts, posters, pamphlets, pictures, models, motion pictures, and apparatus for conducting chemical, physiological, and mental tests portrayed the Church's continuing commitment to this principle of health. In addition, the *Improvement Era* launched a no-liquor and no-tobacco col-

umn, and two members of the Council of the Twelve, John A. Widtsoe
and Joseph F. Merrill, began producing literature on the subject. As
might be expected, some members went to extremes, denouncing many
items not specifically noted in the Word of Wisdom, but the major
emphasis was on health and the general importance of proper diet.
Abstinence from tea, coffee, alcohol, and tobacco were, and still are,
required for faithful membership, but they were only symbols of the
Saints' devotion to the broader principles of physical and spiritual well-
being.

In 1932 Franklin D. Roosevelt ran for president of the United States
on a platform that included repeal of the prohibition amendment. Although they had no desire to involve the Church in political controversy,
the First Presidency and the Council of the Twelve maintained strong
opposition to repeal. Since prohibition was to them a moral issue, it
was of great consequence. "The ground already gained ought not to be
surrendered," the First Presidency declared. "Liquor has always been
and it will continue to be the intimate ally of crime."

The advocates of repeal argued that prohibition had created a situation worse than before. The law was not rigidly enforced, which made
it a mockery, and many young people tried liquor simply because it
was forbidden. Speakeasies, bootleggers, and corruption of public officials were becoming all too common. Church leaders believed that
these things could be overcome and that the force of law should be
used to eliminate liquor traffic. To the chagrin of President Grant,
however, in 1933 Utah became the thirty-sixth state to ratify the repeal
amendment, thus putting it into law. Though many of the Saints had
been persuaded by proponents of repeal, the outcome was, from the
Church's standpoint, not wholly negative: at least this was evidence
to its critics that the Church did not control politics in Utah. After
repeal the Church redoubled its emphasis on the Word of Wisdom.

In other political activities Church leaders continued to demonstrate that they could hold differing political views and still retain love
and harmony as brethren in the gospel. President Grant, for example,
became an outspoken critic of the New Deal, as did his counselor J.
Reuben Clark, Jr. But B. H. Roberts was an open admirer of Roosevelt
and the direction he was taking of involving the federal government
more deeply in social and economic affairs. Utahns generally voted
Democratic in that decade, and Reed Smoot, the longtime senator, was
defeated at the polls in the Roosevelt landslide of 1932. In 1936 President Grant openly endorsed Alf Landon, the Republican candidate for

president, though he quickly made it clear that he was speaking for himself and did not intend to commit Church members. In the ensuing election Roosevelt handily carried Utah and the nation.

Education and the Secular Challenge

Meantime, education was still one of the Church's most expensive continuing programs, and as the Depression cut heavily into Church income the leaders were especially cautious about new expansion. No schools were closed, other than those that the Church had already determined to discontinue or turn over to the states, and no teachers were released because of the Depression. There was, however, a necessary retrenchment of teacher salaries.

After 1933 the Church retained ownership of only four institutions of higher learning: Brigham Young University, Ricks College in Rexburg, Idaho, and the LDS Business College and the McCune School of Music in Salt Lake City. In 1935 Dr. M. Lynn Bennion became supervisor of the seminary system, and through his efforts the curriculum was revised and student-centered instruction enhanced. The programs of the institutes of religion were expanded, with institutes being opened at most major colleges in the Mountain West where substantial numbers of Latter-day Saints attended. The first institute outside the area got its start in 1935 at the University of Southern California. Elder John A. Widtsoe had been invited to give a course on religion at the university, and while there he held meetings with Latter-day Saint students. A regular, full-time institute of religion was established several years later.

The Church was equally interested in the welfare of its college students where there were no institutes. At several universities it authorized establishment of Deseret Clubs designed to bring students together on both a social and religious basis. These clubs became the forerunners of many regular institute programs. At the same time a fraternity-type organization, Lambda Delta Sigma, was founded in 1936 by Dr. Lowell L. Bennion at the institute of religion adjacent to the University of Utah. The organization was designed to bring Latter-day Saint students together in a group that would compete with the attraction of the Greek-letter fraternities and sororities and would sponsor uplifting social activities as well as provide outlets for service. The organization spread rapidly to fifteen different campuses within the next ten years.

Now that the Church was fully committed to an expansion of its

By the 1930s the Church had committed itself to providing institutes of religion adjacent to college campuses. This is the interior of the Pocatello, Idaho, Institute, October 1929. (Church Archives)

religious education programs at both the high school and college level, the need for excellent teachers and for writers to prepare manuals increased. Most teachers were trained at Utah institutions, and there were few high-quality study materials available outside the scriptures themselves. Some Church leaders and educators became concerned with the possibility of excessive educational inbreeding and suggested that a few Latter-day Saint teachers should have the advantage of studying under important scholars outside the Mountain West in order to become more familiar with current insights and knowledge. Biblical studies, for example, was an especially important academic field, and it was felt LDS teachers should be aware of the new discoveries and new ideas about biblical interpretation.

Other persons challenged the idea that Mormon educators should draw on the learning of the world. Higher criticism and other aspects of secular learning, they felt, could raise doubts about the validity of the scriptures. They were not impressed by the argument that a man with a firm testimony would not be hurt by the learning of the world and that a broad, well-disciplined education in which he had been challenged at every turn would make him a better teacher. The idea was pushed, however, by Dr. Adam S. Bennion, Church Commissioner of Education, and Joseph F. Merrill, who succeeded him in 1928. They were strongly supported by John A. Widtsoe. As a result, in the late 1920s and early 1930s, a few Latter-day Saint teachers were encouraged to continue their education at prestigious institutions elsewhere, such as the University of Chicago, and were given leaves of absence to do so. They were encouraged to study religious subjects, and some of them received divinity degrees from the University of Chicago. It was an unusual calling, completely unanticipated by some, but one that demonstrated the Church's continuing interest in gaining knowledge from every available source.

The challenge of secularism in religious education was indeed a real one. The scientific method discounted experiences that could not be tested and demonstrated; therefore, the element of inspiration and revelation in the writing and interpretation of the scriptures was increasingly challenged. On the other hand, the new methodology was producing important information that Church teachers could not ignore if they were to respond intelligently to students' questions.

The theory that received the widest publicity in the 1920s and early 1930s was that of organic evolution. Church leaders did not take an official stand on any specific theories regarding evolution (and there were many), except to reaffirm that the Church would always accept the basic truth that man was created by God, that Adam and Eve were the parents of the human race, and that the destiny of man would be worked out according to the plan of God, which included the reality of the atonement of the Savior. Individually, some Church leaders went further. In 1930, for example, Elder James E. Talmage gave an important radio address, later reprinted and widely circulated, entitled "The Earth and Man." An internationally known scientist, Elder Talmage demonstrated in this address his own ability to reconcile the truths made known both by scientific investigation and by revelation. Church leaders recognized the value of the pursuit of secular knowledge. Their principal concern was that teachers refrain from propounding theories as if they were proven truths and from teaching with such dogmatism that they could disturb the faith of youth.

The Mission of the Church Goes On

Important as such discussions may have been to the intellectual climate of the Church, they did not absorb the principal energy of

Church efforts. As in earlier years, missionary work continued as a major concern. In Europe, for example, the missionary program was augmented by local missionaries serving on a part-time basis, even before the stake missionary program got going well in the United States. Especially noteworthy was the German-Austrian Mission, where at one point there were 138 missionaries from the United States and 152 local missionaries. During the decade, however, membership in all of Europe increased by only a thousand, due partly to the continuing emigration of the Saints.

Several new missions were opened in the 1930s. The Japanese Mission, closed in 1924, was reopened in 1936 with headquarters in Hawaii, though missionaries did not actually return to Japan until after World War II. Eight new missions were opened in Europe and the United States, and the Book of Mormon was published in Czech, Armenian, and Portuguese and translated, though not published, into Hungarian. It was also translated into Braille.

Within the stakes, this decade saw the beginning of more well-organized stake missionary programs. Home missionary work, as it was previously called, had been going on for years, but not with the same kind of institutional support that emerged in the 1930s. As with so many activities eventually adopted churchwide, this program had its beginning at the local level when leaders in some newly formed stakes outside the intermountain region organized efforts to preach to their non-Mormon neighbors. Utah stakes soon caught the spirit, and in 1934 Elder J. Golden Kimball of the First Council of the Seventy reported hundreds of converts had been made through the efforts of local missionaries in Los Angeles, Maricopa, Liberty, Salt Lake, Granite, East Jordan, and other stakes. He emphasized that all who held the office of seventy had a particular duty to preach the gospel and told local seventies that they must be willing to serve as stake missionaries. At the general conference of April 1936, it was announced that supervision of stake missions was being assigned to the First Council of the Seventy and that each stake was to organize a mission immediately.

By the end of 1937 missions had been organized in 105 of the 118 stakes, and 1,757 converts had been baptized. In addition, 2,756 members had been reactivated and one ward reported an overall 50 percent increase in the activity of its members as a result of home missionary work. A powerful new stimulus had been added to the missionary program.

Missionary work was also enhanced by the increased use of radio,

Council of the Twelve, April 1931. Seated, left to right: Rudger Clawson, Reed Smoot, George Albert Smith, George F. Richards, Orson F. Whitney, David O. McKay. Standing: Joseph Fielding Smith, James E. Talmage, Stephen L Richards, Richard R. Lyman, Melvin J. Ballard, John A. Widtsoe. (Church Archives)

which by the 1930s was common in almost every home in America. In 1931 missionaries in the Eastern States Mission delivered more than 212 radio sermons in thickly populated areas, at no cost to the Church.

The Church also continued its efforts to preserve historical landmarks and perpetuate its heritage. In 1933 the Relief Society unveiled a monument at Nauvoo marking the site of the Joseph Smith store, where the Relief Society was organized in 1842. The Winter Quarters monument, dedicated on September 20, 1936, was one of the most impressive markers erected in this era. Located at the cemetery in modern Florence, Nebraska, it was designed by Avard Fairbanks to honor the memory of the hundreds of Saints who suffered and died following the exodus from Nauvoo.

In 1937 the Church purchased eighty-eight acres of the original farm of Martin Harris, one of the witnesses to the Book of Mormon. That same year Wilford C. Wood purchased the original temple site at Nauvoo for the Church. Later he purchased about one-fourth of the original temple block and several homes of leading members.

Probably the best-known activity connected with these historic sites is the annual pageant at the Hill Cumorah, *America's Witness for*

The Church's interest in historic sites was symbolized in 1930 when these prominent leaders were part of a caravan along the Mormon Trail to Independence Rock, Wyoming. Left to right: Oscar A. Kirkham, B. H. Roberts, George Albert Smith, Andrew Jenson, John D. Giles. (Church Archives)

Christ. Pageants and programs had been presented at this important historic site periodically since the early days of the twentieth century. In 1935 President Don B. Colton of the Eastern States Mission met with Professor E. H. Eastmond of Brigham Young University to discuss the possibility of a continuing, Church-sponsored production. They asked Elder Harold I. Hansen, a missionary, to direct the pageant in 1937; under his direction, the production became an annual presentation and was constantly enlarged and improved. Later Elder Hansen joined the Department of Dramatic Arts at Brigham Young University, and BYU students began participating with missionaries and local members in New York in staging the widely acclaimed production.

The New Image

By the 1930s the Church had acquired a new and more favorable public image. It had been steadily improving since the turn of the century, but in that decade the total number of positive articles in American periodicals for the first time exceeded those with a negative viewpoint. Writers became increasingly aware of the positive aspects of Mormon doctrine and practices, and readers caught up in the problems of the Depression followed with great interest the outcome of the

The First Presidency, 1934–45: President Heber J. Grant and counselors David O. McKay and J. Reuben Clark, Jr. (Church Archives)

welfare program. Such widely read periodicals as *Life, Saturday Evening Post, Time, Newsweek, Nation, National Geographic,* and the *New York Times* devoted considerable space to the welfare program. *Nation,* for example, complimented it as the "only project organized solely to free Americans from the burden of government relief, and advertised as such." *Life* published two pages of illustrations dealing with welfare projects and a full-page photograph of President Grant. *Catholic Worker* suggested, "It is a bitter tea that we must swallow," but that Catholics could learn a few lessons in charity from the Latter-day Saints.

A few periodicals paid attention to the Word of Wisdom. *Horizon* in New York published an article reprinted in *Health Digest* in 1936 praising the Mormon health code as "the greatest experiment in correct eating and correct living ever conducted." The new public image of the Church was also spread by the continuing broadcasts of the Tabernacle Choir.

In the first decade of Mormonism's second century, then, the Church built on its historic strengths but also made some new beginnings. The welfare program, the stake missionary program, a new effort at public relations—all represented fresh approaches to the Church's continuing commitment to its traditional values. Very shortly, however, its hopes for promoting those values in a peaceful world would again be dashed.

CHAPTER 18

The Church and World War II, *1939–1950*

In the 1940s the world was at war once more. Again the missionaries were withdrawn from most of the world, the Church retrenched its programs, and Latter-day Saints on both sides fought and suffered. In the end, however, the clouds of war were brightened by a few silver linings, as Mormon servicemen helped introduce the gospel into various parts of the world, and as welfare activities among the Saints in war-torn Europe helped demonstrate that the brotherhood of the gospel was stronger than the politics of international conflict.

War and Response

Many things contributed to the gathering of war clouds in the 1930s, but one of the most important was the rise of several new dictatorships, some with designs for territorial expansion, in Europe and Asia. In Russia, a revolution in 1917 had led to the establishment of a Communist dictatorship. In Japan, a military dictatorship was set up in 1931, and almost immediately invaded Manchuria. In Germany, partly as a result of dissatisfaction with poor economic recovery after the first World War, Adolph Hitler was given dictatorial power after he became chancellor in 1933. He immediately began to rebuild the German war machine and to prepare to carry out his expansionist aims. Democracy was destroyed also in Italy and, later, in Spain, and with the unchecked expansionism of Hitler and of Italy's Benito Mussolini democracy was threatened in all of western Europe. In March 1938 Hitler annexed Austria, and within a year he had seized Czechoslovakia. In August 1939 he signed a "nonaggression" pact with Russia, and on September 1 he attacked Poland, which fell in less than a month. The attack on Poland provoked England and France into honoring their commitments to defend that country's independence, but in 1940 Germany conquered

Denmark, Norway, Belgium, the Netherlands, and France. Hitler also signed a military aid pact with Italy and Japan. The following year he turned on Russia, and also conquered Yugoslavia and Greece.

Even though they deplored these aggressions, Americans, at first, were overwhelmingly isolationist in their sentiment. Only after 1939 was President Franklin D. Roosevelt able to gain enough congressional support to begin to strengthen the armed forces and to provide economic aid to England through a lend-lease agreement. As German submarine warfare increased the threat to U. S. shipping, American policy became one of preparedness, and before December 1941 the United States was doing all it could, short of outright war, to help England in her desperate struggle for survival.

At the same time, U.S. relations with Japan deteriorated because of American efforts to discourage that country's continued aggression in Asia. Then on December 7, 1941, the Japanese attacked the American naval base at Pearl Harbor, Hawaii. Immediately the United States was at war, not just against Japan but also with its allies in Europe.

The nearly 15,000 Latter-day Saints in Germany, meanwhile, faced a cruel dilemma with respect to their response to the Nazi regime. Some, impressed with the Church's teaching that people should be loyal to their existing governments, felt comfortable sympathizing with it, and mission presidents and local church leaders often publicly extolled its virtues. Others found Hitler's aims distasteful, and privately chafed under his dictatorial rule. Some apparently knew something of his atrocities against the Jewish people, but political loyalty, fear, or simply the inability to act kept them from doing anything more than the rest of their countrymen. At the same time, Church programs were affected by the regime, which required the Church to disband the Boy Scout program in favor of the Hitler Youth Movement, disallowed the distribution and/or reading of some Church publications (particularly those with religious ideas that seemed to run counter to Nazi propaganda), monitored Church meetings, and made it difficult for missionaries to obtain funds from America. Such things happened not only in Germany proper, but also among the Saints in Austria after the *anschluss* of 1938.

In 1939 Elder Joseph Fielding Smith of the Council of the Twelve was sent on a tour of the European missions. At the same time President J. Reuben Clark, Jr., a former undersecretary of state, was in daily contact with the U. S. State Department, and through his efforts Church leaders were kept constantly aware of changing European conditions.

On August 24, 1939, just a week before Hitler invaded Poland, the First Presidency instructed Elder Smith to direct the evacuation of all missionaries from Germany and Czechoslovakia.

The task was charged with difficulties. In Germany, Elder Smith and mission president M. Douglas Wood telegraphed all the missionaries to leave for Holland immediately, but they soon discovered that the Netherlands had closed its borders to all foreigners. The alternate destination was Denmark, and after realizing that thirty-one missionaries were stranded somewhere between Frankfurt and the Dutch border, the mission president gave Elder Norman G. Seibold a unique assignment: get on the train, follow his impressions, and somehow find them. Seibold did exactly that. The first place he felt impressed to get off was Cologne and there, in the crowded station, he could think of nothing to do but jump up on a baggage cart and begin whistling a hymn well-known to every missionary, "Do What Is Right." Eight missionaries soon found him. The same thing happened in other towns and in one instance, Elder Seibold reported, "as surely as someone had taken me by the hand, I was guided" into a restaurant and found two more missionaries. On August 28 President Wood learned that fourteen of his missing missionaries had somehow entered Holland safely, and the next day he received a telegram from Elder Seibold reporting that the other seventeen would arrive in Denmark that evening. In Czechoslovakia, meanwhile, before mission president Wallace Toronto could evacuate all his missionaries, he had the task of freeing a few who had been arrested and jailed by the Germans. After he got the final one released, the two boarded the last train to leave the country and, on September 1, the last ferry to cross from Germany to Denmark.

The missionaries could not stay for long in this or any other neutral country, however, and before the end of the year, and with the help of some seemingly miraculous events, all but a handful were back in America. Some crossed the Atlantic on passenger liners, but most found passage in makeshift accommodations on cargo ships. In 1940 all missionaries were withdrawn from South Africa and the Pacific. None were withdrawn from South America, but after 1941 no new missionaries were sent there. After 1943, therefore, proselyting activity was limited to North America and Hawaii, and even there it was drastically curtailed.

Church leaders condemned the use of war for expanding national boundaries, and throughout the crucial year of 1939 they continually warned the Saints to not be blinded by the various arguments used to justify wars of aggression. Most believed that the United States should remain neutral, and President Clark was especially outspoken on the issue. "We would not settle it now by joining the conflict," he counseled in 1939. "This is one of those questions which can be settled only by the parties themselves by themselves."[1] The United States' role, he believed, was to be that of peacemaker, but this could not be achieved by intervention. Rather, America must demonstrate love for humanity, justice, and fair-mindedness before she could exercise her influence for peace.

When the United States entered the conflict, however, General Authorities quickly urged wholehearted support for the nation's war efforts. As in the previous war, they recognized that even though America was fighting to overthrow dictatorships that undermined individual liberty and freedom of worship, there were Latter-day Saints on both sides of the conflict. The official position necessarily became one similar to that of President Joseph F. Smith during World War I. Members were encouraged to retain a spirit of humanity, love, and peacemaking. Latter-day Saint servicemen were told to look upon themselves as ministers of life rather than death; they were fighting to defend liberties rather than to destroy enemies. To Saints who were citizens of enemy countries, Church leaders could only say that, as innocent pawns of war, they had no recourse but to support the government to which they owed allegiance. In a special message delivered on April 6, 1942, the First Presidency declared:

> On each side they believe they are fighting for home, and country, and freedom. On each side, our brethren pray to the same God, in the same name, for victory. Both sides cannot be wholly right; perhaps neither is without wrong. God will work out in His own due time and in His own sovereign way the justice and right of the conflict, but He will not hold the innocent instrumentalities of the war, our brethren in arms, responsible for the conflict.[2]

The war brought many difficulties for the Church. When the missions were closed, the First Presidency charged the mission presidents to keep in touch with local leaders and members as much as possible. For the most part, however, communications between Church leaders and the Saints in most war-affected areas were cut off, and local leaders

---

[1]"In Time of War," *Improvement Era* 42 (November 1939): 657.
[2]Clark, *Messages of the First Presidency*, 6:159.

struggled to hold the members together without direction from any higher authorities.

In America, many activities were cut back. Travel was difficult as automobiles were no longer readily available, and gasoline and tires were strictly rationed. One response was to suspend all auxiliary institutes and stake leadership meetings for the duration of the war. Beginning in 1942, general conferences were closed to the general membership and confined to approximately 500 priesthood leaders. The Relief Society postponed its elaborate centennial celebration scheduled to take place in Salt Lake City in April 1942. Instead, special commemorations were held in wards and branches. Because of paper shortages, publication of instruction manuals and other materials was severely limited. Food rationing led the national government to promote "victory gardens," but many Saints were a jump ahead on that matter, for the Church had long been urging them to grow their own food and to store a year's supply.

Whatever Americans suffered during the war was nothing compared with the nightmare that came upon those in the warring nations of Europe, where the ordeals of the Saints produced some powerful stories of faith, heroism, and political courage. Except in France, Church programs continued in all countries, though meetings were held in partially destroyed buildings or in homes. Local missionaries were called, converts were made, tithes and offerings were paid, and the welfare program was seldom, if ever, more remarkable. In Belgium one elderly sister, whose son died as a result of his efforts to escape to France, dedicated herself to hiding and caring for foreign airmen shot down by the Germans. In Rotterdam, Holland, where 30,000 people were killed and most homes were destroyed, the Saints raised $4,000 in only a few days for the Relief Society to assist the needy. Swiss Saints sent money and food to their brothers and sisters in France, Belgium, Germany, and Austria. In Hamburg, during the horrible devastation of the 1944 Allied bombing attacks, the surviving Saints pooled all their resources to be sure that everyone had food and clothing. Before Belgium was invaded by Germany, Belgian Saints had stored grain and potatoes, planted gardens, and put 3,000 francs in a "Security Plan Fund." After the invasion these preparations proved vital to survival. Free soup became available at Church meetings, and, as elsewhere, the Saints cooperated to see that none were totally deprived. In England, which sustained the most long-lasting and devastating air raids of any country outside Germany, there were about 6,400 Saints. The mission presidency at first suggested the evacuation of the children from London to LDS homes in Canada, but later evacuated them to the English countryside. The tearful farewells between parents and "little boys and girls with labels tied to them" at the railway station was heartrending, but James R. Cunningham, a member of the mission presidency, noted later that "out of [that] crucible came great bishops, stake presidents, patriarchs, regional representatives, and temple presidents."[3] So far as devastation and casualties were concerned, the German and Dutch Saints suffered the most, with a huge percentage of their homes and meetinghouses destroyed, economic privation rampant, and hundreds of German Saints, including soldiers and civilians, killed.

In war few things could be more spiritually frustrating than divided loyalties, and few stories illustrate this better than that of Helmuth Huebener. This sixteen-year-old Church member living in Hamburg, Germany, listened to short-wave radio broadcasts from England and became convinced that Hitler was wrong. He and three friends (two of them also Church members) began secretly duplicating and distributing inflammatory anti-Nazi fliers. They were arrested early in 1942, interrogated, and Huebener was tortured and subsequently sentenced to execution. Huebener believed that in opposing the evils of the Nazi regime he was fighting for the freedoms espoused by the gospel. In the minds of some, Huebener was not only a traitor but also a heretic for disobeying the principle espoused in the Twelfth Article of Faith: "We believe in being subject to kings, presidents, rulers, and magistrates, in obeying, honoring, and sustaining the law." His branch president even decided to excommunicate him from the Church, though after the war church leaders in Salt Lake City posthumously rescinded the action. There is perhaps no "right" answer to the dilemmas presented by Helmuth Huebener's story, where good people, each of them loyal to the Church and the gospel, made opposite political decisions. It only demonstrates how personal such decisions must be.

A Program for Servicemen

By the end of the war nearly 100,000 young Mormon men and women either had been inducted into or had enlisted in the American armed forces. On May 1, 1941, Elder Hugh B. Brown, a former Canadian

---

[3]As quoted in Louis B. Cardon, "War and Recovery, 1939–1950," in *Truth Will Prevail: The Rise of the Church of Jesus Christ of Latter-day Saints in the British Isles 1837–1987*, p. 374.

During World War II Latter-day Saint servicemen made efforts to continue church attendance wherever and whenever possible. These signs on the island of Okinawa were typical of the kind of advertising seen along roads in many places in the world. (Church Archives)

army officer, assumed the newly created position of LDS Servicemen's Coordinator. He was assigned to visit military installations and confer with Mormon servicemen, local leaders, and military officials, and to provide spiritual help for those in the service. As a result of these visits, he received information on the religious and social needs of servicemen, which subsequently led to a new program.

In October 1942, acting upon Elder Brown's recommendations, the LDS Servicemen's Committee was organized. It was headed by Elder Harold B. Lee and included Elder Brown. The committee was responsible for providing Church programs and guidelines to Latter-day Saints in the service and for securing government cooperation in appointing LDS chaplains for all branches of the armed forces. Through the work of the committee the government was persuaded to increase the number of Mormon chaplains, and by the end of the war some servicemen were even allowed to have "LDS," rather than "Protestant," stamped on their identification tags.

A special publications program was particularly important to the success of the servicemen's program. The committee developed directories for LDS servicemen, providing maps and Church addresses worldwide, and published pocket-size editions of the Book of Mormon and

Principles of the Gospel and made them available to all members of the armed forces. Each person in the service was also sent the *Improvement Era* and the "Church News" section of the *Deseret News*. Late in the war the Church published a servicemen's edition of the "Church News." Special homes were established near a number of military bases in the United States where military personnel could relax and socialize when off duty.

One unusual approach to providing leadership among the fighting forces came when the General Authorities authorized setting apart worthy elders, usually returned missionaries, as group leaders, with authority to hold meetings, administer the sacrament, and, under certain circumstances, baptize converts. These group leaders appeared on every battlefront and aboard many ships, helping to make the Church a vital force in the lives of many even in the midst of battle. But the absence of group leaders did not deter other enterprising young Latter-day Saints from holding their own meetings, administering the sacrament, and, regardless of military rank, enjoying the brotherhood and spiritual uplift of the gospel. In addition, forty-five Latter-day Saint chaplains served in the U.S. armed forces.

The appointment of Latter-day Saint chaplains was at first complicated by the fact that chaplains corps required men with three years of ministerial service, yet the Church had no professional ministry. The rule was soon interpreted, however, so that Latter-day Saints who had filled two-year missions and were employed full-time as seminary teachers could qualify. LDS chaplains saw duty in all major theaters of war. Officially they were considered Protestant chaplains, and they performed all such duties. Whenever possible, they also met and counseled with Mormon servicemen, though in most cases this was done on their own time, beyond their regular assignments.

World War II was filled with the hate, horror, and brutality characteristic of any war, but out of it also came dramatic and faith-promoting events that have become part of the tradition of the Saints. Missionary-minded servicemen on military bases, aboard ships, or even in trenches studied their pocket editions of the Book of Mormon and *Principles of the Gospel* and discussed religion with their buddies. Many previously lukewarm LDS servicemen were converted in battle, and many non-Mormons joined the Church as a result of their friends' examples and teaching. These military missionaries frequently bore testimony of the power of the priesthood as they witnessed the preservation of life or the comforting of the wounded through the laying on of hands. Nor was it uncommon for a young Latter-day Saint soldier feeling lonely to suddenly hear someone whistle the familiar tune "Come, Come, Ye Saints," a refrain that gave sure notice of a kindred soul.

The war in Europe finally ended on May 8, 1945, and on August 14 Japan surrendered. The Latter-day Saint servicemen scattered around the globe soon returned home — some to school, many to families, and others to mission calls, sometimes to countries where they had fought. On September 4 the Church sponsored a mass meeting of all faiths in the Salt Lake Tabernacle to give thanks for the return of peace.

A Change of Leadership

On May 14, 1945, President Heber J. Grant died. He was succeeded by George Albert Smith, whose family had distinguished itself in Church service for four generations. His great-grandfather was John Smith, the Prophet Joseph's uncle, who served as Church Patriarch and as president of three stakes. His grandfather, George A. Smith, was ordained an apostle in the days of Joseph Smith and was an outstanding missionary, colonizer, and counselor to Brigham Young. His father, John Henry Smith, was also an apostle and a counselor to President Joseph F. Smith. Born in 1870, George Albert became a member of the Council of the Twelve in 1903. He was active in public life as well as in the Church and worked both in government and business. Especially interested in youth, he won many awards for his contributions to Scouting. Noted for his interest in other people, he was particularly concerned with sharing the gospel.

Reestablishing Contact and Reopening Missions in Europe

As soon as the war was over, Church leaders in America were ready to reestablish contact with the Saints in Europe, resume missionary proselyting, and provide badly needed welfare supplies to destitute members. In January 1946, Elder Ezra Taft Benson of the Council of the Twelve was appointed to preside over the European Mission. His main task was to reestablish missionary work, but he was also assigned to organize distribution of welfare food, clothing, and bedding.

Elder Benson left immediately for what proved to be an arduous but rewarding ten months in Europe. He arrived in England in February and by December had traveled sixty thousand miles. Transportation and communications had been seriously disrupted, and he found it difficult to place telephone calls from London to many missions on the continent. Some countries, such as Holland, Poland, and Czechoslovakia, could not be contacted by phone at all. Traveling on the continent, his party was often delayed by bombed-out bridges and damaged highways. Little groups of Saints often waited for hours past the appointed meeting time in expectation of his arrival.

Elder Benson was gratified at the spirit he felt among the members, most of whom had remained loyal to the Church. Some practices had been slightly altered during the six years of isolation, and a few unauthorized doctrinal interpretations had crept in, but most branches had remained intact and local leaders were anxious to begin gaining strength under the direction of newly appointed mission leaders.

In April 1946 a letter from Elder Benson was read at general conference in Salt Lake City. In it he declared that "nowhere in all the world do members live and sustain their leaders more whole-heartedly than here," and that "never were there more sincere expressions of gratitude and such spirit" than in the meetings he had just completed in the war-torn European nations. Perhaps the spirit of the gospel was no more tenderly expressed than in a report he made of his first meeting in Karlsruhe, Germany, where the Saints had been waiting two hours for his arrival:

> And then for the first time in my life, I saw almost an entire audience in tears as we walked up onto the platform, and they realized that at last, after six or seven long years, representatives from Zion, as they put it, had finally come back among them. Then as the meeting closed, prolonged at their request, they insisted that we go to the door and shake hands with each one of them as we left the bombed-out building. And we noted that many of them, after they had passed through the line, went back and came through a second and third time, so happy were they to grasp our hands. As I looked into their upturned faces, pale, thin, many of these Saints dressed in rags, some of them barefooted, I could see the light of faith in their eyes as they bore testimony to the divinity of this great latter-day work, and expressed their gratitude for the blessings of the Lord.
>
> That is what a testimony does. We saw it in many countries. I say there is no greater faith, to my knowledge, anywhere in the Church than we found among those good people in Europe.[4]

---

[4]*Improvement Era* 50 (May 1947): 293–94.

During the war some European branches had organized their own local missionary activity, and in some cases they seemed more effective at teaching converts than had been the full-time missionaries. Still, it was essential that regular missionary work be reestablished and new mission presidents be appointed. Beginning in 1946 the Church engaged in a concerted effort to send missionaries to all parts of the world from which they had previously been withdrawn, and by the end of the year there were 2,294 in the field, including 311 in Europe. By 1950 the Church counted more than five thousand missionaries, with twelve hundred in Europe. In late 1946 and early 1947 mission presidents began to arrive again from the United States. Local leaders had carried on well during the war, but Church leaders believed it important that they now receive guidance from men more directly familiar with the general programs of the Church.

Aid to European Saints

Economic conditions in some areas of Europe bordered on destitution. Marauding armies had destroyed or stolen much of worth, and recent crop failures had left thousands hungry and vagrant. Fuel supplies and clothing were meager, and many European Saints found themselves without homes. The postwar period was as much a test of their faith as the war itself had been.

Even before Church aid arrived from the United States, continuing welfare efforts by the Saints themselves helped demonstrate what brotherhood across national boundaries really meant. Swedish Saints, for example, sent assistance to their brethren and sisters in Norway and Denmark, while the Danish Saints supplied food and clothing to Norway and Holland. The Swiss Mission also forwarded food and funds to Belgium, Holland, and Germany. The Saints in the Netherlands sent carloads of potatoes to members in Germany, and the Saints in Canada sent them large quantities of wheat.

Official arrangements for Church shipments of goods to Europe began with the visit of President George Albert Smith to President Harry S Truman in November 1945. Pleased at the Church's willingness to ship food and clothing to Europe, the American president asked how long it would take to get it ready. He was surprised when President Smith informed him that the supplies were waiting. The Church leader then had a chance to inform President Truman of some aspects of the welfare program, and of the Relief Society, which had over two thousand

*President George Albert Smith meets with U.S. President Harry S Truman
immediately after World War II. (Church Archives)*

homemade quilts ready to ship. All the Church needed was a pledge
of cooperation and help from the government in arranging transportation, and this the nation's president readily gave.

After Elder Benson's arrival in Europe he immediately began making arrangements for the receipt and distribution of welfare goods, and
on March 14, 1946, he cabled Church headquarters to have the first
shipments sent. Military authorities were amazed at the promptness
with which the goods were shipped. They were distributed initially in
the areas of greatest distress, and the major burden of distribution fell
on the newly appointed mission presidents. It was estimated that as
many as 88 percent of the Saints in some districts were clothed with
goods sent from America. In some cases goods were also shared with
nonmembers.

All this created some interesting situations and provided a unique
opportunity for cooperative work. West German Mission president Jean
Wunderlich and his wife spent a major portion of their first year in
Europe dealing with welfare distribution problems. When it was discovered that American clothes were generally too small for the German
women, they held fashion shows throughout the mission demonstrating
clothing that had been remodeled or even reconstructed by combining
two pieces. Knitted clothing was often unraveled to provide yarn for

Elder Ezra Taft Benson (left) inspects cartons of welfare supplies stacked in a warehouse of the International Red Cross at Geneva, Switzerland, prior to distribution in Germany and Austria after World War II. (Church Archives)

making other clothing. If sweaters could not be used, the sleeves were sometimes refashioned into stockings. Button-sorting parties matched the thousands of buttons that came with the goods, and when it was discovered that there were many men's shoes that could not be matched into pairs, they were donated to a German hospital treating former soldiers who had lost one leg through amputation.

Welfare aid to European Saints continued for two years. In 1947 alone the Church shipped 149,600 pounds of food and clothing to seven missions and helped 6,872 people. By the end of the crisis approximately 140 railroad carloads valued at about two million dollars had been shipped. The European Saints were helped, and church brotherhood worldwide was enhanced.

Revitalizing Other Church Programs

Shortly after Elder Benson began reconstructing the European missions, Elder Matthew Cowley of the Council of the Twelve arrived in the newly established Pacific Mission. His responsibility was to direct missionary efforts in Hawaii, the Central Pacific, Tonga, Tahiti, New Zealand, and Australia. That same year the Book of Mormon was published in Tongan, enhancing missionary possibilities in that island country. In 1947 Elder Cowley announced the long-awaited reopening of the Japanese Mission, and in 1949 he witnessed entrance of the first modern missionaries into Hong Kong. The Pacific soon became one of the most important areas of growth in the Church.

Missionary work in Latin America received a boost in August 1946, when a former Argentina Mission president, Frederick S. Williams, was given a party in Salt Lake City by some returned missionaries. Some members of the group, concerned over the need for more proselyting efforts in South America, obtained an appointment with the First Presidency. As spokesman, President Williams explained much of the political and social structure of South America and the opportunity for preaching the gospel more widely. The First Presidency treated the group with great courtesy and interest, and President Williams was invited to put his message in writing. Eight months later he was called to become the first president of the new Uruguay Mission.[5]

In the United States, missionary work among Native Americans increased. The year 1943 saw the opening of the first formal mission to teach the Zuni and Navajo people. Six years later the mission was extended to all tribes in the area and renamed the Southwest Indian Mission. Elder Spencer W. Kimball directed this expansion in the years after 1945. Elder Matthew Cowley and President Antoine R. Ivins of the First Council of the Seventy were appointed to serve with him on a new Indian Relations Committee. By 1951 Indian missionary work had been organized in all the stakes where Native Americans lived or visited as mobile groups, and by the end of the year nearly 2,500 had been baptized.

The effectiveness of missionary work in this decade was enhanced by several experimental approaches to teaching the gospel. One of the earliest was the "Message of Mormonism," which LeGrand Richards left behind when he completed a term as president of the Southern States Mission in 1937. This mimeographed outline was borrowed by other missions, used by teachers in Church schools, copied by stake missionaries, and finally expanded and published in 1950 as *A Marvelous Work and a Wonder*.

---

[5]From a tape-recorded representation at the Uruguay Mission reunion, April 7, 1972, Church Archives.

Idaho Falls Temple, dedicated September 23, 1945. (Church Archives)

The interest in systematic proselyting plans continued and in the late 1940s led to development of a number of other approaches. Some of these were prepared by missionaries who felt the inadequacy of traditional methods. They organized lesson presentations around certain themes and incorporated well-known salesmanship techniques. Some plans proved so effective that mission presidents adopted them for the use of all the missionaries. In the Northwestern States Mission, for example, Elder Richard L. Anderson developed a plan that was accepted for the mission in 1948. Its effectiveness was demonstrated when baptisms jumped from 158 during the first six months of the year to 348 during the last half. In the Great Lakes Mission, Elder Willard A. Aston, second counselor to President Carl C. Burton, developed a plan based on seven lessons, presented as sample dialogues. The increase in convert baptisms was impressive. These and other plans were so successful that other missions soon began using them.

None of the plans had the official backing of the Church, for they were still experimental in nature. In fact, some mission presidents resisted reliance on memorized dialogue because they felt it hindered the spontaneous promptings of the Spirit. Nevertheless, the systematic approach soon won a closer look from Church leaders and in the 1950s led to a standardized presentation in missions worldwide.

The decade of the 1940s was also a time of change for other programs. Especially significant was the expansion of the number of General Authorities, symbolizing the continuing need to adjust the administrative structure to the needs of an ever-growing Church. In April 1941 five men were selected to become Assistants to the Council of the Twelve. President J. Reuben Clark, Jr., made the announcement during the process of sustaining leaders in general conference:

> The rapid growth of the Church in recent times, the constantly increasing establishment of new Wards and Stakes, the ever widening geographical area covered by Wards and Stakes, the steadily pressing necessity for increasing our missions in numbers and efficiency that the Gospel may be brought to all men, the continual multiplying of Church interests and activities calling for more rigid and frequent observation, supervision, and direction — all have built up an apostolic service of the greatest magnitude.
>
> The First Presidency and the Twelve feel that to meet adequately their great responsibilities and to carry on efficiently this service for the Lord, they should have some help.
>
> Accordingly it has been decided to appoint Assistants to the Twelve, who shall be High Priests, who shall be set apart to act under the direction of the Twelve in the performance of such work as the First Presidency and the Twelve may place upon them.[6]

Seated comfortably in the audience was Marion G. Romney, president of the Bonneville Stake in Salt Lake City, who was shocked to hear his name listed first among the five to be sustained. As he recalled it later, "I hadn't heard about it; nobody else had heard about it. I didn't hear the other four names."[7] The other four were Thomas E. McKay, Clifford E. Young, Alma Sonne, and Nicholas G. Smith. The number of Assistants to the Twelve would later be significantly expanded, but the need for appointing them was dramatically suggested by the fact that during the 1940s sixty-one new stakes were organized, many of them in California.

Seminaries, institutes, and other educational programs also grew during the 1940s. Between 1940 and 1951 thirty-nine new seminaries were opened and five new institute buildings were erected. In 1949

---

[6]*Conference Report*, April 1941, pp. 94–95.
[7]Marion G. Romney, oral history interviews by James B. Allen, 1972–73, Typescript, Interview 2, p. 16, Oral History Program, Archives, Historical Department of The Church of Jesus Christ of Latter-day Saints.

Ricks College became a four-year college. The commitment to education was further dramatized in 1950 by the completion of a two-million-dollar science building on the Brigham Young University campus.

Genealogical activity received special stimulus during the decade. The Genealogical Society of Utah began broadening its program of microfilming important documents and records around the world to make them accessible for study in a central location. Beginning with early county records of Tennessee, the society sent microfilmers to the Southern, Eastern, and New England states. After the war it extended these operations to Great Britain, Holland, Switzerland, Italy, Germany, Finland, and the Scandinavian countries. In 1944, while celebrating its fiftieth anniversary, the society was reincorporated as The Genealogical Society of The Church of Jesus Christ of Latter-day Saints.

The building program was reinvigorated after the war. In 1945 the Idaho Falls Temple, delayed because of shortages in building supplies, was dedicated. During the decade members constructed approximately 450 new chapels, and 400 more were nearing completion in 1950. Many of these reflected a new architectural style characterized by a plain, stucco finish with lack of decoration. It was both an attempt to find an international style and a reflection of the austerity of the war years. President Smith also initiated a program of beautifying and improving older chapels; as part of that program the Salt Lake Tabernacle was renovated with a fresh coat of paint, a new roof, and additional organ pipes.

Finally, in connection with two significant events, the pioneer heritage of the Latter-day Saints received wide publicity in this decade. One was the 1947 centennial celebration of the settlement of the Great Salt Lake Valley. Special parades and celebrations were held throughout Utah and beyond, and the dramatic musical production *Promised Valley* made its first appearance. Written and composed by Arnold Sundgaard and Crawford Gates, it was performed regularly for many years afterward in Salt Lake City and other stakes of the Church. The 1947 celebration was highlighted by the completion and dedication of the huge "This Is the Place" monument at the mouth of Emigration Canyon. Sculpted by Mahonri M. Young, the artist-grandson of Brigham Young, this imposing work commemorates many early explorers and trappers who passed through the region prior to its settlement. Its focal point is a group of statues representing Brigham Young, Wilford Woodruff, and Heber C. Kimball.

Celebrating the centennial of the arrival of the Mormon pioneers in the Salt Lake Valley, the Sons of the Utah Pioneers retraced their steps in 1947 by covering their automobiles to give them the appearance of covered wagons. Here they are camped near Independence Rock, a familiar landmark to their forefathers. (Church Archives)

A second important monument to the Latter-day Saint heritage was a twelve-foot marble statue of Brigham Young, also by Mahonri Young, which was unveiled in the rotunda of the United States Capitol in Washington, D. C., in 1950. More than a thousand people attended the ceremony, and Vice-President Alben W. Barkley honored Brigham Young as a "man of God" and an "advocate of justice and democracy." Congress also recognized his importance and the positive significance of the Latter-day Saint contribution to American history when it authorized permanent placement of the figure in Statuary Hall and called Brigham Young one of Utah's "most eminent citizens, illustrious for his leadership as a colonizer." This was, indeed, a far cry from what national leaders had said a hundred years earlier.

These events represented a century of achievement and increasing public acceptance; however, like the centennial celebration of 1930, they also represented new beginnings. The 1940s had been a decade of war and recovery. The period after the war was one of revitalization and recommitment. The vitality of the Church's welfare system was demonstrated in its program of aid to Europe. Education, missionary work, genealogical activity, and temple work were all stimulated and expanded in the postwar years. This activity, however, was only preliminary to the decade of the 1950s in which the Church made dramatic strides in every direction and laid the groundwork for genuinely becoming an international faith.

In the early evening of his eighty-first birthday, on April 4, 1951, President George Albert Smith died quietly in his home. He was succeeded by David O. McKay, who would lead the Church through the next two decades of remarkable growth.

PART V

Toward Becoming a Universal Church, *1950–1990*

The new Church Office Building, completed in 1972, symbolizes on its facade the worldwide scope of the Church. (LDS Church)

IN 1950 THE PLANET EARTH was a complex, contradictory, and not yet peaceful world. On the one hand the United Nations, founded in 1945, was dedicated to keeping peace; on the other hand, the major world powers were locked in an ideological cold war that would continue for another four decades. Essentially a struggle between competing political and economic ideologies, the cold war created two armed camps. Each possessed awesome nuclear weapons and was capable of destroying the other. Dominated by the Soviet Union on one side and by the United States on the other, the cold war had already turned hot in China where, in 1949, the Communists took over. It heated up again in Korea in 1950, in Vietnam in the 1960s, and in numerous other places around the world, though the superpowers avoided confronting each other directly.

Scores of other wars, revolutions, military coups, and civil conflicts caused death and misery around the world in the last half of the twentieth century. Among them was the bitter conflict between the state of Israel, founded in 1948, and the Arab world around it which, in turn, was divided on almost every issue except that of the legitimacy of the Israeli state. In Asia and Africa, meanwhile, one of the great turning points in world history came with the end of over four hundred years of European colonialism. It was not long before the former colonies found new ties, mostly economic in nature, not only with their prior rulers but also with other world powers, and found themselves newly involved in many global affairs. Decolonization, however, did not mean peace, for continuing political conflict brought violence in many newly independent nations. South American nations, too, saw civil conflict in these years, usually as an ideological struggle between democracy and Communism or some other form of authoritarianism. But whatever the cause, post-World War II political alignments failed to create a peaceful world.

Neither did the postwar world find solutions to wide economic disparity. Western Europe, parts of Asia, and North America saw rapid and amazing economic growth in these years, and even though there were distressing pockets of poverty in each of these areas, the general standard of living soared. But in the so-called third world, the emerging nations of Asia and Africa, life remained difficult and poverty continued to abound. Efforts at industrialization and modernization resulted in considerable economic growth, but burgeoning populations almost negated the impact, and the contrast in living standards between these and other nations seemed only to become more apparent. The United Nations, various churches, and other charitable groups stepped up their efforts to help, especially in times of famine and other disaster, but in general poverty remained.

The world, however, was smaller and closer together than ever before. Jet airplanes made it possible for people to get almost anywhere within twenty-four hours. Improved telephone, radio, and television, especially after space technology put satellite systems in place, made instant communication commonplace. For the people of the industrialized nations, the problems as well as the pleasures of the rest of the world were at their doorsteps.

All this had an important effect on the story of the Latter-day Saints as, in the last half of the twentieth century, world affairs affected the Church and its people more directly than ever before. In 1950 Mormonism was still largely an American religion, but it stood on the threshold of a new international presence.

Outwardly, the history of the Church between 1950 and 1990 was characterized by continuing numerical growth, rapid expansion outside North America, and numerous administrative and program changes. As individuals, however, the Saints faced increasingly serious challenges that could not be solved simply through Church structural and procedural changes. The world around them offered more and more enticements away from the moral and ethical teachings of the gospel of Christ. Rampant sexual permissiveness, eroding ethical values, rising divorce rates, drug abuse, pornography, and other such evils affected the spiritual well-being of people of all ages. The changing culture of youth also was of special concern. In the United States, especially, many young people were disillusioned with the world their parents had created and began seriously to question the traditional values and institutions of their society. Some adopted life-styles that suggested to their worried elders not only nonconformity, but also irresponsibility. The Church faced the continuing challenge of seeing that its young members were headed in proper directions and were keeping uplifting goals in mind.

At a different level, the attitudes of the Saints toward each other and toward the human beings around them were tested more seriously than ever before. The widespread acceptance of the gospel by people of diverse ethnic and cultural origins demanded not just tolerance but, more importantly, a reexamination by some Saints of their personal attitudes toward other races and cultures. As the Church grew more rapidly in Asia, Latin America, and Africa, for example, as well as among highly diverse cultural and ethnic groups in the United States itself, some important questions were raised. Could the traditional American-born, Wasatch-front Latter-day Saint, whose culture tended to dominate the Church, wholly and sincerely accept those of other cultures as brothers and sisters in the fullest sense? Could the Church as an institution adapt its policies and emphases in such a way that people of all cultures felt fully accepted? Conversely, to what degree did some cultural mores violate the essence of the gospel, and what necessary changes would some converts have to make in order to become Saints? Or, to put it another way, what traditional LDS policies, practices, and teachings were *essential* to the gospel of Jesus Christ, and which ones were merely convenient and subject to change? In 1971 Elder Bruce R. McConkie, then a member of the First Quorum of the Seventy, reminded some American Saints that in the New Testament times even the apostles were so indoctrinated with the idea that the plan of salvation was limited to a particular people that they found it difficult to take it to the gentile nations, and he aptly applied the lesson to the modern Church. "There are going to be some struggles and some difficulties, some prejudices, and some uncertainties along the way," he said, but he called upon the American Saints to rise above their biases, as the apostles of old rose above theirs. Other peoples, he said, "have a different background than we have, which is of no moment to the Lord [!] . . . It is no different to have different social customs than it is to have different languages. . . . And the Lord knows all languages."[1]

As the Church progressed through the last half of the twentieth century, the vision of an international, worldwide church was continually reemphasized, but the more important quest was for a *universal* church: one in which people of all nations, all races, and all cultures could act toward each other as brothers and sisters in the truest sense of Christ's teachings. A major step toward a more universal concept of Sainthood was President Spencer W. Kimball's momentous revelation in June 1978 that opened the priesthood to all worthy male Latter-day Saints, regardless of race. It was one of the pivotal events in Church history, not because of what it did for the growth of the Church but because of what it did to build closer bonds of love and brotherhood within the Church and across racial barriers.

Though various problems kept the Church from achieving the full potential of the universal vision, the Spirit was there and President McKay's worldwide call to missionary work — "every member a missionary" — became a favorite Latter-day Saint slogan. By 1990 the Church still was not truly a worldwide church — it had only minimal membership in eastern Europe, for example, and most of Asia and Africa was still without missionaries. When compared with its status forty years earlier, however, the change was dramatic.

The comparative statistics for these four decades provide an important key to what was happening. In 1950 Church membership was about 1,100,000. At the beginning of 1990 it was 7,300,000. In 1950 there were 180 organized stakes, about 47 percent of them in Utah. Forty years later there were 1,700, over half of which had been created in the past twelve years, and only about 23 percent of which were in Utah.

---

[1]Bruce R. McConkie, "To the Koreans and All the People of Asia," address at a special "Korean Night Program," March 15, 1971, Provo, Utah, reproduced in Spencer J. Palmer, *The Expanding Church* (Salt Lake City: Deseret Book, 1978), pp. 143, 147.

In 1950 there were 43 organized missions, compared with 228 at the beginning of 1990. In 1950 the Church was organized in fewer than 50 nations or territories, but in 1990 it was in 128 nations. In 1950 there were fewer than 6,000 missionaries in the field. In 1990 there were nearly 40,000. In 1950 some 7.7 percent of the population of the Church lived outside the United States and Canada, but forty years later this had changed to 40.5 percent. In 1950 most missionaries spent ten days or so in a mission home in Salt Lake City, where they received minimal training. In 1990 they received intensive language and missionary training in fourteen missionary training centers around the world, and 23 percent of all the missionaries went to those outside Provo, Utah. In 1950 the Church was operating eight temples, only one of which was outside the United States. In 1990 it was operating forty-four, twenty-three of them outside the United States. In the 1950s there was no such thing as area and regional organization. There were broad units, such as the European Mission, with various missions as subdivisions of those. In 1991, after a complex series of changes in church administration, the Church was administered through twenty-two area organizations around the world.

There was also a striking decline in the percentage of members living in the missions as compared with membership in the stakes, dropping from 19 percent in 1950 to 7 percent in 1989. This reflected an important effort to organize stakes wherever possible and was probably a better indicator of maturity in a given area than mere growth in numbers. In some areas the continuing division and subdivision of missions and stakes told a dramatic story of growth. In 1955, for example, the Northern Far East and the Southern Far East missions encompassed all of Asia, but by 1990 the Asia Area included forty-four stakes, eighteen missions, two missionary training centers, and 186,000 Latter-day Saints.

The postwar world offered a life of neither peace nor abundance, though it was one in which science and technology provided tools for enriching the life of humankind. People had not learned to share either the human or natural resources of the earth in ways that would uplift and ennoble man. The Church continued to maintain that only the gospel of Christ would bring peace, true brotherhood, and well-being to the people of the world. But with a membership representing less than one-tenth of one percent of the world's population, it had little impact, even in countries where its growth was most dramatic. When seen in this perspective, its universal mission was awesome. Still only a tiny stone cut out of a huge mountain, the latter-day kingdom was boldly rolling forth but had scarcely begun to fill the earth. The Saints, nevertheless, were acting as if accomplishing that dream was their most urgent task. "Lengthen your stride," they were told in the 1970s. The Church must inform "all nations, kindreds, tongues and people" of the restoration of the gospel and the coming Millennium. With nearly forty thousand missionaries in the field in 1990, this historic Mormon sense of mission continued as the heart of its vitality.

CHAPTER 19

Foundations for Expansion, *1951–1959*

David O. McKay was seventy-seven years old when he was sustained as ninth President of the Church on April 9, 1951. An educator by profession, he was a school principal in Huntsville, Utah, at age twenty. He later attended the University of Utah, where he graduated from a three-year teacher education program, and thus was the first President of the Church to hold a college degree. He taught at Weber Stake Academy and became principal of that institution in 1902. This early commitment to education was still strong when, during his administration, the Church's educational program began an unprecedented expansion. President McKay was also well prepared to lead the Church in an era of new internationalism. From 1897 to 1899 he fulfilled a mission in Scotland, and in 1920–21, as a young apostle, he traveled around the world for the Church. Thirty years later, as President, he toured all the European missions and announced that temple building would soon begin there. Between 1953 and 1955 he visited the Saints in Europe, South Africa, Latin America, and the South Pacific. More widely traveled than any previous Church president, and thoroughly dedicated to a broad understanding of the world around him, President McKay was the ideal leader for the Church in the postwar world.

During the first decade of President McKay's leadership, Church membership grew from about 1,100,000 to 1,693,000, and the number of organized stakes increased from 180 to 319. This reflected, in part, a general increase in religious interest that followed World War II. In the United States, 63 percent of the population claimed some religious affiliation in 1958, more than at any previous time in American history. The Church, however, was on the threshold of expanding more rapidly than ever before into other nations — some of them extremely underdeveloped. The challenge would be to spread the gospel and maintain

President David O. McKay. (Church Archives)

its basic values not only in the perplexing industrial society of America but also among the diverse societies of an international church.

Internationalization: The Asian Missions

The idea of a worldwide church was not new, but after World War II various historical forces combined to bring its fulfillment partly within reach—at least in most of the world outside the "iron curtain" that separated much of eastern Europe and Asia from the Western world. President McKay once again spelled out the vision in a general conference address on Sunday, April 3, 1955, when he stressed the need "to put forth every effort within reason and practicability to place within reach of Church members in these distant missions every educational and spiritual privilege that the Church has to offer."[1] The Church was reaffirming its intent not only to convert people around the world but, at long last, to induce them more effectively to remain in their homelands and there to build up Zion.

In 1950 some 7.7 percent of the members lived outside North America; by the end of the decade this had changed to 10.4 percent. Perhaps the most impressive growth was in east Asia. In 1950 only 439 members lived in the Orient. By 1960, some 7,400 members were organized in 51 branches. Though still not great, these numbers represented a new and permanent commitment to Asia.

The task of building the Church in Asia was not easy. In China, for example, the Communist party concluded a twenty-year civil war in 1949 by taking control of the mainland and driving the Nationalist government to the island of Taiwan. At this point a "bamboo curtain" that blocked entrance to Asian communist countries descended around China. The Church opened a Chinese Mission in 1949 with headquarters in the British crown colony of Hong Kong, but lack of access to the mainland made it impossible to work among the vast majority of the Chinese people. The outbreak of the Korean conflict in 1950 forced the withdrawal of all missionaries and the final closing of the mission in 1953.

In Japan, meanwhile, there were perhaps fifty members of the Church remaining after World War II, but LDS servicemen stationed there as part of the American occupation forces helped prepare the way for the reopening of the mission. The conversion of Tatsui Sato was

---

[1]*Conference Report*, April 1955, p. 25.

an inspiring example of how the gospel could bridge the gulf between former enemies. Sato, who lived in Narumi village, already had strong faith in the Christian Bible and could speak English. One day late in 1945, while visiting with friends in a tea shop, he invited three American soldiers into the shop to warm themselves. The villagers were astonished when the soldiers politely declined cups of warm tea. One of them, Ray Hanks, explained to their gracious host, "Our church teaches us that our bodies are a very sacred gift from God, and that we should take special care of our health." In the conversation that followed, the Americans were able to explain much about the gospel, and when they returned to the village they brought a copy of the Book of Mormon and began holding study classes with the Sato family. Tatsui Sato was impressed as he read and reread the book, studied with the soldiers, and prayed. Soon more soldiers came, and a small Sunday School was begun in the Sato home. This continued for several months. Tatsui Sato and his wife became converted to the gospel and on July 7, 1946, the Sato family was baptized. The serviceman who baptized Chiyo Sato, Tatsui's wife, was twenty-one-year-old Boyd K. Packer, who in later years became a member of the Council of the Twelve.

The baptism of Brother Sato and his family began a new era for the Church in Asia. In 1948 the Japanese Mission was reopened, with Edward L. Clissold, a former member of the American occupation forces, as president. The first five missionaries to arrive were also former American servicemen, all of which beautifully symbolized the universal nature of the gospel and the fact that it could bridge the gap between former enemies. In the next few years many more missionaries were sent to Japan and building sites were purchased in Tokyo and Yokohama. In 1955 the Japanese Mission was divided into the Northern Far East and the Southern Far East missions.

The pioneer Latter-day Saint in Korea was Dr. Kim Ho Jik, a vice-minister of education in the South Korean government. As a Ph.D. candidate at Cornell University, Kim had been converted by a fellow graduate student, Dr. Oliver Wayman, and upon his return to Korea he became an avid missionary. At the same time, just as the reestablishment of the Church in Japan was in large part an outcome of the American occupation after World War II, so the establishment of the Church in South Korea was partly due to the efforts of LDS servicemen who were there with American forces sent, in accord with a United Nations resolution, to repel an invasion by North Korea. Some were returned missionaries and others had been called into military service

Missionary activity in Korea began when LDS servicemen from the United States found themselves stationed in that country. Here six servicemen pose with Korean converts at baptismal ceremonies, 1953. (Photograph courtesy Spencer J. Palmer)

before they could serve on missions, but they enthusiastically gave their time and money to share the gospel with the Korean people. In January 1952 they began offering both English language classes and gospel investigator sessions in the port city of Pusan, and on August 2 Kim Ho Jik watched with deep emotion as an American serviceman baptized his son and daughter in the ocean near Pusan. In 1954 Elder Harold B. Lee of the Council of the Twelve visited the country, and in 1955 Korea was dedicated for missionary work by President Joseph Fielding Smith of the Council of the Twelve. The first regular missionaries came from among the American elders laboring in Japan, and a separate Korean Mission was organized in 1962.

The foundations for the expansion of the Church in the Philippines, Okinawa, and other Pacific islands were similar. World War II brought into these areas Mormon servicemen who were faithful in conducting their own church activities and living exemplary lives, and their work laid the foundation for regular missionary activity.

Missionary Work in General

Between 1950 and 1960 the number of full-time missionaries in the field rose from 5,000 to nearly 6,000. In addition, an important administrative change improved supervision of missionary work. For years different phases of the missionary program had been divided among four different committees at Church headquarters, all under the direction of the First Council of the Seventy. In 1951, to eliminate this unwieldy diffusion of responsibility, all missionary functions were consolidated under the newly formed Missionary Committee, with Elder Joseph Fielding Smith as chairman.

At the same time Church leaders were impressed with the effectiveness of various missionary lesson plans adopted by some missions during the late 1940s, and in 1951 the Church Radio, Publicity, and Missionary Literature Committee, headed by Gordon B. Hinckley, decided to develop a churchwide plan. In 1952 the committee introduced a *Systematic Program for Teaching the Gospel*. Essentially the same as a plan developed earlier in the Great Lakes Mission, it consisted of seven lessons in dialogue form, to be memorized by every missionary. By 1955 the Church was also distributing flannelboard material to visually supplement the lessons. Use of the plan was optional and some missions continued to produce their own plans, but the First Presidency finally decided that a single plan should be adopted in order to make it easier to train missionaries in the mission home. In 1961 *A Uniform System for Teaching Investigators* was introduced at the first worldwide seminar for mission presidents, and it was officially adopted churchwide. It changed as experience demonstrated the need for further refinement, and the missionaries were also urged to be sensitive to different needs and responsive to the promptings of the Spirit.

An interesting effort of the 1950s was a special mission to the Jewish people in the United States. Because LDS doctrine emphasized the importance of the Israelite heritage and the eventual gathering of all the scattered tribes of Israel, the Saints felt a special kinship with the Jews and had long been interested in finding ways to reach them. At the same time, most members did not understand modern Jewish faith and culture and therefore found it difficult to communicate.

In 1955 Elder LeGrand Richards of the Council of the Twelve published a book, *Israel! Do You Know?*, which was an effort to show the Jewish people the relationship between their heritage and the faith of the Mormons. That same year a special Jewish Mission was opened on a trial basis in Los Angeles. Soon more stakes in California, Utah, and a few other areas had similar programs, each with its own teaching plan based on an opening approach that directly linked the Mormons to the Jews. By September 1958, some fifty stake missionaries were involved in the Jewish Mission in southern California.

At the same time, other members in southern California became involved in a program called "Understanding Israel," an attempt to promote better Mormon understanding of the Jewish people. Among other things, it taught young Latter-day Saints various aspects of Jewish culture, including modern Israeli folk dancing. Not part of the Jewish Mission, the "Understanding Israel" program nevertheless influenced the missionaries and helped them gain better understanding of what they were about.

The fate of this special mission provided an important lesson on the delicacy of intercultural relations as the Saints attempted to spread the gospel beyond their traditional culture. Although some Jews were converted, the result of four years of effort seemed to suggest that such a specially directed program was unsatisfactory. In 1959 the First Presidency sent a circular to all stake and mission presidents directing that all Jewish missions be dissolved. Henceforth, proselyting among Jews would be a regular part of stake missions, but no missionaries were to confine themselves to work exclusively among them. The Saints were warned, furthermore, not to promote discussions relating to pro- or anti-semitism, for some missionaries apparently had been unwise in making statements with controversial social and political implications. Some were also overzealous in their interpretations of biblical prophecy and had made statements that were not church doctrine and could prove embarrassing. They were warned by the First Presidency of the "unwisdom of any attempt to set dates and times, for the fulfillment is in the unfathomable wisdom of the Lord. It is well to teach all people to be prepared for the fulfillment of prophecy, and leave all else to Him."[2]

Missionaries and Servicemen during the Korean War

During the Korean conflict of the early 1950s many young American men found themselves being drafted into the armed forces, and the Church's missionary corps plummeted from 4,847 in 1951 to a low of 2,189 in 1953. To partially fill the gap, in 1951 the First Presidency called upon the seventies quorums in the stakes to provide one thousand full-time missionaries. Such a call required unusual sacrifice, for the seventies were usually men who had already been on missions, were married and had families, and were becoming settled in their occu-

---

[2]First Presidency, Circular Letter, March 2, 1959, Church Archives.

Council of the Twelve, October 1953. Seated: Joseph Fielding Smith, Harold B. Lee, Spencer W. Kimball, Ezra Taft Benson, Mark E. Petersen, Matthew Cowley. Standing: Henry D. Moyle, Delbert L. Stapley, Marion G. Romney, LeGrand Richards, Adam S. Bennion, Richard L. Evans. (Church Archives)

pations. Nevertheless, with the aid of families, friends, and priesthood quorums, many seventies accepted the challenge and filled short-term missions.

Another emergency innovation was the calling of young women under the age of twenty-three, the minimum age for missionaries at that time. On January 19, 1953, the First Presidency informed stake presidents of the need for stenographers and other office help in the missions and suggested that a few properly trained women who were at least twenty-one could be called. The response was so generous that by July all needs were met and permission to call women under twenty-three was suspended.

The most complicated wartime issue was obtaining draft exemptions for missionaries. The Church did not intend to keep young men from military service altogether, but it made every effort to clarify the fact that missionaries were full-time ministers during their two years of missionary service and that they would be willing to serve in the armed forces when they returned. The problem was complicated in areas heavily dominated by Latter-day Saints, for local draft boards sometimes found themselves unable to meet their quotas and at the same time allow many deferments for missionaries. Both the military and the Church were trying to draw from the same pool. The Church accommodated by not calling young men who had received notices to report for preinduction physical examinations, and in January 1950 the First Presidency required that all prospective missionaries receive prior clearance from draft boards. In July 1953 they also introduced a quota system whereby each ward in the United States could call only one young man in 1953 and perhaps two the following year. By 1955 the crisis was over and the quota system was dropped.

As young Latter-day Saints were called into the military during the Korean conflict, Church leaders revitalized the servicemen's program. In August 1950 local leaders were again instructed to maintain regular contact with men and women in the armed services and to be sure that a pamphlet, *So You Are Going Into Military Service*, was given to all prospective inductees. In 1951 a new *Servicemen's Directory* was printed and distributed. Throughout the decade the Church continued to promote religious activities for servicemen, organize special branches, and hold servicemen's conferences. The servicemen themselves contributed to the stability of the Church in many areas by strengthening local branches and missionary work, helping to build chapels, and, in some cases, providing additional leadership. In 1960 an estimated fifteen thousand Latter-day Saints were still on active duty in the armed services of the United States.

The Building Program as a Symbol of Growth

The growth of the Church in this decade was well illustrated by the building program. The Latter-day Saints erected and dedicated 1,350 chapels, schools, and welfare buildings between 1946 and 1955, and the chapels built in that period constituted more than half of all chapels then in use. In July 1955 Wendell B. Mendenhall was selected to head the new Church Building Committee.

The building program in the South Pacific expanded more rapidly than in any other place, and in 1950 the members in Tonga participated in the unofficial beginnings of new innovation: the labor-missionary program. The Liahona School was under construction, but volunteer laborers were unable to complete it because they lacked the skills needed for the most technical tasks. At that point the president of the Tonga Mission decided to call young men on missions to work until the school was finished and to receive special training. The Church provided housing while local members provided food, and by the end of 1951, with the young missionary-laborers working alongside a few skilled builders, all the school buildings were complete. This work-training program spread to other parts of Tonga, and in 1951 to New Zealand, where another school was under construction. The labor-missionary approach soon became institutionalized and in the 1950s contributed to dozens of buildings, including chapels, schools, the Church College of Hawaii, and the New Zealand Temple. The benefits of the program were seen not only in construction of many fine buildings but also in the training of young men. Many learned new skills and trades and prepared themselves spiritually to contribute more fully to their various branches. Because of its success in the South Pacific, the program was extended throughout the Church during part of the 1960s.

Temple Building and the International Vision

The Church erected four new temples in the 1950s. The most elaborate was the $4,000,000 building at Los Angeles, California, dedicated March 11, 1956, by President David O. McKay. The massive four-story structure had a center spire rising 268 feet above the ground, topped by a gilded statue representing the Angel Moroni. The grounds were gracefully landscaped with a large variety of plants, including palm trees and other tropical foliage, and additional small palm trees were planted atop the annex.[3]

The other three temples constructed in the 1950s were outside the United States, reflecting the international commitment of the Church. In 1955 President McKay dedicated the first European temple, near Bern, Switzerland. Three years later he dedicated a temple near London, England, as well as one in New Zealand. Up to this point the Saints outside North America or Hawaii could never feel that all the blessings of the gospel were available to them, for it was impossible for most of them to get to a temple even once in their lifetimes, let alone with any regularity. For that reason many continued to emigrate to America. This move, however, represented the prophet's serious commitment

---

[3]In a way this architecture was a dramatic reminder of Brigham Young's prediction in 1853 when, speaking of the Salt Lake Temple, he said: "Now do not any of you apostatize because it will have six towers, and Joseph only built one. . . . The time will come when there will be one in the center of Temples we shall build, and on top, groves and fish ponds." *Journal of Discourses*, 1:133.

The New Zealand Temple opened for public visits prior to its dedication in April 1958. (Church Archives)

to make every blessing of the gospel available to the Saints worldwide, and it helped persuade the Saints to remain in their homelands, build up Zion there, and thus contribute even more to helping the kingdom fill the world.

Certain changes in temple design were also reflective of the dynamics of Mormonism as it adapted to the problems of growth in the postwar world. The Los Angeles Temple was the last to be designed with separate rooms for each stage of the endowment ceremony. The Swiss, London, and New Zealand temples each consisted of only one ordinance room in addition to the celestial room. This smaller plan provided a less expensive way to construct temples and made it possible to build more throughout the world. In addition, the Church made use of modern technology to enhance its ability to deliver the message of the endowment. In the Swiss Temple and all those erected since, it has been presented through the use of tape recordings and motion pictures, thus making the presentation not only more efficient and effective but also more adaptable to different languages. Most of the older temples eventually also were adapted to the same procedure, and as the ceremony was translated into many languages patrons from various nations often could enjoy it in their own tongues even when traveling in other countries.

The Involvement of Youth

In the 1950s the Church became increasingly concerned with the winds of social change that tended to sweep many youth from traditional moorings and into a spirit of rebellion against the values and institutions of their society. Changes in the youth programs reflected efforts to keep young people rooted in the Latter-day Saint tradition by giving them a greater sense of involvement. In 1950, for example, responsibility for the girls' program was transferred from the Presiding Bishopric to the Young Women's Mutual Improvement Association. The MIA responded by sponsoring more musical and recreational programs, and in 1954 a huge regional conference in southern California featured music, dance, and drama festivals. Preparation included local activity in all the wards of the region and involved many young people in long hours of planning and practice, under church sponsorship.

For young men, a slight but significant change was made in 1954 when the Presiding Bishopric announced that henceforth worthy boys could be ordained to the office of teacher at age fourteen and to the office of priest at sixteen. Fourteen-year-old boys, they explained, were restless as deacons, and because they did not want to be grouped with the younger boys in deacons quorums, their activity lessened. The earlier advancement was designed to give them a feeling of increased responsibility in the higher quorum. In lowering the age of ordination to the office of priest, young men over sixteen were placed under the direct guidance of the ward bishop, who was president of the priests quorum. The Church also continued its involvement in the Boy Scout program, and in 1955 the "Duty to God" award was established. To achieve this special recognition, a Scout was required to demonstrate unusual achievement in his religious activity as well as in the regular Scouting program.

In the 1950s the Church had a higher proportion of its boys enrolled in Scouting than did any other religious group in America. In 1952 it adopted the national Cub Scout program, to be supervised by the Primary Association. The result was that all kinds of Scouting activity became even more a part of traditional Mormon family life. Women in every ward were mustered into service as den mothers, and fathers found themselves participating in outings as well as regularly helping their Cub Scout sons carve model racing cars for the annual "pinewood derby."

When combined with the regular activities connected with Sunday

School, the Aaronic Priesthood, and the seminaries, the broadened youth program of the 1950s helped large numbers retain a religious commitment that seemed unusual in the context of contemporary society.

The Commitment to Education

The Church's commitment to its various educational programs also expanded in this decade, as seen in part by the commitment of church funds. In 1949 education absorbed 15.8 percent of the total church expenditures; in 1958, the last year such figures were published, it took 21.3 percent.

So far as weekday religious education was concerned, seminary enrollment in the 1950s jumped 220 percent (from 28,600 to 81,400) while enrollment in the LDS institutes of religion increased 150 percent (4,300 to 10,200). One reason for the dramatic increase in seminary students was the early-morning seminary program, a far-reaching innovation resulting from the persistence of imaginative Church leaders in southern California and eventually adopted churchwide.

In April 1950 eleven California stake presidents met with Church Commissioner of Education Franklin L. West, urging the introduction of a seminary program in their region. The idea was approved on a trial basis and Ray L. Jones, a successful seminary teacher in Logan, Utah, was transferred to southern California to direct it and work out the details. The data he gathered, including surveys taken among parents and students in every ward, only emphasized the fact that it would be no easy task. Members were widely scattered; comparatively few Latter-day Saint students attended any one high school; the California released-time law permitted only one hour per week and then ordinarily only for grades four through six, but the Church wanted high school students to attended seminary classes five days a week; seminary could not be held at noon because lunch hours were staggered; texts and reference works would be expensive; if LDS chapels were used for seminary classes there would be transportation problems, for few chapels were within walking distance of the schools; and if early-morning seminaries were held, they would have to begin at 7:00 A.M. or earlier in order to allow students to get to school on time. Despite such obstacles, six early-morning pilot classes with 198 students were opened in September 1950. They soon demonstrated that with proper organization and pioneer-type enthusiasm, such a program could be successful. Teachers were drawn from the ranks of professional men, housewives, public school teachers, and others; transportation was provided through car pools; and with parental cooperation and urging, students attended seminary classes each day before regular school hours. The program spread so rapidly that within a decade nearly 30 percent of all seminary students were enrolled in nonreleased-time programs.

Another important development was the Indian seminary program, which began in Brigham City, Utah, where, in 1949, the United States government opened an off-reservation dormitory school, the Intermountain Indian School. Six Latter-day Saints were among the first six hundred students to arrive, and local leaders not only showed concern for their welfare but immediately began planning for the religious needs of those who would follow. J. Edwin Baird and Boyd K. Packer, both local officials, were placed in charge, and Elder Packer, also a teacher in the seminary at Brigham City, was soon assigned to develop a religious education program for all Latter-day Saint Indian students. In 1955 he became a general supervisor for the seminary system, and three years later he and A. Theodore Tuttle began a survey of all Indian schools in the United States. Their completed report was submitted to the Church Board of Education in 1958 and approved. Under their direction an effort was begun to provide religious instruction for all LDS students at the major Indian schools. In 1959 Elder Baird was appointed full-time director of the program, and by 1966 nearly ten thousand students were enrolled in Indian seminaries at about two hundred schools.

In the South Pacific, limited educational opportunities persuaded Church leaders that they should build and maintain schools that offered academic training in secular subjects as well as religious education. New or enlarged schools included Mapusaga High School in American Samoa; the Church College of Western Samoa and the Pesaga Elementary School with shared facilities at Pesaga; schools in Sauniatu and on the island of Savai'i in Western Samoa; the Liahona High School in Tonga; and the Church College of New Zealand. Elementary and secondary schools had been conducted in some of these areas for many years, but in every case they were mission schools, operated under the direction of the mission president and taught by full-time missionaries. By 1957 it was clear that the educational programs in the Pacific were too extensive to continue under mission operation, and in July of that year the Pacific board of education was established to centralize control. Under the direction of this new board, the change to professionally trained teachers began, and the transition was nearly complete by 1959. The last mission school to close was the one at Vailu'utai, discontinued in 1963 after sixty-five years of operation.

The founding of the Church College of Hawaii was foreshadowed at least as early as 1921 when David O. McKay attended a flag-raising ceremony at the mission school in Laie and was deeply impressed with the need for an institution of higher learning. This vision remained in his mind, and in 1951, as President of the Church, he appointed a special advisory committee to look into the matter. The committee recommended that a school be located in Laie, near the temple, that it be a boarding school, and that it emphasize vocational training. On July 21, 1954, the First Presidency officially announced that a college would be established in Hawaii. Many local Saints wanted it in the Honolulu area, but in the long run Laie, which was practically a Church colony and where the Church owned considerable property, was chosen. By the end of 1958 the new campus was completed and dedicated, and in 1959 the college received accreditation for its two-year program. In 1961 it received four-year accreditation.

Church educational programs in Mexico also grew. An academy had been operating in Juarez since 1887, but by the 1950s more than six thousand Saints lived in Mexico and less than 60 percent of their school-age children had the advantage of an elementary education. In October 1957 the First Presidency appointed a committee to study educational needs of the Mexican Saints, and the committee recommended that a number of primary schools be organized throughout the country. Branch meetinghouses were used at first but the Church moved quickly to construct separate school buildings. In 1959 the committee submitted to the First Presidency a more detailed report observing that the Mexican government had indicated a desperate need for more schools, especially in urban areas, and that private schools were encouraged. There would be 2,085 Latter-day Saint students available for grades one through eight in the fall of 1959, and the committee recommended the establishment of twelve to fifteen elementary schools. In January 1960 the First Presidency approved the plan, and the following September five primary schools were organized. From its beginning the school system drew upon Mexican citizens for its teachers and administrators.

Indian Placement

Another educational innovation with far-reaching consequences was the Indian student placement program. After World War II the

American government expanded its day schools and boarding schools to many reservations. The dropout rate was high, and cultural differences as well as lack of support from parents made it difficult for many Native American children to achieve. It was inevitable that the Church, with its special concern for the descendants of the people of the Book of Mormon, would develop a program for the growing number of Indian children within its ranks.

The roots of this program went back to 1947 when Golden Buchanan, a member of the Sevier Stake presidency and resident of Richfield, Utah, was touched by the predicament of transient Indian workers in county sugar beet fields. He was especially troubled that members of his stake seemed to have no concern for the workers' personal welfare, and he expressed his feelings forcefully at a stake conference. Afterwards a member of his stake told him of a particular Indian girl, Helen John, who spoke English and who had the job of bargaining with the farmers on behalf of the Indian workers. Helen wanted an education and indicated that she was willing to pitch a tent in a backyard if only she could stay and go to school. Buchanan went out to visit Helen. It was late in the fall, and he reported the visit this way:

> You never saw a muddier girl. It was snowing and all the Indians had gone home except a few that were staying to dig out the remaining beets that were frozen in the snow. There were Helen, Helen's older sister Bertha, and Lois Begay. Bertha didn't speak English at all and Lois had been to school only one or two years. These three girls were living in a tent way out in the field in six to eight inches of snow. They were as muddy as could be from the waist down. They were all three typical Indian girls with long hair. Mrs. Avery introduced me to the girls and we talked. Helen said, "I am just going to stay. I am not going home. I am going to get an education."[4]

Touched by such an expression, Buchanan wrote to Elder Spencer W. Kimball of the Council of the Twelve. Two days later he was surprised by a personal visit from the apostle, who asked the Buchanans if they would consider taking Helen into their home while she went to school. After a night to think it over, the Buchanans accepted the

---

[4]As quoted in Clarence R. Bishop, "Indian Placement: A History of the Indian Student Placement Program of the Church of Jesus Christ of Latter-day Saints" (M.A. thesis, University of Utah, 1967), p. 32, from an interview with Golden Buchanan, October 13, 1966.

An Indian family visits with the host family that has taken an Indian child into its home during the school year as part of the Indian placement program. (Church Archives)

challenge, and by January 1948 Helen was settled with them. Two of her friends were placed in the homes of other Richfield families.

From this beginning the program spread, although slowly, so that by 1953 sixty-eight Native American students were living in foster homes while attending school. In the meantime, Buchanan became acquainted with Miles Jensen of Gunnison Stake, who was already deeply involved with the Indian people because of his responsibility to coordinate and recruit migrant laborers for the Gunnison Sugar Company. The Jensen family was one of those persuaded by Buchanan to take in foster children, and in June 1948 Elder Jensen received an assignment to be coordinator of Indian affairs for the Church, under the direction of the Indian Relations Committee headed by Spencer W. Kimball. The placement of Indian children in foster homes was still not officially promoted by the Church, but Buchanan and Jensen were active throughout southern Utah in personally encouraging it. Jensen assumed full responsibility in 1951 when Buchanan was appointed president of the Southwest Indian Mission. By the fall of 1951 Indian student placements had extended to Idaho, Oregon, and southern California.

Even though the Church did not officially participate in the grass-roots beginning of the program, Elder Kimball kept close to it and reported on it to other Church leaders. But it was with difficulty that some Caucasian members accepted the full implications of Indian placement. In April 1954 Elder Kimball began his general conference address by commenting with pleasure on the large number of Saints from various minority groups who were attending the conference, then quoted with outrage an anonymous letter complaining of Indians being allowed to talk in church, go to the temple, and otherwise participate intimately with other Church members.

> If Mrs. Anonymous were the only one who felt that way! However, from many places and different directions I hear intolerant expressions. While there is an ever-increasing number of people who are kind and willing to accept the minority groups as they come into the Church, there are still many who speak in disparaging terms, who priestlike and Levite-like pass by on the other side of the street. . . . In the letter quoted, there is the suggestion of a superior race! From the dawn of history we have seen so-called superior races go down from the heights to the depths in a long parade of exits. . . . Is the implication of Mrs. Anonymous justified that the white race or the American people is superior? . . .
>
> The Lord would have eliminated bigotry and class distinction. He talked to the Samaritan woman at the well, healed the centurion's kin, and blessed the child of the Canaanitish woman. . . .
>
> And now, Mrs. Anonymous, when the Lord has made all flesh equal; when he has accepted both the Gentiles and Israel; when he finds no difference between them, who are we to find a difference and to exclude from the Church and its activities and blessings the lowly Indian?

There could be no better expression of the need for some Latter-day Saints to broaden their racial perspectives as the Church attempted to better serve the needs of various cultures and, in the process, imbue all its members with the universal spirit exemplified by Christ.

In July 1954, many Saints having caught the vision more fully, the Church officially inaugurated the Indian student placement program, with the full expectation that children placed in white foster homes would find genuine love and understanding. Seven stakes in southern Utah were asked to begin the official program, with foster families participating on a strictly voluntary basis. Since Indian families were generally without financial means to provide even the necessary food, clothing, and transportation, the foster families must be willing to shoulder such expenses. In addition, the First Presidency made it clear that "if an Indian child is taken into a home he comes not as a mere guest, nor as a servant, . . . he or she may enter the home as a welcomed member of the household to enjoy the spiritual and cultural atmosphere of the home, and to be given such schooling in the public schools as may be afforded to him."[5]

Under Utah law, the program had to be supervised by a licensed agency, and with the cooperation of the State Department of Public Welfare, the Relief Society was so licensed. Miles Jensen continued as a caseworker and supervisor, and Golden Buchanan, president of the Southwest Indian Mission, assumed responsibility for selecting participating students, who were required to be members of the Church. After passing physical examinations and receiving various immunization shots, the students were introduced to their foster families. Between 1956 and 1966 the number of students enrolled in the program grew from 242 to 1,569. It had expanded to many states, as well as Canada, and included students from sixty-four tribes.

Inevitably, there were problems. Some Native American children found the educational, cultural, and social challenges overwhelming and dropped out of school. Some white families were unable to adapt to foster children, and Indian families were torn by mixed emotions as their children left home each fall. Some members and a few overly enthusiastic missionaries attempted to place children in foster homes without going through proper channels. It became necessary for the First Presidency to warn the Saints that such independent action could not be condoned, for it disregarded the law and jeopardized the well-being of the Indian children.

Complaints about the operation of some parts of the program also began to come from the U.S. Bureau of Indian Affairs and other sources. Critics charged that in some cases the program was used for proselyting and to encourage mass baptisms on the reservations, that it tended to alienate the affection of children from their parents, that it deprived parents of the responsibility of training their own children, that it often took children from reservations when adequate education was available in their own communities, and that some of the caseworkers used in the program were not competent. An early response to such criticism came in a special meeting at Kanab, Utah, in March 1957, when rep-

[5]Stephen L Richards and J. Reuben Clark, Jr., to the presidents of seven southern Utah stakes, August 10, 1954, as quoted in Bishop, "Indian Placement," p. 43.

resentatives of the Church met with officials from state and federal welfare services. As a result, new guidelines were adopted that kept Church representatives in closer contact with state and federal agencies, provided better evaluation procedures, and gave increased attention to the relationship between the foster children and their natural parents. In addition, the student selection process became more professionalized rather than being assigned to missionaries.

Despite the problems, placing Native American children in white homes throughout Utah and other areas had many positive effects. It not only helped hundreds of children gain an education but also contributed to breaking down racial prejudice. In 1967 the annual dropout rate was no higher than that in off-reservation boarding schools, and students often returned to the program after a year back on the reservation. Educational attainment varied, but in 1967 more than 80 percent of the program's graduates had received post-high-school training, and a large number had served missions for the Church.

Higher Education

The growth of Brigham Young University in this decade and the unification of the Church school system were results of the gradual development of a master plan for Church education. Dr. Ernest L. Wilkinson, a noted Washington, D.C., attorney, was inaugurated as president of Brigham Young University in 1951. Almost immediately he launched a program of expansion. His well-designed, forceful presentations were influential in persuading the board of trustees that new buildings and facilities as well as new faculty members were needed at the university. In the ensuing decade enrollment more than doubled, from 4,584 to 10,445. The number of full-time faculty members increased from 196 to 502, and by 1961 at least ten new buildings were completed. This was only the beginning of a physical expansion that continued for many years, and under Wilkinson's guidance Brigham Young University became the largest church-related university in America.

The move toward consolidation of the Church's educational institutions began in 1952 when LDS Business College in Salt Lake City was placed under the administrative direction of Brigham Young University. In July 1953 all of the educational institutions were combined under one administration, except those still under the Pacific board of education, and President Wilkinson was named Administrator of the

Unified Church School System. The position of Commissioner of Education, which directed seminaries and institutes, was discontinued. William E. Berrett was appointed vice-president of Brigham Young University and vice-administrator of the school system with responsibility for religious education. The seminaries and institutes came directly under his jurisdiction.

The growth of the school system promised to receive an important boost in 1954 when the Utah legislature authorized the governor to turn over three junior colleges — Dixie, Snow, and Weber — to the Church. The state was in financial difficulty, and to many people this seemed to be a logical solution to the problem. The Church had given the colleges in question to the state in the 1930s, with the provision that if the state should cease to operate them, the property would return to the Church. Seizing on this opportunity, Governor J. Bracken Lee urged the transfer, but a citizens' reaction put the matter on the ballot as a referendum in the next election. The Church stated its willingness to take the schools and operate them on a sound financial basis, but in the referendum a majority of Utah citizens voted against the proposition, and the schools continued under state sponsorship.

Consolidation and planning for the future did not come without still further controversy, as seen in the fate of a larger plan for Church involvement in higher education proposed by President Wilkinson in 1957. A 1953 study on the growth of the Church had demonstrated that BYU simply could not provide for the rapidly increasing number of LDS college students; and President Wilkinson, supported by the First Presidency, laid plans for a system of junior colleges in areas of high LDS population. Even though institutes of religion adjacent to other colleges and universities could provide religious training, Wilkinson and others pointed out that institutes in most areas attracted only part of the LDS students and that Church colleges would provide all of them not only with religious education but also with a more well-rounded LDS atmosphere. Land for new colleges was purchased in Salt Lake City, Idaho Falls, Idaho, and in various places in California and Arizona.

The plan, however, was controversial. Wilkinson and other advocates emphasized the obvious religious and social values for LDS students, as well as the long-range value to the Church. Opponents pointed to the extremely high cost of operating colleges, and also to the fact that a more vigorous institute system not only was less expensive but also had great missionary potential. The debates continued until, during the 1959–60 academic year, other financial needs caused the Church to trim its proposed educational budget drastically. At that point the First Presidency concluded that a junior-college program simply would not be undertaken until the income of the Church justified it.

Another controversy centered on President Wilkinson's plan for moving Ricks College from Rexburg, Idaho, to Idaho Falls. In 1954 Ricks received the highest accreditation possible for a four-year college, but in that same year it was cut back to a two-year school. The First Presidency had concluded that, in light of plans for the overall development of the Church school system, Ricks would be of more service and "have greater destiny as an integral and permanent part of the school system by being a first class junior college than by continuing as a relatively small four-year college."[6] The First Presidency urged all Latter-day Saint students in the area to obtain their first two years of college at Ricks, then move on to BYU.

In April 1957 the Church Board of Education approved the transfer of the college to Idaho Falls. Factors entering into this decision included the possibility of more employment and better housing opportunities for the growing number of students expected to attend, the greater accessibility of Idaho Falls, and the presence of a temple. Surprised and dismayed leaders from Rexburg, however, protested strongly to Church leaders, pointing out that the existing buildings would go to waste, the cost of providing new facilities in Rexburg would be much less, and that Rexburg could fill all the needs of the students. President McKay, in turn, visited Rexburg, investigated the situation himself, and in July announced that he was convinced of the merits of the Rexburg argument and that moving the school simply was not worth the price. The following year, however, the Church learned that the state of Idaho planned to establish a junior college in Idaho Falls if local residents approved, and this caused Church leaders again to reconsider. All the former considerations, together with the fear that a competing junior college in Idaho Falls would cause enrollment at Ricks to dwindle, led to a new decision to make the transfer, and on November 15, 1958, Elders Marion G. Romney and Hugh B. Brown of the Council of the Twelve explained the decision to Church leaders in Rexburg.

The controversy still did not end, and in February 1959 a local

---

[6]Letter of the First Presidency, April 7, 1954, as quoted in Harvey L. Taylor, "The Story of the LDS Church Schools," 2 vols., typed Ms., prepared for the Church Commissioner of Education, 1971, 2:183, in Church Archives.

Brigham Young University campus, about 1963. In the early twentieth century the campus began to move from downtown Provo to "Temple Hill." The first building to be completed in the new location was the Karl G. Maeser Building, seen in the front center of this view, which was dedicated in 1911. (Brigham Young University Archives)

"Committee of 1,000" even put out a publication that emphasized the history and traditions of the college in Rexburg and noted that the twenty-eight miles between Rexburg and Idaho Falls was not really a significant distance. More important to the final decision, however, were the same financial considerations that stopped the construction of other junior colleges. By June 1960 General Authorities were finally convinced that the Church simply could not afford to move the college, and in 1961 the First Presidency announced that three new buildings would be constructed on the Ricks campus.

Religious Organization and Educational Expansion

The overall Church school system continued to expand, however, and efforts were made to get ward members more directly involved in promoting seminary and institute enrollment. One such step was the organization of ward education committees in 1957. These committees were especially effective in the areas where nonreleased-time or early-morning seminaries were held. They were responsible for encouraging enrollment, organizing transportation pools, and supporting seminary classes in other appropriate ways. In addition, they were instructed to maintain contact with college-age students and to encourage attendance either at a Church college or at a college where an institute of religion was established. By the end of the decade it was clear the efforts of these committees had helped substantially improve the percentage of young people enrolled in Church education programs. They continued to function until 1968, when the new correlation program began.

With the rapid growth in enrollments at colleges and universities, increasing attention was given to the church activity of LDS college students. Often those living away from home were not absorbed into wards and stakes in their college communities. Branches had been organized at BYU and other schools with large Mormon student populations, but they still did not seem to provide the full range of training and activity needed. In other cases, students overcrowded the wards in college areas, dominating the classes and seemingly relegating older residents to the background.

With these problems in mind, administrators of the school system recommended the organization of student wards. In 1956 the first student stake was organized on the Brigham Young University campus. Campus wards were later organized at every location where the number of students justified it. Generally they were supervised by the local stakes, but in Rexburg and at the larger institutes of religion, such as those in Salt Lake City and Logan, Utah, and Pocatello, Idaho, student stakes were also created.

President Wilkinson often remarked that the organization of student wards and stakes was the most important thing to happen during his administration. In terms of the spiritual well-being of the students, he may well have been correct. Immediately students found themselves involved in every aspect of local church administration. Usually a professor or someone from the community served as bishop, but often mature students were called as counselors. Students became ward clerks, presidents of Relief Societies and MIAs, and even, in many cases, members of stake high councils. The student wards demonstrated a certain flexibility in church organization; the Mutual Improvement Association and the Relief Society, for example, were modified to meet students' special needs.

The results were outstanding, especially with regard to Relief Society, which traditionally had been considered an organization for the more mature women of the ward. In the college setting young women met in Relief Society on Sunday morning at the same time the men attended priesthood meeting. Thousands of young women suddenly found themselves not only involved in, but also excited about, the program of religious instruction, cultural training, social relations, and homemaking that the Relief Society sponsored. The spiritual growth of young people under the new program was phenomenal, and in temple marriages and attendance at meetings, as well as most other statistical measurements, student wards led the Church.

Secularism, Stress, and the Public Image

The Church in this age could hardly avoid stresses and strains related to the secular world around it. University students came face-to-face with highly potent discussions of the theory of evolution, higher criticism and other modern approaches to the scriptures; scientific theories concerning the origin of the earth and the ancestry of the American Indian; various sociological theories relating to the nature of man; and new assumptions about the nature of historical evidence. To some observers, such theories and methodologies could challenge the faith of Latter-day Saints, particularly at the college level, as the traditional function of a university was to present all theories in an effort to teach students to think independently — even to question traditional kinds of authority in their independent quest for truth. Although this approach tended to disturb some students, Church colleges and institutes of religion attempted to employ well-educated teachers who were also men and women of faith and who, themselves, had seriously wrestled with such problems. Presumably they could deal with the issues in a well-informed, non-dogmatic, yet faithful and constructive way, and help students over whatever religious-secular hurdles they may face.

In 1957 one nationally recognized non-Mormon scholar expressed great admiration for the way the Church and its students were coping with such stresses. He met with a group of mature Latter-day Saint students who were studying in the social sciences and humanities at one eastern university and asked them what they really thought about the future of the Church as it more frequently confronted these challenges. "The result," he reported, "was more persuasive than any analysis could possibly be." Rather than responding dogmatically without awareness of the implications of their statements, the students discussed the questions intelligently and demonstrated great flexibility in an atmosphere of faith — an ability to distinguish passing tradition from the essential elements of the faith and thus reorient themselves to changing circumstances. He wrote:

They demonstrated that Mormonism was meaningful to them, who were in some way Mormondom's young elite—those sent to bring learning and higher degrees to Utah. Their testimony must be admitted as eloquent.

Strains, yes; conflict, perhaps; but strains and conflict are both signs and sources of vitality. The fact is that the Church of Jesus Christ of Latter-day Saints is still a vital institution. Conflict and strain have not been sufficient to prevent its orderly functioning over the last many decades. It may not be so well adapted or prepared to meet new problems as it was in times in the past; yet all transitions and all reorientations are difficult. That its values still provide a meaningful context to great numbers of its adherents cannot be denied. Its flexibility in the past and its viability under the most adverse conditions do not augur badly for its future.[7]

There were other, more general, images of the Mormons being created in the 1950s. In national periodicals, for example, the 1950s saw a generally favorable public image. The Church was praised for its continuing activities in the welfare program. Successful Mormon businessmen were often favorably publicized, and frequently their church affiliation was pointed out. The continuing national broadcasts of the Tabernacle Choir also contributed to a positive image. The choir achieved special recognition for its successful tour of Europe in 1955 and a tour of the eastern United States in 1958. In 1959 it received the "Grammy" award from the record industry for its recording of the famous Civil War song "Battle Hymn of the Republic," and after the 1950s Mormon Tabernacle Choir records, including sacred and secular music, sold widely. In addition, in 1953 the Church began to televise its general conferences so that certain sessions could be seen in many parts of the United States.

Political Affairs

Because of its predominance in Utah and its growing influence in the United States, the Church continued to become involved in public issues, in at least two ways. On the one hand, whenever individual leaders participated in political life, people asked if their views were endorsed by the Church. They always affirmed that their opinions were strictly personal, but if they were General Authorities the respect members had for them nevertheless helped lend considerable weight to their

---

[7]Thomas F. O'Dea, *The Mormons* (Chicago: University of Chicago Press, 1957), p. 263.

During the Eisenhower administration, Elder Ezra Taft Benson of the Council of the Twelve served as Secretary of Agriculture. (U.S.D.A. photograph, Benson Papers, Church Archives)

views. On the other hand, the Church sometimes found itself directly concerned with public policies, especially when moral issues were involved or when they affected the well-being of the Church itself.

An example of the involvement of a leading Latter-day Saint in public affairs came in 1952 when Elder Ezra Taft Benson of the Council of the Twelve was appointed Secretary of Agriculture by the newly elected President of the United States, Dwight D. Eisenhower (which appointment Elder Benson accepted with President McKay's consent). Elder Benson, whose professional career before he became a General Authority had been in agricultural marketing, had long been opposed to farm subsidies and crop controls. As Secretary of Agriculture he remained loyal to his sometimes controversial political principles and was successful in bringing about several significant reforms. In his first news conference he said that he believed in some price supports, as insurance against farm disaster, but that they should be flexible in order to help adjust each crop to the demands of the market. When Secretary Benson's specific proposals were sent to Congress by the president in 1954, the agricultural committees of both the Senate and House voted against them, but the entire body of Congress approved them. When he left office in January 1961, Elder Benson was highly respected, even by those who had opposed his views.

Other leaders also spoke out on national political affairs. One was President J. Reuben Clark, Jr., a former undersecretary of state, former American ambassador to Mexico, and since 1933 a member of the First Presidency. He was particularly vocal in his opposition to American involvement in the United Nations, which, he believed, could only undermine American sovereignty. In the same spirit as Elder Benson, however, when President Clark delivered an attack on the United Nations in 1952, in a speech entitled "Our Dwindling Sovereignty," he made it abundantly clear that he was speaking only for himself and not in behalf of the Church. Three months earlier he had discussed the forthcoming speech with President McKay, recognizing that it would be controversial. President McKay saw no objection in his airing his personal views in that manner; and when he gave the speech President Clark declared, "For what I shall say tonight I am solely responsible." Interestingly enough, President McKay himself tended to support the United Nations, though he did not make it a public issue.

Another Church leader who spoke out frequently on political affairs was Hugh B. Brown, who became an Assistant to the Twelve in 1953, a member of the Council of the Twelve in 1958, and was a member of the First Presidency from 1961 to 1970. A former Democratic candidate for U.S. senator, Elder Brown frequently spoke in favor of the United Nations as well as some of the social welfare activities of the federal government. His major emphasis when speaking to Church members, however, was on political balance and toleration. On May 31, 1968, he declared at the Brigham Young University commencement exercises: "Strive to develop a maturity of mind and emotion and a depth of spirit which enables you to differ with others on matters of politics without calling into question the integrity of those with whom you differ. Allow within the bounds of your definition of religious orthodoxy variations of political beliefs. Do not have the temerity to dogmatize in issues where the Lord has seen fit to be silent."

Unfortunately some people, both members and nonmembers, sometimes either misinterpreted or misconstrued for their own purposes the political views of such Brethren. Because many prominent Latter-day Saints who were active politically seemed to lean toward the Republican party, some people were persuaded that in some way Latter-day Saint doctrines were more compatible with that party and that faithful Saints should adhere to it. Nothing could have been more contrary to the actual position of the General Authorities, who constantly refused officially to endorse candidates and repeatedly reminded members that the Church would take no official stands on political issues, with a few exceptions on matters that seemed to affect fundamental gospel principles. There were Church leaders active in both principal American parties; their political differences did not keep them from maintaining genuine gospel brotherhood with the rest of their brethren.

Perhaps the feeling of the Brethren with regard to LDS participation in politics was best characterized in a statement by President McKay during the October 1952 general conference:

> Twice, during the conference, reference has been made to the fact that we are approaching a general election, in which tension becomes high; sometimes feelings are engendered; often false reports are made; and innocent people are misjudged.
>
> Recently we heard that in one meeting, for example, it was stated authoritatively by somebody that two members of the General Authorities had said that the General Authorities of the Church had held a meeting and had decided to favor one of the leading political parties over the other, here in this state, particularly. . . .
>
> This report is not true, and I take this opportunity here, publicly, to renounce such a report as without foundation in fact.
>
> In the Church, there are members who favor the Democratic party. There are other members who sincerely believe and advocate the principles and ideals of the Republican party. The First Presidency, Council of the Twelve, and other officers who constitute the General Authorities of the Church preside over members of both political parties.
>
> . . . The welfare of all members of the Church is equally considered by the President, his Counselors, and the General Authorities. Both political parties will be treated impartially.[8]

The decade of the 1950s was another important time of transition for the Church. As the postwar world presented new challenges and opportunities, the Church grew rapidly and augmented its programs. New directions in missionary work, youth programs, temple activity, and educational programs as well as a renewed emphasis on building up the Church outside America laid the foundation for the two most dramatic developments of the next three decades: genuine internationalism and major administrative innovations that would help the Church accommodate both internationalism and growth.

---

[8]*Conference Report*, October 1952, pp. 129–30.

CHAPTER 20

Correlating the International Church, *1960–1973*

As the Church entered the 1960s with over 1,600,000 members around the world, it had long outgrown the simple administrative structure established in the days of Joseph Smith. Three kinds of Church organizations actively served the needs of the Saints. One was the regular ecclesiastical system, with its well-defined chain of priesthood authority. Another consisted of the auxiliaries — the Relief Society, Sunday School, Mutual Improvement Associations, and Primary — each of which had its own general board and officers, published its own manuals, held its own conferences, determined its own courses of study, and published its own magazine. A third type of organization included a multitude of professional services necessary to carry out the normal functions of the Church — and these would continue to burgeon. Thousands of people were employed full-time to carry out the essential day-to-day tasks without which the modern church could not function completely.

As the administrative burden of the Church expanded, the need for examining the interrelationship between all the departments, ecclesiastical and professional, became apparent. By the mid-1970s all Church functions were impressively though not completely correlated under a unique administrative system with the priesthood as its central force. The achievement of this organizational realignment was one of the principal themes of the Church's history for a dozen or so years after 1960. Other themes included its continuing international growth, the more widespread adoption of various technological developments in order to meet the needs of modernization, and the impact of some of the Church's policies on its public image around the world.

Three Modern Prophets

During this period three different men presided, in turn, over the Church. David O. McKay served until his death at age ninety-six in January 1970. As a young apostle he had been appointed in 1908 to the General Priesthood Committee on Outlines, the first group seriously to consider ways to correlate the entire Church program. He was directly involved in all subsequent correlation attempts, and it seemed only natural that a major correlation effort would be conducted during the final decade of his presidency.

Joseph Fielding Smith became President of the Church at age ninety-three, on January 23, 1970. Perhaps the most prolific writer on doctrinal subjects the Church had yet produced, his numerous books and articles were widely read. In 1921 he became Church Historian, and in 1934 he was named president of the Genealogical Society. He also served as president of the Salt Lake Temple, chairman of the General Church Melchizedek Priesthood Committee, member of the Church Board of Education, chairman of the Church Committee on Publications, President of the Council of the Twelve, and after 1965 as a counselor to President McKay. As President of the Church, he oversaw implementation of many administrative procedures recommended by the studies and experiences of the 1960s. Despite his advanced age, President Smith proved that he was still vigorous both mentally and physically. In addition, his kindly leadership demonstrated that he was, indeed, a generous, loving prophet whose basic concern was the well-being of all the Saints.

A few of the important decisions made during President Smith's administration were the reorganization of the educational program, the organization of the Historical Department, the revamping of the publications program, organization of the Social Services Corporation, the inauguration of a training program for bishops, the creation of fourteen new missions, and the expansion of the teacher development program churchwide. He kept up a remarkable pace, including an active speaking schedule, and many who had been critical of a system that allowed aged men to govern had ample reason to change their minds.

The Church was going through a metamorphosis, and President Smith proved capable of responding to the challenge. Earlier he had misgivings about some aspects of rapid expansion, particularly its impact on the gathering to Utah. As President of the Church, however, he not only approved the organization of far-flung stakes but also presided

President David O. McKay, known for his love of horses, often visited his family farm at Huntsville, Utah. (Church Archives)

over the area conference in Manchester, England, the first general conference held outside the United States. At this significant meeting he declared:

> We are members of a world church. . . .
>
> The day is long since past when informed people think of us as a strange group in the tops of the Rocky Mountains in America. . . . We are coming of age as a church and as a people. We have attained the stature and strength that are enabling us to fulfill the commission given us by the Lord through the Prophet Joseph Smith that we should carry the glad tidings of the restoration to every nation and to all people. . . .
>
> Thus the church is not an American church except in America. In Canada it is a Canadian church; in Australia it is an Australian

church; and in Great Britain it is a British church. It is a world church; the gospel is for all men.[1]

Harold B. Lee became President July 7, 1972, and served until his death on December 26, 1973. Never fearful of innovation so long as it was carried out under the clear direction of priesthood authority, he was uniquely suited to encourage correlation. His first general Church assignment was to establish the welfare program in 1936, and after he became a member of the Council of the Twelve in 1941 he continued at the head of the program. In 1948 he was appointed by the First Presidency to head a committee of apostles assigned to recommend changes in the work of the priesthood and auxiliaries—another effort at correlation. His committee's recommendations were not adopted, for they included organizational changes that President George Albert Smith did not think the Church was prepared for, but he remained vitally interested in the problem of effective coordination of all church units.

President Lee had other qualifications for leadership. A teacher by profession, he was concerned not only with the problems of youth but also with the need for constant improvement in both religious and secular training. Before becoming a General Authority he had served Salt Lake City as a city councilman and the Church as a stake president.

Achievements in Correlation

Achieving effective coordination among all units of the modern church was complex and difficult, and in March 1960 the effort was renewed. Harold B. Lee, chairman of the Melchizedek Priesthood Committee, was assigned to conduct a study of church curriculum. He, in turn, appointed Antone K. Romney, dean of the College of Education at Brigham Young University, to head a committee that would make a historical survey of the auxiliaries and correlation efforts. Its final report, completed on July 10, 1961, was adopted by the General Priesthood Committee.

The first public announcement of the new correlation effort came from Elder Lee at a general priesthood meeting on September 30, 1961. He described the formation of an all-Church Coordinating Council consisting of himself as chairman, three additional members of the Council of the Twelve, the Presiding Bishop, the auxiliary heads, and

[1]"To the Saints in Great Britain," *Ensign* 1 (September 1971): 2–3.

representatives from the Melchizedek Priesthood Committee and the education system. In addition, the three apostles on the committee would each preside over one of three new age-group committees: child, youth, and adult. These committees would be responsible for instructional programs relating to their respective groups; but their ultimate goal was to consolidate and simplify all Church curricula, publications, meetings, and other activities. The Coordinating Council's executive committee was called the Correlation Committee, though eventually all plans went to the First Presidency and the Council of the Twelve for approval. As far as final decision-making was concerned, these authorities actually functioned as the ultimate correlation committee.

The three age-group committees went to work with vigor, but the task of creating a fully coordinated curriculum took longer than expected. It was highly complicated and ran into opposition from almost every group affected as each perceived the need to protect some historic special interest. In addition, some task committees presented plans that would mean a restructuring of Church organizations, which the Correlation Committee rejected, for its commission was to work within the existing organizational structure. Gradually, however, efforts at correlation began to affect every program.

The first major innovation came in a refinement of the old ward teaching program. Inaugurated churchwide in 1964, it was renamed home teaching and, in the spirit of correlation, priesthood quorum leaders, rather than the bishop, were made responsible for its supervision. Priesthood holders, moreover, were instructed that henceforth they were to do more than simply make their traditional monthly visits; they were to become personally acquainted with all family members and make visits whenever they could contribute to their spiritual welfare. Conventional monthly lessons were eliminated so that home teachers were more free to use their own initiative and inspiration in determining what was right for the families concerned.

The Correlation Committee also determined that priesthood responsibility fell into four major categories: missionary work, genealogy, welfare, and home teaching. Accordingly, four committees were organized to deal with these responsibilities.

By the mid-1960s the wide sweep of correlation was beginning visibly to affect ward organization and activities. In 1963 each ward was instructed to set up a home-teaching committee, which later became known as the priesthood executive committee. Consisting of the bishopric and priesthood leaders, this agency planned, coordinated, and

President Joseph Fielding Smith at a general conference converses with Harold B. Lee, who succeeded him as President. (Church Archives)

directed ward priesthood activities. Each ward was instructed also to organize a ward council, which met monthly. Comprised of the priesthood executive committee and the heads of the auxiliaries, this body was designed to coordinate ward functions and discuss better ways to focus on individuals and determine which organization or combination of organizations could best assist those who needed help. This local aspect of correlation was designed to assure that no one ever would be lost because of lack of interest or concern on the part of the local members.

Correlating activities at the local level was relatively easy compared with achieving full coordination in the higher echelons. Some auxiliaries, for example, continued to send out instructions to stake and ward workers without clearing them through the Correlation Committee. In addition, reporting procedures tended to emphasize the independence of the auxiliaries, for each had its own system. Such problems were partially solved in 1967 when all ward reports were consolidated into one set of forms, which were then routed through the stake president to the Presiding Bishop's Office, rather than through auxiliary heads to general auxiliary executives. In 1965 the *Priesthood Bulletin* was inaugurated, designed for distribution to all leaders. All organizations and committees were supposed to send their instructions through that correlated and unified publication.

One aspect of correlation that directly affected every member was the family home evening program, formally launched in 1965. The Church had frequently advised families to spend at least one night each week together, but now special home-evening manuals provided suggested lessons and activities. Families were urged to be flexible and to plan those activities best suited to bring them together. Recognizing that Church-sponsored events sometimes stood in the way of achieving this ideal, leaders soon requested that Monday night be left free of all other church activities. The Monday family home evening quickly caught on throughout the Church and by the 1970s was an important and viable tradition — one of the most successful of all the innovations in this era. In some areas where the Latter-day Saints enjoyed a numerical majority, town and school administrators even scheduled athletic and community activities to avoid competing with family night.

Administrative Reforms in the Correlation Era

With the steady growth in Church population and the proliferation of wards and stakes in these years, the administrative burden on the General Authorities inevitably became excessive, especially since they were still trying to visit stake conferences at least twice a year. As early as 1961 it was decided that members of the First Council of the Seventy would be ordained to the office of high priest so that when they attended conferences they could perform ordinations to that office and carry out other duties assigned them by the Council of the Twelve. Because of his advanced age, the administrative burden seemed especially heavy on President McKay, and in 1965 he took the unusual, though not unprecedented, step of appointing two additional counselors in the First Presidency: Joseph Fielding Smith and Thorpe B. Isaacson.[2]

In 1967 the position of Regional Representative of the Twelve was created. Initially sixty-nine men were called, but the number soon expanded. Each Regional Representative was assigned to regularly visit a certain number of stakes. He was not to preside at stake conferences, but he would act as an adviser to the stakes and as liaison officer between

---

[2]For the names of other additional counselors in the First Presidency, see the listing of General Authorities in any issue of the *Deseret News Church Almanac*.

stake presidents and the Council of the Twelve. In 1972 a number of Mission Representatives were appointed with the same responsibility toward missions, but in 1974 this office was combined with that of Regional Representative.

Continued emphasis on correlation, meanwhile, resulted in further administrative reforms. In 1970 a bishops' training program was inaugurated under the direction of the Presiding Bishopric. The following year a churchwide teacher development program was adopted that included a basic eleven-week course plus a correlated in-service training program for all teachers. Also in 1970, as part of the effort to relieve General Authorities from burdensome routine activities, stake presidents were made responsible for setting apart missionaries before they went into the field.

Elder Lee and his associates were still not satisfied that the Saints fully grasped the concept that the directing influence in all Church activity should be the priesthood and that auxiliary organizations were in reality only helps to the priesthood in carrying out its proper function. In 1973, while Elder Lee was President of the Church, a major step toward clarifying this philosophy was taken when the Mutual Improvement Associations and the priesthood were combined. This move had been envisioned as early as 1928 but never fully implemented. The Aaronic Priesthood MIA, as it was called, retained the traditional age-group divisions, but henceforth the deacons quorum adviser served as the Scoutmaster, and the other Aaronic Priesthood advisers assumed responsibility for the same age groups in the former MIA program. The young women were divided into corresponding groups, with a woman appointed to supervise each.

The following year the century-old tradition of having a separate auxiliary known as the Mutual Improvement Association came to an end as the name was dropped and the two groups became known simply as the Aaronic Priesthood and the Young Women. The general presidency of each group was responsible to the Presiding Bishopric of the Church. Three years later the Aaronic Priesthood organization was renamed the Young Men and supervision of both groups was given to the Priesthood Department.

By the 1970s other traditions were also changing. In 1971, for example, the athletic and dance programs were regionalized. In place of all-Church athletic tournaments and dance festivals, each region was instructed to conduct its own events. This was designed to stimulate greater local participation and minimize expenses and logistical prob-

Youth speaker in one of the modern chapels—typical of what was seen regularly in meetings throughout the Church in the mid-twentieth century, and a significant change from the typical Church meeting of a hundred years earlier. (Church Archives)

lems involved in annual treks to Salt Lake City. Another program developed under instructions from the Correlation Committee affected college students. In the late 1960s the Latter-day Saints Student Association (LDSSA) was organized. Its purpose was to upgrade spiritual and social activities for LDS college students as well as to coordinate activities between students and non-student young adults.

At the same time Church leaders began to show more concern for the special needs of unmarried men and women. Traditional Church activity oriented toward couples and families simply did not meet the social and spiritual needs of many unmarried adults. In the 1970s special programs for young single adults as well as older singles were created under the auspices of the priesthood and Relief Society. Through self-directed councils at the ward, stake, and regional level they participated in dances and other cultural activities and found broader opportunities to become acquainted with Saints their own age who shared common interests. In addition, as part of this new emphasis, wards for young singles were organized, first in the Emigration Stake in Salt Lake City and then in other areas.

Adjustments in Central Services

The idea of more fully coordinating the Church's various programs, eliminating overlapping functions, and relieving General Authorities of many day-to-day administrative duties soon affected the whole structure of the Church, including the administration of the ever-expanding professional services.

One of the first steps in the restructuring process came in 1969 when Indian student placement, child adoption, and youth guidance were combined in a unified social service program. In 1971, health, social, and welfare services were involved in a major reorganization under the Presiding Bishopric. Social Services and Health Services both became licensed corporations, and Social Services was given the responsibility for programs relating to Native Americans. The Health Services Corporation took control of all Church-owned hospitals as well as activities such as nurses' training programs and training in preventive medicine for members in underdeveloped areas. In 1971 Health Services also inaugurated, for the first time in Church history, a health-missionary program in which young adults were sent to underdeveloped countries to teach basic principles of nutrition and health care to members. In 1973 a legally separate Social Services Corporation was organized to meet the needs of people requiring special social services, such as adoptions, foster care, and specialized counseling. While all this was a far cry from the original scope of correlation, it indicates that the idea of better integrating and directing programs was affecting all Church services by the 1970s.

Church publications, too, were restructured under the principle of correlation. In December 1970, the last issues of five traditional magazines, most published by and largely for the benefit of particular organizations, came off the presses.[3] In their places three new, correlated magazines designed to carry articles and instructions pertaining to the three basic age groups were inaugurated in January 1971: the *Friend* for children, the *New Era* for youth, and the *Ensign* for adults. Regional and mission publications, including the one-hundred-thirty-year-old *Millennial Star* in England, were also discontinued, some of them earlier than 1970. They were replaced by a unified international magazine,

---

[3]These were the *Children's Friend* (published by the Primary), the *Relief Society Magazine*, the *Instructor* (published by the Sunday School), the *Improvement Era* (originally published by the MIA but later a general Church magazine), and *Impact* (published by the seminaries and institutes).

Health missionaries working with a family in Patzicha, Guatemala. (LDS Church)

begun in 1967. Translated into many languages, the new publication included selected articles from the other three magazines, a few original articles, and local news sections inserted for particular areas.

Publishing for an international and intercultural Church presented serious problems of translation and distribution. Leaders were especially concerned with lesson manuals, which often were not published in non-English editions. Even when available they were usually written from the perspective of American culture, and the examples used and issues raised were not always relevant in other societies. Writing committees were instructed to use universal examples as much as possible and to eliminate references that were unique to the American experience.

In 1965 the Translation Department was organized, and in 1967 it was combined with the Distribution Department. Soon Church distribution centers were established in several places in Europe, North and South America, the Pacific, and Asia to assist in getting Church literature to the wards and branches as quickly as possible.

With such rapid expansion of services and the resulting growth of administrative responsibility, Church leaders also recognized the need for independent, professional examination of the Church's administrative structure. In 1971 they employed two well-known business consulting firms to make in-depth studies of internal operations of the Church. These were Cresap, McCormack, and Paget, Inc., of New York, and Safeway Stores, Inc., of Oakland, California. By August 1971 both companies had completed their studies and submitted comprehensive reports and recommendations. Many of these recommendations were soon adopted.

The Cresap report pointed to the obvious problem that General Authorities had become too heavily burdened with administrative responsibilities, and it recommended that most administrative functions be turned over to full-time managing directors. General Authorities, and especially the First Presidency and Quorum of the Twelve, would thus be freed to attend to their roles as spiritual leaders and policy-makers. Both studies recommended creation of two new departments: External Communications (later changed to Public Communications and then Public Affairs), for matters of public relations; and Internal Communications, to solve the serious problems involved in getting materials out to members. In 1972 both departments were organized and functioning, with full-time managing directors who reported to designated advisors from among the Quorum of the Twelve.

The Department of Internal Communications had the most direct effect on general Church administration and correlation. J. Thomas Fyans (who later became an Assistant to the Quorum of the Twelve) was the first managing director. The old Correlation Committee was dissolved, and its functions were transferred to Internal Communications. Elder Fyans was given full responsibility for planning, preparing, translating, printing, and distributing all communications, instructional materials, and periodicals for members worldwide. Translation and distribution services, the magazines, editorial services, and curriculum planning all were brought together under Internal Communications.

The most effective steps toward genuine correlation of curricula were taken through the Division of Instructional Materials. An elaborate instructional development program was set up to create teaching materials for all organizations. It was directed by full-time professional educators, with each subcommittee manned by individual writers and researchers who were called to devote their Church service time to these assignments. Elder Fyans's office received requests from priesthood or auxiliary organizations, established priorities, and directed the preparation of long-range plans. It was also responsible for eliminating duplication of effort and unnecessary overlapping, and insured that all materials approved for publication conformed to Church doctrine, standards, and procedures.

The original correlation concept thus became, in the 1970s, largely the responsibility of the director of instructional materials, who had the staff and authority to carry it out. By 1974 control of the writing of manuals was completely removed from the auxiliaries. Also in that year the correlation section was made into a separate division of the Department of Internal Communications, with the idea that it could more objectively review the materials produced by the Division of Instructional Materials as well as those written for the magazines. Eventually these functions were separated out into the Correlation Department, Curriculum Department, and Translation Department.

In the spirit of the Cresap report, other departments also were restructured in the early 1970s. One was the Church Historian's office. When Joseph Fielding Smith became President of the Church in 1970, he had been Church Historian for forty-nine years. During the last decade of his service, the administration of the vast and rapidly growing archival holdings of the Church became increasingly complex. By 1972 Church leaders were impressed with the need for the Church itself to engage in more research and writing in the field of Church history. To accomplish these ends the staff must be enlarged, with more professional help added.

Under President Smith's direction, the Church Historian's Office was reorganized in January 1972 as the Historical Department of the Church, with three major divisions. The Church Archives, under the direction of Earl L. Olson, was responsible for acquiring, storing, and managing documents and records relating to Church history. The Church Library, under Donald T. Schmidt, was responsible for acquiring and making available to Church authorities as well as to the public printed materials pertaining to the Church. The History Division, under Leonard J. Arrington as Church Historian, was responsible for writing and publishing Church history. Arrington's appointment was particularly unique, for he was the only non-General Authority ever to be sustained and set apart as Church Historian.

The first managing director of the new department was Elder Alvin R. Dyer, an Assistant to the Quorum of the Twelve, and under his direction it soon began to provide vastly expanded historical services. Later the library and archives were combined into one division, and a new division, the Arts and Sites Division headed by Church Curator Florence S. Jacobsen, was added to look after historical buildings, artifacts, and paintings. Still later, in 1980, after the First Presidency and the Quorum of the Twelve concluded that professional historical writing could be done more freely and effectively in an academic setting, the History Division was transferred to Brigham Young University as the Joseph Fielding Smith Institute for Church History, with Leonard J. Arrington as director. Since that time the managing director of the Historical Department has been designated officially as Church Historian.

These were only some of the changes brought into the administrative structure during the era of correlation which, in a symbolic way, came to a close with the death of President Harold B. Lee in December 1973. Not every objective had been achieved, but the changes made were pivotal in nature and established important new administrative patterns that came close to fulfilling dreams long held, especially by Presidents McKay and Lee. They also helped pave the way for even more extensive changes in the coming decades as the Church more than ever before found itself facing the challenge of becoming a truly international, universal faith.

Church Growth around the World

The need for such far-reaching refinements in administration was in large part a reflection of the Church's dynamic growth. Over a million members were added in the 1960s, bringing the total to more than 2,800,000; 206 new stakes were organized; 2,158 chapels were completed, many of them outside the United States. Sixty-nine school buildings were constructed in South America, Mexico, and the Pacific; and eighty-one new institute of religion and 113 seminary buildings were erected in the United States. The Church began broadcasting around the world from a new shortwave radio transmitter, participated in several international fairs, and opened dozens of new missions.

An important sign of Church maturity in any area is the organization of a stake, the basic unit of local Church administration. Such a move represents not only numerical growth but also the fact that enough local members hold the Melchizedek Priesthood and are trained in Church leadership that the Saints in the area can operate the full program of the Church without constant outside supervision. It was a significant milestone in Church history, then, when the Auckland New Zealand Stake was created on May 18, 1958, the first stake outside North America or Hawaii. By 1973 there were stakes in American

The Tabernacle Choir performs at a general conference in the Tabernacle in Salt Lake City. (Church Archives)

Samoa, South Africa, and seventeen more nations in Latin America, Asia, the South Pacific, and western Europe. As President Harold B. Lee reminded the Saints that year: "No longer might this Church be thought of as the 'Utah Church,' or as an 'American church,' but the membership of the Church is now distributed over the earth in 78 countries, teaching the gospel in 17 different languages at the present time. This greatly expanded Church population is today our most challenging problem."[4]

The 1960s was a special era of growth for Latin America and Asia. Latin American Saints increased in numbers from 18,700 to 135,000 in ten years. The first Latin American stake was organized in Mexico in 1961. By the end of 1973 there were seven stakes in Mexico, nine in Brazil, three in Argentina, and one each in Chile, Peru, Uruguay, and Guatemala. Much of the growth came as the missionaries not only expanded their activities within the major cities but also reached out into underdeveloped rural areas.

Expansion in Latin America was not free from problems. Missionary work was often hampered when it became difficult to obtain or renew visas, not just because of occasional religious intolerance but also because of the concern of some governments that foreign missionaries might prove subversive. In some countries it also became difficult to import Church literature, and partly for that reason printing

---

[4]*Ensign*, July 1973, p. 4.

centers were eventually established in Sao Paulo and Mexico City, along with translation and distribution centers.

The growth in Latin America necessitated further expansion of church education in the area. It was Church policy to establish schools only where local school systems did not provide adequate opportunity for basic education. In 1963 two elementary schools were organized in Chile. A large educational complex, including an elementary and secondary school as well as a normal school for training teachers, was dedicated in Mexico City in 1968. By 1972 more than 11,000 students were enrolled in LDS elementary and secondary schools in Bolivia, Chile, Mexico, Peru, and Paraguay. Home-study seminary programs, an innovation begun in the American Midwest in 1966, were also spread to every country where the Church was located.

The special needs of some Latin American Saints also led to the extension of other programs to their countries. In the 1970s some of the first agricultural missionaries went to Guatemala and other areas, in an effort to improve the farming skills of rural members. In 1972 Brigham Young University began sending students and faculty on "Project Mexico" to help teach agricultural skills. Many of the first health missionaries also went to Latin America; they gave instruction in sanitation, nutrition, and preventive medicine.

There were also a number of unofficial ways in which some North American Saints began to assist Latin American members. In eastern Guatemala, for example, Cordell Anderson, a former missionary, established a large agricultural project that provided employment and self-help opportunities for many members. A different type of program, Ayuda, which means "help" in Spanish, was founded in 1968 as a nonprofit venture by a group of former missionaries from the United States. In 1969 the group opened a medical clinic in Cunen, Guatemala, where volunteers, including doctors, dentists, nurses, educators, builders, and other professional people, gave from two weeks to twelve months of voluntary, unpaid assistance. For about a decade this program continued to help Latin Americans.

In Asia membership rose from 5,100 to 25,900 in the 1960s. The first Asian stake was organized in Tokyo in 1970. Singapore, Indonesia, Vietnam, and other areas were dedicated for preaching the gospel, several new missions were opened, and the Book of Mormon was published in Chinese and Korean. In 1968 the Language Training Mission at the Church College of Hawaii began to offer training in various Asian and

Pacific languages to better prepare missionaries for work in those countries.

Symbolic of the spirit of the Saints in areas where the Church was growing but still had no temples was a heartwarming excursion to the Hawaiian Temple by 166 Japanese Saints in 1965. In order to make the trip they had to raise some $600 per couple—for some, nearly the equivalent of a year's salary. Under the direction of the mission president they had sponsored fund-raising projects, patterned after such practices in America, but the difference in cultures was revealed when some Japanese Saints at first wondered if such fund-raising was either honorable or Christian. The Saints also worked at genealogical research and submitted to the temple at least three family group sheets each so they would have opportunity to do considerable temple work for Japanese people. In the meantime, Tatsui Sato was authorized to go to Hawaii, where he spent six months translating the audio tapes of the temple ceremony into Japanese. "Project Temple" reached its inspiring climax in July when the group arrived in Hawaii and participated in baptism, endowment, and sealing rites. Other excursions in later years strengthened the Saints in Japan and helped them prepare more fully for the day when the full Church program, including a temple, would be provided in their country. Similar stories could be told of Saints in many other nations.

In 1971 the Church's worldwide growth resulted in another important innovation when, on August 27, the first area general conference convened in Manchester, England, with President Joseph Fielding Smith presiding. It had become manifestly impossible for members around the world to attend general conferences in Salt Lake City, so the General Authorities decided to take the conferences to the members. Another area conference was held in Mexico in 1972. These were the forerunners of a series of area conferences in Europe, Latin America, the Pacific, and Asia in subsequent years. For the first time in their lives many members had the opportunity to see and be instructed by the prophet and other General Authorities. The resulting spiritual uplift in those areas was evidence of the Church's essential unity in the midst of growing cultural diversity.

Missionary Work

On June 27, 1961, and continuing for a week, the first world seminar for mission presidents was held in Salt Lake City. There new mission presidents were instructed in new programs and techniques and were told that missionary work must be a cooperative program between full-time and part-time missionaries as well as the auxiliary organizations. They were also introduced to the new proselyting plan, *A Uniform System for Teaching Investigators*. About the same time the eligible age for young men to accept mission calls was lowered from twenty to nineteen, and by the end of 1973 more than seventeen thousand missionaries were in the field—an increase of over six thousand since 1960.

During this era President David O. McKay's motto, "Every Member a Missionary," became a Church ideal. Families were encouraged to invite friends and neighbors to hear the missionaries, and special emphasis was placed on what young people could do to influence nonmember friends. These suggestions resulted in an increase in the number of group meetings attended by missionaries, for members were more enthusiastically sharing the responsibility of finding investigators. One mission president reported that his missionaries were spending 90 percent of their time actually teaching rather than searching for contacts.

Unfortunately, in their enthusiasm for making record numbers of baptisms, a few mission presidents promoted their goals in ways that encouraged missionaries to baptize people before they were truly converted. In some instances young boys were given the chance to participate on athletic teams but told they must be baptized in order to join. Such so-called "baseball baptisms" not only resulted in poor publicity but also created unnecessary problems for branches that were suddenly made responsible for new "converts" who really did not know what the Church was all about.

As Church leaders became aware of what was happening in the mid-1960s, they took steps to change it. They cautioned mission presidents strongly against such proselyting techniques and placed special emphasis on the importance of converting whole families. As a result, about 1965 the surge of baptisms declined but the staying power of the converts increased. The number of baptisms per year began climbing again in 1968.

In addition, the Church paid attention to better missionary preparation. In 1961 a language training program was initiated at Brigham Young University, initially for the benefit of missionaries who were experiencing delays in obtaining visas to enter Argentina and Mexico. It was so successful that two years later it became a formal Language Training Mission, and those who needed language training reported there after the traditional period of instruction in Salt Lake City. At first limited to Spanish and Portuguese, eventually it provided training in every language newly called missionaries needed. Some language training was also provided at Ricks College and at the Church College of Hawaii.

The Church also increased the number of bureaus of information as part of its continuing missionary effort. More use of audio-visual presentations followed the success of the Mormon Pavilion at the World's Fair in New York City in 1964 and 1965, which attracted thousands of visitors and resulted in many important missionary contacts. This was followed by similar pavilions at other expositions, such as those in San Antonio, Texas (1968); Osaka, Japan (1970); and Spokane, Washington (1974). Visitors' centers were expanded at many temples, and those at Church historic sites were reoriented to include films, slide presentations, and more informative literature.

Planting the Seeds in West Africa

Meanwhile, one of the most unusual conversion stories in Church history was taking place in western Africa: a part of the world where the Church was unable, at least for the time being, to open a mission, yet where perhaps thousands of people were literally begging for missionaries to come.

It began in Nigeria when several groups of black Christians somehow obtained Church books, believed them, organized churches patterned after what they read in the literature, and wrote to Church headquarters asking for missionaries. In 1960, at the request of the First Presidency, Glen G. Fisher visited some of them as he returned to Utah from his assignment as president of the South African Mission. He received a sincere and warm welcome and found that members of the various congregations he visited were anxious to be baptized into The Church of Jesus Christ of Latter-day Saints.

This presented a perplexing challenge to Church leaders. It had been Church policy almost from the beginning not to ordain blacks to the priesthood, and Church leaders believed the policy could not be changed without direct revelation. Yet here were whole congregations of sincere, faithful blacks asking to have the Church established among them. President McKay wanted to do something about it, but the question was whether a Church organization could be set up and staffed among the Nigerians when they could not hold the priesthood and therefore could not run it themselves.[5] Ironically, when President Fisher explained the policy to them, the Nigerians were not too concerned; they only wanted more literature, help in building chapels, and to be baptized.

With letters from Nigerians pouring in, by 1961 President McKay concluded that the Church must permit the Nigerians to be baptized and confirmed members of the Church. He cogently observed to his counselors that this problem was even greater than that faced by the Twelve in New Testament times when the question of whether the gentiles should have the gospel shook the Church. The Lord would have to let them know what to do, he said, and when the Lord was ready He would open the door. Until then they could only tell the people they could go so far and no farther.

As a preliminary step, in October the First Presidency sent LaMar S. Williams to Nigeria on a fact-finding trip. After spending a month traveling from village to village through the jungle, meeting with many congregations in mud huts and tiny chapels, and hearing hundreds of fervent testimonies from expectant Nigerians who had been praying for the arrival of missionaries from Utah, Williams returned convinced. The various congregations of "Latter-day Saints" were often quite independent of each other, but, Williams reported, they were sincere and certainly worthy of baptism. Before the end of February 1962, the First Presidency and Quorum of the Twelve decided to open a mission in Nigeria. In March, Williams was called to return there, along with his wife, Nyal, to preside over a district to be established under the umbrella of the West European Mission. Four additional couples were soon selected to assist. On November 21 Williams was set apart by President McKay as the first missionary to the black people of Nigeria and told to establish the Church, conduct missionary work, and organize all the auxiliaries, with local members supervising the auxiliaries.

The would-be Saints in Nigeria were ecstatic but, unfortunately, the long hoped-for mission was not destined to open at that time. Nigeria had only recently gained independence from British colonial

---

[5]Something of President McKay's willingness to make at least some adjustments had been seen in 1954 when he became the first President of the Church ever to visit the South African Mission. One of the things weighing heavily on his mind as he went there was the priesthood policy which, by interpretation, had prohibited anyone who could not trace his lineage out of Africa from being ordained. While there President McKay felt inspired to change the policy, so that any man whose physical appearance did not suggest black ancestry was presumed to be eligible for the priesthood.

rule, and government officials were suspicious of outsiders. When they learned of the priesthood policy they immediately denied visas to LDS missionaries. Williams spent the next three years trying unsuccessfully to obtain visas, and the Nigerian "Saints" mounted their own campaign to try to convince their government that the Church posed no threat. In 1964 one group even had itself officially incorporated under Nigerian law as "The Church of Jesus Christ of Latter Day Saints." Meanwhile, the Nigerians sent a few young people to Brigham Young University, supported in part by scholarship funds raised by Williams and other Saints. Each of them was baptized before returning home. Twice Williams returned briefly on temporary visitor's visas. During his second visit in October 1965, he was suddenly recalled to Salt Lake City. The First Presidency had decided to make no further efforts at that time to open the mission. Only two months later a violent military coup in Nigeria became the opening wedge of a bloody civil conflict, the Biafran War. The war wreaked havoc with the congregations of "Saints," though many people continued to watch, wait, and pray for the day when the Church finally could be established among them. That happy time was about twelve years away.

In nearby Ghana, meanwhile, a similar story was taking place. Sometime in 1962 a missionary tract, the "Joseph Smith Story," found its way into the hands of a black religious leader, Dr. A. F. Mensah, who was converted almost immediately. He soon converted several others, organized a "Church of Jesus Christ of Latter-day Saints," and began to correspond with LaMar Williams at the Missionary Department of the Church. In 1964 he gave a copy of the Book of Mormon as well as other literature to J. W. B. Johnson who, after reading it and receiving a series of dramatic personal revelations, was also converted and became equally successful in spreading the gospel among fellow Ghanians. Eventually Johnson and his followers formed several "Latter-day Saint" congregations, somewhat independent of Mensah. Mensah, Johnson, and others continued through the 1970s to preach the gospel as they understood it, and to plead with the Church for missionaries and for the official establishment of the Church among them. They were helped and encouraged, at times, by a number of Saints from Utah who were in their country on temporary teaching or other professional assignments, or on business. For the time being, however, the Church could make no official response to their continuing requests for missionaries and baptism.

Even though none of this resulted in any numerical growth for the

Church, it is important to an understanding of the 1960s as a time of transition. Many things were changing as the Church faced the myriad challenges of international growth, and in that spirit Church leaders seriously considered opening a unique mission among the blacks of western Africa despite the fact that it could not yet grant them the priesthood. The mission was delayed but the Spirit was at work in Nigeria and Ghana as surely as it was elsewhere, planting seeds that eventually produced a rich harvest after the revelation on priesthood finally came in 1978.

Modernization and Other Signs of Growth

The numerous changes seen in the Church during these and succeeding years reflected not just the necessities of numerical growth but also the impact of modern technologies. As the world entered the computer age in the 1960s and 1970s, for example, the adaptation of computer technology to many needs of the Church proved a Godsend. In 1962 the Financial Department became the first Church unit to make use of the computer, but others soon followed. In 1968 the Church announced that membership records would soon be transferred to a computer system, and it was not long before computer keyboards and silicon chips almost replaced typewriters and filing cabinets in the massive task of keeping track of individual Saints in the ever-expanding Church. In 1970 an automated donation system was inaugurated, whereby all financial contributions sent to Church headquarters were processed weekly, rather than monthly as before, which not only proved more efficient but also began to earn for the Church thousands of dollars per year in added interest. Eventually, membership and financial computer programs were developed for use in wards and stakes, beginning first in the United States and Canada. But even before that happened, local units began to develop their own programs. Two clerks in the Fullerton Fourth Ward in California, for example—both of them systems engineers at a local aircraft plant—developed hardware and software for ward membership records in 1978–80, then shared their findings with headquarters.

Genealogical and temple work also benefitted from the computer, beginning with the adoption of the "R-Tab" (Records Tabulation) program in 1962. For years the rate of name submission to the temples by individual patrons had fallen far behind the number needed to keep pace with the demands of increasing temple attendance. Under the new

The Granite Mountain vaults, carved into a mountain east of Salt Lake City, preserve important Church documents and family history records. Many of them are stored on microfilm. (LDS Church)

Genealogical Society program, individuals were called to Church service assignments to extract names and vital statistics from parish registers and other sources in order to supply names for temple ordinance work. The program became more technologically sophisticated as time went on and was soon renamed the name extraction program. Even though it resulted in more names being available for temple work, the Church did not draw back from continually reminding the Saints of their obligation to continue genealogical research and temple work in behalf of their own families. Eventually, in fact, the computer was harnessed to assist not just in data collection but also in research and linking families together.

In another technological development, in 1966 the Church officially dedicated a huge record vault that had been carved into a granite cliff in Little Cottonwood Canyon, near Salt Lake City. Used primarily for the storage of vital documents and microfilm records of the Genealogical Society, its peculiar structure and location contributed to proper temperature and humidity control.

Beyond the impact of technology, change in every phase of Church activity seemed to come more rapidly than ever. New temples were dedicated in Oakland, California (1964), and in Provo and Ogden, Utah (1972). The unfolding international nature of the Church was reflected in 1968 when the Church Historian's Office authorized the submission of reports in languages other than English. In 1972 a new "prospective elders" program was inaugurated. Previously young men who were not ordained to the office of elder by the time they reached the age of nineteen were placed in the "senior Aaronic Priesthood program," designed to encourage them to become more active and advance in the priesthood. Instead, this often tended to separate them from young men their own age who had become elders. Now, however, they were assigned to the elders quorums even though they may not have been ordained, which meant that the elders were directly responsible for activating and fellowshipping them.

A visible symbol of the growing Church was the new twenty-eight-story Church Office Building, completed in 1972. The First Presidency, Council of the Twelve, and most General Authorities retained offices in the old Church Office Building, later renamed the Church Administration Building, but most of the professional services and administrative units were housed in the towering new structure. Huge cast-stone representations of the world's hemispheres on the building's wings symbolized the international nature of the Church.

In the field of education, programs spread to many places, particularly to Latin America. In 1964 the Pacific board of education was discontinued and the Pacific schools became part of the Unified Church School System. The following year Harvey L. Taylor became administrator of that system when it was separated, at least temporarily, from Brigham Young University. At the same time, discussions continued concerning the feasibility of establishing a chain of two-year junior colleges. Enrollment was expanding so rapidly at BYU that many members feared their children could not get in, and by 1970 the Board of Trustees had established an enrollment ceiling of 25,000 (later increased to 27,000).

It was soon determined that expansion would come only in seminaries and institutes and in areas where secular learning facilities were not otherwise available. In 1970 Church colleges enrolled 32,900 students, while nearly 200,000 Latter-day Saints attended other institutions around the world, and nearly 50,000 of these were enrolled in institutes of religion.

In 1970 the office of Commissioner of Education was reestablished and Neal A. Maxwell, former executive vice-president of the University of Utah, was appointed to the post. The commissioner was made responsible for all phases of Church education, including Brigham Young

University, though each university and college would have its own president. In January 1971 Commissioner Maxwell announced a unified admissions system for all Church colleges. After looking at the basic needs in Church education, he had suggested that many young people, especially in the less advantaged areas of the world, should be encouraged to go into technical and vocational training, and it was suggested that the Church schools would develop increasingly competent programs in those fields.

Social and Cultural Activities

Latter-day Saints became increasingly involved in a variety of social and cultural affairs, and as the Church grew these became better known to the public. The annual dance festivals sponsored by the Mutual Improvement Associations were major events in the Intermountain West and included young people who had previously participated in local festivals. In 1970 both a youth symphony and a youth chorus were organized in Salt Lake City, symbolizing the Church's encouragement to interested youth everywhere to participate in similar activities. The annual Hill Cumorah pageant continued to draw capacity crowds and became known as one of the outstanding theatrical spectacles in the region. Saints in other areas promoted local pageants, such as *The Mormon Miracle* in Manti, Utah, which expressed the Church's story in music and drama. *Promised Valley*, the musical drama initially presented in Salt Lake City in 1947, became an annual production in the 1960s and attracted thousands of visitors. In 1970 alone, an estimated 118,000 persons viewed it, and in 1972 the old Lyric Theater in Salt Lake City was renovated under Church sponsorship and became the Promised Valley Playhouse. Here this drama and other productions appropriate as family entertainment were presented.

One of the outstanding cultural developments of the period was the Polynesian Cultural Center in Hawaii, dedicated in 1963. Students at the Church College of Hawaii represented nearly every group of Polynesian people, and the Cultural Center, developed under Church sponsorship, provided employment for these students as they gave visiting tourists an authentic feeling for their native cultures. Almost immediately it became a major tourist attraction in Hawaii.

A different kind of cultural activity was instituted in 1962 with the founding of Nauvoo Restoration, Incorporated. This nonprofit foundation had the full backing and significant financial support of the

President Spencer W. Kimball and First Counselor N. Eldon Tanner enjoy a tour of the Polynesian Cultural Center, a cultural attraction sponsored by the Church in Hawaii. (LDS Church)

Church and was eventually taken fully under Church auspices. Its objective was to make an authentic restoration of parts of the city of Nauvoo as it appeared in the mid-1840s. The restoration would become an important cultural attraction in Illinois, reminding visitors of the Mormon contribution to the Midwest as well as telling the general story of the Latter-day Saints.

These and other cultural developments were all enhanced by the fact that a growing number of highly trained, professional Latter-day Saints in many fields were dedicated to achieving excellence in portraying the story of the Latter-day Saints. In 1968 Brigham Young University sponsored its first annual Mormon Festival of Art, which placed emphasis on Mormon contributions in music and the visual arts. In literature, *Brigham Young University Studies*, founded in the 1950s and revitalized in the 1960s, provided an outlet for LDS writers who were producing works of literary and scholarly importance in many fields.

Outside the official sponsorship of the Church, private individuals were also concerned with what they could contribute to a greater understanding of the LDS heritage. In the field of history, for example, Leonard J. Arrington's *Great Basin Kingdom* (published in 1958) was among the first of several important new studies that gained wide acceptance because of their scholarly, balanced presentation and new insights into the history of the Church. A number of Latter-day Saints and other interested historians formed the Mormon History Association, designed to promote scholarly research and writing. LDS history increasingly became the subject of articles in national journals and scholarly sessions at national historical conventions. There were other outlets for published treatments of LDS culture, including *Dialogue: A Journal of Mormon Thought, Sunstone,* and, later, the *Journal of Mormon History,* which devoted their pages to various literary, historical, and other scholarly assessments of Latter-day Saint life.

The Church and Public Policy

In the United States the Saints were becoming more visible throughout the nation, and in the 1960s there was more commentary on the involvement of the Church and its leaders in public affairs than in any period since 1920. An unusual number of public issues arose in which the Church seemed to have a direct interest, and for that reason this was not only a period of growth and correlation but also one of controversy and some public criticism.

During the presidential campaign of 1960, the public press seemed insistent upon interpreting the political statements of the President of the Church as somehow reflecting Church policy rather than private opinion. When the Republican candidate, Richard M. Nixon, visited Salt Lake City, President David O. McKay was heard to tell him "we hope you are successful." This comment was quickly picked up in the national press and interpreted as an official endorsement. President McKay quickly clarified his statement by declaring that he was speaking "as a personal voter and as a Republican," but certainly not for the Church as a whole. Unfortunately, the correct explanation did not receive nearly as much publicity as the original news story.

More controversial was the debate over what methods should be employed to combat the growth of communism. Latter-day Saints along with other Americans were convinced that communism posed a threat to the American economic and political system, as well as to religion, and that communists were involved in various subversive activities. President McKay affirmed that the Church was opposed to communism, and encouraged the Saints to help prevent its spread. But a number of nationally prominent Saints were also active in anti-communist groups that seemed to go too far in making unproven accusations and defaming the character of other Americans by implying they were involved in subversive activities. Such groups also tended to oppose any extension of the power of the federal government, on the grounds that this would lead inevitably to communism. Some Saints even created the impression, perhaps unintentionally, that the Church officially endorsed conservative political causes. The First Presidency continually issued statements reiterating that the Church took no position on partisan politics, prohibiting the use of church buildings for political purposes, and making it clear that even though the Church opposed communism, it could not condone the methods sometimes employed by anti-communist individuals and groups.

Despite its efforts to remain aloof from partisan politics, the Church nevertheless took sides on a few significant political issues in the 1960s. In each case Church leaders felt a moral obligation to take a stand, though they were occasionally criticized for "dabbling in politics." One issue was liquor by the drink, which came before Utahns in 1968. The Church not only took a public stand against it but openly used its priesthood organization to distribute literature and circulate petitions. Significantly, opposition to the Church's stand was not construed as disloyalty to the Church. The First Presidency also supported Sunday closing laws, upheld the spirit of civil rights legislation (although it did not take sides on specific bills), and favored the protection of state right-to-work laws.

Perhaps the most delicate public issue involving the Church in the 1960s was civil rights. In the United States racial strife reached a peak as black citizens demanded an end to racial discrimination in every form. Prejudice and the tradition of segregation led to violence in many parts of the country, though in the long run considerable constructive legislation provided a legal basis for an end to discrimination in housing, education, employment opportunity, and all other public aspects of American life. In the turmoil every institution in America was reexamined, and for the first time many people became aware of the Church's policy of not ordaining blacks to the priesthood. This was interpreted by some people in the 1960s as a sign of racial prejudice and discrimination, and the Church quickly came under fire in national periodicals and from civil rights groups. In the late 1960s protest rallies were held in Salt Lake City, and delegates from many civil rights groups sought audiences with Church leaders in an effort to get them to change the policy. Brigham Young University athletic teams were picketed and

The new Church Office Building, completed in 1972. (LDS Church)

harangued while on road trips, and at some games anti-Mormon riots broke out. Some schools severed athletic relations with BYU.

The Church's response was that it could not change the policy without divine revelation authorizing it to do so. Church leaders reminded critics that the issue was a matter of religious faith and that those who did not share that faith should not attempt to dictate policy to the Church. The priesthood policy had nothing to do with the position of individual members on the matter of civil rights; the Saints were duty-bound to support the principle of full civil rights for all people. In 1963 President Hugh B. Brown of the First Presidency declared in October general conference:

> We believe that all men are the children of the same God, and that it is a moral evil for any person or group of persons to deny any human being the right to gainful employment, to full educational opportunity, and to every privilege of citizenship, just as it is a moral evil to deny him the right to worship according to the dictates of his own conscience. . . .
>
> We call upon all men, everywhere, both within and outside the Church, to commit themselves to the establishment of full civil equality for all of God's children.

On December 15, 1969, partly because protests still continued, the

First Presidency issued another official statement. It said, "We believe the Negro, as well as those of other races, should have his full constitutional privileges as a member of society, and we hope that members of the Church everywhere will do their part as citizens to see these rights are held inviolate."[6]

Historic Preservation versus Contemporary Needs

Church policy affected its public relations in various ways. In America, for example, its building projects sometimes came into conflict with the burgeoning interests of historic preservation, especially in Utah. Once programs had outgrown an older chapel or tabernacle — a common occurrence in areas where there had been a ward since the nineteenth century — there was need for an updated facility. In many instances the older building was razed without hesitation and a new one built. There were cases, however, in which public sentiment for a historic building was strong enough to demand action to spare it. A number of buildings were placed on the National Register of Historic Sites, because of their representation of the pioneer heritage. Heber City, Utah's 1889 Wasatch Stake Tabernacle was such a case, and in 1965 the Church turned that building over to the city and the Wasatch County chapter of the Utah State Historical Society for preservation as a public theater and lecture facility.

The most well-publicized controversy concerned the stately Coalville Utah Tabernacle, on which construction had begun in 1879. The building was razed in March 1971 after a struggle that brought national attention. In later years, however, tensions were eased as the Church established a policy of more careful consideration of each case. A noteworthy example was the Bountiful Utah Tabernacle, originally dedicated in 1863. After over a hundred years some people wondered if the adobe structure had outlived its usefulness, but in 1975 the First Presidency designated it for preservation. With great care it was structurally reinforced, restored, and refurbished. It still stands as an impressive example of nineteenth-century LDS religious architecture.

The sixties and early seventies, then, were years of significant development. The Church's growth was impressive, important changes in policy and practice took place, its internationalism became more

---

[6]These comments are published in *Conference Report*, October 1963, p. 91, and *Improvement Era* 73 (February 1970): 70.

clearly apparent, and its efforts at correlation achieved much of what leaders had been seeking for sixty years. The Church's public image suffered slightly because of the overzealousness of some of its missionaries as well as its involvement in public affairs, but most of these were passing questions, and in later years new issues would affect public awareness. New challenges would also face the Saints, as the next few years became a time of both consolidation and innovation as well as a time of even greater determination to extend the gospel worldwide in the spirit of universal brotherhood and sisterhood.

CHAPTER 21

Toward a Universal Church, *1974–1990*

The years 1974 to 1990 were marked by continuing international growth for the Latter-day Saints and also by concern about the problems and commitments involved in building a worldwide Church. During this era many of the most far-reaching decisions and innovations of the twentieth century were made, nearly all of which related to the growth of the Church and its new international and intercultural challenges.

Two Prophets and Their Modern Messages

On December 30, 1973, Spencer W. Kimball was ordained the twelfth President of the Church. Born in Salt Lake City on March 28, 1895, President Kimball grew up in Thatcher, Arizona. The multi-talented young man was a star basketball player, a fine pianist, the student-body president in high school, and an honor graduate. He served as a missionary in the Central States Mission and in 1917 spent a semester attending the University of Arizona. On November 17, shortly after he was informed of his pending induction into the army, Spencer married Camilla Eyring in a quiet ceremony performed by the bishop in her home in Pima. The actual military call never came, however, and seven months later their marriage was sealed in the Salt Lake Temple.

Spencer began his professional career in the banking business, but in 1926 he became part owner and manager of an insurance and real estate firm in Safford, Arizona. Active in both civic and church affairs, he served on two town councils, as a member and officer in Rotary International, on numerous civic committees, and on the governing board of Gila College. In 1938 he became president of the Mount Graham Stake. Known for his kindness, his quiet and unpretentious

President Spencer W. Kimball visits the Mesa Temple on the occasion of its rededication. It was the first temple to be completely renovated and rededicated. Left to right: President Kimball, Temple President C. Bryant Whiting, President N. Eldon Tanner (first counselor to President Kimball), President Marion G. Romney (second counselor), and President Ezra Taft Benson of the Council of the Twelve. (LDS Church)

charity, and his humility, Spencer Kimball was also very much aware of his own weaknesses. This only magnified his personal amazement when, on July 8, 1943, he received a telephone call from President J. Reuben Clark, Jr., informing him of his call to the Quorum of the Twelve. He was ordained on October 7.

As an apostle Elder Kimball traveled extensively to many parts of the world. In 1963 he became chairman of the Missionary Committee and in 1965 he was assigned to supervise the seven South American missions. He also took special interest in the American Indians.

Spencer W. Kimball's life was remarkable, in part, for a series of miraculous recoveries from serious physical problems. At about age seven he nearly drowned. At age ten he was struck on one side of his head by a mysterious paralysis that doctors feared would be permanent and would disfigure his face, but after a priesthood blessing he recovered completely. At age thirteen he lay near death for weeks with typhoid fever, which was followed by a serious case of smallpox. After his call to the Council of the Twelve he suffered a series of heart attacks, and then, in 1957, developed a malignancy of the throat and vocal cords.

He lost one cord and part of another, as well as his voice, and was required to learn to speak again, this time in a softer, less audible tone. Despite all this, after he became President of the Church at age seventy-eight he informed the news media that he was in sound health and felt vigorous. Later a special miniature microphone was constructed for him to better amplify his voice for radio and television audiences.

President Kimball continued to stress messages that had characterized his years as an apostle. Among them was moral cleanliness and chastity, along with renewed emphasis on the principles of repentance and forgiveness. His 1969 book, *The Miracle of Forgiveness*, was widely read among the Saints. He also emphasized honesty, exemplary personal grooming, kindness, and many Christian virtues, while he denounced pornography and other degrading influences in the literature and theaters of the world and preached against the evils of racial prejudice. He passed away quietly on November 5, 1985.

Five days later, Ezra Taft Benson was ordained and set apart as President of the Church by the Quorum of the Twelve.

Ezra Taft Benson's life began with a miracle. He was born on August 4, 1899, in the Mormon farming community of Whitney, Idaho, but his mother, Sarah Dunkley Benson, had great difficulty delivering the 11¾-pound baby. The doctor pronounced him dead at birth and immediately turned to saving his mother's life. His father, George, however, gave the child a priesthood blessing and his two grandmothers rushed to the kitchen and began dipping him alternately in warm and cold water until finally they heard a cry.

The oldest of seven sons and four daughters, Ezra grew up on the family farm and became an energetic, robust, and frugal young man. In 1919 he enrolled at Utah State Agricultural College (now Utah State University) in Logan, and two years later went on a two-year mission to England. Later he enrolled in Brigham Young University, where he pursued a double major in animal husbandry and marketing and graduated with honors in 1926. That same year, on September 28, he married Flora Amussen in the Salt Lake Temple.

On the day of their marriage, Ezra and Flora Benson left Salt Lake City in a Model-T Ford truck and headed for Iowa State College in Ames, where Ezra had a scholarship. There he earned a master's degree in agricultural economics, after which he went back to farming in Whitney. He soon became county agricultural agent and then, in 1929, he was made head of Idaho's newly created Department of Agricultural

Economics and Marketing. He also served for seven years in the Boise, Idaho, stake presidency and became stake president in 1938.

In 1939 he became executive secretary of the National Council of Farmer Cooperatives, with headquarters in Washington, D.C. A year later he was called by Church leaders to be the first president of the newly organized Washington, D.C., Stake. At the outbreak of World War II he was named by U.S. President Franklin D. Roosevelt to a special agricultural advisory committee. In 1943 he was called to the apostleship, and he was ordained on October 7, 1943, the same day as Spencer W. Kimball.

Elder Benson's years as an apostle were punctuated with both Church and public service responsibilities, including two periods as European Mission president (1946 and 1964–65) and eight years (1953–61) as U.S. Secretary of Agriculture. Throughout his remarkable career he received numerous awards and honors, but they were relatively unimportant to him when compared with his devotion to the gospel of Christ. The messages he preached to the world included allegiance to the principles of the American Constitution, emphasis on love and service and, by example as well as in his public teachings, the sanctity and importance of the family. "This is not a day I have anticipated," he said at a press conference the day after he was set apart as President of the Church, but he shouldered his solemn new burden with the spirit of universal brotherhood. "I love all our Father's children of every color, creed, and political persuasion," he continued. "My only desire is to serve as the Lord would have me do."

The Lengthening Stride

Those who predicted that President Kimball's would be a short, "caretaker" administration could not have been more wrong. Instead, he set a pace of physical, spiritual, and mental activity that much younger men found difficult to follow. On October 3, 1974, the seventy-nine-year-old Church leader stood before a seminar for Regional and Mission Representatives. Filled with a vision of the universal mission of the Church, he was concerned with what the Latter-day Saints must do to help it fulfill its destiny worldwide. "If I need a title for what I desire to say this morning," he said, "I think it would be 'Lengthening Our Stride.' " That theme characterized the history of the Church itself for the rest of the decade and throughout the 1980s.

President Kimball demanded no more of the Saints than he did of himself. Early on the morning of Saturday, December 6, 1975, for example, he was at the Logan Temple conducting a solemn assembly for stake and ward priesthood leaders. It lasted all morning, after which he traveled to the Salt Lake Temple for another solemn assembly in the afternoon and still another that night. He preached no new policy or doctrine, but challenged priesthood leaders to show increased spirituality in the days ahead. The signs of spiritual and moral corruption were increasing in the world, he declared, but the Saints must be examples of righteous living. Seldom had this theme been more meaningful than when expressed by the aged Church leader in these impressive and sacred assemblies. His grueling schedule that day was little different from the pace he had maintained since becoming a General Authority. His personal vigor was contagious and seemed to spread a new vitality throughout the Church.

Missionary work received an immediate boost as President Kimball called for more young people from every land to accept mission calls. In April 1974 he declared to the Regional Representatives: "The question is frequently asked: Should every young man fill a mission? And the answer has been given by the Lord. It is 'Yes.' Every young man should fill a mission." The jump in missionary statistics was dramatic. For the previous five years the number of missionaries in the field had increased at a rate of less than a thousand per year, but the number jumped from 18,100 in 1974 to 22,500 in 1975. By 1985 29,300 missionaries were serving.

President Kimball also wanted the missionaries better prepared. "I am asking that we start earlier and train our missionaries better in every branch and every ward in the world," he told the Regional Representatives, and even as he was issuing this challenge several stakes were establishing their own missionary training programs. Effective language training already was taking place, and beginning in 1976, missionaries reported to a new, fifteen-million-dollar Language Training Mission near the BYU Campus. In 1978 the name was changed to Missionary Training Center and the program expanded to serve all missionaries. Later, smaller training centers were established in other areas of the world. In 1986, under President Benson's administration, the Church introduced teaching outlines that encouraged missionaries to explain the restoration of the gospel in their own words and to testify from the heart.

Church leaders also called for more retired married couples to volunteer for full-time missions. Such service varied from six to eighteen

Council of the Twelve, mid-1975. Seated: President Ezra Taft Benson, Mark E. Petersen, Delbert L. Stapley, LeGrand Richards, Hugh B. Brown, Howard W. Hunter. Standing: Gordon B. Hinckley, Thomas S. Monson, Boyd K. Packer, Marvin J. Ashton, Bruce R. McConkie, L. Tom Perry.

months, and the work of missionary couples ranged from regular proselyting to doing mission office work and temple and genealogical work, providing social services in underdeveloped areas, staffing visitors' centers at historic sites and temples, teaching at some Church schools, and many other possibilities. By the end of 1990 there were nearly 3,000 couples serving missions and over 43,000 missionaries in total.

The emphasis on missionary work was contagious in other ways. The Family-to-Family Book of Mormon program, for instance, demonstrated the commitment of many individual Saints. This program began as early as 1969 when Arlene Crawley, a Primary teacher from Kaysville, Utah, began working with hosts at Temple Square to obtain help for her family and her class to "send the Book of Mormon on a mission." Copies were placed with various missionaries and families throughout the world, and in 1975 the program was adopted by the Church. Eventually a full-time employee at the Missionary Department was placed in charge and numerous volunteer workers assisted in sending out the books. Church members who donated to the program had their personal testimonies, and usually their photographs, placed in the

One of the area conferences in 1975 was held in Hong Kong, China. These conferences symbolized the worldwide nature of the Church in the latter twentieth century. (LDS Church)

front of each book. By the end of 1989 over two million copies of the Book of Mormon were being placed annually through the Family-to-Family program. The administrative burden became so complex, however, that at the beginning of 1991 the Church discontinued the program. The Saints could still contribute money for copies of the Book of Mormon for missionary use, but it was no longer possible to place individual photographs and messages in each book.

President Kimball also stepped up the pace of area conferences. Previously one each year had been held, and in August 1974 he presided over a conference in Stockholm, Sweden, where 4,500 Saints from Denmark, Norway, Sweden, and Finland gathered to hear him and other General Authorities. The following year he scheduled seven such conferences in South America and Asia, and in 1976 seventeen in the Pacific and Europe.

Area conferences were all part of what President Kimball called "a great new adventure in taking the whole program of the Church out to the people of the whole world."[1] In each conference there were calls

---

[1]*Church News*, 12 July, 1975.

by President Kimball to greater service, messages from other General Authorities, and outstanding cultural programs by the people of the region involved. Many who attended had saved for months, sometimes at great personal sacrifice, to share the spiritual richness of the occasion. Beginning in 1983 these conferences were replaced by smaller-scale regional (multistake) conferences.

The Church also lengthened its stride in temple building, dedicating twenty-nine new temples (over half the total in operation) in this period alone, most of them outside North America. Near Washington, D.C., the largest temple ever completed by the Church was dedicated by President Kimball in November 1974. In addition, new temples were dedicated in Brazil, Japan, Samoa, Tonga, Chile, Tahiti, Mexico, Australia, the Philippines, Taiwan, Guatemala, the Federal Republic of Germany (West Germany), Sweden, South Africa, Korea, Peru, Argentina, the German Democratic Republic (East Germany), Toronto, Canada, and nine more United States locations: Seattle, Jordan River (Utah), Atlanta, Boise, Dallas, Chicago, Denver, Portland, and Las Vegas.

With additional temples came increased temple work for the dead, and to support this effort several changes were made in the way names were processed for ordinance work. Forms and procedures were simplified, and the Genealogical Library put its entire card catalog on computer to make searching for records easier. In 1985 the department opened a new $8.2 million library, and two years later was renamed the Family History Library. Under the department's supervision, stakes established research centers in meetinghouses where local volunteers could extract names from early records. Automation of name processing reached into the temples themselves, but in 1990 most of the computerized temple record keeping was suspended to save money and because the amount of information needed as a permanent record of ordinances was minimal. A new reference center for general public use was under preparation in the old Hotel Utah Building to open in 1993 to supplement the professional research library on West Temple Street.

The Church also continued to extend its seminary and institute programs worldwide. At the same time, the Church College of Hawaii was merged with BYU in 1974 and became the Brigham Young University—Hawaii Campus. At BYU the J. Reuben Clark, Jr., School of Law was dedicated in September 1975.

Growth and Internationalization: Statistical Observations

Church membership worldwide rose from 2,900,000 at the beginning of 1974 to about 7,600,000 at the end of 1990. Such rapid expansion was nothing new, but a few significant milestones were passed in this period and some interesting statistical observations could be made. In 1979, after 169 years of Church history, President Ezra Taft Benson of the Council of the Twelve organized the one thousandth stake, in Nauvoo, Illinois. By the end of 1990 there were 1,784 stakes, and it was anticipated that the two thousandth would be organized before the year 2000. On June 25, 1989, the Tecalco Mexico Stake was created, making Mexico the first nation outside the United States to reach one hundred stakes. Before the end of 1990, Mexico had 570,000 Latter-day Saints and 121 stakes.

The percentage of local missionaries in areas outside the United States, as opposed to American missionaries, increased remarkably. In 1977 the percentage was 15.2; ten years later that number had jumped to 30.5. In the Mexico Monterey Mission the new proportion was dramatic: 210 of the 240 missionaries were from Mexico itself. In Tonga 93 percent of the missionaries were Tongans. Such statistics plus the fact that stakes were organized in so many nations and an increasing number of missions were being presided over by local mission presidents all suggested the growing strength of the international Church.

The statistical growth of seminaries and institutes was also dramatic. Between 1974–75 and 1988–89, seminary enrollment increased from 174,000 to 250,000, and institute enrollment from 68,100 to 125,500. Much of that growth, particularly in seminaries, was international. In Japan, fifty-nine early-morning seminary classes were begun in 1985 with an enrollment of 334 students. In 1989, a year after classes opened in western Africa, there were 1,800 seminary students in Ghana and 1,300 in Nigeria. In the Caribbean, daily seminary classes began in 1984 and by 1989 there were over a thousand students each in the Dominican Republic and Puerto Rico, about 185 in Haiti, and 141 in Jamaica.

The Revelation on Priesthood

On June 8, 1978, in a letter to all general and local priesthood officers, the First Presidency made one of the most far-reaching announcements of the century.[2] President Spencer W. Kimball had received a revelation extending the priesthood to all worthy male members of the Church. Nothing could have given a greater boost to the Church's

---

[2]The letter is dated June 8, but the public announcement was made on Friday, June 9.

President Spencer W. Kimball. (Drawing by Judith Campion, courtesy Museum of Church History and Art)

universal thrust, and it was clear in the announcement that international expansion was one of the things that led to President Kimball's constant petitions to the Lord in the Salt Lake Temple:

> As we have witnessed the expansion of the work of the Lord over the earth, we have been grateful that people of many nations have responded to the message of the restored gospel, and have joined the Church in ever-increasing numbers. This, in turn, has inspired us with a desire to extend to every worthy member of the Church all of the privileges and blessings which the gospel affords.
>
> Aware of the promises made by the prophets and presidents of the Church who have preceded us that at some time, in God's eternal plan, all of our brethren who are worthy may receive the priesthood, and witnessing the faithfulness of those from whom the priesthood has been withheld, we have pleaded long and earnestly in behalf of these, our faithful brethren, spending many hours in the Upper Room of the Temple supplicating the Lord for divine guidance.
>
> He has heard our prayers, and by revelation has confirmed that the long-promised day has come when every faithful, worthy man in the Church may receive the holy priesthood, with power to

The temple near Washington, D.C., dedicated in 1974, presents an imposing image from certain vantage points outside the American capital city. (LDS Church)

exercise its divine authority, and enjoy with his loved ones every blessing that flows therefrom, including the blessings of the temple. Accordingly, all worthy male members of the Church may be ordained to the priesthood without regard for race or color. (D&C Official Declaration-2.)

Across the United States and Canada the announcement was headline, front-page news. *Time* and *Newsweek* stopped their presses to get it in their weekend editions, and it was picked up internationally. For Latter-day Saints, it was the kind of momentous event that became etched in their memory. Next to what it did for the blacks themselves, perhaps the most important consequence of the revelation was an outpouring of interracial brotherhood and sisterhood. Some Saints found in it an answer to their prayers while others found a spiritual challenge to overcome whatever remaining biases they had. Most, however, responded with an outpouring of joy, relief, gratitude, and genuine enthusiasm for the opportunity the revelation provided to strengthen interracial fellowship. Many received their own spiritual witnesses of the truth of the revelation, and literally cried for joy.

The announcement also gave rise to new discussions about the nature of revelation in the Church and how it contributes to the process of change. On August 17, 1978, Elder Bruce R. McConkie of the Quorum of the Twelve reminded a group of Church teachers that, despite past comments by some General Authorities, the new revelation, verified by powerful spiritual confirmations to all the General Authorities, changed everything:

> I have said the same things, and people write me letters and say "You said such and such, and how is it now that we do such and such?" And all I can say is that it is time disbelieving people repented and got in line and believed in a living, modern prophet. Forget everything I have said, or what President Brigham Young or President George Q. Cannon or whomsoever has said in days past that is contrary to the present revelation. We spoke with a limited understanding and without the light and knowledge that now has come into the world.
>
> We get our truth and our light line upon line and precept upon precept. We have now had added a new flood of intelligence and light on this particular subject, and it erases all the darkness and all the views and all the thoughts of the past. They don't matter any more.[3]

The revelation had an immediate impact on the Church around

---

[3]"All Are Alike Unto God," Address given to Church Education System Religious Education Symposium, BYU, August 18, 1978, p. 12.

the world. Worthy black families began to appear in the temples. Young blacks were called as missionaries, adding a rich dimension to the testimonies borne by all the missionaries. In South America, the tensions and discomforts once caused by the priesthood policy found solutions. In Brazil, for example, because of the high incidence of interracial marriage over several generations, people with black ancestry were difficult to identify; and prior to the revelation local Church policy required prospective priesthood holders to prove their ancestry through clear genealogical evidence before ordination. The policy was eventually liberalized to allow ordination for any who did not have obvious black features or whose patriarchal blessings identified them with one of the tribes of Israel, but it continued to be a test of faith for those who were still denied the priesthood. The new revelation provided a powerful reward for that faith. And in two black African states, Nigeria and Ghana, thousands of citizens who had been praying for years that the Church would send missionaries found their prayers answered before the year was out.

One story from Brazil provides a poignant illustration of the meaning of the new revelation. In 1975 the Church announced that a temple would be built in Sao Paulo, Brazil. General Authorities in Salt Lake City were deeply moved when they learned how black members donated money, assisted in the construction, and helped plan the dedication of a temple they did not expect to enter. Helvécio and Rudá Martins were such a couple. Sister Martins even sold her jewelry to help with the fund-raising. Like many other blacks, the Martinses had such strong faith in a future change that they even set up a missionary fund for their son. One day they visited the temple site and, Brother Martins reported later, "we were overcome by the Spirit. We held each other and wept." President Kimball dedicated the Sao Paulo Temple on October 30, 1978, less than five months after the revelation, and the Martins family was among the first to be sealed there. On March 31, 1990, Elder Martins was sustained to the Second Quorum of the Seventy—the first black to become a General Authority of the Church.

In Africa, meanwhile, the results of the revelation were equally powerful. In August 1978 the First Presidency sent Edwin Q. Cannon and Merrill Bateman on a short fact-finding trip to Nigeria and Ghana, where they met with many blacks who had been waiting for the Church for years. A few already had been baptized in America or elsewhere, but most—almost two thousand in Nigeria and a thousand in Ghana—were still praying for baptism. One of the leaders with whom they met

The matron of the Sao Paulo Temple, Sara B. Paulsen, welcomes Trina Christina, her mother Theresa Tobango, and sister, Miriam Marina, at one of the ten temple dedication services in October 1978. (Church News photo, courtesy Church Archives)

in Ghana was J. W. B. Johnson, who had been waiting for fourteen years and headed seven congregations of those who wanted to become Latter-day Saints. In Nigeria they met, among others, Ime Eduok, who since his baptism in California had been coordinating several groups in his area. After these visits they reported to the First Presidency that the people of these two nations were ready for baptism. In November, Edwin and Janath Cannon and Rendell and Rachel Mabey became the first official representatives of the International Mission in West Africa, and on November 21 nineteen Nigerians were baptized. Johnson became the Church's first district leader in Ghana, and Eduok was the first in Nigeria. Over seventeen hundred Nigerians and five hundred Ghanians were members of the Church when the Cannons and the Mabeys returned to Utah in 1979.

The first person baptized in Nigeria was Anthony Obinna, and his story reflects the outpouring of the Spirit long before the Church was established. It began in the late 1960s when, he reported,

> One night I was sleeping and a tall man came to me . . . and took me to one of the most beautiful buildings and showed me all the rooms. At the end he showed himself in the crucified form. Then in 1970 I found this book to read. It was the September 1958 *Reader's Digest.* There was an article entitled "The March of the Mormons" with a picture of the Salt Lake Temple. It was exactly the same building I had seen in my dreams.[4]

Obinna was one of those who wrote persistently to Salt Lake City seeking Church literature, requesting missionaries, and using what he received to teach his family and friends.

On April 1, 1980, the West African Mission was formally created. Ten years after the priesthood revelation, the first stake in western Africa, the Aba Nigeria Stake, was created on May 15, 1988, with David Eka as stake president. Missions were also organized in Zaire (1986) and Zimbabwe (1987), and the gospel spread rapidly among blacks in those countries. As missionary work continued to spread, branches were organized also in Ivory Coast, Liberia, Sierra Leone, and Swaziland, and by 1990 there was the beginning of activity in other places. In addition, the Church continued its growth in South Africa, where the government's apartheid policy perpetuated racial strife but where missionaries brought increasing numbers of blacks as well as whites into the gospel fold. On October 1, 1990, the Africa Area was created, with an estimated 48,000 Saints. There were five stakes in South Africa, two stakes in Nigeria, and others were scheduled for organization soon.

The International Church

The priesthood revelation gave a dramatic boost to the international nature of the Church, but other developments around the world were also important.

In the United States, members celebrated their nation's bicentennial in 1976. The Church participated, and American Saints were urged to learn and speak proudly of their religious, political, and cultural heritage. Stakes and wards throughout the nation sponsored appropriate

---

[4]Interview by Dale E. LeBaron, June 4, 1988, as quoted in Dale E. LeBaron, *All Are Alike Unto God* (Salt Lake City, Bookcraft, 1990), p. 5.

projects of a patriotic and civic nature, and President Kimball presided at an Independence Day devotional in the Washington, D.C., area.

A number of general conference addresses between October 1975 and October 1976 expressed appreciation for America, its Constitution, and its divine destiny, but in April 1976 President N. Eldon Tanner, first counselor in the First Presidency, also encouraged Latter-day Saints in every nation to take pride in their own heritage and demonstrate loyalty toward their own countries. "We are all reading and hearing much concerning the events connected with the founding of this country," he said, then reminded the Saints, "We would expect every man to be loyal to his native land—the land in which he was born, the land in which he lives, works, and rears his family. . . . All countries are greatly blessed by the Lord, and each is uniquely different in its beauties, its people, customs, and traditions." This comment symbolized the momentous transition through which the Church was passing: from an organization with a basic American orientation to an international Church in which one crucial challenge was for all Saints to separate their own political, racial, or cultural traditions from the essentials of the gospel. The goal was to fill the world not just with members of the Church but with Saints who loved and felt comfortable with each other, regardless of their individual backgrounds.

That goal was emphasized by President Kimball in his opening address at general conference in April 1975, when he explained what the term "gathering of Israel" meant in modern times.

> The "gathering of Israel" is effected when the people of the faraway countries accept the gospel and remain in their native lands. The gathering of Israel of Mexicans is in Mexico; in Scandinavia, for those of the northern countries; the gathering place for Germans is in Germany; and the Polynesians, in the islands; for the Brazilians, in Brazil, for the Argentines, in Argentina.[5]

The countries that held most of the world's population still had not opened their doors to the missionaries, however, and there was no immediate prospect that they would. In June 1975 President Kimball placed the responsibility squarely on the Saints themselves when he asked members worldwide to join in "a serious, continuous petition to the Lord" and pray for two things: that the Church could obtain all the missionaries needed to "cover the world as with a blanket," and

---

[5]*Conference Report*, April 1975, p. 4

that when the Church was ready to carry the gospel to inaccessible nations, the gates would be opened. The possibility of filling the entire world may have seemed remote to some, but President Kimball's determination knew no bounds. As he told the Regional Representatives in April 1975: "Sometimes it seems impossible, but again remember the little stone cut out of the mountain without hands which was destined to roll forth and fill the whole earth. It has gone a long way but it must go farther."

Church leaders increasingly encouraged American Saints to re-examine their cultural baggage. In 1974, President Kimball appointed David M. Kennedy as the First Presidency's international representative — an innovative position that had no defined place in the hierarchy of the Church. A man of broad experience in American business, government, and foreign affairs, David Kennedy's new Church assignment was to be an ambassador to the world and to work with various governments in order to resolve problems that had hindered the Church's activities within their borders. No one was better suited for the task, for he was acquainted with the principal political and financial leaders in nearly every country of the world and they, in turn, respected him for his honesty, directness, intelligence, and human decency. He remained in this position until his release on March 31, 1990.

The challenge was complex, partly because of restrictions on religious freedoms in countries where the Church was not yet established. Some governments recognized the right of members to worship together and teach their families and friends, but did not allow active proselyting. Others allowed for no personal religious expression. Under President Kimball's direction, Elder Kennedy visited many such countries including, in his first two years, Lebanon, Greece, Portugal, Thailand, India, Pakistan, Yugoslavia, the Philippines, Hungary, Poland, the German Democratic Republic, Iran, and Egypt. He met with government officials, explained Church policies, answered objections, explained how respected the Church was in other nations, and emphasized that the Church taught its members to obey and sustain the law in every nation. In some countries, such as Portugal in 1974, he was able to gain both recognition and the right to send missionaries.

In eastern and central Europe, some nations, such as Poland, liberalized their laws in the 1970s at least enough to allow recognition of the Church. In the meantime, local Latter-day Saints maintained contact with each other, and small groups of members continued to meet privately and tried to hold their struggling branches together. In addition, mission presidents in Switzerland and Austria, as well as other Church members and representatives, maintained what contact they could. In Poland, the Church was able to establish a small visitors center in Warsaw at the place where Sunday services were held, and it was manned by a Polish-speaking couple called to go into Poland as Church representatives. The same thing was true in Athens, Greece. It was a milestone in Church history when, on August 24, 1977, President Kimball, accompanied by Elder Kennedy and others, dedicated Poland for preaching the gospel and establishing the Church.

By 1988 the Church enjoyed an open presence not only in Poland but also in Yugoslavia, Hungary, and East Germany. Significantly, the communist government of the German Democratic Republic even allowed the Church to build a temple in Freiberg and dedicate it in 1985. This seemingly amazing concession was the result of good relations built up by General Authorities, as well as David Kennedy, who convinced the government that the Latter-day Saints would be good citizens, would not clamor to leave their country permanently, and would always, in the spirit of the twelfth Article of Faith, obey, honor, and sustain the law.

The effort to build goodwill extended around the world. In the People's Republic of China, Elder Russell M. Nelson of the Council of the Twelve was named an honorary professor by a medical school, and he and Elder Dallin H. Oaks had many discussions with Chinese leaders in the late 1980s. In November 1988, they were assured that the Latter-day Saints were free to practice their religious beliefs in China. On February 21, 1990, after a devastating earthquake in China, Elder Nelson presented a check on behalf of the First Presidency for $25,000 to the Chinese ambassador to the United States to help in reconstruction. In January 1990, Elder Oaks was invited to present an hour-and-a-half lecture about the Church to the Chinese Academy of Social Sciences. Important bridges were being built.

Such activities were vital to the eventual fulfillment of the world-wide mission of the Church, but even more essential were the continuing faith and struggles of Latter-day Saints in countries where the Church was not fully recognized or well established. "The [second world] war cost us everything," said one East German Saint. "But there was something they couldn't take—our testimonies." In 1981 a mission was organized to help direct the activities of Church members in the countries near Austria, and in 1987 it was reorganized as the Austria Vienna East Mission. Mission presidents visited neighboring countries when they could, local Church officers were appointed, and the Saints maintained the Church the best they could. The faithful Saints in Poland, along with couples who came in as Church representatives, kept the Church together. In Czechoslovakia the Saints often had to meet privately, but they managed to maintain their unity and faith and there was some small growth each year. In Yugoslavia the efforts of the Saints were enhanced by national basketball star Kresimir Cosic, who joined the Church while playing basketball at Brigham Young University and who later not only played basketball in Yugoslavia but coached the national Olympic team. He also served as president of the Church's Yugoslavian District. In the mid-1980s the Church gained recognition and built a small chapel in that country.

Then in 1989–90, central and eastern Europe went through a series of democratic revolutions that, among other things, resulted in more popularly elected governments, more freedom of the press, and, in most cases, new laws allowing more freedom of religion. The wall that had separated East and West Berlin since 1961 came down in 1989, and with this and other political developments it appeared as if the forty-five-year-old cold war had come to an end.

These changes led to official recognition for the Church in many previously restricted countries, some new missions were opened, and the number of young full-time missionaries grew. The German Democratic Republic Dresden Mission was organized on July 1, 1989, and then, on October 3, 1990, the two Germanies were reunified. In Czechoslovakia, recognition of the Church had been withdrawn for forty years, but in March 1990 it was restored. On July 1, 1990, twenty-eight new missions were created around the world, among them the Czechoslovakia Prague Mission, the Poland Warsaw Mission, the Hungary Budapest Mission, the Greece Athens Mission, and the Finland Helsinki East Mission. In the Soviet Union, where the Church had been seeking legal recognition since 1987, the parliament adopted a new freedom of religion law in 1990 that eased prohibitions and improved the legal status of all religious organizations. In September 1990 the Church gained recognition for the Leningrad Branch, a unit of the Baltic District of the new Finland Helsinki East Mission. Many of the missionaries already were trained in the Russian language, and missionary work in the Leningrad (renamed Saint Petersburg in 1991) area was proceeding on a limited basis.

The vision of a worldwide Church was still far from reality, for there were still many nations where the Church was not able to function

Missionaries in the Finland Helsinki East Mission gather with President Gary Browning and his family in Moscow, Russia, for their first mission conference, December 14–15, 1990. (Courtesy Bill McKane)

fully and which would not allow proselyting missionaries. Nevertheless, citizens who had been converted elsewhere often returned and formed the nucleus for local groups of Saints. Active Latter-day Saints from America and other countries came as businessmen, government representatives, foreign employees of local governments, or in some special service capacity. Such people maintained an active faith, often converted families and friends through private contacts, and helped create positive feelings for the Church. In India, for example, some national and state laws made proselyting by non-nationals illegal, but a few small branches existed and local missionaries were sometimes called. In 1977 Edwin and Elsie Dharmaraju of Hyderabad were converted to the Church while living in Samoa. The next year they returned to India on a short-term mission to teach the gospel to their family, and on December 27 eighteen family members were baptized. Though Edwin and Elsie returned to Samoa, their family became the nucleus for a branch in Hyderabad. Elsie's father, the Reverend P. Sreenivasam, was not a member of the

The BYU Jerusalem Center for Near Eastern Studies sponsors educational programs in biblical and contemporary studies in its handsome facility on the Mount of Olives near the Mt. Scopus campus of Hebrew University. (Brigham Young University Jerusalem Center)

Church, but he nevertheless translated the Book of Mormon into Telgu, one of India's major languages. It was printed in 1982, along with another full translation in Hindi. Total membership of the Church in India was eight hundred at the beginning of 1990.

There was a different kind of LDS presence in China where, under an agreement between the government of the People's Republic of China and the David M. Kennedy Center for International Studies at Brigham Young University, a number of people were teaching English in various universities. Most of these individuals were retired couples who had volunteered to live and teach in China for a year and who understood that they were not missionaries.

A Church presence was felt also in Israel, where BYU's Jerusalem Center for Near Eastern Studies, dedicated in 1989, provided classes for university students spending a semester there. Again, no missionary work was attempted, but to the degree that BYU could establish a positive image for itself through its educational programs, the attitudes of residents toward the Church, too, would be enhanced.

International growth was sometimes accompanied by public image problems, especially in areas where anti-American sentiment was rampant. In Latin America there were incidents of violence against the

Saints themselves or upon Church buildings, but these were usually seen as attacks upon a visible sign of American influence rather than upon the Church itself. In May 1989 two American missionaries serving in the Bolivia La Paz Mission were murdered; in July a chapel in Santa Cruz, Bolivia, was bombed; and that same month a group of Saints were held hostage in a chapel in Chile. In August 1990 two Peruvian missionaries were shot and killed in Peru. Similar incidents happened elsewhere and only increased Church concerns for divorcing itself from any political overtones that might accompany its presence in countries around the world. In June 1989, with no advance notice, all LDS missionaries as well as those of the Jehovah's Witnesses were expelled from Ghana. The reasons were not clear, though there was some feeling that a perceived threat of Americans dominating Ghanian people was among them. For a time the doors of LDS meetinghouses were closed and members were not allowed to assemble. Over the next year Church representatives met with Ghanian officials and gave assurances on the integrity of LDS intent. In December 1990 the Church was allowed to open its buildings and function normally. The official government announcement expressed satisfaction that the Church taught its people to honor the flag and promoted racial harmony.

The Intercultural Challenge

The challenge of crossing national boundaries was one thing, but crossing cultural boundaries was another challenge entirely. Many cultural challenges were facing the Church in the late twentieth century, largely because the gospel was still often transmitted and interpreted in American terms. One priesthood manual, for example, admonished husbands to treat their wives with love and respect, certainly an appropriate universal theme, but then urged them to kiss their wives each time they left the house or returned home. This created a cultural conflict that most American manual writers would never perceive. In Japan, for example, public kissing was not culturally acceptable. If a father followed all the suggestions in the priesthood manual his children might well want to know why he was "biting" their mother. On a different level, American manual writers were traditionally enthralled with capitalism, but many Latin American Saints identified capitalism with wealthy upper classes and economic and political oppression. Such problems suggested that the Church as an institution, as well as the Saints as individuals, still had a ways to go in their efforts to teach and practice the gospel in universal terms.

One response of the Church was to instruct those who produced manuals to simplify them. Texts were to focus on essential gospel principles and avoid illustrations that represented peculiarly American, or Utah, cultural values. The result was a new genre of manuals for many Church organizations that were short, focused on the scriptures and basic principles. This approach left ample opportunity for local teachers to expand according to their own concerns and inspiration. In addition, the international magazines translated and published articles from the *Ensign* and other Church periodicals but also printed articles more specifically directed to people of specific language areas. Beyond that, the effort to replace American mission presidents in non-American countries with native leaders, as well as the effort to increase the percentage of local missionaries, helped avoid misunderstandings and miscommunication.

The intercultural problem involved more than moving between countries, for within the United States itself a myriad of cultural differences existed. In large urban areas the Church grew among a variety of ethnic groups who, though loyal American citizens, were trying to cling to the language and cultural traditions of their ancestral heritage. America itself was no longer idealized as the "melting pot," in which peoples of all nations would be amalgamated into a common culture. The new metaphor was that of a salad bowl, where there was loyalty to common principles but also a rich variety because of identifiable and desirable differences within the common boundary. The Church, too, might be thought of as a huge salad bowl, particularly in America, where white Americans, Native Americans, blacks, hispanics, Asian-Americans, and a variety of other cultural groups were all united in the common goals of the restored gospel but were also attempting to maintain their distinctive characteristics while appreciating those of others.

What happened in the Los Angeles area in the 1970s and 1980s is illustrative of the challenges. Literally millions of immigrants from other nations, particularly Asian and Central and South American nations, reshaped the ethnic composition of Los Angeles and many surrounding communities. In addition, the growing black population gradually dominated many former middle- and upper-class white neighborhoods, and this, together with a rising crime rate, caused many whites, including Mormons, to leave. Because of the flight from the center of Los Angeles, one ward was dissolved in 1971 and the population of the Los Angeles Stake continued to decline.

By the end of the 1970s a sizeable number of Korean Saints were

A small group of Relief Society sisters meet in Puerto Rico. (Church Archives)

residing within the stake boundaries. John K. Carmack, a counselor to stake president Winfield Q. Cannon, had served with the American military in Korea and learned to love the Korean people. At President Cannon's direction, Carmack organized a Korean Sunday School that consisted initially of about fifty members. Soon the mission president assigned two full-time missionaries to work with the Koreans, through an interpreter, and they helped the group begin to grow. Then, early in the 1970s, a proposal was made for organizing a Korean branch, but this raised policy questions both locally and at Church headquarters. Some felt that such language group branches only resulted in built-in segregation and second-class citizenship for the minority groups. They preferred the advantages of an integrated ward. Others believed that special units for minorities provided better training in leadership and better opportunities to teach gospel principles unencumbered by language and cultural barriers. The proposed unit was not immediately approved, but in 1977 a dependent Korean branch was finally organized at the Wilshire Ward. About the same time Korean-speaking missionaries were called to work in Los Angeles, and in December the branch became the Los Angeles Second Branch. By 1987 it had around 250 members.

In 1972 John K. Carmack was named president of the Los Angeles

Stake, and shortly thereafter he and his counselors felt inspired that contemplated plans for abandoning the central city Wilshire Ward chapel were wrong. Immediately they set about changing directions, fired by a vision of what the stake could become: a kind of microcosm of the worldwide Church. The result was a new viability for the Church in an area where some people once predicted it would practically disappear. It seemed almost providential that the restored and refurbished Wilshire Ward chapel was dedicated on June 11, 1978, just two days after the announcement of the priesthood revelation. The Saints wept with gratitude as they began to foresee the future intercultural potential of the Church in that area.

Meanwhile, the number of Spanish-speaking Saints in the Los Angeles area slowly grew, but efforts to integrate with the Anglo wards met with only mixed success. Many wanted to be taught in their own language, and belong to a Church community in which they could preserve some of their own cultural traditions. By the end of 1964 hispanic Saints were holding their own sacrament meetings, and eventually a small dependent branch was created for them. Stake leaders worked to stamp out prejudice among Anglo members and to strengthen the Spanish-speaking people. The branch grew, a seminary program for Spanish-speaking youth was initiated, and Mexican Americans were encouraged to continue their annual folk festivals and other cultural activities. Finally, in 1984, the Huntington Park West Stake was created, completely staffed by Spanish-speaking people.

Blacks in the Los Angeles area, meanwhile, faced problems of racial discrimination, poverty, and growing violence. In 1965 a series of devastating riots in Watts, center of the black community, brought turmoil and stress to everyone in the area. While the riots were not aimed at the Church, it was, nevertheless, an object of hate and abuse because of its priesthood policy. Following the revelation on priesthood, however, missionary work among blacks increased dramatically, and eventually the Southwest Branch of the Huntington Park Stake was established in Watts. Unfortunately, when some people encouraged blacks from other areas to attend the Southwest Branch, it was interpreted by some as another attempt at segregation. William W. Tanner, the new Los Angeles Stake president, supported the Watts area branch for local residents, but encouraged other blacks to seek full integration into their own wards. Soon blacks in Watts as well as the other wards were receiving the full blessings of the gospel and feeling less discrimination. And black membership grew.

There was also a growing Chinese population, and in 1980 the Los Angeles Fifth Branch, the first independent Chinese branch in southern California, was organized. It was small, but by the end of the 1980s it was viable and had strong priesthood leadership.

Los Angeles was not the only metropolitan area with such challenges, for they occurred in many other parts of the United States, including San Francisco, Chicago, and New York City, where similar approaches were taken. Nowhere were all the problems of cultural diversity within the Church solved, but Church leaders and members themselves were moving toward greater intercultural understanding.

Among the dilemmas faced by Church leaders in their continuing effort to respond to the needs of various groups was the question of whether to continue special programs for American Indians. As the Bureau of Indian Affairs began closing government schools and shifting Native American students to the public schools, for example, the need for Indian seminaries declined; by the end of the 1980s this thirty-year-old program had been phased out. In addition, the Indian student placement program was greatly cut back and special Indian education programs at BYU were eliminated. Some scholarship funds were still specifically earmarked for Indian students, and a Native American Studies program continued to offer classes related to Indian history and culture, but special admittance requirements and classes designed specifically for Indian students were discontinued. All these programs had served the Native American Saints well, but as educational opportunities and other circumstances changed, so also did Church policy.

Unfortunately, such changes were not well received by some people, and they even led one General Authority, Elder George P. Lee of the Seventy, into direct disagreement and confrontation with the First Presidency and Quorum of the Twelve. A Navajo Indian himself, Elder Lee argued that through these and other changes the Church was abandoning its divine obligation to the Lamanites. Church leaders, on the other hand, felt that in their effort to take the full Church program to all the native people of North and South America, as well as to the rest of the world, they could no longer maintain specialized programs for a few. The discussions went on privately for months; but finally, after it was clear that he could not be reconciled to the decisions of the leaders, Elder Lee was excommunicated on September 1, 1989.

Course Corrections: Major Changes in Administrative Policies and Programs

Like the captain of a ship at sea, headed toward some predetermined destination but often confronted by winds and storms, Church leaders in this era found the need for course corrections coming with increasing frequency. In nearly every instance these administrative and program changes were a response to the rapidly changing needs of members created by growth and by changing social and economic challenges. Only a brief summary of some of those not already discussed speaks volumes about what was happening.

In 1975 the Church divested itself of the fifteen hospitals it had operated for many years in Utah, Idaho, and Wyoming. It was felt that the Church could more wisely spend its money on the health needs of members around the world rather than in a few intermountain states. The hospitals were turned over to a nonprofit corporation, Intermountain Health Care, Inc. Other Church-sponsored health services were soon expanded. More health-services missionaries, for example, were called to augment the 120 already serving on Indian reservations in the United States and among members in twenty foreign countries.

Another sign of growth came when President Kimball announced that, as President of the Church, he no longer had time to act as board chairman of various businesses in which the Church held substantial interest. His lengthening stride was in the direction of more vigorous church activity, and he left the business world in other hands. Other General Authorities remained as chairmen and/or board members for Church-owned corporations.[6]

Because of declining income, the Church contracted out the operation of the historic Hotel Utah, then, in August 1987, closed it for good. The building was extensively renovated for use as a meetinghouse

---

[6]At the end of 1990 these included Beneficial Development Company, Beneficial Life Insurance Company, Bonneville International Corporation (which, in turned, owned various broadcast facilities), Deseret Book Company, Deseret News Publishing Company, Deseret Trust Company, Farm Management Company, Temple Square Hotel Corporation, Utah Home Fire Insurance Company, and Zions Securities Corporation (a holding company for Church real estate). The Church also owned Laie Resorts, Inc., a small motel, restaurant, and service station located adjacent to the Polynesian Cultural Center in Hawaii. All these came under the umbrella of Deseret Management Company, which performed audits, generated consolidated financial statements, and filed consolidated income tax returns. Church businesses contributed significantly to the tax base of their states and communities. In addition, the Church was a minor stockholder in several other businesses, and a major stockholder in ZCMI.

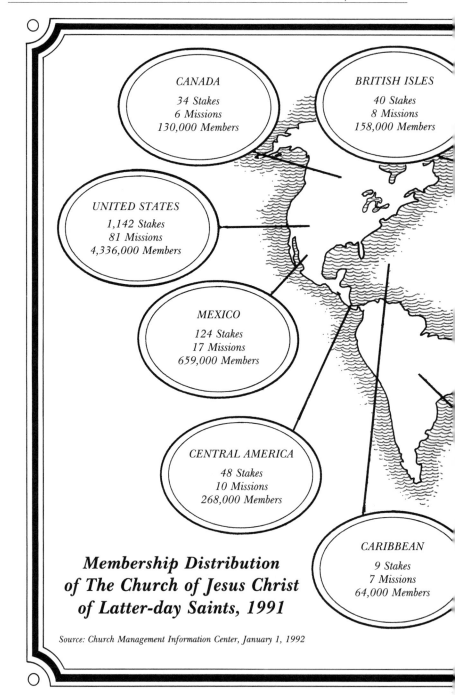

CANADA
34 Stakes
6 Missions
130,000 Members

BRITISH ISLES
40 Stakes
8 Missions
158,000 Members

UNITED STATES
1,142 Stakes
81 Missions
4,336,000 Members

MEXICO
124 Stakes
17 Missions
659,000 Members

CENTRAL AMERICA
48 Stakes
10 Missions
268,000 Members

CARIBBEAN
9 Stakes
7 Missions
64,000 Members

**Membership Distribution
of The Church of Jesus Christ
of Latter-day Saints, 1991**

Source: Church Management Information Center, January 1, 1992

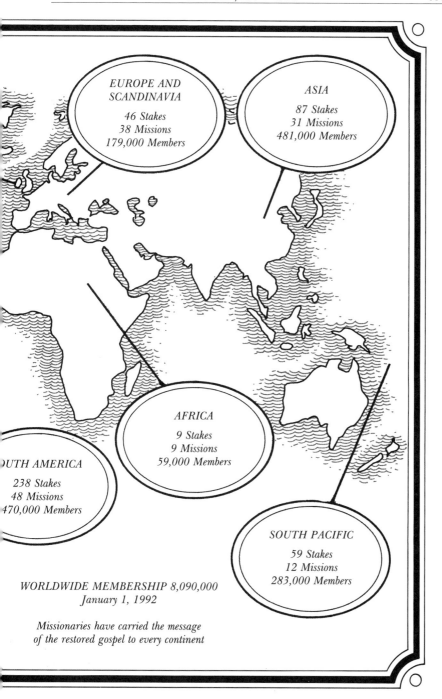

EUROPE AND
SCANDINAVIA

46 Stakes
38 Missions
179,000 Members

ASIA

87 Stakes
31 Missions
481,000 Members

AFRICA

9 Stakes
9 Missions
59,000 Members

SOUTH AMERICA

238 Stakes
48 Missions
470,000 Members

SOUTH PACIFIC

59 Stakes
12 Missions
283,000 Members

WORLDWIDE MEMBERSHIP 8,090,000
January 1, 1992

Missionaries have carried the message
of the restored gospel to every continent

and Church office building. But closure did not entirely remove the Church from the hotel business. In 1990 it reopened the remodeled Hotel Temple Square as the Inn at Temple Square.

In 1974 the names of stakes and missions were changed to reflect their geographic locations. Each now carried the name of a city and a state or country and could be identified alphabetically by this location-title. The former New Zealand North Mission, for example, head-quartered in Auckland, was renamed the New Zealand Auckland Mission. With over seven hundred stakes and nearly 140 missions by the end of 1975, a more convenient and understandable designation system was necessary.

After 1975 annual churchwide conferences for the Primary, Sunday School, and Relief Society were no longer held, and in 1986 Relief Society boards were greatly reduced in size. The traditional June Conference for YWMIA and YMMIA was also discontinued, and the instructions and cultural activities associated with these meetings were thereafter conducted on a regional and local level. Beginning in 1977, coordination of cultural arts and sports programs was given to new activities committees.

Early in 1976 a new Correlation Department was organized, separate from the Department of Internal Communications. The latter, renamed the Curriculum Department in 1978, would continue to prepare and plan instructional materials and supervise Church magazines and other publications, including the scriptures. The new Correlation Department would be responsible for long-range planning, review of published materials, and evaluation of Church programs.

In May 1975 a new area supervisory program was adopted for the Church outside North America, but in January 1984 the First Presidency announced an even more significant shift. At that point the world was divided into thirteen supervisory areas that included both stakes and missions. A presidency chosen from among the General Authorities presided over each. In 1991 there were twenty-two such areas headed by members of the Quorums of the Seventy. In a church faced with the increasingly serious challenge of maintaining unified direction as it grew in unprecedented numbers around the world, this new organizational development was a necessity.

The area supervisory program was made possible partly because of another major administrative change introduced by President Kimball. During the October 1975 general conference he announced the reconstitution of the First Quorum of the Seventy, which had not been filled since the Saints left Nauvoo. Now, with a burgeoning church creating a need for more top-level supervision, it was decided to recall it into being. Members would be General Authorities of the Church, having the same authority as Assistants to the Twelve (who were called into the Seventies a year later). One of the assignments given to them was to serve as department and general priesthood and auxiliary heads at Church headquarters. In 1989 the Second Quorum of the Seventy was organized, with still another innovation. The members of that quorum would be General Authorities, but they would be called for temporary terms, usually five years.

All seventies quorums in the stakes of the Church were discontinued in October 1986, and local seventies joined the elders quorums or were ordained to the office of high priest. Henceforth the only seventies in the Church would be General Authorities. Holding the office of high priest, their major function would be to assist the First Presidency and the Quorum of the Twelve in spreading the gospel and supervising the affairs of the kingdom of God around the world.

In 1978 the Church began the practice of placing members of the First Quorum of the Seventy on emeritus status for reasons of age or health, and the following year the Patriarch to the Church, Eldred G. Smith, also became an emeritus General Authority. Because stake and other specially appointed patriarchs were readily available to carry out his previous churchwide functions, no replacement was appointed.

In 1977 the First Presidency made a distinction between ecclesiastical and temporal affairs. Ecclesiastical affairs and the Church Education System were to be administered by the Quorum of the Twelve and temporal affairs by the Presiding Bishopric. One important result was that youth programs, formerly the responsibility of the Presiding Bishopric, came under the wing of the Twelve.

In 1980 a consolidated meeting schedule was inaugurated, in which meetings were placed into a three-hour block on Sunday rather than the former pattern of holding sacrament meeting, Sunday School, priesthood meeting, Primary, and Relief Society at various times throughout the day and week. The Young Women also began meeting on Sunday morning for the first time in history. The immediate catalyst was the need for energy savings during a time of crisis, but the First Presidency also hoped to give families more time for scripture study, service, and other activities at home.

A revision of the hymnal used since 1950 was completed and published in 1985. Most of the familiar hymns were retained and new ones were added. Some were written by Latter-day Saints and expressed distinctive doctrines and practices of the restored Church, while others were adopted from the rich musical traditions of other Christian churches. This mixture continued a song-practice begun by Emma Smith in 1835. The new compilation also incorporated extensive indexes and scriptural annotations. In 1988, to encourage the learning of new hymns, the Sunday School reintroduced a song-practice time when Sunday School opening exercises were incorporated into the block meeting format.

In 1987 the International Mission was discontinued. Originally organized in 1972 to look after the needs of Saints who lived in places not specifically assigned to other missions or stakes, its vast area of responsibility was divided among the various administrative areas.

In the 1980s and early 90s, three major modifications affecting financial contributions were announced. The first came in April 1982, when the local share of costs for meetinghouse construction was reduced to 4 percent and, for a time, made contingent on tithing faithfulness. Eventually the full cost of new buildings was shifted to general Church funds.

In the second adjustment, ward and stake budget donations were no longer required after January 1, 1990. Instead, all operating expenses of local units were paid from tithes and offerings. As Elder Boyd K. Packer explained in a satellite-broadcast "Member Finances Fireside" in February, the new policy was intended to save money for the Saints and also to increase their spiritual strength by encouraging members to do more as families rather than rely on ward and stake programs. Previously some wards comprised of affluent individuals had collected large sums of money for such things as expensive youth excursions or parties. Other wards had few if any such activities, for their people simply could not afford them. Under the new program ward budgets would be tied to sacrament meeting attendance, and no extra funds could be solicited for any purpose. "It is my personal conviction," Elder Packer declared, "that this change in budgeting will have *enormous* reactivating influence on those who have held back because they could not afford the cost of Church activities." Finally, he said, "I could not express to you, my brethren and sisters, the depths of my feeling about what has been announced. It is a course correction; it is an inspired move."

The third major financial change came on the heels of a May 22, 1990, ruling by the U.S. Supreme Court that money given directly to missionaries was not a deductible donation under federal tax law. The Church had previously urged members supporting missionaries to donate their money to the ward missionary fund for distribution by the bishop. Now this became the standard procedure. At the same time, the Brethren had long been considering what to do about drastic variations in missionary expenses around the world: from $100 per month to $750, depending on the mission. With the court's decision acting as a possible catalyst, the First Presidency announced that beginning January 1, 1991, the contributions required to support missionaries called from the United States and Canada would be equalized at $350 U.S. or $400 Canadian. Families with missionaries in the field were to contribute directly to the ward missionary fund. Collected at Church headquarters, these funds were sent to mission presidents, who distributed them as they deemed appropriate. Like the course correction a year earlier, this one also had great spiritual potential and could encourage members generally to donate to the ward missionary fund, whether or not they had missionaries in the field.

The Compassionate Church: Community and World Involvement

Latter-day Saints continued to be involved in their communities and in compassionate service around the world, and there were numerous examples of direct Church involvement in humanitarian undertakings. When the Teton Dam in Idaho's Snake River Valley burst in 1976, thousands of Saints in nearby areas and from as far away as central Utah flocked to help clear debris, clean up homes, and replace goods destroyed in the resulting flood. In July 1980, the First Presidency requested members of the Church to contribute to a special LDS refugee relief fund. Food, medical supplies, and building materials were shipped to Ghana, Colombia, and Tahiti in 1983 when these areas were hit by food shortages, an earthquake, and hurricanes, respectively.

In January 1985 a special fast day was held throughout the Church and the Saints were urged to contribute funds for famine relief in Ethiopia and elsewhere. More than $6 million was collected, and a second fast day in November brought in an additional $3.8 million. Funds from the first fast were used primarily for immediate famine relief efforts, and after the second fast money became available also for long-term development projects. In Nigeria, for example, in 1987, the Church joined hands with Africare, a nonprofit volunteer organization, to help

The Christus *by Bertel Thorvaldsen is the central point of the Visitors Center on Temple Square in Salt Lake City. It reminds all visitors of the central focus of the LDS faith. (Church Archives)*

develop two demonstration farm plots, wells to provide rural villages with pure drinking water, the development of fifteen acres of virgin land for small-plot farming, and training for young people in agriculture. Many of the volunteer workers on the Africare projects were Latter-day Saints, and the first farm demonstration project was established within the LDS meetinghouse compound at Aboh Mbaise.

In 1991 the Church shipped tents, sleeping bags, and other supplies to Iran to help victims of a devastating earthquake.

Members of the Church were also reminded that they should become personally involved in compassionate service wherever needed. In October 1990 Bishop Glenn L. Pace, second counselor in the Presiding Bishopric, urged members to not wait for the Church itself to designate ways in which they could take part in worthy causes, and to not assume that their responsibilities ended with their Church donations. "Wherever we live in the world," he said, "there is pain and sorrow all around us," and as individuals the Saints should take the initiative in compassionate service in their own neighborhoods and communities. "The fact that a particular activity is not sponsored by the Church does not mean it is not worthy of a Church member's support," he cogently reminded them. "We must reach out beyond the walls of our own church. In humanitarian work, as in other areas of the gospel, we cannot become the salt of the earth if we stay in one lump in the cultural halls of our beautiful meeting houses." As a result of such service, he assured the Saints, and through the power of the Holy Ghost, "a sanctification takes place within our souls and we become more like our Savior."[7]

Politics and Public Policy

Church leaders continued to urge the Saints to participate responsibly in the political process, but it also continued to refuse to support particular political parties or to take sides officially on political issues unless they were considered to be issues also of morality. A Special Affairs Committee, organized in 1974, gathered information on various questions that affected the Church and helped formulate a Church response.

Perhaps the most controversial issue was connected with the rising tide of American feminism, and particularly the proposed Equal Rights Amendment to the U.S. Constitution. Like other American women, LDS women were divided on the issue. Those who supported the amendment felt this was the best way to move toward more realistic political, economic, and social equality for women. Opponents, even if they supported the objectives, felt that the federal government should not be involved. In October 1976 the First Presidency issued an official statement recognizing that there had been injustices to women before the law and that many rights still needed to be achieved, but vigorously opposing the ERA as the means to reach the objective. The effect was divisive, but eventually not enough states ratified the amendment to make it part of the Constitution. In Utah the influence of the Church contributed strongly to the defeat of the amendment, and in several other states, particularly Florida, Virginia, and Illinois, Latter-day Saints, with encouragement from the Church, worked effectively with other groups opposed to it.

Other public issues also directly concerned Church leaders, who opposed legalized abortion and gambling, called for stronger measures against child abuse, urged parental control of sex education, and opposed the move for homosexual "rights." General Authorities repeatedly urged members to become involved in efforts to stop the spread

---

[7]*Ensign*, November 1990, pp. 9–10.

of pornography, and such efforts were particularly successful in Utah, Arizona, and California. In California the Church joined with religious and family-oriented organizations and was effective in helping to promote passage of a law prohibiting the possession of child pornography. When the law went into effect in 1990, the Church received public commendation for its help.

At another level, Church leaders were concerned with the arms race that characterized the cold war, and particularly with the potentially devastating possibility of nuclear armament. In 1981 the United States was considering basing its mobile multiple warhead missile system, the MX system, in the Utah-Nevada desert. In May the First Presidency issued a strongly worded statement decrying the idea of "the building of vast arsenals of nuclear weaponry. . . . Our fathers came to this western area to establish a base from which to carry the gospel of peace to the peoples of the earth," the statement said. "It is ironic, and a denial of the very essence of that gospel, that in this same general area there should be constructed a mammoth weapons system potentially capable of destroying much of civilization."[8] Ultimately the MX site was moved to Wyoming, partly, some observers believed, because of U.S. President Ronald Reagan's respect for the Church.

The Church and the Changing Role of Women

The role of women in society changed rapidly in the last part of the twentieth century, particularly in the United States. Women became more deeply involved in business, law, medicine, and all the other professions, and a larger proportion of mothers than ever before found their way into the working place. Inflation and other financial problems associated with the changing economic structure of the nation made two-income families commonplace, but many married women and mothers worked for personal enrichment and to make meaningful professional contributions. The number of women enrolling in colleges and universities, including graduate schools, increased dramatically.

All this presented a dilemma to the Church for, in some cases, it seemed to fly in the face of the traditional emphasis on the importance of having mothers in the home. Church leaders became concerned, also, when radical feminists included sexual emancipation, abortion

---

[8]"Statement of the First Presidency on Basing of the MX missile," *Church News*, 9 May 1981, p. 2.

Members of the general presidencies of the Relief Society, Young Women, and Primary offer counsel in an annual General Women's Meeting in the Tabernacle. (Photo printed in the November 1991 Ensign, *© The Church of Jesus Christ of Latter-day Saints. Used by permission.)*

on demand, public sex education, and birth control in their agendas. Such rhetoric, they felt, tended to belittle motherhood, which was considered sacred. Some Mormon women were satisfied with the way things were. Others sought a new synthesis that would preserve the best of the old values, including the sacredness of the family, but at the same time recognize and accommodate new needs and perspectives. The latter feeling gave rise to *Exponent II*, a privately published periodical begun in 1974 by a few Mormon women in Boston. It provided an unofficial forum for discussing women's concerns of every sort.

Church leaders continued to stress the values associated with motherhood, the family, and home, though they also began more frequently to emphasize the broader concept of parenthood (which included more serious consideration of the role of the father in the home), Christian service, personal development, and sisterhood. Also, in 1978 an annual General Women's Meeting was inaugurated. In the long run each Mormon woman had to make her own decisions and, if married, work out with her husband their common goals. By 1990 it appeared that many young couples were cultivating a relationship based on a commitment to the family, religious testimony, and Church activity but also on a new synthesis of these values with a recognition of the need some women felt to find individual self-fulfillment through education, employment, and service. The Relief Society provided continued opportunity for receiving spiritual strength, building homemaking skills, and participating in meaningful compassionate service. It also provided a broad-based sisterhood for women around the world. At the same time, many Mormon women found increasing opportunity to involve themselves in public service outside the structure of the Church, and their endeavors increased public understanding of the Latter-day Saints in general.

The Public Image

The Church's image was enhanced in many other ways, including its own public relations programs and the involvement of members in public life. Church television spots, especially the "Home Front" series dealing with family values and used by numerous stations as public service features, promoted positive attitudes toward the Church. Inserts on similar themes in *Reader's Digest* in 1978 brought thousands of inquiries for information. Brigham Young University's achievements in sports also brought the Church considerable positive attention.[9]

One of the most well-known agents in making friends for the Church continued to be the Mormon Tabernacle Choir, with its weekly broadcasts and regular tours. In July 1976, for example, the choir presented several concerts in connection with the U.S. bicentennial celebration. In 1979 it toured Japan and Korea, presenting thirteen concerts in six cities. In 1987, in connection with the bicentennial of the U.S. Constitution, it joined with the internationally known barbershop chorus "Vocal Majority" and the Constitution Symphony Orchestra for two concerts in Dallas, Texas, attended by an estimated 25,000 people. The following summer it made a 25,000–mile tour to Hawaii, New Zealand, and Australia, performing seventeen concerts. Something of its enduring attraction was suggested when, on February 15, 1987, it performed its 3,000th radio broadcast, and on July 16, 1989, it commemorated sixty years of continuous network radio broadcasting on the Sunday-morning program, "Music and the Spoken Word."

The Church's visitors centers at temples and historic sites contin-

---

[9]BYU received national attention in, among other things, gymnastics, golf, track, football, and basketball. In 1984 its football team achieved a Number 1 ranking in the nation for its 13–0 season, and in 1990 quarterback Ty Detmer received the coveted Heisman Trophy.

ued to attract visitors, including 4.2 million who came to Temple Square in Salt Lake City in 1988. An updated version of the film "Man's Search for Happiness" was released a year earlier for use in visitors centers. The public relations value of temple dedications was illustrated in July 1989 when over 314,000 people, more than half of them non-LDS, visited the Portland, Oregon, Temple during its three-week prededication open house, which was publicized by eighty radio spots and sixty television spots. Pictures of Christ displayed throughout the temple reaffirmed to visitors that the Savior was at the center of LDS worship.

For Latter-day Saints, the years leading up to and beyond the Church's 150th anniversary in 1980 brought forth an expanded interest in its history and historic sites. Monuments and markers, historic restorations, publications, and activities of many kinds helped strengthen members in their understanding of their religious heritage.

The story of pioneering in the American West was one of the subjects highlighted during this period. The trail from Nauvoo to Salt Lake City received national attention in 1978 when the U.S. Congress added the "Mormon Pioneer National Historic Trail" to the network of significant historical trails. In Utah, the Church acquired the Brigham Young Winter Home in St. George and the Jacob Hamblin Home in Santa Clara in 1978 and historic Cove Fort ten years later. The restoration of these places along with the renovation to preservation standards of several magnificent tabernacles, including those in Paris, Idaho, Honolulu, Hawaii, and Brigham City, Provo, and Logan, Utah, reemphasized the importance of enriching contemporary life through remembering past accomplishments. In Nauvoo in 1978, the Relief Society celebrated women's roles in the Church with a "Monument to Women" sculpture garden funded by donations from women worldwide. Nauvoo Restoration, Inc., in the late 1980s, sponsored a major renovation of the Carthage Jail and adjacent visitors center and rebuilt and furnished several important buildings in Nauvoo. Farther east, the Church acquired and partially restored in 1982 the Grandin Printing Building, where the first edition of the Book of Mormon was printed. A year after celebrating its fiftieth anniversary in 1987, the Hill Cumorah Pageant, "America's Witness for Christ," was given a new script and new music.

The eighties also witnessed a steady outpouring of articles and books on the history of the Church. Deseret Book Company, the *Ensign*, and other Church magazines, as well as numerous non-Church magazines, journals, and book publishers, fed public interest with new

The Bountiful (Utah) Tabernacle, dedicated in 1863, is an impressive
example of nineteenth-century LDS architecture. In 1975 it was designated
for preservation by the First Presidency. (Utah State Historical Society)

information about many specialized topics, and especially the early
years of LDS history. Increasingly, historians outside the Church looked
to Mormon studies as a legitimate field for intellectual inquiry. This
helped encourage LDS writers in their own research and brought new
respect for the Church as publications from many perspectives avoided
polemical writing in favor of serious inquiry. It also contributed to a
vigorous, ongoing debate on the nature of historical writing.

This active interest in early Church history had one tragic consequence. Spurred on by increasing attention to original documents from
the Joseph Smith years, collectors and dealers in early manuscripts
rejoiced initially when Salt Lake documents dealer Mark W. Hofmann
"discovered" several rare and important manuscripts that altered or
added to certain known details in the historical records. Some of them
related to such things as the origin of the Book of Mormon, but eventually many of the items sold to the Church, including all of the most
noteworthy documents, proved to be skillful forgeries. In October 1985,

in an attempt to avoid exposure, Hofmann planted pipe bombs that killed two persons and ultimately drew attention to the fact that he was the creator of the fabricated records. In January 1987, after a long and complex investigation and, finally, a plea-bargaining agreement, he formally confessed to the scheme. Subsequent testimony and investigation revealed that the Church was not the only victim of Hofmann's deceit. He had forged and sold hundreds, perhaps thousands, of manuscripts and printed documents relating to American history.

Many of Hofmann's lucrative creations appeared during a decade when interest in Church history was heightened by numerous anniversary celebrations. They centered around the sesquicentennial of the organization of the Church, noted with special observances during the April 1980 general conference. On April 6, President Kimball dedicated a restored log home on the Whitmer farm where the Church was organized in 1830. He spoke to the Church from the farmhouse by satellite transmission linked to the Salt Lake Tabernacle during a conference session. Other anniversaries noted in the following years included the 1987 centennial of Mormon settlement in western Canada and sesquicentennial of the opening of the British Mission. Anniversaries for Church colleges, temples, missions, and other events filled out an eventful decade.

For more than a century, Church members had been donating treasured artifacts to Church-sponsored museums, beginning with the Deseret Museum in 1869 and continuing through a half century on Temple Square at the LDS Museum and Bureau of Information. In April 1984, President Benson dedicated a modern facility just west of Temple Square where educational exhibits using historical artifacts, memorabilia, and art could be installed. The Museum of Church History and Art sponsored both permanent and changing exhibits and in 1990 opened a major historical installation, "A Covenant Restored," to interpret important themes in Church history.

Despite these and numerous other events and activities that helped provide public information about the Church, the libraries and schoolrooms of the world still housed few works about the Latter-day Saints, and much of what they had was either anti-Mormon in nature, highly inaccurate, or inadequate. Even many of the Saints were at a loss to know where to go for some kinds of information. This problem promised to be at least partly solved when the Macmillan publishing company of New York proposed publication of an encyclopedia of Mormonism. In August 1988 a contract was finalized with Brigham Young Univer-

The Museum of Church History and Art opened in 1984 with exhibits on Presidents of the Church and Latter-day Saint art and later added this Church history exhibit, "A Covenant Restored." (Museum of Church History and Art)

sity. With Daniel H. Ludlow as editor-in-chief, the five-volume *Encyclopedia of Mormonism* contained over 1,100 essays on a myriad of topics, an intensive index, and a handsome reprinting of the LDS scriptures. It was published late in 1991 and promised to become an important reference tool for general audiences and libraries.

The Scriptures

The First Presidency and Council of the Twelve also enlarged the canon of Latter-day Saint scripture. Two additions to the Pearl of Great Price were accepted in the April 1976 general conference. One was Joseph Smith's vision of the celestial kingdom, received in the Kirtland Temple on January 21, 1836, dealing with the salvation of those who died without hearing the gospel. The other was President Joseph F. Smith's 1918 vision of the redemption of the dead. These were the first additions to the scriptures in seventy years.

In the meantime, Church leaders were considering the publication of new editions of all the scriptures, along with improved study helps. Many Saints, for example, were anxious for a Bible that was cross-referenced to the other standard works of the Church. As early as 1972

President Harold B. Lee appointed a Scripture Study Committee consisting of Elders Thomas S. Monson and Boyd K. Packer. Elder Bruce R. McConkie was soon added, and other members of the Twelve served for short periods. The committee's initial charge was to prepare Bible study aids, but soon plans were made for an LDS edition of the King James Version. At one time at least a hundred faculty members and students at BYU assisted with the project. Printing was done at Cambridge University in Great Britain, and the work came from the press in August 1979. New editions of the other standard works appeared in 1981.

The LDS edition of the Bible made no alteration at all to the text of the King James version. New explanatory chapter headings were added to more clearly represent an LDS perspective. It also included cross-references to all the standard works; an extensive topical guide, referenced to all the standard works; over three hundred excerpts from the Joseph Smith Translation; a new 195–page Bible dictionary that included many entries specifically written for LDS use; a simplified footnote system; and twenty-four newly designed maps, with a gazetteer.

The new edition of the Book of Mormon also contained new interpretive chapter headings as well as some modified introductory material. More importantly, it incorporated at least 265 corrections in the text, reflecting long, painstaking research by LDS scholars. Researchers examined available manuscripts, the original edition, and Joseph Smith's own corrections in the 1840 version that had not been reflected in later editions. In 1982 an important phrase was added to the title page, making it read: "The Book of Mormon: Another Testament of Jesus Christ."

The Doctrine and Covenants contained important new explanatory material and two new sections: the revelations published in the 1979 edition of the Pearl of Great Price became Sections 137 and 138. In addition, supplementary material from President Wilford Woodruff regarding the Manifesto was added, and the First Presidency statement regarding President Kimball's 1978 revelation on priesthood became Official Declaration-2. The Pearl of Great Price was changed the least, but the "Introductory Note" gave historical information concerning the origin and development of the book itself.

President Benson and the Book of Mormon

President Ezra Taft Benson's first general conference address as President of the Church, on April 5, 1986, provided a fitting reminder

The First Presidency in November 1985, President Ezra Taft Benson and his counselors Gordon B. Hinckley (left) and Thomas S. Monson (right), stand by a globe in the Church Administration Building symbolizing the international growth of the Church. (LDS Church)

of the powerful continuity between administrations and, at the same time, his distinctive prophetic concerns. "As I have sought direction from the Lord," he said with humility, "I have had reaffirmed in my mind and heart the declaration of the Lord to 'say nothing but repentance unto this generation.' " (D&C 6:9; 11:9.) Reminding the Saints that this had been President Kimball's major theme, he then issued his own powerful call for repentance. He also introduced what would become one of his predominant messages: the importance of constant scriptural study, and particularly study of the Book of Mormon. He reminded the Saints of the new editions of the scripture and asked, "Are we taking advantage of them?" "The Book of Mormon has not been, nor is it yet, the center of our personal study, family teaching, preaching, and missionary work," he lamented. "Of this we must repent." He also denounced pride in this forceful initial sermon and then reminded the Saints of what they were capable of doing: "We have made some wonderful strides in the past. We will be lengthening our stride in the future. To do so, we must first cleanse the inner vessel by awaking and arising, being morally clean, using the Book of Mormon . . . , and finally conquering pride by humbling ourselves. We can do it. I know we can."

At the next general conference President Benson's introductory address was devoted fully to the Book of Mormon, and wherever he went throughout the Church he made it one of his constant themes. By July 1989 he had delivered thirty-nine public addresses on the Book of Mormon, including fourteen at general conferences. His message was effective, for throughout the Church people increasingly bore witness of what reading or rereading the book had done for them, and young people's groups eagerly took up the challenge to read it within a specified period of time. "I have a vision of homes alerted, of classes alive, and of pulpits aflame with the spirit of the Book of Mormon messages. . . . Indeed, I have a vision of flooding the earth with the Book of Mormon," he proclaimed in October 1988. "I do not know fully why God has preserved my life to this age, but I do know this: That for the present hour He has revealed to me the absolute need for us to move the Book of Mormon forward now in a marvelous manner. You must help with this burden and with this blessing which He has placed on the whole Church."

In the early years of President Benson's administration, the translation and distribution of the Book of Mormon expanded rapidly. From 1985 to 1989 fifteen new translations of a shortened version and five complete new translations (Arabic, Aymara, Czech, Greek, and a revised Braille edition) appeared, and by the end of that year it could be read by approximately 90 percent of the world's population. To help meet the increased demand for missionary editions of the Book of Mormon, and to produce Church magazines and manuals more efficiently, a new 186,000–square-foot printing facility was dedicated in Salt Lake City in December 1987. In addition, the Church produced an hour-long movie on the Book of Mormon, entitled "How Rare a Possession," and unveiled it in time for the 1988 gospel doctrine class.

The Book of Mormon was not President Benson's only theme. He gave prophetic advice to parents, commemorated the bicentennial of the U.S. Constitution with a general conference address on its inspiration, called upon the Saints to love the Lord, denounced the evil of pride, spoke to children about their responsibilities, encouraged the elderly, and reminded the Saints of their duty toward the aged. He also had the same expansive vision of the future of the Church as his predecessors.

Looking to the Future

As President Benson and other leaders looked to the future, they knew that the worldwide Church would continue to face difficult challenges as well as great opportunities. During 1991 many important things happened that seemed to be portends for the future. The eighteen hundredth stake was organized in the Dominican Republic. The Church was officially recognized in the Ivory Coast, suggesting the continuing opportunity for growth in Africa. Though the Church continued to receive negative publicity in some places, in many more instances the lives of its members and the programs of the Church itself continued to win the admiration of people. In June the Tabernacle Choir made a three-week tour of Russia and eastern Europe, leaving an outstanding trail of goodwill. That same month the government of Armenia (one of the Soviet republics) donated land to the Church in appreciation for its humanitarian aid after a disastrous earthquake in 1988. Late in the summer the Soviet Union began to break up into a number of republics, Russia being the largest, and later a mission was officially opened in St. Petersburg (formerly Leningrad). As political change continued to install democratic governments in eastern Europe, more religious restrictions fell and the opportunity for missionary work was enhanced even more. The genuinely international flavor of the Church was beautifully symbolized by the Second International Art Competition. During the summer the Museum of Church History and Art displayed 200 entries from forty-one countries.

The Church also continued to respond to public issues in America that seemed to present direct challenges to society's ethical and moral standards. In January, for example, it issued a statement strongly opposing the practice of abortion. It did not take a position with respect to specific legislative proposals, but encouraged members individually to "let their voices be heard in appropriate and legal ways that will evidence their belief in the sacredness of life."

In April, President Gordon B. Hinckley gave an address on "The State of the Church" in the priesthood session of General Conference. "We are far from that state of perfection for which we work," he said as he looked to the future, "but we are making substantial progress." After reporting on several aspects of the Church and its programs, he

asked the question, "What is the future of the Church?" His answer
emphasized that the charge to preach the gospel in all the world was
"almost beyond comprehension," but that it must be fulfilled. The
Church, he said, is concerned with the "eternal welfare of all generations
who have lived upon the earth. No other organizations, in my judgment,
faces so great a challenge."[10] In October, Elder Howard W. Hunter,
President of the Quorum of the Twelve, captured the continuing challenge by emphasizing again the universality of the gospel of Jesus Christ.
It is "a global faith," he said, "with an all-embracing message. It is
neither confined nor partial nor subject to history or fashion. Its essence
is universally and eternally true. Its message is for all the world."[11]

---

[10]*Ensign*, May 1991, pp. 51–54.
[11]*Ensign*, November 1991, p. 18.

General Bibliography

The annotated list below identifies some of the books, articles, and reference works most valuable and useful in the study of LDS Church history. As a selection, it has two purposes. First, it will guide the reader who wishes to learn more about the topics discussed in this book. Second, because we have used footnotes only to identify direct quotations in the narrative, it will indicate the principal sources we consulted and, in part, express our debt to other historians.

Most of the items listed here are readily available in major libraries with collecting interests in Latter-day Saint history or by inter-library loan. Additional readings can be located in specialized bibliographies. We have not included most dissertations and theses, most published ward and stake histories, many biographies, and numerous articles on aspects of Mormon studies outside of history. We have often excluded references to historical articles when books adequately treat the same topic. Many of these books go beyond the scope of our narrative and offer, as well, suggestions for further reading.

In this General Bibliography are sections titled General Works, Biography and Autobiography, Collected Works, Bibliographies, and Historiography. This general listing is followed by separate chapter bibliographies. Included in the General Bibliography are sources covering a broader period than any one chapter or section and works helpful in other ways not directly related to the chronological framework of the chapters. Works identified with full bibliographic citation in these general sections are listed by shortened title in all subsequent citations. This selected bibliography covers publications issued or announced by March 1, 1992.

GENERAL WORKS

Broad Surveys

Comprehensive Overviews. The most extensive overview of Church history published to date, B. H. Roberts's *A Comprehensive History of The Church* *of Jesus Christ of Latter-day Saints, Century I,* 6 vols. (Salt Lake City: The Church of Jesus Christ of Latter-day Saints, 1930), though half a century old, remains a valuable resource for information and commentary. Joseph Smith's *History of the Church* (7 vols.), because of its documentary approach, is cited below under "Published Documents."

One-volume Overviews. While *The Story of the Latter-day Saints* looks at Church history in a chronological format and pays attention to questions of most interest to LDS members, *The Mormon Experience: A History of the Latter-day Saints,* by Leonard J. Arrington and Davis Bitton (New York: Alfred A. Knopf, 1979), offers a valuable thematic discussion of issues of concern to a non-Mormon audience. For young readers a good survey weighted toward the nineteenth century is Dean Hughes, *The Mormon Church: A Basic History* (Salt Lake City: Deseret Book, 1986).

Textbooks. Most surveys written for LDS use were prepared as textbooks. The most up-to-date of these is Church Educational System, *Church History in the Fulness of Times: The History of The Church of Jesus Christ of Latter-day Saints* (Salt Lake City: The Church of Jesus Christ of Latter-day Saints, 1989), written for institute of religion classes. Joseph Fielding Smith's *Essentials in Church History,* 26th ed. (Salt Lake City: Deseret Book Co., 1973), first published in 1922 for Melchizedek Priesthood quorums, became the standard reference for general use for a half century. A widely published seminary text, William E. Berrett's *The Restored Church . . .* (1936, and numerous later printings) is now available as *The Latter-day Saints: A Contemporary History of the Church of Jesus Christ* (Salt Lake City: Deseret Book, 1985).

Illustrated Histories. Useful for their historic photographs are Nelson B. Wadsworth, *Through Camera Eyes* (Provo: Brigham Young University Press, 1975); and Douglas F. Tobler and Nelson B. Wadsworth, *The History of the Mormons in Photographs and Text: 1830 to the Present* (1987; New York: St. Martin's Press, 1989). A contemporary visual examination is Scot Facer Proctor, *Witness of the Light: A Photographic Journey in the Footsteps of the American Prophet Joseph Smith* (Salt Lake City: Deseret Book, 1991).

Topical Histories

Economic History. The standard monograph on nineteenth-century economic programs is Leonard J. Arrington, *Great Basin Kingdom: An Economic History of the Latter-day Saints, 1830–1900* (Cambridge: Harvard University Press, 1958). With this seminal work utilizing scholarly research standards, Arrington launched a new era in the writing of Church history. No comparable study exists for twentieth-century Church economic activities.

Political and Legal History. Many of the general histories of the Church adopt a political framework for events, especially of the nineteenth century. For a fresh scholarly look at the late Utah period, see E. Leo Lyman, *Political Deliverance: The Mormon Quest for Utah Statehood* (Urbana: University of

Illinois Press, 1986). Several other studies are listed in chapter bibliographies. Broader studies, blending insights from political and economic history, theology, and other disciplines, include the highly interpretive *Quest for Empire: The Political Kingdom of God and the Council of Fifty in Mormon History* (East Lansing: Michigan State University Press, 1967), by Klaus J. Hansen; and a contrasting interpretation by Marvin S. Hill, *Quest for Refuge: The Mormon Flight from American Pluralism* (Salt Lake City: Signature Books, 1989). Still another view is offered by Kenneth H. Winn, *Exiles in a Land of Liberty: Mormons in America, 1830–1846* (Chapel Hill: University of North Carolina Press, 1989). For a thorough examination of legal issues, see Edwin Brown Firmage and Richard Collins Mangrum, *Zion in the Courts: A Legal History of the Church of Jesus Christ of Latter-day Saints, 1830–1900* (Urbana: University of Illinois Press, 1988).

Social History. Useful introductions to Mormon values and social institutions are Thomas F. O'Dea, *The Mormons* (Chicago: University of Chicago Press, 1957); and Dean L. May, "Mormons," in Stephen Thernstrom, ed., *Harvard Encyclopedia of American Ethnic Groups* (Cambridge: Harvard University Press, 1980). Commenting on the book is Robert S. Michaelson, "Thomas F. O'Dea on the Mormons: Retrospect and Assessment," *Dialogue: A Journal of Mormon Thought* 11 (Spring 1978): 44–57. For perspectives of sociocultural anthropology, see the analysis by Rex E. Cooper, *Promises Made to the Fathers: Mormon Covenant Organization* (Salt Lake City: University of Utah Press, 1990); and the companion study by Steven L. Olsen, "The Mormon Ideology of Place: Cosmic Symbolism of the City of Zion, 1830–1846" (Ph.D. diss., University of Chicago, 1985).

Religious Studies. Various recent works treat LDS religious activities and ideas through the lens of religious studies or broadened historical perspectives. Important analytical work includes Klaus J. Hansen, *Mormonism and the American Experience* (Chicago: University of Chicago Press, 1981); and Jan Shipps, *Mormonism: The Story of a New Religious Tradition* (Urbana: University of Illinois Press, 1985). For examinations of major themes, see Thomas J. Alexander, "Wilford Woodruff and the Changing Nature of Mormon Religious Experience," *Church History* 45 (March 1976): 50–69; and Jan Shipps, "The Reality of the Restoration and the Restoration Ideal in the Mormon Tradition," in Richard T. Hughes, ed., *The American Quest for the Primitive Church* (Urbana: University of Illinois Press, 1988), pp. 181–95. Doctrinal developments are examined in Thomas G. Alexander, "The Reconstruction of Mormon Doctrine: From Joseph Smith to Progressive Theology," *Sunstone* 5 (July-August 1980): 24–33; Alexander, "The Word of Wisdom: From Principle to Requirement," *Dialogue: A Journal of Mormon Thought* 14 (Autumn 1981): 78–88; Martin R. Gardner, "Mormonism and Capital Punishment: A Doctrinal Perspective, Past and Present," ibid., 12 (Spring 1970): 9–26; and Philip L.

Barlow, *Mormons and the Bible: The Place of the Latter-day Saints in American Religion* (New York: Oxford University Press, 1991).

Mormon Family Life

Plural Marriage. The most complete study of plural marriage is Richard S. Van Wagoner, *Mormon Polygamy: A History* (1985; 2nd ed., Salt Lake City: Signature Books, 1989). Jessie L. Embry, *Mormon Polygamous Families: Life in the Principle* (Salt Lake City: University of Utah Press, 1987), examines interviews with participants. Comparisons with marriage practices in other religions are made by Lawrence Foster, *Religion and Sexuality* (New York: Oxford University Press, 1981).

Demography and Family History. The new fields of demography and family history are expanding traditional examinations of the Latter-day Saint past. Demographic studies include: Dean L. May, "People on the Mormon Frontier: Kanab's Families of 1874," *Journal of Family History* 1 (December 1976): 169–92; and Larry M. Logue, *A Sermon in the Desert: Belief and Behavior in Early St. George, Utah* (Urbana: University of Illinois Press, 1988), which offers new insights into plural marriage. Family life is examined further in Lawrence Foster, "Between Heaven and Earth: Mormon Theology of the Family in Comparative Perspective—The Shakers, the Oneida Perfectionists, the Mormons," *Sunstone* 7 (July-August 1982): 6–13, with commentary by Marybeth Raynes, "Between Heaven and Earth: A Response to Larry Foster," ibid., pp. 14–15.

Women's History. The field of women's history has expanded rapidly in the past two decades. Among the fine recent studies is Jill Mulvay Derr's reliable overview, " 'Strength in Our Union': The Making of Mormon Sisterhood," which appears in Maureen Ursenbach Beecher and Lavina Fielding Anderson, eds., *Sisters in Spirit: Mormon Women in Historical and Cultural Perspective* (Urbana and Chicago: University of Illinois Press, 1987), pp. 153–207, along with ten other useful essays. Selected personal documents are collected in Kenneth W. Godfrey, Audrey M. Godfrey, and Jill Mulvay Derr, *Women's Voices: An Untold History of the Latter-day Saints, 1830–1890* (Salt Lake City: Deseret Book, 1982). See also Leonard J. Arrington, "Blessed Damozels: Women in Mormon History," *Dialogue: A Journal of Mormon Thought* 6 (Summer 1971): 22–31, one of several pieces in a special issue on women. Appearing elsewhere are Anne Firor Scott, "Mormon Women, Other Women: Paradoxes and Challenges," *Journal of Mormon History* 13 (1986–87): 3–20; Lawrence Foster, "From Frontier Activism to Neo-Victorian Domesticity: Mormon Women in the Nineteenth and Twentieth Centuries," ibid., 6 (1979): 3–21; Carol Cornwall Madsen, " 'Feme Covert': Journey of a Metaphor," ibid., 17 (1991): 43–61; and Jill Mulvay Derr, "Woman's Place in Brigham Young's World," *Brigham Young University Studies* 18 (Spring 1978): 377–95. Offering a broader context are Beverly Beeton, *Women Vote in the West: The Woman*

Suffrage Movement, 1869–1896 (New York: Garland Publishing, 1986); and Lawrence Foster, *Women, Family, and Utopia: Communal Experiments of the Shakers, the Oneida Community, and the Mormons* (Syracuse, N.Y.: Syracuse University Press, 1992). See also the biographical works listed below. An extensive bibliography is available from the Women's Research Center at Brigham Young University.

Medical History. A general overview by Robert J. Divett, *Medicine and the Mormons: An Introduction to the History of Latter-day Saint Health Care* (Bountiful, Utah: Horizon Publishers, 1981), is supplemented with histories of selected issues: Lester E. Bush, Jr., "Birth Control among the Mormons: Introduction to an Insistent Question," *Dialogue: A Journal of Mormon Thought* 10 (Autumn 1976): 12–44; and Bush, "Ethical Issues in Reproductive Medicine: A Mormon Perspective," ibid., 18 (Summer 1985): 41–66.

Mormon Migration

The Mormon Trail. Readers can begin a study of the Mormon Trail with the detailed account by Wallace Stegner, *The Gathering of Zion: The Story of the Mormon Trail* (New York: McGraw-Hill, 1964); and Gustive O. Larson's pathbreaking history, *Prelude to the Kingdom: Mormon Desert Conquest, A Chapter in American Cooperative Experience* (Francestown, N.H.: Marshall Jones Co., 1947). Reference works on this subject include Stanley B. Kimball's *Discovering Mormon Trails* (Salt Lake City: Deseret Book, 1979), and *Historic Sites and Markers along the Mormon and Other Great Western Trails* (Urbana: University of Illinois Press, 1988). Additional sources on Latter-day Saint migration are cited in chapter bibliographies.

British Migration. The early British migration is recounted in P. A. M. Taylor, *Expectations Westward: The Mormons and the Emigration of Their British Converts in the Nineteenth Century* (Edinburgh and London: Oliver & Boyd, 1965). Another group is studied in Ronald D. Dennis, *The Call of Zion: The Story of the First Welsh Emigration* (Provo: Religious Studies Center, 1987). Immigrant contributions in Utah are discussed in Frederick S. Buchanan, "Scots among the Mormons," *Utah Historical Quarterly* 36 (Fall 1968): 328–52. For migration from Australia, see John Devitry-Smith, "The Wreck of the *Julia Ann*," *Brigham Young University Studies* 29 (Spring 1989): 5–29.

Scandinavian Migration. The classic work on Scandinavian migration is William Mulder, *Homeward to Zion: The Mormon Migration from Scandinavia* (Minneapolis: University of Minnesota Press, 1957). Also useful are Mulder's analysis, "Mormonism's 'Gathering': An American Doctrine with a Difference," *Church History* 23 (September 1954): 248–64; and "Utah's Ugly Ducklings: A Profile of the Scandinavian Immigrant," *Utah Historical Quarterly* 23 (July 1955): 233–60.

Migration Sources. Important primary sources on migration include James Linforth, ed., *Route from Liverpool to Great Salt Lake Valley, Illus-*

trated . . . from *Sketches made by Frederick Piercy* . . . (Liverpool, 1855; reprint
ed., Cambridge: Belknap Press, Harvard University Press, 1962), as edited by
Fawn M. Brodie; and William Clayton, *The Latter-day Saints' Emigrants'
Guide . . . from Council Bluffs to the Valley of the Great Salt Lake* . . . (St. Louis,
1848; reproduced in Roberts, *Comprehensive History of the Church*, vol. 3,
and more recently by Stanley B. Kimball, ed., Gerald, Mo.: Patrice Press, 1983).
The earliest extant journal of a transatlantic voyage by Mormons is published
as James B. Allen and Thomas G. Alexander, eds., *Manchester Mormons: The
Journal of William Clayton, 1840 to 1842* (Santa Barbara and Salt Lake City:
Peregrine Smith, 1974).

The Church in the American West

State Histories. Much information on the Saints as pioneers and settlers
is contained in state and local histories. Especially useful are histories of Utah's
territorial period, 1847 to 1896. Many histories of other states tell the story of
the Latter-day Saints within their borders, specifically those of Ohio, Missouri,
Illinois, Iowa, Nebraska, Nevada, Arizona, Idaho, and Wyoming. Focused on
the Mormon experience are newspaper articles collected in Leonard J. Arrington,
The Mormons in Nevada (Las Vegas: Las Vegas Sun, 1979).

Utah Territorial Histories. The early standard about the Utah Territory,
prepared with help from the Church Historian's Office, is Hubert Howe Bancroft, *History of Utah, 1540–1886* (1889; reprint ed., Salt Lake City: Bookcraft,
1964). Anticipating statehood was the historical and biographical work of Orson
F. Whitney, *History of Utah*, 4 vols. (Salt Lake City: George Q. Cannon &
Sons, 1892–1904). Whitney's short survey, *Popular History of Utah* (Salt Lake
City: Deseret News, 1916), was used as a school text. Surveys prepared for
college classroom use are: Levi Edgar Young, *The Founding of Utah* (New York:
Charles Scribner's Sons, 1923); Andrew Love Neff, *History of Utah, 1847–
1869*, ed. Leland H. Creer (Salt Lake City: Deseret News Press, 1940); and
Leland H. Creer, *Founding of an Empire: The Exploration and Colonization
of Utah, 1776–1856* (Salt Lake City: Bookcraft, 1947).

A widely recognized and readable study is Nels Anderson, *Desert Saints:
The Mormon Frontier in Utah* (Chicago: University of Chicago Press, 1942).
Another useful work is Milton R. Hunter, *Brigham Young the Colonizer* (1940;
4th ed. rev., Santa Barbara and Salt Lake City: Peregrine Smith, 1973). An
overview of the period to 1877 is Ray B. West, Jr., *Kingdom of the Saints: The
Story of Brigham Young and the Mormons* (New York: Viking Press, 1957).

Recent Utah Textbooks. The best topical textbook treatment about Utah
is the college-level *Utah's History* (Provo: Brigham Young University Press,
1978; reprinted, Logan: Utah State University Press, 1989), edited by Richard
D. Poll, Thomas G. Alexander, Eugene E. Campbell, and David E. Miller. A
concise, interpretive essay is Charles S. Peterson, *Utah: A Bicentennial History*,
The States and the Nation series (New York: W. W. Norton, and Nashville,

Tenn.: American Association for State and Local History, 1977). Dean L. May, *Utah: A People's History* (Salt Lake City: University of Utah Press, 1987), beautifully supplements a popular television course. S. George Ellsworth, *The New Utah's Heritage* (1972; rev. ed., Salt Lake City: Peregrine Smith, 1985), ably serves junior high schools.

Utah Community Studies. Essays on aspects of the topic are collected in Jessie L. Embry and Howard A. Christy, eds., *Community Development in the American West: Past and Present Nineteenth and Twentieth Century Frontiers* (Provo: Charles Redd Center for Western Studies, 1985). Helpful analyses are Dean L. May, "The Making of Saints: The Mormon Town as a Setting for the Study of Cultural Change," *Utah Historical Quarterly* 45 (Winter 1977): 75–92; Charles S. Peterson, "Life in a Village Society, 1877–1920," ibid., 49 (Winter 1981): 78–96; Peterson, "Utah's Regions: A View from the Hinterland," ibid., 47 (Spring 1979): 103–109; and Peterson, "A Mormon Village: One Man's West," *Journal of Mormon History* 3 (1976): 3–12. A geographer's assessment of settlement is D. W. Meinig, "The Mormon Culture Region: Strategies and Patterns in the Geography of the American West, 1847–1964," *Annals of the Association of American Geographers* 55 (June 1965): 191–220.

Utah Society and Economy. Ethnic groups, many including Latter-day Saints, are described in historical essays in Helen Z. Papanikolas, ed., *The Peoples of Utah* (Salt Lake City: Utah State Historical Society, 1976). Labor history, including mining, is detailed in J. Kenneth Davies, *Deseret's Sons of Toil: A History of the Workers Movements of Territorial Utah, 1852–1896* (Salt Lake City: Olympus Publishing, 1977). A critical period is examined in Thomas G. Alexander and Leonard J. Arrington, *A Dependent Commonwealth: Utah's Economy from Statehood to the Great Depression*, Charles Redd Monographs in Western History, no. 4 (Provo: Brigham Young University Press, 1974). Agricultural ideals are assessed in Donald H. Dyal, "Mormon Pursuit of the Agrarian Ideal," *Agricultural History* 63 (Fall 1989): 19–35.

The International Church

For the history of the Church in most countries, the reader must consult graduate theses and dissertations on missions. All except those of broad, general coverage are excluded from the list below. Where published histories are available, as is increasingly the case, they are listed instead.

Membership. An indication of the spread of membership can be seen in Dean R. Louder, "A Distributional and Diffusionary Analysis of the Mormon Church, 1850–1970" (Ph.D. diss., University of Washington, 1972); and the patterns of missionary service in Gordon Irving, "Numerical Strength and Geographical Distribution of the LDS Missionary Force, 1830–1974," *Task Papers in LDS History*, no. 1 (Salt Lake City: Historical Department of The Church . . . , 1975).

North and South America. A careful and highly important study for a specific period is S. George Ellsworth, "A History of Mormon Missions in the United States and Canada, 1830–1860" (Ph.D. diss., University of California, Berkeley, 1951).

Published histories of specific North and South American areas include Brigham Y. Card, Herbert C. Northcott, John E. Foster, Howard Palmer, and George K. Jarvis, eds., *The Mormon Presence in Canada* (Edmonton, Alberta: University of Alberta, 1987; reissued, Logan, Utah: Utah State University Press, 1990); Donald G. Godfrey, " 'Canada's Brigham Young': Charles Ora Card, Southern Alberta Pioneer," *American Review of Canadian Studies* 18 (Summer 1988): 223–38; LaMond F. Tullis, *Mormons in Mexico: The Dynamics of Faith and Culture* (Logan, Utah: Utah State University Press, 1987); and Frederick S. Williams and Frederick G. Williams, *From Acorn to Oak Tree: A Personal History of the Establishment and First Quarter [Century] Development of the South American Missions* (Fullerton, California: Et Cetera, 1987). The Church within states or regions is examined in Wallace R. Draughton, *History of the Church . . . in North Carolina* (Durham, N.C.: James L. Bennett, 1974). The Department of Church History and Doctrine, Brigham Young University, has issued essays in a *Regional Studies in Latter-day Saint Church History* series, with works to date including: Donald Q. Cannon, ed., *New England* (1988); H. Dean Garrett and Clark V. Johnson, eds., *Arizona* (1989). Unpublished mission and regional histories (theses) exist for the Southern States, California, South America, and Southwestern U.S. Indian missions.

Great Britain. The sesquicentennial in 1987 brought forth several offerings: V. Ben Bloxham, James R. Moss, and Larry C. Porter, eds., *Truth Will Prevail: The Rise of the Church . . . in the British Isles, 1837–1987* (Solihull, England: The Church of Jesus Christ of Latter-day Saints, 1987); Derek A. Cuthbert, *The Second Century: Latter-day Saints in Great Britain, Volume 1, 1937–1987* (Cambridge, England: Cambridge University Press, 1987); Richard L. Jensen and Malcolm R. Thorp, eds., *Mormons in Early Victorian Britain* (Salt Lake City: University of Utah Press, 1989); and James R. Moss and LaVell Moss, *Historic Sites of the Church of Jesus Christ of Latter-day Saints in the British Isles* (Salt Lake City: Publishers Press, 1987). These works supercede the centennial volume, Richard L. Evans, *A Century of Mormonism in Great Britain: A Brief Summary* (Salt Lake City: Deseret News Press, 1937). Focused on Wales is Douglas J. Davies, *Mormon Spirituality: Latter-day Saints in Wales and Zion* (Nottingham, England: University of Nottingham, 1987). Early missionary labors of members of the Twelve in England are detailed in James B. Allen, Ronald K. Esplin, and David J. Whittaker, *Men with a Mission 1837–1841: The Quorum of the Twelve Apostles in the British Isles* (Salt Lake City: Deseret Book, 1992).

Articles detailing British history include Leonard J. Arrington, "Mormon Women in Nineteenth-century Britain," *Brigham Young University Studies* 27 (Winter 1987): 67–83; Robert D. Hales, "The British Contribution to the

Restored Gospel," ibid., pp. 13–24; Ronald W. Walker, "Cradling Mormonism: The Rise of the Gospel in Early Victorian England," ibid., pp. 25–36; Jan G. Harris, "Mormons in Victorian Manchester," ibid., pp. 47–56; Tim B. Heaton, Stan L. Albrecht, and Randal J. Johnson, "The Making of British Saints in Historical Perspective," ibid., (Spring 1987): 119–35; Madison H. Thomas, "The Influence of Traditional British Social Patterns on LDS Church Growth in Southwest Britain," ibid., pp. 107–17; Bruce A. VanOrden, "The Decline in Convert Baptisms and Member Emigration from the British Mission after 1870," ibid., pp. 97–115.

Europe and the Middle East. Published works about the Church in Europe and the Middle East include Andrew Jenson, *History of the Scandinavian Mission* (Salt Lake City: Deseret News Press, 1927); Gilbert W. Scharffs, *Mormonism in Germany: A History of the Church . . . in Germany* (Salt Lake City: Deseret Book, 1970); and Gerald M. Haslam, *Clash of Cultures: The Norwegian Experience with Mormonism, 1842–1920* (New York: Peter Lang, 1984). Helpful articles are Richard L. Jensen, "Without Purse or Scrip? Financing Latter-day Saint Missionary Work in Europe in the Nineteenth Century," *Journal of Mormon History* 12 (1985): 3–14; and James R. Christiansen, "Early Missionary Work in Italy and Switzerland," *Ensign* 12 (August 1982): 35–46. For additional information see unpublished mission histories listed in the first edition of this work, p. 644.

Pacific. A comprehensive survey for the Pacific area is R. Lanier Britsch, *Unto the Islands of the Sea: A History of the Latter-day Saints in the Pacific* (Salt Lake City: Deseret Book, 1986). Focused on one country is Brian W. Hunt, *Zion in New Zealand . . .* (Temple View, N.Z.: Church College of New Zealand, 1977). Presenting an analysis in a broader context is Peter Lineham, "The Mormon Message in the Context of Maori Culture," *Journal of Mormon History* 17 (1991): 62–93. Other incidents are reported in John Devitry-Smith, "William James Barratt: The First Mormon 'Down Under,'" *Brigham Young University Studies* 28 (Summer 1988): 53–66; and Carol Cornwall Madsen, "Mormon Missionary Wives in Nineteenth Century Polynesia," *Journal of Mormon History* 13 (1986–87): 61–88.

Asia. The Church in Asia is outlined in Spencer J. Palmer, *The Church Encounters Asia* (Salt Lake City: Deseret Book, 1970), with one country highlighted by Don W. Marsh, comp., *"The Light of the Sun": Japan and the Saints* (Tokyo: Japan Mission, 1968). Graduate theses treat missions in South and East Asia; India, 1849–1856; Korea, 1950–1985; Japan, 1901–1924; and the Philippines.

Africa. See bibliography for chapter 21.

Church Government and Organizations

As yet no single book covers the subject of Church government and organizations; see preliminary overviews by David J. Whittaker, "An Introduction to Mormon Administrative History," *Dialogue: A Journal of Mormon Thought* 15 (Winter 1982): 14–20; D. Michael Quinn, "The Evolution of the Presiding Quorums of the LDS Church," *Journal of Mormon History* 1 (1974): 21–38; and Neil K. Coleman, "A Study of the Church . . . as an Administrative System, Its Structure and Maintenance" (Ph.D. diss., New York University, 1967). Insights from institutional studies are in Jill Mulvay Derr and C. Brooklyn Derr, "Outside the Mormon Hierarchy: Alternative Aspects of Institutional Power," *Dialogue: A Journal of Mormon Thought* 15 (Winter 1982): 21–43. Administrative practices of the time are described in John A. Widtsoe, comp., *Priesthood and Church Government* (Salt Lake City: Deseret Book Co., 1939). Disciplinary practices are traced in Lester E. Bush, Jr., "Excommunication and Church Courts: A Note from the General Handbook of Instructions," *Dialogue: A Journal of Mormon Thought* 14 (Summer 1981): 74–98.

Succession. Members of the First Presidency and Council of the Twelve from 1832 to 1970 are ranked by seniority in Reed C. Durham, Jr., and Steven H. Heath, *Succession in the Church* (Salt Lake City: Bookcraft, Inc., 1970). Further discussion is in Steven H. Heath, "Notes on Apostolic Succession," *Dialogue: A Journal of Mormon Thought* 20 (Summer 1987): 44–57; and in items referenced for chapter 6.

Priesthood Offices. General studies of specific offices in the Church are William G. Hartley, "Ward Bishops and the Localizing of LDS Tithing," in Bitton and Beecher, *New Views of Mormon History* (1987), pp. 96–114; Dale Beecher, "The Office of Bishop," *Dialogue: A Journal of Mormon Thought* 15 (Winter 1982): 103–15; D. Gene Pace, "Changing Patterns of Mormon Financial Administration: Traveling Bishops, Regional Bishops, and Bishops' Agents, 1851–1888," *Brigham Young University Studies* 23 (Spring 1983): 183–95; E. Gary Smith, "The Office of Presiding Patriarch: The Primacy Problem," *Journal of Mormon History* 14 (1988): 35–47; Thomas Jay Kemp, *The Office of the Patriarch to the Church in the Church of Jesus Christ of Latter-day Saints* (Stamford, Conn.: Thomas J. Kemp, 1972); and Richard D. Ouellette, "Seventies Quorums 1835–1986," *Sunstone* 11 (January 1987): 35–37. Studies narrower in scope are included in appropriate chapter bibliographies.

Relief Society. The sesquicentennial in 1992 encouraged production of an excellent general history to replace older commemorative studies: Jill Mulvay Derr, Janath R. Cannon, and Maureen Ursenbach Beecher, *Women of Covenant: The Story of Relief Society* (Salt Lake City: Deseret Book, 1992). Other publications include the photographic collection *Something Extraordinary: Celebrating Our Relief Society Sisterhood* (Salt Lake City: Deseret Book, 1992); and Janet Peterson and LaRene Gaunt, *Elect Ladies: Presidents of the Relief Society* (Salt Lake City: Deseret Book, 1990).

Sunday School. The published *Jubilee History of Latter-day Saint Sunday Schools, 1849–1899* (Salt Lake City: Deseret Sunday School Union, 1900) must be supplemented with articles. A good short account is A. Hamer Reiser, "Latter-day Saint Sunday Schools," *Improvement Era* 38 (April 1935): 241, 262–63. More detailed is the "Sunday School Centennial Edition, 1849–1949," *Instructor* 84 (December 1949), part of a special issue. See also the year-long series, J. N. Washburn, " 'Ye Have Need That One Teach You': A History of the Sunday Schools of the Church . . . ," *Instructor* 84 (January through November 1949).

Mutual Improvement Associations. A combined history of the Mutual Improvement Associations for a selected period is Scott Kenney, "The Mutual Improvement Associations: A Preliminary History, 1900–1950," *Task Papers in LDS History*, no. 6 (Salt Lake City: Historical Department of The Church . . . , 1976).

Young Women. The early years of the Young Women are narrated in Susa Young Gates, *History of the Young Ladies Mutual Improvement Association* (Salt Lake City: Deseret News Press, 1911). The story is continued in a topical account by Marba C. Josephson, *History of the YWMIA* (Salt Lake City: Young Women's Mutual Improvement Association of The Church . . . , 1955), and is illustrated with photographs in *A Century of Sisterhood: Chronological Collage, 1869–1969* (Salt Lake City: Young Women's Mutual Improvement Association, 1969). A brief summary is Clarissa A. Beesley, "The Young Women's Mutual Improvement Association," *Improvement Era* 38 (April 1935): 243, 264–66, 271.

Young Men. The most comprehensive treatment of the Young Men is in Leon M. Strong, "A History of the Young Men's Mutual Improvement Association, 1877–1938" (M.S. thesis, Brigham Young University, 1939), and John Kent Williams, "A History of the Young Men's Mutual Improvement Association, 1939 to 1974" (M.A. thesis, Brigham Young University, 1976). A note on origins is Henry W. Naisbitt, " 'Polysophical' and 'Mutual,' " *Improvement Era* 2 (August 1899): 741–47. Useful especially for what they reveal about the periods in which they were written are Edward H. Anderson, "The Past of Mutual Improvement," ibid., 1 (November and December 1897): 1–10, 85–93; Junius F. Wells, "Historic Sketch of the Y.M.M.I.A., First Period," ibid., 8 (June 1925): 712–29; and Richard R. Lyman, "The Young Men's Mutual Improvement Association," ibid., 28 (April 1935): 242, 253, 259–62.

Primary. The history of the Primary is best told in Carol Cornwall Madsen and Susan Staker Oman, *Sisters and Little Saints: One Hundred Years of Primary* (Salt Lake City: Deseret Book, 1979). An early look at the founding years is Aurelia S. Rogers, *Life Sketches of Orson Spencer and Others, and History of Primary Work* (Salt Lake City: George Q. Cannon & Sons, 1898).

Historical Department. Early historical activities are traced in Charles P. Adams and Gustive O. Larson, "A Study of the LDS Church Historian's Office, 1830–1900," *Utah Historical Quarterly* 40 (Fall 1972): 370–88; while more recent projects are noted in Ronald K. Esplin and Max J. Evans, "Preserving Mormon Manuscripts: Historical Activities of the LDS Church," *Manuscripts*

27 (Summer 1975): 166–67. A reflection on the History Division in the 1970s is Davis Bitton, "Ten Years in Camelot: A Personal Memoir," *Dialogue: A Journal of Mormon Thought* 16 (Autumn 1983): 9–33.

Family History Department. On organized genealogical work, see Merrill S. Lofthouse, "A Glance Backward: Historical Sketch of the Genealogical Society," *Improvement Era* 72 (July 1969): 14–17; and his "A History of the Genealogical Society of The Church . . . to 1970" (M.A. thesis, Brigham Young University, 1971). A newer study, James B. Allen and Jessee Embry, "Hearts Turned to the Fathers: A History of the Genealogical Society of The Church of Jesus Christ of Latter-day Saints" (unpublished manuscript, 1991) is available at the libraries of Brigham Young University, the LDS Church Historical Department, and the Family History Library.

Music. For a probing analysis of music in the Church, see Michael Hicks, *Mormonism and Music: A History* (Urbana: University of Illinois Press, 1989). The most recent guide to the hymnbook is Karen Lynn Davidson, *Our Latter-day Hymns: The Stories and Messages* (Salt Lake City: Deseret Book, 1988). Also see articles in a theme issue of *Dialogue: A Journal of Mormon Thought* 10 (Spring 1975).

The Tabernacle Choir is celebrated in Charles Jeffrey Calman, *The Mormon Tabernacle Choir* (New York: Harper & Row, 1979); and in Gerald A. Petersen, *The Mormon Tabernacle Choir: More Than Music* (Provo: Brigham Young University Press, 1979); and chronicled in J. Spencer Cornwall, *A Century of Singing: The Salt Lake Mormon Tabernacle Choir* (Salt Lake City: Deseret Book Co., 1958).

Church Publishing. A history of the Church-owned *Deseret News* is Wendell J. Ashton, *Voice in the West: Biography of a Pioneer Newspaper* (New York: Duell, Sloan & Pearce, 1950). Adding the pre-Utah period is Monte B. McLaws, *Spokesman for the Kingdom: Early Mormon Journalism and the Deseret News, 1830–1898* (Provo: Brigham Young University Press, 1977); and articles cited in chapter bibliographies. The first 125 years of Deseret Book Company are chronicled in Eleanor Knowles, *Deseret Book Company: 125 Years of Inspiration, Information, and Ideas* (Salt Lake City: Deseret Book, 1991).

Temples. Early temple-related accomplishments are described in James E. Talmage, *The House of the Lord: A Study of Holy Santuaries, Ancient and Modern* (1912; reprinted with additions; Salt Lake City: Deseret Book, 1976). For further information see temple dedication issues of Church magazines. Master's theses treat many of the older temples. See also Nolan Porter Olsen, *Logan Temple: The First 100 Years* (Providence, Utah: Keith W. Watkins and Sons, 1978). Richard O. Cowan, *Temples to Dot the Earth* (Salt Lake City: Bookcraft, 1989) gives the subject a contemporary focus.

Temple ordinance history is traced in a controversial article, David John Buerger, "The Development of the Mormon Temple Endowment Ceremony,"

Dialogue: A Journal of Mormon Thought 20 (Winter 1987): 33–76. A related study is Buerger's " 'The Fulness of the Priesthood': The Second Anointing in Latter-day Saint Theology and Practice," ibid., 16 (Spring 1983): 10–44.

Education

Very few published sources on Church educational activities are available, but graduate students in history and education have completed a large number of theses and dissertations on aspects of the Church educational program.

Philosophy of Education. Background influences on a key Mormon educator are examined by Douglas F. Tobler, "Karl G. Maeser's German Background, 1828–1856: The Making of Zion's Teacher," *Brigham Young University Studies* 17 (Winter 1977): 155–75. Broader studies include Wendell O. Rich, "Certain Basic Concepts in the Educational Philosophy of The Church . . . , 1830–1930" (Ph.D. diss., Utah State Agricultural College, 1954); and James R. Clark, "Church and State Relationships in Education in Utah" (Ed.D., Utah State University, 1958).

Historical Overviews. A standard reference is the concise history by M. Lynn Bennion, *Mormonism and Education* (Salt Lake City: [Church] Department of Education, 1939). For more recent information see William E. Berrett, *A Miracle in Weekday Religious Education: A History of the Church Educational System* (Salt Lake City: Author, 1988). Utah beginnings are discussed in Frederick S. Buchanan, "Education among the Mormons: Brigham Young and the Schools of Utah," *History of Education Quarterly* 22 (Winter 1982): 435–59; and Charles S. Peterson, "The Limits of Learning in Pioneer Utah," *Journal of Mormon History* 10 (1983): 65–78. A specialized effort is traced in D. Michael Quinn, "Utah's Education Innovation: LDS Religion Classes, 1890–1929," *Utah Historical Quarterly* 43 (Fall 1975): 379–89.

School Histories. On specific schools see Ernest L. Wilkinson, ed., *Brigham Young University: The First One Hundred Years*, 4 vols. (Provo: Brigham Young University Press, 1975–76), the official history; and an alternative perspective in Gary James Bergera and Ronald Priddis, *Brigham Young University: A House of Faith* (Salt Lake City: Signature Books, 1985). Other schools are examined in David L. Crowder, "Ricks College: A Centennial Sketch, 1888–1988," *Snake River Echoes* 29 (Fall 1989): 7–22; and in other material listed in chapter bibliographies.

Public Image

Overviews. The image of the Church in periodicals, novels, and other popular media continues to attract the attention of qualified researchers. General overviews are found in unpublished works by Richard O. Cowan, Dennis L. Lythgoe, and Jan Shipps.

Nineteenth Century. Concentrating on the public image in the nineteenth century are Gary L. Bunker and Davis Bitton, *The Mormon Graphic Image,*

1834–1914 (Salt Lake City: University of Utah Press, 1983); David Brion Davis, "Some Themes of Counter-Subversion: An Analysis of Anti-Masonic, Anti-Catholic, and Anti-Mormon Literature," *Mississippi Valley Historical Review* 47 (September 1970): 205–24; D. L. Ashliman, "The Image of Utah and the Mormons in Nineteenth-Century Germany," *Utah Historical Quarterly* 35 (Summer 1967): 209–27; and in Gail Farr Casterline's thesis.

Twentieth Century. Broadening the question of image is Jan Shipps, "Beyond the Stereotypes: Mormon and Non-Mormon Communities in Twentieth Century Mormondom," in Bitton and Beecher, *New Views of Mormon History* (1987), pp. 342–60.

Mormons in Fiction. The image of the Saints in fiction is treated in Neal Lambert, "Saints, Sinners and Scribes: A Look at the Mormons in Fiction," *Utah Historical Quarterly* 36 (Winter 1968): 63–76; Lambert and Richard H. Cracroft, "Through Gentile Eyes: A Hundred Years of the Mormons in Fiction," *New Era* 2 (March 1972): 14–19; Leonard J. Arrington and Jon Haupt, "Intolerable Zion: The Image of Mormonism in Nineteenth Century American Literature," *Western Humanities Review* 22 (Summer 1968): 243–60; Arrington and Haupt, "Community and Isolation: Some Aspects of 'Mormon Westerns,'" *Western American Literature* 8 (Spring and Summer 1973): 15–31; and Arrington, "Mormonism: Views from Without and Within," *Brigham Young University Studies* 14 (Winter 1974): 40–54.

BIOGRAPHY AND AUTOBIOGRAPHY

Biographical studies of Latter-day Saints are numerous, though few are professionally done and many give only a selective look at the life of the individual. For assessments of the historiographical implications of the task, see Ronald W. Walker, "The Challenge and Craft of Mormon Biography," *Brigham Young University Studies* 22 (Spring 1982): 179–92; and David J. Whittaker, "The Heritage and Tasks of Mormon Biography," in Cannon and Whittaker, *Supporting Saints* (1985), chapter 1. The titles listed below represent a small portion of those available in libraries of Latter-day Saint history. Many of these works contain background information useful in understanding Church history.

Collective Biography

Reference Works. For the essential details on prominent Latter-day Saints in the nineteenth and early twentieth centuries, the standard references are Andrew Jenson, *Latter-day Saint Biographical Enyclopedia: A Compilation of Biographical Sketches of Prominent Men and Women in The Church . . .*, 4 vols. (1901–1936; reprinted, Salt Lake City: Western Epics, 1971); and Frank Esshom, *Pioneers and Prominent Men of Utah* (Salt Lake City: Utah Pioneers Book Publishing Co., 1913).

Chapter-length Biographies. Leonard J. Arrington, *The Presidents of the Church* (Salt Lake City: Deseret Book, 1986), has replaced Preston Nibley, *The Presidents of the Church*, 13th ed. rev. (Salt Lake City: Deseret Book Co., 1974), and Emerson Roy West, *Profiles of the Presidents* (rev. ed.; Salt Lake City: Deseret Book, 1980), as the standard reference. Other Church leaders are introduced by the brief personality portraits in Lawrence R. Flake, *Mighty Men of Zion: General Authorities of the Last Dispensation* (Salt Lake City: Karl D. Butler, 1974). A scholarly study in group biography is D. Michael Quinn, "Organizational Development and Social Origins of the Mormon Hierarchy, 1832–1932: A Prosopographical Study" (M.A. thesis, University of Utah, 1973). Of related interest is Leonard J. Arrington and Susan Arrington Madsen, *Mothers of the Prophets* (Salt Lake City: Deseret Book, 1987).

Women: Biographical Sketches. An interest in women's studies is encouraging biographies of Latter-day Saint women. Full-length studies are listed below with other books. A collection of sketches is Leonard J. Arrington and Susan Arrington Madsen, *Sunbonnet Sisters: The Stories of Mormon Women and Frontier Life* (Salt Lake City: Bookcraft, 1984). Other studies include Maureen Ursenbach Beecher, "Three Women and the Life of the Mind," *Utah Historical Quarterly* 43 (Winter 1975): 26–40; Jill Mulvay, "The Two Miss Cooks: Pioneer Professionals for Utah Schools," ibid., 43 (Fall 1975): 396–409; Sherilyn Cox Bennion, "Enterprising Ladies: Utah's Nineteenth-century Women Editors," ibid., 49 (Summer 1981): 291–304; Beecher, "The Eliza Enigma: The Life and Legend of Eliza R. Snow," *Essays in the American West 1974–75*, Charles Redd Monographs in Western History, no. 6 (Provo: Brigham Young University Press, 1976), pp. 29–46; Beecher, "The 'Leading Sisters': A Female Hierarchy in Nineteenth Century Mormon Society," *Journal of Mormon History* 9 (1982): 25–39; and Leonard J. Arrington, "The Legacy of Early Latter-day Saint Women," *John Whitmer Historical Association Journal* 10 (1990): 3–17.

Older biographies of women are found in Augusta Joyce Crocheron, *Representative Women of Deseret: A Book of Biographical Sketches . . .* (Salt Lake City: J. C. Graham, 1884); and Edward W. Tullidge, *Women in Mormondom* (1877; reprinted., Salt Lake City: n.p., 1966).

Biographies of Church Presidents

Book-length biographies on all Church presidents have been published, with the greatest interest focusing on the lives of Joseph Smith and Brigham Young.

Joseph Smith. For many Latter-day Saints the most satisfying history of Joseph Smith is John Henry Evans, *Joseph Smith, An American Prophet* (New York: Macmillan, 1933; reprinted, Salt Lake City: Deseret Book, 1946 and 1989). Other positive assessments include the carefully detailed recounting by Donna Hill, *Joseph Smith, The First Mormon* (Garden City, N.Y.: Doubleday,

1977); the older Daryl Chase, *Joseph the Prophet, As He Lives in the Hearts of His People* (Salt Lake City: Deseret Book Co., 1944); and the more recent work for LDS readers, Francis M. Gibbons, *Joseph Smith: Martyr, Prophet of God* (Salt Lake City: Deseret Book, 1977).

The most analytical biography is Fawn M. Brodie, *No Man Knows My History: The Life of Joseph Smith, the Mormon Prophet* (1945; 2nd ed. rev., New York: Alfred A. Knopf, 1971). Though widely accepted by U.S. historians, LDS readers disagree with Brodie's naturalistic assumptions. For assessments of the book see Marvin S. Hill, "Brodie Revisited: A Reappraisal," *Dialogue: A Journal of Mormon Thought* 7 (Winter 1972): 72–84; and Hill's "Secular or Sectarian History? A Critique of 'No Man Knows My History,' " *Church History* 43 (March 1974): 78–96. Other perspectives are Newell G. Bringhurst, "Fawn M. Brodie: Her Biographies as Autobiography," *Pacific Historical Review* 59 (1990): 203–29; Louis Midgley, "The Brodie Connection: Thomas Jefferson and Joseph Smith," *Brigham Young University Studies* 20 (Fall 1979): 59–67; Hugh Nibley, *No, Ma'am, That's Not History: A Brief Review . . .* (Salt Lake City: Bookcraft, 1946); and a book prepared at the request of Church leaders, John A. Widtsoe, *Joseph Smith: Seeker after Truth, Prophet of God* (Salt Lake City: Deseret News Press, 1951).

Another widely read study is Preston Nibley, ed., *History of Joseph Smith by His Mother, Lucy Mack Smith* (Salt Lake City: Bookcraft, 1954), based on the "corrected Utah version," issued by the *Improvement Era* (1902). The original work is Lucy Smith, *Biographical Sketches of Joseph Smith the Prophet and His Progenitors for Many Generations* (Liverpool: S. W. Richards for Orson Pratt, 1853), reprinted by Herald House (Independence, Mo., 1969) and Arno Press (New York, 1969). Readers of the work should consult Richard Anderson, "The Reliability of the Early History of Lucy and Joseph Smith," *Dialogue: A Journal of Mormon Thought* 4 (Summer 1969): 13–28.

Drawn from Lucy Mack Smith's account and from Joseph Smith, *History of the Church*, is Preston Nibley, *Joseph Smith, the Prophet* (Salt Lake City: Deseret News Press, 1944). Another detailed study is George Q. Cannon, *Life of Joseph Smith* (Salt Lake City: Deseret News Press, 1907). The work by Edward W. Tullidge, *Life of Joseph Smith the Prophet* (New York: Tullidge & Crandall, 1878), was discredited by Church leaders (see John Taylor's comments in James R. Clark, *Messages of the First Presidency*, 2:315–30). Incidents from the Prophet's life are compiled in Hyrum L. Andrus, *Joseph Smith, the Man and the Seer* (Salt Lake City: Deseret Book, 1960); the recollections of associates are in Hyrum L. Andrus and Helen Mae Andrus, *They Knew the Prophet* (Salt Lake City: Bookcraft, 1974); while the Prophet's character is profiled in Truman G. Madsen, *Joseph Smith the Prophet* (Salt Lake City: Bookcraft, 1989).

Articles on aspects of the Prophet's life are compiled in Larry C. Porter and Susan Easton Black, eds., *The Prophet Joseph: Essays on the Life and*

Mission of Joseph Smith (Salt Lake City: Deseret Book, 1988). Included are LaMar C. Berrett, "Joseph, a Family Man," pp. 36–48; and others cited in chapters 1–6.

Brigham Young. The standard, a biography marked by thorough scholarship and good writing, is Leonard J. Arrington, *Brigham Young: American Moses* (New York: Alfred A. Knopf, 1985). Written mainly for a national audience is Newell G. Bringhurst, *Brigham Young and the Expanding American Frontier* (Boston: Little, Brown, 1986). Written for Latter-day Saint readers is Francis M. Gibbons, *Brigham Young: Modern Moses, Prophet of God* (Salt Lake City: Deseret Book, 1981). Aspects of his life are examined in Richard F. Palmer and Karl D. Butler, *Brigham Young: The New York Years* (Provo: Charles Redd Center for Western Studies, 1983); and Ronald W. Walker and Ronald K. Esplin, "Brigham Himself: An Autobiographical Recollection," *Journal of Mormon History* 4 (1977): 19–34. See also the works cited earlier by Ray B. West *(Kingdom of the Saints)* and Milton R. Hunter *(Brigham Young the Colonizer)*.

Now dated are Morris R. Werner, *Brigham Young* (New York: Harcourt, Brace & Co., 1925); and Preston Nibley, *Brigham Young, the Man and His Work* (Salt Lake City: Deseret News Press, 1936); and the older biographies by Edward H. Anderson, *The Life of Brigham Young* (Salt Lake City: George Q. Cannon & Sons, 1893); and Edward W. Tullidge, *Life of Brigham Young or, Utah and Her Founders* (New York: Tullidge & Crandall, 1876). Less reliable is a work based heavily upon biased newspaper reports, Stanley P. Hirshson, *The Lion of the Lord: A Biography of Brigham Young* (New York: Alfred A. Knopf, 1969). Family members have written admiring tributes: Susa Young Gates, in collaboration with Leah D. Widtsoe, *The Life Story of Brigham Young* (New York: Macmillan Company, 1930); S. Dilworth Young, *"Here is Brigham": Brigham Young, the Years to 1844* (Salt Lake City: Bookcraft, 1964); and Clarissa Young Spencer with Mabel Harmer, *Brigham Young at Home* (Salt Lake City: Deseret Book Co., 1940), first published as *One Who Was Valiant* (Caldwell, Ida.: Caxton Printers, 1940).

Other Presidents. An increasing number of biographers have examined the lives of presidents since John Taylor. Some of these studies were intended as full biographies; others are extracted from first-person documents or merely recapitulate highlights, but with little analysis. For short biographies consult Leonard Arrington's *Presidents of the Church* (1986).

John Taylor. Quite comprehensive is B. H. Roberts, *The Life of John Taylor, Third President of the Church* . . . (1892; reprinted, Salt Lake City: Bookcraft, 1963). Francis M. Gibbons has written *John Taylor: Mormon Philosopher, Prophet of God* (Salt Lake City: Deseret Book, 1985) for LDS readers. A descendant's dramatic interpretation is Samuel W. Taylor, *The Kingdom or Nothing: The Life of John Taylor, Militant Mormon* (New York: Macmillan, 1976). The early years are examined by G. St. John Stott, "John Taylor's Religious

Preparation," *Dialogue: A Journal of Mormon Thought* 19 (Spring 1986): 123–28.

Wilford Woodruff. The scholarly biography by Thomas G. Alexander, *Things in Heaven and Earth: The Life and Times of Wilford Woodruff, A Mormon Prophet* (Salt Lake City: Signature Books, 1991), offers the most complete examination and only interpretive study of Woodruff's life. A narrative treatment is Francis M. Gibbons, *Wilford Woodruff: Wondrous Worker, Prophet of God* (Salt Lake City: Deseret Book, 1988). First-person diary entries are welded together in Matthias F. Cowley, *Wilford Woodruff, Fourth President of the Church . . . History of His Life and Labors as Recorded in His Daily Journals* (Salt Lake City: Deseret News, 1909).

Lorenzo Snow. The documentary approach is used in Eliza R. Snow Smith, *Biography and Family Record of Lorenzo Snow, One of the Twelve Apostles of The Church . . .* (1884; reprinted, Salt Lake City: Zion's Book Store, 1975); while a more thorough treatment is Thomas C. Romney, *The Life of Lorenzo Snow: Fifth President of The Church . . .* (Salt Lake City: Nicholas G. Morgan, Sr., 1955). More recent is Francis M. Gibbons, *Lorenzo Snow: Spiritual Giant, Prophet of God* (Salt Lake City: Deseret Book, 1982).

Joseph F. Smith. Another in his series on Church presidents is Francis M. Gibbons, *Joseph F. Smith: Patriarch and Preacher, Prophet of God* (Salt Lake City: Deseret Book, 1984). A lengthy section on ancestors introduces the fairly complete biography in Joseph Fielding Smith, *Life of Joseph F. Smith* (Salt Lake City: Deseret Book Co., 1938).

Heber J. Grant. The most complete overview to date of Heber J. Grant's life is Francis M. Gibbons, *Heber J. Grant: Man of Steel, Prophet of God* (Salt Lake City: Deseret Book, 1979). A brief account is Bryant Hinckley, *Heber J. Grant: Highlights in the Life of a Great Leader* (Salt Lake City: Deseret Book, 1951). Selected experiences are examined in the following essays by Ronald W. Walker: "Jedediah and Heber Grant," *Ensign* 9 (July 1979): 47–52; "Young Heber J. Grant's Years of Passage," *Brigham Young University Studies* 24 (Spring 1984): 131–49; "Young Heber J. Grant and His Call to the Apostleship," ibid., 18 (Fall 1977): 121–26; "Strangers in a Strange Land: Heber J. Grant and the Opening of the Japanese Mission," *Journal of Mormon History* 13 (1986–87): 21–44; "Heber J. Grant and the Utah Loan and Trust Company," ibid., 8 (1981): 21–36; and "Young Heber J. Grant: Entrepreneur Extraordinary," in Alexander, Christy, and Colonna, eds., *The Twentieth Century American West* (1983), pp. 85–119.

George Albert Smith. A full-length life story of the eighth President is Francis M. Gibbons, *George Albert Smith: Kind and Caring Christian, Prophet of God* (Salt Lake City: Deseret Book, 1990). Other fine studies are Merlo J. Pusey, *Builders of the Kingdom: . . . George Albert Smith* (Provo: Brigham Young University Press, 1981); and the Ph.D. dissertation of Glen R. Stubbs (1974).

David O. McKay. David O. McKay's life is reviewed by David Lawrence McKay, *My Father, David O. McKay* (Salt Lake City: Deseret Book, 1989); while selected episodes are recounted by a sister in Jeannette McKay Morrell, *Highlights in the Life of President David O. McKay* (Salt Lake City: Deseret Book, 1966).

Joseph Fielding Smith. A brief background report by Joseph F. McConkie, *True and Faithful: The Life Story of Joseph Fielding Smith* (Salt Lake City: Bookcraft, 1971), has been supplanted by the work of Joseph Fielding Smith, Jr., and John J Stewart, *The Life of Joseph Fielding Smith, Tenth President of the Church* . . . (Salt Lake City: Deseret Book, 1972).

Harold B. Lee. A complete biography by a son-in-law is L. Brent Goates, *Harold B. Lee: Prophet and Seer* (Salt Lake City: Bookcraft, 1985). Essays by 52 persons influenced by President Lee are assembled in Goates, *He Changed My Life: Personal Experiences with Harold B. Lee* (Salt Lake City: Bookcraft, 1988).

Spencer W. Kimball. Setting a new standard in presidential biographies, and issued while President Kimball was still living, is Edward L. Kimball and Andrew W. Kimball, *Spencer W. Kimball: Twelfth President of the Church* . . . (Salt Lake City: Bookcraft, 1977). Additional insights are found in the following writings and compilations by Edward L. Kimball: *The Story of Spencer Kimball: A Short Man, A Long Stride* (Salt Lake City: Bookcraft, 1985); "I Sustain Him As a Prophet, I Love Him As an Affectionate Father," *Dialogue: A Journal of Mormon Thought* 11 (Winter 1978): 48–62; "Spencer W. Kimball at College," *Brigham Young University Studies* 25 (Fall 1985): 139–45; and "Spencer W. Kimball: A Man of Good Humor," ibid., pp. 59–71. Also see Ronald W. Walker, "Mesquite and Sage: Spencer W. Kimball's Early Years," ibid., 24 (Fall 1985): 19–41.

Ezra Taft Benson. A sympathetic overview of Ezra Taft Benson's life through the date of publication is Sheri L. Dew, *Ezra Taft Benson: A Biography* (Salt Lake City: Deseret Book, 1987). Stories of his life are compiled in Elaine Cannon, *Boy of the Lord, Man of the Lord* (Salt Lake City: Bookcraft, 1989). The post-World War II welfare efforts are told in first-person accounts in Ezra Taft Benson, *A Labor of Love: The 1946 European Mission of Ezra Taft Benson* (Salt Lake City: Deseret Book, 1989). For an assessment of his service as U.S. Secretary of Agriculture, see Edward L. Schapsmeier and Frederick H. Schapsmeier, *Ezra Taft Benson and the Politics of Agriculture: The Eisenhower Years, 1953–1961* (Danville, Ill.: Interstate Printers, 1975).

Wives of Presidents. A much-needed, balanced treatment is offered by Linda King Newell and Valeen Tippetts Avery, *Mormon Enigma: Emma Hale Smith, Prophet's Wife, Elect Lady, Polygamy's Foe, 1804–1870* (New York: Doubleday, 1984). (See also the commentary by Paul M. Edwards, "An Enigma Resolved: The Emma Smith of Newell and Avery," *Journal of Mormon History* 11 [1984]: 119–124.) A memorable biography of a recent Church president's wife is Edward L. Kimball and Caroline Eyring Miner, *Camilla: A Biography of Camilla Eyring Kimball* (Salt Lake City: Deseret Book, 1980). Shorter sketches include Lynda W. Harris, "The Legend of Jessie Evans Smith," *Utah Historical Quarterly* 44 (Fall 1976): 351–64; and Derin Head Rodriguez, "Flora Amussen Benson: Handmaiden of the Lord, Helpmeet of a Prophet, Mother in Zion," *Ensign* 17 (March 1987): 15–20.

Other Biographies

Selected Books. Only a few of the many life studies of Latter-day Saints can be listed here.

Autobiographies. Two classic autobiographies are Parley P. Pratt, ed., *Autobiography of Parley Parker Pratt* (1874; 3rd ed., 1938; reprinted, Salt Lake City: Deseret Book, 1961); and Annie Clark Tanner, *A Mormon Mother: An Autobiography* (1941; rev. ed., Salt Lake City: Tanner Trust Fund, University of Utah Library, 1973). Other noteworthy autobiographies are Juanita Brooks, *Quicksand and Cactus: A Memoir of the Southern Mormon Frontier* (Salt Lake City: Howe Brothers, 1982); Scott G. Kenney, ed., *Memories and Reflections: The Autobiography of E. E. Ericksen* (Salt Lake City: Signature Books, 1987); and Margery W. Ward, ed., *A Fragment: The Autobiography of Mary Jane Mount Tanner* (Salt Lake City: Tanner Trust Fund, University of Utah Library, 1980).

Biographies: Nineteenth-century Figures. Notable publications include the classic by Juanita Brooks, *John D. Lee: Zealot, Pioneer Builder, Scapegoat* (1961; rev. ed., Glendale, Calif.: Arthur H. Clark Company, 1972); Harold Schindler's balanced *Orrin Porter Rockwell: Man of God, Son of Thunder* (1966; 2nd ed., Salt Lake City: University of Utah Press, 1983); the comprehensive study by Andrew Karl Larson, *Erastus Snow: The Life of a Missionary and Pioneer for the Early Mormon Church* (Salt Lake City: University of Utah Press, 1971); and the well-written family biography by Merlo J. Pusey, *Builders of the Kingdom: George A. Smith, John Henry Smith, George Albert Smith* (Provo: Brigham Young University Press, 1981).

Other important works include: Leonard J. Arrington, *Charles C. Rich: Mormon General and Western Frontiersman* (Provo: Brigham Young University Press, 1974); Howard H. Barron, *Orson Hyde: Missionary, Apostle, Colonizer* (Bountiful, Ut.: Horizon, 1977); Truman G. Madsen, *Defender of the Faith: The B. H. Roberts Story* (Salt Lake City: Bookcraft, 1980); Stanley B. Kimball, *Heber C. Kimball: Mormon Patriarch and Pioneer* (Champaign: University of Illinois Press, 1981); Gene A. Session, *Mormon Thunder: A Documentary History of Jedediah Morgan Grant* (Urbana: University of Illinois Press, 1982); Susan Evans McCloud, *Not in Vain: The Inspiring Story of Ellis Shipp, Pioneer Woman Doctor* (Salt Lake City: Bookcraft, 1984); Breck England, *The Life and Thought of Orson Pratt* (Salt Lake City: University of Utah Press, 1985); James B. Allen, *Trials of Discipleship: The Story of William Clayton, a Mormon* (Urbana, Ill.: University of Illinois Press, 1987); and S. George Ellsworth,

Samuel Claridge: Pioneering the Outposts of Zion (Logan, Utah: S. George Ellsworth, 1987).

General Authorities: Twentieth Century. Church leaders are profiled in numerous recent books. An influential counselor in the First Presidency is examined in Frank W. Fox, *J. Reuben Clark: The Public Years* (Salt Lake City: Deseret Book, 1980); and D. Michael Quinn, *J. Reuben Clark, the Church Years* (Provo: Brigham Young University Press, 1983). Other counselors' lives are unfolded in Eugene E. Campbell and Richard D. Poll, *Hugh B. Brown: His Life and Thought* (Salt Lake City: Bookcraft, 1975), with additional insight in Edwin B. Firmage, ed., *An Abundant Life: The Memoirs of Hugh B. Brown* (Salt Lake City: Signature Books, 1988); Edwin B. Firmage, ed., "Hugh B. Brown: The Early Years," *Dialogue: A Journal of Mormon Thought* 21 (Summer 1988): 17–28; G. Homer Durham, *N. Eldon Tanner: His Life and Service* (Salt Lake City: Deseret Book, 1982); and F. Burton Howard, *Marion G. Romney: His Life and Faith* (Salt Lake City: Bookcraft, 1988). Biographies of other leaders include David S. Hoopes and Roy Hoopes, *The Making of a Mormon Apostle: The Story of Rudger Clawson* (Lanham, Md.: Madison Books, 1990); Peggy Petersen Barton, *Mark E. Petersen: A Biography* (Salt Lake City: Deseret Book, 1985); Lucile C. Tate, *LeGrand Richards: Beloved Apostle* (Salt Lake City: Bookcraft, 1982); Lucile C. Tate, *David B. Haight: The Life of a Disciple* (Salt Lake City: Bookcraft, 1987); and George P. Lee, *Silent Courage, An Indian Story: The Autobiography of George P. Lee, a Navajo* (Salt Lake City: Deseret Book, 1987).

Selected Articles: Nineteenth-century People. Useful for information about early Church figures and their families are Frederick G. Williams III, "Frederick Granger Williams of the First Presidency of the Church," *Brigham Young University Studies* 12 (Spring 1972): 243–61; Valeen Tippetts Avery and Linda King Newell, "Lewis C. Bidamon, Stepchild of Mormondom," ibid., 19 (Spring 1979): 375–88; Paul Edwards, "The Sweet Singer of Israel: David Hyrum Smith," ibid., 12 (Winter 1972): 171–84; Ronald G. Watt, "Sailing 'The Old Ship Zion': The Life of George D. Watt," ibid., 18 (Fall 1977): 48–65; Carol Cornwall Madsen, "Emmeline B. Wells, 'Am I Not a Woman and a Sister,' " ibid., 22 (Spring 1982): 161–78; Carol Cornwall Madsen, "A Fine Soul Who Served Us: The Life of Emmeline B. Wells," *Journal of the John Whitmer Historical Association* 2 (1982): 11–21; Valeen Tippetts Avery, "Irreconcilable Differences: David H. Smith's Relationship with the Muse of History," *Journal of Mormon History* 15 (1989): 3–13; John Quist, "John E. Page: An Apostle of Uncertainty," ibid., 12 (1985): 53–68; Loretta L. Hefner, "Amasa Mason Lyman, The Spiritualist," ibid., 6 (1979): 75–87; Hefner, "From Apostle to Apostate: The Personal Struggle of Amasa M. Lyman," *Dialogue: A Journal of Mormon Thought* 16 (Spring 1983): 90–104; Ronald W. Walker, "Martin Harris: Mormonism's Early Convert," ibid., 19 (Winter 1986): 29–43; Irene Bates, "Uncle John Smith, 1781–1854: Patriarchal

Bridge," ibid., 20 (Fall 1987): 79–89; Peter Crawley, "Parley P. Pratt: Father
of Mormon Pamphleteering," ibid., 15 (Autumn 1982): 13–26; and Steven
Pratt, "Eleanor McLean and the Murder of Parley P. Pratt," *Brigham Young
University Studies* 15 (Winter 1975): 225–56; and Paul L. Anderson, "William
Harrison Folsom: Pioneer Architect," *Utah Historical Quarterly* 43 (Summer
1975): 240–59.

Articles: Twentieth-century Church Leaders. In addition to the important
books listed above, see the following articles on other twentieth-century Church
leaders: Ray C. Hillam, comp., "J. Reuben Clark, Jr.: Diplomat and Statesman,"
a collection of essays by various authors, *Brigham Young University Studies*
13 (Spring 1973): 231–456; and Richard D. Poll, "Apostle Extraordinary: Hugh
B. Brown (1883–1975)," *Dialogue: A Journal of Mormon Thought* 10 (Spring
1975–76): 68–71.

Published Diaries. Diaries covering the founding years and early Utah are
Stanley B. Kimball, ed., *On the Potter's Wheel: The Diaries of Heber C. Kimball*
(Salt Lake City: Signature Books and Smith Research Associates, 1987); S.
George Ellsworth, *The Journals of Addison Pratt* (Salt Lake City: University of
Utah Press, 1990). Others are listed at appropriate points in the chapter bib-
liographies.

COLLECTED WORKS

Useful for general reference are a number of publications in which essays,
sermons, statistics, and important documents are collected.

Articles and Essays

The most important sources for articles are the professional journals,
usually issued quarterly, from which we have cited many titles throughout this
bibliography.

Collected Essays. Historical essays are collected in Marvin S. Hill and
James B. Allen, eds., *Mormonism and American Culture* (New York: Harper
& Row, 1972); and Mark F. McKiernan, Alma R. Blair, Paul M. Edwards, eds.,
The Restoration Movement: Essays in Mormon History (Lawrence, Kans.: Co-
ronado Press, 1973). A variety of topics appear in Davis Bitton and Maureen
Ursenbach Beecher, *New Views of Mormon History: Essays in Honor of Leonard
J. Arrington* (Salt Lake City: University of Utah Press, 1987); and in Lyndon
W. Cook and Donald Q. Cannon, *A New Light Breaks Forth: Essays in Mormon
History* (Salt Lake City: Hawkes, 1980). Many of the articles in these books
are cited in chapter bibliographies.

Useful for background information are the articles by Leonard J. Arrington
and Thomas G. Alexander in *A Dependent Commonwealth: Utah's Economy
from Statehood to the Great Depression*, ed. Dean May, Charles Redd Monographs in Western History, no. 4 (Provo: Brigham Young University Press,

1974); and Clark Knowlton, ed., *Social Accommodation in Utah* (Salt Lake City: American West Center, University of Utah, 1975).

DUP Books. Lesson booklets issued monthly by the Daughters of Utah Pioneers, Salt Lake City, often contain historical and biographical information. These are collected into annual volumes, compiled by Kate B. Carter and her successors: *Heart Throbs of the West*, 12 vols. (1939–51); *Treasures of Pioneer History*, 6 vols. (1952–57); *Our Pioneer Heritage*, 20 vols. (1958–77); and *An Enduring Legacy*, 12 vols. to date (1978–).

Sermons

A vast resource for talks given by early Church leaders is the serial publication issued by British Mission officials from transcriptions provided by George D. Watt and other reporters, *Journal of Discourses* . . . , 26 vols. (London: Latter-day Saints' Book Depot, 1854–1886), available in facsimile editions. Issued semiannually in 1880 and the years since 1898 is the *Conference Report* of general conferences of the Church. Older volumes (1898–1921) were reprinted by Hawkes Publishing (Salt Lake City, 1974–75). The Church also published separate reports of the area general conferences. The discourses of many individual General Authorities appear in convenient compilations.

Reference Works

A modern reference work is *Deseret News Church Almanac* (Salt Lake City: Deseret News, annual, 1972–83; biannual, 1985–). It contains a selective chronology, data on current and former General Authorities, useful facts, and statistical information. An older reference work is Andrew Jenson, *The Historical Record: A Monthly Periodical Devoted Exclusively to Historical, Biographical, Chronological, and Statistical Matters*, 9 vols. (Salt Lake City, 1882–1890). Jenson's *Encyclopedic History of The Church* . . . (Salt Lake City: Deseret News Publishing Co., 1941) contains details from the manuscript histories of wards, branches, stakes, missions, and mission conferences on file in the Church Archives. Useful for dating events is Jenson's *Church Chronology: A Record of Important Events* . . . (1886; 2nd ed. rev., Salt Lake City: Deseret News Press, 1914), which consolidates the 2nd edition (1889) and two supplements (covering 1899–1905 and 1906–1913), with indexes.

Useful on the ocean-crossings is Conway B. Sonne, *Saints on the Seas* (Salt Lake City: University of Utah Press, 1983), and Sonne's *Ships, Saints, and Mariners: A Maritime Encyclopedia of Mormon Migration, 1830–1890* (Salt Lake City: University of Utah Press, 1987).

Published Documents

To make the vast resources of the Church Archives and other repositories more widely available, scholars have edited diaries, letters, and other manuscript materials for publication.

Joseph Smith's History. The principal source for the period through 1846 is Joseph Smith, *History of the Church of Jesus Christ of Latter-day Saints. Period I: History of Joseph Smith, the Prophet, and . . . Period II: From the Manuscript History of Brigham Young and Other Original Documents,* ed. B. H. Roberts, 7 vols. (Salt Lake City: published by The Church of Jesus Christ of Latter-day Saints, 1902–1932). Sometimes referred to as the "Documentary History," it is more properly cited by the short title, *History of the Church.* For background on the method of its compilation, see Dean C. Jessee, "The Writing of Joseph Smith's History," *Brigham Young University Studies* 11 (Summer 1971): 439–73; Richard L. Anderson, "New Data for Revising the Missouri 'Documentary History,' " ibid., 14 (Summer 1974): 488–501; Jessee, "The Reliability of Joseph Smith's History," *Journal of Mormon History* 3 (1976): 23–46; and Howard C. Searle, "Authorship of the History of Joseph Smith: A Review Essay," *Brigham Young University Studies* 21 (Winter 1981): 101–22; and Searle, "Authorship of the History of Brigham Young," ibid., 22 (Summer 1982): 367–74.

Early Records. The record of the first Church historian is published as F. Mark McKiernan and Roger D. Launius, *An Early Latter Day Saint History: The Book of John Whitmer; Kept by Commandment* (Independence, Mo.: Herald House, 1980). Early minutes are now published as Lyndon W. Cook and Milton V. Backman, Jr., *Kirtland Elders' Quorum Record, 1836–1841* (Provo: Grandin Book Co., 1985); and Donald Q. Cannon and Lyndon W. Cook, comp., *Far West Record* (Salt Lake City: Deseret Book, 1983).

Selected Documents. Official circulars, letters, and other documents are available in James R. Clark, ed., *Messages of the First Presidency of the Church . . . ,* 6 vols. (Salt Lake City: Bookcraft, 1965–75). A variety of published and unpublished material is brought together in William E. Berrett and Alma P. Burton, comps., *Readings in L.D.S. Church History, from Original Manuscripts,* 3 vols. (Salt Lake City: Deseret Book Co., 1953–58). For valuable personal accounts, see William Mulder and A. Russell Mortensen, eds., *Among the Mormons: Historic Accounts by Contemporary Observers* (1958; Lincoln: University of Nebraska Press, 1973). The period from 1830 to 1844 is included in Keith C. Huntress, ed., *Murder of an American Prophet: . . . Materials for Analysis* (San Francisco: Chandler Publishing, 1960). Individual documents also appeared for a time in "The Historian's Corner," in *Brigham Young University Studies.*

Joseph Smith. The authoritative edition of Joseph Smith's published documents is Dean C. Jessee, ed., *The Papers of Joseph Smith, Volume I: Autobiographical and Historical Writings* (Salt Lake City: Deseret Book, 1989), and other volumes to follow. This edition will prove more useful than Scott H. Faulring, ed., *An American Prophet's Record: The Diaries and Journals of Joseph Smith* (1987; Salt Lake City: Signature Books in Association with Smith Research Associates, 1989). Other useful publications include: Lyndon W. Cook,

The Revelations of the Prophet Joseph Smith (Provo: Seventy's Mission Bookstore, 1981); Andrew F. Ehat and Lyndon W. Cook, comps., *The Words of Joseph Smith* (Salt Lake City: Bookcraft, 1980); Dean C. Jessee, ed. and comp., *The Personal Writings of Joseph Smith* (Salt Lake City: Deseret Book, 1984); and Robert L. Millet, ed., *Joseph Smith: Selected Sermons and Writings* (Mahwah, N.J.: Paulist Press, 1989). Melvin J. Peterson offers helpful observations on "Preparing Early Revelations for Publication," *Ensign* 15 (February 1985): 14–20.

Other Leaders. Published documents include: Dean C. Jessee, *Letters of Brigham Young to His Sons* (Salt Lake City: Deseret Book Co., 1974); Everett L. Cooley, ed., *Diary of Brigham Young, 1857* (Salt Lake City: Tanner Trust Fund, University of Utah Library, 1980); Dean C. Jessee, ed., "The John Taylor Nauvoo Journal," *Brigham Young University Studies* 23 (Summer 1983): 1–105; Elden J. Watson, comp., *The Orson Pratt Journals* (Salt Lake City: Elden J. Watson, 1975); Hyrum M. Smith, ed., *From Prophet to Son: Advice of Joseph F. Smith to His Missionary Sons* (Salt Lake City: Deseret Book, 1981); and David H. Yarn, ed., *J. Reuben Clark: Selected Papers on Religion, Education, and Youth* (Provo: Brigham Young University Press, 1984).

Other Documents. Only a few of the many published personal documents of other Latter-day Saints can be cited. Those pertinent to general topics include Andrew Karl Larson and Katharine Miles Larson, eds., *The Diary of Charles Lowell Walker* (Logan: Utah State University Press, 1980); Mary Ann Hafen, *Recollections of a Handcart Pioneer of 1860: A Woman's Life on the Mormon Frontier* (Lincoln, Neb.: University of Nebraska Press, 1983); and Frederick Stewart Buchanan, ed., *A Good Time Coming: Mormon Letters to Scotland* (Salt Lake City: University of Utah Press, 1988).

BIBLIOGRAPHIES

Guides to further reading and research can be found in most of the general Church histories listed in this bibliography. For sources on specialized topics, see the monographs, theses, and dissertations.

Comprehensive Bibliographies. Of major significance is the union catalog of more than ten thousand publications by and about Latter-day Saints: Chad J. Flake, ed., with an introduction by Dale L. Morgan, *Mormon Bibliography, 1830–1930* (Salt Lake City: University of Utah Press, 1978), and 1,800 additional entries in a . . . *Ten Year Supplement* (1989). A specialized listing is Susan L. Fales and Chad J. Flake, *Mormons and Mormonism in U.S. Government Documents* (Salt Lake City: University of Utah Press, 1989). Published and unpublished materials are listed in Davis Bitton, ed., *Guide to Mormon Diaries and Autobiographies* (Provo: Brigham Young University Press, 1977), a descriptive listing of nearly three thousand items. A concise listing of guides is Susan L. Fales and Lanell M. Reeder, "Mormonism: Bibliography of Bibliographies," *Mormon History Association Newsletter*, no. 72 (April 1989): 5–8, and no. 74 (October 1989): 4–7. Marvin E. Wiggins, *Mormons and Their Neighbors* (Provo: Brigham Young University Library, 1984), indexes 75,000 biographical sketches.

General Bibliographical Essays. Now dated are articles by Thomas G. Alexander and James B. Allen, eds., "The Mormons in the Mountain West: A Selected Bibliography," *Arizona and the West* 9 (Winter 1967): 365–84; Marvin S. Hill, "The Historiography of Mormonism," *Church History* 28 (December 1959): 418–26; and P.A.M. Taylor, "Recent Writing on Utah and the Mormons," *Arizona and the West* 4 (Autumn 1962): 249–60. A discussion and listing of dissertations is Leonard J. Arrington, "Scholarly Studies of Mormonism in the Twentieth Century," *Dialogue: A Journal of Mormon Thought* 1 (Spring 1966): 15–32.

Other Bibliographies. Listing both historical and other types of studies is *A Catalogue of Theses and Dissertations Concerning The Church . . . , Mormonism, and Utah* (complete to January 1970), compiled by the College of Religious Instruction at Brigham Young University (Provo: College of Religious Instruction, BYU, 1971). Other specialized lists are Peter Crawley, "A Bibliography of the Church . . . in New York, Ohio, and Missouri," *Brigham Young University Studies* 12 (Summer 1972): 465–537; Mark L. Grover, *The Mormon Church in Latin America: A Periodical Index, 1830–1976* (Provo: Brigham Young University Press, 1977); and Hyrum L. Andrus and Richard E. Bennett, comps., *Mormon Manuscripts to 1846: A Guide to the Holdings of the Harold B. Lee Library* (Provo: Archives and Manuscripts, Harold B. Lee Library, Brigham Young University, 1977).

Periods in History. Focused on specific periods in Mormon history are Richard D. Poll, "Nauvoo and the New Mormon History: A Bibliographical Survey," *Journal of Mormon History* 5 (1978): 105–123; and Glen M. Leonard, "Recent Writing on Mormon Nauvoo," *Western Illinois Regional Studies* 11 (Fall 1988): 69–93.

Regions. Regional listings include David J. Whittaker, "Mormonism in Victorian Britain: A Bibliographic Essay," in Jensen and Thorp, *Mormons in Early Victorian Britain* (1989), pp. 258–71; Lannon W. Mintz, *The Trail: A Bibliography of the Travelers on the Overland Trail to California, Oregon, Salt Lake City, and Montana during the Years 1841–1864* (Albuquerque: University of New Mexico Press, 1987); Ronald D. Dennis, *Welsh Mormon Publications from 1844 to 1862: A Historical Bibliography* (Provo: BYU Religious Studies Center, 1988); and Russell T. Clement, *Mormons in the Pacific: A Bibliography* (Laie, Hawaii: Institute for Polynesian Studies, 1981).

Topics. Topical bibliographies include Richard O. Cowan and Frank A. Bruno, *Bibliography on Temples and Temple Work* (Provo: Brigham Young University, 1982); Davis Bitton, "Mormon Polygamy: A Review Article," *Journal of Mormon History* 4 (1977): 101–108; Carol Cornwall Madsen and David

J. Whittaker, "History's Sequel: A Source Essay on Women in Mormon History," ibid., 6 (1979): 123–45; Steven L. Shields, *The Latter Day Saint Churches: An Annotated Bibliography* (New York: Garland Publishing, 1987); Chester L. Hawkins, comp., *Selected and Annotated Bibliography on the History and Status of Blacks in the Church . . , 1830–1985* (n.p.: n.p., 1987), available in BYU Special Collections; Wayne L. Wahlquist, "A Review of Mormon Settlement Literature," *Utah Historical Quarterly* 45 (Winter 1977): 3–21; William A. Wilson, "A Bibliography of Studies in Mormon Folklore," ibid., 44 (Fall 1976): 389–94; and Max J. Evans and Ronald G. Watt, "Sources for Western History at the Church . . . , " *Western Historical Quarterly* 8 (July 1977): 303–12.

Concise selected listings are published regularly in *Mormon History Association Newsletter.* They include Roger D. Launius, "A Bibliographical Review of the Reorganized Church in the Nineteenth Century," no. 64 (January 1987): 5–8; David J. Whittaker, "Mormonism in Great Britain, 1837–1987," no. 66 (July 1987): 1–4; Whittaker, "History—Educational System of the LDS Church," no. 68 (April 1988): 2–5; Whittaker, "Bibliography, LDS Missionary Work, Part I," no. 69 (July 1988): 5–8.

Selective rankings are offered by Kent L. Walgren, *The Scallawagiana Hundred: A Selection of the Hundred Most Important Books about the Mormons and Utah* (Salt Lake City: Scallawagiana Books, 1982).

Current Bibliographies. The most helpful current bibliographies are the annual listing, "Mormon Bibliography," compiled by Chad J. Flake, and later by Scott H. Duvall, for *Brigham Young University Studies*, and the three compilations a year initiated by Ralph W. Hansen and continued by Stephen W. Stathis, "Among the Mormons: A Survey of Current Literature," in *Dialogue: A Journal of Mormon Thought.*

HISTORIOGRAPHY

How Mormon history has been and should be written is a subject that has blossomed in interest since the mid-1970s. An increasing number of professionally trained historians are at work in LDS history, and they have engaged in an active discussion of the topic.

The Historians. One way to study how history is written is to look at those who write history. A fine overview is Davis Bitton and Leonard J. Arrington, *Mormons and Their Historians* (Salt Lake City: University of Utah Press, 1988). An unpublished study is Howard C. Searle, "Early Mormon Historiography: Writing the History of the Mormons, 1830–1858" (Ph.D. diss., University of California, Los Angeles, 1979). A shorter overview is David J. Whittaker, "Historians and the Mormon Experience: A Sesquicentennial Perspective," in *Eighth Annual Sidney B. Sperry Symposium* (1980), pp. 293–327. Specific LDS historians are discussed by Ronald W. Walker, "The Stenhouses and the Making of a Mormon Image," *Journal of Mormon History* 1 (1974): 51–71; Walker, "Edward Tullidge: Historian of the Mormon Commonwealth," ibid., 3 (1976): 55–72; James B. Allen, "Since 1950: Creators and Creations of Mormon History," in Bitton and Beecher, *New Views of Mormon History* (1987), pp. 407–38; Dean C. Jessee, "Joseph Smith and the Beginning of Mormon Record Keeping," in Porter and Black, *The Prophet Joseph* (1988), pp. 136–60; Jerald F. Simon, "Thomas Bullock as an Early Mormon Historian," *Brigham Young University Studies*, 30 (Winter 1990): 71–88; and Ted J. Warner, "B. H. Roberts on a Non-Mormon Topic: An Exercise in Historiography," ibid., 16 (Spring 1976): 409–14. A biography of an important student of Mormonism's early Utah period is Levi S. Peterson, *Juanita Brooks: Mormon Woman Historian* (Salt Lake City: University of Utah Press, 1988). Also see Peterson's "Juanita Brooks as a Mormon Dissenter," *John Whitmer Historical Association Journal* 8 (1988): 13–29 and "Juanita Brooks: The Mormon Historian as Tragedian," *Journal of Mormon History* 3 (1976): 47–54. Another influential historian is examined in David J. Whittaker, "Leonard J. Arrington: His Life and Work," *Dialogue: A Journal of Mormon Thought* 11 (Winter 1978): 23–32, to which is appended a list of Arrington's work.

    Historians' Approaches. Commentaries on how specific historians have applied professional techniques in writing religious history include Mario S. DePillis, "Bearding Leone and Others in the Heartland of Mormon Historiography," *Journal of Mormon History* 8 (1981): 79–97; Marvin S. Hill, "Richard L. Bushman: Scholar and Apologist," ibid., pp. 125–33; Klaus J. Hansen, "Jan Shipps and the Mormon Tradition," ibid., pp. 135–45; Newell G. Bringhurst, "Fawn M. Brodie, 'Mormonism's Lost Generation,' and *No Man Knows My History*," ibid., 16 (1990): 11–12; Thomas G. Alexander, "Historiography and the New Mormon History: A Historian's Perspective," *Dialogue: A Journal of Mormon Thought* 19 (Fall 1986): 25–49; M. Gerald Bradford, "The Case for the New Mormon History: Thomas G. Alexander and His Critics," ibid., 21 (Winter 1988): 143–50; and "Coming to Terms with Mormon History: An Interview with Leonard Arrington," ibid., 22 (Winter 1989): 39–54.

    Critiques, 1959–79. Comments on how Mormon history has been written, with suggestions for correcting imbalances, include the survey by Marvin S. Hill, "The Historiography of Mormonism," *Church History* 28 (December 1959): 418–26; and essays by Leonard J. Arrington, "The Search for Truth and Meaning in Mormon History," *Dialogue: A Journal of Mormon Thought* 3 (Summer 1968): 55–66; Robert B. Flanders, "Writing the Mormon Past," ibid., 1 (Autumn 1966): 47–61; and Fawn M. Brodie, *Can We Manipulate the Past?* (Salt Lake City: Center for Studies of the American West, 1970), reviewed by Marvin S. Hill, "The Manipulation of History," in *Dialogue: A Journal of Mormon Thought* 5 (Autumn 1970): 96–99.

    Continuing the discussion are Leonard J. Arrington, "Centrifugal Tendencies in L.D.S. History," in Truman Madsen and Charles Tate, Jr., eds., *To the Glory of God: Mormon Essays on Great Issues* (Salt Lake City: Deseret Book, 1972), pp. 165–77; Richard L. Bushman, "The Historians and Mormon Nauvoo," *Dialogue: A Journal of Mormon Thought* 5 (Spring 1970): 51–61; Robert A. Rees, " 'Truth Is the Daughter of Time': Notes Toward an Imaginative Mormon History," ibid., 6 (Autumn-Winter 1971): 15–22; and Robert Flanders, "Some Reflections on the New Mormon History," ibid., 9 (Spring 1974): 34–42. Offering suggestions for making religion and naturalistic history compatible are Richard L. Bushman, "Faithful History," ibid., 4 (Winter 1969): 11–25; Richard D. Poll, "God and Man in History," ibid., 7 (Spring 1972): 101–109; and Paul M. Edwards, "The Irony of Mormon History," *Utah Historical Quarterly* 41 (Autumn 1973): 393–409; Marvin S. Hill, "The 'Prophet Puzzle' Assembled; or, How to Treat Our Historical Diplopia toward Joseph Smith," *Journal of Mormon History* 3 (1976): 101–105; Thomas G. Alexander, "The Place of Joseph Smith in the Development of American Religion: A Historiographical Inquiry," ibid., 5 (1978): 3–17; Dean L. May, "Thoughts on Faith and History," *Sunstone* 3 (September-October 1978): 35–36; Jan Shipps, "Writing about Modern Mormonism," ibid., 4 (March-April 1979): 42–48; and James B. Allen, "Line upon Line: Church History Reveals How the Lord Has Continually Added to His People's Knowledge and Understanding," *Ensign* 9 (July 1979): 32–39. An early study of the professionalization movement is Richard S. Marshall, "The New Mormon History" (Honors thesis, University of Utah, 1977). Articles by Arrington, Bushman, Clayton, Flanders, Gaustad, Marty, Midgley, Quinn, Robson, and others are collected in George D. Smith, ed., *Faithful History: Essays on Writing Mormon History* (Salt Lake City: Signature Books, 1992).

Comments on Mormon historiography in its western American setting are Moses Rischin, "The New Mormon History," *American West* 6 (March 1969): 49; Rodman W. Paul, "The Mormons as a Theme in Western Historical Writing," *Journal of American History* 54 (December 1967): 511–23; and Thomas G. Alexander, "Toward the New Mormon History: An Examination of the Literature on the Latter-day Saints in the Far West," in Michael P. Malone, ed., *Historians and the American West* (Lincoln: University of Nebraska Press, 1983), pp. 344–68.

Critiques, 1980–91. More recent discussions on how best to write religious history include Boyd K. Packer, "'The Mantle Is Far, Far Greater Than the Intellect," *Brigham Young University Studies* 21 (Summer 1981): 269–78; Louis Midgley, "Faith and History," in Robert L. Millet, ed., *To Be Learned Is Good If . . .* (Salt Lake City: Bookcraft, 1987), pp. 219–26; Leonard J. Arrington, "The Writing of Latter-day Saint History: Problems, Accomplishments, and Admonitions," *Dialogue: A Journal of Mormon Thought* 14 (Autumn 1981): 199–29; Melvin T. Smith, "Faithful History/Secular Faith," ibid., 16 (Winter 1983): 65–71; Kent E. Robson, "Objectivity and History," ibid., 19 (Winter 1986): 87–97; Marvin Hill, "The 'New Mormon History' Reassessed in Light of Recent Books on Joseph Smith and Mormon Origins," ibid., 21 (Autumn 1988): 115–27; Melvin T. Smith, "Faithful History: Hazards and Limitations," *Journal of Mormon History* 9 (1982): 61–69; Edwin S. Gaustad, "Historical Theology and Theological History: Mormon Possibilities," ibid., 11 (1984): 99–111; Henry Warner Bowden, "From the Age of Science to an Age of Uncertainty: History and Mormon Studies in the Twentieth Century," ibid., 15 (1989): 105–19; Grant Underwood, "The New England Origins of Mormonism Revisited," ibid., pp. 15–25; Richard P. Howard, "The Nauvoo Heritage of the Reorganized Church," ibid., pp. 41–52; Edwin S. Gaustad, "History and Theology: The Mormon Connection," *Sunstone* 5 (November-December 1980): 44–50; Jan Shipps, "The Mormon Past: Revealed or Revisited?" ibid., 6 (November-December 1981): 55–57; Ronald K. Esplin, "How Then Should We Write History?" ibid., 7 (March-April 1982): 41–45; Lawrence Foster, "New Perspectives on the Mormon Past," ibid., 7 (January-February 1982): 41–45; Richard D. Poll, "Dealing with Dissonance: Myths, and Faith," ibid., 12 (May 1988): 17–21; Grant Underwood, "Re-visioning Mormon History," *Pacific Historical Review* 55 (August 1986): 403–26; Don H. Compier, "History and Theological Implications of the 'New Mormon History,'" *John Whitmer Historical Association Journal* 8 (1988): 45–53; Thomas Morain, "Mormons and Nineteenth-century Iowa Historians," ibid., 1 (1981): 34–42; and Paul M. Edwards, "A Time and a Season: History as History," ibid., 10 (1990): 85–90.

Personal Reflections. These are contained in William Mulder, "Mormon Angles of Historical Vision: Some Maverick Reflections," *Journal of Mormon History* 3 (1976): 13–22; Joe J. Christensen, "The Value of Church History and Historians: Some Personal Impressions," in *Church Educational System Religious Educators' Symposium, August 22, 1977* (Provo: Brigham Young University Press, 1977), pp. 12–17; Gordon B. Hinckley, "150 Year Drama: A Personal View of Our History," *Ensign* 10 (April 1980): 10–14; Davis Bitton, "Ten Years in Camelot: A Personal Memoir," *Dialogue: A Journal of Mormon Thought* 16 (Autumn 1983): 9–33; Jan Shipps, "An 'Inside-Outsider' in Zion," ibid., 15 (Spring 1982): 138–61; and Richard D. Poll, *History and Faith: Reflections of a Mormon Historian* (Salt Lake City: Signature Books, 1989). An unfinished history and reflections on the writing of Mormon history are collected in John Phillip Walker, ed., *Dale Morgan on Early Mormonism: Correspondence and a New History* (Salt Lake City: Signature Books, 1986).

Chapter Bibliographies

CHAPTER 1
The Historical Setting for the Restoration

Most general histories of the Church listed above comment on the religious setting of the Restoration. Locating historic sites of the Restoration is made easier by Richard Neitzel Holzapfel and T. Jeffery Cottle in their *Old Mormon Palmyra and New England: Historic Photographs and Guide* (Santa Ana, Calif.: Fieldbrook Productions, 1991).

Religious Background. Much information important to Latter-day Saint history is conveniently assembled in Milton V. Backman, Jr., *American Religions and the Rise of Mormonism*, rev. ed. (Salt Lake City: Deseret Book Co., 1970); and summarized in De Lamar Jensen, "Seventeen Centuries of Christianity," *Ensign* 8 (September 1978): 50–57. For more detail on major religious trends, consult standard histories such as Sydney E. Ahlstrom, *A Religious History of the American People* (New Haven: Yale University Press, 1972), parts 1–4; Edwin Scott Gaustad, *A Religious History of America* (New York: Harper & Row, 1966), chaps. 5–12; or Clifton E. Olmstead, *History of Religion in the United States* (Englewood Cliffs, N.J.: Prentice-Hall, 1960), chaps. 1–17.

Putting Mormonism into context is the interpretive work of Marvin S. Hill, *Quest for Refuge: The Mormon Flight from American Pluralism* (Salt Lake City: Signature Books, 1989). An alternative view is presented by Grant Underwood, "The New England Origins of Mormonism Revisited," *Journal of Mormon History* 15 (1989): 15–25. See also John G. Gager, "Early Mormonism and Early Christianity: Some Parallels and Their Consequences for the Study of New Religions," ibid., 9 (1982): 53–60; Timothy L. Smith, "The Book of Mormon in a Biblical Culture," ibid., 7 (1980): 3–21; James R. Christianson, "Puritanism and Mormonism: Parallel Paths, A Parting of Ways," in Cannon, ed., *Regional Studies . . . : New England* (1988), pp. 14–32; Gordon S. Wood, "Evangelical America and Early Mormonism," *New York History* 61 (October 1980): 359–86; Nathan O. Hatch, *The Democratization of American Chris-*

tianity (New Haven: Yale University Press, 1989); and Jan Shipps, "The Reality of the Restoration and the Restoration Ideal in Mormon History" in Richard T. Hughes, ed., *The American Quest for the Primitive Church* (Urbana: University of Illinois Press, 1988), pp. 181–95.

Social Origins. For a brief overview of the political and social setting, see Richard L. Anderson, "1830: Pivotal Year in the Fulness of Times," *Ensign* 8 (September 1978): 9–13. Extensive detail, though partly controversial, on the early American folk setting in which the Smith family lived is presented in D. Michael Quinn, *Early Mormonism and the Magic World View* (Salt Lake City: Signature Books, 1987). See also Ronald W. Walker, "The Persisting Idea of American Treasure Hunting," *Brigham Young University Studies* 24 (Fall 1984): 430–59; Alan Taylor, "Rediscovering the Context of Joseph Smith's Treasure Seeking," *Dialogue: A Journal of Mormon Thought* 19 (Winter 1986): 18–28; and Howard Kerr and Charles L. Crow, eds., *The Occult in America* (Urbana: University of Illinois Press, 1983), especially pp. 58–78. Information on religious activities is in Whitney R. Cross, *The Burned-over District: The Social and Intellectual History of Enthusiastic Religion in Western New York, 1800–1850* (1950; New York: Harper & Row, 1965), chaps. 1–8; with alternative observations in Marvin S. Hill, "The Rise of Mormonism in the Burned-over District: Another View," *New York History* 61 (October 1980): 411–30. See also Hill's "Quest for Refuge: An Hypothesis as to the Social Origins and Nature of the Mormon Political Kingdom," *Journal of Mormon History* 2 (1975): 3–20; Hill, "Counter-Revolution: The Mormon Reaction to the Coming of American Democracy," *Sunstone* 13 (June 1989): 24–33; and Laurence M. Yorgason, "Preview on a Study of the Social and Geographical Origins of Early Mormon Converts, 1830–1845," *Brigham Young University Studies* 10 (Spring 1970): 279–82.

Background on Revivals. See general histories and studies of the Burned-over district listed above and the biographies of Joseph Smith named in the General Bibliography. For discussion, see Wesley P. Walters and Richard L. Bushman, "Roundtable: The Question of the Palmyra Revival," *Dialogue: A Journal of Mormon Thought* 4 (Spring 1969): 59–100; and Peter Crawley, "A Comment on Joseph Smith's Account of His First Vision and the 1820 Revival," ibid., 6 (Spring 1971): 106–7. A good summary is Milton V. Backman, Jr., *Joseph Smith's First Vision: Confirming Evidences and Contemporary Accounts*, 2nd ed. (Salt Lake City: Bookcraft, 1980), chaps. 1–4, which is supplemented by Backman's "Awakenings in the Burned-over District: New Light on the Historical Setting of the First Vision," *Brigham Young University Studies* 9 (Spring 1969): 301–20; Backman, "Lo, Here! Lo, There! Early in the Spring of 1820," in Porter and Black, *The Prophet Joseph* (1988), pp. 19–35; and Backman, "The New England Background to the Restoration," in Cannon, ed., *Regional Studies . . . : New England* (1988), pp. 33–41. A controversial interpretation is Dan Vogel, *Religious Seekers and the Advent of Mormonism*

(Salt Lake City: Signature Books, 1988). A number of articles listed in chapter 2 are also useful.

Joseph Smith's Family. Biographical information and documents on the Prophet's ancestors are in Richard Lloyd Anderson, *Joseph Smith's New England Heritage: Influences of Grandfathers Solomon Mack and Asael Smith* (Salt Lake City: Deseret Book, 1971). Also see Richard L. Bushman, "Joseph Smith's Family Background," in Porter and Black, eds., *The Prophet Joseph Smith* (1988), pp. 1–18; Bushman's *Joseph Smith and the Beginnings of Mormonism* (Urbana: University of Illinois Press, 1984), chap. 1; Gary A. Anderson, "The Mack Family and Marlow, New Hampshire," in Cannon, ed., *Regional Studies . . . : New England* (1988), pp. 43–52; LaMar E. Garrard, "Traditions of Honesty and Integrity in the Smith Family," ibid., pp. 53–64; Richard Lloyd Anderson, "The Alvin Smith Story: Fact and Fiction," *Ensign* 17 (August 1987): 58–72; and biographies of the Prophet. Also pertinent is Reed C. Durham, Jr., "Joseph Smith's Own Story of a Serious Childhood Illness," *Brigham Young University Studies* 10 (Summer 1970): 480–82; LeRoy S. Wirthlin, "Nathan Smith (1762–1828): Surgical Consultant to Joseph Smith," ibid., 17 (Spring 1977): 319–37; Wirthlin, "Joseph Smith's Boyhood Operation: An 1813 Surgical Success," ibid., 21 (Spring 1981): 131–54; Richard L. Anderson, "Joseph Smith's Home Environment," *Ensign* 1 (July 1971): 56–59; Donald L. Enders, "A Snug Log House: A Historical Look at the Joseph Smith, Sr., Family Home in Palmyra, New York," ibid., 15 (August 1985): 14–23; and James B. Allen, "Joseph Smith as a Young Man," *New Era* 1 (January 1971): 19–23.

CHAPTER 2
The Restoration Commences, 1820–1831

Standard Treatments. The best scholarly study of the New York period is Richard L. Bushman, *Joseph Smith and the Beginnings of Mormonism* (Urbana: University of Illinois Press, 1984), a sympathetic account based on primary sources. See also the pertinent chapters in the general works listed in the General Bibliography and the specialized studies listed below.

Concise overviews are Leonard J. Arrington, "Mormonism: From Its New York Beginnings," *New York History* 61 (October 1980): 387–410; and Larry C. Porter, "The Church in New York and Pennsylvania, 1816–1831," in McKiernan et al., *Restoration Movement* (1973), pp. 27–61. For greater detail on the people involved and the historic sites, see Milton V. Backman, *Eyewitness Accounts of the Restoration* (1983; Salt Lake City: Deseret Book, 1986); Holzapfel and Cottle, *Old Mormon Palmyra and New England* (1991); and Larry C. Porter, "A Study of the Origins of The Church . . . in the States of New York and Pennsylvania, 1816–1831" (Ph.D. diss., Brigham Young University, 1971).

First Vision. Several early accounts are discussed in Backman, *Joseph*

Smith's First Vision, cited in chapter 1, and Dean C. Jessee, "The Early Accounts of Joseph Smith's First Vision," *Brigham Young University Studies* 9 (Spring 1969): 275–94. James B. Allen presents a convenient summary and analysis in "Eight Contemporary Accounts of Joseph Smith's First Vision: What Do We Learn from Them?" *Improvement Era* 73 (April 1970): 4–13, and examines public knowledge of the vision in "The Significance of Joseph Smith's First Vision in Mormon Thought," *Dialogue: A Journal of Mormon Thought* 1 (Autumn 1966): 28–45. A related study is Richard L. Anderson, "Circumstantial Confirmation of the First Vision Through Reminiscences," *Brigham Young University Studies* 9 (Spring 1969): 373–404. On the minister who is thought to have influenced Joseph Smith's search for religion, see Larry C. Porter, "Reverend George Lane: Good 'Gifts,' Much 'Grace,' and Marked 'Usefulness,' " ibid., pp. 321–40. Marvin S. Hill offers assessments in "A Note on Joseph Smith's First Vision and Its Import in the Shaping of Early Mormonism," *Dialogue: A Journal of Mormon Thought* 12 (Spring 1979): 90–99; and "The First Vision Controversy: A Critique and Reconciliation," ibid., 15 (Summer 1982): 31–46; as do Neal Lambert and Richard H. Cracroft, "Literary Form and Historical Understanding: Joseph Smith's First Vision," *Journal of Mormon History* 7 (1980): 31–42. For another viewpoint, see Richard P. Howard, "Joseph Smith's First Vision: The RLDS Tradition," ibid., pp. 23–29.

Detractors and Defenders. A good introduction to detractors and defenders is James B. Allen and Leonard J. Arrington, "Mormon Origins in New York: An Introductory Analysis," *Brigham Young University Studies* 9 (Spring 1969): 241–74. See also Marvin S. Hill, "The Historiography of Mormonism," *Church History* 28 (December 1959): 418–26. Discussion of specific issues can be found in Hill, "Joseph Smith and the 1826 Trial: New Evidence and New Difficulties," *Brigham Young University Studies* 12 (Winter 1972): 223–33; Gordon A. Madsen, "Joseph Smith's 1826 Trial: The Legal Setting," ibid., 30 (Spring 1990): 91–108; Richard Lloyd Anderson, "Joseph Smith's New York Reputation Reappraised," ibid., 10 (Spring 1970): 283–314; Rodger I. Anderson, *Joseph Smith's New York Reputation Reexamined* (Salt Lake City: Signature Books, 1990); Marvin S. Hill, "Money-Digging Folklore and the Beginnings of Mormonism: An Interpretive Suggestion," *Brigham Young University Studies*, 24 (Fall 1984): 473–88; Richard Lloyd Anderson, "The Mature Joseph Smith and Treasure Searching," ibid., pp. 489–560; Ronald W. Walker, "The Persisting Idea of American Treasure Hunting," ibid., 24 (Fall 1984): 427–59; Walker, "Joseph Smith: The Palmyra Seer," ibid., pp. 461–72; Richard L. Bushman, "Treasure-seeking Then and Now," *Sunstone* 11 (September 1987): 5–6; Leonard J. Arrington, "James Gordon Bennett's 1831 Report on 'The Mormonites,' " *Brigham Young University Studies* 10 (Spring 1970): 353–64; and Jan Shipps, "The Prophet Puzzle: Suggestions Leading toward a More Comprehensive Interpretation of Joseph Smith," *Journal of Mormon History* 1 (1974): 3–20. Also pertinent are Backman's study on the First Vision cited above; Richard L. Anderson, "The Reliability of the Early History of Lucy and Joseph Smith" *Dialogue: A Journal of Mormon Thought* 4 (Summer 1969): 13–28; and Hugh Nibley, *The Myth Makers* (Salt Lake City: Bookcraft, 1961).

Historical Context. Two important early essays by non-Mormon historians are David Brion Davis, "The New England Origins of Mormonism," *New England Quarterly* 27 (June 1953): 148–53; and Mario S. DePillis, "The Quest for Religious Authority and the Rise of Mormonism," *Dialogue: A Journal of Mormon Thought* 1 (Spring 1966): 68–88. Both have been reprinted in Hill and Allen, *Mormonism and American Culture* (1972), pp. 13–28 and 29–34. Continuing the discussion are Klaus J. Hansen, "Mormonism and American Culture: Some Tentative Hypotheses"; McKiernan et al., *Restoration Movement* (1973), pp. 1–26; Marvin S. Hill, *Quest for Refuge* (1989); Mario DePillis, "The Social Sources of Mormonism," *Church History* 37 (March 1968): 50–79; and Hansen, "The Millennium, the West, and Race in the Antebellum Mind," *Western Historical Quarterly* 3 (October 1972): 373–90. Placing the Book of Mormon into a nineteenth-century cultural setting is Timothy L. Smith, "The Book of Mormon in a Biblical Culture," *Journal of Mormon History* 7 (1980): 3–21; and Dan Vogel, "Mormonism's 'Anti-Masonick Bible,' " *John Whitmer Historical Association Journal* 9 (1989): 17–30.

Book of Mormon. On events leading to publication, see Richard Lloyd Anderson, *Investigating the Book of Mormon Witnesses* (Salt Lake City: Deseret Book, 1980); and four articles in the Spring 1970 issue of *Brigham Young University Studies*: Russell R. Rich, "Where Were the Moroni Visits?" pp. 255–58; Dean C. Jessee, "The Original Book of Mormon Manuscript," pp. 259–78; Russell R. Rich, "The Dogberry Papers and the Book of Mormon," pp. 315–19; and Stanley B. Kimball, "The Anthon Transcript: People, Primary Sources, and Problems," pp. 325–52. Also see Brent Ashworth, ed., "Acquiring the Manuscript," ibid., 23 (Winter 1983): 114–19; Richard Van Wagoner and Steven C. Walker, "Joseph Smith: 'The Gift of Seeing,' " *Dialogue: A Journal of Mormon Thought* 15 (Summer 1982): 49–68; Richard L. Anderson, " 'By the Gift and Power of God,' " *Ensign* 7 (September 1977): 79–85; and Richard L. Bushman, "The Book of Mormon and the American Revolution," *Brigham Young University Studies* 17 (Autumn 1976): 3–20. The book's impact is assessed in Richard L. Bushman, "The Book of Mormon in Early Mormon History," in Bitton and Beecher, *New Views of Mormon History* (1987), pp. 3–18. Another useful study is Richard P. Howard, *Restoration Scriptures: A Study of Their Textual Development* (Independence, Mo.: Herald Publishing House, 1969), chaps. 1–4.

Restoration of the Priesthood. In addition to Bushman, *Joseph Smith and the Beginnings of Mormonism* (1984), see William G. Hartley, " 'Upon You My Fellow Servants': Restoration of the Priesthood," in Porter and Black, eds., *The Prophet Joseph* (1988), pp. 49–72; Larry C. Porter, "Dating the Restoration of the Melchizedek Priesthood," *Ensign* 9 (June 1979): 5–10; Roberts, *Com-*

prehensive History (1930), vol. 1, chap. 15; Richard L. Anderson, "The Second Witness of Priesthood Restoration," *Improvement Era* (September 1968): 15–24; and Hill, *Quest for Refuge* (1989), pp. 25–26.

Organization of the Church. Supplementing standard sources are Carter E. Grant, "Peter Whitmer's Log House," *Improvement Era* 62 (May 1959): 349, 365–66, 369; Larry C. Porter, "The Colesville Branch and the Coming Forth of the Book of Mormon," *Brigham Young University Studies* 19 (Spring 1970): 365–86; Porter, "Was the Church Legally Incorporated at the Time It Was Organized in the State of New York?" *Ensign* 8 (December 1978): 26–27; and Richard L. Anderson, "Who Were the Six Who Organized the Church on 6 April 1830?" *Ensign* 10 (June 1980): 44–45. An important letter is reproduced in D. Michael Quinn, "The First Months of Mormonism: A Contemporary View by Rev. Diedrich Willers," *New York History* 54 (July 1973): 317–33.

Early Missionary Work. Information can be found in Larry C. Porter, " 'The Field is White Already to Harvest': Earliest Missionary Labors and the Book of Mormon," in Porter and Black, *The Prophet Joseph* (1988), pp. 73–89; Richard L. Anderson, "The Impact of the First Preaching in Ohio," *Brigham Young University Studies* 11 (Summer 1971): 474–96; Richard E. Bennett, " 'Plucking Not Planting': Mormonism in Eastern Canada, 1830–1850," in Card et al., eds., *The Mormon Presence in Canada* (1990), pp. 19–34; and Warren A. Jennings, "The First Mormon Mission to the Indians," *Kansas Historical Quarterly* 38 (Autumn 1971): 288–99.

Other Topics. Useful on doctrine are Philip L. Barlow, "Before Mormonism: Joseph Smith's Use of the Bible, 1820–29," *Journal of the American Academy of Religion* 57 (Winter 1989): 739–71; and Marvin S. Hill, "The Shaping of the Mormon Mind in New England and New York," *Brigham Young University Studies* 9 (Spring 1969): 351–72. Also see the studies of Grant Underwood: "Millenarianism in the Early Mormon Mind," *Journal of Mormon History* 9 (1982): 41–51; "Book of Mormon Usage in Early LDS Theology," *Dialogue: A Journal of Mormon Thought* 17 (Autumn 1984): 35–74; and "Saved or Damned: Tracing a Persistent Protestantism in Early Mormon Thought," *Brigham Young University Studies* 24 (Summer 1985): 85–103. Preliminary comments on identifying locations are in T. Edgar Lyon, "How Authentic Are Mormon Historic Sites in Vermont and New York?" ibid., pp. 341–50.

CHAPTER 3
Unfolding Latter-day Zion, 1831–1836

Details on the important events transpiring in the areas surrounding both Kirtland, Ohio, and Jackson County, Missouri, can be found in the relevant chapters of the general works cited in the General Bibliography.

Descriptions. For settings for the two gathering places, see Robert L. Layton, "Kirtland: A Perspective on Time and Place," *Brigham Young University Studies* 11 (Summer 1971): 423–38; Richard L. Anderson, "Jackson County in Early Mormon Descriptions," *Missouri Historical Review* 65 (April 1971): 270–93; and Anderson's "New Data for Revising the Missouri 'Documentary History,' " *Brigham Young University Studies* 14 (Summer 1974): 488–501. Also of interest is Max H. Parkin, "The Courthouse Mentioned in the Revelation on Zion," ibid., pp. 451–57.

Ohio. For a comprehensive overview on Ohio see Milton V. Backman, Jr., *The Heavens Resound: A History of the Latter-day Saints in Ohio, 1830–1838* (Salt Lake City: Deseret Book, 1983). Supplementing this basic synthesis are Backman, "The Quest for a Restoration: The Birth of Mormonism in Ohio," *Brigham Young University Studies* 12 (Summer 1972): 346–64; Mark R. Grandstaff and Backman, "The Social Origins of the Kirtland Mormons," ibid., 30 (Spring 1990): 47–66; and Backman, *A Profile of Latter-day Saints of Kirtland, Ohio, and Members of Zion's Camp, 1830–1839* (Provo: BYU Department of Church History and Doctrine, 1982). Max H. Parkin summarizes his M.A. thesis in "Kirtland, a Stronghold for the Kingdom," in McKiernan et al., *The Restoration Movement* (1973), pp. 63–98; and offers additional insight in his "Mormon Political Involvement in Ohio," *Brigham Young University Studies* 9 (Summer 1969): 484–502. Other interpretations include Keith W. Perkins, "The Prophet Joseph Smith in 'the Ohio': The Schoolmaster," in Porter and Black, *The Prophet Joseph* (1988), pp. 90–114; and Robert Kent Fielding, "The Growth of the Mormon Church in Kirtland, Ohio" (Ph.D. diss., University of Indiana, 1957).

Personal glimpses into Mormon life are in Dean C. Jessee, ed., "The Kirtland Diary of Wilford Woodruff," *Brigham Young University Studies* 12 (Summer 1972): 365–99; Leonard J. Arrington, ed., "Oliver Cowdery's Kirtland, Ohio, 'Sketch Book,' " ibid., pp. 410–26; Linda King Newell and Valeen Tippetts Avery, "Sweet Counsel and Seas of Tribulation: The Religious Life of the Women in Kirtland," ibid., 20 (Fall 1979): 151–62; Karl R. Anderson, *Joseph Smith's Kirtland: Eyewitness Accounts* (Salt Lake City: Deseret Book, 1989); and Richard N. Holzapfel and T. Jeffrey Cottle, *Old Mormon Kirtland and Missouri* (Santa Ana, Calif.: Fieldbrook Productions, 1991). An important figure is examined in Hans Rollmann, "The Early Baptist Career of Sidney Rigdon in Warren, Ohio," *Brigham Young University Studies*, 21 (Winter 1981): 37–50.

Missouri. Besides narratives in general histories, see Warren A. Jennings, "The Expulsion of the Mormons from Jackson County, Missouri," *Missouri Historical Review* 64 (October 1969): 41–63, drawn from his Ph.D. dissertation. Important essays seeking to understand the Missouri problems are Jennings, "The City in the Garden: Social Conflict in Jackson County, Missouri," in McKiernan et al., *Restoration Movement* (1973), pp. 99–119; Richard L. Bushman, "Mormon Persecutions in Missouri, 1833," *Brigham Young University*

Studies 3 (Autumn 1960): 11–20; and R. J. Robertson, Jr., "The Mormon Experience in Missouri, 1803–1839," *Missouri Historical Review* 68 (April and July 1974): 280–98 and 393–415. An important survey of the Latter-day Saint image is David Brion Davis, "Some Themes of Counter-Subversion: An Analysis of Anti-Masonic, Anti-Catholic, and Anti-Mormon Literature," *Mississippi Valley Historical Review* 47 (September 1960): 205–24, reprinted in Hill and Allen, *Mormonism and American Culture* (1972), pp. 59–73. Events are given a religious interpretation in B. H. Roberts, *The Missouri Persecutions* (1900; reprinted, Salt Lake City: Bookcraft, 1965); and Clark V. Johnson, "Let Far West Be Holy and Consecrated," in Porter and Black, *The Prophet Joseph* (1988), pp. 226–45.

Conflict. One aspect is examined in Warren A. Jennings, "Factors in the Destruction of the Mormon Press in Missouri, 1833," *Utah Historical Quarterly* 35 (Winter 1967): 56–76. Useful for background reading is Donnie D. Bellamy, "Free Blacks in Antebellum Missouri, 1820–1860," *Missouri Historical Review* 67 (January 1973): 198–226. The race issue and its implications are traced beyond this period in Stephen Taggart, *Mormonism's Negro Policy: Social and Historical Origins* (Salt Lake City: University of Utah Press, 1970); and in Lester Bush, Jr., "Mormonism's Negro Doctrine: An Historical Overview," *Dialogue: A Journal of Mormon Thought* 8 (Spring 1973): 11–68. The 1832 mob incident is described in Susan Easton Black, "Hiram, Ohio: Tribulation," in Porter and Black, *The Prophet Joseph* (1988), pp. 161–74.

Zion's Camp. The basic story of the attempt to reinstate the Saints on their Jackson County lands is in Peter Crawley and Richard L. Anderson, "The Political and Social Realities of Zion's Camp," *Brigham Young University Studies* 14 (Summer 1974): 406–20; and, from an RLDS perspective, Roger D. Launius, *Zion's Camp: Expedition to Missouri, 1834* (Independence: Herald House, 1984). Useful also are Bruce A. Van Orden, "Zion's Camp: A Refiner's Fire," in Porter and Black, *The Prophet Joseph* (1988), pp. 192–207; and Stanley B. Kimball, "Zion's Camp March from Ohio to Missouri, 1834," *Ensign* 9 (April 1979): 45–49. An interesting incident is examined in Kenneth W. Godfrey, "The Zelph Story," *Brigham Young University Studies* 29 (Spring 1989): 31–56. For other items of interest see Warren A. Jennings, "The Army of Israel Marches into Missouri," *Missouri Historical Review* 62 (January 1968): 107–35.

Cooperative Economics. Basic economic studies are Leonard J. Arrington's careful analysis, "Early Mormon Communitarianism: The Law of Consecration and Stewardship," *Western Humanities Review* 7 (Autumn 1953): 341–69; his *Great Basin Kingdom* (1958), chap. 1; and Lyndon W. Cook, *Joseph Smith and the Law of Consecration* (Orem, Utah: Grandin Books, 1985). Selected aspects of the conflict and comments on economic activities are in T. Edgar Lyon, "Independence, Missouri, and the Mormons, 1827–1833," *Brigham Young University Studies* 13 (Autumn 1972): 10–19; and Ronald E. Romig and John H. Siebert, "First Impressions: The Independence, Missouri, Printing Operation, 1832–33," *John Whitmer Historical Association Journal* 10 (1990): 51–66. Differing assessments on the law of consecration and economic policies are in Kent W. Huff, "The United Order of Joseph Smith's Times," *Dialogue: A Journal of Mormon Thought* 19 (Summer 1986): 146–49; Mario S. DePillis, "The Development of Mormon Communitarianism, 1826–1846" (Ph.D. diss., Yale University, 1960); and R. Kent Fielding, "The Mormon Economy in Kirtland, Ohio," *Utah Historical Quarterly* 27 (October 1959): 331–56. See also the bibliography for chap. 4.

Administrative History. To supplement standard histories, see D. Michael Quinn, "The Evolution of the Presiding Quorums of the LDS Church," *Journal of Mormon History* 1 (1974): 21–38; Robert J. Woodford, "Jesse Gause, Counselor to the Prophet," *Brigham Young University Studies* 15 (Spring 1975): 362–64; Quinn, "Jessee Gause: Joseph Smith's Little-known Counselor," ibid., 23 (Fall 1983): 487–93; Donald Q. Cannon, "Licensing in the Early Church," ibid., 22 (Winter 1982): 96–105; and Richard L. Anderson, "What Changes Have Been Made in the Name of the Church?" *Ensign* 9 (January 1979): 13–14.

Church Activities. On proselyting, see Davis Bitton, "Kirtland as a Center of Missionary Activity, 1830–1838," *Brigham Young University Studies* 11 (Summer 1971): 497–51; Larry C. Porter, "Beginnings of the Restoration: Canada: An 'Effectual Door' to the British Isles," in Bloxam et al., *Truth Will Prevail* (1987), pp. 3–43; F. Mark McKiernan, "The Conversion of Sidney Rigdon to Mormonism," *Dialogue: A Journal of Mormon Thought* 5 (Summer 1970): 71–78; a chapter on the Kirtland School in John A. Patrick, "The School of the Prophets: Its Development and Influence in Utah Territory" (M.A. thesis, Brigham Young University, 1970); and Louis C. Zucker, "Joseph Smith as a Student of Hebrew," *Dialogue: A Journal of Mormon Thought* 3 (Summer 1968): 41–55.

Kirtland Temple. See Talmage, *House of the Lord* (1920, 1976), chap. 5; and Lauritz G. Peterson, "The Kirtland Temple," *Brigham Young University Studies* 12 (Summer 1972): 400–409. An RLDS view is Roger D. Launius, *The Kirtland Temple: A Historical Narrative* (Independence: Herald House, 1986). Another context is offered in Laurel B. Andrew, *The Early Temples of the Mormons* (1978); and by Clarence L. Fields, "History of the Kirtland Temple" (M.S. thesis, Brigham Young University, 1963).

Joseph Smith's Revision of the Bible. The Prophet's work is described in Robert J. Matthews, *"A Plainer Translation": Joseph Smith's Translation of the Bible; A History and Commentary* (Provo: Brigham Young University Press, 1975), and in Howard, *Restoration Scriptures* (1969), chaps. 5–9.

Book of Mormon Critiques. E. D. Howe, *Mormonism Unvailed* (Painesville, N.Y.: E. D. Howe, 1834) raised the question of Joseph Smith's reputation in New York (see the writings on detractors and defenders in the bibliography for chap. 2) and introduced the Spaulding-Rigdon theory of the origin of the *Book of Mormon*. This theory has long been discredited by writers, among them George Reynolds, *The Myth of the "Manuscript Found"; or, The Absurdities of the "Spaulding Story"* (Salt Lake City: Juvenile Instructor Office, 1883); Brodie, *No Man Knows My History* (1945), pp. 442–56; and Kirkham, *New Witness for Christ* (1942, 1967), 1:299–336. It is discussed in its historical context in Arrington and Allen, "Mormon Origins in New York: An Introductory Analysis," *Brigham Young University Studies* 9 (Spring 1969): 245–48; and at length in Lester E. Bush, Jr., "The Spaulding Theory Then and Now," *Dialogue: A Journal of Mormon Thought* 10 (Autumn 1977): 40–69. Another early critique of Mormonism is explained in Dennis Rawley, "The Ezra Booth Letters," ibid., 16 (Autumn 1983): 133–39.

Doctrine and Covenants. To supplement general histories and commentaries, see the detailed historical treatises by Howard, *Restoration Scriptures*, chaps. 10–11; and Robert J. Woodford, "The Historical Development of the Doctrine and Covenants" (Ph.D. diss., Brigham Young University, 1974). Also useful is Earl E. Olson, "The Chronology of the Ohio Revelations," *Brigham Young University Studies* 11 (Summer 1971): 329–49; and Woodford, "The Story of the Doctrine and Covenants," *Ensign* 14 (December 1984): 32–39.

Book of Abraham. The history of the Book of Abraham is described in Jay M. Todd, *The Saga of the Book of Abraham* (Salt Lake City: Deseret Book, 1969); and Walter L. Whipple, "The St. Louis Museum and the Two Egyptian Mummies and Papyri," *Brigham Young University Studies* 10 (Autumn 1969): 57–64. Closer looks at the translation include Hugh Nibley, *Message of the Joseph Smith Papyri: An Egyptian Endowment* (Salt Lake City: Deseret Book, 1975); and several articles by Nibley: "Phase One," *Dialogue: A Journal of Mormon Thought* 3 (Summer 1969): 99–105; "The Meaning of the Kirtland Egyptian Papers," *Brigham Young University Studies* 11 (Summer 1971): 350–99; and "A New Look at the Pearl of Great Price," 22 installments, *Improvement Era* 71–73 (January 1968–May 1970).

Doctrine. Studies on specific LDS teachings originating in this period are Lester E. Bush, Jr., "The Word of Wisdom in Early Nineteenth-Century Perspective," *Dialogue: A Journal of Mormon Thought* 14 (Winter 1981): 46–65; Leonard J. Arrington, "An Economic Interpretation of the 'Word of Wisdom,' " *Brigham Young University Studies* 1 (Winter 1959): 37–49; Robert J. Matthews, "The 'New Translation' of the Bible, 1830–33: Doctrinal Development during the Kirtland Era," ibid., 11 (Summer 1971): 400–423; Gordon Irving, "The Mormons and the Bible in the 1830s," ibid., 13 (Summer 1973): 473–88; Danel W. Bachman, "New Light on an Old Hypothesis: The Ohio Origins of the Revelation on Eternal Marriage," *Journal of Mormon History* 5 (1978): 19–32; and Peter Crawley, "The Passage of Mormon Primitivism," *Dialogue: A Journal of Mormon Thought* 13 (Winter 1980): 26–37.

CHAPTER 4
The Saints Move On, 1836–1839

The last years in Ohio and Missouri have been portrayed by historians as years of conflict. The most up-to-date overviews are in Backman, *The Heavens Resound* (1983), and the CES textbook, *Church History in the Fulness of Times* (1989), chaps. 14–16. The story is told in the general surveys cited in the General Bibliography. On the beginnings of the British Mission, see James R. Moss, "The Gospel Restored to England," in Bloxham et al., eds., *Truth Will Prevail* (1987), pp. 71–103.

Additional insights include articles in special summer issues of *Brigham Young University Studies*, 1972, 1973, and 1974. See also Leland H. Gentry, "A History of the Latter-day Saints in Northern Missouri from 1836 to 1839" (Ph.D. diss, Brigham Young University, 1965). Events at key places are discussed in Floyd C. Shoemaker, "Clay County," *Missouri Historical Review* 52 (October 1957): 25–34; Robert J. Matthews, "Adam-ondi-Ahman," *Brigham Young University Studies* 13 (Autumn 1972): 27–35; Leland H. Gentry, "Adam-ondi-Ahman: A Brief Historical Survey," ibid., 13 (Summer 1973): 553–76; and F. Mark McKiernan, "Mormonism on the Defensive: Far West," in McKiernan et al., *Restoration Movement* (1973), pp. 121–40. Davis Bitton examines the neglected years after Joseph Smith's departure in "The Waning of Mormon Kirtland," *Brigham Young University Studies* 12 (Summer 1972): 455–64.

Kirtland Economy. A combination of historical and economic research techniques has produced significant reinterpretations of Latter-day Saint financial affairs in Ohio, reported in D. Paul Sampson and Larry T. Wimmer, "The Kirtland Safety Society: The Stock Ledger Book and the Bank Failure," *Brigham Young University Studies* 12 (Summer 1972): 427–36; Scott H. Partridge, "The Failure of the Kirtland Safety Society," ibid., pp. 437–54; Marvin S. Hill, "Cultural Crisis in the Mormon Kingdom: A Reconsideration of the Causes of Kirtland Dissent," *Church History* 49 (September 1980): 286–97; and an important study by Marvin S. Hill, Larry T. Wimmer, and Keith C. Rooker, "The Kirtland Economy Revisited: A Market Place Critique of Sectarian Economics," *Brigham Young University Studies* 17 (Summer 1977): 391–472 (and issued by BYU Press separately in 1978). Another treatment is D. A. Dudley, "Bank Born of Revelation: The Kirtland Safety Society Anti-Banking Co.," *Journal of Economic History* 30 (December 1971): 848–53.

Missouri Difficulties. One thorough analysis of the Missouri conflict is Stephen C. LeSueur, *The 1838 Mormon War in Missouri* (Columbia: University of Missouri Press, 1987). Supplementing general sources are the following articles in *Brigham Young University Studies*: Peter Crawley, "Two Rare Missouri Documents," 14 (Summer 1974): 502–27, which reproduces the *Evening and the Morning Star* Extra of February 1834 and Sidney Rigdon's July 4, 1838, oration; F. Mark McKiernan, "Sidney Rigdon's Missouri Speeches," 11 (Autumn 1970): 90–92; Leland H. Gentry, "The Danite Band of 1838," 14 (Summer 1974): 421–50; Dean C. Jessee and David J. Whittaker, eds., "The Last Months of Mormonism in Missouri: The Albert Perry Rockwood Journal," 28 (Winter 1988): 1–41; Paul C. Richards, "Missouri Persecutions: Petitions for Redress," 13 (Summer 1973): 520–43; Reed C. Durham, Jr., "The Election Day Battle at Gallatin," 13 (Autumn 1972): 36–61; Alma Blair, "The Haun's Mill Massacre," ibid., pp. 62–67; and Clark V. Johnson, "Missouri Persecutions: The Petitions of Isaac Leany," 23 (Winter 1983): 94–103. Also pertinent are Monte B. McLaws, "The Attempted Assassination of Missouri's Ex-Governor, Lilburn W. Boggs," *Missouri Historical Review* 60 (October 1965): 50–62; Schindler, *Orrin Porter Rockwell* (1966), chap. 2; and David J. Whittaker, "The Book of Daniel in Early Mormon Thought," in John M. Lundquist and Stephen D. Ricks, eds., *By Study and Also by Faith* (Salt Lake City: Deseret Book; and Provo: Foundation for Ancient Research and Mormon Studies, 1990), pp. 155–99. Also see Leonard J. Arrington, "The Colloquial Term 'Jack-Mormon': Where Does It Come From?" *Ensign* 4 (March 1974): 25.

Exile. On the final months in Missouri see Gregory Maynard, "Alexander Doniphan: Man of Justice," *Brigham Young University Studies* 13 (Summer 1973): 462–72; Leonard J. Arrington, "Church Leaders in Liberty Jail," ibid., 13 (Autumn 1972): 20–26; and Dean C. Jessee, " 'Walls, Grates and Screeking Iron Doors': The Prison Experience of Mormon Leaders in Missouri, 1838–1839," in Bitton and Beecher, *New Views of Mormon History* (1987), pp. 19–42. That Nauvoo was not the only place of refuge for exiles from western and northern Missouri is pointed out in Stanley B. Kimball, "The Saints and St. Louis, 1831–1857: An Oasis of Tolerance and Security," *Brigham Young University Studies* 13 (Summer 1973): 489–519.

CHAPTER 5
Building the City Beautiful, 1839–1842

Most histories of this period focus on events in Nauvoo and, except for the British Mission, say little of the Church outside the central gathering place. For the general histories, see the listings in the General Bibliography.

Two monographs focusing on the whole period are especially useful: Robert B. Flanders, *Nauvoo: Kingdom on the Mississippi* (Urbana: University of Illinois Press, 1965), analyzes political and economic life in depth; while David E. Miller and Della S. Miller, *Nauvoo: The City of Joseph* (Santa Barbara and Salt Lake City: Peregrine Smith, 1974), offers a narrative survey, with useful sections on land purchases, religious activities, and the operations of city government. See also Allen, *Trials of Discipleship: The Story of William Clayton* (1987), chaps. 1–7. Useful brief overviews are Janath Cannon, *Nauvoo Panorama: Views of Nauvoo before, during, and after Its Rise, Fall, and Restoration* (Salt

Lake City: Nauvoo Restoration, Inc., 1991); Donald Q. Cannon, "The Founding of Nauvoo," in Porter and Black, *The Prophet Joseph* (1988), pp. 246–60; Stanley B. Kimball, "The Mormons in Illinois, 1838–1846: A Special Introduction," *Journal of the Illinois State Historical Society* 64 (Spring 1971): 4–21; and, with a perspective on social history, Kenneth W. Godfrey, "Some Thoughts Regarding an Unwritten History of Nauvoo," *Brigham Young University Studies* 15 (Summer 1975): 417–24. The expansion of settlements is examined in Stanley B. Kimball, "Nauvoo West: The Mormons of the Iowa Shore," ibid., 18 (Winter 1978): 132–42; and Hamilton Marshall, " 'Money-Diggersville': The Brief, Turbulent History of the Mormon Town of Warren," *John Whitmer Historical Association Journal* 9 (1989): 49–58. Buildings for which photographs survived are identified in Richard N. Holzapfel and T. Jeffery Cottle, *Old Mormon Nauvoo and Southeastern Iowa, 1839–1846: Historic Photographs and Guide*, 2nd ed. (Santa Ana, Calif.: Fieldbrook Productions, 1991). Further information on the settlement process is in Donald L. Enders, "Platting the City Beautiful: A Historical and Archaeological Glimpse of Nauvoo Streets," *Brigham Young University Studies* 19 (1979): 409–15; and James E. Smith, "Frontier Nauvoo: Building a Picture from Statistics," *Ensign* 9 (September 1979): 16–19.

British Mission and Emigration. The sesquicentennial in 1987 of the British Mission's beginning brought forth many new studies. A detailed account which includes important documents is James B. Allen, Ronald K. Esplin, and David J. Whittaker, *Men with a Mission: The Quorum of the Twelve Apostles in the British Isles, 1837–1841* (Salt Lake City: Deseret Book, 1992). See also the following in Bloxham et al., *Truth Will Prevail* (1987); Ben V. Bloxham, "The Call of the Apostles to the British Isles," pp. 104–20; and "The Apostolic Foundations, 1840–41," pp. 121–62. Also of interest are John F. C. Harrison, "The Popular History of Early Victorian Britain: A Mormon Contribution," *Journal of Mormon History* 14 (1988): 3–15; Richard L. Jensen, "Transplanted to Zion: The Impact of British Latter-day Saint Immigration upon Nauvoo," *Brigham Young University Studies* 31 (Winter 1991): 77–87; and relevant sections of Allen and Alexander, *Manchester Mormons* (1974); P.A.M. Taylor, *Expectations Westward* (1965); and Flanders, *Nauvoo: Kingdom on the Mississippi* (1965). George D. Watt's claim to being the first baptized is examined in Garth N. Jones, "Who Came in Second?" *Dialogue: A Journal of Mormon Thought* 21 (Summer 1988): 149–54.

Government in Nauvoo. Besides the books by Flanders and the Millers, see two articles by James L. Kimball, Jr., "The Nauvoo Charter: A Reinterpretation," *Journal of the Illinois State Historical Society* 64 (Spring 1971): 66–78; and "A Wall to Defend Zion: The Nauvoo Charter," *Brigham Young University Studies* 15 (Summer 1975): 491–97. On the city militia, see Hamilton Gardner, "The Nauvoo Legion, 1840–1845: A Unique Military Organization," *Journal of the Illinois State Historical Society* 65 (Summer 1961):

181–97, a concise chronicle of the Legion's legal basis, activities, and uniqueness; and John Sweeney, Jr., "A History of the Nauvoo Legion in Illinois" (M.A. thesis, Brigham Young University, 1974), a year-by-year account with lists of officers and charts of organization.

Economic Life. The subject receives adequate treatment in Flanders and Miller and Miller. The economic impact of the Mississippi is examined in Dennis Rowley, "Nauvoo: A River Town," *Brigham Young University Studies* 18 (Winter 1978): 255–72. Two projects reported by Donald L. Enders are "A Dam for Nauvoo: An Attempt to Industrialize the City," ibid., pp. 246–54; and "The Steamboat 'Maid of Iowa': Mormon Mistress of the Mississippi," ibid., 19 (Spring 1979): 321–35. Additional insights are in T. Edgar Lyon, "The Account Books of the Amos Davis Store at Commerce, Illinois," ibid., 19 (Winter 1979): 241–43; Arrington, *Great Basin Kingdom* (1958), pp. 3–35; and M. Hamblin Cannon, ed., "Bankruptcy Proceedings against Joseph Smith in Illinois," *Pacific Historical Review* 14 (December 1945): 424–33, and 15 (June 1946): 214–15.

Nauvoo Society. For a systematic presentation of facts, see George W. Givens, *In Old Nauvoo: Everyday Life in the City of Joseph* (Salt Lake City: Deseret Book, 1990). Kenneth W. Godfrey offers a comparative approach in "The Nauvoo Neighborhood: A Little Philadelphia or a Unique City Set upon a Hill," *Journal of Mormon History* 11 (1984): 79–97. Useful also is Guy M. Bishop, "Sex Roles, Marriage, and Childrearing at Mormon Nauvoo," *Western Illinois Regional Studies* 11 (Fall 1988): 30–45; Terence A. Tanner, "The Mormon Press in Nauvoo, 1839–1846," ibid., pp. 5–29; and Kenneth W. Godfrey, "Some Thoughts Regarding an Unwritten History of Nauvoo," *Brigham Young University Studies* 15 (Summer 1975): 417–24, a brief sampling from firsthand sources.

Biographical Studies. In addition to the biographies listed in the General Bibliography, see the following profiles by Lyndon W. Cook: "Isaac Galland: Mormon Benefactor," *Brigham Young University Studies* 19 (Spring 1979): 261–84; "James Arlington Bennett and the Mormons," ibid., 19 (Winter 1979): 247–49; "Lyman Sherman: Man of God, Would-be Apostle," ibid., 19 (Fall 1978): 121–24; and "William Law, Nauvoo Dissenter," ibid., 22 (Winter 1982): 47–72.

Freemasonry. For an introduction, see Kenneth W. Godfrey, "Joseph Smith and the Masons," *Journal of the Illinois State Historical Society* 64 (Spring 1971): 79–90. Extensive research by Mervin B. Hogan is reported in a series of booklets published by the author in Salt Lake City, including: *Mormonism and Free Masonry: The Illinois Episode* (1980); *Freemasonry and Civil Confrontation on the Illinois Frontier* (1982); and *Joseph Smith's Embracement of Freemasonry* (1988); and in Hogan's "The Milieu of Mormonism and Freemasonry at Nauvoo: An Interpretation," *Transactions: The American Lodge of Research, Free, and Accepted Masons* 13 (1976): 188–202. A related study is James B. Allen, "Nauvoo's Masonic Hall," *John Whitmer Historical Association Journal* 10 (1990): 39–49.

Church Organization and Doctrine. Basic sources include Miller and Miller, *Nauvoo: City of Joseph* (1975), chap. 3; Joseph Smith, *History of the Church* (1902–32), vols. 4–5; and two useful articles by T. Edgar Lyon: "Nauvoo and the Council of the Twelve," in McKiernan et al., *The Restoration Movement* (1973), pp. 167–205; and "Doctrinal Development of the Church during the Nauvoo Sojourn, 1839–1846," *Brigham Young University Studies* 15 (Summer 1975): 435–46. For a helpful overview see Marvin S. Hill, "The Mormon Religion in Nauvoo: Some Reflections," *Utah Historical Quarterly* 44 (Spring 1976): 170–80. Focused looks at doctrinal development include D. Michael Quinn, "The Practice of Rebaptism at Nauvoo," *Brigham Young University Studies* 18 (Winter 1978): 226–32; M. Guy Bishop, " 'What Has Become of Our Fathers?' Baptism for the Dead at Nauvoo," *Dialogue: A Journal of Mormon Thought* 23 (Summer 1990): 84–97; David J. Whittaker, "Orson Pratt: Prolific Pamphleteer," ibid., 15 (Autumn 1982): 27–31; Whittaker, "Early Mormon Pamphleteering," *Journal of Mormon History* 4 (1977): 35–49; Steve Epperson, "Jews in the Columns of Joseph's *Times and Seasons*," ibid., 22 (Winter 1989): 135–42; Charles R. Harrell, "The Development of the Doctrine of the Preexistence, 1830–1844," *Brigham Young University Studies* 28 (Spring 1988): 75–96; Linda Wilcox, "The Mormon Concept of a Mother in Heaven," *Sunstone* 5 (September-October 1980): 9–15; Stanley B. Kimball, "Kinderhook Plates Brought to Joseph Smith Appeared to be a Nineteenth Century Hoax," *Ensign* 11 (August 1981): 66–74; David J. Whittaker, " 'The Articles of Faith' in Early Mormon Literature and Thought," in Bitton and Beecher, *New Views of Mormon History* (1987), pp. 63–92; and Thomas G. Alexander, " 'A New and Everlasting Covenant': An Approach to the Theology of Joseph Smith," ibid., pp. 43–62. Kathryn M. Daynes looks at plural marriage as a way to cement loyalty in "Family Ties: Belief and Practice in Nauvoo," *John Whitmer Historical Association Journal* 8 (1988): 63–75.

King Follett Discourse. This influential funeral sermon is examined in Donald Q. Cannon, "The King Follett Discourse: Joseph Smith's Greatest Sermon in Historical Perspective," *Brigham Young University Studies* 18 (Winter 1978): 179–92; Stan Larson, "The King Follett Discourse: A Newly Amalgamated Text," ibid., pp. 193–208; Van Hale, "The Doctrinal Impact of the King Follett Discourse," ibid., pp. 209–25; and Hale, "The King Follett Discourse: Textual History and Criticism," *Sunstone* 8 (September-October 1983): 5–12.

Nauvoo Temple. For information beyond that in histories of the period, see Stanley B. Kimball,"The Nauvoo Temple," *Improvement Era* 66 (November 1963): 974–84, for a physical description; J. Earl Arrington, "William Weeks, Architect of the Nauvoo Temple," *Brigham Young University Studies* 19 (Spring 1979): 337–59; and for detail on the construction, Don F. Colvin's

M.S. thesis (BYU, 1962). The temple's impact on the Church is examined in Ronald K. Esplin, "The Significance of Nauvoo for Latter-day Saints," *Journal of Mormon History* 16 (1990): 71–86; and Lisle G. Brown, "The Sacred Departments for Temple Work in Nauvoo: The Assembly Room and the Council Chamber," *Brigham Young University Studies* 19 (Spring 1979): 361–74.

CHAPTER 6
Difficult Days: Nauvoo, 1842–1845

The specialized studies on the Nauvoo period by Flanders, Miller and Miller, and Roberts listed earlier contain much information on developments leading to the death of Joseph Smith. The period as a whole, political strains, the martyrdom, and the process of succession also receive substantial treatment in general Church histories cited in the General Bibliography.

Political Conflict. Important interpretive studies are Klaus J. Hansen, *Quest for Empire: The Political Kingdom of God and the Council of Fifty in Mormon History* (East Lansing: Michigan State University Press, 1967); and Annette P. Hampshire, *Mormonism in Conflict: The Nauvoo Years* (New York: Edwin Mellen Press, 1985). Further discussion is in Robert B. Flanders, "The Kingdom of God in Illinois: Politics in Utopia," *Dialogue: A Journal of Mormon Thought* 5 (Spring 1970): 26–36; and Flanders, "Dream and Nightmare: Nauvoo Revisited," in McKiernan et al., *The Restoration Movement* (1973), pp. 141–66. Details are offered by D. Michael Quinn, "The Council of Fifty and Its Members, 1844 to 1945," *Brigham Young University Studies* 20 (Fall 1979): 163–97. Other interpretations are presented in Marvin S. Hill, *Quest for Refuge* (1989); George R. Gayler, "The Mormons and Politics in Illinois: 1839–1844," *Journal of the Illinois State Historical Society* 49 (Spring 1956): 48–66; and John E. Hallwas, "Mormon Nauvoo from a Non-Mormon Perspective," *Journal of Mormon History* 16 (1990): 53–69. Kenneth W. Godfrey presents a topical analysis in his dissertation (BYU, 1967) and a summary of political events in "The Road to Carthage Led West," *Brigham Young University Studies* 8 (Winter 1968): 204–15. The Prophet's political ideas are examined in Andrew F. Ehat, " 'It Seems Like Heaven Began on Earth': Joseph Smith and the Constitution of the Kingdom of God," ibid., 20 (Spring 1980): 253–70; Dean C. Jessee, ed., "Joseph Smith's 19 July 1840 Discourse," ibid., 19 (Spring 1979): 390–94; and "J. Keith Melville, "Joseph Smith, the Constitution, and Individual Liberties," ibid., 28 (Spring 1988): 65–74.

For the political debate in newspapers, see Jerry C. Jolley, "The Sting of the 'Wasp': Early Nauvoo Newspaper, April 1842 to April 1843," ibid., 22 (Fall 1982): 487–96. A chief opponent's views are examined in Annette P. Hampshire, "Thomas Sharp and Anti-Mormon Sentiment in Illinois," *Journal of the Illinois State Historical Society* 72 (May 1979): 82–100; Marshall Hamilton, "Thomas Sharp's Turning Point: Birth of an Anti-Mormon," *Sunstone*

13 (October 1989): 16–22; and Roger D. Launius, "Anti-Mormonism in Illinois: Thomas C. Sharp's Unfinished History of the Mormon War, 1845," *Journal of Mormon History* 15 (1989): 27–45. Early plans for western settlement are recounted in Lewis Clark Christian, "A Study of Mormon Knowledge of the American Far West Prior to the Exodus (1830–February 1846)" (M.A. thesis, BYU, 1972).

Presidential Campaign. On the 1844 campaign see Richard D. Poll, "Joseph Smith and the Presidency, 1844," *Dialogue: A Journal of Mormon Thought* 3 (Autumn 1968): 17–21; and Martin B. Hickman, "The Political Legacy of Joseph Smith," ibid., pp. 22–27, which introduces a reprint of Joseph Smith's *Views of the Powers and Policy of the Government of the United States* (pp. 28–36). Additional comments on the issues are in James B. Allen, "The American Presidency and the Mormons," *Ensign* 2 (October 1972): 46–56.

Expositor. A thorough study of legal questions is Dallin H. Oaks, "The Suppression of the Nauvoo Expositor," *Utah Law Review* 9 (Winter 1965): 862–903. Thomas G. Alexander, "The Church and the Law," *Dialogue: A Journal of Mormon Thought* 1 (Summer 1966): 123–28, comments on Oaks. A social context is set in James B. Allen, "One Man's Nauvoo: William Clayton's Experience in Mormon Illinois," *Journal of Mormon History* 6 (1979): 37–59.

Martyrdom. Two views of the Illinois governor's role are Keith Huntress, "Governor Thomas Ford and the Murderers of Joseph Smith," *Dialogue: A Journal of Mormon Thought* 4 (Summer 1969): 41–52; and George R. Gayler, "Governor Ford and the Death of Joseph and Hyrum Smith," *Journal of the Illinois State Historical Society* 50 (Winter 1957): 391–411. Useful for background is David Grimsted, "Rioting in Its Jacksonian Setting," *American Historical Review* 77 (April 1972): 361–97; and Paul D. Ellsworth, "Mobocracy and the Rule of Law: American Press Reaction to the Murder of Joseph Smith," *Brigham Young University Studies* 20 (Fall 1979): 71–82. Joseph Smith's perspective is examined in Ronald K. Esplin, "Joseph Smith's Mission and Timetable: 'God Will Protect Me until My Work Is Done,' " in Porter and Black, *The Prophet Joseph* (1988), pp. 280–319; and Richard Lloyd Anderson, "Joseph Smith's Final Self-Appraisal," in ibid., pp. 320–32.

Historiographical articles on the martyrdom of Joseph Smith include Dean C. Jessee, "Return to Carthage: Writing the History of Joseph Smith's Martyrdom," *Journal of Mormon History* 8 (1981): 3–19; Kenneth W. Godfrey, "Non-Mormon Views of the Martyrdom: A Look at Some Early Published Accounts," *John Whitmer Historical Association Journal* 7 (1987): 71–82; and Richard C. Poulsen, "Fate and the Persecutors of Joseph Smith: Transmutations of an American Myth," *Dialogue: A Journal of Mormon Thought* 11 (Winter 1978): 63–70. Contemporary descriptions are Dan Jones, "The Martyrdom of Joseph Smith and His Brother Hyrum," *Brigham Young University Studies* 24

(Winter 1984): 78–109; and examples cited in Davis Bitton, "The Martyrdom of Joseph Smith in Early Mormon Writings," *John Whitmer Historical Association Journal* 3 (1983): 29–39.

After the Martyrdom. Events can be traced in general histories. A useful analysis is Annette P. Hampshire, "The Triumph of Mobocracy in Hancock County, 1844–1846," *Western Illinois Regional Studies* 5 (1982): 17–37. Dallin H. Oaks and Marvin S. Hill, *Carthage Conspiracy: The Trial of the Accused Assassins of Joseph Smith* (Urbana: University of Illinois Press, 1975), is a balanced study of legal affairs. An important primary source for the late Nauvoo and early Utah periods is Juanita Brooks, ed., *On the Mormon Frontier: The Diary of Hosea Stout, 1844–1861*, 2 vols. (Salt Lake City: University of Utah Press and Utah State Historical Society, 1964).

Succession. A useful outline is Durham and Heath, *Succession in the Church* (1970), chap. 4. Interpretive essays on Brigham Young's role include Ronald K. Esplin, "Joseph, Brigham, and the Twelve: A Succession of Continuity," *Brigham Young University Studies* 21 (Summer 1981): 301–41; which responds to D. Michael Quinn, "The Mormon Succession Crisis of 1844," ibid., 16 (Winter 1976): 187–233; Esplin, "Inside Brigham Young: Abrahamic Tests as Preparation for Leadership," ibid., 20 (Spring 1980): 300–310; and Valeen Tippetts Avery and Linda King Newell, "The Lion and the Lady: Brigham Young and Emma Smith," *Utah Historical Quarterly* 48 (Winter 1980): 81–97. On Joseph Smith's brother, see Irene M. Bates, "William Smith, 1811–93: Problematic Patriarch," *Dialogue: A Journal of Mormon Thought* 16 (Summer 1983): 11–23; E. Gary Smith, "The Patriarchal Crisis of 1845," ibid., pp. 24–35; and Paul M. Edwards, "William R. Smith: The Persistent Pretender," ibid., 18 (Summer 1985): 128–39. Other contenders are profiled in Lawrence Foster, "James J. Strang: The Prophet Who Failed," *Church History* 50 (June 1981): 182–92; Davis Bitton, "Mormons in Texas: The Ill-fated Lyman Wight Colony, 1844–1858," *Arizona and the West* 1 (Spring 1969): 5–26; Richard E. Bennett, "Lamanism, Lymanism, and Cornfields," *Journal of Mormon History* 13 (1986–87): 45–59; and Roger D. Launius, "Joseph Smith III and the Mormon Succession Crises," *Western Illinois Regional Studies* 6 (1983): 5–22.

CHAPTER 7
Exodus to a New Zion, 1846–1850

The story of the migration of the Saints to the Great Basin has been told in detail in most general histories of the Church and in histories of Utah. Also consult specialized migration and settlement studies in the General Bibliography.

The most comprehensive recent examination is Eugene E. Campbell, *Establishing Zion: The Mormon Church in the American West, 1847–69* (Salt Lake City: Signature Books, 1988), chaps. 1–4. For additional detail see *Church*

History in the Fulness of Times (1989), chaps. 25–27; Leland H. Creer, *Founding of an Empire* (1947), chaps. 9–13; and Leonard J. Arrington, *Great Basin Kingdom* (1958), chaps. 2–3. Expanding upon the usual story is Richard E. Bennett, *Mormons at the Missouri, 1846–52: "And Should We Die"* (Norman: University of Oklahoma Press, 1987). Useful documentary collections are Joseph Smith, *History of the Church* (1902–32), vol. 7, chaps. 38–41; Elden J. Watson, ed., *Manuscript History of Brigham Young, 1846–1847* (Salt Lake City: Elden J. Watson, 1971); and Gregory R. Knight, ed., "Journal of Thomas Bullock (1816–1885): 31 August 1845 to 5 July 1846," *Brigham Young University Studies* 31 (Winter 1991): 5–75.

Exodus from Nauvoo. A helpful narrative is Richard E. Bennett, *Mormons at the Missouri* (1987), chaps. 1–2. On the final evacuation, see Andrew Jenson, "The Battle of Nauvoo," *Historical Record* 8 (June 1889): 845–47. The early stages of the trek are outlined in Stanley B. Kimball, "The Iowa Trek of 1846," *Ensign* 2 (June 1972): 36–45; Richard E. Bennett, "Eastward to Eden: The Nauvoo Rescue Missions," *Dialogue: A Journal of Mormon Thought* 19 (Winter 1986): 100–108; Paul E. Dahl, " 'All Is Well . . . ': The Story of 'the Hymn That Went Around the World,' " *Brigham Young University Studies* 21 (Fall 1981): 515–27; and Susan W. Easton, "Suffering and Death on the Plains of Iowa," ibid., pp. 431–39. Other aspects are treated in Reed C. Durham, Jr., "The Iowa Experience: A Blessing in Disguise," ibid., pp. 463–74; Leland H. Gentry, "The Mormon Way Stations: Garden Grove and Mt. Pisgah," ibid., pp. 445–62; Ronald K. Esplin, "A 'Place Prepared': Joseph, Brigham, and the Quest for Promised Refuge in the West," *Journal of Mormon History* 9 (1982): 85–111; and Lorin K. Hansen, "Voyage of the Brooklyn," *Dialogue: A Journal of Mormon Thought* 21 (Autumn 1988): 46–72.

Mormon Battalion. For a scholarly analysis, see John F. Yurtinus, "A Ram in the Thicket: A History of the Mormon Battalion in the Mexican War" (Ph.D. diss., BYU, 1975); and Bruce A. Van Orden, "The March of the Mormon Battalion in Its Greater American Historical Setting," in Garrett and Johnson, *Regional Studies . . . : Arizona* (1989), pp. 159–76. The march is logged on small-scale maps in Charles S. Peterson, John F. Yurtinus, David E. Atkinson, and A. Kent Powell, *Mormon Battalion Trail Guide* (Salt Lake City: Utah State Historical Society, 1972); and discussed in Harlan Hague, "The First California Trail: The Southern Route," *Overland Journal* 5 (Winter 1987): 41–50; and Stanley B. Kimball, "The Mormon Battalion March, 1846–47," *Ensign* 9 (July 1979): 57–61. Four articles by John F. Yurtinus explore details: "The Mormon Volunteers: The Recruitment and Service of a Unique Military Company," *Journal of San Diego History* 25 (Summer 1979): 242–61; " 'Here Is One Man Who Will Not Go, Dam'um': Recruiting the Mormon Battalion in Iowa Territory," *Brigham Young University Studies* 21 (Fall 1981): 475–87; "Colorado, Mormons, and the Mexican War," *Essays and Monographs in Colorado History* (1983): 109–145; and "The Battle of the Bulls," *Military History of Texas and* *the Southwest* 14 (1978): 99–106. Probing important aspects of the topic are W. Ray Luce, "The Mormon Battalion: A Historical Accident?" *Utah Historical Quarterly* 42 (Winter 1974): 27–38; Eugene E. Campbell, "Authority Conflicts in the Mormon Battalion," *Brigham Young University Studies* 8 (Winter 1968): 127–42; and Hamilton Gardner, "The Command and Staff of the Mormon Battalion in the Mexican War," *Utah Historical Quarterly* 29 (October 1952): 331–52. Daniel Tyler, *A Concise History of the Mormon Battalion in the Mexican War, 1846–47* (1881; reprint, Chicago: Rio Grande Press, 1964), is a standard reference.

Migration. Eugene E. Campbell, "A History of the Church . . . in California" (Ph.D. diss., Univ. of Southern Calif., 1952), presents useful histories of the *Brooklyn* Saints (chap. 2), the Mormon Battalion (chap. 3), and Mormons and the Gold Rush (chap. 4). The Mississippi Saints and Battalion sick detachment are carefully followed in Leroy R. Hafen and Frank M. Young, "The Mormon Settlement at Pueblo, Colorado, during the Mexican War," *Colorado Magazine* 9 (July 1932): 121–36; and in LaMar C. Barrett, "History of the Southern States Mission, 1831–1861" (M.S. thesis, BYU, 1960), part 5. See Ronald G. Coleman, "Utah's Black Pioneers: 1847–1869," *Umoja: A Scholarly Journal of Black Studies* 2 (1979): 95–110, for a summary of another aspect of the migration. Lavina Fielding Anderson, "Mary Fielding Smith: Her Ox Goes Marching On," *Dialogue: A Journal of Mormon Thought* 14 (Winter 1981): 71–80, looks at a popular story of the exodus.

Dissension. On dissenters, see the helpful overviews in Russell Rich, *Those Who Would Be Leaders (Offshoots of Mormonism)*, 2nd ed. (Provo: Brigham Young University Extension Publications, 1967); Rich, "Nineteenth Century Break-offs," *Ensign* 9 (September 1979): 68–71; and Steven L. Shields, *Divergent Paths of the Restoration: A History of the Latter Day Saint Movement*, 3rd ed. (Bountiful, Utah: Restoration Research, 1982). The standard reference on James J. Strang is Milo M. Quaife, *The Kingdom of Saint James: A Narrative of the Mormons* (New Haven: Yale University Press, 1930). Among many newer studies are Roger Van Noord, *King of Beaver Island: The Life and Assassination of James Jesse Strang* (Urbana: University of Illinois Press, 1988); and Doyle C. Fitzpatrick, *The King Strang Story: A Vindication of James J. Strang, the Beaver Island Mormon King* (Lansing, Mich.: National Heritage, 1970). Shorter assessments include Klaus J. Hansen, "The Making of King Strang: A Reexamination," *Michigan History* 46 (September 1962): 201–29; John Quist, "Polygamy among James Strang and His Followers," *John Whitmer Historical Association Journal* 9 (1989): 31–48; and William D. Russell, "King James Strang: Joseph Smith's Successor?" in McKiernan et al., *The Restoration Movement* (1973), pp. 231–56.

Two sympathetic views of a major group are Alma R. Blair, "The Reorganized Church of Jesus Christ of Latter Day Saints: Moderate Mormons," in ibid., pp. 207–30; and Richard P. Howard, "The Reorganized Church in Illinois,

1852–1882: Search for Identity," *Dialogue: A Journal of Mormon Thought* 5 (Spring 1970): 63–75. Religious activities of a former leader are treated in Thomas J. Gregory, "Sidney Rigdon: Post Nauvoo," *Brigham Young University Studies* 21 (Winter 1981): 51–67. Alpheus Cutler's beliefs and following are analyzed in Danny L. Jorgensen, "The Fiery Darts of the Adversary: An Interpretation of Early Cutlerism," *John Whitmer Historical Association Journal* 10 (1990): 67–83. Additional details on the Rigdon and Cutler groups are presented in Ian G. Barber, "The Ecclesiastical Position of Women in Two Mormon Trajectories," *Journal of Mormon History* 14 (1988): 63–79. Religious views are compared in Grant Underwood, "Apocalyptic Adversaries: Mormonism Meets Millerism," *John Whitmer Historical Association Journal* 7 (1987): 53–61.

Council Bluffs Area. The once neglected period in Council Bluffs has received thorough attention in Bennett, *Mormons at the Missouri* (1987). See also Robert A. Trennert, Jr., "The Mormons and the Office of Indian Affairs: The Conflict over Winter Quarters, 1846–1848," *Nebraska History* 53 (Fall 1972): 381–400; Lawrence G. Coates, "Refugees Meet: The Mormons and Indians in Iowa," *Brigham Young University Studies* 21 (Fall 1981): 491–514; Donald Q. Cannon, ed., "Thomas L. Kane Meets the Mormons," ibid., 18 (Fall 1977): 126–28; Maureen Ursenbach Beecher, "Women at Winter Quarters," *Sunstone* 8 (July-August 1983): 11–19; and Michael W. Homer, "After Winter Quarters and Council Bluffs: The Mormons in Nebraska Territory, 1854–1867," *Nebraska History* 65 (Winter 1984): 467–83.

Mormon Trail. For background on western wagon roads, see Merrill J. Mattes, *The Great Platte River Road: The Covered Wagon Mainline via Fort Kearny to Fort Laramie* (Lincoln: Nebraska State Historical Society, 1969); and John D. Unruh, Jr., *The Plains Across: The Overland Emigrants and the Trans-Mississippi West, 1840–60* (Urbana: University of Illinois Press, 1979). The story of the pioneer journey is well told in general histories, but see Guy E. Stringham, "The Pioneer Roadometer," *Utah Historical Quarterly* 42 (Summer 1974): 258–77, and Norman E. Wright, "Answers to Gospel Questions," *Ensign* 11 (August 1981): 30–31, for correctives on a well-known artifact. The standard account of the 1847 trek is *William Clayton's Journal: A Daily Record of the Journey of the Original Company . . .* (Salt Lake City: Clayton Family Association, 1921). Another published diary of the journey is Leland H. Creer, ed., "Journey to Zion: From the Journal of Erastus Snow," *Utah Humanities Review* 2 (April and July 1948): 107–28, 264–84. For a sense of the trail itself, see Stanley Kimball, *Heber C. Kimball* (1981), chaps. 12–14.

Early Utah Period. Supplementing Campbell and other listed sources are Ellsworth, *Utah's Heritage* (1972), chaps. 9–12; Dale L. Morgan, *The Great Salt Lake* (1947; reprint, Albuquerque: University of New Mexico Press, 1973), chaps. 10–12; and Hansen, *Quest for Empire* (1967), chap. 7. Specialized studies include William Hartley, "Mormons, Crickets, and Gulls: A New Look at an Old Story," *Utah Historical Quarterly* 38 (Summer 1970): 224–39; Davis Bitton and Linda P. Wilcox, "Pestiferous Ironclads: The Grasshopper Problem in Pioneer Utah," ibid., 46 (Fall 1978): 336–55; Lawrence L. Linford, "Establishing and Maintaining Land Ownership in Utah Prior to 1869," ibid., 42 (Spring 1974): 126–43; and Brigham D. Madsen, "Stansbury's Expedition to the Great Salt Lake, 1949–50," ibid., 56 (Spring 1988): 148–59. Looking at the California gold rush are J. Kenneth Davies, *Mormon Gold: The Story of California's Mormon Argonauts* (Salt Lake City: Olympus Publishing, 1984); Davies, "Mormons and California Gold," *Journal of Mormon History* 7 (1980): 83–95; and Brigham D. Madsen, *Gold Rush Sojourners in Great Salt Lake City, 1849 and 1850* (Salt Lake City: University of Utah Press, 1983). Another topic is examined in Richard H. Jackson, "Righteousness and Environmental Change: The Mormons and the Environment," in Thomas G. Alexander, ed., *Essays on the American West, 1973–74*, Charles Redd Monographs in Western History, no. 5 (Provo: Brigham Young University Press, 1975), pp. 21–42.

Early Utah Government. Background on the Latter-day Saint role in government for the Great Basin before 1850 can be gleaned from Dale L. Morgan's careful overview, "The State of Deseret," *Utah Historical Quarterly* 8 (April, July, October 1940): 65–239; and from Peter Crawley, "The Constitution of the State of Deseret," *Brigham Young University Studies* 29 (Fall 1989): 7–22; Hansen, *Quest for Empire* (1967), chaps. 6–7; Leland H. Creer, "The Evolution of Government in Early Utah," *Utah Historical Quarterly* 27 (January 1958): 23–44; Gwynn W. Barrett, "Dr. John M. Bernhisel: Mormon Elder in Congress," ibid., 36 (Spring 1968): 143–67; and Wayne K. Hinton, "Millard Filmore, Utah's Friend in the White House," ibid., 48 (Spring 1980): 112–28.

Early Utah Life. Information on domestic life is in Maureen Ursenbach Beecher, "Women's Work on the Mormon Frontier," *Utah Historical Quarterly* 49 (Summer 1981): 276–90. Summarizing the life of the mind is Joseph Heinerman, "Early Utah Pioneer Cultural Societies," ibid., 47 (Winter 1979): 70–89.

CHAPTER 8
Establishing an Ensign, 1851–1856

Basic sources for this chapter include the standard histories of the Church, histories of Utah, and several specialized studies. Events at Winter Quarters are covered in Richard Bennett, *Mormons at the Missouri* (1987). For the most complete recent monograph on western settlement, see Campbell, *Establishing Zion* (1988), chaps. 6–13. Economic policy is detailed in Arrington, *Great Basin Kingdom* (1958), chaps. 4–5. Much data not contained elsewhere is in Hunter, *Brigham Young the Colonizer* (1940), chaps. 9–34.

Territorial Government. Specialized studies on the Church and territorial government include: Michael W. Homer, "The Judiciary and the Common

Law in Utah Territory, 1850–61," *Dialogue: A Journal of Mormon Thought* 21 (Spring 1988): 97–108; Raymond T. Swenson, "Resolution of Civil Disputes by Mormon Ecclesiastical Courts," *Utah Law Review* (1978): 573–95; James B. Allen, "Ecclesiastical Influence on Local Government in the Territory of Utah," *Arizona and the West* 8 (Spring 1966): 35–48; P.A.M. Taylor, "Early Mormon Loyalty and the Leadership of Brigham Young," *Utah Historical Quarterly* 30 (Spring 1962): 102–32; Hansen, *Quest for Empire* (1967), chaps. 7–8; James R. Clark, "The Kingdom of God, the Council of Fifty, and the State of Deseret," *Utah Historical Quarterly* 26 (April 1958): 130–48.

Settlement. In addition to the basic references noted above, see Joel E. Ricks, *Forms and Methods of Early Mormon Settlement in Utah and Surrounding Region, 1847 to 1877* (Logan: Utah State University Press, 1964); Lowry Nelson, *The Mormon Village: A Pattern and Technique of Land Settlement* (Salt Lake City: University of Utah Press, 1952); Richard H. Jackson, "The Mormon Village: Genesis and Antecedents of the City of Zion Plan," *Brigham Young University Studies* 17 (Winter 1977): 233–40; and Jackson, "Mormon Perception and Settlement," *Annals of the Association of American Geographers* (1978): 317–34. Robert Alan Goldberg compares Mormon settlement successes with a Jewish failure at Clarion, Utah, in "Building Zions: A Conceptual Framework," *Utah Historical Quarterly* 57 (Spring 1989): 165–79. On Mormon outposts, see Eugene E. Campbell, "Brigham Young's Outer Cordon: A Reappraisal," *Utah Historical Quarterly* 41 (Summer 1973): 220–53; Edward Leo Lyman, "The Demise of the San Bernardino Mormon Community, 1851–1857," *Southern California Quarterly* 65 (Winter 1983): 321–39; Lyman, "The Rise and Decline of Mormon San Bernardino, *Brigham Young University Studies* 29 (Fall 1989): 43–63; M. Guy Bishop, "Politics, Land, and Apostasy: The Last Days of the San Bernardino Mormon Colony, 1855–57," *Pacific Historian* 30 (Winter 1986): 18–31; Bishop, " 'We Are Rather Weaker in Righteousness Than in Numbers': The Mormon Colony at San Bernardino, California, 1851–1857," in Carl Guarneri and David Alvares, eds., *Religion and Society in the American West: Historical Essays* (Lanham, Maryland: University Press of America, 1987), pp. 171–93; Fred R. Gowans, "Fort Bridger and the Mormons," *Utah Historical Quarterly* 42 (Winter 1974): 49–67; Gowans and Campbell, *Fort Bridger: Island in the Wilderness* (Provo, Utah: Brigham Young University Press, 1975); and Gowans and Campbell, *Fort Supply: Brigham Young's Green River Experiment* (Provo: Brigham Young University Press, 1976).

Economic Life. Ronald W. Walker analyzes Brigham Young's utopian dream of a labor-driven, agrarian, cooperative theocracy as expressed in a lifetime of public discourses: "Brigham Young and the Social Order," *Brigham Young University Studies* 28 (Summer 1988): 37–52. In addition to general works, see an assessment of Mormon contributions in Leonard J. Arrington and Dean May, " 'A Different Mode of Life': Irrigation and Society in Nineteenth-Century Utah," *Agricultural History* 49 (January 1975): 3–20; and studies by Charles L. Schmalz, "The Failure of Utah's First Sugar Factory," *Utah Historical Quarterly* 56 (Winter 1988): 36–53; Kirk Henrichsen, "Pioneer Pottery of Utah and E. C. Henrichsen's Provo Pottery Company," ibid., 56 (Fall 1988): 360–95; and Norman K. Johnson, "Early Mormon and Utah Holographic Scrip," *Utah Historical Quarterly* 57 (Summer 1989): 216–39.

Indian Relations. The subject is summarized in Charles S. Peterson, "Jacob Hamblin, Apostle to the Lamanites, and the Indian Mission," *Journal of Mormon History* 2 (1975): 21–34; and Leonard J. Arrington, "The Mormons and the Indians: A Review and Evaluation," *The Record* (Friends of the Library, Washington State University, Pullman) 31 (1970): 5–29. Reassessments include articles by Ronald W. Walker, "Toward a Reconstruction . . . ," and Howard A. Christy, "Open Hand and Mailed Fist," both cited in chap. 7; and Floyd A. O'Neil and Stanford J. Layton, "Of Pride and Politics: Brigham Young as Indian Superintendent," *Utah Historical Quarterly* 46 (Summer 1978): 236–50. Other studies include Peterson's "The Hopis and the Mormons, 1858–1873," ibid., 39 (Spring 1971): 179–93; Beverly Beeton, "Teach Them to Till the Soil: An Experiment with Indian Farms, 1850–1862," *American Indian Quarterly* 3 (Winter 1977–78): 299–320; Charles E. Dibble, "The Mormon Mission to the Shoshoni Indians," *Utah Humanities Review* (January, April, and July 1947): 53–73, 166–77, and 279–93; the broad overview by Lawrence G. Coates, "Mormons and Social Change among the Shoshoni, 1853–1900," *Idaho Yesterdays* 15 (Winter 1972): 3–11; and studies of the mission at Limhi by John D. Nash, "The Salmon River Mission of 1855," ibid., 11 (Spring 1967): 22–31; and by Lawrence G. Coates, "The Spaulding-Whitman and the Lemhi Missions: A Comparison," ibid., 31 (Spring-Summer 1987): 38–46. An important firsthand account is Thomas D. Brown, *Journal of the Southern [Utah] Indian Mission: Diary of Thomas D. Brown*, ed. Juanita Brooks (Logan: Utah State University Press, 1972).

Religious Life. On polygamy see general studies on the topic and David J. Whittaker, "The Bone in the Throat: Orson Pratt and the Public Announcement of Plural Marriage," *Western Historical Quarterly* 18 (July 1987): 293–314; Whittaker, "Early Mormon Polygamy Defenses," *Journal of Mormon History* 11 (1984): 43–63; Dana Bennett, "Mormon Polygamy in Early Southeastern Idaho," *Idaho Yesterdays* 28 (Spring 1984): 24–30; and the statistical analysis by Stanley S. Ivins, "Notes on Mormon Polygamy," *Western Humanities Review* 10 (Summer 1956): 229–39, reprinted twice: *Utah Historical Quarterly* 35 (Fall 1967): 309–21, and Hill and Allen, *Mormonism and American Culture* (1972), pp. 101–11.

On the movement for spiritual uplift, see Gustive O. Larson, "The Mormon Reformation," *Utah Historical Quarterly* 26 (January 1958): 45–63; Paul H. Peterson, "The Mormon Reformation of 1856–1857: The Rhetoric and the Reality," *Journal of Mormon History* 15 (1989): 59–87; Robert J. McCue, "Did the Word of Wisdom Become a Commandment in 1851?" *Dialogue: A Journal of Mormon Thought* 14 (Autumn 1981): 66–77; and Howard C. Searle, "The Mormon Reformation of 1856–1857," (M.S. thesis, Brigham Young University, 1956).

Comparative insights are presented in R. Laurence Moore, "Learning to Play: The Mormon Way and the Way of Other Americans," *Journal of Mormon History*, 16 (1990): 89–106. Administrative matters are examined in Gordon Irving, "Encouraging the Saints: Brigham Young's Annual Tours of the Mormon Settlements," *Utah Historical Quarterly* 45 (Summer 1977): 233–51; R. Collin Mangrum, "Furthering the Cause of Zion: An Overview of the Mormon Ecclesiastical Court System in Early Utah," *Journal of Mormon History* 10 (1983): 79–90; and William G. Hartley, "Ordained and Acting Teachers in the Lesser Priesthood, 1851–1883," *Brigham Young University Studies* 16 (Spring 1976): 375–98. A broad overview is Richard L. Jensen, "Forgotten Relief Societies, 1844–67," *Dialogue: A Journal of Mormon Thought* 16 (Spring 1983): 105–25.

Glimpses into local worship are in Ronald W. Walker, " 'Going to Meeting' in Salt Lake City's Thirteenth Ward, 1849–1881: A Microanalysis," in Bitton and Beecher, *New Views of Mormon History* (1987), pp. 138–61; Jessie Embry, "Little Berlin: Swiss Saints of the Logan Tenth Ward," *Utah Historical Quarterly* 56 (Summer 1988): 222–35; and William G. Hartley, "LDS Pastors and Pastorates, 1852–55," in Jensen and Thorp, *Mormons in Early Victorian Britain* (1989), pp. 194–210.

Missions. Convenient sources on specific missions are R. Lanier Britsch, "Church Beginnings in China," *Brigham Young University Studies* 10 (Winter 1970): 161–72; Britsch's "The Latter-day Saint Mission to India, 1851–1856," ibid., 12 (Spring 1972): 262–77; Richard W. Sadler, "Franklin D. Richards and the British Mission," *Journal of Mormon History* 14 (1988): 81–95; Evans, *A Century of Mormonism in Great Britain* (1984); Jenson, *History of the Scandinavian Mission* (1927); and Michael W. Homer, "The Italian Mission, 1850–67," *Sunstone* 7 (May-June 1982): 16–21.

Migration. To supplement general histories see Robert Flanders's account of the Mutual Benefit Association in *Nauvoo: Kingdom on the Mississippi* (1965), pp. 78–86; Marjorie Newton, "The Gathering of the Australian Saints in the 1850s," *Brigham Young University Studies* 27 (Spring 1987): 67–78; Jens P. Wilde, "Bleeding Feet, Humble Hearts: Danish Mormon Migration, 1850–1860," *The Bridge: Journal of the Danish American Heritage Society* 3 (August 1980): 6–19; and the useful summary by William G. Hartley, "Coming to Zion: Saga of the Gathering," *Ensign* 5 (July 1975): 14–18. LeRoy R. Hafen, "Handcarts to Utah, 1856–1860," *Utah Historical Quarterly* 24 (October 1956): 309–17, is a convenient summary of the main themes of his and Ann W. Hafen's *Handcarts to Zion: The Story of a Unique Western Migration 1856–1860* (Glendale, Calif.: Arthur H. Clark Co., 1960). Additional information is in Leonard J. Arrington and Rebecca Cornwall, *Rescue of the 1856 Handcart Companies* (Midvale, Utah: Signature Books, 1984); and Richard L. Jensen, "By Handcart to Utah: The Account of C. C. A. Christensen," *Nebraska History* 64 (Winter 1985): 333–48.

CHAPTER 9
In the National Spotlight, 1857–1863

These challenging years have received careful attention in the political histories covering the Utah War period and in a number of specialized works, as well as in most of the general works listed in the General Bibliography. A basic treatment is Campbell, *Establishing Zion* (1988), especially chaps. 11–19. Additional insights into the social and economic life can be found in Anderson, *Desert Saints* (1942), chaps. 7–8, and Arrington, *Great Basin Kingdom* (1958), chaps. 6–7. The story is given a secular setting in Bancroft, *History of Utah* (1889), chaps. 18–22. See also Whitney, *History of Utah* (1892–1904), vol. 1, chaps. 28–32, and vol. 2, chaps. 1–4.

Fiction. For an analysis of the way Latter-day Saints were depicted in popular novels of the time, see Leonard J. Arrington and Jon Haupt, "The Missouri and Illinois Mormons in Ante-Bellum Fiction," *Dialogue: A Journal of Mormon Thought* 5 (Spring 1970): 37–50. The political effect of this image is traced in Richard D. Poll, "The Mormon Question Enters National Politics, 1850–1856," *Utah Historical Quarterly* 25 (April 1957): 117–31.

Utah Expedition. Thorough accounts are Donald R. Moorman with Gene A. Sessions, *Camp Floyd and the Mormons: The Utah War* (Salt Lake City: University of Utah Press, 1992); and Norman F. Furniss, *The Mormon Conflict, 1850–59* (New Haven: Yale University Press, 1960). Supporting documents are collected in LeRoy R. Hafen and Ann W. Hafen, eds., *The Utah Expedition, 1857–58: A Documentary Account . . .* (Glendale, Calif.: Arthur H. Clark, 1958). Additional insights are in Leonard J. Arrington, "Mormon Finance and the Utah War," *Utah Historical Quarterly* 20 (July 1952): 219–37; William F. Mackinnon, "The Buchanan Spoils System and the Utah Expedition: Careers of W.M.F. Magraw and John M. Hockaday," *ibid.*, 31 (Spring 1963): 127–50; Mackinnon, "The Gap in the Buchanan Revival: The Utah Expedition of 1857–58," *ibid.*, 45 (Winter 1977): 36–46; and Mackinnon, "125 Years of Conspiracy Theories: Origins of the Utah Expedition of 1857–1858," *ibid.*, 52 (Spring 1984): 212–30. For the reaction of the *Deseret News,* see A. R. Mortensen, "A Local Paper Reports on the Utah War," *ibid.*, 25 (October 1957): 297–318. The impact on residents is described in Richard D. Poll, "The Move South," *Brigham Young University Studies* 29 (Fall 1989): 65–88; and William G. Hartley, ed., "The Miller, the Bishop, and the 'Move South,'" *ibid.*, pp. 99–105. Another incident is explored in Clifford L. Stott, *Search for Sanctuary: Brigham Young and the White Mountain Expedition* (Salt Lake City: University of Utah Press, 1984). The aftermath of the military arrival is studied in Thomas G. Alexander and Leonard J. Arrington, "Camp in the Sagebrush: Camp Floyd, Utah, 1858–1861," *Utah Historical Quarterly* 34 (Winter 1966): 3–21; and Davis Bitton, "The Cradlebaugh Court (1859): A Study in Early Mormon-Gentile Misunderstanding," in Knowlton, *Social Accommodation in Utah* (1975), pp. 71–97.

For studies of two personalities who played key roles, see Charles S. Peterson, " 'A Mighty Man was Brother Lot': A Portrait of Lot Smith, Mormon Frontiersman," *Western Historical Quarterly* 1 (October 1970): 393–414; Albert L. Zobell, "Thomas L. Kane, Ambassador to the Mormons," *Utah Humanities Review* 1 (October 1947): 320–46; and Michael W. Homer, "The Federal Bench and Priesthood Authority: The Rise and Fall of John Fitch Kinney's Early Relationship with the Mormons," *Journal of Mormon History* 13 (1986–87): 89–110. Among several published diaries is one of a Mormon soldier, Hamilton Gardner, ed., "A Territorial Militiaman in the Utah War: Journal of Newton Tuttle," *Utah Historical Quarterly* 22 (October 1954): 297–320. Audrey M. Godfrey, "A Social History of Camp Floyd, Utah Territory, 1858–1861" (M.A. thesis, Utah State University, 1989), is instructive; as is Richard D. Poll, "The British Mission during the Utah War, 1857–58," in Jensen and Thorp, *Mormons in Early Victorian Britain* (1989), pp. 224–42.

Massacres and Murder. The thorough research of Juanita Brooks, *The Mountain Meadows Massacre* (1962; new ed., Norman: University of Oklahoma Press, 1991), has made this balanced account the standard on the subject, though other re-examinations are in process. One of these is Morris Shirts, *Mountain Meadows Massacre: Another Look* (Cedar City, Utah: Author, 1992). Also of interest is the speech of Juanita Brooks and the response by Ralph R. Rea at the dedication of a monument to the victims: "An Historical Epilogue," *Utah Historical Quarterly* 24 (January 1956): 71–77. The standard on the Indian massacre in northern Utah is Brigham M. Madsen, *The Shoshone Frontier and the Bear River Massacre* (Salt Lake City: University of Utah Press, 1985). For the tragic event in Arkansas see Steven Pratt, "Eleanor McLean and the Murder of Parley P. Pratt," *Brigham Young University Studies* 15 (Winter 1975): 225–56.

Civil War. On the Civil War period consult the overviews by E. B. Long, *The Saints and the Union: Utah Territory during the Civil War* (Champaign: University of Illinois Press, 1981); Gustive O. Larson, "Utah and the Civil War," *Utah Historical Quarterly* 33 (Winter 1965): 55–57; and Ray C. Colton, *The Civil War in the Western Territories: Arizona, Colorado, New Mexico, and Utah* (Norman: University of Oklahoma, 1959), pp. 180–90. Special topics include George U. Hubbard, "Abraham Lincoln as Seen by the Mormons," *Utah Historical Quarterly* 31 (Spring 1963): 91–108; and Tom Generous, "Over the River Jordan: California Volunteers in Utah during the Civil War," *California History* 63 (1984): 200–211.

Morrisites. The most comprehensive investigation of Joseph Morris and his schism is C. LeRoy Anderson, *For Christ Will Come Tomorrow: The Saga of the Morrisites* (Logan: Utah State University Press, 1981). Also see G. M. Howard, "Men, Motives, and Misunderstandings," *Utah Historical Quarterly* 44 (Spring 1976): 112–32.

Visitors. The accounts of those who observed Latter-day Saint society in these years include the biased accounts of Benjamin G. Ferris, *Utah and the Mormons.* . . . (1854; reprint, New York: AMS Press, 1971), and his wife, *The Mormons at Home.* . . . (1856; reprint, New York: AMS Press, 1971); the delightful observations of Elizabeth Randall Cumming, "The Governor's Lady: A Letter from Camp Scott, 1857," A. R. Mortensen, ed., *Utah Historical Quarterly* 22 (April 1954): 165–73; the descriptions of world travelers Jules Remy and Julius Brenchley, *A Journey to Great-Salt-Lake City,* 2 vols. (1861; reprint, New York: AMS Press, 1971); and Richard F. Burton, *The City of the Saints and across the Rocky Mountains to California,* ed. by Fawn M. Brodie (1861; New York: Alfred A. Knopf, 1963); and the letters collected in Harold D. Langley, ed., *To Utah with the Dragoons and Glimpses of Life in Arizona and California, 1858–1859* (Salt Lake City: University of Utah Press, 1974). For a summary of selected visitors, see Edwina J. Snow, "British Travelers View the Saints, 1847–1877," *Brigham Young University Studies* 31 (Spring 1991): 63–81.

CHAPTER 10
Challenges and Cooperatives, 1864–1872

This important period of economic and cultural adjustment surrounding the completion of the transcontinental railroad has been thoroughly examined with respect to political and economic activities, less thoroughly concerning religious and cultural developments.

General and Topical Histories. Basic information is in Campbell's careful overview, *Establishing Zion* (1988), chaps. 15–19. The best economic survey remains Arrington, *Great Basin Kingdom* (1958), chaps. 7–10. Of great use are the general works and Utah histories identified in the General Bibliography.

The Quest for Economic Self-sufficiency. For background beyond basic sources, see Leonard J. Arrington, "Abundance from the Earth: The Beginnings of Commercial Mining in Utah," *Utah Historical Quarterly* 31 (Summer 1963): 192–219; and his "The Deseret Agricultural and Manufacturing Society in Pioneer Utah," ibid., 24 (April 1956): 165–70. Specialized industries are examined in M. Guy Bishop, "Building Railroads for the Kingdom: The Career of John W. Young, 1867–91," ibid., 48 (Winter 1980): 66–80; Chris Rigby Arrington, "The Finest of Fabrics: Mormon Women and the Silk Industry in Early Utah," ibid., 46 (Fall 1978): 376–96. For the development of two Church-owned businesses, see Martha S. Bradley, *ZCMI: America's First Department*

Store (Salt Lake City: ZCMI, 1991), and Eleanor Knowles, *Deseret Book Company: 125 Years of Inspiration, Information, and Ideas* (Salt Lake City: Deseret Book, 1991).

The southern Utah-Nevada economic mission is described in a classic local history, Andrew Karl Larson, *"I Was Called to Dixie": The Virgin River Basin, Unique Experiences in Mormon Pioneering* (Salt Lake City: The Deseret News Press, 1961); in a special issue of *Utah Historical Quarterly*, edited by Juanita Brooks, "Utah's Dixie: The Cotton Mission," 29 (July 1961): 193–302; in L. A. Fleming, "The Settlements on the Muddy, 1865 to 1871: 'A Godforsaken Place,'" ibid., 35 (Spring 1967): 147–72; S. George Ellsworth, *Mormon Settlement on the Muddy* (Ogden: Weber State College Press, 1987); Monique E. Kimball, "A Matter of Faith: A Study of the Muddy Mission," *Nevada Historical Quarterly* 30 (Winter 1987): 291–303; Carolyn Grattan-Aiello, "New St. Joseph, Nevada: The Muddy Mission Experience Revisited," ibid., 29 (Spring 1986): 31–52; and in Leonard J. Arrington, "Mormon Trade on the Colorado River, 1864–1867," *Arizona and the West* 8 (Autumn 1966): 239–50. Other cooperative activities are detailed in Dean L. May, "Mormon Cooperatives in Paris, Idaho, 1869–1896," *Idaho Yesterdays* 19 (Summer 1975): 20–30.

Challenges to the defensive economic programs are examined in Brigham D. Madsen, *Glory Hunter: A Biography of Patrick Edward Connor* (Salt Lake City: University of Utah Press, 1990). A related question is discussed in Gustive O. Larson, "Land Contest in Early Utah," *Utah Historical Quarterly* 29 (October 1961): 3–25; and in Lawrence R. Linford, "Establishing and Maintaining Land Ownership in Utah Prior to 1869," ibid., 42 (Spring 1974): 126–43. Also useful on the 1860s and '70s is Kenneth J. Davies, "The Secularization of the Utah Labor Movement," in Knowlton, *Social Accommodation in Utah* (1975), pp. 19–64; and John K. Hulmston, "Mormon Immigration in the 1860s: The Story of Church Trains," *Utah Historical Quarterly* 58 (Winter 1990): 32–48.

Schismatic Groups. An early treatment of schismatic groups is in Bancroft, *History of Utah* (1889), chap. 23. A religious interpretation of the Godbeites is set forth in four articles by Ronald W. Walker, "The Commencement of the Godbeite Protest: Another View," *Utah Historical Quarterly* 42 (Summer 1974): 216–44; "When the Spirits Did Abound: Nineteenth-Century Utah's Encounter with Free-Thought Radicalism," ibid., 50 (Fall 1982): 304–24; "The Liberal Institute: A Case Study in National Assimilation," *Dialogue: A Journal of Mormon Thought* 19 (Autumn 1977): 74–85; and "The Stenhouses and the Making of a Mormon Image," *Journal of Mormon History* 1 (1974): 51–72. The Godbeites are placed in a broader context in Davis Bitton, "Mormonism's Encounter with Spiritualism," ibid., pp. 39–50. Relations between RLDS and LDS leaders are examined in Linda King Newell, "Cousins in Conflict: Joseph Smith III and Joseph F. Smith," *John Whitmer Historical Association Journal* 9 (1989): 3–16; and Roger D. Launius, "Methods and Motives: Joseph Smith

III's Opposition to Polygamy, 1860–90," *Dialogue: A Journal of Mormon Thought* 20 (Winter 1987): 105–20. For a useful introduction, see Paul M. Edwards, *Our Legacy of Faith: A Brief History of the Reorganized Church of Jesus Christ of Latter Day Saints* (Independence: Herald House, 1991). A localized study of a later period is A. J. Simmonds, *The Gentile Comes to Cache Valley: A Study of the Logan Apostasies of 1874 and the Establishment of Non-Mormon Churches in Cache Valley, 1873–1913* (Logan: Utah State University Press, 1976).

Walter Murray Gibson. The traditional interpretation of Walter Murray Gibson's life is set forth by assistant Church historian Andrew Jenson, "Walter Murray Gibson: A Sketch of His Life in Two Chapters," *Improvement Era* 4 (November and December 1900): 5–13, 86–95; and writer Samuel W. Taylor, "Walter Murray Gibson: Great Mormon Rascal," *American West* 1 (Spring 1964): 18–27. This view has been challenged by Gwynn Barrett, "Walter Murray Gibson: The Shepherd Saint of Lanai Revisited," *Utah Historical Quarterly* 40 (Spring 1972): 142–62; but the older interpretation is sustained by R. Lanier Britsch, "Another Visit with Walter Murray Gibson," *Utah Historical Quarterly* 46 (Winter 1978): 65–78.

Church Programs and Auxiliaries. For information on the auxiliaries, see the standard histories listed in the General Bibliography. Administrative insights are in Gary James Bergera, "The Orson Pratt-Brigham Young Controversies: Conflict within the Quorums, 1853–1868," *Dialogue: A Journal of Mormon Thought* 13 (Summer 1980): 7–49. The history of an important Salt Lake City landmark is told in Stewart L. Grow, *A Tabernacle in the Desert* (Salt Lake City: Deseret Book, 1958). An educational innovation is described in Douglas D. Alder, Paul J. Goodfellow, and Ronald G. Watt, "Creating a New Alphabet for Zion: The Origin of the Deseret Alphabet," *Utah Historical Quarterly* 52 (Summer 1984): 275–86; "The Deseret Alphabet," ibid., 12 (January and April 1944): 99–102; and S. S. Ivins, "The Deseret Alphabet," *Utah Humanities Review* 1 (July 1947): 223–39.

Other Religions in Utah. On the non-Mormon challenge, see Robert Joseph Dwyer, *The Gentile Comes to Utah: A Study in Religious and Social Conflict (1862–1890)*, (1941; 2nd ed. rev., Salt Lake City: Western Epics, 1971). A related article is C. Merrill Hough, "Two School Systems in Conflict, 1867–1890," *Utah Historical Quarterly* 28 (April 1960): 112–28. Juanita Brooks tells the story of another religious group among the Mormons in *History of the Jews in Utah and Idaho* (Salt Lake City: Western Epics, 1973).

Political Challenges. For the beginnings of the crusade against Mormonism — to supplement the general histories — see the detailed account in Gustive O. Larson, *The "Americanization" of Utah for Statehood* (San Marino, Calif.: Huntington Library, 1971), chaps. 2–3; the discussions of Hansen, *Quest for Empire* (1967), chaps. 7–9; and S. George Ellsworth, "Utah's Struggle for Statehood," *Utah Historical Quarterly* 31 (Winter 1963): 60–69. Useful articles include Lola Van Wagenen, "In Their Own Behalf: The Politicization of Mormon Women and the 1870 Franchise," *Dialogue: A Journal of Mormon Thought* 24 (Winter 1991): 31–43; Thomas G. Alexander, "An Experiment in Progressive Legislation: The Granting of Woman Suffrage in Utah in 1870," *Utah Historical Quarterly* 38 (Winter 1970): 20–30; James B. Allen, "The Unusual Jurisdiction of County Probate Courts in the Territory of Utah," ibid., 36 (Spring 1968): 132–42; and Jay E. Powell, "Fairness in the Salt Lake County Probate Court," ibid., 38 (Summer 1970): 256–62.

CHAPTER 11
Close of a Career, 1872–1877

Most of the themes that dominated the last years of Brigham Young's life have been examined in specialized studies listed below. The broader story is outlined in Utah and LDS general histories noted in the General Bibliography.

Education. For information on Latter-day Saint educational policies and programs see publications listed in the General Bibliography, plus James R. Clark, "Church and State Relationships in Education in Utah" (Ed.D. diss., Utah State University, 1958); the multivolume history prepared under the direction of Ernest L. Wilkinson, *Brigham Young University: The First One Hundred Years* (1975–76), vol. 1 , chaps. 2–3; the pioneering work of Stanley S. Ivins, "Free Schools Come to Utah," *Utah Historical Quarterly* 22 (October 1954): 321–42; and the analysis of C. Merrill Hough, "Two School Systems in Conflict, 1867–1890," ibid., 28 (April 1960): 112–28. Another glimpse is Ronald W. Walker, "Growing Up in Early Utah: The Wasatch Literary Association, 1874–1878," *Sunstone* 6 (November-December 1981): 44–51.

The Crusade. The judicial and political crusade against the Saints is given most thorough examination in Larson, *The "Americanization" of Utah* (1971), chaps. 3–4; and in the works of Roberts and Whitney noted above. Legal actions are traced in Thomas G. Alexander, "Federal Authority versus Polygamic Theocracy: James B. McKean and the Mormons, 1870–1875," *Dialogue: A Journal of Mormon Thought* 1 (Autumn 1966): 85–100. The involvement of journalists is told in O. N. Malmquist, *The First 100 Years: A History of "The Salt Lake Tribune," 1871–1971* (Salt Lake City: Utah State Historical Society, 1971), chaps. 1–4. Three articles listed in the bibliography for chap. 10 add additional insights: see Walker's article on the Stenhouses in the "Schismatic Groups" listing and those by Allen and Powell on the role of probate courts in the "Political Challenges" section.

United Orders. For information on United Orders, see the overview in Arrington, *Great Basin Kingdom* (1958), chaps. 10–11. Tracing the movement from its beginning is Arrington, Dean L. May, and Feramorz Fox, *Building the City of God: Community and Cooperation Among the Mormons* (Salt Lake City: Deseret Book, 1976). Four articles in *Utah Historical Quarterly* examine the order in individual communities: Mark A. Pendleton, "The Orderville United Order of Zion," 7 (October 1939): 141–59; Arrington, "Cooperative Community in the North: Brigham City, Utah," 33 (Summer 1965): 198–217; Fox, "Experiment in Utopia: The United Order of Richfield, 1874–1877," 32 (Fall 1964): 355–80; and P. T. Reilly, "Kanab United Order: The President's Nephew and the Bishop," 42 (Spring 1974): 144–64. A sympathetic 1874 travel account by Mrs. Thomas L. [Elizabeth Wood] Kane is *Twelve Mormon Homes Visited in Succession on a Journey through Utah to Arizona*, ed. Everett L. Cooley (Salt Lake City: Tanner Trust Fund, University of Utah Library, 1975).

Arizona Mormons. The history of the Arizona Mormon settlements is assessed in Charles S. Peterson, *Take Up Your Mission: Mormon Colonizing along the Little Colorado River, 1870–1900* (Tucson: University of Arizona Press, 1973). Additional insights are in Melvin J. Peterson, "The Little Colorado Settlements of 1876," in Garrett and Johnson, *Regional Studies . . . : Arizona* (1989), pp. 113–32; and Gary A. Anderson, "Events at Lee's Ferry, or Lonely Dell, 1864–1928," ibid., pp. 17–37.

Temples. On temple design and construction, see David S. Andrew and Laurel B. Blank, "The Four Mormon Temples in Utah," *Journal of the Society of Architectural Historians* 30 (March 1971): 51–65; and Kirk M. Curtis, "History of the St. George Temple" (M.S. thesis, BYU, 1964).

Transition. An important administrative reform is recounted in William G. Hartley, "The Priesthood Reorganization of 1877: Brigham Young's Last Achievement," *Brigham Young University Studies* 20 (Fall 1979): 3–36. Lester E. Bush, "Brigham Young in Life and Death: A Medical Overview," *Journal of Mormon History* 5 (1978): 79–103, reviews health history and the cause of death.

CHAPTER 12
A Turbulent Decade, 1877–1887

In addition to the general accounts in standard histories listed in the General Bibliography, look for new insights on the political story in Lyman, *Political Deliverance* (1986), and a helpful overview in Lowell C. Bennion, "Mormon Country a Century Ago: A Geographer's View," in Thomas G. Alexander, ed., Charles Redd Monographs, no. 10, *The Mormon People: Their Character and Traditions* (Provo: BYU Press, 1980), pp. 1–26.

Succession. On the transfer of authority following Brigham Young's death, see the useful outline in Durham and Heath, *Succession in the Church* (1973), chap. 6; and a discussion of the principle of succession in John Taylor, *Succession in the Priesthood* (Salt Lake City: Deseret News Press, 1902).

Priesthood and Auxiliaries. For one quorum's revitalization, see William G. Hartley, "The Seventies in the 1880s: Revelations and Reorganizing," *Dia-*

logue: A Journal of Mormon Thought 16 (Spring 1983): 62–88. Histories of the Primary and other auxiliaries are listed in the General Bibliography. See also Susan Staker Oman, "Nurturing LDS Primaries: Louie Felt and May Anderson, 1880–1940," *Utah Historical Quarterly* 49 (Summer 1981): 262–75.

Economics. A broad economic overview that goes beyond this period is Davis Bitton and Linda Wilcox, "The Transformation of Utah's Agriculture, 1847–1900," in Thomas G. Alexander et al., eds., Charles Redd Monographs, no. 12, *The Twentieth Century American West* (Provo: Charles Redd Center for Western History, 1983), pp. 57–84. Church-related events are detailed in Leonard J. Arrington, "The Settlement of the Brigham Young Estate, 1877–1879," *Pacific Historical Review* 21 (February 1952): 1–20; and his "Zion's Board of Trade: A Third United Order," *Western Humanities Review* 5 (January 1951): 1–20. The economic impact of Church construction programs is outlined in Arrington and Melvin A. Larkin, "The Logan Tabernacle and Temple," *Utah Historical Quarterly* 41 (Summer 1972): 301–14.

Colonization. The expansion of settlement is summarized with detail in Richard Sherlock, "Mormon Migration and Settlement after 1875," *Journal of Mormon History* 2 (1975): 53–68. The drama of opening a route into extreme southeastern Utah is told in David S. Miller, *Hole-in-the-Rock: An Epic in the Colonization of the Great American West* (Salt Lake City: University of Utah Press, 1959); the story of Arizona settlement in Peterson, *Take Up Your Mission* (1973); George S. Tanner, *Colonization of the Little Colorado: The Joseph City Region* (Flagstaff, Ariz.: Northland Press, 1977); and of a town in southeastern Idaho in Ronald R. Boyce, "The Mormon Invasion and Settlement of the Upper Snake River Plain in the 1880s: The Case of Lewisville, Idaho," *Pacific Northwest Quarterly* 78 (January-April 1987): 50–58. Other areas are examined in Carleton Q. Anderson et al., eds., *The Mormons: 100 Years in the San Luis Valley of Colorado, 1883–1983* (La Jara, Colo.: La Jara Stake, 1982); and in Dean L. May, "Between Two Cultures: The Mormon Settlement of Star Valley, Wyoming," *Journal of Mormon History* 13 (1986–87): 125–40.

Missionaries. Insights on the times are found in David Buice, " 'All Alone and None to Cheer Me': Excerpts from the Southern States Mission Diaries of J. Golden Kimball, 1883–1885," *Journal of Mormon History* 16 (1990): 40–56; and Frederick S. Buchanan, "Mormons Meet the Mennonites: A View from 1884," *Mennonite Quarterly Review* 62 (April 1988): 159–66.

Canada. On the thrust beyond United States borders, see Leonard J. Arrington, "Historical Roots of the Mormon Settlement in Southern Alberta," in Card et al., *The Mormon Presence in Canada* (1990), pp. 3–18; Robert J. McCue, "British Columbia and the Mormons in the Nineteenth Century," ibid., pp. 35–52; Brigham Young Card, "Charles R. Card and the Founding of the Mormon Settlements in Southwestern Alberta, North-West Territories," ibid., pp. 77–107; Maureen Ursenbach Beecher, "Mormon Women in Southern Alberta: The Pioneer Years," ibid., pp. 211–30; Robert J. McCue, "The 'Restoration' in British Columbia: The LDS and RLDS Churches in Canada's West Coast," *Dialogue: A Journal of Mormon Thought* 22 (Spring 1989): 142–51. Other studies of the northern frontier include the fine article by Lawrence B. Lee, "The Mormons Come to Canada, 1887–1902," *Pacific Northwest Quarterly* 59 (January 1968): 11–22, and Melvin S. Tagg, *A History of the Mormon Church in Canada* (Lethbridge, Alberta: Lethbridge Herald Co., 1968).

Mexico. Studies of the Mormon refugees in Mexico include F. LaMond Tullis, *Mormons in Mexico* (1987), chaps. 1–4; Tullis, "Early Mormon Exploration and Missionary Activities in Mexico," *Brigham Young University Studies* 22 (Summer 1982): 289–310; Thomas H. Naylor, "The Mormons Colonize Sonora: Early Trials at Colonia Oaxaca," *Arizona and the West* 20 (Winter 1978): 325–42; Thomas C. Romney, *The Mormon Colonies in Mexico* (Salt Lake City: Deseret Book, 1938); and Carmon Hardy, "The Mormon Colonies of Northern Mexico: A History, 1885–1912" (Ph.D. diss., Wayne State University, 1963).

Immigration. Useful are Richard L. Jensen, "Steaming Through: Arrangements for Mormon Emigration from Europe, 1869–1887," *Journal of Mormon History* 9 (1982): 3–23; and William Mulder, "Immigration and the 'Mormon Question': An International Episode," *Western Political Quarterly* 9 (June 1956): 416–33; as well as other titles by Mulder and P.A.M. Taylor listed in the General Bibliography.

Southern United States. The Church in the American South is discussed in Gene A. Sessions, "Myth, Mormonism, and Murder in the South," *South Atlantic Quarterly* 75 (Spring 1976): 212–25; Ken Driggs, " 'There Is No Law in Georgia for Mormons': The Joseph Standing Murder Case of 1879," *Georgia Historical Quarterly* 73 (Winter 1989): 745–72; David Buice, "A Stench in the Nostrils of Honest Men: Southern Democrats and the Edmunds Act of 1882," *Dialogue: A Journal of Mormon Thought* 21 (Autumn 1988): 100–113; and William Whiteridge Hatch, *There Is No Law: A History of Mormon Civil Relations in the Southern States, 1865–1905* (New York: Vantage Press, 1968).

Plural Marriage. Careful studies of the subject during the crusade are Van Wagoner, *Mormon Polygamy* (1985); Phillip R. Kunz, "One Wife or Several? A Comparative Study of Late Nineteenth-century Marriage in Utah," in Thomas G. Alexander, ed., *The Mormon People* (Provo: Brigham Young University Press, 1980), pp. 53–74; Lowell Bennion, "The Incidence of Mormon Polygamy in 1880: 'Dixie' versus Davis Stake," *Journal of Mormon History* 11 (1984): 27–42; Jessie L. Embry, " 'Two Legal Wives': Mormon Polygamy in Canada, the United States, and Mexico," in Card et al., *The Mormon Presence in Canada* (1990), pp. 170–85; B. Carmon Hardy, "Mormon Polygamy in Mexico and Canada: A Legal and Historiographical Review," ibid., pp. 186–209; John C. Lehr, "Polygamy, Patrimony, and Prophecy: The Mormon Colonization of Cardston," *Dialogue: A Journal of Mormon Thought* 21 (Winter 1988): 114–21; Robert J. McCue, "Anthony Maitland Stenhouse, Bachelor

Polygamist," ibid., 23 (Spring 1990): 108–25. Also helpful are the overview by Arrington and Bitton, "Marriage and Family Patterns," *The Mormon Experience* (1979), chap. 10; and studies cited in the General Bibliography by Anne Scott ("Mormon Women"), Maureen Beecher ("The 'Leading Sisters' "), and Carol Madsen ("Missionary Wives").

    Anti-Polygamy Legislation. The history of federal legislation and legal prosecution against the Saints is assessed by Kenneth D. Driggs, "The Mormon Church-State Confrontation in Nineteenth Century America," *Journal of Church and State* 30 (Spring 1988): 273–89; and in the thorough analysis by Carol Cornwall Madsen, " 'At Their Peril': Utah Law and the Case of Plural Wives, 1850–1900," *Western Historical Quarterly* 21 (November 1990): 425–43. The subject forms a central part of Larson's monograph, *The "Americanization" of Utah* (1971), chaps. 4–10. See Richard D. Poll, "The Political Reconstruction of Utah Territory, 1866–1890," *Pacific Historical Review* 27 (May 1958): 111–26, for information on the crusade. Its beginnings are examined in Ken Driggs, "The Prosecution Begins: Defining Cohabitation in 1885," *Dialogue: A Journal of Mormon Thought* 21 (Spring 1988): 109–25.

    Legal aspects of the crusade are explored further in Joseph H. Groberg, "The Mormon Disfranchisements of 1882 to 1892," *Brigham Young University Studies* 16 (Spring 1976): 399–408; Ken Driggs, "Lorenzo Snow's Appellate Court Victory," *Utah Historical Quarterly* 58 (Winter 1990): 81–93; and Orma Linford, "The Mormons and the Law: The Polygamy Cases," *Utah Law Review* 9 (Winter 1964 and Summer 1965): 308–70, 543–91. Linford is critiqued in Thomas G. Alexander, "The Church and the Law," *Dialogue: A Journal of Mormon Thought* 1 (Summer 1966): 123–28. An excellent study of the judge behind the prosecutions is Alexander's "Charles S. Zane, Apostle of the New Era," *Utah Historical Quarterly* 34 (Fall 1966): 290–314. See also Leonard J. Arrington, ed., "Crusade against Theocracy: The Reminiscences of Judge Jacob Smith Boreman of Utah, 1872–1877," *Huntington Library Quarterly* 24 (November 1960): 1–45; and M. Paul Holsinger, "Senator George Graham Vest and the 'Menace' of Mormonism, 1882–1887," *Missouri Historical Review* 65 (October 1970): 23–36. An examination of the crusade on moral grounds is Charles A. Cannon, "The Awesome Power of Sex: The Polemical Campaign against Mormon Polygamy," *Pacific Historical Review* 43 (February 1974): 61–82.

    For the impact on individuals, see Larson's, "An Industrial Home for Polygamous Wives," *Utah Historical Quarterly* 38 (Summer 1970): 263–75; William C. Seifrit, "The Prison Experience of Abraham H. Cannon," ibid., 53 (Summer 1985): 222–36; James B. Allen, " 'Good Guys' vs. 'Good Guys': Rudger Clawson, John Sharp, and Civil Disobedience in Nineteenth-century Utah," ibid., 48 (Spring 1980): 148–74; Kimberly Jensen James, " 'Between Two Fires': Women on the 'Underground' of Mormon Polygamy," *Journal of Mormon History* 8 (1982): 49–61; and Constance L. Lieber and John Sillito, eds., *Letters from Exile: The Correspondence of Martha Hughes Cannon, 1886–1889* (Salt Lake City: Signature Books, 1989).

Prosecution Outside Utah. For the political actions against Latter-day Saints in Idaho, see Merle W. Wells, *Anti-Mormonism in Idaho, 1872–1892* (Provo: Brigham Young University Press, 1978); A. J. Simmonds, "Idaho's Last Colony: Northern Cache Valley under the Test Oath, 1872–1896," *Idaho Yesterdays* 32 (Summer 1988): 2–14; Eric N. Moody, "Nevada's Anti-Mormon Legislation of 1887 and Southern Idaho Annexation," *Nevada Historical Society Quarterly* 22 (Spring 1979): 21–32; and the studies concerning Fred T. Dubois listed in the bibliography for chap. 14. On action elsewhere, see JoAnn Bair and Richard L. Jensen, "Prosecution of the Mormons in Arizona Territory in the 1880s," *Arizona and the West* 19 (Spring 1977): 25–46.

CHAPTER 13
The End of an Era, 1887–1896

This pivotal decade in Church history is traditionally examined in terms of church-state relationships, and can be followed in general works listed in the General Bibliography. The story of institutional and administrative developments is interpreted with breadth of detail in Thomas G. Alexander, *Mormonism in Transition: A History of the Latter-day Saints, 1890–1930* (Urbana: University of Illinois Press, 1986).

Political Issues. A fresh look at the Mormon question in national politics is E. Leo Lyman, *Political Deliverance* (1986), based on previously unused primary sources. Other useful treatments are Larson, *The "Americanization" of Utah* (1971), chaps. 11–14; Richard Poll, "The Political Reconstruction of Utah Territory, 1866–1890," *Pacific Historical Review* 27 (May 1958): 111–26; and his "The Americanism of Utah," *Utah Historical Quarterly* 44 (Winter 1976): 76–93. Other excellent analyses are Howard R. Lamar, "Statehood for Utah: A Different Path," ibid., 39 (Fall 1971): 307–27; and S. George Ellsworth, "Utah's Struggle for Statehood," ibid., 31 (Winter 1963): 60–69.

Legal questions are examined by Edwin B. Firmage, "The Judicial Campaign against Polygamy and the Enduring Legal Questions," *Brigham Young University Studies* 27 (Summer 1987): 91–117; James L. Clayton, "The Supreme Court, Polygamy and the Enforcement of Morals in Nineteenth Century America: An Analysis of Reynolds v. United States," *Dialogue: A Journal of Mormon Thought* 12 (Winter 1979): 46–61; Randal Gyunn and Gene C. Schaerr, "The Mormon Polygamy Cases," *Sunstone* 11 (September 1987): 8–17; and Mark S. Lee, "Legislating Morality: Reynolds v. the United States," ibid., 10 (April 1985): 8–12. The economic effects of the raid are dealt with in Arrington, *Great Basin Kingdom* (1958), chap. 12; while M. Hamblin Cannon, ed., "The Prison Diary of a Mormon Apostle," *Pacific Historical Review* 16 (November 1947): 393–409, preserves the 1888 account kept by George Q.

Cannon; and Michael E. Christensen, "Charles W. Nibley: A Case Study of Polygamy," *Journal of Mormon History* 7 (1980): 101–114, examines one family's experience.

The Manifesto. Important studies of millennial expectations and the Manifesto are Thomas G. Alexander, "Wilford Woodruff and the Changing Nature of Mormon Religious Experience," *Church History* 45 (March 1976): 50–69; and Alexander, "The Odyssey of a Latter-day Prophet: Wilford Woodruff and the Manifesto of 1890," *Journal of Mormon History* 17 (1991): 169–206. Interpretations of events in the late 1880s include Henry J. Wolfinger, "A Reexamination of the Woodruff Manifesto in the Light of Utah Constitutional History," *Utah Historical Quarterly* 39 (Fall 1971): 328–49; Kenneth W. Godfrey, "The Coming of the Manifesto," *Dialogue: A Journal of Mormon Thought* 5 (Autumn 1970): 11–25; Gordon C. Thomasson, "The Manifesto Was a Victory," ibid., 6 (Spring 1971): 37–45; Jan Shipps, "The Principle Revoked: A Closer Look at the Demise of Plural Marriage," *Journal of Mormon History* 11 (1984): 65–77; and Charles A. Cannon, "The Awesome Power of Sex: The Polemical Campaign against Mormon Polygamy," *Pacific Historical Review* 43 (February 1974): 61–82. Examining the impact of plural marriage is Eugene E. Campbell and Bruce L. Campbell, "Divorce among Mormon Polygamists: Extent and Explanations," *Utah Historical Quarterly* 46 (Winter 1978): 4–23. Comments on turn-of-the-century events by a participant are preserved in James Henry Moyle, *Mormon Democrat: The Religious and Political Memoirs of James Henry Moyle,* ed. Gene A. Sessions (Salt Lake City: James Moyle Genealogical and Historical Association, 1975).

Utah Statehood. The involvement of Church leaders in the Utah statehood movement is analyzed in Lyman, *Political Deliverance* (1986), and his "The Political Background of the Woodruff Manifesto," *Dialogue: A Journal of Mormon Thought* 24 (Fall 1991): 21–39. Jean Bickmore White has studied the activities of the constitutional convention itself in two articles, "The Making of the Convention President: The Political Education of John Henry Smith," *Utah Historical Quarterly* 39 (Fall 1971): 350–69; and "Woman's Place Is in the Constitution: The Struggle for Equal Rights in Utah in 1895," ibid., 42 (Fall 1974): 344–69. The impact on women is examined in Carol Cornwall Madsen, "Schism in the Sisterhood: Mormon Women and Partisan Politics, 1890–1900," in Bitton and Beecher, *New Views of Mormon History* (1987), pp. 211–41; and Linda Thatcher, ed., " 'I Care Nothing for Politics,': Ruth May Fox, Forgotten Suffragist," *Utah Historical Quarterly* 49 (Summer 1981): 239–53. For applications of the Church's "Political Rule," see J. D. Williams, "Separation of Church and State in Mormon Theory and Practice," *Dialogue: A Journal of Mormon Thought* 1 (Summer 1966): 30–54; and E. Leo Lyman, "The Alienation of an Apostle from His Quorum: The Moses Thatcher Case," ibid., 18 (Summer 1985): 67–91.

Church Activities. On the Iosepa immigrant colony in western Utah see

Leonard J. Arrington, "The L.D.S. Hawaiian Colony at Skull Valley," *Improvement Era* 57 (May 1954): 314–15; and Dennis A. Atkin, "A History of Iosepa, the Utah Polynesian Colony" (M.A. thesis, Brigham Young University, 1958). Auxiliary programs are described in the several histories of those organizations listed in our General Bibliography. On educational programs, see Stanley S. Ivins, "Free Schools Come to Utah," *Utah Historical Quarterly* 22 (October 1954): 321–42; D. Michael Quinn, "Utah's Educational Innovation: LDS Religion Classes, 1890–1929," ibid., 43 (Fall 1975): 379–89; and Quinn's "The Brief Career of Young University at Salt Lake City," ibid., 41 (Winter 1973): 69–89.

Religious Practices. Significant topics are discussed in Gordon I. Irving, "The Law of Adoption: One Phase of the Development of the Mormon Concept of Salvation, 1830–1900," *Brigham Young University Studies* 14 (Spring 1974): 291–314; and Arthur Dean Wengreen, "The Origin and History of the Fast Day in The Church of Jesus Christ of Latter-day Saints, 1830–1896" (M.A. thesis, Brigham Young University, 1955).

Economic Policies. The transition in Latter-day Saint economic policies in the post-Manifesto era is examined in Arrington, *Great Basin Kingdom* (1958), chap. 13. An important Church-supported industry is described in Arrington's *Beet Sugar In the West: A History of the Utah-Idaho Sugar Company, 1891–1966* (Seattle: University of Washington Press, 1966). LDS welfare activities are discussed in Arrington's "Utah and the Depression of the 1890s," *Utah Historical Quarterly* 29 (January 1961): 2–18. The impact of the 1893 depression is examined in Ronald W. Walker, "Crisis in Zion: Heber J. Grant and the Panic of 1893," *Arizona and the West* 21 (Autumn 1979): 257–78 (reprinted in shortened form in *Sunstone* 10 [May 1985]: 70–78).

CHAPTER 14
A Time of Transition, 1897–1907

The period of adjustment that bridged the centuries is given thorough treatment in Alexander, *Mormonism in Transition* (1986), with briefer surveys in selected general works cited in the General Bibliography.

Jubilee. Events connected with the fiftieth anniversary celebration of Mormon arrival in the Great Basin are recited in Horace Whitney, "A Jubilee Review," *Improvement Era* 1 (December 1897): 65–76; and Spencer Clawson, "The Pioneer Monument," ibid., 3 (October 1900): 881–85.

Presidents. Supplementing biographies of Wilford Woodruff and Lorenzo Snow listed in our General Bibliography are Franklin D. Richards, "Wilford Woodruff," *Improvement Era* 1 (October 1898): 865–80; and Nephi Anderson, "Life and Character Sketch of Lorenzo Snow . . . ," ibid., 2 (June 1899): 561–70. The continuity between administrations is demonstrated in Joseph F. Smith, "The Last Days of President Snow," *Juvenile Instructor* 36 (November

15, 1901): 688–91; while the mechanics of the transfer of authority are outlined in Durham and Heath, *Succession in the Church* (1970), chaps. 8–9. A helpful source on the years after 1901 is the *Life of Joseph F. Smith* (1972), by his son Joseph Fielding Smith and John J. Stewart.

Political Life. In addition to Alexander's solid treatment, several article-length studies examine the Latter-day Saint role in American political life. Surveying the transitional years is Jan Shipps, "Utah Comes of Age Politically: A Study of the State's Politics in the Early Years of the Twentieth Century," *Utah Historical Quarterly* 35 (Spring 1967): 91–111. Attitudes toward war are analyzed in D. Michael Quinn, "The Mormon Church and the Spanish-American War: An End to Selective Pacifism," *Pacific Historical Review* 43 (August 1974): 342–66.

Post-Manifesto Polygamy. Besides information in Van Wagoner, *Mormon Polygamy* (1985), see Kenneth L. Cannon II, "After the Manifesto: Mormon Polygamy, 1890–1906," *Sunstone* 8 (January-April 1983): 27–35; D. Michael Quinn, "LDS Church Authority and New Plural Marriages, 1890–1904," *Dialogue: A Journal of Mormon Thought* 18 (Spring 1985): 9–105; and Cannon, "Beyond the Manifesto: Polygamous Cohabitation among LDS General Authorities after 1890," *Utah Historical Quarterly* 46 (Winter 1978): 24–36.

B. H. Roberts. A careful study of "The B. H. Roberts Case of 1898–1900," by Davis Bitton, appears in *Utah Historical Quarterly* 25 (January 1957): 27–46; with another viewpoint examined in William Griffin White, Jr., "Feminist Campaign for the Exclusion of Brigham Henry Roberts from the Fifty-sixth Congress, *Journal of the West* 17 (January 1978): 45–52. The public life of Roberts is examined in D. Craig Mikkelsen, "The Politics of B. H. Roberts," *Dialogue: A Journal of Mormon Thought* 9 (Summer 1974): 25–43.

Reed Smoot. T. Edgar Lyon, "Religious Activities and Development in Utah, 1847–1910," *Utah Historical Quarterly* 35 (Fall 1967): 292–306, is helpful in understanding the setting for ministerial opposition to the election of Roberts and of Senator Reed Smoot. On the latter's fight for his seat, see M. Paul Holsinger, "For God and the American Home: The Attempt to Unseat Senator Reed Smoot, 1903–1907," *Pacific Northwest Quarterly* 60 (July 1969): 154–60. Smoot's career is summarized in Milton R. Merrill, *Reed Smoot, Apostle in Politics* (Logan, Utah: Utah State University Press and Department of Political Science, Utah State University, 1990), and is given fresh treatment in Harvard S. Heath, "Reed Smoot: The First Modern Mormon" (Ph.D. diss., Brigham Young University, 1990). Smoot's contributions in Washington are analyzed in Thomas G. Alexander, "Reed Smoot and the Development of Western Land Policy, 1905–1920," *Arizona and the West* 13 (Autumn 1971): 245–64; and in Alexander, "Reed Smoot, the L.D.S. Church, and Progressive Legislation, 1903–1933," *Dialogue: A Journal of Mormon Thought* 7 (Spring 1972):47–56. Another perspective is offered in Jan Shipps, "The Public Image of Senator Reed Smoot, 1902–32," *Utah Historical Quarterly* 45 (Fall 1977): 380–400.

On the opponents of Smoot, see the journalistic treatment in Malmquist, *The First 100 Years* (1971), chaps. 13–20; and two portraits by M. Paul Holsinger: "J.C. Burrows and the Fight against Mormonism, 1903–1907," *Michigan History* 52 (Fall 1968): 181–95; and "Philander C. Knox and the Crusade against Mormonism, 1904–1907," *Western Pennsylvania History Magazine* 51 (January 1969): 47–56. Smoot's political antagonist Fred T. Dubois is studied in Jay R. Lowe, "Fred T. Dubois, Foe of the Mormons . . . , 1903–1907," (M.A. thesis, Brigham Young University, 1960); Merle W. Wells, "Fred T. Dubois and the Idaho Progressives, 1900–1914," *Idaho Yesterdays* 3 (Summer 1960): 24–31; and in Leo William Graff, "The Senatorial Career of Fred T. Dubois of Idaho, 1890–1907" (Ph.D. diss., University of Idaho, 1968). The official Church response, the *Address . . . to the World* was first published as a supplement to the April 1907 *Conference Report* and appears also in *Improvement Era* 10 (May 1907): 481–95; and in Clark, *Messages of the First Presidency*, 4: 142–55. Also see the studies on plural marriage by Hilton and Jessee that are cited in the bibliography for chap. 17.

Public Image. Information can be found in the Holsinger articles cited above and in studies by Lambert, Cracroft, Lythgoe, and Shipps, all noted in the General Bibliography.

Historic Sites. Supplementing Roberts on historic sites are Darel P. Bartschi, "The Joseph Smith Memorial: A 1905 Tribute to the Prophet and His Work," *Ensign* 18 (February 1988): 7–10; "Bureau of Information and Church Literature," *Improvement Era* 5 (September 1902): 899–901; Junius F. Wells, "The Birthplace of the Prophet Joseph Smith," *Contributor* 16 (February 1895): 203–11; and Susa Young Gates, "Memorial Monument Dedication," *Improvement Era* 9 (February and March 1906): 308–19, 375–89.

Financial Affairs. See Arrington, *Great Basin Kingdom* (1958), chap. 13, and Roberts, *Comprehensive History of the Church* (1930), vol. 6, chap. 180. Useful background is Arrington's, "The Commercialization of Utah's Economy: Trends and Developments from Statehood to 1910," in Arrington and Alexander, *A Dependent Commonwealth* (1974), pp. 3–34. For the story of a Church-owned resort, see Nancy McCormick and John McCormick, *Saltair* (Salt Lake City: University of Utah Press, 1984). The tithing reform is described in LeRoi C. Snow, "The Lord's Way Out of Bondage . . . ," *Improvement Era* 41 (July 1938): 400–401, 439–42, which is reprinted in Berrett and Burton, *Readings in LDS Church History* (1953–58), 3: 258–66, as "Lorenzo Snow and the Law of Tithing"; and in sermons published in *Conference Report*, 1899–1901.

Social Problems. An important statement on social problems of the time is [Joseph F. Smith], "Editor's Table: Attitude of the Church Towards Reform-Political Parties," *Improvement Era* 2 (February 1899): 310–12. Discussions concerning liquor at Saltair are reported in Stan Larson, "Synoptic Minutes of a Quarterly Conference of the Twelve Apostles: The Clawson and Lund Diaries of July 9–11, 1901," *Journal of Mormon History* 14 (1988): 97–119. Instances of humanitarian concern are retold in Allen Kent Powell, "Tragedy at Scofield," *Utah Historical Quarterly* 41 (Spring 1973): 182–94; and in William G. Hartley, "That Terrible Wednesday: The Saints and the San Francisco Earthquake," *Brigham Young University Studies* 23 (Fall 1983): 431–59.

Church Education. Programs are well documented in sources listed under Education in the General Bibliography. An important contemporary statement of Church attitudes is Karl G. Maeser, *School and Fireside* (Provo: Skelton & Co., 1898). The writings of a BYU professor are analyzed in Davis Bitton, "N. L. Nelson and the Mormon Point of View," *Brigham Young University Studies* 13 (Winter 1973): 157–71.

Missionary Work. Supplementing standard sources listed earlier are reports from mission presidents published in *Conference Report* for this period and documents in Clark, *Messages of the First Presidency* (1965–75), vol. 4. For beginnings in Japan, see Ronald W. Walker, "Strangers in a Strange Land: Heber J. Grant and the Opening of the Japanese Mission," *Journal of Mormon History* 13 (1986–87): 21–44; R. Lanier Britsch, "The Closing of the Early Japan Mission," *Brigham Young University Studies* 15 (Winter 1975): 171–90; and Gordon A. Madsen, comp., *A Japanese Journal [of Heber J. Grant]* (Salt Lake City: n.p., 1970). A new beginning is summarized in F. LaMond Tullis, "Reopening the Mexican Mission in 1901," *Brigham Young University Studies* 22 (Fall 1982): 441–53. Attempts between 1889 and 1928 to establish a gathering place in Palestine are traced in Rao H. Lindsay, "The Dream of a Mormon Colony in the Near East," *Dialogue: A Journal of Mormon Thought* 1 (Winter 1966): 50–67. A mission president's experiences are detailed in Ronald W. Walker, "Heber J. Grant's European Mission, 1903–1906," *Journal of Mormon History* 14 (1988): 17–33. Beginnings in eastern Europe are examined in Kahlile Mehr, "The 1903 Dedication of Russia for Missionary Work," *Journal of Mormon History* 13 (1986–87): 111–24.

Auxiliaries. See the works listed in our General Bibliography for information on the auxiliaries. Priesthood activities are described in William G. Hartley, "The Priesthood Reform Movement, 1908–1922," *Brigham Young University Studies* 13 (Winter 1973): 137–56; and in general conference talks and *Improvement Era* articles of the period.

CHAPTER 15
Consolidating for Growth, 1908–1918

During the last decade of Joseph F. Smith's presidency, Church programs underwent significant adjustment, and the focus of Latter-day Saint history turns perceptively inward to follow institutional developments. The most complete treatment is Alexander, *Mormonism in Transition* (1986), where all of the topics identified below are given careful analysis. The outlines of the story can be found in most other general works listed in the General Bibliography.

Administrative Matters. Useful statistical and financial reports spanning the decade are in *Improvement Era* 13 (May 1910): 657–59; and 19 (May 1916): 653–54. Background reading for Church economic activities is Thomas G. Alexander, "The Burgeoning of Utah's Economy, 1910–1918," published in Arrington and Alexander, *A Dependent Commonwealth* (1974), pp. 35–56. A new Church publishing venture is described briefly in "New Home of Zion's Printing and Publishing Company at Independence, Jackson Co., Missouri," *Liahona: The Elders' Journal* 13 (November 2, 1915): 289–91; and another business in Leonard J. Arrington and Heidi S. Swinton, *The Hotel: Salt Lake's Classy Lady, the Hotel Utah, 1911–1986* (Salt Lake City: Westin Hotel Utah, 1986). A description of the Administration Building by the architect, J. D. C. Young, is "The Latter-day Saint Church Headquarters Building," *Utah Genealogical and Historical Magazine* 8 (April 1917): 57–60. Meetinghouse design is characterized in a survey by Allen D. Roberts, "Religious Architecture of the LDS Church: Influences and Changes Since 1847," *Utah Historical Quarterly* 43 (Summer 1975): 301–27. The administration of charity is examined in Bruce D. Blummell, "Welfare before Welfare: Twentieth Century LDS Church Charity before the Great Depression," *Journal of Mormon History* 6 (1979): 89–106. An issue introduced in chapter 14 is explored in Victor W. Jorgensen and B. Carmon Hardy, "The Taylor-Cowley Affair and the Watershed of Mormon History," *Utah Historical Quarterly* 48 (Winter 1980): 4–36.

Public Image. To supplement B. H. Roberts's treatment of the magazine crusade (*Comprehensive History of the Church* [1930], vol. 6, chap. 179), see Dennis L. Lythgoe, "The Changing Image of Mormonism in Periodical Literature" (Ph.D. diss., University of Utah, 1969); and Malmquist, *The First 100 Years* (1971), chaps. 20–23. Theodore Roosevelt's reaction to the anti-Mormon magazine campaign (Isaac Russel, ed., "Mr. Roosevelt to the 'Mormons,'" *Colliers*, April 15, 1911), is reprinted in *Improvement Era* 14 (June 1911): 712–18. European opposition is described in the thorough study by Malcolm R. Thorp, " 'The Mormon Peril': The Crusade against the Saints in Britain, 1910–1914," *Journal of Mormon History* 2 (1975): 69–88; in Thorp, "The British Government and the Mormon Question, 1910–22," *Journal of Church and State* 21 (1979): 305–23; and in a contemporary report by George F. Richards, "Why Are 'Mormon' Missionaries Expelled from Germany?" *Improvement Era* 13 (September 1910): 1004–7. Historic preservation issues are presented in Ronald W. Walker and Alexander M. Starr, "Shattering the Vase: The Razing of the Old Salt Lake Theater," *Utah Historical Quarterly* 57 (Winter 1898): 64–88. The Tabernacle Choir tour is chronicled in J. Spencer Cornwall, *A Century of Singing* (1958), chap. 8.

Organization. Priesthood activities can be traced in Bumgarten's thesis on the seventies listed in the General Bibliography; in Hartley's study of "The Priestood Reform Movement, 1908–1922," cited above (chap. 14); and in Gary L. Phelps, "Home Teaching: Attempts by the Latter-day Saints to Establish an Effective Program during the Nineteenth Century" (M.A. thesis, Brigham Young University, 1975). We also benefited from a study of "Priesthood Programs of the Twentieth Century" by Richard O. Cowan of Brigham Young University and other members of a task committee under the direction of Dean C. Jessee, then of the Church Historical Department.

Histories of the auxiliaries cited in the General Bibliography furnish information on activities in those organizations. An effort at rejuvenation of the MIA is described in A. Glen Humpherys, "Missionaries to the Saints," *Brigham Young University Studies* 17 (Autumn 1976): 74–100. Jessie L. Embry, "Grain Storage: The Balance of Power between Priesthood Authority and Relief Society Autonomy," *Dialogue: A Journal of Mormon Thought* 15 (Winter 1982): 59–66, examines one aspect of welfare activities. For other issues, see Thomas G. Alexander, "Between Revivalism and the Social Gospel: The Latter-day Saints Social Advisory Committee, 1916–1922," *Brigham Young University Studies* 23 (Winter 1983): 19–39; and James B. Allen and Jesse L. Embry, " 'Provoking the Brethren to Good Works': Susa Young Gates, the Relief Society, and Genealogy," ibid., 31 (Spring 1991): 115–38.

Doctrine. The "Doctrinal Exposition on the Father and the Son" appears in *Improvement Era* 19 (August 1916): 934–42, and has been published as well in Talmage, *Articles of Faith* (1901, 1975), pp. 465–73; and in Clark, *Messages of the First Presidency* (1965–75), 5: 26–33. President Smith's "Vision of the Redemption of the Dead" is canonized as Doctrine and Covenants, Section 137. For a deletion from scripture, see Richard S. Van Wagoner, Steven C. Walker, and Allen D. Roberts, "The 'Lectures on Faith': A Case Study in Decanonization," *Dialogue: A Journal of Mormon Thought* 20 (Fall 1987): 71–77.

Education. On Church educational programs, consult sources listed in the General Bibliography and Quinn's article on religion classes cited in the listing for chapter 13. The controversy over scientific modernism is examined in Wilkinson, *Brigham Young University* (1975–76), vol. 1, chaps. 13–17; Mark K. Allen, *The History of Psychology at Brigham Young University* (Provo: Brigham Young University Psychology Department, 1975), chaps. 5–7; and in Richard Sherlock, "Campus in Crisis: BYU, 1911," *Sunstone* 4 (January-February 1979): 10–16 (reprinted in 10 [May 1985]: 30–35). The issue is placed in broader historical perspective in Duane E. Jeffrey, "Seers, Savants, and Evolution: The Uncomfortable Interface," *Dialogue: A Journal of Mormon Thought* 8 (Autumn-Winter 1973): 41–75; and Richard Sherlock, "A Turbulent Spectrum: Mormon Reactions to the Darwinist Legacy," *Journal of Mormon History* 5 (1978): 33–59. A biographical approach is Steven H. Heath, "The Reconciliation of Faith and Science: Henry Eyring's Achievement," ibid., 15 (Autumn 1982): 86–99.

Political Issues. Discussions from the Progressive Era are found in Shipps's article cited with sources on "Political Life" for chapter 14; in John R. Sillito and John S. McCormick, "Socialist Saints: Mormons and the Socialist Party in Utah, 1900–1920," *Dialogue: A Journal of Mormon Thought* 18 (Spring 1985): 121–31; and in Reuben Joseph Snow, "The American Party in Utah: A Study of Political Party Struggles during the Early Years of Statehood" (M.A. thesis, Univ. of Utah, 1963). See also comments on William Howard Taft's candidacy in Joseph F. Smith, "The Presidential Election," *Improvement Era* 15 (October 1912): 1120–21; and Jean Bickmore White, ed., *Church, State, and Politics: The Diaries of John Henry Smith* (Salt Lake City: Signature Books and Smith Research Associates, 1990).

Prohibition. Latter-day Saint involvement in the prohibition movement is treated in Larry E. Nelson, "Utah Goes Dry," *Utah Historical Quarterly* 41 (Fall 1973): 340–57; in Brent G. Thompson, " 'Standing between Two Fires': Mormons and Prohibition, 1908–17," *Journal of Mormon History* 10 (1983): 35–52; and in Bruce T. Dyer, "A Study of the Forces Leading to the Adoption of Prohibition in Utah in 1917" (M.S. thesis, Brigham Young University, 1958).

Mexican Revolution. Effects of the Mexican Revolution on Mormon colonists are recounted in the histories by Hardy and Romney listed in our bibliography for "Mexico" in chap. 12, and in Joseph Flake Boone, "The Roles of the Church . . . in relation to the United States Military" (Ph.D. diss., BYU, 1975), chap. 3. Other sources include B. Carmon Hardy, "Cultural 'Encystment' as a Cause of the Mormon Exodus from Mexico in 1912," *Pacific Historical Review* 34 (November 1965): 439–54; Thomas H. Naylor, "Colonia Morelos and the Mexican Revolution: Consul Dye Inspects an Evacuated Mormon Colony, 1912," *Journal of Arizona History* 20 (Spring 1979): 101–20; and Karl E. Young, *The Long Hot Summer of 1912* (Provo: Brigham Young University Press, 1967).

World War I. B. H. Roberts devotes two chapters to LDS participation in the war in *Comprehensive History of the Church* (1930), vol. 6, chaps. 182–83. For additional details, consult Louis B. Cardon, "The First World War and the Great Depression, 1914–39," in Bloxham et al., *Truth Will Prevail* (1987), pp. 335–60; Leonard J. Arrington, "Modern Lysistratus: Mormon Women in the International Peace Movement, 1899–1939," *Journal of Mormon History* 15 (1989): 89–104; and chap. 4 of Boone's dissertation (noted above). General attitudes toward the war are discussed in Robert J. Stott, "Mormonism and War": An Interpretative Analysis of Selected Mormon Thought Regarding Several American Wars" (M.A. thesis, Brigham Young University, 1974), chap. 5. Its impact on the Saints in one European country is described in Scharffs, *Mormonism in Germany* (1970), chap. 5.

CHAPTER 16
Change and Continuity in the Postwar Decade, 1919–1930

The early years of Heber J. Grant's presidency marked the beginning of a dispersion of Church membership beyond the concentration in the Rocky Mountain West. As the Church approached its centennial, it experienced important membership growth and adjustments in programs. Alexander gives thorough treatment to this period in his *Mormonism in Transition* (1986); and Roberts covers it in *Comprehensive History of the Church* (1930), vol. 6, chaps. 184–89. The decade gets brief treatment in some other general works cited in the General Bibliography.

Growth Patterns. Helpful in charting growth in the decade after World War I are appropriate sections in studies by Dean R. Louder, "A Distributional and Diffusionary Analysis of the Mormon Church, 1850–1970" (Ph.D. diss., Univ. of Washington, 1972); and D. W. Meinig, "The Mormon Culture Region: Strategies and Patterns in the Geography of the American West, 1847–1962," *Annals, Association of American Geographers* 55 (June 1965): 191–220.

Correlation. Especially helpful in understanding the coordination of priesthood and auxiliary activities is the study of "Priesthood Programs of the Twentieth Century" by Cowan and Jessee noted earlier ("Organization," chap. 15); standard auxiliary histories; William G. Hartley, "The Priesthood Reform Movement, 1908–1922," *Brigham Young University Studies* 13 (Winter 1973): 137–56; and D. Michael Quinn, "Utah's Educational Innovation: LDS Religion Classes, 1890–1929," *Utah Historical Quarterly* 43 (Fall 1975): 379–89.

Church Education. Developments are traced in the literature cited in the General Bibliography. A new program begun in this period is discussed in Leonard J. Arrington, "The Founding of the LDS Institutes of Religion," *Dialogue: A Journal of Mormon Thought* 2 (Summer 1967): 137–47.

Missionary Activities. Additional information about missionary activities is in three articles in *Brigham Young University Studies*: Dale F. Beecher, "Rey L. Pratt and the Mexican Mission," 15 (Spring 1975): 293–307; R. Lanier Britsch, "The Closing of the Early Japan Mission," 15 (Winter 1975): 171–90; and J. Christopher Conkling, "Members without a Church: Japanese Mormons in Japan from 1924 to 1948," ibid., pp. 191–214.

Temples and Meetinghouses. An overview of the period is Paul L. Anderson, "The Early Twentieth Century Temples," *Dialogue: A Journal of Mormon Thought* 14 (Spring 1981): 9–19. On the Idaho Falls and and some later temples, see Anderson, "Mormon Moderne: Latter-day Saint Architecture, 1925–1945," *Journal of Mormon History* 9 (1982): 71–84. The meaning of the temple at Mesa to Indians in the Southwest is examined in Richard O. Cowan, "The Arizona Temple and the Lamanites," in Garret and Johnson, *Regional Studies . . . : Arizona* (1989), pp. 53–69.

Radio and TV. Histories of Church use of the electronic media are Heber

G. Wolsey, "The History of Radio Station KSL from 1922 to Television" (Ph.D. diss., Mich. State Univ., 1967), and David Jacobs, "The History of Motion Pictures Produced by the Church . . . " (M.A. thesis, BYU, 1967). The dissertations by Cowan and Lythgoe, listed in the General Bibliography, are helpful on the Latter-day Saint public image in the 1920s. Also see Richard Alan Nelson, "From Antagonism to Acceptance: Mormons and the Silver Screen," *Dialogue: A Journal of Mormon Thought* 10 (Spring 1977): 59–69.

Public Issues. For topics of interest to the Church, see Dan E. Jones, "Utah Politics, 1926–1932" (Ph.D. diss., Univ. of Utah, 1968); James B. Allen, "Personal Faith and Public Policy: Some Timely Observations on the League of Nations Controversy in Utah," *Brigham Young University Studies* 14 (Autumn 1973): 77–98; Larry E. Nelson, "Problems of Prohibition Enforcement in Utah, 1917–1933" (M.S. thesis, Univ. of Utah, 1970); John S. H. Smith, "Cigarette Prohibition in Utah, 1921–23," *Utah Historical Quarterly* 41 (Autumn 1973): 358–72; and Allan Kent Powell, "Mormon Influence on the Unionization of Eastern Utah Coal Miners, 1903–33," *Journal of Mormon History* 4 (1977): 91–100. Two articles by Loretta L. Hefner explore social issues: "The National Women's Relief Society and the U.S. Sheppard-Towner Act," *Utah Hisotrical Quarterly* 50 (Summer 1982): 255–67; and "This Decade Was Different: Relief Society's Social Services Department, 1919–1929," *Dialogue: A Journal of Mormon Thought* 15 (Autumn 1982): 64–73. An interpretation of intellectual conflicts within the Church is Ephraim Edward Ericksen, *Psychological and Ethical Aspects of Mormon Group Life* (1922; reprint ed., Salt Lake City: University of Utah Press, 1975).

CHAPTER 17
The Church and the Great Depression, 1930–1938

Scholars are beginning to give this critical period attention, but reference to primary sources is still necessary to fill in many aspects of the story. The most complete accounts are Cowan, *The Church in the Twentieth Century* (1985), chaps. 7–9; and CES, *Church History in the Fulness of Times* (1989), chap. 39.

Depression Era. Useful for background is John F. Bluth and Wayne K. Hinton, "The Great Depression," in Richard D. Poll et al., eds., *Utah's History* (1978), pp. 481–96; Wayne K. Hinton, "Some Historical Perspective on Mormon Responses to the Great Depression," *Journal of the West* 24 (October 1985): 19–26; and Hinton, "The Economics of Ambivalence: Utah's Depression Experience," *Utah Historical Quarterly* 54 (Summer 1986): 268–85. Statements on the effects of the Great Depression on Latter-day Saints can be found in J. H. Paul, "Land Poor!" *Improvement Era* 35 (January 1931): 135–36; Joseph F. Merrill, "Can the Depression Be Cured?" ibid., 36 (November 1932): 5–6; and Lowry Nelson, "The Next Hundred Years," ibid., 36 (December 1932):

71–73, 117. For early reactions by Church leaders, consult *Conference Report*, October 1932; First Presidency, "An Important Message on Relief," *Deseret News*, April 7, 1936 (reprinted in Clark, *Messages of the First Presidency* [1965–75], 6:9–13); and "A Message from the First Presidency Concerning Preparation for Relief Measure," July 1933, in ibid., 5: 330–34.

Welfare Plan. Useful histories are Leonard J. Arrington and Wayne K. Hinton, "Origin of the Welfare Plan of The Church of Jesus Christ of Latter-day Saints," *Brigham Young University Studies* 5 (Winter 1964): 67–85; Paul C. Child, "Physical Beginnings of the Church Welfare Program," ibid., 14 (Spring 1974): 383–85; and Betty L. Barton, "Mormon Poor Relief: A Social Welfare Interlude," ibid., 18 (Fall 1977): 66–88. Administrative adjustments are examined in Jill Mulvay Derr, "Changing Relief Society Charity to Make Way for Welfare," in Bitton and Beecher, *New Views of Mormon History* (1987), pp. 242–72. Early guides to the program are Henry D. Moyle, "Some Practical Phases of Church Security," *Improvement Era* 40 (June 1937): 354–55, 390; and Albert E. Bowen, *The Church Welfare Plan* (Salt Lake City: Deseret Sunday School Union, 1946). Operations are also explained in a pamphlet, *What Is the "Mormon" Security Program* (Independence, Mo.: Zion's Printing and Publishing Co., [ca. 1930]).

Temperance. A good overview on temperance is John Kearnes, "Utah, Sexton of Prohibition," *Utah Historical Quarterly* 47 (Winter 1979): 5–21. New emphasis on observance of the Word of Wisdom and opposition to the prohibition repeal movement are discussed in Thomas G. Alexander, "The Word of Wisdom: From Principle to Requirement," *Dialogue: A Journal of Mormon Thought* 14 (Autumn 1981): 78–88; and in several contemporary statements. See First Presidency and the Twelve, "Prohibition: How We Stand," *Improvement Era* 35 (September 1932): 642 (reproduced in Clark, *Messages of the First Presidency*, 5:308–10); Mutual Improvement Associations, "In the Name of Temperance . . . ," *Improvement Era* 36 (October 1933): 707; and James H. Wallis, "President Grant: Defender of the Word of Wisdom," ibid., 39 (November 1936): 696–98.

Plural Marriage and Fundamentalism. President Grant's April 1931 general conference statement countering Fundamentalist teachings on plural marriage is reproduced in Clark, *Messages of the First Presidency*, 5:292–303. The issue is discussed in Martha S. Bradley, "Changed Faces: The LDS Position on Polygamy, 1890–1990," *Sunstone* 14 (February 1990): 26–33; Ken Driggs, "After the Manifesto: Modern Polygamy and Fundamentalist Mormons," *Journal of Church and State* 32 (Spring 1990): 367–89; and Driggs, "Twentieth-century Polygamy and Fundamentalist Mormons in Southern Utah," *Dialogue: A Journal of Mormon Thought* 24 (Winter 1991): 44–58. Life among those still involved in plural families after the Manifesto is examined in Jessie L. Embry, *Mormon Polygamous Families: Life in the Principle* (Salt Lake City: University of Utah Press, 1987). Fundamentalist groups are examined in Clair

L. Wyatt, *"Some That Trouble You": Subcultures in Mormonism* (Salt Lake City: Bookcraft, 1974); Martha S. Bradley, "The Women of Fundamentalism: Short Creek, 1953," *Dialogue: A Journal of Mormon Thought* 23 (Summer 1990): 15–37; and Ken Driggs, "Fundamentalist Attitudes toward the Church: The Sermons of Leroy S. Johnson," ibid., pp. 39–60. The question is explored as well in Van Wagoner, *Mormon Polygamy* (1989).

Church Education. Information is scattered in many histories, published and unpublished. Consult the General Bibliography for titles. On the issue of higher criticism, see the studies listed for chap. 14; Russel B. Swensen, "Mormons at the University of Chicago Divinity School," *Dialogue: A Journal of Mormon Thought* 7 (Summer 1972): 37–47; Richard Sherlock, "Faith and History: The Snell Controversy," ibid., 12 (Spring 1979): 27–41; Sherlock, "We Can See No Advantage to a Continuation of the Discussion: The Roberts/Smith/Talmage Affair," ibid., 13 (Fall 1980): 63–78; and Jeffrey E. Keller, "Discussion Continued: The Sequel to the Roberts/Smith/Talmage Affair," ibid., 15 (Spring 1982): 79–98.

Church Programs. Consult the general surveys and histories of the missions for outlines. Administrative and auxiliary reform is studied in Richard O. Cowan, "The Priesthood-Auxiliary Movement, 1928–38," *Brigham Young University Studies* 19 (Fall 1978): 106–20. Also useful is John A. Widtsoe, "The Japanese Mission in Action," *Improvement Era* 42 (February 1939): 88–89, 125–27; and Joseph M. Dixon, "Mormons in the Third Reich: 1933–1945," *Dialogue: A Journal of Mormon Thought* 7 (Autumn-Winter 1971): 70–78. One leader's experiences are retold in Richard L. Bushman, "The Crisis in Europe and Hugh B. Brown's First Mission Presidency," ibid., 21 (Summer 1988): 51–59.

CHAPTER 18
The Church and World War II, 1939–1950

The years during which Church programs were dramatically curtailed by the world war are summarized in Cowan, *The Church in the Twentieth Century* (1985), chaps. 10–12, and in the more recently published general works in our General Bibliography. Helpful for understanding the setting on the home front is John E. Christensen, "The Impact of World War II," in Poll et al., *Utah's History* (1978), pp. 497–514. Documents pertaining to the period are collected in Berrett and Burton, *Readings in LDS Church History* (1958), vol. 3.

Isolationism. Contemporary Latter-day Saint expressions supportive of the isolationist viewpoint are J. Reuben Clark, Jr., "In Time of War," *Improvement Era* 42 (November 1939): 656–57, 693–703; First Presidency, "Editorial: Comment on War," ibid., p. 672 (reproduced in Clark, *Messages of the First Presidency* [1965–75], 6: 92–93); and First Presidency, "To a World at

War," *Improvement Era* 43 (December 1940): 712 (reprinted in Clark, *Messages*, 6: 115–17).

The War. For an overview, see James R. Moss, R. Lanier Britsch, James R. Christianson, and Richard Cowan, *The International Church* (Provo: Brigham Young University Publications, 1982), pp. 71–83. After Pearl Harbor, Church leaders threw their support behind the war effort in official statements read to the general conference by J. Reuben Clark, Jr., "Message of the First Presidency to the Church," *Improvement Era* 45 (May 1942): 272–73, 343–50; and David O. McKay, "The Church's Part in Defense: Message from the First Presidency," ibid., p. 274. These are also published in Clark, *Messages*, 6:148–63, 163–65. Other contemporary statements are John A. Widtsoe, "Evidences and Reconciliations, 48: Should a Soldier Love His Enemy?" *Improvement Era* 45 (April 1942): 225; and David O. McKay, "The Church and the Present War," ibid., (May 1942): 276, 340–42.

The impact on members is told in Joseph M. Dixon, "Mormons in the Third Reich: 1933–1945," *Dialogue: A Journal of Mormon Thought* 7 (Spring 1962): 70–78; and William G. Hartley, "War and Peace and Dutch Potatoes," *Ensign* 8 (July 1977): 18–23. The personal challenge of a German Saint is the focus in Karl-Heinz Schnibbe, Alan F. Keele, and Douglas F. Tobler, *The Price: The True Story of a Mormon Who Defied Hitler* (Salt Lake City: Bookcraft, 1984); and in Keele and Tobler, "The Fuhrer's New Clothes: Helmuth Huebner and the Mormons and the Third Reich," *Sunstone* 5 (November-December 1980): 20–29. Also see Campbell and Poll, *Hugh B. Brown: His Life and Thought* (1975), chap. 11.

Postwar Europe. On the subject of reopening the European missions, see Frederick W. Babbel, "Europe's Valiant Saints Forge Ahead," *Improvement Era* 49 (October 1946): 622–23, 664–67; Babbel, *On Wings of Faith* (Salt Lake City: Bookcraft, 1972); and Louis B. Cardon, "War and Recovery, 1939–1959," in Bloxham et al., *Truth Will Prevail* (1987), pp. 361–93. Additional firsthand accounts of postwar Europe are preserved in the typewritten transcripts of interviews conducted under the Oral History Program of the Church Historical Department, including interviews with Jean Wunderlich, Scott Taggart, A. Hamer Reiser, and others identified in the *Guide to the Oral History Program . . . , 1975* (Salt Lake City: Historical Department of The Church . . . , 1975).

Postwar Welfare. The task of aiding the Saints is recounted in Ezra Taft Benson, *A Labor of Love: The 1946 European Mission of Ezra Taft Benson* (Salt Lake City: Deseret Book, 1989); and reported in "The Church Welfare Program Helps European Saints," *Improvement Era* 48 (December 1945): 747; Arthur Gaeth, "The Saints in Central Europe," ibid., 49 (March 1946): 148, 185; Henry D. Moyle, "Ten Years of Church Welfare," ibid., (April 1946): 207–9, 244–55; and Alma Stone, "The Church in Europe," ibid., 51 (July 1948): 426.

Other Church Programs. See the overview in Milton R. Hunter, "Unparalleled Growth Marks All Phases of Church Endeavor," *Deseret News*, Church News section, December 12, 1951. New missions are described in "The China Mission," *Improvement Era* 52 (December 1949): 784, 863; and Albert L. Zobell, Jr., "Uruguay: New Mission Field," ibid., 51 (January 1948): 47–48. David F. Boone describes "The Worldwide Evacuation of Latter-day Saint Missionaries at the Beginning of World War II" (M.A. thesis, Brigham Young University, 1981). The impact of isolation is recounted in J. Christopher Conkling, "Members without a Church: Japanese Mormons in Japan from 1924 to 1948," *Brigham Young University Studies* 15 (Winter 1975): 191–214. An official statement on Selective Service, December 14, 1945, is "Letter of the First Presidency Concerning Military Training," *Improvement Era* 49 (February 1946): 76–77 (reprinted in Clark, *Messages*, 6: 239–42). A personal reflection on the 1940s building program is Claudia L. Bushman, "Sunset Ward," *Dialogue: A Journal of Mormon Thought* 22 (Summer 1989): 119–30.

Other Topics. See McBride's study of LDS higher education and other studies on education listed in the General Bibliography. Other events of interest to the Church are described in Albert L. Zobell, Jr., "The Temple at Idaho Falls," *Improvement Era* 50 (September 1947): 569; David O. McKay, "The Meaning of 'This Is the Place' Monument," ibid., 573, 601; and Charles W. Whitman, "The History of the Hill Cumorah Pageant, 1937–1964" (M.A. thesis, Univ. of Minnesota, 1967). Davis Bitton, "The 'Ritualization' of Mormon History," *Utah Historical Quarterly* 43 (Winter 1975): 67–85, describes how parades, pageants, historic sites, and other activities function as an expression of a people's celebration of their heritage.

CHAPTER 19
Foundations for Expansion, 1951–1959

The years of postwar growth after David O. McKay became President of the Church are introduced with some detail by Cowan, *The Church in the Twentieth Century* (1985), chaps. 12–16; and highlighted in many general works cited in the General Bibliography.

Members. For information on the social profile of the mid-century Saints, see John A. Widtsoe, "How Is Church Membership Divided as to Ages?" *Improvement Era* 55 (February 1952): 78–79; Widtsoe, "What Are the Occupations of Latter-day Saints?" ibid. (March 1952): 142–43, 167; Widtsoe, "Are Latter-day Saints Homeowners?" ibid. (April 1952): 222–23; "What Are the Educational Attainments of the Latter-day Saints?" ibid. (May 1952): 310–11; and two unpublished reports found in the Church Archives: Howard C. Nielson, "Membership of the Church . . . by Areas" (Salt Lake City, 1971) and Daniel H. Ludlow, "A Study Comparing the Recent Growth of the

Church . . . with Other Selected Christian Groups in the United States" (prepared for Institute of Mormon Studies, Brigham Young University, ca. 1963).

Missions. On the Asian missions see the overview by Spencer J. Palmer, *The Church Encounters Asia* (1970); and the analysis by Paul V. Hyer, "Revolution and Mormonism in Asia: What the Church Might Offer a Changing Society," *Dialogue: A Journal of Mormon Thought* 7 (Spring 1972): 88–93. Derek A. Cuthbert, "Church Growth in the British Isles, 1937–1987," *Brigham Young University Studies* 27 (Spring 1987): 13–26, examines one rapidly growing area. Apostasy and other difficulties among missionaries are examined in Kahlile Mehr, "The Trial of the French Mission," *Dialogue: A Journal of Mormon Thought* 21 (Autumn 1988): 27–45. Copies of selected missionary teaching plans are on file at the Church Historical Department.

Change and Expansion. The expansion of physical facilities in one part of the world is told in David W. Cummings, *Mighty Missionary of the Pacific: The Building Program of the Church . . . : Its History, Scope, and Significance* (Salt Lake City: Bookcraft, 1961). This study and Harvey Taylor's "Story of L.D.S. Church Schools" (manuscript, 1971, Church Archives) explain educational expansion and administrative reorganization, as do other sources listed in the General Bibliography. A study extending through the late 1950s is Ruben D. Law, *The Founding and Early Development of the Church College of Hawaii* (St. George, Utah: Dixie College Press, 1972).

Indian Student Placement Program. Helpful sources are Spencer W. Kimball, "The Expanded Indian Program," an October 1956 conference talk, in *Improvement Era* 59 (December 1956): 937–40; and Clarence R. Bishop's history (M.A. thesis, Univ. of Utah, 1967).

Public Affairs. Events in this period are discussed in O'Dea, *The Mormons* (1957); Ezra Taft Benson, *Crossfire: The Eight Years with Eisenhower* (Garden City, N.Y.: Doubleday, 1962); Edward L. Schapsmeier and Frederick H. Schapsmeier, *Ezra Taft Benson and the Politics of Agriculture: The Eisenhower Years, 1953–1961* (Danville, Ill.: Interstate Printers and Publishers, 1975); Dennis L. Lythgoe, "A Special Relationship: J. Bracken Lee and the Mormon Church," *Dialogue: A Journal of Mormon Thought* 11 (Winter 1978): 71–87; and Stan A. Taylor, "J. Reuben Clark and the United Nations," *Brigham Young University Studies* 13 (Spring 1973): 415–25, which is one of nine essays in this special issue on Clark.

CHAPTER 20
Correlating the International Church, 1960–1973

The significant developments of the 1960s and early 1970s are receiving increased attention from historians and have produced a rich store of commentary by persons who have lived through these eventful years. General surveys include Cowan, *The Church in the Twentieth Century* (1985), chaps.

16–20; and CES, *Church History in the Fulness of Times* (1989), chap. 43. The period can be approached as well through appropriate sections in the biographies of Presidents McKay, Smith, and Lee and in the sketches in Arrington's *Presidents of the Church* (1986). Also useful are the "Journal History of the Church," articles in Church periodicals, and statistical information in the biannual *Deseret News Church Almanac*.

Correlation. Background on this and earlier periods can be found in Jerry J. Rose, "The Correlation Program of the Church . . . during the Twentieth Century" (M.A. thesis, Brigham Young University, 1973). A convenient summary is John P. Fugal, comp., *A Review of Priesthood Correlation* (Provo: Brigham Young University Press, 1968). Contemporary statements include Harold B. Lee, "New Plan of Coordination Explained," *Improvement Era* 65 (January 1962): 34–37; and numerous other references listed in *Index to Periodicals of the Church . . .* , 1961–1970 (Salt Lake City: The Church . . . , 1972). We benefitted from preliminary research reports by Bruce D. Blumell, formerly of the Church Historical Department, and Robert G. Mouritsen of the Department of Seminaries and Institutes. Many of the committees and programs mentioned in the text have generated guides, manuals, and handbooks that give information on their activities. Also see "MIA as a Priesthood Function," *Ensign* 3 (June 1973): 48–54; and the announcement in ibid., 3 (January 1973): 135–36.

Church Growth. The meaning of Church growth outside North America is explored in F. LaMond Tullis, ed., *Mormonism: A Faith for All Cultures* (Provo: Brigham Young University Press, 1978); John Sorenson, "Mormon World View and American Culture," *Dialogue: A Journal of Mormon Thought* 8 (Summer 1973): 17–29; Tullis, "Three Myths about Mormons in Latin America," ibid., 7 (Spring 1972): 79–87; and Tullis, "Politics and Society: Anglo-American Mormons in a Revolutionary Land," *Brigham Young University Studies* 13 (Winter 1973): 126–34. Reports on Asian growth are in Desmond L. Anderson, "Meeting the Challenges of the Latter-day Saints in Vietnam," ibid., 10 (Winter 1970): 186–96; and Seiji Katanuma, "The Church in Japan," ibid., 14 (Autumn 1973): 16–28. For one part of Europe, see Kahlile Mehr, "The Eastern Edge: LDS Missionary Work in Hungarian Lands," *Dialogue: A Journal of Mormon Thought* 24 (Summer 1991): 27–45. The impact of the New York World's Fair exhibit on proselyting methods is told in Brent L. Top, "Legacy of the Mormon Pavilion," *Ensign* 19 (October 1989): 22–28.

Church Education. Further information can be found in Wilkinson, *Brigham Young University* (1975–76), vol. 3, and Taylor, "The Story of L.D.S. Church Schools" (manuscript, 1971, Church Archives). One region is examined in R. Lanier Britsch, "Latter-day Saint Education in the Pacific Islands," in Bitton and Beecher, *New Views of Mormon History* (1987), pp. 197–211.

Family. The modern Latter-day Saint family is examined in Harold T. Christensen, "Stress Points in Mormon Family Culture," *Dialogue: A Journal* *of Mormon Thought* 7 (Winter 1972): 11–19; and in special theme sections of two publications: "Women, Family, Home," from talks given in Relief Society conference, *Ensign* 2 (February 1972): 47–74; and "The Mormon Family in the Modern World," a series of ten articles, *Dialogue: A Journal of Mormon Thought* 2 (Autumn 1967): 41–108.

The Church and Public Policy. The subject can be approached through articles by Dennis L. Lythgoe, "The Changing Image of Mormonism," *Dialogue: A Journal of Mormon Thought* 3 (Winter 1968): 45–58; Thomas F. O'Dea, "Sources of Strain in Mormon History Reconsidered," in Hill and Allen, *Mormonism ard American Culture* (1972), pp. 147–67; and Leonard J. Arrington, "Crisis in Identity: Mormon Responses in the Nineteenth and Twentieth Centuries," in the same work, pp. 168–84. Also relevant are many of the articles in a special issue, "Mormons in the Secular City," *Dialogue: A Journal of Mormon Thought* 3 (Autumn 1968): 39–108; and Milton Hollstein, "The Church as Media Proprietor," ibid., 10 (Spring 1977): 21–24.

Political Issues of the 1960s. The relationship of church and state in Utah during the 1960s is discussed in Frank H. Jonas, ed., *Politics in the American West* (Salt Lake City: Univ. of Utah Press, 1969), pp. 327–80; and in a broader context in Armand L. Mauss, "Assimilation and Ambivalence: The Mormon Reaction to Americanization," *Dialogue: A Journal of Mormon Thought* 22 (Spring 1989): 30–67. See Dennis L. Lythgoe, "The 1968 Presidential Decline of George Romney: Mormonism or Politics?" *Brigham Young University Studies* 11 (Spring 1971): 219–40, on a prominent Latter-day Saint's campaign for the U.S. presidency; and four articles on "The Church and Collective Bargaining in American Society," *Dialogue: A Journal of Mormon Thought* 3 (Summer 1968): 106–33, in a "Roundtable" discussion by Garth L. Mangum, Vernon H. Jensen, H. George Frederickson, Alden J. Stevens, Richard B. Wirthlin, and Bruce D. Merrill; and a response by Ken W. Dyal in "Letters to the Editors," ibid., 3 (Autumn 1968): 11–14. An issue of global concern is discussed by Ray C. Hillam, Eugene England, and John L. Sorenson, in "Roundtable: Vietnam," *Dialogue: A Journal of Mormon Thought* 2 (Winter 1970): 65–100. Gordon C. Thomasson, ed., *War, Conscription, Conscience, and Mormonism* (Santa Barbara: Mormon Heritage, 1971), reproduces miscellaneous articles and documents on Mormon attitudes toward war in the Vietnam years.

Race Relations. Attitudes are discussed in two articles by Armand L. Mauss: "Mormonism and Secular Attitudes towards Negroes," *Pacific Sociological Review* 9 (Fall 1966): 91–99, and "Mormonism and the Negro: Faith, Folklore, and Civil Rights," *Dialogue: A Journal of Mormon Thought* 2 (Winter 1967): 19–39; and in Brian Walton, "A University Dilemma: B.Y.U. and Blacks," ibid., 6 (Spring 1971): 31–36. Historical perspective is contributed in the studies by Taggart and Bush cited in the bibliography for chap. 3. Commenting on Bush's article are Gordon C. Thomasson, "Lester Bush's Historical

Overview: Other Perspectives," ibid., 8 (Spring 1973): 69–72; Hugh Nibley, "The Best Possible Test," ibid., pp. 73–77; and Eugene England, "The Mormon Cross," ibid., pp. 78–86. For the statement of December 15, 1969, on blacks and the priesthood see "Letter of First Presidency Clarifies Church's Position on the Negro," *Improvement Era* 73 (February 1970): 70–71. Collected essays appear in Lester E. Bush, Jr., and Armand L. Mauss, eds., *Neither White nor Black: Mormon Scholars Confront the Race Issue in a Universal Church* (Midvale, Utah: Signature Books, 1984).

CHAPTER 21
Toward a Universal Church, 1974–1990

The story is told in CES, *History of the Church in the Fulness of Times* (1989), chaps. 44–47; and in Cowan, *The Church in the Twentieth Century* (1985), chaps. 19–24. A convenient chronology of recent events in Church history is the "Year in Review" section in the biannual issues of *Deseret News Church Almanac*. Filling in details are Hoyt W. Brewster, Jr., "The '80s—Looking Back; the '90s—Looking Ahead," *Ensign* 20 (January 1990): 8–13; and other accounts in the *Ensign*, the Church News section of the *Deseret News*, and other newspaper and magazine articles compiled in the "Journal History of the Church."

Church Presidents. Supplementing the full-length biographies listed in the General Bibliography are chapters in Arrington, *Presidents of the Church* (1986). For President Kimball, additional profiles include: Boyd K. Packer, "President Spencer W. Kimball: No Ordinary Man," *Ensign* 4 (March 1974): 2–13; and Spencer W. Kimball, *One Silent Sleepless Night* (Salt Lake City: Bookcraft, 1975). Assessing accomplishments are Edward L. Kimball, "The Administration of Spencer W. Kimball," *Sunstone* 11 (March 1987): 8–14; and a special issue of *Brigham Young University Studies* 25 (Fall 1985), containing: Dennis L. Lythgoe, "Lengthening Our Stride: The Remarkable Administration of Spencer W. Kimball," pp. 5–17; Eugene England, "A Small and Piercing Voice: The Sermons of Spencer W. Kimball," pp. 77–90; and other articles.

Missionary and Temple Work. Much information can be gleaned from entries in the International Church section below. Origins of one popular effort are recounted in Arlene Crawley, "The Beginning of the Family to Family Program," in Eugene England, ed., *Converted to Christ through the Book of Mormon* (Salt Lake City: Deseret Book, 1989), pp. 10–19. On the Washington Temple and its dedication, see the special issue of the *Ensign* 4 (August 1974), and J. M. Heslop, "Majestic Temple Dedicated," *Church News*, November 23, 1974.

International Growth. Membership growth is examined in Dean L. May, "A Demographic Portrait of the Mormons, 1830–1980," in Alexander and

Embry, eds., *After 150 Years* (Charles Redd Monograph, no. 13, 1983), pp. 37–70. The story is outlined in Leonard J. Arrington, "Historical Development of International Mormonism," *Religious Studies and Theology* 7 (January 1987): 9–22. Another interpretive overview is Jan Shipps, "The Mormons: Looking Forward and Outward," in Martin E. Marty, ed., *Where the Spirit Leads: American Denominations Today* (Atlanta: John Knox Press, 1980), pp. 25–40.

The Priesthood Revelation. Historical perspectives offering background to the revelation on priesthood are in Ronald K. Esplin, "Brigham Young and Priesthood Denial to the Blacks: An Alternate View," *Brigham Young University Studies* 19 (Spring 1979): 394–402; Armand L. Mauss, "The Fading of the Pharaoh's Curse: The Decline and Fall of the Priesthood Ban against Blacks in the Mormon Church," *Dialogue: A Journal of Mormon Thought* 14 (Autumn 1981): 10–45; "Saint without Priesthood: The Collected Testimonies of Ex-slave Samuel D. Chambers," ibid., 12 (Summer 1979): 13–21; James B. Allen, "Would-Be Saints: West Africa before the 1978 Priesthood Revelation," *Journal of Mormon History* 17 (1991): 207–47; and Newell G. Bringhurst, *Saints, Slaves, and Blacks: The Changing Place of Black People within Mormonism* (Westport, CT: Greenwood Press, 1981).

Discussing the revelation and its impact are Alexander B. Morrison, *The Dawning of a Brighter Day: The Church in Black Africa* (Salt Lake City: Deseret Book, 1990); Dale E. LeBaron, *"All Are Alike unto God"* (Salt Lake City: Bookcraft, 1990); Bruce R. McConkie, "All Are Alike unto God," Address to CES Religious Education Symposium, Brigham Young University, August 18, 1978; Mark L. Grover, "Religious Accommodation in the Land of Racial Democracy: Mormon Priesthood and Black Brazilians," *Dialogue: A Journal of Mormon Thought* 17 (Autumn 1984): 23–34; Grover, "The Mormon Priesthood Revelation and the Sao Paulo, Brazil, Temple," ibid., 23 (Spring 1990): 39–53; Newell G. Bringhurst, "An Ambiguous Decision: The Implementation of Mormon Priesthood Denial for the Black Man: A Reexamination," *Utah Historical Quarterly* 46 (Winter 1978): 45–64; Bringhurst, "Mormonism in Black Africa: Changing Attitudes and Practices, 1830–1981," *Sunstone* 6 (May-June 1981): 15–21; Dale LeBaron, "Revelation on the Priesthood: The Dawning of a New Day in Africa," in *Doctrines for Exaltation: The 1989 Sperry Symposium on the Doctrine and Covenants* (Salt Lake City: Deseret Book, 1989), pp. 127–38; and O. Kendall White, Jr., "Boundary Maintenance: Blacks and the Mormon Priesthood," *The Journal of Religous Thought* 37 (Fall-Winter 1980–81): 30–44.

The International Church. An important study of the intercultural challenges is LaMond Tullis, ed., *Mormonism: A Faith for All Cultures* (Provo: Brigham Young University Press, 1978). Thoughtful looks at international expansion are Spencer J. Palmer, *The Expanding Church* (Salt Lake City: Deseret Book, 1978); and Garth N. Jones, "Expanding LDS Church Abroad: Old Realities Compounded," *Dialogue: A Journal of Mormon Thought* 13 (Spring

1980): 8–22. A useful general summary for specific areas is James R. Moss, R. Lanier Britsch, James R. Christianson, and Richard O. Cowan, *The International Church* (Provo: Brigham Young University Publications, 1982). For David M. Kennedy's special role in establishing the Church among the nations, see Martin B. Hickman, *David Matthew Kennedy: Banker, Statesman, Churchman* (Salt Lake City: Deseret Book, 1987), especially chap. 19, "Ambassador to the World," pp. 334–65. Examining challenges are Lee Copeland, "From Calcutta to Kaysville: Is Righteousness Color-coded? *Dialogue: A Journal of Mormon Thought* 21 (Autumn 1988): 89–99; Joseph G. Stringham, "The Church and Translation," *Brigham Young University Studies* 21 (Winter 1981): 69–90; and Sterling M. McMurrin, "Problems in Universalizing Mormonism," *Sunstone* 4 (December 1979): 9–17.

Growth in Africa is told in Alexander B. Morrison, "The Dawning of a New Day in Africa," *Ensign* 17 (November 1987): 25–26 (and in his book cited above); E. Dale LeBaron, "Gospel Pioneers in Africa," ibid., 20 (Aug. 1990): 40–43; and Marjorie Wall Folsom, *Golden Harvest in Ghana* (Bountiful, Utah: Horizon Publishers, 1989). The opening of eastern Europe is reported in Kahlile Mehr, "The Gospel in Hungary: Then and Now," *Ensign* 20 (June 1990): 8–13; Garold and Norma Davis, "Behind the Wall: The Church in Eastern Germany," *Ensign* 21 (April 1991): 22–27; and (June 1991): 32–36. The Church in Asia and the Pacific is explored in Jiro Numano, "How International Is the Church in Japan?" *Dialogue: A Journal of Mormon Thought* 13 (Spring 1980): 85–91; Garth N. Jones, "Spreading the Gospel in Indonesia: Organizational Obstacles and Opportunities," ibid., 15 (Winter 1982): 79–90; and Marjorie Newton, " 'Almost Like Us': The American Socialization of Australian Converts," ibid., 24 (Fall 1991): 9–20. For yet another area see F. LaMond Tullis, "The Church Moves Outside the United States: Some Observations from Latin America," ibid., 13 (Spring 1980): 63–73.

Examining the impact of growth are Garth N. Jones, "Spiritual Searchings: The Church on Its International Mission," *Dialogue: A Journal of Mormon Thought* 20 (Summer 1987): 58–74; C. Brooklyn Derr, "Messages from Two Cultures: Mormon Leaders in France, 1985," ibid., 21 (Summer 1988): 98–111; James B. Allen, "On Becoming a Universal Church: Some Historical Perspectives," ibid., 25 (March 1992): 13–36; "Mormonism Becomes a Mainline Religion: The Challenge," essays by Mario De Pillis, Marie Cornwall, Marjorie Newton, Richard P. Howard, and Helen Papanikolas, ibid., 24 (Winter 1991): 59–96; De Pillis, "The Persistence of Mormon Community into the 1990s," *Sunstone* 15 (October 1991): 28–49; and David Knowlton, "Missionaries and Terror: The Assassination of Two Elders in Bolivia," *Sunstone* 13 (August 1989): 10–15.

Native Americans and Ethnic Groups. The life of the first Native American general authority is told in George P. Lee, *Silent Courage, An Indian Story: The Autobiography of George P. Lee, A Navajo* (Salt Lake City: Deseret Book,

1987). Responses to ethnic needs in urban areas are recounted in Chad M. Orton, *More Faith than Fear: The Los Angeles Stake Story* (Salt Lake City: Bookcraft, 1987); Robert G. Larsen and Sharyn H. Larsen, "Refugee Converts: One Stake's Experience," *Dialogue: A Journal of Mormon Thought* 20 (Fall 1987): 37–55; and Jessie L. Embry, "Separate but Equal?: Black Branches, Genesis Groups, or Integrated Wards?" ibid., 23 (Spring 1990): 11–37.

Church Administration. An historical overview is offered in James B. Allen, " 'Course Corrections': Some Personal Reflections," *Sunstone* 14 (October 1990): 34–40; and D. Michael Quinn, "From Sacred Grove to Sacral Power Structure," *Dialogue: A Journal of Mormon Thought* 17 (Summer 1984): 9–34. Simplification of programs is examined in J. Lynn England, "The Importance of Programs in Our Religious Community," *Sunstone* 14 (October 1990): 41–43; and Marie Cornwall, "The Paradox of Organization," *Sunstone* 14 (October 1990): 44–47. Changes in the seventies are given a setting in S. Dilworth Young, "The Seventies: A Historical Perspective," *Ensign* 6 (July 1976): 14–21. Douglas D. Alder, "The Mormon Ward: Congregation or Community?" *Journal of Mormon History* 5 (1978): 61–78, compares groups in two centuries. Sesquicentennial essays include Kenneth W. Godfrey, "150 Years of General Conference," *Ensign* 11 (February 1981): 66–71; and six articles in Thomas G. Alexander and Jessie L. Embry, eds., *After 150 Years: The Latter-day Saints in Sesquicentennial Perspective* (Provo: Charles Redd Center for Western Studies, 1983). The new Church magazines are discussed in Jay M. Todd, "A Status Report on Church Magazines: A Look at How They Came to Be," *Ensign* 6 (February 1976): 70–75; while the history of the Curriculum Department is outlined in Julie A. Dockstader, "Curriculum: Helping Members Apply Gospel to Daily Lives," *Deseret News*, December 29, 1990, "Church News" section, pp. 6, 10. Financial policy changes are reported in "New Meetinghouse Financing Policy Considers Tithing Faithfulness," *Ensign* 12 (May 1982): 101–102. Two accounts of disaster assistance are Bruce D. Blummell, "The LDS Response to the Teton Dam Disaster in Idaho," *Sunstone* 5 (March-April 1980): 35–42; and F. Ross Peterson, *The Teton Dam Disaster: Tragedy or Triumph!* (Logan: Utah State University Press, 1982).

Public Issues. Eugene England, "Hanging by a Thread: Mormons and Watergate," *Dialogue: A Journal of Mormon Thought* 9 (Summer 1974): 9–18, is one of several articles on the subject in this periodical. An overview prompted by the war in Vietnam is Ronald W. Walker, "Sheaves, Bucklers, and the State: Mormon Leaders Respond to the Dilemmas of War," *Sunstone* 7 (July-August 1982): 43–56; with other views in Edwin Brown Firmage, "Allegiance and Stewardship: Holy War, Just War, and the Mormon Tradition in the Nuclear Age," *Dialogue: A Journal of Mormon Thought* 16 (Spring 1983): 47–61; and D. Michael Quinn, "Christian Soldiers or Conscientious Objectors?" *Sunstone* 10 (March 1985): 14–23. For reports on Brigham Young University's opposition to federal antidiscrimination regulations, see "Journal

History" entries for October 16 and 27, 1975. On other issues, see Steven A. Hildreth, "The First Presidency Statement on MX in Perspective," *Brigham Young University Studies* 22 (Spring 1982): 215–25; Hildreth, "Mormon Concern over MX: Parochialism or Enduring Moral Theology," *Journal of Church and State* 26 (1984): 255–72; Joan Elbert, "Mormons and the MX Missile," *Christian Century* 98 (July 15–22, 1981): 725–26; Richard Sherlock, "Abortion, Politics, and Policy: A Deafening Silence in the Church," *Sunstone* 6 (July-August 1981): 17–19; and Donald G. Hill, Jr., "Abortion, Politics, and Policy: The Beginning of Actual Human Life," ibid., pp. 25–27.

Equal Rights Amendment. Assessing LDS involvement in the issue are Dixie Snow Huefner, "Church and Politics and the IWY Conference," *Dialogue: A Journal of Mormon Thought* 11 (Spring 1978): 58–75; Linda Sillitoe, "Women Scorned: Inside Utah's IWY Conference," *Utah Holiday* 6 (August 1977): 26; Sillitoe, "Church Politics and Sonia Johnson: The Central Conundrum," *Sunstone* 5 (January-February 1980): 35–42; O. Kendall White, Jr., " 'A Feminist Challenge': Mormons for ERA as an Internal Social Movement," *Journal of Ethnic Studies* 13 (Spring 1985): 29–50; White, "Overt and Covert Politics: The Mormon Church's Anti-ERA Campaign in Virginia," *Virginia Social Science Journal* 18 (Winter 1980); and White, "Mormonism and the Equal Rights Amendment," *Journal of Church and State* 31 (Spring 1989): 249–67. Comments on the equal rights amendment include Rex E. Lee, *A Lawyer Looks at the Equal Rights Amendment* (Provo: Brigham Young University Press, 1980); those of Relief Society President Barbara B. Smith, reported in *Deseret News*, December 13, 1974, and *Church News*, December 21, 1974; and editorials in the *Church News*, January 11, 1975, and *Deseret News*, January 22, 1975. Copies of these and other discussions on the issue can be found in "Journal History of the Church," for the dates specified.

LDS Women and Men. For broad historical overviews, see Jill Mulvay Derr, " 'Strength in Our Union': The Making of Mormon Sisterhood," in Beecher and Anderson, *Sisters in Spirit* (1987), pp. 153–207; and Leonard J. Arrington, "Persons for All Seasons: Women in Mormon History," *Brigham Young University Studies* 20 (Fall 1979): 39–58. Examining contemporary issues are Francine Bennion, "Mormon Women and the Struggle for Definition: What Is the Church?" *Sunstone* 6 (November-December 1981): 17–20; Carol Cornwall Madsen, "Mormon Women and the Struggle for Definition," *Dialogue: A Journal of Mormon Thought* 14 (Winter 1981): 40–47; and Eugene England, "On Being Male and Melchizedek," *Dialogue: A Journal of Mormon Thought* 23 (Winter 1990): 64–79.

Single Adults. Program adjustments are explained in *Ensign* 3 (January 1973): 135–36; 4 (March 1974): 17–21; 5 (February 1975): 74–76; and 7 (August 1977): 66–74. The role of singles is explored in Lavina Fielding Anderson and Jeffrey O. Johnson, "Endangered Species: Single Men in the Church," *Sunstone* 2 (Summer 1977): 2–7; Lavina Fielding Anderson, "Mormon Women and the Struggle for Definition: Contemporary Women," ibid., 6 (November-December 1981): 12–16; and Jeffery O. Johnson, "On the Edge: Mormonism's Single Men," *Dialogue: A Journal of Mormon Thought* 16 (Autumn 1983): 48–58; and Marybeth Raynes, "Getting Unmarried in a Married Church," ibid., 14 (Winter 1981): 75–90.

Public Image. Public relations efforts are described in Fred C. Esplin, "The Church as Broadcaster," *Dialogue: A Journal of Mormon Thought* 10 (Spring 1977): 25–45; and discussed in Stephen W. Stathis, "Mormonism and the Periodical Press: A Change is Underway," ibid., 14 (Summer 1981): 48–73; Stathis and Dennis L. Lythgoe, "Mormonism in the Nineteen-seventies: The Popular Perception," ibid., 10 (Spring 1977): 95–113; and Peggy Fletcher, "A Light unto the World: Issues in Mormon Image Making," *Sunstone* 7 (July-August 1982): 16–23. An outside perspective is Rodman Paul, "The Mormons: From Poverty and Persecution to Prosperity and Power," *American Heritage* 28 (June 1977): 74–83.

Historic Preservation and Museums. An overview of Church sites activities is Paul L. Anderson, "Heroic Nostalgia: Enshrining the Mormon Past," *Sunstone* 5 (July-August 1980): 47–55; and Florence S. Jacobsen, "Restorations Belong to Everyone," *Brigham Young University Studies* 18 (Spring 1978): 275–85. The history of an early Church museum is Lila Carpenter Eubanks, "The Deseret Museum," *Utah Historical Quarterly* 50 (Fall 1982): 361–76. Contemporary museum activities are noted in Gerry Avant, "Museum to Display LDS History, Art," *Deseret News*, Church News Section, Oct. 18, 1990, pp. 8–10; "New Museum First to Emphasize Arts," ibid., March 25, 1984, pp. 4, 10; and Golden A. Buchmiller, "Museum: 'A House of Appreciation,' " ibid., April 8, 1984, pp. 3, 10. Commentaries on a controversial decision are Edward Geary, "The Last Days of the Coalville Tabernacle," *Dialogue: A Journal of Mormon Thought* 5 (Winter 1970): 42–49; and Mark Leone, "Why the Coalville Tabernacle Had to be Razed: Principles Governing Mormon Architecture," ibid., 8 (Summer 1973): 30–39.

History and Historical Documents. Histories of the Hofmann forgeries and murders are Linda Sillitoe and Allen D. Roberts, *Salamander: The Story of the Mormon Forgery Murders* (Salt Lake City: Signature Press, 1988); and Robert Lindsey, *A Gathering of Saints: A True Story of Money, Murder, and Deceit* (New York: Simon & Schuster, 1988). Analyzing these works is David J. Whittaker, "The Hofmann Maze: A Book Review Essay with a Chronology and Bibliography of the Hofmann Case," *Brigham Young University Studies* 29 (Winter 1989): 67–124. Richard E. Turley, Jr., examines the documents story within the Church: *Victims: The LDS Church and the Mark Hofmann Case* (Urbana: University of Illinois Press, 1992). Discussing the forgeries are Roberts, " 'The Truth Is the Most Important Thing': The New Mormon History According to Mark Hofmann," *Dialogue: A Journal of Mormon Thought* 20 (Winter 1987): 87–96; Roberts, "The Hofmann Case: Six Issues," ibid., 19

(Winter 1986): 47–52; Linda Sillitoe, "The Sucessful Marketing of the Holy Grail," ibid., pp. 97–104; Jeffery O. Johnson, "The Damage Done: An Archivist's View," ibid., 19 (Winter 1986): 52–60; Sillitoe, "The Mormon Documents' Day in Court," *Sunstone* 10 (1986): 23–29; and Allen Roberts and Fred Esplin, "When the Dealing's Done: Bombs and Historical Bombshells," *Utah Holiday*, January 1986, pp. 42–43, 47–58. A comparative view is Edward L. Kimball, "The Artist and Forger: Han van Meegeren and Mark Hofmann," *Brigham Young University Studies* 27 (Fall 1987): 5–14. The event's impact on the RLDS Church is presented in Richard P. Howard, "Under the Cloud of Mark Hofmann," *Saints' Herald* 134 (December 1987): 15–16, 18.

Scriptures. Analyzing the most significant changes in the new LDS editions is Robert J. Matthews, "The New Publication of the Standard Works, 1979, 1981," *Brigham Young University Studies* 22 (Fall 1982): 387–423. See also, Boyd K. Packer, "The Library of the Lord," *Ensign* 20 (May 1990): 36–38.

Ezra Taft Benson and the Book of Mormon. President Benson introduced the Book of Mormon as a major emphasis for his administration during closing remarks at the April 1986 conference. He opened the October 1986 conference with a major address on the subject, and in his opening remarks in October 1988 called upon the Saints to "flood the earth" with this scripture. See the published *Official Report* of these conferences or the respective May and November issues of the *Ensign*.

Index